INTERPERSONAL BEHAVIOR

Communication and Understanding in Relationships

ANTHONY G. ATHOS
Graduate School of Business Administration
Harvard University

JOHN J. GABARRO
Graduate School of Business Administration
Harvard University

with the assistance of
JANE LYMAN HOLTZ

PRENTICE-HALL, INC., Englewood Cliffs, New Jersey 07632

Library of Congress Cataloging in Publication Data

ATHOS, ANTHONY G.
Interpersonal behavior.

Includes bibliographical references.
1. Interpersonal relations. 2. Interpersonal communication. I. Gabarro, John J., joint author.
II. Title.
HM132.A84 301.11 77-28090
ISBN 0-13-475004-7

Printed in the United States of America

10 9 8 7 6 5 4 3 2 1

Case material of the Harvard Graduate School of Business Administration is made possible by the cooperation of business firms who may wish to remain anonymous by having names, quantities, and other identifying details disguised while maintaining basic relationships. Cases are prepared as the basis for class discussion rather than to illustrate either effective or ineffective handling of administrative situations.

PRENTICE-HALL INTERNATIONAL, INC., *London*
PRENTICE-HALL OF AUSTRALIA PTY. LIMITED, *Sydney*
PRENTICE-HALL OF CANADA, LTD., *Toronto*
PRENTICE-HALL OF INDIA PRIVATE LIMITED, *New Delhi*
PRENTICE-HALL OF JAPAN, INC., *Tokyo*
PRENTICE-HALL OF SOUTHEAST ASIA PTE. LTD., *Singapore*
WHITEHALL BOOKS LIMITED, *Wellington, New Zealand*

Dedicated with Our Thanks to Two Men Who Preceded Us

George F. F. Lombard

and

Arthur N. Turner

Contents

PART TWO
UNDERSTANDING ANOTHER PERSON 131

PART THREE
UNDERSTANDING PERSONS IN RELATIONSHIP *265*

PART FOUR
DEVELOPING SKILLS IN UNDERSTANDING AND HELPING ANOTHER PERSON *393*

Preface for Teachers

This book is an outcome of an elective MBA course known as Interpersonal Behavior, which has been offered in one form or another at the Harvard Business School for over twenty years. The text is made up of materials currently used in that course, most of which have been developed within the last five years. These materials have been used not only in this course, but also in the school's programs for executives, in outside training programs, and by faculty in other universities. As a result of this classroom experience, much of the material has been subjected to many revisions, and thus this current version has been thoroughly tested by many teachers in varied settings with different students. We believe that the text, cases, and readings are ready for even wider use. We hope they will prove as helpful to others' learning as they have to ours.

The text is in many respects different from most books we have seen on interpersonal behavior. First, our focus is on interpersonal behavior in two-person relationships, rather than on the dynamics of group behavior. There are many excellent texts on behavior in group settings, but relatively few deal with individual relationships and the problems people experience in "one-to-one" settings. Much of a manager's work and personal life takes place in relationships of this kind, and we have felt for some time that this focus has been neglected in the field. We hope this text will help fill that gap.

A second respect in which this text is somewhat different from others is that our emphasis is on the interpersonal behavior of managers as people rather than on their behavior as "role occupants." We have found that our students' learning improved significantly as we shifted our emphasis away from the specific role-related interpersonal tasks of managers and toward the more universal human dilemmas that managers face in all their interpersonal relationships. Focusing upon the managerial role *per se* seemed to distance our students from the immediacy and power of the ideas and skills we valued. This was the case whether our students were 24-year-old MBAs or 42-year-old executives. The more we considered both the *experiencing and the behavior* of managers in their important relationships *at and away from work*, the more we found that managerially relevant learning increased. That's not very surprising, in retrospect. The people who use these materials do not compartmentalize themselves into roles, whether or not curriculums do. We have come to believe that when students engage learning as whole persons in the present and not just as roles anticipated in the future, the impact of that learning is more powerful and lasting.

The implications of this shift in focus, we felt, are important. It meant that our goal as teachers becomes one of enhancing the learning of people *as such* who also *wanted to be managers*. Yet we did not want to lose sight of the managerial implications of what we were doing. Thus, while much of this text is useful to students in education, counselling, or communication, we have chosen to retain the occupational setting of the manager. As you can imagine, this multiple focus on personal and professional relationships was the cause of dozens of revisions. We think the current balance between the two works better than any other we have tried.

A third respect in which this book is different from most on interpersonal behavior is that it provides a combination of descriptive chapters, selected readings and cases. These materials are organized into five parts described in the introduction to the book. The chapters provide the conceptual content and central themes of the book while the readings have been chosen to supplement or elaborate on them. The cases provide real life situations and dilemmas with which to "ground" and explore the ideas presented in the text and readings. This combination lends itself to a variety of classroom processes including case discussion, experiential work, and lecture/discussions. We suspect that this blend of cases, readings and descriptive chapters will strongly appeal to instructors who may be tiring of predominantly analytical or experimental approaches to teaching interpersonal behavior.

It occurs to us, however, that in some educational settings, additional managerial emphasis may be useful; in others, more experiential activities may help; and in still others, more behavioral science findings could be added. Our experience suggests that such additions are useful only when they are in response to the demonstrated needs of learners. Every time we met our *own needs* by adding more management theory, behavioral science, or experience, the personally relevant learning of our students seemed to decline. This taught us more than a few things we weren't eager to know.

There are other implications beyond the mix of materials. We found that the text worked best when it was written in more colloquial, everyday language, in a style that was more personal than academic. Indeed, we worked hard to eliminate as much jargon as possible, and to use a minimum number of necessary abstractions. We have chosen concepts that are as simple as possible but that do not lend themselves to being used mechanistically. Thus, they are deliberately less than what is needed to account for all the data in all the cases in some rote way. In short, the text is written to encourage instructors and students to use their own concepts, and especially their own metaphors, *in addition to* the ideas provided. Experienced teachers will grasp immediately the advantage of such an approach.

But of course, this in turn asks for the involvement of the teacher as a person, and not just as a role, much as it does for learners.

The orientation of this book is phenomenological, humanistic and pragmatic. Our purpose has *not* been to provide an exhaustive review of theories and concepts about relationships. Rather, it has been to convey a set of ideas, values and attitudes about what makes relationships effective and satisfying. We have opted for fewer concepts, rather than more, and greater depth rather than breadth. Thus, the book does not deal with all the issues in or approaches to interpersonal behavior. Instead, our primary emphasis has been on developing interpersonal understanding and effective communication. Some facets of relationships (such as power, loneliness, negotiation, etc.) are not dealt with explicitly although they are implicit issues in most of the text and cases.

This focus has a number of specific implications that are best expressed at the outset. The first is that we have chosen to use a client-centered approach as our primary vehicle for developing skills in helping relationships and understanding others. We have used this approach so exclusively in Part Four of the book that the sophisticated teacher may find our unilateral reliance on it somewhat surprising and disconcerting. This focus has not been a result of ignorance or an assumption that other approaches are not useful. Indeed, most of the text, readings and cases, as well as our own values, are very congenial to the use of transactional analysis, gestalt techniques and other confrontation approaches to improving interpersonal understanding and communication.

We have chosen, however, to use a Rogerian approach as a basis for skill development for three reasons. First, we believe that an in-depth treatment of one approach has greater pay-off for student learning than a broader but more superficial treatment of several. Second, we believe that the client-centered approach is more effective than other models for developing in students a capacity to understand and respond to another person's meanings. And we believe that this skill is basic to working and living with others. Finally, we believe that the Rogerian approach provides a very solid foundation for proceeding to other approaches, particularly transactional analysis. In fact, our assumption is that many instructors will use Part Four of the book as a basis from which to teach transactional analysis or other approaches within their own course.

The second area that needs commenting is the book's focus on two-person relationships. Our heavy emphasis on behavior in one-to-one encounters assumes that the student has previously developed an understanding of how group norms and culture affect the context within which two-person relationships exist. Where students have not had this prior background, the instructor may wish to supplement Part Three of the book with a reading on group norms or groups as social system.

The materials in the book provide a basis for many different kinds of classroom activities and processes. In our own classes we have aimed for a classroom process that is not intellectually distant or "public." Nor is it, as in an encounter group, emotional, intimate and "private." Rather, the materials in this text work best when the classroom process is engaging, close and personal—much like a compelling personal exploration among friends. We found that most classes moved fairly rapidly toward this personal tone of voice and that the resulting learnings were important to the students and the teachers. Former students often testified to their continued use of what they had begun to learn with us. Faculty who have taught this material have also reported important growth as persons and in their skills as teachers. Generally, most people have found their involvement with these materials rewarding—and for some of us it was a transforming experience. We hope they will turn out to be important to you too.

Anthony G. Athos
San Francisco, California

John J. Gabarro
Cambridge, Massachusetts

Acknowledgments

This book, perhaps more than some, is the outcome of the contributions of a great many people. We first want to express our gratitude to the hundreds of students whose response to the materials in this book provided ideas on the direction the work should take, as well as continuing evidence of the need for revision. In a real way, this text is a result of a long collaboration with learners, and we remain grateful for their help.

We thank George F. F. Lombard and Arthur N. Turner for the fundamental concepts from which we proceeded. Their basic work has stood the test of time, and they encouraged us to take the course that resulted in this book in new directions. Their support was both freeing and appreciated.

We are grateful too for the excitement and ideas we gained from the work of Fritz J. Roethlisberger, Carl Rogers, Arthur Combs, Donald Snygg, James F. T. Bugental, and Abraham Maslow, each of whom is represented by readings or reflected in the text. But their importance to our learning and thus to the book far exceeds their visible presence here. Also important to us was the work of Rollo May, Allen Wheelis, and Paul Tillich, whose writings altered our way of thinking about power, change, and choice. All these men were our teachers, and we are grateful to them.

We owe special thanks to Eileen Morley, who worked with us for several years and helped us in preparing earlier drafts of several chapters. She brought her clinical training to bear not only in a deft redesign of a troublesome section of the course, but also in her insightful observations of class process. She was so much a part of the adventure of building these materials, and such a warmly supportive colleague and friend, that the two of us regard her as our third.

It is with similar affection that we thank Jane Lyman Holtz, long-time assistant, whose patient revisions of materials over time made them more accessible to learners. Her commitment to the students, to the teaching group, and to her own learning led her to contribute in many ways that were important. She began a subordinate, became a peer, and would have been our coauthor except for other demands on her time.

J. B. Kassarjian and Michael McCaskey, who both taught the course with us and contributed to its development, were welcomed and valued colleagues. Many of their suggestions are reflected in this text, and several materials developed by Professor McCaskey have been included.

We are grateful too to Fernando Bartolome, Jay Norman, and Luise Dittrich, who as course assistants helped immeasurably in furthering our work over several years. They were especially helpful in keeping us close to the learner's viewpoint, a crucial contribution.

We also benefited greatly from the useful criticisms of Louis Barnes, Cyrus Gibson, Anne Harlan, Robert Le Duc, and Richard Walton all of whom taught some of the materials and gave us careful feedback.

We are particularly grateful to Richard Johnson, Stanford University; David A. Kolb, Case Western Reserve; Richard T. Pascale, Stanford University; Roy J. Lewicki, Dartmouth College; and Preston Probasco, San Jose State, for their useful suggestions and criticisms, many of which we have incorporated in the book. We are also indebted to David Bradford of Stanford University and Alan Cohen of the University of New Hampshire who with David Kolb offered several ideas for the teacher's manual that accompanies this text (*Teaching Interpersonal Behavior* by Michael McCaskey, John Gabarro, and Luise Dittrich).

We are especially grateful to Joyce Gaida for her editorial assistance and unflagging support. Her critical eye and cheerful disposition have made this a substantially more readable book.

We also thank Kay Smith, Denise Sareyan, and Cathy Tendler for their superb secretarial support. Only they and God know all they have done for us. Their competence and kindness were so apparent that we are truly grateful.

We thank the President and Fellows of Harvard College, Dean Lawrence Fouraker, and Charles Gebhard for permission to publish the text and to use certain cases and readings.

We are also indebted to the following men and women for permission to use their materials in this volume: John Anderson, Alex Bavelas, Luise Dittrich, Gareth Evans, Fred Foulkes, Charles Hampton-Turner, George Lombard, Bertha Maslow, Eileen Morley, Jay Norman, Charles D. Orth, Arthur Turner, and Jack Weber.

Finally, we mention Marilyn Gabarro, Gerald Holtz, and Carmen Strickler—three people who were very important to us. Marilyn Gabarro critically read several chapters and offered many useful suggestions. All three tolerated interminable discussion of the book, especially kind since they were most aware of our opportunity to personally benefit from what we were writing. Thanks.

Introduction for Students

This text is intended to serve as the basis for a classroom course in interpersonal behavior. It has been written, however, so that it also can be of value to individual readers who are not taking a course but are interested in learning more about interpersonal relations.

What is this book about? Our own students have often asked this and other questions: What will their experience be like? How can studying interpersonal behavior help them be better managers? Will it be an intellectual "head-trip"? How can anybody *learn* anything useful about the ways they relate to others? and so on. We've tried valiantly over the years to develop answers to such questions, but we've found it's a lot like trying to describe the taste of lobster to someone who has never eaten one.

There are a number of reasons why it is difficult to describe at the outset what this text is about. First, a simple description of the issues this book covers would merely provide a list of the book's topics; it would give only the smallest hint of the dilemmas and problems that are at the core of these issues, and it is only by exploring these dilemmas and problems in depth that important learnings emerge. Second, our experience in teaching the materials in this book has shown us that although most students arrive at a number of commonly shared learnings, their *important personal* learnings vary significantly, depending upon what their individual needs and interests are. We suspect that the same will apply to you as you work with this text.

The best we can do in this introduction is to provide a rough road map of what we will cover and to tell you as best we can what our intentions are. In briefest terms, this book is about interpersonal behavior in relationships. Its primary focus is on two-person relationships of the kind that people develop, for good or bad, in their personal and professional lives. It will explore the problems of interpersonal behavior in terms of "one-to-one" encounters as well as the dynamics of relationships as they develop (or fail) over time. The text is not about the dynamics of group behavior, nor is it a book about management theory (although the ideas presented are obviously applicable to working in groups and managing people). We will be concerned mainly with understanding people in relationships, the interpersonal problems that typically occur between people, and how interpersonal relationships can be made more vital, effective, and satisfying.

The text has been written primarily for people who are preparing to become or already are managers. We believe that the ideas presented in this book can be of value to people in other vocations as well, and we have in fact used these materials in programs for educators, health-care professionals, and counselors. However, the book's occupational context is principally managerial. At the same time, the concepts and ideas we will develop are intended to be of value in all types of relationships—personal as well as professional. Many of the cases are about personal decisions or problems, and we will urge you throughout the book to use what you learn from it in your own personal relationships.

Having given the context and focus of the book, we would like to describe briefly what we see as some of its purposes. These intentions can be simply summarized as follows:

- *To increase your awareness of the process of communication* so that you can see and hear more of what is taking place in your relationships with others.

- *To refine your ability to understand another person* and deepen your capacity to "imagine the real" of another's experiencing.

- *To develop your insight into yourself* so that you are more in touch with your own needs, aspirations, and experiencing.

- *To deepen your understanding of the dynamics of relationships as they evolve over time*, how they are formed, the roles that people tacitly agree to play in them, and the unstated "contracts" that often are at the core of relationships.

- *To develop your skills in listening to and responding to others* and thus develop your capacity to understand, help, and work with others.

- *To sharpen your awareness of some of the important questions and dilemmas of interpersonal relationships*, notably those related to the values and life choices common to many of us.

In short, we hope to help you become more aware of what is going on inside other people, inside yourself, and between you and others, as well as develop more skill in working and living with others.

The book is organized into five parts, each with chapters, readings, and case studies. Part One focuses on communication and covers the many languages through which people intentionally or unintentionally "talk" to each other. It also deals with some common sources of communication problems and what can be done to prevent them. Part Two focuses more deeply on understanding another person (and also one's own self). It introduces the idea of self concept as a way of understanding another person's behavior, and also explores the powerful effects of personal identifications, expectations and people's needs for mastery and approval. Part Three looks at the development of relationships over time, how they grow or fail. It considers the topics of interpersonal attraction, complementarity and the notion of "interpersonal contracts." Part Four presents an approach for developing skills in listening and responding to others: Skills which can help you become more interpersonally competent. Finally, Part Five addresses some choices and dilemmas inherent in working and living with others.

The organization of the book is somewhat different from most texts in that the five parts of the book are not sharply differentiated from each other. All of the book is about interpersonal relations, but the specific focus shifts from one part to the next. There is also some overlap within each individual section of the book. Many of the readings, for example, elaborate on ideas or themes presented in the chapters, and some chapters use case-like examples to illustrate concepts.

Moreover, not all of the chapters are written in text book style. Some chapters are intentionally informal and conversational, especially those which deal with developing awareness of what takes place in everyday interactions. Chapters which concern personal issues tend to be written in a personal tone of voice, while those which explicate concepts tend to be more structured and instructional in their presentation. This variation in style reflects our belief that different topics are best discussed in different ways.

It has been our intention to keep the concepts pretty simple and the cases increasingly complex. The book proceeds in a step-by-step process that often temporarily focuses upon a part at the expense of the whole. The materials are sequenced so that each part builds on what precedes it. As you go further with the material, more and more of it will become integrated for you.

Our approach to this subject matter is a synthesis of clinical psychology (especially those ego psychologies with phenomenological and existential orientations), organizational behavior (largely relying upon a social systems approach), and a number of other intellectual sources, including general semantics. The resulting synthesis is rooted in humanistic values. If you are familiar with the work of the people thanked in the acknowledgments, you have a pretty good idea of what our approach will be like. The book is not a traditional "psych" text, however, for, among other things, it was written with present and future executives very much in mind. However, our hope is that you will find the book useful in your current life, whether you are an executive or not.

Our experience has been that the more a person attempts to use what is learned in his or her daily life, the more ideas come alive in an exciting and personally relevant way. We have often recommended that students ask after each chapter, reading, or case, "So what?"—"So what for *my* life," that is. To the extent that relevance is apparent, there is likely to be learning that lasts.

And we hope the learning that results is not just a stockpile of abstractions, or a miscellany of awareness, or a gaggle of specific techniques. Rather, we hope it is an interactive relationship of ideas, awareness, and techniques that is practiced carefully enough to become a natural, intuitive, and "second-nature" skill. This goal is ambitious. It requires of you detailed attention to ideas and the data in cases, as well as courage to practice what may be some new ways of being in your world. And that means that at times, you may feel a bit self-conscious, inadequate, or perhaps even somewhat threatened. It's much like learning to drive a car. At first it can be exasperatingly complex and difficult. But with practice, the necessary set of ideas, awareness, and skills become second nature, and the process of driving becomes intuitive. So it can be with this material. If you are motivated to learn, you will find that many of the concepts, once used, will soon recede from your consciousness but will remain a part of the way you are in relationships.

We have done what we can to provide you with written materials that will be useful. Your instructor can help you use those materials more effectively. But in the end, the learning we hope for you will result from what you do. We hope you will suspend any disbelief you may have, at least temporarily, and dig into these materials. Others have found that they have learned a lot they valued greatly. We wish you such outcomes too.

PART ONE

PROBLEMS OF COMMUNICATION

Introduction

"They're having a communication problem"; "We just can't seem to communicate"; "I wish I could get them to communicate with each other." People often use the term "communicate" to describe interpersonal problems or conflicts. Sometimes, "poor communication" is not at all the source of an interpersonal problem, but much of the time it is at least part of the problem. Indeed, it is almost impossible to talk about interpersonal relations without also talking about communication between people. The process of communication and the forms it takes are basic to how interpersonal relationships develop, grow, or fail.

Communication is so fundamental a part of interpersonal behavior that we will begin this book with it as the first topic. The chapters, readings, and cases in this section of the book will focus on the process of communication. We will be concerned with how people communicate and miscommunicate, and how the quality and effectiveness of communication can be improved. The purposes of these materials are threefold: (1) to help you develop an increased awareness of how people communicate, intentionally *and unintentionally*; (2) to help you gain a better appreciation of the problems that occur in communicating; and (3) to provide you with some concepts and a way of thinking that can help you improve your own effectiveness and skill in communicating with others.

We will begin by focusing on the different languages people use to "talk" to each other. We don't mean the word *languages* literally. Rather, we are using the term metaphorically to mean the different media through which people communicate with each other. Chapter 1 will discuss the use of time, space, and things as languages of communication. These are nonverbal languages but nonetheless potent ones in which people "talk" to each other, consciously or unconsciously. People are constantly giving off messages to others by the way they use their time, the space they work and live in, and their objects. In the same vein, Chapter 2 will discuss another nonverbal medium of communication, "body language." Although body language is a more obvious form of communication than time, space, or things, most of us are seldom aware of how our own body behavior speaks, and we are often only partially aware of the body behavior of others. The reading on "Place, Imagery, and Nonverbal Clues" goes beyond these nonverbal languages and focuses on the settings in which we work and live. It describes how physical settings communicate and influence the nature of interactions that take place among people. Chapter 3 focuses on the most obvious, and perhaps the most troublesome, language of communication: the use of words.

Each of these chapters will ask you to consider small and subtle details of interaction in much more depth than you are normally accustomed to. You may even find yourself becoming temporarily "hyperaware" of your own and other people's behavior. Many of our students have experienced an initial period of being overly sensitized to nonverbal and verbal behavior, but this is part of the learning process. In our experience, this is a brief transitionary period, which passes. Going through this process, however, will result in your becoming more intuitively aware of how you interact and communicate with others. The outcome, we hope, is that you will develop better skills in perceiving what is taking place in normal as well as difficult interactions, and become more conscious of how your own actions affect others.

You may also find that the chapters on languages of communication present you with a double message. On the one hand, these chapters and readings wll urge you to pay attention to small details and nuances of how people behave. Their tacit message is, "Pay attention—how you and others communicate is important." On the other hand, these same chapters will also be saying, "Yes, but be careful not to be too certain about the meanings you take from observations of verbal and nonverbal behavior, because the same symbols, actions, and words may mean different things to different people." Although these messages appear contradictory, both are true. It *is* important to attend to the subtleties of verbal and nonverbal communication, and you will not develop greater awareness unless you do so. However, the inferences you draw from what others say and do must be considered in the total context of who those others are as persons and what their words and actions are likely to mean to them.

The implicit assumption in the three chapters on languages of communication is that people are communicating all the time, even when they haven't uttered a word. Our facial expressions, posture, and use of space and time are "saying" things to others, whether or not we intend them to. The important task, of course, is to be aware of these languages so that what you "say" to others is what you mean, and so that you are more effective in understanding the meanings of others.

PROBLEMS OF COMMUNICATION

The chapters on languages of communication deal indirectly with miscommunication, but Chapter 4 will address problems of communication more explicitly. This chapter explores and identifies how the unarticulated assumptions we carry around with us influence our ability to communicate effectively and understand what another person is trying to say or do. It also presents some concepts for thinking about how different people can experience the same situation differently. These ideas can be helpful in recognizing what is taking place when a misunderstanding occurs, particularly when you yourself are part of the problem. The chapter also describes some attitudes and behaviors that, if learned and practiced, can improve effectiveness in communicating and working with others.

In many respects, Chapter 4 pulls together several of the ideas that underlie the readings that follow and the chapters on languages of communication. It also lays the groundwork for what will follow in remaining sections of the book, so it is a chapter that should be read carefully.

THE READINGS IN THIS SECTION

The readings in this section of the book were chosen to supplement the chapters. "Place, Imagery, and Nonverbal Clues" provides a concise review of the psychology of place and of the effect of verbal imagery and nonverbal clues on communication and interpersonal behavior. "Barriers and Gateways to Communication" treats the question of what impedes and what facilitates communication. It presents some simple but powerful ideas for improving communication in general. The reading on "Giving and Receiving Feedback" deals with the important question of how you can give or receive feedback in a way that is helpful and useful.

THE CASES IN THIS SECTION

The cases in this section of the book have been chosen to allow you to test and explore your own ideas and learnings using descriptions of real situations. These cases cannot substitute for "live" behavior, particularly in terms of nonverbal communication. The best laboratory for exploring these ideas and learnings is in your own experience in the classroom and particularly in your own relationships outside of class. However, the cases do provide a useful way of beginning the process.

The cases provide a number of different contexts: a confrontation between a manager and a group of protestors; a developing intimate relationship between a man and a woman, and how it is affected by their physical surroundings; an exchange of letters between a job candidate and a potential employer; an escalating interpersonal conflict between a principal and a teacher; an exit interview between an expatriate manager in a developing country and his successor who is a native of that country; and a strained relationship between a project manager and a gifted scientist in a laboratory.

As a collection, these cases also describe situations in which the people are in a variety of relationships: boss–subordinate, peers, lovers, and adversaries. In some of these cases, the people involved are faced with the problem of communicating across powerful barriers, including differences in generations and age, in race and culture, in personal style and predispositions, and in ideologies.

The cases, like the text and readings, are meant to trigger and develop awareness. The most powerful learning takes place when you try out these ideas and test them in your own relationships and experience. For example, as you work with these materials, consider how *you* use time, space, things, and body language in your own relationships. How do your instructors (intentionally or unintentionally) communicate, and to what effect? What are the sources of misunderstandings or interpersonal conflicts you are currently experiencing, and what can you do about them?

Chapter One

Communication: The Use of Time, Space, and Things

TIME

It is amazing to discover how many ways we have of talking about time. We have time, keep time, buy time, and save time; we mark it, spend it, sell it, and waste it; we kill time, pass time, give time, take time, and make time. With so many ways of dealing with time in the English language, we must be as sensitive to it as Eskimos are to snow, for which they have many words and no small respect.

Our American concepts of time are that it is continuous, irreversible, and one-dimensional.[1] Recent movies that shuffle the sequence of events so that they do not proceed in the same order as they do in "real" time, including "flashaheads" as well as the old standard flashbacks, are effective in powerfully disturbing us precisely because they deny our long-standing assumptions about time. We often seem to experience tomorrow as spatially in front of us and yesterday as almost

Some of the ideas in this chapter were developed in a lecture given by Anthony G. Athos, which was first published in A.G. Athos and R.E. Coffey, *Behavior in Organizations: A Multidimensional View* (Englewood Cliffs, N. J.: Prentice-Hall, 1968). The author is greatly indebted to the stimulation of Edward T. Hall's *The Silent Language* (New York: Doubleday, 1959), and *The Hidden Dimension* (New York: Doubleday, 1966). Hall's work is much recommended to those who find that this brief discursive introduction stimulates further interest in a different and more systematic approach.

[1] "United States" and "American" refer here to the whole country, ignoring the considerable differences in the "cultures" of Hawaii, Alaska, Texas, and other parts of the whole.

literally behind us. With some effort we might be able to think of today as the space we were just in and the space we will very soon be in as we walk in a straight line. "Now" is even harder for many Americans, and it seems we experience it as the space filled by our bodies.

Perhaps that is why such interesting variations exist in different parts of the United States in orientations toward time. My personal experience in New England leads me to see people here as more oriented toward the past and the future than toward the present. Southern Californians seem more present-and-future oriented, with some important emphasis upon now (and thus greater familiarity with their bodies). The Latin Americans I know seem more past-and-present oriented. My point here is that we differ in our experiencing of time (as contrasted with our ways of thinking about it), focusing upon different aspects of it. Yet there is a tendency for us to assume it is linear in space—that is, as a "straight line" from the past through the present into the future.

Of course, these who live more in touch with nature—say, farmers or resort operators—might also see time as cyclical. The earth makes its daily round of the sun; the seasons, like circles, "each mark to the instant their ordained end" and cycle again. And many of us—on an island vacation, for example—"unwind" like a corkscrew from what we left behind, slowly lose our concerns for tomorrow, and relax into letting days happen so that each merges with the one before and into the one after as an experienced, continuous present. The loosening delight of such vacations is in contrast with our more usual patterns, wherein our concerns about time can easily become compulsive.

Accuracy

I can recall being in Athens, Greece, and asking my Greek cousin, "How long does it take to walk from here to the library?" I was staying with her family, and I wanted to spend the afternoon at the library and leave there in time to get back home for a 6 P.M. appointment with an American friend. She said, "Not long." I replied with some irritation, "No. I need to know, so I can stay there as long as possible. How long does it take?" She shrugged and said, "It's a short walk." I said with a frown, "Come on! I want to know exactly. How long?" With great exasperation, she finally dismissed me with, "A cigarette!" Well, I felt a bit defeated, if a little amused, for to her a ten- or even twenty-minute error in estimate would have been simply irrelevant. Any greater precision would confine her. Yet we Americans want to know *exactly*. Our concern for accuracy is enormous. Where else but in the Western industrialized world would watches be advertised as not being off more than a few seconds a month? Where else would people have timepieces literally strapped to their bodies so they can be sure they "keep on time"? Because of our concern for accuracy, the way we use time in our culture "talks" to other people.

Many men can remember the first time they ever drove to pick someone up for a date. It's not surprising that many of us got there a bit early and drove around the block a while so as not to communicate our anxiety or eagerness too openly. To arrive at 7:00 for a 7:30 date is to "tell" the other about these feelings and may result in seeming naive, unless you can explain it away. To arrive at 8:00 for a 7:30 date "says" you feel somewhat indifferent, and a decent explanation is required if the evening is to make any sense at all. Similarly, it is not uncommon for professors to assume that a student who is frequently late for class "doesn't care," and to get angry as a result. Students also tend to assume that professors who are late to class don't care very much. Thus, time often "tells" about caring, whether accurately or not.

We also use time to tell how we feel about and see others in terms of relative status and power. If the president of the United States called you to Washington to talk with him next Tuesday at 3 P.M., it is unlikely that you would arrange your flight to arrive at National Airport at 2 P.M. You would most likely want very much to be sure you were at the White House no later than 3 P.M., and might very well get to Washington on Monday to be certain nothing would go wrong. Because of the great difference between the status of the president and that of the rest of us, we would probably feel that any inconvenience in waiting ought to be ours.

The same can be true in companies. If the president of a large organization calls a young salesman to his office for a 3 P.M. meeting, the chances are awfully good that the salesman will arrive before 3 P.M., even if he has to walk around the block for an hour so as not to arrive too early.

Imagine two men who are executives in the same large company, whose respective status is virtually the same but who are very competitive in many ways. One calls the other on the phone and asks him to come to his office for a meeting at 1:00 that afternoon. (Notice that one is initiating, which generally indicates higher status; that he is specifying the place and the time, which diminishes the other's influence on those decisions; and that the "invitation" comes only a few hours before the intended meeting, which may imply that the other has nothing more important to do.) The chances are good that the second man will not arrive before or even *at* 1:00 for the meeting, unless his compulsiveness about time in general is so great that it overcomes his feelings about being "put down" (in which case he has lost a round in their competition and may be searching for a "victory" during the meeting). He might well arrive late, perhaps five minutes, which is enough to irritate but not openly insult, and then offer either no apology or only a very casual one. The way he handles time in this setting will communicate something to the first executive, and so he may plan his response as carefully as a choreographer plans a ballet. Yet little of the process may be fully conscious for him. As Hall says in the title of his book, these are often truly "silent languages" for many of us.

The longer people are kept waiting, the worse they feel. If the young salesman who was invited to his company president's office for a 3 P.M. meeting arrives at a "respectful" 2:50 and is told by the secretary to have a seat, he remains relatively comfortable until 3:00. If the secretary waits until 3:10 to phone the president and remind him the salesman is there, she may communicate (that is, the salesman may "hear") that she thinks a ten-minute wait is about all she can handle without sensing that the salesman will be feeling the first pangs of being unwanted. If she hangs up the phone and says, "He'll be right with you," and the clock continues to tick until 3:25, she might feel impelled to say something about how busy the president is today (in other words, "Don't feel bad. It's nothing personal"). By 3:45, the salesman is apt to be somewhat angry, since he is likely to assume that the president doesn't really care about seeing him. If the president comes out of his office (note this use of space) to get the salesman, apologizes for being late, and explains why (especially if the explanation includes information about "the top" that the salesman is not usually aware of), the salesman may "forgive" his boss ("That's all right. I don't mind at all. Your time is more important than mine") and all can go well. If the president buzzes his secretary, tells her to send the salesman in, and then proceeds directly to the business at hand, the salesman is likely to be torn between the anger he feels and the fear of expressing it, which may affect their meeting without either knowing why. In short, then, the longer a person is kept waiting, the more "social stroking" is required to smooth ruffled feathers. Awareness of the process can reduce its power to discomfort when you are on the receiving end, and can increase your skill at helping others to realize that you were not deliberately, with intent, trying to "put them down." Being "thoughtless" and thus hurting others' feelings is all too often just what we call it: thoughtless. Thinking about our uses of time can, after an awkward self-consciousness, lead to an increase in intuitive, out-of-awareness skill in dealing with self and others.

Using time to manipulate or control others is common, even if we who do so are unaware of it. I once hired a gardener on a monthly contract to care for my yard. When we were discussing the arrangements, I felt somewhat uncertain that he would do all I wanted done or do it to my satisfaction. My feelings of mistrust were expressed by focusing upon time. I wanted to know precisely what day of the week he would come and how many hours he would stay. He seemed to understand and said, "Thursday. Four hours." Well, he actually did come on Thursday once in a while, but he also came on any other day of the week except Sunday and Monday. He never to my knowledge stayed four hours, even when I happened to be home. I was sure I was being "taken"—until it occurred to me that the yard had never looked so good and everything really needing to be done was done.

The gardener apparently thought in terms of planting and cutting and fertilizing cycles. He felt his duty was to the yard, not to me. He sent me bills about every three or four months, and then he often had to ask me what I owed him. He trusted me completely to pay him what he deserved. He worked in terms of seasons of the year, and I was trying to pin him down to an hourly basis. Any attempt I made to replace my mistrust with the brittle satisfaction of controlling another person in regard to time would eventually have led him to quit or me to fire him. I was lucky to see what was happening, and I left him alone. We got along fine.

Time is viewed as both precious and personal, and when we allow someone to structure our time, it is usually in deference to his or her greater status or power. This is especially true when we would rather be doing something else, as is the case with some employees in many organizations who "put in their time" from nine to five. Many people today are looking for an opportunity to "do their own thing" (when they can figure out what that is), and their reluctance to be controlled vis-à-vis a dimension as personal as time is reflected in such questions as, "How much of your time is yours?" "Did you take time to smell the flowers?" and "Do you own your life?" "Private time" (such as weekends) is often "intruded upon" by work, with the notable exception of the Pacific Northwest, where it is generally regarded more strongly as nonwork time.

The use of time to define relationships can also be seen in most marriages. How many Americans do you know who work through the dinner hour or into the night without calling their spouses? By contrast, people in other cultures often handle the time of their arrival home differently. In Greece, I found that dinner was served at my uncle's house whenever he came home—and that might be anywhere from 6 P.M. to 9 P.M. This variation in the use of time, as well as my dealings with the gardener, introduces still another major notion about time.

Scarcity

We seem to see time as a limited resource for each person, so we think that what people choose to do with what time they have is a signal about how they feel about us.

You have already experienced the application of this notion. We all feel the obligation to see certain people with a certain frequency in order to express a suitable amount of affection. Take visits home to see your parents: some students go home every weekend, some only on vacations, some only on holidays, some every few years, and some never. But almost all parents are pleased, assuming they like their children, to find that their offspring choose to visit them rather than do something else. There is a mutual exclusivity operating here. If you go home to see your parents, they know you do so at the expense of some other option. If your other options are attractive, they "hear" that you care enough about your relationship with them to forego some other pleasure. Your choosing to spend your time with them is thus a gift of sorts and a signal about your sentiments. The same is true with other people, of course, especially subordinates in an organization.

Even when the choice of how or with whom we spend our time is not really our own, others may "hear" a communication about our feelings. If you and two other people begin to meet after class once a week for a beer, and then you take a part-time job that forces you to go directly from class to work, your absence in the pub will be "understood" as out of your control (given the choice you made to work). But the loss of interaction must be made up elsewhere, or your friends will probably feel that you "withdrew."

Some people are really tough on this one. You may have three final exams to study for plus a broken leg, and yet, like most professors, some friends will insist you come to the appointed meeting and bring your leg with you. On the other hand, there need be no unreasonable demands involved for misunderstandings to occur. Perfectly reasonable people can think we don't care for them because we do something else rather than see them. They can misjudge the importance to us of the something else and be ignorant of the conditions that made it important. A supervisor who spends more time per day with one subordinate because the tasks being done temporarily require closer supervision may communicate to other subordinates, especially if time with them is temporarily reduced, that the supervisor "cares" more about what the first subordinate is doing and perhaps will come to care more about that person than about them. There may be more than a little truth in this. Sociologists have noted that it is not uncommon for positive sentiment to increase as the frequency of interaction increases, albeit with several important exceptions (including the problem of formal authority).

We sometimes experience with a new friend an increase in frequency of interaction that accelerates beyond a point of equilibrium, given the importance the relationship comes to have for one or both persons. Then, if one person begins to withdraw a bit in order to adjust the frequency of contact to the kind and amount of sentiment, the other person—especially if he or she is desirous of more frequent interaction—tends to feel hurt. This hurt can lead him to react by further reducing or demanding increases in the frequency of contact, and until someone says openly what he is feeling, the cycle can proceed to the destruction of the relationship.

The scarcity of time for a person at a given moment is also his or her "cost" of time. When two people spend time together in any activity, communication will be strained and difficult unless the time being spent has approximately the same value for each participant. This is obvious when we by chance meet a friend in the street or hallway; if one begins to chat and the other is in a hurry, the encounter is bound to be a little awkward even if the person "short of time" explains why.

Our notion that time is scarce fits most Americans' feelings that things should be ordered, and that earlier is better than later. First born, first position, number-two man, fourteenth in a class of 655, top 10 percent—all assume meaning because of their position.

Early promotions in business or an advanced degree in two years instead of three are seen as praiseworthy, even if some run right by what they are trying to catch. These notions of time sequence are not inborn; they are culturally conditioned. Edward Hall reports that it takes the average child a little more than twelve years to master time and the concepts of order. I am constantly reminded of this by my young daughter, who recently asked, "But how long away is Friday?"

The point of this is, again, that time is seen as scarce, and thus, whom or what you choose to "give your time to" is a way of measuring your sentiments. Just being more aware of this can help you recognize the usefulness of simply saying, out loud, what the meaning of your choice is for you. And of course, such awareness also helps prevent you from assuming (without awareness of the assumption) the meanings of other persons without checking their intent.

Repetition

Finally, time has meaning for us in terms of repetition of activities. Some of our personal rhythms are so intimate and familiar to us that we are unaware of them. Most of us eat three meals a day, for example, not two, not five. The culture assumes that lunch is at noon for the most part, and this was probably defined originally in response to people's experience of hunger. But the convention also becomes a structure to which we adapt and with which we become familiar. When we experience an interrruption of our pattern, we often become irritated. I can recall, for example, that I found it difficult to adjust to a change in schedule on my first teaching job. For several years as a doctoral candidate, I had had coffee at 10 o'clock with a group of congenial colleagues. The coffee hour became one of the central social functions of my day, in addition to a means of getting some caffeine into my reluctantly awakening body. When I began teaching, I had a 9 o'clock and a 10 o'clock class three days a week; I was troubled by the 10 o'clock class and adjusted by bringing a cup of coffee into class with me. The pattern was so well developed and so valued within me that I was willing to break a norm (and, in fact, a rule) against food in the classrooms in order to have my 10 o'clock coffee. It sounds like a small matter, and in one sense it is, but it makes my point. There are daily cycles we are used to, and while there are many we share, there are others relatively unique to each of us. The closer to the body any repetitions of activity come, the more important they are to us.

Take seasons of the year, for example. In areas that have weather rather than climate—say, New England rather than southern California—the use of time varies from season to season as activities change. People in Boston not only put away their silver and use their stainless steel in August, but they give different kinds of parties with different time rules than they do in winter. In general, the rules are relaxed, more variety is "allowed," and time is less carefully measured for meaning.

Our rhythms are also influenced by our feasts and holidays and rituals. Christmas, Easter, Rosh Hashonah, Chanukah, Father's Day, Thanksgiving, Memorial Day, and the like, all have their "time" in the year. It has been hypothesized that Christ was really born in August, and the December celebration of His birth came about because the people of northern Europe had long had a pagan winter festival that they were used to. In any event, we are accustomed to certain activities and feelings in connection with each "special day."

For example, most businesspeople know there will be less work than usual done just prior to and just after Christmas. People experience a need for closeness, for family, for ritual, for the nostalgia of past Christmases, for gift giving and midnight services. They eat more and drink more and even get fond of their old Aunt Minny. It is a time set aside for warmth, affection, children, family, friends, and ritual.

The Greeks, however, celebrate their Easter much as we do our Christmas, and mark their Christmas almost as casually as we do our Easter. If you were to spend Christmas in Athens, you would probably sense something missing. If you were there on Easter, you would get a "bonus." If you were in the United States, working on a job that peaked in volume between December 20 and January 3—say, in a post office—and you had to work long hours, the chances are that you would feel quite resentful. The rhythms of our days, our weeks, our months, our years are all deeply familiar to us even if we are unaware of them. Any serious disruption of any of them is felt as deprivation. Just being aware of this can help you in many ways—planning changes, for example. Can you see why major changes in work design or location or personnel are particularly resented during the Christmas holidays?

Then, for students (and nowadays, nearly everyone in the country spends at least twelve years as one, and more are spending sixteen or even eighteen), certain rhythms that matter are established. Where else in our culture do people get promoted every year for anything better than dreadful work? Where else can people choose their bosses (professors) so as to avoid certain ones, and where else can they drop one of them with no penalty after several weeks work? If you look at the assumptions students naturally take with them to work from school, you can see why the yearly immigration of graduates into business is such a trauma for both students and companies. Subculture shock is what it is.

A subsummary may help here. Basically, all I am saying is that time is important to us in many ways, that *when* you do what you do says things to others about what you feel, and that the "rules" about time vary from setting to setting. If you will just watch for one day what is going on in your life vis-à-vis time, I think you will see some interesting things. How you and others use time to communicate would make a terrific din if "talking" with time made noise.

SPACE

Space is a language just as expressive as time. Indeed, as hinted above, it is hard to separate it from the language of time, but it is useful to try.

More Is Better Than Less

The chances are good that you have seen various business organizations. The chances are even better that you found the size of offices related to the status of people there. It is rare indeed to find a company president occupying a smaller office than his subordinates, and it is not uncommon to find the top person ensconced in a suite of rooms. One of the ways we "tell" about the importance of people is by the amount of space we assign to them. Space, like time, is a scarce and limited resource.

I recall a distinguished senior professor returning to school after a long and nearly fatal illness. He was being moved from his old office to a new one in an air-conditioned new building, largely because the dean of his school believed the air-conditioning would be of help to him. The professor may have thought he "heard" something else, for as I passed his office one day, I found him on his hands and knees measuring his new office with a twelve-inch ruler. It was a good deal smaller than his prior office, and from how he behaved later, I think he was "learning" that his illness had diminished his importance to the school, so that he was reduced to a smaller office. It would have been amusing if it were not so painful.

Another time, I was being shown through a new and beautiful office building of a large corporation. The president's office was handsome indeed, but when I was taken next door to the executive vice-president's office, I realized that the VP had a larger and recognizably more stunning space in which to work. I later asked my guide, an officer of the company, if the president and executive vice-president had been vying for power. He looked surprised and said defensively, "Why do you ask?" I told him what I saw in the use of space. He laughed and said, "Another theory bites the dust! The VP's office is better because he has charge of sales in this district, and his office is our best example of what we can do for customers."

A year later, the VP and president came into open conflict in seeking the support of the board of directors, and the VP left the organization. Of course, the offices were not the cause; but they were a signal that something was off. There are few organizations that can accept incongruence in the use of space when it communicates so clearly to hundreds of employees. In the company mentioned, I heard later, a frequent question in the executive ranks prior to the VP's departure was, "Who is running this place?"

Of course we observe this in everyday life. We want larger houses on more land. We want lots with a view. (Although I notice few people with a picture window looking out at the view. What we want, I suspect, is mostly the illusion of an enlargement of our space.) Yet other people are more comfortable in smaller spaces. Latin people love to be awed by cathedrals and vistas in parks, but they seem to enjoy being "hugged" by smaller rooms at home and at work. The smaller space is apparently associated with warmth and touch and intimacy, while larger spaces are associated with status and power and importance. Perhaps this is why entering a huge office intimidates many of us. We almost physically inflate the person who occupies it. In any event, there is a strong tendency in organizational subcultures to relate the amount of space assigned to individuals to their formal status or organizational height. Check this out around school or in any business. When the pattern doesn't hold, something interesting may be going on.

Private Is Better Than Public

As a doctoral candidate, I was first given a desk in a large room with many other desks, then was "upgraded" to a cubicle with six-foot walls and an open top, then to a private office. It was minuscule, but I could close it and be alone or private within it. When I began working as a professor, I shared an office with two others, then I shared it with one other, and now once again I have my own private office, roughly twice as big as my last one. Sequence and size are what matter here. It is "better" to have your own space than to share it, and it is "better" if it can be closed off for privacy than if it is open to the sight or hearing of others. And each "advantage" was distributed by rank, and by seniority within rank.

We use much the same thinking about country clubs or pools or university clubs. By excluding some others, on whatever criteria, we make it feel more private to us. And we apparently like that. The very process of exclusion marks the boundaries of our space, both physically and socially—and, of course, psychologically. When we say a person is "closed," we mean we are excluded from him or her, and vice versa. Thus, the process of defining the extent to which our various spaces are private is complex. As we set our boundaries, we also exclude. And we need our own space, as we also at times need to be "open." Yet in organizations, it is clearly the rule that private offices are better than public ones. To go from a large but public office to a smaller but private one is a mixed blessing, but often the balance is favorable. For we are not like Miss Garbo, wanting to be alone, but we do want *to be able* to be alone or private when we wish.

A powerful illustration of the value we place on privacy took place in the 1920s. A coal company in West Virginia owned the houses in which its miners lived. When the miners struck, the company took the doors off the houses. It is not hard to imagine the wrath of the miners. Another example is the automobile company that took the doors off the men's room stalls in the 1950s to discourage workers from long toilet breaks. The response in this instance was also very strong, and understandably so. When a space is designed for activity that is close to our body, we value its privacy all the more. Our free-flowing modern houses almost always have doors on at least two rooms—the bedroom and the bathroom. Perhaps that infamous "key to the executive men's room" is of more utility than arbitrary status.

Given the importance we attach to privacy, the way we use the space we have "talks" to others. If we have a private office and shut its door to speak with someone, we announce a message to that person and to those outside. We are saying, "This conversation is important and not to be overheard or casually interrupted." Neither the person nor those outside know whether the news is good or bad, but they do know that you care about it, and they may make unwarranted assumptions. For we close off our space for more private or personal behavior. Whether it is angry or loving, we intend to focus importantly.

Higher Is Better Than Lower

A few years ago, I watched my three-year old daughter playing "King of the Castle" with friends. They laughingly fought each other for position at the top of a small steep hill. Each wanted to be on top, to be higher up than the others—in this instance, quite literally, in space. When they grow up, I fell to musing, they'll jockey for height with less laughter and more discomfort.

Perhaps our desire to be higher rather than lower is inherited from our primitive ancestors, or perhaps it comes from such childlike games—or rather, from the important business of being little for so long, and thus less powerful than we might wish. In any event, houses higher on the hill, from Hong Kong to Corning, are "better" (and usually more expensive) than those below. The view is often cited as the reason, but I doubt it. It's more likely a residue of our childhood that probably reaches back in evolution far beyond the Greeks, who built the Acropolis on a sharp-rising rock for protection as much as grandeur. Much as dogs still circle about before they lie down to sleep (a still-visible link to their wild forebears, who circled to crush tall grass into a kind of nest), we seek height for reasons in large part lost to us.

We move up in organizations, or "climb the ladder." We go up to the head office and down to the shop. We call the wealthiest people the upper classes and the poorest the lower classes. Much of our imagery for what we value is in terms of up and down. People from Boston go "down" to Maine, although it is north of Boston. Allegedly this is because early travelers were referring to tides, but it also fits the notion of some Bostonians that Boston is the apex from which one can only go down.

On a more concrete level, the ground-floor, walk-in legal aid centers that have opened their doors in deprived neighborhoods are less frightening to prospective clients partly because of their ground-level location. Here again, space speaks. To be higher than you is to be better than you.

Near Is Better Than Far

Really, this one can be just the reverse of what it says. It depends upon whether sentiments are positive or negative. Near is better if the sentiments are positive. Far is better if the sentiments are negative.

In a business organization, it is not uncommon for the offices near the boss to be more highly valued than those farther away. If the chief executive officer is on the third floor, the others on that floor are also assumed to be privileged. They are closer to the top person and thus have more opportunities for informal interaction, as well as the formal designation of spatial assignment near the boss's space.

The same principle holds at formal dinner parties, where nearness to the host is valued. The farther down the table one is placed, the lower one's status at the dinner. In branch organizations that cover large territories, a common problem is that each branch develops internal loyalties greater than the loyalty to the head office. The distance from the center of the organization impedes communication.

Thus, when the sentiments are positive, being near is better than being far away. As I mentioned, the reverse can also be true. People prefer to increase distance when their sentiments are negative.

In Is Better Than Out

We seem to assume that people who work inside are better than those who work outside, perhaps because of the respective associations with mental and manual work. Baseball teams prefer to be in their own field, their most familiar space. Often, when we are uneasy or anxious, we move to our own space. In it we feel more secure.

The basic difference between in-out and near-far is that the former works from a specific point, whereas the latter is a matter of degree. But they are closely related. For example, a few years ago, a wedding was to take place in the side chapel off the main seating area of a church. The number of guests exceeded the number of seats in the chapel. So decisions needed to be made about who sat in the chapel and who sat outside it. There were thus created two "classes" of guests—those sitting inside and those sitting outside—yet within each class, there was a sliding scale at work. How close to the front of your class were you seated? I can tell you, those who sat at the back of the second class felt like relative outsiders. Certainly, they were not among the "in" group.

Interpersonal Space

Naturally, the five dimensions of space above are related. An office that is small but private and near an important executive may be highly desirable in spite of its size. When you consider the impact of space, you must look at the possible influence of each of the five dimensions, and how they can balance each other in specific settings, as well as how they influence the use of time as a language.

But on a more personal level, we have another silent language related to space. We have the general notion that we own the space around us, much like an invisible bubble. Others are to stay outside the bubble except when powerful feelings—of intimacy or anger—are being expressed. Touch is especially to be avoided in our culture, with the same exceptions. How many times have you sat next to a stranger in a movie theater and jockeyed for the single armrest? Since touching is out, it often ends up under the arm of the bolder person who risks touch.

I recall an amusing yet painful incident at a recent cocktail party. A woman newly arrived from Israel was talking with an American male of Swedish descent. Her conception of the proper distance from her face to his was about half the distance he apparently felt comfortable with. She would step in, he would step back. She virtually chased him across the room before they both gave up. She dismissed him as "cold." He saw her as "pushy." Each had a different notion of the appropriateness of distance given their relationship, and neither could feel comfortable with the other's behavior.

When someone with a different notion of the use of interpersonal space steps into our bubble, we feel either uncomfortable and crowded, aggressed against and threatened, or expectant of affection. Getting that close in the USA is for many a hit-or-kiss affair.

In addition, in our mouthwashed, deodorant-using culture, the idea of smelling another's body or breath is often thought to be repugnant. The experience is avoided except in lovemaking, and even there, many perfume away all traces of personal odor. Yet some people enjoy being close enough to others in public settings to feel their body warmth and smell their natural odors, and they touch others more often then we do. When we meet such people, we have a terrible time because they "say" things, in the way they use space, that we do not appreciate or understand. They, in turn, find us as difficult as we find them.

Within this huge country, there are many subgroups with variations in their use of interpersonal space. Men in the Italian district of

Boston often walk down the street arm in arm, something one would seldom, if ever, see around most universities in the Boston area. And in any large business organization, you can see the effects of variations in the use of space complicating relationships. A warm, expressive executive who feels comfortable touching the arm or shoulder of a subordinate may make him exceedingly uncomfortable if he is the non-touch, keep-your-distance type. You can watch your own behavior here to see how you use your own space and how you react to others who behave differently. Just being aware of it helps a great deal.

Since the American experience of smell, body warmth, and touch is so poorly developed, most of what we say to each other using these media does not take place in our awareness. But it does take place. Communication by smell, largely a chemical process, is far more extensive than we think. Edward Hall reports that in discussing olfactory messages with a psychoanalyst, a skillful therapist with an unusual record of success, he learned that the therapist could clearly distinguish the smell of anger in patients at a distance of six feet or more. Schizophrenic patients are reputed to have a characteristic odor, and Dr. Kathleen Smith of St. Louis has demonstrated that rats readily distinguish between the smells of a schizophrenic and a non-schizophrenic. If chemical messages are this powerful, one wonders how many of what we consider to be well-hidden feelings are being "telegraphed" by the smells we are unable to disguise.

If smell as a communicator is out of awareness, how much more so is the skin as a major sense organ. Yet the skin has remarkable thermal characteristics; it apparently has an extraordinary capacity to both emit and detect infrared heat. Under stress or strong emotion, we can send out thermal messages that can be "read" by perceptive people (usually spouses, lovers, or children) who can get within two feet. Getting "red in the face" in anger or embarrassment or sexual arousal is so common we hardly think about it. Yet the coloration of skin talks too.

In summary, remember that people use space to say things they are often unaware of, but highly responsive to. To the extent that you can become more aware of your own behavior and that of others, you can be more skillful at "saying" what you mean to others and "hearing" what they mean. It is a fascinating exploration.

THINGS

This aspect of communication is so easily grasped that I will just briefly present ten rather obvious generalizations. Each points to what I see as a major assumption operating in our culture. Each naturally has exceptions, and each interacts with the others much as the various dimensions of space modify outcomes, and relate to time.

Bigger Is Better Than Smaller. The automobile is a good example in the United States. Except for small sports cars, bigger cars (which, see below, are often more expensive) have been generally regarded as better than smaller; giving up the use of a "gas guzzler" during a fuel shortage is considered a brave sacrifice.

More Is Better Than Fewer. Two cars, two houses, and so on, are better than one.

Clean Is Better Than Dirty. The American fetish under attack.

Neat and Orderly Is Better Than Messy and Disorderly. A clean desk may communicate efficiency, while a messy one may "say" you are disorganized in many settings.

Expensive Is Better Than Cheap. Original works of art are "better" than reproductions.

Unique Is Better Than Common. Ditto.

Beautiful Is Better Than Ugly. Ditto.

Accurate Is Better Than Inaccurate. Back to Acutron.

Very Old or Very New Is Better Than Recent. Victorian furnishings are now old enough to be of increasing value, after sixty years of being "recent."

Personal Is Better Than Public. One's own object—say, chair or desk—is valued as a possession. In offices, as in homes, the boss or host often has "his" chair, and others usually stay out of it. The news photo of a student sitting in the chair of the president of Columbia University during the 1969 uprising was used so often because it showed someone breaking this "rule."

SUMMARY

Just as the various aspects of space are interrelated (remember the small but private office near the boss?) and influence the uses of time as language, so, too, do both overlap with our use of things. If that same office near the boss has an expensive, one-of-a-kind Persian rug and antique furniture, it can become even more valued even though it is small.

The way we and others use time and space and things talks. If you are deaf to the messages, you miss much of the richness of what is being said by you and others. If you start "listening" consciously, you can begin to appreciate more of the subtle languages that are in use and thus gradually increase your personal intuitive skill in being with other people in and out of organizations.

BIBLIOGRAPHY

HALL, EDWARD J., *The Hidden Dimension.* New York: Doubleday, 1966.

———, *The Silent Dimension.* New York: Doubleday, 1959.

SOMMER, ROBERT, *Personal Space: The Behavioral Basis of Design.* Englewood Cliffs, N.J.: Prentice Hall, 1966.

STEELE, FRED I., *Physical Settings and Organization Development.* Reading, Mass.: Addison-Wesley, 1973.

Chapter Two

Communication: The Use of Body Languages

A firm moved its offices from an old building to one of the new skyscrapers that define Atlanta's skyline. Putting aside for the moment the many considerations of space design and their implications, the firm concerned itself with the most up-to-date means of communications, among them an interoffice intercom system. The intercom was indeed efficient, for it cut down the need for traveling between one person's office and another, which, in these considerably larger quarters, could mean a long walk. Access to one another involved simply the buzz of an intercom. Group discussions could be initiated at a moment's notice. Those who were unavailable or otherwise occupied could be quickly determined. The intercom also provided flexibility, for it did not tie people to the phone receiver but rather allowed them to move around their offices, perhaps to locate relevant files while carrying on a conversation. In short, it saved time and served to "close the space" between people—a noteworthy use of time, space, and things. It was greeted with enthusiasm.

Over time and after a number of misunderstandings, however, a major drawback became apparent. Communication was largely dependent on *words.* Tone of voice helped the message along, but the people communicating with words couldn't see one another. Verbal messages were being sent and received while their nonverbal counterparts were effectively ignored. And so a whole dimension of communication was virtually omitted.

Living and working with others is a process of communication, and most of us think communicating is largely a process of saying and hearing, reading and writing, *words*. Yet we communicate with one another in a number of languages that are not verbal. Communication includes the use of five "language systems": words, time, space, things, and the use of the body. The combination of these forms a fugue that has different meanings to different people. In this chapter, we will consider how body language "talks." But before we get into the specifics of body language, we will look at how body language, as one means of communication, relates to behavioral communication as a whole. First, we will consider our need for increased awareness of a language that we use largely unconsciously and largely unintentionally, and thus overlook or take for granted. Second, we will consider body language as an *interdependent* part of a scheme of communication, which we *learn* in our process of socialization—although, once again, we are largely unaware of doing so. Third, we will consider the relationship between perception and communication—the process by which we make meanings from how we "see" another person.

TOWARD INCREASED AWARENESS

Much of what we communicate to others is through the use of our bodies. The movement of our eyes, hands, legs, our facial expressions, our overall stance, all send signals for others to interpret. Not only *can* we express nonverbally just about every important emotion experienced by human beings, but we do so all the time, even if we are largely unaware that we and others are doing so.

Communication involves the sending and receiving of a message. Although we can shut our mouths and send no verbal message, it is hard to shut off the nonverbal messages we send or shut out those we receive. Further, the problem of "hearing" or "being heard" can be even greater for nonverbal messages than for verbal ones, owing to our tendency to be relatively unaware of how we send them and how we interpret others' use of them. A nonverbal message can be sent and/or received with relative awareness, with relative lack of awareness, or any degree between the two extremes. A nonverbal message may be sent but completely missed by the intended receiver. Or the receiver may "hear" a nonverbal message that was never intended by the sender. It is important to remember that *message* can refer to the meaning that a person intends to send, the form the communication takes, the form in which it is received, or the meaning the communication has to the receiver (see Exhibit I-1). On the other hand, the nonverbal aspect of a message may help to clarify the verbal message, but will not necessarily ensure that the meanings taken by the receiver will duplicate the intended meanings of the sender. Any messages received will be interpreted by the receiver and given *his or her* meanings. The amount of distortion possible is great, and in this respect,

Exhibit I-1

Sending and Receiving Nonverbal Messages

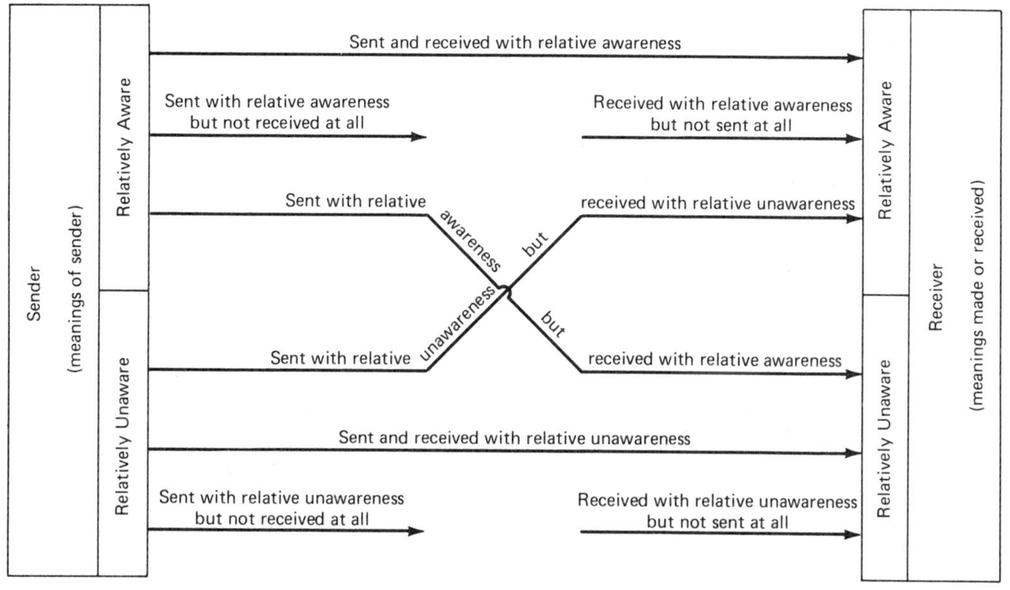

nonverbal communication is troublesome. One step in the direction of increasing understanding of others and ourselves is to increase our awareness of how we send and receive nonverbal messages, as well as how we each take different meanings from the messages we receive.

The trouble is that as we grow, we are much more aware of learning a verbal language than we are of learning nonverbal language. Yet research by Ray L. Birdwhistell and Albert E. Scheflen indicates that languages of movement are often as ordered as those of speech. And a child must learn the "patterned interdependence"[1] of both before gaining acceptance into our society at large. The emphasis here is on the *pattern* involved, for Birdwhistell has thoroughly demolished the notion that communication is the building of a vocabulary of words and movements:

> Communication control is not achieved through a simple additive process which involves the accumulation of parcels of sound or body motion which carry encapsulated chunks of meaning. Nor is it the slightly more complex matter of hooking together these pieces called "words" and "gestures" into little meaning trains called sentences. I use the word "simple" here in derision, for if this were the way we had to incorporate our communicational system, the human life span would not be long enough to permit us ever

[1]Ray L. Birdwhistell, "There Was a Child Went Forth," in *Kinesics and Context,* p. 5. Philadelphia: University of Pennsylvania Press, 1970.

> to achieve such control. Human culture is possible because we do not have to do it this way—because we learn in a patterned way.[2]

That is not to say that we all communicate in exactly the same way. Far from it. Patterns differ across cultures, ethnic groups, geographical regions, families, age groups, and sex. What is important is to be aware of these differences and be able to "translate" their meanings.

One starting point in the process toward awareness is perception. How we perceive others and how others perceive us is, in large part, a function of our use of body language. We all emit so many cues about ourselves simultaneously via our clothes, hair styles, facial expressions, body movements, postures, and positioning that we are a kind of "walking ad" of how we *wish* to be seen. Either intentionally or unintentionally, we "express" ourselves, and others are "impressed" in some way.[3] Impressions are formed on the basis of the expression we "give" *and* the expression we "give off."[4] These are two very different types of symbolic expression, the former consisting of the words we speak, the latter consisting of nonverbal signs, more subtle and vague, which we often communicate unintentionally or unconsciously. We then feed these signals into our personal scheme of impression formation, interpreting them through a kind of veil of our prior experience, preconceptions, or stereotypes. Whatever our impressions, we use them to make *judgments* from which we respond to the other person. The other in turn responds to us, setting in motion a cycle of expressing and impressing that forms the basis for our gathering information about each other—information that helps define the situation and, given the situation, our expectations of one another. In effect, from perceptions made through some pattern of nonverbal communication, we make meanings about who we are, who others are, and how we stand in relation to them.

Our relationships with others determine our body language at times; at other times, our body language determines the nature of our relationships. Closely related is the context in which the relationship is set at the moment. Depending on the situation and our reaction to it, our body language almost automatically falls in line. Again closely related to the way in which we use our body is our emotional investment in, or our attitude toward, a given situation. We can nonverbally indicate acceptance or rejection, approval or disapproval, like or dislike, respect or lack of it, fear, impatience, anxiety, suspicion, embarrassment, anger, hostility, repulsion, affection, and on and on and on, and we do so with remarkable effectiveness. We can initiate, maintain, change, and otherwise structure and control a relationship or situation with the help of nonverbal cues. For example, an astute salesman may

[2]*Ibid.*, pp. 6, 7.

[3]Gustav Ichheiser, "Misunderstandings in Human Relations," Supplement to *The American Journal of Sociology* September 1949, pp. 6–7, as found in Erving Goffman, *The Presentation of Self in Everyday Life* (New York: Doubleday, 1959), p. 2.

[4]Goffman, *The Presentation of Self in Everyday Life*, p. 2.

intuitively mirror his customers' gestures to help establish an atmosphere of congeniality. A conference leader can indicate the end of a meeting in many ways, depending on the body signals he gives—turning away, getting up, or just looking bored. And as relationships vary and situations change, so do the meanings we attach to them. It is impossible to consider the meanings attached to body language apart from the relationship, the context, and the people involved. There is no *one* meaning that any sublanguage can be regarded as communicating with certainty to all people. Therefore, some caution should always be used in inferring intentions or mood solely from a person's body behavior. Inferences need to be made, obviously, in the context of what is being said, the people involved, and the situation.

Let us next consider some of the basics of body language and the generalizations people tend to make from them.

THE BASICS OF BODY LANGUAGE

The ways in which we use our body to send messages are more extensive than we might think at first glance. Following are some of the ways we most commonly communicate via body language.

"It Was Written All Over His Face"

The face is the most richly expressive part of our body. Our facial expressions, as well as specific facial cues, qualify and amplify the spoken word. Because understanding is increased by the availability of facial expressions and cues, it is no wonder that we like to see as well as hear the person with whom we are talking. For this reason, we sometimes feel uncomfortable dealing with certain transactions by telephone (recall the earlier example of the intercom). Likewise, television has changed the nature of political campaigns. Disagreement over which presidential candidate is trustworthy centers on the "look in the eye" or the "smile on the face." Certain situations call for a certain facial expression—consider the "look" associated with a funeral as compared to that for a wedding.

Moving from overall facial expressions to specifics, every feature of our face communicates. A furrowed forehead can indicate concern, anger, frustration. Raised eyebrows together with a wide-eyed look express surprise or astonishment. A wrinkling nose can point to mild dislike or displeasure. Flared nostrils are usually interpreted as a sign of anger, but in another context, one of sexual arousal. Lips clamped, tightly drawn, or pursed can signal anything from uncertainty or hesitancy to secrecy, depending on the context and other accompanying body cues.

The smile is a complicated gesture, capable of expressing obvious pleasure or subtle cynicism, innocent embarrassment or the promise of attack. The smile of the Mona Lisa is probably the most famous example of such ambiguity. Birdwhistell has shown that the meaning of smiles varies across geographical regions of the United States and is closely tied to regional assumptions about relationships.

> "In New England you're likely to have more smiling among familiars and less with strangers," Professor Birdwhistell suggested. "A Southerner or a Midwesterner will be noticed in New England and in the Great Lakes region for his extraordinary propensity to smile.
>
> "Southerners think they're friendlier because they smile, and New Englanders think they're more reserved because they don't," he went on. "I'm not sure either is true. I think the smile is used a good deal in the South as a device for reducing aggression and anger. The so-called reserve in New England doesn't mark unfriendliness but a hesitancy to engage in personal relationship which seems inappropriate.
>
> "Southerners are probably not more hospitable than New Englanders are; they are simply more willing to remind you of the fact they're being hospitable.
>
> "In Manhattan," the professor suggested, "the mask of nonparticipation is fixed, and New Yorkers are stereotyped as an unmannerly group. A New Yorker outside New York who smiles a great deal is considered as 'selling.' If he doesn't smile a great deal it won't surprise anyone."[5]

A person's eyes are a powerful means of communicating, for they can signal everything from intimacy to rejection. As such, *when we look* and *when we don't* have meanings that can vary dramatically with relationships, situations, and cultures.

> A woman who had taken part in a civil rights demonstration reported that she was advised, if a policeman confronted her, to look straight into his eyes. "Make him *see* you as another human being and he's more likely to treat you as one," she was told.[6]

Looking acknowledges the other as a person. It generates a "special kind of human-to-human awareness."[7] Catching the eye of a stranger—a hitchhiker, for example—recognizes his presence but limits the relationship to a fleeting one, at best. Holding someone's eye can be an invitation to extend a relationship in a variety of ways. Looking patterns differ when we talk and when we listen, when we initiate an interaction or accept the consequences. It is a way of giving and receiving feedback, both positive and negative. It is a way of establishing control. Golda Meir, former prime minister of Israel, described her visit with the Pope:

> "Everything went off in meticulous quiet, in holiness. But we gazed at each other frankly. His eyes bored deep into me, and I looked back with an

[5] Israel Shenker, "What's in a Smile," *New York Times*, July 13, 1972.

[6] Flora Davis, "How to Read Body Language," *Glamour*, September 1969.

[7] *Ibid.*

open, strong, honest gaze, and I decided I would not lower my eyes under any circumstances. And I didn't."[8]

How we look and how we are looked at has a lot to do with our needs for approval, acceptance, trust, and love—and we usually react accordingly. Looking is a nontactile way to "touch" another.

Looking away or not looking at all is a clear-cut sign of lack of interest, of distancing oneself from another. Avoiding eye contact is a way of hiding true feelings, especially discomfort or guilt. People who feel insecure about themselves will avoid eye contact in a threatening situation but seek it when the situation is to their advantage. In such a way, characteristics of self-concept can be expressed through body language.[9] However, some caution must be used in making inferences about eye contact. Scheflen points out that these meanings differ across culture and social class.[10]

Hand Talk

Hand gestures have won the Italians due fame, but they are used by other cultures to a greater or lesser extent.[11] But the meanings of hand gestures differ across cultures so much so that the unsuspecting tourist can convey unintended messages. A Thai friend winced whenever I pointed my index finger at the children when reprimanding them. The pointing finger is a gesture of extreme insult in Thailand. Studies have shown that poking is a frequent and accepted gesture among Jewish Americans for maintaining a listener's attention.[12] Scheflen has pointed to the ethnic variations in hand gestures among immigrant Americans and how these serve to differentiate—in fact, separate—them from what he terms the "mainstream British-American system of communicational behaviors and meanings. . . . WASPs of the middle class do not gesture broadly like Italian-Americans or as frequently as eastern European Jewish-Americans. Many middle-class WASP children are actually taught not to gesticulate because it looks 'foreign' or is 'impolite.' "[13] Further, because gestures take long to "unlearn," telltale cultural signs persist as long as three generations, despite attempts to assimilate.

Some hand gestures are more obvious and less ambiguous in meaning than others—the hitchhiker's thumb is a prime example. The

[8]*New York Times,* Saturday, January 20, 1973.

[9]Michael Argyle, "Eye Contact and the Direction of Gaze," in *The Psychology of Interpersonal Behavior* (Baltimore: Penguin, 1970), pp. 105–16.

[10]Albert Scheflen, *Body Language and the Social Order* (Englewood Cliffs, N.J.: Prentice-Hall, 1972), pp. 95–96.

[11]Many of the examples in this and the next two sections were drawn from Gerard I. Nierenberg and Henry H. Calero, *How to Read a Person Like a Book* (New York: Cornerstone, Febuary 1971).

[12]Scheflen, *Body Language,* p. 44.

[13]*Ibid.,* p. 88.

handshake is almost universally a gesture of greeting, but its general meaning breaks down quickly when we consider variations in kind and appropriateness from one country, situation, or sex to another. The confusion over whether or not a man should initiate a handshake when meeting a woman, or vice versa, can prove amusing, depending on one's point of view. We tend to associate strength of character and a sense of decisiveness with a firm handshake. A clenched fist in normal interaction is a pretty clear indication of hostility or anger. Under other circumstances, depending on the context, it can be a sign of determination. And among some subgroups, it has come to signify feelings of solidarity. Hand-wringing usually signals worry—concern combined with a sense of stress and expectancy.

Other hand gestures are somewhat less obvious but nonetheless reveal an inner state or attitude. Opening one's hands to another can indicate openness, sincerity, and acceptance. Punching your own palm is an emphatic gesture. Joining fingertips to form a "church steeple" can indicate confidence or superiority. Tapping one's fingertips can indicate nervousness or tension. A hand-to-mouth gesture can be read as surprise, while covering one's mouth can be read as concealment or nervousness. Resting a hand on one's face can point to boredom or extreme interest, depending on how it is done and the expression on the person's face. Placing hands on hips can be an expression of readiness or aggression.

From Hands to Arms . . .

Raising one's hands in a surrender gesture means just that. It expresses an "I give up," "What more can I say or do?" feeling. Folding your arms across your chest (aside from being a comfortable way to sit) is also a protective or defensive gesture—consider the traditional image of a baseball umpire. Both arms behind the back, combined with locked hands, can command authority or indicate an attempt at self-control. Sitting with your arms up and your hands supporting the back of your head is a comfortable, relaxing position, which can indicate a degree of informality and also a degree of superiority, depending on the context.

From Arms to Legs . . .

In our culture, crossed legs are probably the most observable leg gesture. It is curious to note that the ways Americans cross their legs differ from the ways Europeans do, and the ways males cross their legs differ from those of females. People tend to be self-conscious about how they cross their legs, and this is related to the feelings associated with the gesture—formality, competition, tension. Crossed legs combined with crossed arms may be the epitome of an adversary or defensive pose. In contrast, an informal, cooperative, relaxed, and unconcerned atmosphere can be signaled by sitting with one leg draped over the arm of a chair.

Foot-shaking, like finger-tapping, indicates boredom, impatience, or nervousness. Further, studies of body behavior show that people use their bodies to define territorial rights. For example, considerable research has shown that a boss whose feet are on the desk signals authority, dominance, superiority, and ownership of space, as well as comfort and ease. If we look around us, we can find many more examples in our everyday living. The next step is to put them together in relation to the person as a whole.

From the Parts to the Whole

A person's total appearance—even when he remains motionless—can communicate. The size and form of another's body can affect the inferences we make about that person's character, attitudes, and temperament—in short, personality. A former student, well over six feet in height, had a very large head with a prominent bone structure especially noticeable in the jaw, and a long and very thick neck. His arms were longer than seemed "average" and his legs a bit shorter than his torso and arms seemed to require. Arms, legs, and torso were very muscular. And he had played football in college. His complaint was that fellow students just looked at him and assumed he was "a jock," which often meant to them "stupid" as well as "athlete," and consequently they ignored him. The fact that he majored in religion, wrote poetry that had been published, and seemed an unusually sensitive, aware, and intelligent person was apparently discovered by relatively few of his fellow students. His body "said" all that many apparently needed to "hear." Unfortunately, whether or not the stereotypic judgments people make are correct, these judgments influence communication.

The way we carry ourselves, our posture, can give away feelings about us. For example, a student's body posture as well as the expression on his face can tell the instructor if the student is "with" the discussion or someplace else. Similarly, our way of walking can vary with our mood. A hands-in-pockets shuffle can signal dejection or preoccupation, and a bouncing step can signal carefree happiness. Birdwhistell claims that our postures, as with our facial expressions, are *learned* responses reflecting our inner state of being, as well as our culture and inheritance. However subtle, they are a way of asking others to respond to us according to the way we see ourselves. More often than not, it works.

Posture often influences the perception of both liking and status. When talking, leaning toward the other is often felt or seen as an indication of positive feelings. Relaxation of posture is a good indicator of both attitude and status, and can be observed by focusing on a number of body clues, including muscular tension in the hands, amount of forward lean, sideways lean, and, for women, open or closed arm position. Some studies suggest that a person relaxes either very little or a great deal when speaking with someone he dislikes, and that a person relaxes to a moderate degree when speaking with someone he likes. It seems that extreme tension occurs in the presence of threatening persons, and extreme relaxation with those who are both nonthreatening and disliked. As for status, both research and common sense tell us that people relax most with a low-status addressee, second most with a peer, and least with someone of higher status than their own.[14]

Clothes are an extension of self. The manner in which we choose to dress is closely related to how we hope others will see us. Our perception of the demands of a situation is probably the greatest influencing factor in our choice of dress. A businesswoman described to me how her conservative, well-tailored wardrobe gives way to jeans and a body shirt immediately upon her arrival home. In some respects, she "changes people" when she changes clothes.

Even our sense of direction or path motion sends signals. Studies have shown that judgments about personality and character are made on the basis of how an individual moves. A straight-line path was associated with everything from direct, well-reasoned, logical, and ambitious to dogmatic, narrow-minded, and preoccupied. A "meandering pattern" was associated with everything from happy-go-lucky, curious, and sociable to careless, untrustworthy, and immature.[15] Consider these jumps from seemingly simple events to inferences and the variability of the meanings made from them. It seems that, in viewing another, we put together all these signals—specific gestures, posture, physique, and movement, and make judgments from these behaviors. Furthermore, we tend to respond to another person as if our judgments were valid.

INTERACTING NONVERBALLY

Body language is promissory in nature; "it signals something about the relationship that is to follow."[16] Nonverbal cues often represent elements of an entire action that may or may not ever be carried through.[17] For example, "courting gestures," such as hair-smoothing on the part of a woman, or a hands-on-hips stance and squared shoulders on the part of a man, *may* be a promise of things to come. What we call "flirting" is a mixture of courting gestures and qualifiers that in effect set the boundaries of a relationship. Such cues give those

[14]A. Mehrabian, "Communication without Words," *Psychology Today*, September 1968, pp. 53–55.

[15]Renato Tagiuri, "Movement as a Cue in Person Perception," in H.P. David and J.C. Brengelman, eds., *Perspectives in Personality Research* (New York: Springer, 1960).

[16]Scheflen, *Body Language*, p. 64.

[17]The ideas in this paragraph come from Scheflen, *Body Language*, Part I, Chap. 1.

involved an opportunity to encourage or discourage the suggested relationship. If a woman touches her hair in such a way that she attracts a particular man's attention, he, in effect, has her permission to take the next step forward. If he reciprocates her cue, the relationship can progress. "Reciprocal" behaviors can also be used to communicate dominance and submission, can point to a real threat of hostility or to a playful warning to "watch your step." The next time you see a police officer giving a ticket, watch the nonverbal language going on. Humans (as well as other forms of animal life) engage either consciously or unconsciously in such "reciprocal interchanges," in which symbolic gestures are responded to in kind by two people in a face-to-face interaction.

Reciprocal interchanges can serve many purposes.[18] When we are completely in tune with another, we may adjust our body movements to the other person's words as well as gestures. When this occurs, it is called "interactional synchrony."[19] When synchrony wanes, so does our level of rapport. We can shut out or shut off another by a frown, gaze avoidance, or defensive body cues. We can encourage, maintain, modify, or change a relationship by sending cues that simply don't belong to the situation at hand. Consider a member of a discussion group who shifts away from the others, casts her eyes to the floor, and dangles the report under consideration. Part of the person is somewhere else. She may be tuned out, bored, or preoccupied. Whatever, the message is that something is "off."

It has often been said that it is easier to lie with words than with our body. Our body language tends to betray our true feelings. Freud wrote:

> He that has eyes to see and ears to hear may convince himself that no mortal can keep a secret. If his lips are silent, he chatters with his fingertips; betrayal oozes out of him at every pore.[20]

Body language and verbal language can complement or contradict each other. As an example, consider a person who expresses anger through eyes, hands, and body stance, but denies it verbally. Once, while driving with my mother, I stopped short—but not short enough—and hit a truck in front of me. Although I expressed a lack of concern, my shaking and sudden paleness belied the restraint of my words. On the other hand, a former professor of mine expresses his interest or annoyance with a class discussion quite congruently. When he is pleased, a subtle smile may come over his face, which is matched by his eagerness to respond to student comments. But the circles under his eyes seem to grow literally larger as the discussion wanders from the point at hand. It is the interplay between body

[18]The ideas in this paragraph come from Scheflen, *Body Language,* Part II.

[19]Defined and studied by William Condon.

[20]Flora Davis, "How to Read Body Language," *Glamour,* September 1969.

language and words that is crucial to an understanding of what is going on within an individual.

So far, we have dealt with two of our five senses, sight and hearing. But we experience the world and communicate messages through our sense of touch and, to a somewhat lesser extent, smell and taste as well. Touching is the meeting point between our use of space and body language. We all have a sense of the personal space we need between us and another individual. The situation at hand and our relationship with the other person are important variables in determining how much space is appropriate. Touching, in our culture, conveys intimacy and so is carefully governed by "rules and regulations." However, these are informal rules of which we are not always aware.

When we are forced to touch in a public space, we respond by keeping within the context. On a crowded street or subway, we turn the other into a thing, a "nonperson," to defend against what might be interpreted by one or the other as inappropriate intimacy. In the context of this situation, the touching is perfectly permissible (but not always comfortable for those involved). In a private space, touching is usually by choice and meant to communicate feelings. When I greet a friend with a hug, my feelings of warmth and closeness are quite literally expressed. Messages conveyed by touch communicate in very immediate and powerful ways.

Touching varies with status and age. The touch of a doctor is impersonal and professional. Adults feel free to touch children—pick them up, hug them, ruffle their hair—although the child may not always appreciate this adult liberty. Our 4-year-old was once whisked up and hugged by a former high school teacher of mine whom we happened to meet on the street. To Jackie, this man was a total stranger, and I should not have been surprised when he asked why "that man who doesn't know me loves me so much." The message sent by my teacher and the message received by Jackie were quite different. Adolescents tend to be sensitive to and about touch, both across and within sexes. American women tend to touch tentatively and American men largely avoid touching one another except in the context of sports. Birdwhistell comments on the need to touch:

> Behavioral scientists sometimes speak these days of a phenomenon called skin-hunger. And certainly the young in their great ritual gatherings at places such as Woodstock seemed to need and take comfort in what one man called "the warmth of assembled animal bodies." But anthropologist Paul Byers speculates that it's actually the old who suffer most from skin-hunger in our society. They're touched perhaps less than anyone—in fact, it sometimes seems as if people are afraid old age might be contagious—and this literal loss of concept must add greatly to the old person's sense of isolation.[21]

Americans are not a touching people. But touching and the messages it conveys vary greatly across cultures. Latin Americans and

[21]Flora Davis, "Touching and Smelling," *Glamour,* January 1972.

southern Europeans are known to be much freer than we are in their sense of touch. It is interesting to note that the high school teacher in the story above is a first-generation American of Italian descent.

IN CONCLUSION, A WORD OF CAUTION

Any attempt to interpret body language must be tempered with caution. Birdwhistell warns us, "... no position, expression, or movement ever carries meaning in and of itself."[22] Its meanings are *within* the person, the person as a *whole*. To assume we know what a gesture "means" is overstepping the bounds of usefulness, for meanings drawn from body cues are ambiguous and, oftentimes, multiple. Progress by Birdwhistell, Scheflen, and others toward the codification and analysis of body movements has carried us far in our awareness and understanding of nonverbal communication.

No position, expression, or movement can be considered in isolation. Communication is a "multichannel system"—body language is but one channel, interdependent with our use of time, space, things, and verbal language.

> We get an entirely different picture of communication if we recognize that communication is not just what happens in one channel. . . . Communication, upon investigation, appears to be a system which makes use of the channels of all the sensory modalities. By this model, communication is a continuous process utilizing the various channels and the combinations of them as appropriate to the particular situation.[23]

Thus, body language is an inextricable part of a network of communication expressed from within the context of a *particular* individual in a given situation and relationship.

Perhaps what can best be carried over from this review of body language to our everyday world of interpersonal relationships is a greater awareness of the many ways in which we use our body to communicate—the similarities and differences from person to person, and culture to culture. This awareness of body language as a means of communication can sharpen our understanding of the judgments we make, as well as sensitize us to what we intentionally or unintentionally communicate to others.

BIBLIOGRAPHY

ARGYLE, MICHAEL, *The Psychology of Interpersonal Behavior.* Baltimore: Penguin Books, 1970.

BIRDWHISTELL, RAY L., *Kinesics and Context.* Philadelphia: University of Pennsylvania Press, 1970.

[22]Birdwhistell, "There Was a Child," p. 45.

[23]*Ibid.,* p. 70.

DAVIS, FLORA, "Body Music," *Glamour,* February 1972.

———, "How to Read Body Language," *Glamour,* September 1969.

———, "Touching and Smelling," *Glamour,* January 1972.

———, "Why Husbands and Wives Look Alike," *Woman's Day,* September 1972.

FAST, JULIUS, *Body Language.* New York: M. Evans & Co., 1970. Distributed in association with J. B. Lippincott, Phila. and N.Y.

GOFFMAN, ERVING, "On Face-Work: An Analysis of Ritual Elements in Social Interaction," in *The Self in Social Interaction,* Vol. I, Chad Gordon and Kenneth J. Gergen, eds. New York: John Wiley, 1968.

———, "The Presentation of Self to Others," in *Symbolic Interaction,* Jerome G. Manis and Bernard N. Meltzer, eds. Boston: Allyn & Bacon, 1972.

MEHRABIAN, A., "Communication without Words," *Psychology Today,* September 1968.

NIERENBERG, GERARD L. and HENRY H. CALERO, *How to Read a Person Like a Book.* New York: Cornerstone Library, 1971.

SCHEFLEN, ALBERT E., M.D., and ALICE SCHEFLEN, *Body Language and the Social Order.* Englewood Cliffs, N.J.: Prentice-Hall, 1972.

SECORD, PAUL F. "Facial Features and Inference Processes in Interpersonal Perception," in *Person Perception and Interpersonal Behavior,* eds. Renato Tagiuri and Luigi Petrullo. Stanford, Calif.: Stanford University Press, 1958.

TAGIURI, RENATO, "Movement as a Cue in Person Perception," *Perspectives in Personality Research,* H.P. David and J.C. Brengelman, eds. New York: Springer Publishing Company, 1960.

Chapter Three

Communication: The Use of Words

I
know
you believe
you understand
what you think
I said
but I'm not sure
you realize
that
what you heard
is not what I meant.

—Religious Public Relations Council, Inc., New York

WORDS ARE SYMBOLS . . .

A word may be defined as a symbol that stands for something and should convey the meaning of the thing. Words become meaningful symbols when the relationship between the word and the thing it stands for can be agreed upon by two or more people. We have all as children played the original word game,[1] whereby we learn by trial and error, by imitation and repetition, to fit the correct name to the correct thing. My son, aged 2, still uses "words" that remain meaning-

[1]Roger Brown, *Words and Things* (New York: Free Press, 1958), p. 194.

less noises to me, for I cannot determine the things corresponding to his words. On the other hand, lovers the world over can testify to the creation and use of a private language, agreed upon between them for intimate communication. A word needs a thing to turn a meaningless noise into a meaningful symbol, and users of that symbol must be in agreement on the relationship between the word and the thing in order to communicate well.

. . . But the Word Is NOT the Thing

The artist Magritte made a graphic representation of a pipe used for smoking and, as part of his painting, wrote underneath the pipe, "*Ceci n'est pas une pipe*" ("This is not a pipe"). His point is well made and crucial. Neither his picture of the pipe nor the word standing for it can be smoked. "The symbol is not the thing symbolized; the word is not the thing; the map is not the territory it stands for."[2] I dread following directions to someone's house because their verbal map often does not fit my view of the actual territory. If told to "turn east," I feel lost. If told to "turn right off Chestnut Hill Avenue onto Beacon Street," I'm fine. Giving directions serves as a constant reminder that my map is not the territory, but at best merely a more or less useful description of it. To conclude the analogy, words are like maps. The map is not the territory it represents; nor is the word the thing it stands for.

This deceptively simple "first commandment of semantics" is mislearned early and put into frequent practice. Consider the following examples:

- S.I. Hayakawa, a general semanticist, reports the following vignette in his book: "I asked my eight year old, could the sun have been called 'moon' and the moon 'sun?'[3] He answered, No, we'd be confused between the morning and the night." Here the word was confused with his experience of the thing.

- "When you're out of Schlitz, you're out of beer" is a recent example. Advertising directly encourages us to react to the word as if it were the thing.

- A child who is called "stupid" long enough may come to think of himself as such. Another's judgment becomes reality. Another's word become the thing. In this regard, clear denial of reality is present in the chant, "Sticks and stones may break my bones but words can never hurt me."

- A friend, active in the feminist movement, was describing her endeavor in the area of part-time work. "We're going to do away with the term 'part-

[2]S.I. Hayakawa, *Language in Thought and Action* (New York: Harcourt Brace Jovanovich, 1964), p. 30.

[3]Jean Piaget, "The Child's Conception of the World," in S.I. Hayakawa, *op. cit.*, p. 33.

time work'; we're changing it to 'readjusted hours.'" Words alone cannot change the thing. But if words are sufficiently confused with the thing, we can then use them as powerful tools to change *our thinking* and *feeling* about the thing.

. . . and What We Say Is NOT What We Experience

Just as the word is not the thing, what we say is not what we experience. However accurately our words report our experience, the words can never *be* that experience. Words can never fully express all that can be said about anything. We could continue ad infinitum to speak words about words, to give reports about reports, to react to our reactions without ever fully describing our experiencing.[4] That is not to say that words are not an important tool in communicating what we can of our experience—they are. But they are only a partial expression of that experience. What actually takes place is not at the verbal level, but at an "unspeakable level."[5] The unspeakable level is the first-order experience; thinking about it, the second-order experience; words, the third-order experience. The words, "I love you," for example, have a hollow ring in comparison with the experiencing of those words. It is like trying to describe the color blue or the taste of lobster. The often-used expressions, "I simply can't describe it," and, "I can't tell you how I felt," are accurate reflections of the ultimate futility of putting experience accurately or completely into words. Words can never express all that can be said. Nonverbal communication helps, but eventually our capacity to describe and define runs out, and we reach a point at which "we 'know' somehow, but cannot tell."[6] Our words are not containers for our experiences; they are not boxes into which our experiencing can be poured. For experience flows and, in comparison, words are static.

The problem is that we tend to take the words we use for granted. We hardly notice them at all. We take them as givens as we assume that they accurately capture what the other means, or is experiencing. This is especially true of the words we use daily, which we accept without question, while we tend to be more analytical about technical language. We tend to use words automatically, with little or no awareness of how their uses can limit or hurt us and others. This tendency stems in part from the basis that words have in the common experiencing of many. Yet much of the complexity of communication, as we shall see, stems from the fact that the same word often has different meanings for different people.

[4]S.I. Hayawaka, ed., *Language, Meaning and Maturity* (New York: Harper & Row, 1954), p. 27.

[5]Alfred Korzybski, *Science and Sanity*, 4th ed. (Lakeville, CT: The International Non-Aristotelian Library Publishing Co., 1962), p. 34.

[6]*Ibid.*, p. 21.

In many ways, words are a kind of "conditioned stimuli, and successful communication depends on complementary conditioning or . . . complementary experience."[7] In the broadest historical sense, man passes on his culture through the use of words. Konrad Lorenz describes the "invention" of language:

> The truth is that one day a little ape suddenly began to reflect, to form conceptual thoughts, to invent words—and, little by little, conceptual thought and tradition were integrated into an immense system that now permits all the miracles of culture. . . . The appearance of language made it possible to maintain a tradition independent of environment.[8]

People have the capacity to use words to recall the past and capture the present—to bind themselves from one generation to another over time.[9] Within a culture, words are developed from common experience and used to shape subsequent common experience.

In a more practical, everyday context, our common experiencing makes it possible for us to reach a basic agreement upon the relationship between a word and a thing. Our agreement then makes it possible for us to share some of our experience. The most obvious example is that of a child who expands his or her world by relating words to experiences common to the culture. When children learn that "snow" is "cold" and "fire" is "hot," they in effect match their experience with ours in a way that can be shared with nearly all English-speaking people.

Common conditioning may be a fine springboard toward successful communication, but it only carries us so far. For while we may often agree on a common language and largely share a common experience, the *meanings* I draw from the experience and attach to the words I use may be very different from yours. "Snow," for example, may mean "sledding" and "snowmen" to a child, "skiing" to my neighbors, and "nuisance" to me. At some point, common conditioning gives way to individual experience, and the shared meaning of words gives way to the personal meanings we make inside of us. While common experience within a culture makes communication possible, individual experience varies enough to make it difficult.

Words are personal. They are the symbolic expression of events inside our skin. Even the most simple word takes on different images for different people, depending on their past and present experienc-

[7]Alfred Upton, *Design for Thinking* (Stanford, Calif.: Stanford University Press, 1961), p. 85.

[8]"A Talk with Konrad Lorenz," *New York Times Magazine*, July 5, 1970.

[9]Alfred Korzybski, the father of general semantics, called this capacity of people "time-binding."

ing. Consider the word "chair." The mental images people create in response to that word can range from a simple wooden kitchen chair to the Eames chair, a molded, wood-and-leather architectural extravaganza. Although there is some common cultural agreement on the meaning of "chair," there are also vast differences in the particular meanings different people attach to that symbol at any given moment.

Extensional Meanings

In the language of semantics, the symbol "chair" when used to refer to a specific thing illustrates the *extensional* meaning of a word: the physical reality the word stands for. The extensional meaning of a word is that which we can verify by fact or observation. If we point to a chair and keep silent, we rely on a gesture and the thing—not the symbol for the thing. When we use a word to stand for the same thing, we can give the word "chair" its extensional meaning.

Intensional Meanings

The *intensional* meaning of a word is the image the word evokes in our mind. Intensional meaning refers to the goings-on inside us, which cannot be verified by external physical presence. Intensional meaning centers on the *word and our reaction* to it, rather than the word and a physical reality outside us. "Chair" has extensional as well as intensional meanings; "democracy" has only intensional meaning. Consider the different intensional meanings illustrated by the very different forms of government that are called democracies. The ways in which "democracy" has been used and misused are largely based on divergent intensional meanings.

Because each of us has a rich and complex collection of intensional meanings, we have, in effect, our own internal "semantic environment."[10] The words we use are not merely "a bundle of sounds," but "a bundle of associations."[11] These associations grow from experience, both common and individual. Common experience will provide an overlap in meanings; personal experience will provide differences that will vary the meanings for any two people. The trouble is that we tend to go about ignoring the differences and assuming the similarities. Listening to another's words and providing them with only *your* meanings is a near-perfect formula for some degree of misunderstanding.

Listening for another's meanings as well as your own is a difficult

[10]Hayakawa, *Language, Meaning and Maturity,* p. 18.

[11]Mario Pei, *The Story of Language* (Philadelphia: Lippincott, 1965), p. 139.

task. It requires, to some extent, entering someone else's world, and sensing and sharing what the other is experiencing. At the same time, listening hard enough to narrow the gap between another's meaning and your own requires an awareness of what your own "semantic reactions" are. To consciously assume that differences exist in meanings is by far a safer rule of thumb in communicating than to unconsciously assume similarities.

Contextual Meanings

Making meanings is a complicated affair, for it is not only a function of *what* we refer to and *who* uses a word, but *how* it is used as well. *What* points to the physical reality of the symbol used (extensional meaning). *Who* points to the differences in meaning attributable to personal input (intensional meaning). *How* points to the differences in meaning attributable to the context and form of usage. A dictionary will provide you with technical differences in usage—what a word has stood for over time. But words standing alone have little functional meaning. It is their usage in a sentence, their context and connotation, that give them an intended, *contextual* meaning.

Some words may stand for almost anything until context narrows the range of possible meanings. Examples are "business," "deal," "thing," "matter," "concern." Recently, the Gay Activists Alliance of New York was denied a request to be certified as a nonprofit organization. One basis for the rejection stated by the court was, "The name of the corporation is not acceptable since it is not an appropriate name for a corporation when one considers the connotation in which the words are being used."[12] The word "gay," in this context, became unacceptable to the court. Just as context can account for change in the meanings of words, it can also imply the correct meaning. There are times when the relation between context and meaning is so direct that we may omit or incorrectly use the word and our meaning will still be clear. Typographical errors are hard to catch because we tend to read the correct word contextually. A friend reports proceeding through a reception line murmuring, "Dreadful, isn't it?" while smiling and shaking hands, only to be smiled at and told, "So nice to see you."

Context makes the difference between definition and meaning. To presuppose the meaning of a word, given its definition, is at best guesswork. Making meaning is a process in which we react to, interpret, and evaluate the word, the thing, the idea, the event, the context—*extensional, intensional* and *contextual* meanings all rolled into one. We, in effect, make our own meanings in a complex way. These meanings do not come to us like a present, gift-wrapped in a word. We are our own "meaning makers" to a large extent.

[12]*New York Times,* February 25, 1971.

The power of words operates on many levels in many ways. As we have already seen, words can help and words can hurt. Jean-Paul Sartre wrote:

> The serious error . . . is to think that the word is a gentle breeze which plays lightly over the surface of things, which grazes them without altering them, and that the speaker is a pure *witness* who sums up with a word his harmless contemplation. To speak is to act; anything which one names is already no longer the same; it has lost its innocence.[13]

"Playing around with words" is not a harmless game. The use of figurative language, directive language, and "social noise" can be powerful tools in influencing what we and others feel, do, and think.

Figurative language encourages us in many ways to confuse the word with the thing. The simile, defined as a form of description that makes use of comparison, is so common that we hardly notice its use. Simile makes it easy to slip from the figurative to the literal and act as if the comparison were the thing.

- Believing a dog is "gentle as a lamb" could prove to be painfully inaccurate.
- Andy, aged 11, describes his school as "like a prison" and then proceeds to act as if the simile *were* his school. His (presumably) exaggerated value judgment could serve to alter his *perception* of reality, and thus influence significantly his subsequent *experiencing* of school.

The similes we make out of our awareness can distort our experience. Yet the similes we become aware of can broaden and deepen our experience. Alexander Portnoy reports one of the more innocent but, to him, surprising events in his life:

> Did I have a good night's sleep? I don't really know, I have to think—the question comes as something of a surprise. Did I Have A Good Night's Sleep? Why, yes! I think I did! Hey—did you? "Like a log," replies Mr. Campbell. And for the first time in my life I experience the full force of a simile. This man, who is a real estate broker and an alderman of the Davenport town council, says that he slept like a log and I actually *see* a log.[14]

Metaphors place words in unexpected contexts. The common meaning of the word suggests one meaning; its use (or context) quite another. Some metaphors have become so common that the word's

[13]Whit Burnett, ed., "The World's Best," p. 727, in J. Samuel Bois, *Explorations in Awareness* (New York: Harper & Row, 1957), p. 200.

[14]Philip Roth, *Portnoy's Complaint* (New York: Random House, 1969), pp. 220–21.

contextual meaning ceases to seem a metaphor to us any longer—we seldom think of the original meaning of the word:

- Benjy, aged 5, asked the other night at supper if he were sitting at the "head" or "foot" of the table. The metaphor at the moment "went over our heads."

- A friend told me that she casually mentioned to her child one evening that "Daddy was tied up at the office." The child, obviously concerned and rather indignant, asked, "Who did that? Let's go untie him!"

- Baseball is filled with metaphoric language: He flied to center, popped the ball to the infield, shot it to second base.

- Churchill's use of the phrase, "Iron Curtain," captured the imagination of the English-speaking world and influenced the thinking of a generation.

Metaphors can serve to add emotional impact to the word itself:

- Consider the personification of a nation—"motherland," "fatherland." Aldous Huxley makes the point: "In the form of a person, the idea of nation can arouse much stronger feelings than it can evoke when it is spoken in more sober and accurate language."[15]

- From poetry, e.e. cummings was a master of semantic surprise:

  "this young question mark man"[16]

  "My sweet old etcetera
  aunt lucy during the recent war . . ."[17]

  "All knowledge toboggans into know
  and trudges up to ignorance again"[18]

Directive language—choosing words for the purpose of directing behavior—is a revealing example of the power of words.

- Hitler used "verbal ritual" to spellbind a nation. His word became a people's thing. "All the savagery and brutality of which men are capable can be released once they believe in the word as spoken or written, without regard for what that word represents."[19]

- Advertising campaigns and much of our social and political system depend upon the directive power of words charged with meanings: "radical," "democrat," "establishment," "right-wing," "revenue sharing," "housewife," "career woman," "working mother," "success," "power elite," "the system," "the corporation," "remember the name, because you will never forget the taste," "be a drop-in," etc., etc.

[15]Aldous Huxley, "Words and Their Meaning," in *The Importance of Language,* ed. Max Black (Englewood Cliffs, N.J.: Prentice-Hall, 1962), p. 11.

[16]e.e. cummings, *Poems 1923–1954* (New York: Harcourt Brace Jovanovich, 1954), p. 177.

[17]*Ibid.,* p. 197.

[18]*Ibid.,* p. 412.

[19]Irving Lee, *Language Habits in Human Affairs* (New York: Harper & Row, 1941), p. 172.

Being aware of how words are used permits us to modulate the power that words can have over us. Words themselves are simply the innocent symbols for the not-necessarily innocent meanings we or others impose on them. But as long as we are naive about their use, we permit them to be agents of manipulation, misunderstanding, and even violence.

Some Special Uses of Language

Social noise is talking simply for the sake of saying something. It can be synonymous in some instances with talking non-sense, but in other instances, it can perform useful, sometimes powerful functions. First, talking for the sake of talking can prevent an awkward silence. Think of a dinner party at which the conversation suddenly dies. Assuming that this dinner party aims to provide pleasant conversation among a group of people who come together as casual acquaintances, silence is socially and psychologically unacceptable. Silence in such a setting can seem very loud and long. The words that revive the conversation will be welcome almost without regard for what they say. Words, almost any words, will be welcome for the silence they fill.

Second, social noise can pave the way for more significant conversation and more meaningful relationships. When we "pass the time of day," we may be filling the silence gap or we may be using words to grow accustomed to and feel comfortable with another's presence. Often, in the time it takes to exchange "Hi, how are you?" "Terrible weather, isn't it?" we can pick up enough nonverbal cues to decide whether to proceed with more meaningful talk or not. In an interview situation, for example, the preliminary remarks provide a testing ground, a chance to "get a feel for the other," to set the tone for the ensuing conversation. When we meet a friend after a long absence, the "How have you been?" and "How's the family?" simply give each other a chance to "re-touch," to reestablish a past relationship. Hayakawa characterized such social noise as "presymbolic,"[20] since its purpose is not the transfer of information, but rather creating the sense of being together.

Social noise is sometimes expected in given cultures, and there are forms for it. Knowing the "proper" responses can be important, ignoring them insulting. For example, in the United States, "We must get together sometime" usually calls for a "Yes, let's do that." An Israeli friend of mine would respond instead, "When?" and expect a time and date to follow. In fact, she considered the vagueness to which we are accustomed a sign of insincerity. She was initially unaware of our use of this form of social noise, which by its very tentativeness allows the flexibility of meeting again or not (depending on the wishes of those involved) while at the same time making "friendly" noises.

[20]Hayakawa, *Language in Thought and Action,* p. 72.

Social noises can become a ritual. My next-door neighbor and I almost always greet one another with a three-minute discussion about how the grass is doing, how the children are, or how his golf game is this season. This ritual has become established to the extent that its inadvertent omission could amount to a downright snub. Or if you always greet the elevator operator with, "Good morning, nice day," but one day pass silently, the silence might prove troubling. On the other hand, another neighbor of mine is always so much on the go that my conversations with her tend to cut through all the social noise and come right to the point at hand. Depending on how a relationship develops, social noise can be a valuable ritual or an unnecessary bother.

Talking simply for the sake of saying something performs useful social functions. We can limit or expand the boundaries to a relationship, depending on our use of social noises. The usefulness of social noises is hard to accept by those who believe they should always have something significant to say or stay silent. Sometimes we can "say" a great deal by saying very little.

Slang is the special use of a word or expression that sometimes becomes as common as the more general meaning of the word. But the general meaning can be very different indeed.

- A college student from Thailand who baby-sat for us was really thrown (note the metaphor) by our use of such words as "buck" for dollar, "bellyache" for complain, and "kid" for child.

- Slang usage can load a word with value judgment; take the transfer of "pig" to describe a policeman or other authority figure, as an example.

Jargon refers to the specialized vocabulary of a trade, profession, area of business, or study. Its use makes communicating within an area easier and more efficient, and this is a most important advantage indeed. But it also increases the difficulties of outsiders' understanding what is meant. Partly as a result, it is sometimes used to enhance an insider's standing with outsiders, as some lawyers' clients will testify. It can also be used among insiders for much the same effect. "Buzz words" "make a pleasant buzzing sound in our ears when we roll them on our tongues but communicate very little to the hearer about the subject under discussion."[21] Consider the following sentence:

- "An in-depth resource analysis will reveal how the strategic plans should interface with the tactical plan."[22] Even an insider might wonder what that means, but feel hesitant to ask. Somehow the use of currently chic jargon implies that another *ought* to know what is meant—even when it is inappropriately overused and thus simply "impressively saying nothing."[23]

[21]T.H. Barton, "Eloquently Put, Sir . . . But How's That Again?" *Think*, March–April 1970.

[22]*Ibid.*

[23]*Ibid.*

• Sometimes, previously existing phenomena, seen by someone in a new and different way, call for the specialized use of an old word or a completely new word. Sociologists, for example, used the word "norm" not in the sense of its common meaning (i.e., "average behavior"), but rather in terms of a specialized meaning (i.e., "what one ought to do under given circumstances").

Cant refers to the supposedly secret, or at least relatively private, vocabulary of groups of people who are usually somewhat informally organized and partially bound together by their special language. Cant characterizes such groups as the organized crime syndicate, fraternal lodges, religious groups, and some subcultures. Adolescents seem especially inventive in this regard, and keeping up with their vocabulary is sometimes difficult.

• An article in the *New York Times Magazine* entitled, "If You Think It's Groovy to Rap, You're Shucking,"[24] presents a glossary of terms divided into three categories: "Archaic" (dating back to the mid-1960s), "Standbys," and "New." The article points to the fads that words rapidly go through, and how cant can give away your place in a spectrum the author labels "beat-hippie-freak."

• The secret word begins to spread, being used awkwardly at first and then more naturally by others outside the "in" group. Young addicts, for a time, had the relatively private use of "smack" for heroin. A few years ago, a middle-aged man talking about "grass" could seem to others of his age group to be "putting them on." Then again, two children I know, after a drug education course in school, refer to "grass" as naturally as those who smoke it. The word is no longer cant, having spread widely in usage.

Cant is valued particularly because of its function in excluding others and binding its users closer together. Perhaps that's why we enjoy stealing others' cant and turning it into our own slang.

LANGUAGE IN PROCESS

So far, we have considered how the *meanings* of words can change as a function of personal experience and context. We have considered how the *power* of words can change owing to figurative and directive usage and social noise. However, both the power and the meanings of words change over time because of technical or colloquial specialization.

Words are related to and are a reflection of the time. The meanings of old words change as we make them change.

• Some words keep their old meanings and take on additional ones—"cool" and "grass" are obvious examples.

[24]Mike Jahn, "If You Think It's Groovy to Rap, You're Shucking," *New York Times Magazine*, June 6, 1971.

- Others, over time, reverse their original meanings. "Manufacture," now associated with machinery, originally meant "to make by hand."[25] "Administration," now associated with authority and control, comes from the Latin "to serve." "Nice" comes from the Old French *niais,* meaning "silly," and originally from the Latin *nescius,* meaning "stupid" or "not knowing."[26]

- Given enough time, words can almost change their sex. The word "virtue," from the Latin *vir* ("man"), began by meaning "manliness," then specialized to mean "fortitude" or "warlike prowess," and later varied to mean "power," even "magical power."[27] The most commonly retained English usage of "virtue" is "conformity of life and conduct with the principle of morality," with the interesting specialization, "chastity, sexual purity, especially in women." [The Shorter Oxford English Dictionary]

- New and sometimes surprising insights can come from a look into the history of a word. For example, "manage" comes from an Italian word, with one early meaning being "to lead horses." (Contrasting this archaic usage with the original definition of "administration" can trigger new insights.)

- New words come into being as we need them to describe new phenomena. For example, "supermarket" combined two old words into one new one.

The point of this is that the words we use to speak about other things also tell much about ourselves as human beings. Walt Whitman wrote:

> Language is not an abstract construction of the learned or of dictionary makers, but is something arising out of work, needs, ties, joys, affections, tastes of long generations of humanity, and has its basis broad and low, close to the ground.[28]

The meanings we bring to words, the powers we give them, the words we create, and the words we abandon reflect our social behavior and in turn influence it. Common experience may imply "true" meaning, and social convention may prefer it. But *a* "true" meaning is a fiction. Meaning is plural. And thus, communication is complex. The problem of such complexity is perhaps to be valued as part of the wonder of the diversity of human beings.

BIBLIOGRAPHY

BARTON, T.H., "Eloquently Put, Sir . . . But How's That Again?" *Think,* March–April 1970.

BROWN, ROGER, *Words and Things.* New York: Free Press, 1958.

BURNETT, WHIT, ed., "The World's Best," in J. Samuel Bois, *Explorations in Awareness.* New York: Harper & Row, 1957.

[25]Example from Pei, *The Story of Language,* p. 143.

[26]*Ibid.,* p. 145.

[27]Example from S. Robertson and F. Cassidy, "Changing Meanings and Values of Words," in Leonard F. Dean and Kenneth G. Wilson, *Essays on Language and Usage* (New York: Oxford University Press, 1959), p. 56.

[28]Walt Whitman, *Complete Prose Works* (Philadelphia: David McKay, 1897).

CUMMINGS, E.E., *Poems 1923–1959,* First Complete Edition. New York: Harcourt Brace Jovanovich, 1954.

HAYAKAWA, S.I., *Language in Thought and Action.* New York: Harcourt Brace Jovanovich, 1964.

———, ed., *Language, Meaning and Maturity.* New York: Harper & Row, 1954.

HUXLEY, ALDOUS, "Words and Their Meaning," in *The Importance of Language.* ed. Max Black. Englewood Cliffs, N.J.: Prentice-Hall, 1962.

JAHN, MIKE, "If You Think It's Groovy to Rap, You're Shucking," *New York Times Magazine,* June 6, 1971.

KORZYBSKI, ALFRED, *Science and Sanity,* 4th ed. Lakeville, Conn.: The International Non-Aristotelian Library Publishing Co., 1962.

LEE, IRVING, *Language Habits in Human Affairs.* New York: Harper & Row, 1941.

PEI, MARIO, *The Story of Language.* Philadelphia: Lippincott, 1965.

PIAGET, JEAN, "The Child's Conception of the World," in S.I. Hayakawa, *Language in Thought and Action.* New York: Harcourt Brace Jovanovich, 1964.

ROBERTSON, S., AND F. CASSIDY, "Changing Meanings and Values of Words," in Leonard F. Dean and Kenneth G. Wilson, *Essays on Language and Usage.* New York: Oxford University Press, 1959.

ROTH, PHILIP, *Portnoy's Complaint.* New York: Random House, 1969.

"A Talk with Konrad Lorenz," *New York Times Magazine,* July 5, 1970.

UPTON, ALFRED, *Design for Thinking.* Stanford, Calif.: Stanford University Press, 1961.

WHITMAN, WALT, *Complete Prose Works.* Philadelphia: David McKay, 1897.

Chapter Four

Problems of Communication in Interpersonal Behavior

Most people who work in organizations, and particularly managers, are in relationships with a wide range of people. Typically, a manager works with subordinates and important peers whose input, support, and cooperation are vital to his effort. Others he works with include his own boss and other important seniors who are in positions to allocate scarce resources, influence important decisions, and provide advice and support. Even a portfolio manager in a financial institution (who is likely to have few, if any, direct subordinates) must rely heavily on analysts, researchers, and outside contacts to perform effectively.

The value of interpersonal effectiveness and communication seems fairly apparent. Not so obvious, however, is what a person can do to develop and maintain effective interpersonal relationships.

PROBLEMS OF COMMUNICATION

Almost everyone has experienced interpersonal conflicts and misunderstandings in both his personal and professional life. So pervasive is this phenomenon that it takes up a disproportionately large amount

Several of the ideas presented in this chapter draw heavily from "A Note on Communication," 4-474-013, by Prof. Renato Tagiuri of Harvard University; and *Interpersonal Behavior and Administration* by Arthur N. Turner and George F.F. Lombard (New York: Free Press, 1969). Special acknowledgement is given to Eileen Morley, who assisted in preparing an earlier draft of this chapter.

of space in the literature written for and by managers. Indeed, the expression "communication problem" is now used so commonly that it is often applied to just about any difficulty that exists between people, whether or not a communication problem actually exists. Not all interpersonal problems or conflicts are communication problems. Two managers may have difficulty working with each other for many different reasons. They may understand each other extremely well (and therefore not have a communication problem), but one of them may not act as the other wishes. Take, for example, the following possibilities:

- Political infighting and power struggles: Two people do not really want to reach a resolution, because each wants the other to "lose" for political or other reasons. Each might understand the other's intentions and needs quite well. The real agenda in such a situation is to increase one's own power and resources at the expense of the other.
- "Personality conflicts": For reasons of a psychodynamic and unconscious nature, two people may have a propensity to dislike each other's personal styles, personality predispositions, or personal techniques. Again, each person may understand what the other wants, but they may still have difficulty working together.
- Conflicting goals: Two people may have goals that are so much in conflict that it is difficult for them to collaborate. This may not be because they do not understand each other's position, or have failed to communicate needs. Indeed, they may understand and communicate very well; it is just that neither likes what the other does, says, or wants.

Many other examples could be given of interpersonal problems that are not, strictly speaking, problems of communication. The problems listed above involve influence, trust, intention, and competition over scarce resources. However, many, if not most, of the interpersonal difficulties managers face actually do involve problems in communication or in understanding another person's point of view. This chapter will focus explicitly on problems of communication.

"Effective" Communication vs. "Good" Communication

Renato Tagiuri, a specialist in interpersonal perception and communication, has presented a useful distinction between "effective communication" and "good communication."[1]

> The major common concern is with effective communication. And it is a suitable concern for people in management and administration who are constantly trying to use communication to obtain specific results. When a communication does obtain the intended outcomes, it can be properly called "effective." But effective communication requires in most instances "good" communication, which means that party B has understood a concept that party A wished to convey to B.

[1]Renato Tagiuri, "A Note on Communication," 4-475-013, ICCH, 1972.

> "Good communication" is a prerequisite but does not insure "effective" communication. If A said to B, "Jump out the fourth floor window," B would probably not do it unless there were a fire and no other escape alternatives. Yet if we can assume that B has understood A perfectly well, this communication was "good" but not "effective." It is important not to confuse "good" with "effective" communication, for the latter includes aspects of behavior such as persuasion, motivation, power, coercion and the like. . . .
>
> In practice it is not easy to separate the communication process itself from other processes involved in effective communication. But the "communicator" should be alert to this distinction.

If we assume that "effective" communication depends, at least in part, on "good" communication, it is worth considering what gets in the way of good communication and causes misunderstandings. As a way of doing this, let us look at an actual situation in which good communication did not occur and carefully examine what took place. The situation involved two people in a work situation, and although the setting and names have been changed, the important elements of the story remain the same. The relationship between these two people was not an intimate one, but it was nonetheless important in each of their lives. As you read about what took place in this situation, imagine if you will that it is not just a case, but that it involves a company in which you are employed, that you are well acquainted with the men concerned, that you like them both, and that you care about the outcome.

Tom, Steve, and an "Opportunity"

Tom Ellery was vice-president of sales and Steve Watson was a regional sales manager in charge of four district managers. Steve reported to one of three area managers who, in turn, reported to Tom. Tom had followed Steve's career with interest and considered him one of the best sales managers in the company. It was not surprising, then, that Steve's name came immediately to mind when Tom received a memo from the marketing VP asking for recommendations for someone to take over the marketing services department.

Marketing services employed about 400 people and provided promotional support and special services to the sales division. In terms of salary grade, the position was one level higher than regional sales manager, so it would offer Steve a promotion. Tom thought Steve was the ideal candidate for the job for several reasons. First, people in both the marketing and sales divisions felt marketing services had become unresponsive to the sales division's needs. The department was now more of a bottleneck than a service, and Steve's extensive experience as a sales manager would give him a clear idea of what kind of support the department ought to be giving. Second, the department had begun to suffer from an "image problem," which Steve's transfer could do much to correct. Marketing services had developed a reputation for being a place where people were assigned when they ceased being effective in product management or in field sales. Putting an acknowledged "comer" like Steve in charge of the department would go far toward dispelling that image. The position would also provide Steve with an opportunity for wider corporate exposure and the ability to influence total company marketing and sales efforts.

After consulting with the marketing VP, Tom sent Steve a copy of the original memo, with the added note, "Are you interested? I think you're the best person for the job. Come by and let's talk about it." Tom was pleased that his own division was finally strong enough to allow him the flexibility to offer one of his best men to another division. It had taken three years of systematically identifying weak spots and moving strong new people like Steve into them to provide this luxury, and he planned to make the most of it.

Pause for a moment before you read on and consider what assumptions Steve might make on receiving the memo, and what his feelings might be. Note them briefly on a separate paper.

A few days later, Steve came by to discuss the memo. Tom was surprised to find Steve uninterested in the transfer, and slightly curt and ill at ease as well. Steve began by saying he didn't think he had the background to do the job and that he still had a lot to do in the region before he felt he could move on to another position. Sensing that Steve might be a little anxious about moving into the marketing division, Tom went into more detail on the reasons why he thought Steve could handle the job and do it well. Steve remained unconvinced, however, and as a last resort Tom suggested that Steve talk with the marketing VP before making a final decision. Tom couldn't help feeling annoyed at the end of the conversation, and found himself questioning his original judgments about Steve's flexibility and adaptability.

Pause for a moment more and consider what inferences and assumptions Tom is making about Steve's response, and why they lead to feelings of annoyance.

To Tom's continued disappointment, Steve's talk with the marketing VP failed to change his mind, and Tom began to feel his relationship with Steve becoming strained. Soon Tom noticed Steve was avoiding him in the company cafeteria, and seemed especially silent in his presence. About a month later, Tom received a call from Steve's area manager saying that Steve had resigned to take a position with a competitor.

Consider what perceptions and assumptions could lie behind Steve's action. How do you sense Steve feels in taking such an action?

Tom later learned from a mutual friend that Steve had left because he had concluded that his career with the company was finished when Tom offered him the marketing services job.

Did you deduce this from what went before? How do you think Tom felt when he heard the news?

A Case of Misunderstanding

A misunderstanding had taken place, the roots of which we can't begin to understand without getting a better sense of what Steve was experiencing before and during his dealings with Tom. To begin with, Steve had no serious intention of moving to another company until after the memo from Tom arrived. On the contrary, he was very satisfied with his career in the company. He had enjoyed his work and had received two promotions within three years. Why then, did his interpretation of the transfer differ so much from Tom's intention?

While Tom saw the transfer as a recognition of Steve's performance, Steve saw it as a sign that his past performance was not good enough. Steve had reasons on which to base this supposition. As long as Tom Ellery had been in charge of sales, he had never transferred an *effective* sales manager out of the division—only ineffective managers. Steve, like other sales managers, was very much aware of Tom's practice of identifying weak areas and bringing new life to them in the form of new managers. Indeed, he had been a major beneficiary of this policy and was one of the people who had advanced rapidly as a result. But now he wondered if it was his turn to be replaced as a regional sales manager. He had accepted his promotions and Tom's praise as clear signs of approval, but now he wondered if Tom had been less satisfied than he had seemed. The thought that this might have been the case angered him especially because neither Tom nor his area manager had given Steve any indication they were unhappy with his results.

The more Steve thought about the situation, the more suspicious and angry he became. If they wanted to get him out of the way, he could not think of a better place to send him than marketing services. Hadn't he joked with other sales managers about its being the burial ground for old product managers?

Steve's talk with Tom failed to dispel any of these suspicions. All Steve heard were Tom's attempts to sell him on the marketing services job and Tom's obvious annoyance when he refused the transfer. The whole series of events left him so suspicious and uncertain of his status that he decided to leave the company.

Understanding the Misunderstanding

The sources of this and other misunderstandings can be made clearer if we are able to describe and understand what each person *experienced* before and during the events described above. One relatively simple but effective way of doing this is by thinking about what each person experienced in terms of important *assumptions* he brought to the interaction, what he *perceived* as taking place, and what his *feelings* were during this series of episodes.[2] By *assumptions,* we mean the

[2]Arthur N. Turner and George F.F. Lombard, *Interpersonal Behavior and Administration* (New York: Free Press, 1969).

values, attitudes, and beliefs that a given person has about how things "ought" to be in a given situation. By *perceptions,* we mean what the person actually sees, hears, or otherwise perceives as taking place in a given situation (as compared to what he thinks ought to be occurring). By *feelings,* we mean the emotive and affective responses of a person in reaction to what happens in a given situation. In simplest terms, feelings are the emotions a person has that are triggered by what he or she sees taking place. These concepts of assumptions, perceptions, and feelings constitute what we will refer to in later chapters as an "assumptive frame of reference," and are closely related to both a person's self-concept and his individual frame of reference. (This relationship will be elaborated on in greater detail in subsequent chapters.)

What Tom Assumed, Perceived, and Felt. Tom's initial assumption was that he ought to recommend an outstanding man with sales experience for the job. He decided to recommend Steve, based on his perceptions of Steve's past effectiveness. He further assumed that Steve *ought* to see the transfer as an opportunity for further advancement and as recognition of his past achievements. Given these assumptions, it was not surprising that he further assumed that Steve *ought* to be pleased and interested in the transfer. When Tom perceived Steve reacting negatively to the offer, he felt surprised, because Steve's behavior was inconsistent with his own assumptions. When Steve failed to respond to his arguments for taking the transfer, Tom felt annoyed, and ended up questioning his original assumptions about Steve's flexibility and adaptability. Very possibly, Steve's behavior also may have threatened some of Tom's assumptions about his own ability as a manager and judge of people. Tom's annoyance no doubt reflected itself in his nonverbal behavior with Steve.

What Steve Assumed, Perceived, and Felt. Steve's assumptions (based on past perceptions) were that "effective" sales managers didn't get transferred from the sales division and that marketing services was an assignment for people the company wanted out of the way. Both these assumptions/perceptions were based on observations of what had taken place in the past and provided the basis for concluding that the transfer was a sign of Tom's dissatisfaction with Steve's past performance. But this conclusion was inconsistent with his own assumption about himself, "I am a good manager," and his perceptions of the feedback Tom and his boss had given him earlier. This conflict between his own assumptions and what he saw as the meaning of the transfer led him to feel surprise, anxiety, and threat.

Tom's behavior in the meeting (from Steve's point of view) gave Steve little reason to change his new assumptions; rather, it gave him further basis to reinforce them. Tom tried to "sell" the transfer, and appeared annoyed when Steve was not interested—behavior that could reasonably be expected from a man who wanted him out of the division. This led Steve to conclude that he no longer had a future in sales, and he resigned in anger to take another job. (The assumptions, perceptions, and feelings of these two men have been diagrammed in Exhibits I-2 and I-3, and it may be useful to look at these figures before proceeding.)

You may wonder how such a misunderstanding could possibly have occurred between two reasonably bright and probably sensitive people. Why didn't Tom explain his intentions better or anticipate how Steve's assumptions may have differed from his own? How could Steve so seriously misinterpret the offer? Admittedly, these were some of the same questions that first came to my mind. But these questions are reactions from *our* point of view about what took place. They deny the actuality of what each person must have experienced for the situation to develop the way it did.

Before thinking about how the problem could have been avoided,

Exhibit I-2

Tom's Experience

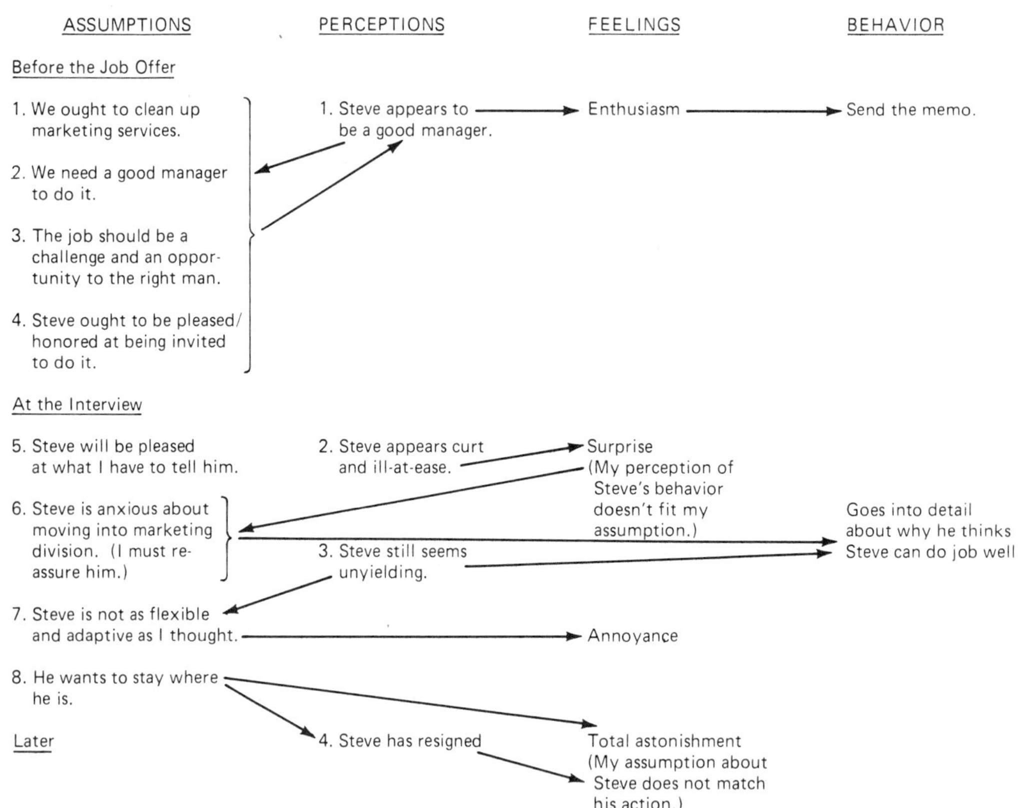
ASSUMPTIONS
PERCEPTIONS
FEELINGS
BEHAVIOR
Before the Job Offer
1. We ought to clean up marketing services.
2. We need a good manager to do it.
3. The job should be a challenge and an opportunity to the right man.
4. Steve ought to be pleased/honored at being invited to do it.
1. Steve appears to be a good manager.
Enthusiasm
Send the memo.
At the Interview
5. Steve will be pleased at what I have to tell him.
6. Steve is anxious about moving into marketing division. (I must reassure him.)
7. Steve is not as flexible and adaptive as I thought.
8. He wants to stay where he is.
2. Steve appears curt and ill-at-ease.
3. Steve still seems unyielding.
Surprise
(My perception of Steve's behavior doesn't fit my assumption.)
Goes into detail about why he thinks Steve can do job well
Annoyance
Later
4. Steve has resigned
Total astonishment
(My assumption about Steve does not match his action.)

Exhibit I-3

Steve's Experience

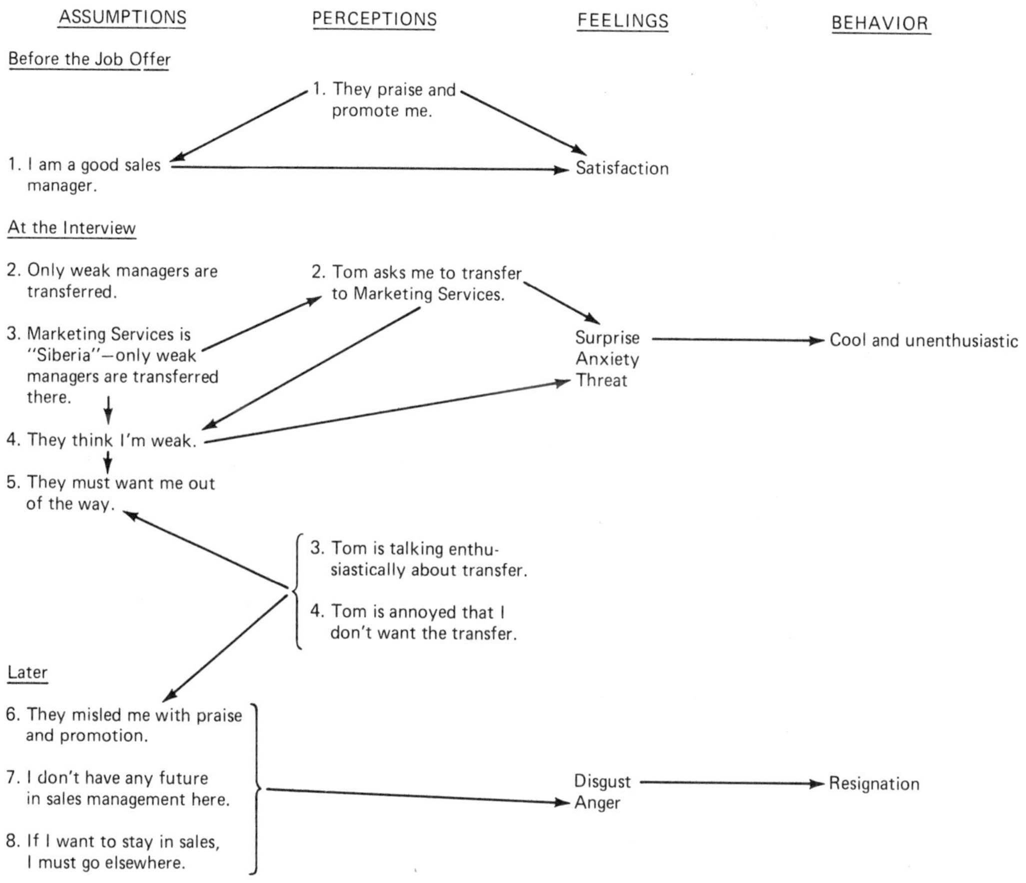
ASSUMPTIONS
PERCEPTIONS
FEELINGS
BEHAVIOR
Before the Job Offer
1. They praise and promote me.
1. I am a good sales manager.
Satisfaction
At the Interview
2. Only weak managers are transferred.
2. Tom asks me to transfer to Marketing Services.
3. Marketing Services is "Siberia"—only weak managers are transferred there.
Surprise
Anxiety
Threat
Cool and unenthusiastic
4. They think I'm weak.
5. They must want me out of the way.
3. Tom is talking enthusiastically about transfer.
4. Tom is annoyed that I don't want the transfer.
Later
6. They misled me with praise and promotion.
7. I don't have any future in sales management here.
8. If I want to stay in sales, I must go elsewhere.
Disgust
Anger
Resignation

try to develop an emphatic understanding of how each person was experiencing his feelings and perceptions in the relationship and how this influenced their behavior in relation to each other.

Try to imagine for a moment how each person might have experienced the situation. Imagine Tom's sense of surprise when Steve refused an offer that seemed to him a compliment and an opportunity; how it must have conflicted with his assumptions about himself as well as about Steve; how this surprise slowly turned to annoyance and possibly anger as he experienced what he saw as irrational behavior on Steve's part. Consider the strength of Steve's feelings in terms of the extent to which his self-concept as an effective sales manager was in jeopardy, and in terms of his expectations about his future, his sense of identity in the organization, and his ability to master a complex situation effectively; and how all were being challenged by his perceptions and assumptions about Tom's view of him.

FACILITATING UNDERSTANDING IN COMMUNICATION

Having had a glimpse of how each of the two people experienced the situation, it becomes easier for us to understand the misunderstanding. The actual situation as it was experienced by Tom and Steve was no doubt a great deal more subtle and complicated than this simple description implied. For example, our understanding of what happened would be sharper if we knew more about the personal histories of the two men and the expectations they had of their careers and broader lives.

However, even with the little information we have about the episode, we know a great more than either man knew at the time about some of the important differences in the way each was experiencing it. We have had the advantage of seeing some of the points of view and assumptions of *both* men, an advantage which unfortunately neither of them had until it was too late. The ability to recognize when important and disabling differences exist in assumptions is a skill that people seldom cultivate in their relationships with others. It is easy to do when the data are laid out as in a case, a film, or a story, or when they are "out there." But what do you do when you are one of the people in the relationship? Even more important, what do you do when you are part of the problem, as Tom and Steve were? What do you do when your own assumptions structure your perceptions and create feelings that prevent you from hearing or seeing how the other person's views and feelings differ from your own?

The simple, although not easy, answer to this question is to increase your awareness of what the other person is experiencing, of what his or her important assumptions, perceptions, and feelings are. This takes practice in trying to imagine the reality of the other person, and trying to keep separate your own point of view from how you think the other person might see it. Developing awareness is like any other skill; it requires practice in everyday interactions. There are also other actions you can take to minimize problems in communication that have to do with understanding the process of communication itself.

Assumptions about Communication that Impede Understanding

Much of the misunderstanding between Steve and Tom stemmed from their different sets of assumptions. Many of these assumptions were about the other's intentions and the specifics of what they were talking about—the transfer, what it symbolized, and its implications.

In a sense, these were assumptions about the *content* of what they were communicating to each other. To a great extent, all of us constantly make such assumptions in our relations with others. It could be argued that such "content" assumptions enable us to operate in a world in which we can never know in any total sense what the other person is experiencing, or how his or her specific meanings may vary from our own.

However, we also make assumptions of a somewhat different kind—assumptions about the *process* of communication itself. These are assumptions about what is taking place when two people talk to each other, rather than the specifics of what is being talked about. These "process" assumptions can be much greater barriers to communication than content assumptions, because they keep us from discovering that our content assumptions may differ;[3] and for this reason, they can be especially dangerous. For example, consider the following process assumptions we often make in day-to-day communication with others:

- That the other person perceives the situation the way we do.
- That the other person is making the same inferences and assumptions we are.
- That what is taking place should be logical from our point of view.
- That the other person is experiencing, or ought to experience, the same feelings we do.
- That the communication process in a given situation has little or no relation to other events in the situation, or to past history.
- That the other person's understanding of the situation ought to be based on our logic rather than the other's feelings.

Most of these process assumptions were implicit in Tom's behavior. They were more critical in impeding his understanding of how Steve experienced the situation than were the set of content assumptions in Exhibit I-2, because these process assumptions kept him from discovering how different his content assumptions were from Steve's.

The Tendency to Evaluate and Judge

One of the reasons why both content and process assumptions impede understanding is that we tend to pass judgments, based on these assumptions, on what we think others are saying without ever getting to hear *the other person's* underlying assumptions.

Carl Rogers, a therapist who has spent much of his career studying the process of increasing understanding and communication, has postulated that "the major barrier to mutual interpersonal communica-

[3]Carl R. Rogers and F.J. Roethlisberger, "Barriers and Gateways to Communication," *Harvard Business Review,* July–August 1952.

tion is our very natural tendency to judge, to evaluate, to approve (or disapprove)" of what the other person is saying. We approve when our perceptions of the other person's behavior fit our assumptions about how he or she *should* behave. We disapprove when they do not.

It is interesting to note that both Tom and Steve were most judgmental when they were experiencing strong emotions, and this is where the "rub" is. It is most difficult to listen nonevaluatively and refrain from passing judgment when feelings are strongest. And feelings are strongest when important assumptions are being violated. This is especially the case when what the other person is saying threatens us, because our defenses against anxiety are highest at those times. It is only by listening nonevaluatively that we can hear enough from the other person's frame of reference to begin to understand his or her assumptions, perceptions, and feelings. If, for example, Tom had been able to suspend his judgments and inferences about why Steve was reluctant and instead had inquired about Steve's lack of enthusiasm for the job, the misunderstanding might have ended there. If Steve had been able to suspend judgment of Tom's intentions long enough to hear him out, he might have discovered that Tom's intentions were quite different from what he assumed they were.

The difficulty, of course, is to be aware that our own *feelings* are signaling us that we are not really hearing the other person, and to shift our emphasis from focusing on our own reactions to focusing on the other person's concerns as well. Trying to hear the other's concerns is the first step toward listening less evaluatively and improving communication. This nonevaluative stance is a precondition to understanding another person from his or her point of view and for imagining what that person's reality is like. This does not necessarily mean that your view must agree with the other person's view of the situation, but it does mean suspending judgments in order to understand the other's point of view. For example, try putting yourself into the shoes of Tom first and then of Steve.

Sit back for a moment, and feel your way through Tom's experience:

- His initial enthusiasm for Steve's transfer.
- His hopes for the marketing services group.
- His surprise and disappointment at Steve's lack of enthusiasm and curtness.
- His need to reassure Steve about his ability.
- His irritation when Steve remained unresponsive.
- His disappointment when Steve's interview with the marketing VP failed to influence Steve's decision.
- His gradual estrangement from Steve around the company.
- His final astonishment when Steve resigned.

Now put yourself in Steve's shoes and follow the same process. Try to recreate within yourself a sense of the flow of Steve's feelings, beginning with his sense of pride and confidence in his performance as an effective manager. Try to imagine the sequence of his feelings so that you begin to share some sense of what this experience meant to him. Then, if you can, try to use this approach in a relationship that you are currently involved in and that is important to you.

SOME FINAL POINTS

To anticipate and deal with problems of communication, three things are necessary: First, a person must develop a sense of awareness of what the other is experiencing, as well as an awareness that difficulties in communication arise more often than we assume. (This is a matter of attitude.)

Second, a person needs a conceptual understanding of how and why people are apt to see the same thing differently. (This requires finding a useful framework.) The simple concepts of assumptions, perceptions, and feelings, and how they might differ for two people, can be very useful in gaining this understanding.

Third, a person needs a way of examining and acting upon what is taking place in the process of communication. This requires an understanding of some of the process assumptions that get in the way of good communication and understanding. (This is a matter of both attitude and behavior.)

Tagiuri suggests the following strategies and attitudes as useful guides in preventing and anticipating communication problems:

- Suspend judgment of right vs. wrong—at least temporarily, until you have understood the other person's point of view (attitude and behavior).
- Assume the legitimacy of the other's views (attitude).
- Try to see the situation from the other's point of view (behavior).
- Define terms (behavior).
- Deal with facts rather than interpretations or inferences (behavior).
- Take the other person's and your own emotions and feelings into account as being important, and if appropriate, recognize them (behavior).
- Reopen communication (balance between telling and listening) (behavior).
- Restate issues as the other party sees them (feedback to the other person and a check on your own understanding) (behavior).
- Attend to and stimulate feedback in terms of consequences of the communication (behavior).

BIBLIOGRAPHY

The ideas presented in this chapter draw heavily from several sources on facilitating understanding in communication. These articles are recommended to the interested reader who finds this brief discussion stimulating and would like to pursue the issues in more detail.

BENNIS, WARREN R., "Interpersonal Communication," in *The Planning of Change: Readings in Applied Behavioral Sciences,* eds. Warren G. Bennis, Kenneth D. Benne, and Robert Chin. New York: Holt, Rinehart & Winston, 1961.

GABARRO, J.J., with E. Morley, "Increasing Understanding of Persons in Relationship," 4-473-019, Intercollegiate Case Clearing House, 1972.

GIBB, JACK R., "Defensive Communication," in *Interpersonal Dynamics: Essays and Readings on Human Interaction,* rev. ed., eds. Warren G. Bennis, Edgar H. Schein, Fred I. Steele, and David E. Berlew. Homewood, Ill.: Dorsey, 1968.

NILSEN, T.R., "Some Assumptions That Impede Communications," *General Semantics Bulletin,* Winter–Spring 1954, reprinted in Arthur N. Turner and George F.F. Lombard, *Interpersonal Behavior and Administration.* New York: Free Press, 1969.

ROGERS, CARL R., and F.J. Roethlisberger, "Barriers and Gateways to Communication," *Harvard Business Review,* July-August 1952.

TAGIURI, RENATO, "A Note on Communication," 4-475-013, Intercollegiate Case Clearing House, 1972.

TURNER, ARTHUR N., and George F.F. Lombard, *Interpersonal Behavior and Administration.* New York: Free Press, 1969.

Readings

Place, Imagery, and Nonverbal Clues

Michael B. McCaskey

People have many simultaneous ways of communicating their meanings to others. In addition to the obvious message they send by the words they say, people also convey messages through their use of time and place, their manner and clothing, their gestures and tone of voice. This paper will explore three of the ways in which a person communicates with another. First, we will discuss the psychology of place—how a physical setting impacts interaction between two people. Next we will examine the way people use words and imagery to convey their meanings. Finally, we will see what messages are sent nonverbally, through body language and tone of voice.

The messages sent through place, words, and nonverbal behavior are subtle, which makes their reading a complex and slippery endeavor. In a manner of speaking, "clues" is a more accurate description than messages for these three areas. They provide a starting point for tentatively trying to appreciate the richness, the contradictory elements, the simultaneously rational and irrational world of another. This note is an amalgamation of research findings, common experience, and personal experience, selected and focused according to what I think you might find useful for understanding another person.

This paper was prepared with the assistance of Luise Cahill Dittrich.

THE PSYCHOLOGY OF PLACE

People use physical settings in distinctive ways that can communicate messages to the people with whom they interact. Yet often the messages about place are only haphazardly sent and received. If we become a little more careful, we can better read what someone is saying through his or her use of place. We can also examine our own physical settings and see what messages we might be sending about ourselves, and how we want to interact with others.

Our first basic notion is that physical settings often represent *territory* for a person. Most animals mark off the range of their territory and defend it against intruders, and it appears that we are not much different from these other animals. Fences and doors separate what is mine from the rest of the world. These boundaries give me security and privacy, protecting me from unwanted encroachments by others. Even in public spaces such as movie theaters, classrooms, or the beach, we often use personal belongings to establish temporary ownership of a place.

For people to have a sense of "home" seems quite important. The basketball team's home court advantage is well known. "Home" is familiar, predictable, and "mine." The importance of having one's own territory shows up in a study of communal space in Coventry, England. Contrary to what you might expect, those families with their own yards fraternized more than the families who shared a communal yard. In analyzing this finding one commentator suggested, "In suburbs and small towns, people are more likely to talk across their backyards if the property line is indicated by a fence. Because this boundary helps them maintain territoriality, it actually brings neighbors closer together."[1] This observation seems to agree with Robert Frost's famous line, "Good fences make good neighbors."

The importance of place as territory shows in the office as well. When a boss and a subordinate meet, whose office is used? If a boss is sensitive to place as territory, the purpose of the meeting will decide the question. To conduct an adversary discussion, to emphasize hierarchy, authority, or giving directions, the boss should probably hold the meeting in his office. If, on the other hand, the boss wants to reach out to the subordinate, to have a conversation more on the other's terms, he might well consider traveling to the subordinate's office.

A second important aspect of setting is how setting can be used to *communicate status*. Fritz Steele is a consultant who has studied the way an organization's physical setting impacts the interaction between people in the organization. He notes the many ways that organizations use space and things to signal an organizational member's status:

> Various facilities and patterns of facilities form the basis for a visual language by which insiders and knowledgeable outsiders can tell at a glance an individual's status level in the system. Some of the elements used as status indicators are:
>
> • Size in square feet of personal space (more space usually signifies higher status).
>
> • Luxuriousness of appointments (carpet, thickness of carpet).
>
> • A private office (being less visible to others usually signifies higher status).
>
> • Desk (having one, size, design, and materials out of which it is made).
>
> • Location of office (on "executive row," in a central place, or in a "backwater," etc.).
>
> • Windows (having one or more, distance to them).
>
> • Decorations (quality, whether provided by company or not).
>
> • Secretary (private one or sharing with others).
>
> • Location of secretary (in a pool, inside or outside one's office).

[1]David Dempsey, "Man's Hidden Environment," *Playboy*.

> As I am sure most readers know, the list is as long as people's ingenuity in devising visual differentiations.[2]

Another consultant recommends that a manager use this visual language to enhance power and authority. According to this device, a manager should try for as big an office as possible. The desk should be wood and imposing (but not so large as to overwhelm the space). If the floor is wood, there should be area rugs. If the floor is tile or linoleum, wall-to-wall carpeting is the only solution. The walls should be off-white or light beige. And, finally, the manager should arrange the office so that, in the view of visitors, he or she is "framed" by a window or a large painting.[3]

In a more facetious tone, a columnist for the *Boston Globe* recommends the following office furniture for an MBA on the make. First, one should have a chair with arms: "You're not going any place in the business world until you can rest elbows on chair arms, clasp hands together, put chin on hands, and say, 'hmmm.' "[4] Next you should have a spare chair or couch so people realize that you are important enough to have visitors. Another important office feature is a work table; it says you have so much work, so many important papers, that your desk can't hold them all. (Others disagree, arguing that an uncluttered desk signals a manager who is efficient and has everything under control.) In the same spirit, the columnist also recommends outfitting an office with shelving, memorabilia, and a grandfather clock.

[2]Fred I. Steele, *Physical Settings and Organization Development* (Reading, Mass.: Addison-Wesley, 1973).

[3]John T. Molloy, *Dress for Success* (New York: Wyden, 1975), Chap. 10.

[4]Susan Trausch, "Things HBS Won't Tell You," *Boston Evening Globe,* December 15, 1975, p. 20.

Using settings to communicate status is a subtle maneuver that many top executives seem to have intuitively learned. Place becomes a means to reinforce other messages they wish to send. But, of course, how settings communicate status is not limited to the office. I remember a recent Thanksgiving feast at a friend's house which culminated a season of Sunday morning touch football games. The players ranged in age from the mid-twenties to the mid-forties, and those at the dinner included children, spouses, and grandparents, so that the total number of people reached about forty. Naturally there were several tables, and people were free to choose where they sat. As part of the generally festive air, someone noted that the heads of *all* the tables had been occupied by the "young Turks." Without consciously planning it, those who were beginning their professional careers and feeling the first surge of career accomplishment had accorded themselves the positions of highest status at the tables. This observation amused most of the diners, and was unusual only in that such status arrangements are not often consciously noticed or publicly announced.

In addition, most of us use settings to communicate more than just status about ourselves. When I enter a person's place for the first time, I often look at how much he or she has personalized it with pictures of family, mentors, friends, or favorite places. How much does that person declare about himself? Who are the special people, what kinds of things does he or she enjoy having around? When you first walk into an office or a home, you might notice the textures. If the person had a choice, did he or she use tactile fabrics, long-haired rugs, coverings that invite a visitor to run a hand over it? This person may be signaling a desire to "be in touch," to interact at a closer distance. Or are the surfaces clean, polished, and smooth? Does the owner seem to prefer orderliness, to keep interactions at more of a distance? In the same way, you might look at your own spaces and try to read the messages that others find there about you and your preferred styles of interacting.

Both the notions of territory and of communicating status combine in a third aspect of the psychology of place: how settings can *influence* the amount and type of interaction between people. Steele quotes a woman whose office had recently been moved:

> My social life has changed drastically since my desk was moved to the end of the corridor. I used to be right near the entrance to the whole place, and saw almost everyone as they came in and out. I don't have so many interruptions now, but I also have fewer conversations. I also eat lunch by myself more, when groups forget to include me. I like the whole feeling less than before.[5]

Mindful of the dynamics of propinquity, some managers try to locate their office as near to the boss as possible.

A manager can use the spaces in his office to influence the character of interactions there. For instance, his office can have two different areas. In one, the manager talks across his desk to a person seated at the other side. Such an arrangement makes for an interaction emphasizing the manager's authority and position. A subordinate is likely to feel that here the boss exercises a "home court" advantage. In a second sitting area, chairs are grouped around a coffee table or are placed at right angles to each other. This arrangement makes for more sociable encounters because it signals a willingness to downplay or disregard differences in hierarchical positions.

Physical settings can be used in other ways to control interactions between people. A buyer for an electronics firm deliberately located his office on the third floor of a building which lacked an elevator. A salesman coming to the reception desk on the first floor would invariably be told that the buyer "could see you immediately." He would then trek the 40 steps to the buyer's office and be greeted by the buyer while still out of breath and somewhat disoriented.[6] Physical setting in this case was designed to control the interaction, beginning it on terms which put the salesman at a disadvantage.

The impact of these arrangements on people is related to what cultural anthropologists have observed concerning people's sense of personal space. For example, Edward T. Hall has studied how people in different cultures vary in what constitutes a comfortable distance for talking. His research shows that while Germans and the English stand further apart when talking, Arabs and Japanese stand closer together than Americans. Hall also identifies four basic distances for interaction: intimate space (touching to 18 inches); personal space (18 inches to four feet); social space (four feet to 12 feet); and public space (12 feet and beyond).[7] With chairs at right angles, both people are likely to be in each other's personal space. Placing a desk between the two people moves the interaction from a personal space to a social space. The content and the nature of speaking between two people change markedly moving from one space to the other. As a result of furniture arrange-

[5]Steele, *Physical Settings*, p. 38.

[6]Luise Cahill Dittrich, "The Psychology of Place," Harvard Business School, ICCH 9-476-086 (1975).

[7]Edward T. Hall, *The Hidden Dimension* (New York: Doubleday, 1966).

ment, then, people often do become "more distant" in both senses of the term.

Before closing this section, I would like to mention the advantages of an office tour when first getting to know a company. A skilled consultant can often read the visual language of a company in a first on-site visit. When you are invited to a company for a job interview, or when you are sizing up a company for any reason, you might find it useful to ask yourself similar questions to the ones consultants ask. How much of the space (and information) is locked up? Files, phones, and offices can all be fastened shut. How carefully is status marked by differences in the size, location, appointments of offices? Look at the bulletin boards. If they are extremely neat and if notices must be initialed, employees will feel less free to scrawl their own notices. Is there a coffee urn or something else that serves as a "watering hole," or are people isolated from one another by the office layout? An informed reading of place can tell you a lot about how tight the company is, how hierarchical, how rule-conscious, whether or not individual expression is encouraged, and what the company values.

Of course, none of these items alone gives you a clearcut message about a place or the people in it. But cumulatively, they can be the basis for impressions and hunches to be checked out through further inquiry. Place has symbolic meanings that can often be picked up by a careful reading. Our physical settings, like the clothes we wear, the words we utter, and the actions we take, communicate to others about us, and influence others with regard to us. Our interactions with people can be affected by what they learn about us through our settings, and by what we learn about them through theirs.

WORDS AND IMAGERY

In addition to the message of place, another major help in understanding another's world is to look at the words he or she uses. The importance of understanding the words of another can hardly be overestimated, especially in managerial life. Fritz Roethlisberger explains why:

> That a good portion of the executive's environment is verbal seems hardly open to question. In discussions, meetings, and conferences the verbal atmosphere is thick. The executive is dealing largely with words, symbols, and abstractions. Of course, all this applies to any one of us. We are all responding to words and other stimuli involving meaning. It seems to me obvious, however, that the higher the executive goes in an organization the more important it becomes for him, if he is to handle effectively one aspect of his job, to deal competently with his verbal environment.[8]

In this section we will take up some features of the verbal environment useful in trying to understand another person.

The first point is that *words are symbols*, the meanings of which greatly depend upon the person using the words. This point is troublesome, both because it seems so obvious and because it counters an assumption we usually make in our everyday behavior. In many situations we assume that words are entities in themselves and that the process of communicating with another is essentially a logical ordering of those entities. We try to get the words right and to present a logically structured train of thought in order to persuade. However, much communication between two people involves

[8]Fritz J. Roethlisberger, *Management and Morale* (Cambridge, Mass.: Harvard University Press, 1941).

sentiments and feelings, albeit not explicitly acknowledged. So a typical conversation bumps along without either party paying close attention to the different experiences, and therefore the different meanings, which lie behind the words. We tend to assume that we are all referring to the same thing when we say "the media," "a report," "socialism," and "a workable solution."

As we examine interpersonal misunderstandings, we often see these common assumptions fouling the channels of communication. The same symbol or word does not necessarily have the same meaning for two persons; differing backgrounds, personal histories and values all lead to our using and hearing words in personally distinctive ways. What makes communication problematical is our failure either to recognize this in ourselves or to hear it in others. As Roethlisberger has put it, "As a result, we fail to notice the differences, and we read into our experiences similarities where differences exist."[9]

If we begin to listen to both the words *and* the person speaking them, one of the first things we notice is *imagery*. Most people have characteristic verbal pictures for describing their own experences and for expressing their points of view. In listening to a person you might consider what metaphors he or she uses most frequently. These vivid kernels of speech can be drawn from the sports world, from literature, from religion, and from other fields of interest or background. They are clues to the world the other person inhabits. The imagery can show what's valued, what's feared, and what the other person's rules for behaving are.

Consider the following examples of imagery:

"Here is the game plan."

"I am prepared to wait until hell freezes over."

"One more snide comment, and I would have exploded."

Recurrent metaphors might suggest that a person sees life as a game, or is fatalistic about outcomes. Metaphors can also reflect an optimistic, pessimistic, or even confused outlook. Think of your own metaphors. Can they be characterized as sensual, poetic, violent? Taken in context, words in the form of imagery can be clues to how another is feeling and what he or she views as important.

The following is a brief checklist of some other features of the verbal environment; with these in mind, you might listen to some conversations somewhat differently than usual:

• *Labeling* assigns a pejorative word ("a Casanova," "brown-nose," "Commie") to another's point of view. It is a quick put-down without making the effort to appreciate the other person's meanings, and it often cuts off any thoughtful response.

• *"I" or "We":* With whom does a person identify? For what groups is he or she willing to say, "We need to . . ."? In addition, there can be an element of pomposity in using the royal or editorial "we" for referring to an action that the speaker has obviously performed alone (royalty and editors excepted).

• Different people are comfortable with different *levels of abstraction.* Some people use homespun expressions from down home; others favor "-ism" and "-ion" words which describe states and conditions. The difficulty here is that we might reject out of hand someone who is more comfortable talking at a more concrete, or a more abstract, level than we are.

• *Filled pauses,* such as "uhhh," fill the spaces between words. Goffman notes that

[9]*Ibid.*

filled pauses are used to "provide continuity, showing that the speaker is still in the business of completing a reply even though he cannot immediately muster up the right words to effect this."[10] A filled pause is a signal that preserves the speaker's right to talk, since it says, in effect, "Don't interrupt. I'm still talking."

• *Joking, kidding* (considered a favored form of interaction among Americans, especially American males), in which there is greater leeway in what is acceptable content than in polite talk. The aphorism, "Many a true word is said in jest," is quite true, since joking is one of the few ways of permitting otherwise questionable statements to be made.

• *Imperatives* in conversation: My ears prick up when I hear myself or others frequently using phrases like, "I have to . . ." or "I must . . ." or "I should. . . ." And I begin to look at where these obligations come from, whether they are all burdens, and if the speaker is conveying a passive acceptance of all he must do. A second common way of using imperatives is to tell others what they should do. Here again, I ask where the sense of obligation is coming from.

Another particularly intriguing area for me is when words are used in the form of *questions.* Questions are not always what they appear to be—many are really disguised statements. In fact, Gestalt psychologist Fritz Perls would sometimes refuse to answer questions that patients put to him. He thought of them as traps, inviting him to be the power figure; but he wanted people to acknowledge their own power and face up to the statements they needed to make without hiding them as questions. Roethlisberger has pointed out that some (perhaps many) questions are so silly they don't deserve to be answered. Yet in America we feel obliged to answer a question, even though answering should depend upon whether the question is a good one, whether it is the right time, and whether you want to answer. You might find it revealing to pay attention to the questions you and others ask in conversations. See how many of the questions are really statements. What a question "is" is not as simple as it seems.

A final area for considering the persons along with the words is *either/or thinking.* Some people habitually frame discussions in either/or terms. Something is either right or wrong, one is either innocent or guilty, a job is either good or bad. Of course, much of life is multidimensional and doesn't fit into two neat categories. However, it is not often that many of us examine the assumptions behind problems posed in either/or terms. Emotions often run high in dichotomized thinking, and so it becomes time to "throw the crooks out" without investigating whether "they" really are "crooks." It is so much easier for us to stereotype the opposition and let thinking and efforts to understanding end there.

So when you hear yourself or someone else discuss a situation in either/or terms, you might examine whether a two-value framework is, in this situation, posing false choices. There may be ways to synthesize a new solution which incorporates something of both sides. The discussion then moves from thinking in either/or terms to thinking in both/and terms.

In sum, we have briefly outlined some important features of the ways people use language. We can improve our understanding of ourselves and others by listening for imagery, labeling, imperatives, questions, either/or thinking, and other features of the verbal environment. What we are looking for are the meanings, the important values, assumptions, and experiences which lie behind a person's choice of words.

[10]Erving Goffman, *Frame Analysis: An Essay on the Organization of Experience* (New York: Harper Colophon, 1974).

NONVERBAL COMMUNICATION

In addition to the words that another person uses, a further set of clues for understanding that person is nonverbal communication. A person often accompanies and accentuates his verbal language with body movements, tone of voice, and visual interaction. Such nonverbal communication has become the subject of a number of popular books.[11] Unfortunately, we must start by sounding a notion of caution. The popular books on body language run the risk of being taken too simple-mindedly. The authors sometimes sound as if one gesture always means the same feeling. However, you yourself know that crossing your arms across your chest, for example, does not always mean that you are resisting the speaker. One can mistakenly attribute meaning to a gesture unless this language is read more wisely. The meaning of any gesture depends upon cultural norms, the style of the individuals involved, the particular physical setting, what has gone before, and what both people anticipate for the future. So the meaning of gesture can only be interpreted as the intersection of cultural, historical, personal, and interactional forces.

Often scholars study nonverbal communication by rerunning film clips of short episodes of behavior thousands of times. One renowned scholar in the field has spent four years charting and analyzing a thirty-minute episode from a therapy session! Repeatedly viewing the same film episode remains the best way to study nonverbal communication. A second possibility is to watch television with the sound turned off. Talk shows are particularly useful in this regard because the interaction is usually limited to two or three people, and the nonverbal communication is closer to a person's natural style than acting is. (Incidentally, observing politicians with the sound turned off is great fun for watching studied sincerity.)

In one of the better popular books on nonverbal communication, Flora Davis relates the ability to read this language with what we normally call "intuition." She also sets a nice tone for how we might go about learning in this area:

> We all have the ability to decode [nonverbal behavior] to some degree. We call it intuition. We learn it in babyhood and use it all of our lives on a subconscious level, and that's much the most efficient way to do it. In a flash, we interpret a body movement or react to a tone of voice, and we read it in as part of the whole message, which is clearly better than consciously juggling several dozen different message components, some of which may actually contradict one another. . . . When I have an impression that someone is secretly angry, for example, I know some of the things he has done with his body that gave me that impression. I still go by an overall feeling for the situation and not by any intellectual analysis, but for my own satisfaction, and much to my delight, I can often partially explain that feeling. I found I'd gained a very special kind of awareness: a new sensitivity to what others were feeling and even an occasional surprising insight into my own reactions.[12]

This is the spirit in which we will review research on nonverbal communication. What additional meanings might we become aware of by becoming more sensitive to the subtleties of this language?

Visual interaction is one of the most direct, powerful forms of nonverbal communication. In American culture the social rules suggest short eye contact for

[11]Judith Hall Koivumaki, "Body Language Taught Here," *Journal of Communication,* Winter 1975, pp. 26–30.

[12]Flora Davis, *Inside Intuition* (New York: Signet, 1975).

most situations. Prolonged eye contact is usually taken to be either threatening or, in another context, a sign of romantic interest. Weitz suggests that authoritarian relationships and sexual encounters are often initiated and maintained through eye contact.[13] Furthermore, a person shows he is listening, providing deference or encouragement to a speaker, by looking at the speaker. A listener who does not look at a speaker is often taken to be inattentive. In most conversations eye contact is broken by the speaker, who finds an excuse to glance away and thereby break eye contact. In this regard it is instructive to observe William Buckley's style of interacting on television. When he is speaking he will look away for long periods, seeming to concentrate on forming thoughts and words very carefully, and then he will dart a glance to his listener in order to make a point or demand agreement. His pattern is a skillful use of looking behavior to establish control.

Like the eyes, the face is an obvious conveyor of feeling, so obvious, in fact, that we have the expression, "It was written all over his face." I know I prefer to have an important conversation in person, rather than over the telephone, because I feel I have a better chance to estimate how the other person is responding. Both his facial expressions and mind help to convey the meaning we intend, and to signal the need to readjust when miscommunication occurs.

We are all familiar with interpretations of common facial expressions. A furrowed forehead can indicate concern or puzzlement or sadness. A wrinkled nose may signal displeasure or disgust. Tight lips and mouth may indicate an attempt to reign in or restrain powerful feelings. Upon greeting, most people show an eyebrow flash of recognition; but eyebrows raised during a conversation often show surprise or astonishment. A mouth pulled down at the corners may say the person is contemptuous or disgusted. Teeth bared and clenched may be a facial expression we share with primates for anger and preparation to fight.[14] One has only to look at several pictures of facial expressions to realize how much meaning we attach to "reading" another's face. What makes this reading complex is that a face often shows a "blend" of several of these different feelings at once.[15]

Another powerful means of tuning into another's feelings is the paralinguistic features of speech, that is, *how* something is said. Paralanguage includes tone and quality of voice, pitch, pacing of speech, and sounds such as sighs or grunts. Research in this area has concentrated on paralanguage as clues to personality and feelings. With respect to personality, people generally have been able to accurately identify the age, sex, and surprisingly the social class of the speaker through paralinguistics. However, in general people are less able to use these clues to judge another's occupation, body type, or personality traits.[16] With respect to feelings, on the other hand, voice can be quite an accurate indicator. In fact, studies on interracial communication have shown the paralinguistic channel often carries more accurate information about emotional responses than the verbal channel. Researchers are developing theories to explain this finding. One widely held view is that expression in words is more likely to be constrained by social norms, but feelings can still be expressed, often un-

[13]Shirley Weitz, *Nonverbal Communication* (New York: Oxford University Press, 1974).

[14]Jane Lyman Holtz, "Communication: The Use of Body Languages," Harvard Business School, ICCH 4-474-058 (1973).

[15]Mark L. Knapp, *Nonverbal Communication in Human Interaction* (New York: Holt, Rinehart & Winston, 1972).

[16]*Ibid.*

consciously, through nonverbal channels.[17] A person may be unwilling to verbally acknowledge, for example, that he is prejudiced or scared or excited; but he may still convey that feeling through his tone of voice or the pacing of his speech.

Paralanguage, then, is like music in its ability to convey and inspire feelings. Good listeners are quite skillful at hearing these cues. And, fortunately for a course on interpersonal behavior, it is clear that skill in this area can be developed through informed effort and practice.

Researchers have been exploring the relationship between body language (movement and gestures) and speech patterns. Condon found that the two work together in effective communication.[18] Smaller movements like dropping the head, the hands, or eye gaze often mark a pause, emphasize a point, or express some doubt or irony in one's speech. To mark larger transitions in thought, the speaker will often change his body position altogether.[19]

Also interesting is Birdwhistell's finding that the movement of a listener is often rhythmically coordinated to the speech and movements of the speaker.[20] Especially in moments of intense emotion and close rapport, the body language of one will mirror the body language of the other. Both seem to move in a dance of similar gestures and postural changes, moving in time with each other and the music.

However, when one person violates the other's expectations or values, interactional trouble is often signaled by "stumbles" which break the dance.[21] Instead of a smooth mirroring, there will often be a burst of movement, almost as if both are losing balance. Arms and legs may be thrust out, the whole body posture changed in order to regain balance. These moments of roughness in the interaction are especially important. They signal that one person has gone against the "rules of relevance" for the interaction, that is, the personal attributes or the topics that will be noticed in the interaction. Some rules derive from the culture; others are established ad hoc by the participants in the situation. In rough spots, the two people quickly move to determine whether the attribute or topic will now be discussed or not. In effect, they decide whether the rules of relevance will be enlarged. This happens very quickly and subtly, and most of the interactive decision making is carried out nonverbally. In short, exploration of the dance and stumbles of nonverbal communication show that the definition of the situation is not stable. Rather, it is a dynamic feature negotiated in the process of interaction. Rough spots, as indicated by bursts of body movement, signal differences of opinion between two people, thus also signaling the need for renegotiation.

Erickson, who has studied and coined the descriptor "stumbles," has done important work on the nonverbal communication between college counselors and undergraduates. He has concluded, "Each counselor must decide, consciously or not, *who he is to be* with each student. I believe this decision is worked out interactionally and depends in part on the counselor's judgment of *who the student is*."[22] This is all part of tuning into and

[17]Weitz, *Nonverbal Communication.*

[18]W.S. Condon and W.D. Ogston, "A Segmentation of Behavior," *Journal of Psychiatric Research,* Vol. 5 (1967), 221–35.

[19]Albert E. Scheflen, *How Behavior Means* (Garden City, N.Y.: Anchor/Doubleday, 1974).

[20]Ray L. Birdwhistell, *Kinesics and Context* (Philadelphia: University of Pennsylvania Press, 1970).

[21]Frederick Erickson, "Gatekeeping and the Melting Pot: Interaction in Counselling Encounters," *Harvard Educational Review,* Vol. 45 (February 1975), 44–70.

[22]*Ibid.*

understanding another person's world. We bring many possibilities in ourselves to every encounter with another. The first moments of a meeting help two people decide the tone and content of their interaction. Perhaps what makes us somewhat anxious in meeting new people is that the rules of relevance have not yet been worked out. With friends, on the other hand, we are likely to have comfortable, established patterns.

The use of body movement to show attention and rapport is very important, therefore, in actively listening to another's meanings. A good listener is very active while someone else is speaking. He or she will often move body and head in rhythm with the movements the speaker is making. His grunts, sighs, and other extralinguistic signals indicate that he is listening and understanding. Even without saying words, we are sending nonverbal messages about the depth of our understanding and the degree of our empathy.

CONCLUDING REMARKS

We have briefly surveyed how we might use place, imagery, and nonverbal behavior to better understand another person. Each of these areas has been the subject of many books. This paper can touch upon only some of the more important features for our hearing and seeing the messages another person may be sending. The aim is to begin increasing our sensitivity to another's meanings, to better tune into that other person's world. Such increased understanding is not quickly gained, and an increase in cognitive understanding is just the beginning of developing greater skill and sensitivity in practice.

Barriers and Gateways to Communication

Carl R. Rogers and F.J. Roethlisberger

PART I

It may seem curious that a person like myself, whose whole professional effort is devoted to psychotherapy, should be interested in problems of communication. What relationship is there between obstacles to communication and providing therapeutic help to individuals with emotional maladjustments?

Actually the relationship is very close indeed. The whole task of psychotherapy is the task of dealing with a failure in communication. The emotionally maladjusted person, the "neurotic," is in difficulty, first, because communication within himself has broken down and, secondly, because as a result of this his communication with others has been damaged. To put it another way, in the "neurotic" individual parts of himself which have been termed unconscious, or repressed, or denied to awareness, become blocked off so that they no longer communicate themselves to the conscious or managing part of himself; as long as this is true, there are distortions in the way he communicates himself to others, and so he suffers both within himself and in his interpersonal relations.

The task of psychotherapy is to help the person achieve, through a special relationship with a therapist, good communication within himself. Once this is achieved, he can communicate more freely and more effectively with others. We may say then that psychotherapy is good communication, within and between men. We may also turn that statement around and it will still be true. Good communication, free communication, within or between men, is always therapeutic.

It is, then, from a background of experience with communication in counseling and psychotherapy that I want to present two ideas: (1) I wish to state what

Reprinted from *Harvard Business Review,* July—August 1952, pp. 28—34,

I believe is one of the major factors in blocking or impeding communication, and then (2) I wish to present what in our experience has proved to be a very important way of improving or facilitating communication.

Barrier: The Tendency to Evaluate

I should like to propose, as a hypothesis for consideration, that the major barrier to mutual interpersonal communication is our very natural tendency to judge, to evaluate, to approve (or disapprove) the statement of the other person or the other group. Let me illustrate my meaning with some very simple examples. Suppose someone, commenting on this discussion, makes the statement, "I didn't like what that man said." What will you respond? Almost invariably your reply will be either approval or disapproval of the attitude expressed. Either you respond, "I didn't either; I thought it was terrible," or else you tend to reply, "Oh, I thought it was really good." In other words, your primary reaction is to evaluate it from *your* point of view, your own frame of reference.

Or take another example. Suppose I say with some feeling, "I think the Republicans are behaving in ways that show a lot of good sound sense these days." What is the response that arises in your mind? The overwhelming likelihood is that it will be evaluative. In other words, you will find yourself agreeing, or disagreeing, or making some judgment about me such as "He must be a conservative," or "He seems solid in his thinking." Or let us take an illustration from the international scene. Russia says vehemently, "The treaty with Japan is a war plot on the part of the United States." We rise as one person to say, "That's a lie!"

This last illustration brings in another element connected with my hypothesis. Although the tendency to make evaluations is common in almost all interchange of language, it is very much heightened in those situations where feelings and emotions are deeply involved. So the stronger our feelings, the more likely it is that there will be no mutual element in the communication. There will be just two ideas, two feelings, two judgments, missing each other in psychological space.

I am sure you recognize this from your own experience. When you have not been emotionally involved yourself and have listened to a heated discussion, you often go away thinking, "Well, they actually weren't talking about the same thing." And they were not. Each was making a judgment, an evaluation, from his own frame of reference. There was really nothing which could be called communication in any genuine sense. This tendency to react to any emotionally meaningful statement by forming an evaluation of it from our own point of view is, I repeat, the major barrier to interpersonal communication.

Gateway: Listening with Understanding

Is there any way of solving this problem, of avoiding this barrier? I feel that we are making exciting progress toward this goal, and I should like to present it as simply as I can. Real communication occurs, and this evaluative tendency is avoided, when we listen with understanding. What does that mean? It means to see the expressed idea and attitude from the other person's point of view, to sense how it feels to him, to achieve his frame of reference in regard to the thing he is talking about.

Stated so briefly, this may sound absurdly simple, but it is not. It is an approach which we have found extremely potent in the field of psychotherapy. It is the most effective agent we know for altering the basic personality structure of an individual and for improving his relationships and his communications with others. If I can listen to what he can tell me, if I can understand how it seems to him, if I can see its personal meaning for him, if I can sense the emotional flavor which it has for him, then I will be releasing potent forces of change in him.

Again, if I can really understand how he hates his father, or hates the company, or hates Communists—if I can catch the flavor of his fear of insanity, or his fear of atom bombs, or of Russia—it will be of the greatest help to him in altering those hatreds and fears and in establishing realistic and harmonious relationships with the very people and situations toward which he has felt hatred and fear. We know from our research that such empathic understanding—understanding *with* a person, not *about* him—is such an effective approach that it can bring about major changes in personality.

Some of you may be feeling that you listen well to people and yet you have never seen such results. The chances are great indeed that your listening has not been of the type I have described. Fortunately, I can suggest a little laboratory experiment which you can try to test the quality of your understanding. The next time you get into an argument with your wife, or your friend, or with a small group of friends, just stop the discussion for a moment and, for an experiment, institute this rule: "Each person can speak up for himself only *after* he has first restated the ideas and feelings of the previous speaker accurately and to that speaker's satisfaction."

You see what this would mean. It would simply mean that before presenting your own point of view, it would be necessary for you to achieve the other speaker's frame of reference—to understand his thoughts and feelings so well that you could summarize them for him. Sounds simple, doesn't it? But if you try it, you will discover that it is one of the most difficult things you have ever tried to do. However, once you have been able to see the other's point of view, your own comments will have to be drastically revised. You will also find the emotion going out of the discussion, the differences being reduced, and those differences which remain being of a rational and understandable sort.

Can you imagine what this kind of an approach would mean if it were projected into larger areas? What would happen to a labor–management dispute if it were conducted in such a way that labor, without necessarily agreeing, could accurately state management's point of view in a way that management could accept; and management, without approving labor's stand, could state labor's case in a way that labor agreed was accurate? It would mean that real communication was established, and one could practically guarantee that some reasonable solution would be reached.

If, then, this way of approach is an effective avenue to good communication and good relationships, as I am quite sure you will agree if you try the experiment I have mentioned, why is it not more widely tried and used? I will try to list the difficulties which keep it from being utilized.

Need for Courage. In the first place, it takes courage, a quality which is not too widespread. I am indebted to Dr. S.I. Hayakawa, the semanticist, for pointing out that to carry on psychotherapy in this fashion is to take a very real risk, and that courage is required. If you really understand another person in this way, if you are willing to enter his private world and see the way life appears to him, without any attempt to make evaluative judgments, you run the risk of being changed yourself. You might see it his way; you might find yourself influenced in your attitudes or your personality.

This risk of being changed is one of the most frightening prospects many of us can face. If I enter, as fully as I am able, into the private world of a neurotic or psychotic individual, isn't there a risk that I might become lost in that world? Most of us are afraid to take that risk. Or if we were listening to a Russian Communist, or Senator Joe McCarthy, how many of us would dare to try to see the world from each of their points of view? The great majority of us could not *listen;* we would find ourselves compelled to *evaluate,* because listening would seem too dangerous. So the first requirement is courage, and we do not always have it.

Heightened Emotions. But there is a second obstacle. It is just when emotions are strongest that it is most difficult to achieve the frame of reference of the other person or group. Yet it is then that the attitude is most needed if communication is to be established. We have not found this to be an insuperable obstacle in our experience in psychotherapy. A third party, who is able to lay aside his own feelings and evaluations, can assist greatly by listening with understanding to each person or group and clarifying the views and attitudes each holds.

We have found this effective in small groups in which contradictory or antagonistic attitudes exist. When the parties to a dispute realize that they are being understood, that someone sees how the situation seems to them, the statements grow less exaggerated and less defensive, and it is no longer necessary to maintain the attitude, "I am 100% right and you are 100% wrong." The influence of such an understanding catalyst in the group permits the members to come closer and closer to the objective truth involved in the relationship. In this way mutual communication is established, and some type of agreement becomes much more possible.

So we may say that though heightened emotions make it much more difficult to understand *with* an opponent, our experience makes it clear that a neutral, understanding, catalyst type of leader or therapist can overcome this obstacle in a small group.

Size of Group. That last phrase, however, suggests another obstacle to utilizing the approach I have described. Thus far all our experience has been with small face-to-face groups—groups exhibiting industrial tensions, religious tensions, racial tensions, and therapy groups in which many personal tensions are present. In these small groups our experience, confirmed by a limited amount of research, shows that this basic approach leads to improved communication, to greater acceptance of others and by others, and to attitudes which are more positive and more problem-solving in nature. There is a decrease in defensiveness, in exaggerated statements, in evaluative and critical behavior.

But these findings are from small groups. What about trying to achieve understanding between larger groups that are geographically remote, or between face-to-face groups that are not speaking for themselves but simply as representatives of others, like the delegates at Kaesong? Frankly, we do not know the answers to these questions. I believe the situation might be put this way: As social scientists we have a tentative test-tube solution of the problem of breakdown in communication. But to confirm the validity of this test-tube solution and to adapt it to the enormous problems of communication breakdown between classes, groups, and nations would involve additional funds, much more research, and creative thinking of a high order.

Yet with our present limited knowledge we can see some steps which might be taken even in large groups to increase the amount of listening *with* and decrease the amount of evaluation *about.* To be imaginative for a moment, let us suppose that a therapeutically oriented international group went to the Russian leaders and said, "We want to achieve a genuine understanding of your views and, even more important, of your attitudes and feelings toward the United States. We will summarize and resummarize these views and feelings if necessary, until you agree that our description represents the situation as it seems to you."

Then suppose they did the same thing with the leaders in our own country. If they then gave the widest possible distribution to these two views, with the feelings clearly described but not expressed in name-calling, might not the effect be very great? It would not guarantee the type of understanding I have been describing, but it would make it much more possible. We can understand the feelings of a person who hates us much more readily when his attitudes are accurately described to us by a neutral third party than we can when he is shaking his fist at us.

Faith in Social Sciences. But even to describe such a first step is to suggest another obstacle to this approach of understanding. Our civilization does not yet have enough faith in the social sciences to utilize their findings. The opposite is true of the physical sciences. During the war when a test-tube solution was found to the problem of synthetic rubber, millions of dollars and an army of talent were turned loose on the problem of using that finding. If synthetic rubber could be made in milligrams, it could and would be made in the thousands of tons. And it was. But in the social science realm, if a way is found of facilitating communication and mutual understanding in small groups, there is no guarantee that the finding will be utilized. It may be a generation or more before the money and the brains will be turned loose to exploit that finding.

Summary

In closing, I should like to summarize this small-scale solution to the problem of barriers in communication, and to point out certain of its characteristics.

I have said that our research and experience to date would make it appear that breakdowns in communication, and the evaluative tendency which is the major barrier to communication, can be avoided. The solution is provided by creating a situation in which each of the different parties comes to understand the other from the *other's* point of view. This has been achieved, in practice, even when feelings run high, by the influence of a person who is willing to understand each point of view empathically, and who thus acts as a catalyst to precipitate further understanding.

This procedure has important characteristics. It can be initated by one party, without waiting for the other to be ready. It can even be initiated by a neutral third person, provided he can gain a minimum of cooperation from one of the parties.

This procedure can deal with the insincerities, the defensive exaggerations, the lies, the "false fronts" which characterize almost every failure in communication. These defensive distortions drop away with astonishing speed as people find that the only intent is to understand, not to judge.

This approach leads steadily and rapidly toward the discovery of the truth, toward a realistic appraisal of the objective barriers to communication. The dropping of some defensiveness by one party leads to further dropping of defensiveness by the other party, and truth is thus approached.

This procedure gradually achieves mutual communication. Mutual communication tends to be pointed toward solving a problem rather than toward attacking a person or group. It leads to a situation in which I see how the problem appears to you as well as to me, and you see how it appears to me as well as to you. Thus accurately and realistically defined, the problem is almost certain to yield to intelligent attack; or if it is in part insoluble, it will be comfortably accepted as such.

This then appears to be a test-tube solution to the breakdown of communication as it occurs in small groups. Can we take this small-scale answer, investigate it further, refine it, develop it, and apply it to the tragic and well-nigh fatal failures of communication which threaten the very existence of our modern world? It seems to me that this is a possibility and a challenge which we should explore.

PART II

In thinking about the many barriers to personal communication, particularly those that are due to differences of background, experience, and motivation, it seems to me extraordinary that any two persons can ever understand each other. Such reflections provoke the question of how communication is possible when people do not see and assume the same things and share the same values.

On this question there are two schools of thought. One school assumes that communication between A and B, for example, has failed when B does not accept what A has to say as being fact, true, or valid; and that the goal of communication is to get B to agree with A's opinions, ideas, facts, or information.

The position of the other school of thought is quite different. It assumes that communication has failed when B does not feel free to express his feelings to A because B fears they will not be accepted by A. Communication is facilitated when on the part of A or B or both there is a willingness to express and accept differences.

As these are quite divergent conceptions, let us explore them further with an example. Bill, an employee, is talking with his boss in the boss's office. The boss says, "I think, Bill, that this is the best way to do your job." Bill says, "Oh yeah!" According to the first school of thought, this reply would be a sign of poor communication. Bill does not understand the best way of doing his work. To improve communication, therefore, it is up to the boss to explain to Bill why his way is the best.

From the point of view of the second school of thought, Bill's reply is a sign neither of good nor of bad communication. Bill's response is indeterminate. But the boss has an opportunity to find out what Bill means if he so desires. Let us assume that this is what he chooses to do, i.e., find out what Bill means. So this boss tries to get Bill to talk more about his job while he (the boss) listens.

For purposes of simplification, I shall call the boss representing the first school of thought *"Smith"* and the boss representing the second school of thought *"Jones."* In the presence of the so-called same stimulus each behaves differently. Smith chooses to *explain;* Jones chooses to *listen.* In my experience, Jones's response works better than Smith's. It works better because Jones is making a more proper evaluation of what is taking place between him and Bill than Smith is. Let us test this hypothesis by continuing with our example.

What Smith Assumes, Sees, and Feels

Smith assumes that he understands what Bill means when Bill says, "Oh yeah!" so there is no need to find out. Smith is sure that Bill does not understand why this is the best way to do his job, so Smith has to tell him. In this process let us assume Smith is logical, lucid, and clear. He presents his facts and evidence well. But, alas, Bill remains unconvinced. What does Smith do? Operating under the assumption that what is taking place between him and Bill is something essentially logical, Smith can draw only one of two conclusions: either (1) he has not been clear enough, or (2) Bill is too damned stupid to understand. So he either has to "spell out" his case in words of fewer and fewer syllables or give up. Smith is reluctant to do the latter, so he continues to explain. What happens?

If Bill still does not accept Smith's explanation of why this is the best way for him to do his job, a pattern of interacting feelings is produced of which Smith is often unaware. The more Smith cannot get Bill to understand him, the more frustrated Smith becomes and the more Bill becomes a threat to his logical capacity. Since Smith sees himself as a fairly reasonable and logical chap, this is a difficult feeling to accept. It is much easier for him to perceive Bill as uncooperative or stupid. This perception, however, will affect what Smith says and does. Under these pressures, Bill comes to be evaluated more and more in terms of Smith's values. By this process, Smith tends to treat Bill's values as unimportant. He tends to deny Bill's uniqueness and difference. He treats Bill as if he had little capacity for self-direction.

Let us be clear. Smith does not see that he is doing these things. When he is feverishly scratching hieroglyphics on the back of an envelope, trying to explain to Bill why this is the best way to do his job, Smith is trying to be helpful. He is a man of goodwill, and he wants to set Bill straight. This is the way Smith sees himself and his behavior. But it is for this very reason that Bill's "Oh yeah!" is getting under Smith's skin.

"How dumb can a guy be?" is Smith's attitude, and unfortunately Bill will hear that more than Smith's good intentions. Bill will feel misunderstood. He will not see Smith as a man of goodwill trying to be helpful. Rather he will perceive him as a threat to his self-esteem and personal integrity. Against this threat, Bill will feel the need to defend himself at all cost. Not being so logically articulate as Smith, Bill expresses this need, again, by saying, "Oh yeah!"

What Jones Assumes, Sees, and Feels

Let us leave this sad scene between Smith and Bill, which I fear is going to terminate by Bill's either leaving in a huff or being kicked out of Smith's office. Let us turn for a moment to Jones and see what he is assuming, seeing, hearing, feeling, doing, and saying when he interacts with Bill.

Jones, it will be remembered, does not assume that he knows what Bill means when he says, "Oh yeah!" so he has to find out. Moreover, he assumes that when Bill said this, he had not exhausted his vocabulary or his feelings. Bill may not necessarily mean one thing; he may mean several different things. So Jones decides to listen.

In this process, Jones is not under any illusion that what will take place will be eventually logical. Rather he is assuming that what will take place will be primarily an interaction of feelings. Therefore, he cannot ignore the feelings of Bill, the effect of Bill's feelings on him, or the effect of his feelings on Bill. In other words, he cannot ignore his relationship to Bill; he cannot assume that it will make no difference to what Bill will hear or accept.

Therefore, Jones will be paying strict attention to all of the things Smith has ignored. He will be addressing himself to Bill's feelings, his own, and the interactions between them.

Jones will therefore realize that he has

ruffled Bill's feelings with his comment, "I think, Bill, this is the best way to do your job." So instead of trying to get Bill to understand him, he decides to try to understand Bill. He does this by encouraging Bill to speak. Instead of telling Bill how he should feel or think, he asks Bill such questions as, "Is this what you feel?" "Is this what you see?" "Is this what you assume?" Instead of ignoring Bill's evaluations as irrelevant, not valid, inconsequential, or false, he tries to understand Bill's reality as he feels it, perceives it, and assumes it to be. As Bill begins to open up, Jones's curiosity is piqued by this process.

"Bill isn't so dumb; he's quite an interesting guy" becomes Jones's attitude. And that is what Bill hears. Therefore Bill feels understood and accepted as a person. He becomes less defensive. He is in a better frame of mind to explore and reexamine his own perceptions, feelings, and assumptions. In this process he perceives Jones as a source of help. Bill feels free to express his differences. He feels that Jones has some respect for his capacity for self-direction. These positive feelings toward Jones make Bill more inclined to say, "Well, Jones, I don't quite agree with you that this is the best way to do my job, but I'll tell you what I'll do. I'll try to do it that way for a few days, and then I'll tell you what I think."

Conclusion

I grant that my two orientations do not work themselves out in practice in quite so simple or neat a fashion as I have been able to work them out on paper. There are many other ways in which Bill could have responded to Smith in the first place. He might even have said, "O.K., boss, I agree that your way of doing my job is better." But Smith still would not have known how Bill felt when he made this statement or whether Bill was actually going to do his job differently. Likewise, Bill could have responded to Jones in a way different from my example. In spite of Jones's attitude, Bill might still be reluctant to express himself freely to his boss.

The purpose of my examples has not been to demonstrate the right or wrong way of communicating. My purpose has been simply to provide something concrete to point to when I make the following generalizations:

1. Smith represents to me a very common pattern of misunderstanding. The misunderstanding does not arise because Smith is not clear enough in expressing himself. It arises because of Smith's misevaluation of what is taking place when two people are talking together.

2. Smith's misevaluation of the process of personal communication consists of certain very common assumptions, e.g., (a) that what is taking place is something essentially logical; (b) that words in themselves apart from the people involved mean something; and (c) that the purpose of the interaction is to get Bill to see things from Smith's point of view.

3. Because of these assumptions, a chain reaction of perceptions and negative feelings is engendered which blocks communication. By ignoring Bill's feelings and by rationalizing his own, Smith ignores his relationship to Bill as one of the most important determinants of the communication. As a result, Bill hears Smith's attitude more clearly than the logical content of Smith's words. Bill feels that his individual uniqueness is being denied. His personal integrity being at stake, he becomes defensive and belligerent. As a result, Smith feels frustrated. He perceives Bill as stupid. So he says and does things which only provoke more defensiveness on the part of Bill.

4. In the case of Jones, I have tried to show what might possibly happen if we made a different evaluation of what is taking place when two people are talking together. Jones makes a different set of

assumptions. He assumes (a) that what is taking place between him and Bill is an interaction of sentiments; (b) that Bill—not his words in themselves—means something; (c) that the object of the interaction is to give Bill an opportunity to express freely his differences.

5. Because of these assumptions, a psychological chain reaction of reinforcing feelings and perceptions is set up which facilitates communication between Bill and him. When Jones addresses himself to Bill's feelings and perceptions from Bill's point of view, Bill feels understood and accepted as a person; he feels free to express his differences. Bill sees Jones as a source of help; Jones sees Bill as an interesting person. Bill in turn becomes more cooperative.

6. If I have identified correctly these very common patterns of personal communication, then some interesting hypotheses can be stated:

a. Jones's method works better than Smith's, not because of any magic, but because Jones has a better map than Smith of the process of personal communication.

b. The practice of Jones's method, however, is not merely an intellectual exercise. It depends on Jones's capacity and willingess to see and accept points of view different from his own, and to practice this orientation in a face-to-face relationship. This practice involves an emotional as well as an intellectual achievement. It depends in part on Jones's awareness of himself, in part on the practice of a skill.

c. Although our colleges and universities try to get students to appreciate intellectually points of view different from their own, very little is done to help them to implement this general intellectual appreciation in a simple face-to-face relationship—at the level of a skill. Most educational institutions train their students to be logical, lucid, and clear. Very little is done to help them to listen more skillfully. As a result, our educated world contains too many Smiths and too few Joneses.

d. The biggest block to personal communication is man's inability to listen intelligently, understandingly, and skillfully to another person. This deficiency in the modern world is widespread and appalling. In our universities as well as elsewhere, too little is being done about it.

7. In conclusion, let me apologize for acting toward you the way Smith did. But who am I to violate a long-standing academic tradition!

Giving and Receiving Feedback

John Anderson

PURPOSE

The purpose of this article is to discuss a few considerations involved in telling another person how you feel about him—"how to do it" considerations that are apt to be important, if your objective is to help him become a more effective person, and also to arrive at a more effective working relationship between him and yourself.

BACKGROUND

One of the central purposes of group experience in a Managerial Grid or sensitivity training lab is to help the participant become more clearly aware of the impact he has on others. That is, during the laboratory experience, the participant has an opportunity to talk with others, solve problems with others, and in general interact with others in ways that are characteristic for him. The image he projects, then—the impression that others have of his behavior—is communicated back to him by other group members. And this sort of exchange is usually a good deal more open than what is common in everyday life. The intent, at least so far as the objectives of the program are concerned, is that this feedback will be helpful to the recipient—that he may see, for example, some discrepancies between the effect he wished to create (and in fact thought he was creating) and what actually took place, with the hope that he will be able to use this information in making a more intelligent choice of behavior with which to deal with similar situations in the future.

Unfortunately, such feedback (for reasons of content, timing, and the way it is given) does not always turn out to be use-

This paper was originally written as an internal document of the Procter & Gamble Company. Reproduced by permission.

ful to the recipient. And, although the very large majority of managers who participate in public sensitivity or Grid training labs return saying that overall the experience was a very helpful one for them personally, still many have felt that "this is a kind of thing you sure couldn't do with people you work next to all the time!" The fear is that if the members of a work team did attempt to enter into an experience of this kind together, either:

1. They would not dare to be open and candid with one another, and the result, therefore, would be a superficial and useless experience, or

2. They would dare to be open with one another, and the result would be one of disruption in team working relationships, escalation of bad feelings carried over from old grievances, etc.

Several companies have now experimented with some sort of team lab. In my own, Procter & Gamble, the design we have used has varied considerably depending on the needs of the particular group. But in no instance have the two fears mentioned above (organized slumber or total destruction) materialized. Each has turned out to be, in judgment of the large majority of participants, a very useful and very worthwhile experience from the standpoint of building more effective working relationships on the job. In general, people seem to be both concerned enough for one another and trusting enough of one another that they are able to be *appropriately* open in exchanging feedback during a team lab situation. It's my belief that instances in which people have only hurt or confused one another in exchanges of this kind have been the result not so much of motivational problems, as problems of skill in giving feedback—that is, knowing *how* to do it well, and what kinds of pitfalls to watch out for. So, so much for background. What follows, then, is a summary of what I feel are some of the more important considerations drawn from a fairly limited and scattered literature on the subject, and from my own personal observation of some of the holes people seem to dig themselves into in experiences like this. I think it is particularly important that these thoughts be given some attention in groups that are to be conducted without the benefit of outside help—that is, where a trained, skilled, experienced, outside observer will not be available to get things back on track if they should begin to wander off in un-useful directions. I'm thinking of Managerial Grid, or other instrumented, trainerless lab designs. No doubt the following considerations also have some application to the conduct of "performance appraisal" discussions as well as other informal exchanges that often take place between people in or out of the workplace.

THE FIRST GENERAL TEST

I think the first, most general, and most significant criterion that "helpful feedback" must meet is simply that it be *intended* to be helpful to the recipient. That is, the sender of the message should ask himself beforehand, "Do I really feel that what I am about to say *is likely to be helpful to the other person*?" I need to examine my own motivation, that is, and be sure that I am not simply about to unload a burden of hostility from my own breast and for my own personal benefit, quite regardless of the expected effect on the receiver. Otherwise, I may convince myself that my only obligation is to be open and honest—that the name of the game is "candor"—and that so long as I am truly and completely "level," I have fulfilled the only necessary obligation. If my objective is to *help* the recipient of the feedback, then, three things are necessary:

1. The other person must *understand* what I am saying.

2. He must be willing and able to *accept* it.

3. He must be *able to do* something about it if he chooses to.

Getting Understanding

Two most important considerations in getting understanding of the message sent are:

1. Feedback should be specific rather than general. If I can give the man I am talking to specific examples of instances in which he has behaved in the way I am describing, it will be much easier for him to understand what I am talking about than it will if I speak only in terms of generalizations about "what he is like." For example, if I tell him that I think he talks too much, or doesn't express his thoughts very clearly, this is likely to be *less* helpful to him than if I am able to cite a particular situation, tied to time and place, where I thought he exhibited this behavior. If I can recall vividly to his mind a particular instance in which he rambled on long after I had gotten the idea of what he was trying to say, or when he had gone on and on and on without ever getting across clearly the idea of what he was trying to say to me or to a group, he is more likely to be able to get a handle on what it is I am trying to tell him. Or at least I will have opened up an area for him that we can then explore further to try to understand what was going on in the situation, so that he can come out of it with a clearer idea of some specific things he might consider doing differently in the future. The key here is, don't just generalize about what kind of a person he is. Give examples.

2. Another important factor in getting understanding is this: Other things equal, recent examples of behavior are better than old ones. To understand what was happening in the situation, a person obviously has to be able to recall the situation somewhat vividly. What happened two minutes ago will be more vividly recallable than what happened an hour ago, which will in turn be more easily remembered that what happened yesterday, last week, last year, five years ago, etc.

Getting Acceptance

There are circumstances in which anyone will find it most difficult to accept critical negative feedback--times at which it will be very difficult for anyone to face what is being said to him in an open, objective frame of mind. I think these things are most important in getting this acceptance:

1. There needs to be a minimum foundation of trust among members of the group before this sort of experience is entered into. If A is to accept critical feedback from B, A must be somewhat convinced, from his previous associations with B, that B's motivations where A is concerned aren't entirely self-serving—that is, that B *does care* for A and can be trusted to be saying what he is saying because he really feels that it will benefit A to do so. Where B has a deep distrust of A going into this situation, there is probably very little that A can do to get B's voluntary acceptance of what he is telling him.

2. How A addresses himself to B in this specific situation, however, can also be an important factor. If A's tone of voice, the expression on his face, his choice of words, and everything about him communicates directly to B the impression that "I value you, and I really would like to help you, and that is the only reason I am telling you this," then B is more likely to attend to the

message with an open mind than if A simply rattles off a list of intellectual observations about B's behavior, perhaps without even looking directly at him while he does so.

3. In sending negative feedback to another person, he will also be more likely to receive it in an accepting frame of mind if I am descriptive rather than evaluative in what I say to him—that is, if I simply describe what happened as I saw it in a particular situation and tell him of the effect it had on me, as opposed to evaluating in more general terms the goodness or badness, rightness or wrongness, of what he did. If I tell you, for example, "This may not be your problem; it may be mine. However, I want you to know that when you act toward me the way you do sometimes [describe a situation, in time and place] it is very difficult for me to [think straight, keep from getting mad, keep my mind on what we are talking about, keep from going to sleep, etc.—whatever fits the situation that I am trying to describe]," you are much more likely to be able to accept this message in an open frame of mind than if I tell you, "I think it is just terrible when you act toward people that way, I think you ought not to be that way, that's a completely senseless way to act, why don't you grow up, etc. . . ."

4. Before giving a person negative feedback of any kind, I ought to ask myself whether *now* is a good time to do it—whether he *appears* to be in a condition of readiness to receive information of this kind. If he appears, for example, to be angry, confused, upset, highly distraught, defensive, etc., the answer is probably no. I ought not to load any more on him right now. Perhaps in a way it is for this reason that feedback which is solicited by the recipient is somewhat more likely to be received in an open state of mind than feedback which is simply sent at him whether he has asked for it or not. And the more specific the area in which feedback is solicited, the more likely it is to be expected and received in an open frame of mind. For example, suppose the leader of a group says to his people, "How about the X decision I made last Friday? Do you feel that that was one I arrived at in an appropriate way, or do you feel that I should have involved you all more before arriving at a conclusion?" As a member of the group, I would feel that this solicitation of feedback was more genuine and could be responded to more openly and with more confidence that it would be received in an open frame of mind, than I would feel when the leader of the group, perhaps a bit too intensely or with a laugh that is a little too loud, says something like, "OK men, this is my turn in the barrel! Really level with me now! I want to hear everything you don't like about me!" He may or he may not. All I am suggesting is that if overt solicitation is indicative of probable acceptance, the former sort is apt to be more meaningful than the latter, all by itself.

5. There is always the problem that feedback sent one man by another will be accepted as valid when in fact it ought *not* to be. For example, if I tell you that there is a particular thing you do in our relationship that I find most upsetting, it may be that the problem isn't yours at all, but rather that it's mine. One of the values of entering into this sort of exchange in a group, as opposed to doing so only in a one-to-one relationship, is that the feedback that each man gives another can be checked around the group to see whether anyone else has common experience of this kind which would support or clarify the meaning of what is being said. This should always be done, both as a check on the validity of the observation and to be sure that the recipient gets as many examples as are available to help him understand what is being said.

Assessing Receiver's Ability to Use the Particular Feedback

The third criterion I mentioned that "useful" feedback should meet is that the recipient be able to do something with it.

1. Suppose I feel that a man does not present his ideas as forcefully and persuasively

as he ought to, to get the attention they deserve from the group; and I decide I want to tell him about this. This is still a pretty general feeling, and before saying anything, therefore, I should consider what specifically there is about his delivery that makes me feel that way. Now if I think, for example, that he doesn't organize his thoughts as well under some circumstances as I know he is capable of (from other experiences I've had with him), this is an example of something I might assume he could do something about, and so I probably should tell him I feel that way, especially if I can give him specific examples of instances in which he had done this. Or suppose I feel that he gets his ideas out all right, but that as soon as he receives any static from anyone about them, he withdraws, either from indifference, lack of confidence in his own ideas, or whatever. This too I might choose to tell him about, because I could expect that he might be able to do something about it.

On the other hand, suppose I feel that one of the key things that interferes with his ability to persuade, to carry his ideas over to a group forcefully, is that he is physically a very little fellow, and with a high squeaky voice, or possibly an even more pronounced speech impediment. If I am really trying to be helpful to him, there obviously is no point in calling these to his attention.

So, by this criterion, you might or might not decide it would be helpful to tell the other person you felt he did not project his ideas in the group as forcefully or persuasively as he might. Whether you chose to do so or not would depend on your best estimate of his ability to do something about the particular barriers you saw to his effectiveness in this particular area.

2. During a group session in which members are exchanging their views of and feelings about one another in this way, there may be a tendency to feel that you haven't really done a man justice unless you have told him "everything that bothers you" about him. It is not at all necessarily desirable, however, to be "complete" in the negative feedback you might give a person. It may be quite a large enough task, for example, for me to understand, accept, and consider doing something about my characteristic ways of behaving in two or three key areas. To give me more than this to think about may be simply spreading my attention beyond what I am capable of dealing with at this particular time. Also, other things equal, the more you unload on me, the more threatening the experience is liable to be, and the more difficulty I am likely to have accepting any of it in an open frame of mind.

Summary

So, to summarize, to be maximally useful to the recipient, feedback should meet the following criteria. It should be:

1. Intended to help the recipient.

2. Given directly and with real feeling, and based on a foundation of trust between the giver and receiver.

3. Descriptive rather than evaluative.

4. Specific rather than general, with good, clear, and preferably recent examples.

5. Given at a time when the receiver appears to be in a condition of readiness to accept it.

6. Checked with others in the group to be sure they support its validity.

7. It should also include only those things that the receiver might be expected to be able to do something about.

8. And he should not be told more than he can handle at any particular time.

RISK OF EXCESSIVE CAUTIOUSNESS

Finally, the question might be asked, "Isn't there some risk that if all these cautions are followed, people might be induced to be overly cautious, and decline to take any risks (and what would probably be desirable risk) in being open with one another?" This is a reasonable question, and I think the answer is yes—this is a risk in itself. Many of us have a tendency to feel that we couldn't possibly share with other people the negative feelings we have about them. They would be crushed if we did so. Or they would never forgive us. All of the criteria listed above are simply considerations that should be given some attention by the sender of feedback. But it will no doubt be impossible to meet all of them, all of the time, and still have something to say. And so, I think in such cases it is appropriate to take prudent risks—to be open more than closed, experimentally, and see what happens. If you at least really *intend* to help—and there is no doubt that you intend to help by the manner in which you say what you say—then a good deal of clumsiness is almost certain to be overlooked by the receiver. Even if he doesn't understand or agree with what you are saying, he at least will probably not hold it against you. And if his defenses stay down, together you may be able to clarify meanings, draw out essentials, and in general compensate for your initial clumsiness in trying to help.

RECEIVING FEEDBACK

I think there is less to say to the recipient of feedback about ways in which he might approach this opportunity:

1. First of all, he should make a sincere effort not to be defensive. This has as much to say about what he allows to go on inside him as about what he allows himself to say overtly to those who are giving him feedback. He should try to look at what is being said with an open mind, trying to understand it, and not all the while explaining to himself and others, "They simply don't understand; it isn't what I meant at all."

2. If the recipient of feedback is having difficulty understanding what people are trying to tell him and they are unable to come up with examples that clarify things for him, he should begin to seek and speculate on possible examples himself with the group—to say, for example, "Remember the time we met last Friday, and I did such and so. Is that the kind of thing you are talking about?"

3. To be sure he understands, I think it is a good idea for the recipient of feedback to try to summarize briefly for the group what he understands them to be saying. This gives them a final opportunity to check misunderstandings that might have taken place.

4. I think it can be very helpful to an individual and to a group if the recipient of feedback from others is allowed, and encouraged, to share his feelings with the group about the kind of thing they have been discussing—that is, his behavior in certain situations. The risk of defensiveness is one that all should be alert to. However, if a man can explore openly some of his feelings about why he tends sometimes to behave in "that" way, two things can happen. First, he may arrive at a better understanding himself of why he behaves in the way he does, simply in talking it through, and thereby be in a better position to consider what he might do about it. Secondly, if he does find it difficult or impossible to do anything about the behavior that has been negatively described to him by the group, even though he tries, if he has genuinely shared with them some of his concerns and some of the internal struggles he has in these situations, they may at least find it a little easier to understand and accept that behavior from him in the future.

5. As a final point, I believe some people react negatively to the very idea of doing this sort of thing—that is, meeting as a work team and exchanging in a quite open fashion our views of how we see one another, positively and negatively. The feeling may be that "I am what I am, and I have a right to be that. And no group of people has a right to dictate to me what I should be like." My feeling is that this is

exactly right. It remains, and should remain, the right of each individual to evaluate what he hears, decide what he believes of it, and decide in what respects, if any, he feels it is personally worth his while to make the effort to change. The purpose of a team lab of the kind described here, and of the kind of information that is exchanged in it, is simply to give a man better and clearer information than he ordinarily receives on which to make his own judgment of his personal effectiveness in working with others, and of how or whether he wishes to further develop that effectiveness.

Cases

Polar Star Beverages Co. (A)

Ken Kirk and three other Polar Star managers had just settled down in Kirk's office. Kirk had returned to the San Francisco plant from San Eduardo, where a regional preview of the company's soft-drink promotion plans had been held. Kirk had made the forty-mile trip back because he wanted to meet with an executive from the Seattle home office who was in town for the meeting. He and Kirk had been joined by two other managers who wanted to talk about some current concerns of the San Francisco plant.

Although it was only 3:30, it had been a long day, and it felt good to sit back and rehash the day's events. Kirk had almost gone directly home from San Eduardo, but changed his mind so that he and the others could meet with the visitor.

The conversation was interrupted by a phone call from a supplier, which Kirk answered at his desk. Suddenly, Kirk heard the sound of bottles falling on the sidewalk below. When he looked out the window, he saw a group of young people gathered on the sidewalk carrying placards and sacks of bottles and cans. He could also see TV cameras and what seemed to be newsmen on the street.

By this time, all four men had joined him at the window. The signs indicated that the kids were from Montview High School in a nearby town that Kirk knew well. Many of the students were the same age as his children, and knowing the high school, he imagined that they were a pretty bright and articulate group. The kids were all wearing worn and faded jeans and all seemed to have long hair.

The plant was on one of the busiest intersections in the Bay Area, and the rush-hour traffic was beginning to swell the normally heavy traffic on both streets. Kirk asked Ed Hall, the plant superintendent and one of the men in the room, to go down and bring them around to the side door. "At least they'll be away from some of the traffic," he thought. "Invite them in for a Polar

Star," he added, almost automatically. Kirk tried to finish the phone conversation as quickly as possible; he noticed that the crowd had begun to move around the side of the building at Hall's request.

Before Kirk could finish, Hall returned to say that the students demanded to talk "to the top man in the company." Kirk immediately ended the phone conversation. As general manager of the San Francisco bottling plant and a vice-president of the Bay Area subsidiary, Kirk was the "top man."

Polar Star Beverages Co. (B)

The four men started down the corridor, and Kirk tried to imagine what the students had on their minds. They were probably protesting Polar Star's one-way, nonreturnable containers, he guessed, because of the bottles and cans they had brought with them. Although he had become very conscious of the ecology movement and shared its goals, he also knew that it was a practical impossibility for Polar Star to go out of the nonreturnable business and survive in the Bay Area market. The Bay Area's consumers preferred nonreturnable bottles and cans, and all the large-volume chains reflected that preference. None of the chains sold returnables for this reason. In addition, the chains did not like the extra work that returnables entailed for store personnel. But this was not the kind of statement that could be made in front of TV cameras without offending the chains, who were Polar Star's largest customers, and other independent dealers.

Yet at the same time, he thought, Polar Star also relied heavily on the Bay Area youth market. Local universities, colleges, and high schools were an important part of the market. Also, the company's reputation for having an honest, quality product had been basic to its success and expansion. It was crucial not to have the company's image damaged by such a confrontation.

When they reached the bottom of the stairs, Kirk could see the students through the garage doors, chanting, "Recycle now, recycle now." Plant employees had begun to close the garage doors, and Kirk could sense their uneasiness. He knew that most of the inside men as well as the driver-salesmen had little sympathy for protestors, and the possibility of a physical confrontation could not be taken lightly. He also realized that within half an hour, a class for supervisors being held in the plant would be breaking up. They, like the plant employees, were apt to be antagonistic to the protestors. He could also see that Polar Star trucks were beginning to return from their day's deliveries and would continue to do so for the next couple of hours.

Kirk stepped outside and found 75 or 80 kids shouting and chanting. They had begun to empty their sacks of bottles and cans. The TV cameras had come around, and he also noticed several people with still cameras and tape recorders. The students had lined up the bottles and cans against the building; the pile included all brands of soft drinks, including national brands and private labels, as well as Polar Star products. Kirk looked into the crowd and wondered what to do.

Polar Star Beverages Co. (C)

The last student protestor had left, and Kirk returned to his office to try and reconstruct what had happened. No outbreak of hostility or violence had occurred, and he felt a sense of relief for that reason alone. He knew that he and the students remained far from agreement on some issues, but it seemed to him that everyone, including himself, had gained a better understanding of the problem. It certainly could have been worse, he thought.

Seattle would want a report on the protest and on the way in which it was handled. The whole episode had come up so suddenly, and everything had happened so rapidly; it could have taken a very different course. So Kirk settled back to retrace the events of the two hours that had just passed.

It was not easy to sort out what had happened and what it meant. In a way, he thought, he had seen it coming. He had tried to keep up on the latest developments in the ecology crisis and had thought a great deal about its implications for companies like Polar Star, but he had never really organized his thoughts into either a defensive or an offensive position. In fact, he found that he agreed with the protestors on most of what they had to say. His responses to them, he thought, were more or less intuitive, but what they had talked about was certainly not new to him.

In an effort to reconstruct what had happened, Kirk tried to review the events as they had occurred. He remembered the men closing the garage doors when he had started out to meet the protest group, and he could feel the tension in the building. His first reaction was to instruct Hall not to have anyone talk to the students except himself. He also recalled seeing the television cameras and the large group of kids and placards. It was hard to tell who their spokesman was because of all the activity and shouting. Kirk remembered walking into the crowd and asking if he could meet their spokesman. He sensed that they were somewhat surprised by his presence, possibly because he had come out of the building so quickly.

Kirk also remembered introducing himself to the group's leader and extending his hand to him. The boy pointedly ignored the gesture and immediately launched into reading a statement. He seemed well-spoken and articulate, but with a certain sharpness in his voice. Kirk found it hard to describe the boy's reaction. It was not really belligerent, but definitely hostile and aggressive. The boy read the prepared statement, and when he finished, the crowd cheered. Then he gave Kirk a copy of it and asked him to pass it along to his superiors, which Kirk assured him he would do. Another student gave Kirk a "Fact Sheet" and he paused for a moment to read it. (See Exhibits I-4 and I-5.) Kirk also remembered being asked who he was and what his title was by a woman reporter. Somehow, he felt that his answer was important to the group, because he remembered stressing the fact that he was a vice-president.

He also remembered the barrage of questions that followed. Some of the questions were asked so rapidly that they could not possibly be answered. It almost seemed as if their purpose was more to harass him than to get answers. Several kids in particular seemed to be pushing him, repeating the same question over and over again. It felt as if they were trying to get him to say something he didn't want to say. After several minutes, however, the group seemed to settle down and there was less shouting. As they talked, he began to sense that they were pretty well informed and appeared to know what they were talking about. It almost seemed more important to understand what they were saying then to respond with answers. Maybe it had something to do with having kids of his own who were the same age, he thought. The students seemed to be not only knowledgeable about ecological problems but also sincerely concerned about them. Possibly for this reason, he tried not to dodge their questions, but to be honest and candid, and to let the "chips fall where they may."

Several times he did not know how to answer a question, and he had to stop and collect this thoughts. But he remembered three of the kids as being real needlers. Even when he tried to answer a question as well as he could, and the subject moved to something else, one of them would bring the question back into the discussion and push him further on it. He remembered feeling harassed at these times, as if they were trying to get him to say something out of context. He also sensed that some of them felt frustrated, and he wondered if his basic agreement with them on much of what they were saying didn't underlie this frustration.

Kirk also remembered that after things had settled down, he asked the group to move off the street and into the building where they could see the plant. Part of his reason was to get them out of the way of the rush-hour traffic. Delivery trucks were beginning to return to the plant, making the situation even more hazardous. Moving them into the building required stopping the truck traffic so that they could all file in. He also remembered being aware of the continued presence of the television cameras and lights, and wondering why they were still there. He couldn't help speculating that they were expecting something dramatic to happen that he could not foresee. However, he also sensed that the TV reporters didn't like his moving the students inside.

Angrily, one of the reporters asked him why he was bringing them into the building, and Kirk answered by saying

Exhibit I-4

Polar Star Beverages Co. (C)

DUMP-IN

The use of non-returnable cans and bottles is a blatant example of poor ecological planning. The use of disposable aluminum cans is an unnecessary, if not a serious, waste of our natural resources. Non-returnable bottles add conspicuously to the accumulation of garbage in urban areas. This act of protest is not belligerent in nature. We realize that the Polar Star Company is not solely responsible for adding to the country's refuse problems, but it is a prime offender. If this amount of bottles can be collected in only a week and a half among such a small group, it is obvious that the amount of trash that could build up in a longer period of time is excessive. We hope that today's Dump-In will serve notice to all consumer industries, and to the packaging industries on which they depend, that people in this community want to see the recycling of metal, glass, and paper. We hope that profit-motive will not blind manufacturers to their social responsibilities and that our presence here today will stiumulate cooperation between industries themselves and between industries and the people, in an effort to improve our environment.

We strongly suggest that the Polar Star Company be the first to return to the use of returnable bottles and cans in the hope that other manufacturers will also realize their responsibility to our environment.

Montview Students for
Ecology Action

that he was going to show them one of Polar Star's recycling machines. "What kind of a recycling machine?" he was asked. Kirk answered, "A paper recycling machine." The machine's purpose was to compress and bale paper products such as cartons and boxes. Kirk brought the group over to the machine and tried to explain that it was, in effect, a recycling machine that Polar Star had developed long before recycling became an important issue.

Inside, the questions still continued to come, and they were hard questions. The group asked about the landfill problem and biodegradable products. Kirk told

Exhibit I-5

Polar Star Beverages Co. (C)

Recycle

Fact Sheet

Recycle

RECYCLE

"Each family in the United States discards, on the average, a ton of empty packages each year." Environment Nov. '69

"Packaging wastes are increasing at the rate of six percent a year, against a one percent increase in population." Environment Nov. '69

"It costs the U.S. taxpayer over one and a half billion dollars a year to dispose of refuse." Boys' Life March '70

"It costs from 20 to 30 cents to dispose of the "disposable" can of 10-cent soda." Boys' Life March '70

"We are rapidly running out of 'sanitary landfill' space." Boys' Life March '70

"Reusable bottles can be reused about 20 times, so they cost the bottler almost nothing." Forbes Aug. 1, '69

"Although there is an abundant supply of aluminun for the foreseeable future, the fact remains that the supply is not unlimited - and aluminum usage has doubled roughly every ten years." Scientific American Sept. '69

"Aluminum scrap offers a worthwhile incentive, a ton of aluminum brings $200 from dealers." Scientific American Sept. '69

"The average American throws away each day about 4½ pounds of trash-cans, bottles, paper, foodstuffs, etc." Boys' Life March '70 them about the biodegradable plastic bottle that Polar Star was trying to develop. This seemed to surprise most of them. Other questions were not quite as easy to answer, such as why Polar Star simply did not stop making nonreturnable bottles. He remembered trying to explain that it was impossible for Polar Star to take that step by itself, because all its competitors emphasized one-way bottles, and the consumer preference in the Bay Area was overwhelmingly for nonreturnables. Polar Star could not dictate to a market that wanted nonreturnables without going out of business. The Bay Area, he added, was one of the first markets in the country to demand nonreturnables. He also pointed out that the pile of bottles they had brought showed that the problem was one that Polar Star alone could not solve. The bottles included chain-store private labels, as well as other brands. He remembered explaining how everyone would be ahead economically if they used returnables and that Polar Star had always supplied dealers with returnable bottles and would continue to do so.

There were several questions Kirk felt he could not answer, because they dealt with confidential information of potential value to competitors, such as the plant's production by bottle type. Kirk explained this and tried to answer giving only percentages. He also felt he could not say anything about whether the company would support proposed state legislation banning nonreturnables, because he had not seen any of the legislation. They asked him this question several times, and he felt that they wanted him to either endorse it or take a stand against it. Although he didn't feel he could comment on the matter, he assured them that the company would comply with any legislation that was passed.

The group moved through the plant as they talked, and Kirk showed them the stacked cases of returnable empties waiting to be reused, as well as the empty fountain and vending-machine syrup containers, which were also continually recycled. Several times during the tour, Kirk had to stop traffic while the group moved within the building. He also remembered pointing out the returnable empties coming back on the trucks. At one point, one of the girls lost her contact lens, and again traffic had to be stopped while they found it. At another point the supervisors' class let out, and Kirk wondered what would happen. Fortunately, the men simply stood around and watched. Similarly, the plant workers and the returning drivers had also kept at a distance, somewhat to Kirk's relief. It had been quite an afternoon, he thought.

During all this, it was apparent that there were several issues on which he and they did not agree. However, he also sensed that he was more aware of some problems that they pointed out, and that they had also begun to see some of the problems facing Polar Star. Much of the hostility he had sensed earlier had gone. In fact, when the students started to leave, he remembered going up and shaking hands with them. Several who had started out the door returned to wish him well.

It had all happened quickly, and he felt a considerable sense of relief that it was over. Yet some of the questions they had raised, and the episode itself, posed a number of questions. Kirk decided that it might be useful to just sit down and try to write out what had happened and what implications it might have for the San Francisco plant as well as other Polar Star bottlers.

Walter Marin

Sherry and I went out a couple of times last fall and really began hitting it off—really changed my thinking. I can remember driving home after an especially soul-searching conversation with her. I was really wound up and thinking about bringing her home sometime soon. As I drove down my street, even the neighborhood looked different, or at least I was seeing new sides of it. I had lived here for about a year, on a back street in an ethnic section of Watertown. The style of the neighborhood was settled, lower middle class, made up of many recent immigrants who were making it in the skilled trades and who had moved here to raise families away from the hectic environs of downtown Boston. Fathers worked as clerks, mechanics, civil servants. Mothers stayed at home and tended kids, house, and husbands. All very orderly and settled. I was kind of odd-man-out on the street, and although the neighbors were friendly, it was hard to establish myself in the neighborhood. People were constantly giving me advice and clucking their tongues a bit when I discussed my life and interests. They were sure I was unhappy as a single person, and I could hear them thinking, "Wouldn't it be nice if he could find some nice woman to take care of him and give him children." Needless to say, my late hours and my companions were the cause of many raised eyebrows.

I was attracted to this place because of its seclusion from city bustle and the relief it provided after hard days at the office. I was in charge of a staff group of about 15 people at a medium-sized consulting firm downtown. It was the job of my staff to see that all departments were coordinating their presentations properly and that all material going to the clients was complete. As a result, I spent much of my day listening to people argue, mediating interpersonal conflicts, and coordinating large volumes of report data. Since I was also studying at night, I needed a quiet and isolated environment.

After living in the city for several years, I had learned that even the most insulated apartment could not block out the traffic noise or provide distance from fellow city dwellers. Early childhood habits developed in the country finally drove me to the suburbs, and, believe me, the quiet was worth the commuting time.

So I ended up on this street, in a somewhat shabby two-family house, living among people with whom I had little in common. I was here because of the space in the apartment, the price (dirt cheap compared to the same square footage in Cambridge), the off-street parking, and the yard that provided the very important distance from one's neighbors.

Well, anyway, I remember driving home that night after seeing Sherry, and I just couldn't wind down. The rest of the street was asleep at midnight, and I walked around my apartment for several hours thinking about Sherry, looking at the books on the wall, shuffling through the papers on my desk and the floor surrounding it, wondering how it all had ended up here. All this recognizable stuff in an apartment that certainly wasn't *mine*—the arsenic-and-old-lace wallpaper, the dusty white venetian blinds, the goddamn flamingos on the bathroom wall. It all hadn't bothered me until now, but tonight it began intruding.

Sherry and I would soon be spending time here, or at least this is what my instincts told me. I wanted her to see the "real" me, not the image this place conveyed. The next day I set in motion a scheme of redecoration. Ordered a new rug, new furniture, new bookshelves, and some wall hangings to blot out the wallpaper.

By January, I was seeing Sherry several times a week, and we had started doing nothing together—a significant action and one that caused a little readjusting. It's somehow easy to have a date or pick someone up or some other socially defined thing, but just doing nothing is serious business. There's no ostensible purpose for being together, so the pressure is on to be casual and noncommittal perhaps, or to be cool and halfway hard to get—all those little games people play when they're first getting to know each other at home.

We tended to do nothing at Sherry's place, because it was the "safest." There was a roommate around to fill gaps in conversation and minimize the amount of attention we would have been forced to pay each other had we been alone. The apartment itself was one of those new garden apartments that you can never quite mess up or change around. Built-in closets and fixtures, all the conveniences, wall-to-wall carpeting, right in the middle of hundreds of other units just like it. Everything was new and clean—the walls were starkly white, the kitchen cabinets plastic veneer. Three white rooms with sliding glass doors opening onto the terrace. Sliding steel closet doors. Not a bit of wood anywhere. I mean, it was a nice place and all, but it was really hard to make it feel like home. I remember Sherry remarking that she always felt "temporary" there. She couldn't make her furniture fit, or find wall hangings that could soften the corners. And, God, the walls were thin! You could hear what was going on in apartments above, below, and beside. That's what really got to us—it felt something like being in a transparent cage, like always being in public or something.

Even though we didn't like the place, we seemed to feel more comfortable there when we first started getting serious. Somehow we just didn't feel isolated as a couple there, we didn't feel self-conscious about being alone together, because there were so many other single people in the apartment complex who were going through the same things we were. Going through the little embarrassments of getting to know people, feeling up or down depending upon whether relationships were working or not. It was also comfortable because we had not really worked out a pattern of sexual behavior yet, and it was often convenient to use "disturbing the roommate" as an excuse for separating at night.

Soon, however, Sherry and I began to want nights alone, and disturbing the roomate became a real problem, so my place became a much better idea. I remember feeling a little nervous as we approached my house for the first time, and we both spontaneously made comments about how quiet the street was for 11 P.M. Sherry seemed a little surprised that I would live in a place so settled. I remember also feeling a little macho—something like the bachelor-pad scenes in 1950s movies—and once we were inside, we began acting a little withdrawn. I think Sherry felt a bit threatened by being so alone with me, and I must admit I felt less sure of myself than at any time before during our dating. We both admitted later that we had been feeling out of character that night, and we couldn't figure out why our feelings had changed so swiftly.

After our first night there, we returned one or two times, but we really couldn't shake that uneasiness. As a result, over the following month, we spent more of our time at Sherry's. Her roommate would be away many nights, and on these occasions we would stay there. As I think back now, I can't figure out why we stayed there. We really didn't like the style of the place, but it was simply less threatening than my place. I don't think we spent any appreciable time at my house until later in February.

Time together convinced us that our relationship was not like many of the passing ones we had had, and in fact we knew it was more serious than some of the longer-term ones we had enjoyed. Both of us were starting to feel like more effective adults, professionally and personally. I was seeing more direction at work, sensing what interests would be long-term ones, getting used to some of the hassles that seemed so worthless and stifling right after college. Sherry was becoming established as a young doctor and starting to feel effective and useful after six years of graduate study and training. We had both changed in recent years and were now discovering that our goals and interests were remarkably compatible. Each of us had found that our ambitions had caused problems in our earlier relationships, and we had grown away from several close partners in painful stages. Needless to say, we weren't very trusting in general about the ability of young professionals to get together and stay together despite demands placed on each partner and the stresses common to this type of life-style. We discussed at length the problems faced by normally stable people who would grow exponentially at work, leaving partners behind—and about the opportunities for meeting new and interesting people that often pushed professional couples apart. We knew that we were getting very close to each other, and that we were satisfying each other's needs to a very great extent.

One night, after several months of commuting between apartments, we were sitting at Sherry's and the subject of people's living together came up. Both of us had lived with partners before, and we had several close friends who had been doing this for some time. Sherry asked if I had thought about living with her. I had, so we got involved in some serious talking, ultimately deciding that we had enough time to try it before our own leases ran out in September.

It was obvious that we should settle at my house so we wouldn't crowd out Sherry's roommate. Sherry began moving her clothes into my house, and we arranged closets and furniture to accommodate the two of us. We were a bit apprehensive at first, but after several weeks we began to feel markedly different. I remember feeling more relaxed because we weren't hopping from one apartment to the other, and I also remember feeling good about being able to see Sherry more conveniently. Both of us worked a lot at home, and it was very nice to be able to share work breaks together. We had been worried about getting into a routine, but living together actually increased our spontaneity at first. We did discover some problems, though, largely due to the size and layout of my apartment. It was impossible to isolate ourselves in any way. We could see each other at all times from any spot in the two main rooms, unless one of us worked at the kitchen table. This meant we couldn't dictate, type, or work too late at night, or listen to music—and sometimes, just knowing that someone was sitting within eyesight could destroy our concentration. Too often we would give in and talk instead of work. Our performances at work began to reflect this.

Also, Sherry needed to practice ballet exercises every day, and she felt constrained by my presence. We could feel the early signs of frustration building, and we knew that living together on a permanent basis would require much more room, and *private* space.

One of the reasons we had chosen this time to test living together was the opportunity to house-sit in a large Cambridge house. In early May, we had arranged with friends, the Campbells, to occupy their house while they were on vacation in Europe. This made temporary quarters in Watertown seem bearable, because we knew we would soon be moving into neutral territory in a dwelling constructed for more than one person.

Before moving into the mansion, Sherry and I scheduled a vacation, which would help us get away from the severe strain at work and also test our developing abilities to live together in close quarters on some kind of committed basis. We visited close friends of Sherry's in the mountains of Georgia for a little more than a week. Despite long hours on the road, suspicious looks from several rural motel owners, and isolation in the mountains, our vacation was very enjoyable and reinforced our intentions to occupy the mansion together upon returning to Boston.

The last week in May, we moved in. It was a huge Tudor house of about twenty rooms, with walk-around gardens, sculptured walls enclosing the property, and incredible cooking facilities. Sherry and I have some 1960s hang-ups about decadent bourgeois taste and conspicuous consumption, and we had been a bit shaky about appearing too settled to ourselves. Well, this house brought out all these feelings at first, and we had some trouble fitting into the spirit of this place for a few days. We were afraid of breaking things, and we limited ourselves to living in two rooms—a bedroom and the kitchen. Both these rooms were larger than my Watertown apartment. We joked around a lot during the first week here, teasing each other about providing ourselves with this style of living, and I was actually nervous at times about being in such a settled place. Some bad feelings about previous "living together" filtered up through my mind, and once in a while I felt myself drawing back from Sherry. She sensed this, and we began to discuss the permanence we could now see as potentially real, trying to bring some of our fears into the open. Some things we had been keeping below the surface came out in these discussions—it was somehow easier to talk about permanent relationships here. When dealing with these thoughts, we could look around us at the life the Campbells lived and somehow joke about long-term living. The real examples around us seemed so unattainable that the whole topic became a bit imaginary. It was strange. We had never before asked questions like, Could we be together when we're 50? Do we want to settle into something like this? We were talking about permanence in very real terms, but it seemed detached.

Work became easier, both because we had more space and because we were secure in demanding less attention from each other. Earlier, we had often "checked each other out" before getting to work to make sure we wouldn't be ignoring each other. Now that we were feeling more at home with each other, we could start working more naturally, without worrying about pulling at the other person. It also helped greatly to have different study spaces. Dr. Campbell had a study in what had once been the servant's quarters, secluded at the back of the second floor. I could completely isolate myself there and think, talk out ideas, or do anything in complete freedom. Sherry moved around more. Sometimes she would study in the "writing room" attached to the bedroom suite we used, at the front of the second floor; at other times she used the living room or even the kitchen table. The kitchen and the bedroom suite were both incredible places, each actually made up of several rooms. The "bedroom" had a sleeping room, an even larger writing room, and a very large, plush-carpeted bathroom. The kitchen was one huge space divided by a counter separating cooking space and informal dining space. Cooking was great fun there, because there were enough appliances and space to serve large banquets—we often cooked and studied there at the same time. We soon noticed that we accomplished more at night and worked more relaxedly at work, because life at the mansion was easier.

While living in the mansion, we began to actively search for a place of our own. We were quite convinced that we should stop messing around and get a reasonable place with enough room and proper atmosphere to accommodate both of us. One of my earlier experiences of living with someone had been severely strained because of space and "ownership" problems (I had moved into her place), and I wanted no part of this kind of hassle now. If Sherry and I didn't make it together, I didn't want any thoughts of "it must have been the environment" to cloud the issue of interpersonal compatibility. Adults simply shouldn't crowd themselves into places meant for pets.

By this time, we had established ourselves as a couple socially and were visiting together largely with other couples. This was sometimes trying, because some unmarried people were having troubles that often came to the surface in front of us. Sherry and I were sure we could handle any pressures of this type, but we were very concerned that we shouldn't place undue stress on our relationship. We knew that for the next several years, professional duties would be more taxing than any we had experienced to this point, and our resources would be limited because I wanted to go back to school, so we felt careful planning would be necessary to make incidental problems as small as possible. We would have to devote most of our energies to careers and our relationship, so we didn't want things like a crappy apartment, extreme living expenses, high fixed costs, lack of vacations, and so on, to occupy too much of our attention. We began to monitor our financial resources and think carefully about what elements of life-style had priority over others. We were becoming more and more interdependent, and we realized that making our relationship work would mean satisfying each other's basic needs. I remember it was hard to talk about anything but finding an apartment and setting up a life-style in such a way that we could meet our growing adult needs in an economical manner. This began to be a real pain in the ass, and since the two of us were prone to anxiety, our emotions began to fly around a bit. The good thing to come of all this planning and tension was the recognition that despite our disagreements and push-pull, we were handling stress in a very healthy way. We began to have little tiffs, something we had avoided almost totally to this point, but we weren't getting destructive or self-serving—we would often remark after a release of emotion that it was great to fight with someone so understanding. This kind of paradox increased our hopes of making it under stress.

We canvassed our unmarried-couple friends to see if they had any unique problems in finding places to live, and learned to our surprise that many people in Boston were still uptight about unmarried couples. Our friends seemed to feel that most of the bad sentiment was economically induced—supposedly, unmarried couples, being less stable, would be more likely to cop out on the rent. One or two people had run into moral objections to cohabitation, though.

After several visits and talks to landlords, Sherry and I decided that we would at least imply the married routine, unless the landlords seemed able to cope with an honest statement of our intentions. It was actually quite easy to convey the impression of being married without actually having to say it—owners were very ready and willing to assume we were married. By this time, Sherry and I could each sense how the other was reacting in many different situations without verbal expression, and we even put on different "acts" for the different styles of landlord we were seeing. Outside of work, apartment hunting had become our major activity by mid-June, and it was even great fun for a while. We weren't turning up any great apartments, but we were sure learning how to go about the interview process, and we found interesting the variety of judgments that landlords passed on us. Sometimes we would react to these negatively, most often because I was forced into the provider-protector role by landlords, and Sherry was forced out of the conversation. This really bugged me. Sherry was first of all in a higher-status professional position than I and would be bringing in more money during the next few years. Also, we both felt that our relationship should not fall along the traditionally conceived lines of sexual stereotypes. One of the prime attractions between us was the ease with which we assumed divisions of labor, and the minimal attention we tried to pay to either traditional or revolutionary roles.

While living in the mansion, we really began settling into the coupled life-style, dividing cooking, shopping, and cleaning; and we were enjoying it even more than we could have anticipated. We began feeling fulfilled in ways that once seemed lost in the memories of adolescence—it wasn't all that "love at first sight" euphoria, but a richer sense that we were accomplishing something, or building something. We still expressed fears of living together and once in a while backed off from each other, but the freedom of the mansion helped us dispel many of these tensions easily. It seemed as if there was a place in that house to match or change any mood you could feel. The living room was gracious and regal, with all those antiques and paintings. It must have been 35 feet long, and it opened onto the terrace, so it seemed even larger. It was obvious that the designer had been riding a fine line between perfect design and comfortable living—the layout was exquisite, but you felt that you could sit down on everything. Dr. Campbell had an office on the first floor with everything finished in suede or velvet. I felt more comfortable there than Sherry did, and I guess this room had a very masculine flavor. I could sit in that room for hours, doing absolutely nothing but thinking, and I couldn't walk in there without becoming philosophical about something. For pure enjoyment, I liked that room better than any in the house.

We often ate out on the patio or in the front garden. It was somehow "illicit" to sit so close to city traffic yet be so isolated. We felt as if we were carrying on some courtly affair on those lazy Sunday mornings. I don't really know how to explain the enchantment of this place, except that it was OK to play out fantasies there—like being adult and kid all at once. Toward the end of our stay in the mansion, we began to feel the pressure of not having a proper place of our own to return to, and we pushed harder in our apartment hunting.

At the end of June, we moved back into my place in Watertown, and we became depressed and irritable despite our best efforts to adapt. We both remarked how much we had grown accustomed to the mansion, and every apartment we saw that week seemed smaller than those we had seen the week before. Now we were stopping some of our social activities in favor of apartment hunting, getting angry that we were willing to sacrifice summer weekends to look at apartments, but finally concluding that's what we had to do. We realized now that we were firmly committed to our permanence, and fleeting thoughts that we might separate seemed absurd.

We joked around a bit about marriage in these days, but rejected it for all the reasons we had before—"it seems to ruin so many good relationships, who needs it with a strong commitment?" and so on. Pressure on Sherry at work was getting out of hand, and we finally concluded it was best to shuck off some of the responsibilities we had set for ourselves and get away from it all in Vermont. As we pulled away from the city, the tensions began to slack off, and we discovered again some of the peace we had known before all hell broke loose two months earlier. That was one great weekend; we came back to the city with renewed enthusiasm and the conviction that no matter what happened in the near future, if the pressure got too much, we would shut down and get away from the world together.

About a week after we got back from Vermont in mid-July, we found an apartment that we truly liked without any reservation. We almost couldn't believe that it fit so many of our desires so well. It was in a two-family house about halfway between my office and Sherry's, in a secluded section of Newton. The street was quiet and full of trees; the house had a large yard, a two-car garage, and a huge basement. No more of that cheap wallpaper—these walls were a nice stucco with natural-finish wood trim. The living room had a large fireplace, and all rooms had clean wooden floors. If you opened the doors to all five rooms, the apartment became a large, semi-open living space. With the doors closed, you could seclude yourself almost anywhere in privacy. This place had character and a sympathetic mood. Both Sherry and I relaxed in the place within seconds after walking in.

Of course, Boston had plenty of others who wanted this place, and about twenty other couples were there to see it. We all lined up outside the kitchen and went in, couple by couple, to an interview with the owners. Sherry and I wanted the place with a passion, so we were nervous as hell and actually quite angry for having to be so competitively sweet for so long (we had been looking for more than six weeks). Everyone was smiling nicely but staring daggers and trying to figure out how to beat all the other couples. After our interview was over, Sherry and I were sure we had blown it, and we argued over what each of us had said wrong and how this or that couple were sure to get the place. We had been willing to lose other apartments, but this one really meant something to us. We could see ourselves enjoying it very much.

Several days later, the owner made up his mind and offered us the place. We couldn't believe it. We just sat down after the phone call and collapsed. Relief. My God, didn't that feel good? We had a home now—even though it took about two days for this to sink in.

I think it was just about the same day that we took a second house-sitting job in Cambridge, with some people we knew through mutual friends. We had never seen the house, and we made all arrangements over the phone, so we didn't know what to expect. Our primary aim was to find a place to stay until we could move into our new apartment. Life at my house in Watertown was bearing down on us, especially in the heat, and we really wanted some room to spread out in, so we would move into the Bartows' house in a week.

Without the bustle of apartment hunting, life seemed almost silent now. I remember that we began changing, becoming more quiet—feeling some of those "pregnant silences" people talk about. We were thinking a lot about what was right for us, what we were doing together, what we really wanted out of life. I think I felt embarrassed and even slightly afraid of how close we had gotten, and although I felt we were surely doing the right thing, I could feel some tensions building up.

One night, our reflecting got so oppressive that we sat down and performed one of our regrouping maneuvers—asking just what the hell we were all about. We were pretty wound up that night, and it was obvious we couldn't sleep, so we just talked, letting emotions rise to the surface, recognizing them, and questioning each other about them. We were pretty hard on each other—something we had learned to do if we were confused. Something powerful was happening, because we were misinterpreting what was said and sometimes drawing back in fear from the other, as if this whole thing was crazy, and who the hell are you, and aren't you really going to leave me anyway no matter how good a person you are? Sometime around 1 A.M., the question arose, Should we get married? Are you serious? I don't know! This is crazy! Well, I don't know, is it? What do you think about it? You're sure you're not kidding? No, dammit! My God, I think we can! I mean . . . yes . . . I think . . . well, yes. . . . Silence. There was no way in the world one of us could have proposed to the other—that would have brought too many images of bad marriages and sexual dominance to the fore—but now we were facing a mutual question, posed equally, and we couldn't back off.

We gave ourselves a day to think about it and try it out after some sleep, and when we found the idea even more attractive, we started the wheels in motion. Both of us had strong aversions to ceremonies, and we weren't willing to put up with much formality. This was our affair, and what we really wanted was a low-key event at which a wide variety of people could enjoy themselves. Our first instinct was to find a location outside the city—outdoors, away from crowds. We scouted and rejected a number of locations, but then we found an opportunity to use a house on the water in Beverly for a week, and as soon as we saw it, we jumped at the chance.

It had been a carriage house of a large ocean-front estate, hanging on a point of land about 50 feet above the water. Two lawns faced the water on either side of the house, and hedges cut it off from the mainland. We could get married on a large flat rock jutting out into the waves, and our friends could sit or stand almost anywhere. Outside, this was the most beautiful yard I had seen in a long time. Inside, the house was even better. The living room ceilings were about 12–15 feet high, because the first floor had actually been a stable. This room was L-shaped, about 40 by 30 feet. One wall facing the ocean was almost entirely glassed in. All the wood was natural wormwood, with a classy rustic flavor. The whole design was a tasteful contrast of rough planking and elegant furniture. There was a large fireplace opposite the ocean wall. Off to one side, the kitchen extended about 30 feet beyond the living room—again, a mixture of rough wood and modern appliances. A master bedroom and a bathroom with the highest ceiling I've ever seen were both tucked away behind one corner of the living room. The hayloft second floor could be reached through a very steep ladder stair. Up there were three uniquely shaped bedrooms. I couldn't picture a more relaxed place to have a wedding, even if it *was* going to be my own.

We called our friends and relatives and told them that if they wanted, they could drop by in comfortable clothes at this Beverly estate and join us in a relaxed afternoon. I really got a kick out of that. Of course, we got some resistance from our immediate families, but they knew how independent-minded we both were, and they backed off quickly and got into the spirit of it all. We were very surprised at the number of relatives and friends who were willing to come from all over the country for such a swift and casual affair.

Just as we were announcing our marriage, we moved into the Bartows' Cambridge house. What a jolt that was. I guess we had been expecting the same atmosphere of the first house we had stayed in, but the whole feeling at the Bartows' was different. Everything was clean and well-kept, of course, but it seemed musty—not in smell or anything, it was more the color or tone of the place. Too much dark, dark wood. A heavy grand piano, covered with lace and pictures in stand-up frames. Ponderous antiques. Heavy, black-bound books, and those stiffly starched thin curtains stretched over the french doors. Even with all the lights on, the place seemed too dark to read in. Upstairs was much the same, except it was covered with heavily ivied wallpaper.

This was truly another century, and Sherry and I drew back quickly. I remember feeling afraid of growing old and feeling compassion for people who only had a few years left. I couldn't believe the place made me feel so somber and pessimistic. Sherry and I stayed in Watertown the first three nights we should have stayed in Cambridge.

Events moved quickly now, and our pace got hectic again—making arrangements for food, reserving motel rooms, renting tables, trying to get some work done during the day. People were calling in from all over, and it seemed as though this simple wedding was going to roll right over us. I really don't have much perspective on that last week. It was call here, drive there, write here, move this, push, push, push. Faster, faster, faster. And then the stream of relatives and friends began arriving—and it was, "Hi. How are you? You don't know me but I'm the groom, I guess, and I'm pleased to meet you, and yes, I'm very happy." And the wedding day. All those people. And I was standing on the rocks in Beverly, looking at the waves, and I was getting married. Talking to the people—"So glad to see you. So glad you could make it. How nice. Yes, it's beautiful here." Lots of talking and lots of fun and very little comprehension of it all. And slowly they are leaving. Only a few close friends left late at night on the lawn, and it is calm. Very calm. The lights in the harbor. The boats. A cool breeze.

The next morning, and we are married. But it doesn't really feel any different. We wake up and the estate is ours—like we have lived here forever. Friends come over for breakfast, and we all sit around knowing everyone will be moving to different parts of the country soon, but today is ours and nothing can break it up right now.

Sherry and I had to be back at work on Monday, and we had to move into the new apartment in a couple of days, but the house in Beverly was ours for a week. We didn't care about any of the places we could stay back in the city—the Bartows', my place in Watertown, Sherry's garden apartment. We were carrying the quiet of our ocean estate into the city each day, and no one was going to mess that up for a week. At Beverly each night we could spread out, open up our minds, and just come to a complete stop. I remember sitting in that huge living room, staring at the ocean and letting the sound of the waves pull me away. The damp sea air soothed everything. I don't think we talked much at all there, and when we did, it was slower and much calmer than usual. We didn't move much beyond the living room, because it was so large and well-shaped that we could get all the space we wanted without moving upstairs. Also, the outside of the house was really only an extension of the inside—with the french doors and windows open, the grass, rocks, and sea became part of the living room. I turned off the stereo several times to let the sound of waves and buoy bells float in. Sherry and I felt almost no physical bounds during our stay there, and we were very sorry to have to return to the city.

We started coming back to earth again, and centered ourselves in the Bartows' house because that's where our strongest obligation lay. We weren't exactly exhausted, but we certainly were detached from any regular schedule. I felt a bit displaced and cut loose from my moorings. There were times when I just couldn't stand sitting in the mansion any more, and I would return to my Watertown apartment to sort through my accumulation of junk. I needed to think a lot about the past, and this spot seemed best. I guess I was trying to gain some perspective on being married, and tracing through memories was one way of doing it. Sometimes I would go over to our new place to see what kind of work it would need when we moved in. I remember staying there several afternoons, again deep in thought about the future and what my new commitments would mean. I think Sherry was doing something similar, because she spent several afternoons and evenings at her old garden apartment, which she was still renting but to which she had not returned for some time. As I think back on that period, I don't remember much specifically, but I do recall flipping through emotions as I moved from place to place. Hope in our new place. A sense of growth and some painful nostalgia at my old one. Depression and discomfort at the Bartows'.

In the second week of August, I moved all my stuff from Watertown to our new place in Newton. This day took on all kinds of symbolic meaning, because I was literally moving out of an old life into a new. Most of my collected or fabricated junk seemed out of place in the new apartment, and I spent the day throwing away a lot of memories. When I pulled away from Watertown for the last trip, I remember feeling almost overwhelmed at cutting off an old part of my life and somewhat silly for feeling so attached to such an ugly house.

Sherry and I gradually began spending time in the new apartment—painting and cleaning in small steps, and finally moving her possessions in. When we first saw our new place empty, it looked much worse than we had remembered. Without the furniture and wall hangings, we could see that, yes, this wall was really orange and that one was really blue. The hall wasn't paneled where the washer and dryer had been. The kitchen floor was really filthy, and there were small holes in all the walls. We were a bit down, but the atmosphere and style were still just what we wanted, and work was fun. We spackled and painted the orange walls off-white. We polished the floors and scrubbed everything in sight. Much of our old furniture didn't fit the style we wanted for this place, so we started giving it away.

We agreed totally on how things should be cleaned and polished, but when it came time to fill up the empty rooms we found that we really had strong differences of opinion on the use of our living space. Sherry wanted the living room light and airy; I wanted it close and cozy. I wanted the study filled with books; Sherry was convinced this made the room look too crowded. Resolving these differences was interesting because we could no longer "escape" to a spare apartment—we had no safety valve like that any more, and any problems had to be worked out right here.

One solution was to designate territory in the place. I was allowed to do whatever I felt like to the study, but I had to defer to Sherry's judgment in the living room (something I'm glad I did). We negotiated priorities on furniture purchases, since our resources were limited, and shopped around extensively to find pieces that would span our tastes. One top-priority item was study space, and we set up several areas in our apartment where one could study in peace. If the pressure is on at work, we can retreat to separate ends of the apartment and do whatever we wish. The new place rather soon became our place.

John Martin

John Martin, a second-year student at a graduate business school, was invited by Jerome L. Anderson, president of Marshall Industries, to come to New Orleans to discuss potential employment. Anderson had heard from a mutual friend of Martin's desire to locate in New Orleans, and had written to Martin on January 6, 1969. Arrangements were made, and Martin visited Anderson in New Orleans on January 24, 1969.

On January 30, 1969, Martin sent the following letter to Anderson:

Dear Mr. Anderson:

I was anxious to let you know how very pleased I was with the day we spent together and with your generous offer. It was a very good trip for me, and I wish to thank you again.

From our discussion I can visualize the position you offered as having tremendous potential for my own personal development. The opportunities with Marshall Industries, and as your assistant, appear to be very significant. I want to assure you that I consider this one of my top two offers, and I will be giving this my utmost consideration during the next month. I have already thought of several questions and I am sure that many more will come up in the next few weeks.

I am most interested in the growth opportunities for Marshall—how strong is the company's and your own commitment to grow, and what do you consider the goals for the next five to ten years? Where will the emphasis on growth be focused—earnings, stock price, sales, etc.? What are the real strengths and weaknesses of the company that could affect the attainment of the goals? What is the distinctive characteristic of Marshall that will help it in the future? How many employees does the whole company have, and what are the backgrounds of the men who head each of the subsidiaries? These are the primary questions that I have now, and I feel that the answers will help me in making my decision.

My wife reminded me to ask you about two other things—holiday and vacation schedules, and medical and insurance coverage. I consider these minor points, and they will in no way affect my decision, but they would be helpful to know.

I will anxiously await hearing from you, and I do appreciate your consideration and cooperation.

You told me to inform you of the additional cost I incurred on my trip; these came to $28.00 and included cab fares in New York and New Orleans plus two breakfasts. Thank you for having me down.

Very truly yours,

Jack

John Martin

On February 10, 1969, Anderson replied as follows:

Dear Mr. Martin:

I have your letter of January 30, 1969. Frankly, it raises a substantial question in my mind as to whether the job we have here is the right one for you. I know this is an important matter to each of us and I would suggest that we should discuss it again.

I plan to be in Washington, D.C., February 25 through 27 and could arrange some free time in the late afternoon and evening of the 27th.

Would you like to join me in Washington one of these days?

Yours very truly,

J. L. Anderson

Jerome L. Anderson

John Martin planned to go to Washington to discuss the situation with Mr. Anderson. He thought it would be useful to study carefully the letter he had sent to Anderson to see if he could uncover what might have led to Anderson's response.

Mr. Dale

The situation reported in this case occurred in a small elementary school with a staff of ten, four men and six women. One of the men was Chester Dale, the principal. The school system had a teachers' union that had a reputation within the state of being especially militant. Mr. Dale had been principal of the school for nearly two years.

This case presents a statement of Dale's view of a conflict he was having with one of his teachers. The statement summarizes a conversation Dale had with the casewriter.

Say, I think you should be in on this. My dear little friend "Teddy" is heading himself into a showdown with me. Recently, one of the teachers brought to my attention that he's using the history book as a reading text, and by prolonging the history period by a half an hour, he uses the period to also teach reading. This gives him a free half hour at the end of the day that he lets his pupils use as study time, or for whatever he happens to think is a "cool" thing for them to do. In effect, he's giving them less reading than they ought to be getting, since they would have to read the history lessons anyway. And I'm not convinced the "supplementary" materials he uses in the extra half hour make up for not using the reading text. In my mind, he's cheating the students and making it easier for himself under the disguise of being innovative. He's not fulfilling the curriculum requirements, which are to teach an hour of history *and* an hour of reading. In effect, it's cheating, and I've called him down on it. A few days ago, I was told he was doing it again, and when I spoke to him about it, he didn't deny it. He said he was fulfilling the requirements called for by the curriculum guide and, therefore, the union contract.

Ted's been getting away with this for too long, and I think he's taking advantage of the situation. I know he didn't like my calling him on it, because the

This case is a redisguised version of "Mr. Hart," originally prepared by Fritz J. Roethlisberger.

next day I got a call from the teachers' union representative and had him breathing down my back. But you know what it's like talking to those people; they'll defend a teacher even if he's being nonprofessional. Well, anyway, I let them both know that I wouldn't tolerate the practice any longer, and I let Ted know that if he continues to do this kind of thing, I would take official action. This kind of thing has to be curbed. Actually, I'm inclined to think that he may have a personality problem, because talking to him has no meaning whatsoever. I've tried just about every approach to jar some sense into that guy's head, and I've just about given it up as a bad deal. I just can't seem to make any kind of an impression on him. It's an unpleasant situation for everyone concerned, and I'm at a loss to know what more I can do about it.

I don't know what it is about the guy, but I think he's harboring some deep feelings against me. For what, I don't know, because I've tried to handle that bird with kid gloves. But his whole attitude around here on the job is one of indifference, and he certainly isn't a good influence on the rest of the staff. Frankly, I think he purposely tried to agitate them against me at times, too. It also seems to me that he's suffering from delusions of grandeur. He plays his guitar in the lunchroom and sings folk songs. He thinks he's Bob Dylan. Even though there are no formal rules against it, I think that a teacher playing a guitar in the lunchroom is unprofessional. Fortunately, most of the children go home for lunch. He claims that the pupils and teachers enjoy it, but I think it's part of an ego trip he's on. I understand he takes singing lessons and is working with some of the local rock bands in the city. All of which is OK by me; but when his outside interests start interfering with his professionalism and effectiveness in the school, then I have to pay close attention to the situation. For this reason, I've been keeping my eye on that bird, and if he steps out of line once more, he and I will part ways.

I feel quite safe in saying that I've done all I can rightfully be expected to do by way of trying to show him what's expected of him. You know there's an old saying, "You can't make a silk purse out of a sow's ear." The guy is simply unscrupulous. He feels no obligation to do a real day's work. Yet I know the guy can do a good job, because for a long time he did. But in recent months, he's slipped for some reason, and his whole attitude on the job has changed. Why, it's even getting to the point now where I think he's inducing other teachers to goof off and leave ten minutes early at the end of the day. It's not that I'm hard-nosed about it, but he should remain available until 4:30 in case a parent calls, or to talk with other staff. But sometimes he goes down to the teachers' room at quarter past, and invariably a couple will follow him out ten minutes early. I've called him on it several times, but words just don't seem to make any lasting impression on him. Well, if he keeps it up much longer, he's going to find himself on the way out. He's asked me for a transfer to an opening at Sarah Blake Elementary next year, so I know he wants to go. But I didn't give him an answer when he asked me, because I was so steaming mad at the time, and I may have told him to go somewhere else.

I think it would be good for you to talk with him. It'll give him a chance to think the matter through a little more carefully. There may be something that's troubling him in his personal life, although I've made every effort to find out if there was such a thing, and I've been unsuccessful. Maybe you'll have better luck.

Mr. Schumann

The situation reported in this case occurred in a small elementary school with a staff of ten teachers, four men and six women, and a principal, Chester Dale. One of the teachers was Theodore Schumann, who taught fourth grade. Schumann had been teaching at the school for three years and had tenure. The school system had a teachers' union with a reputation within the state of being especially militant.

This case presents a statement of Schumann's view of a conflict he was having with Mr. Dale, the principal. The statement summarizes a conversation Schumann had with the casewriter.

According to the union contract, as I understand it, I'm meeting my responsibilities as long as I fulfill or exceed the requirements of the curriculum guide, which I am doing. My kids don't learn less, they learn more than what the guide outlines. The guide requires an hour of history and an hour of reading. The way I've designed the lesson plans, I combine the two subjects for half an hour of the period. I use the history text as a reader because it is 4.5 to 5.5 level, the same as the reading text. I give them the exercise and growth sequences from the regular reading text in the extra half hour. The history text is better reading and more exciting than the reading text. Using a half hour of history for reading frees up time that we can use better as a class in other ways—which we do.

Mr. Dale is all uptight about it because it "offends" his sense of how it should be done. All he has to do is look at the Metro[1] scores for my class last year, the year before, and this year. They've gone up every year, and they will this year, too. So you see, what I'm doing is not only legal by the contract, it also causes better learning and more excitement,

This case is a redisguised version of "Bing," originally prepared by Fritz J. Roethlisberger.

[1]"Metro" was an abbreviation used within the school system for the Metropolitan Achievement Test, a standardized test with national norms. Schumann was referring to the scores on the reading part of the test.

which I think is what really rattles his cage.

Mr. Dale, as you know, has other ideas about it, and claims it's cheating and not meeting the contract requirements.

We really had a confrontation a few days ago. He came over to my classroom and let me know how he felt about it. Man, what a hassle. I've never seen anyone like him before. He's not content to say what's on his mind in a manlike way, but he prefers to do it in a way that makes you want to crawl inside a crack in the floor. What a guy! I don't mind being called down by the principal, but I like to be treated like a man, and not humiliated like he does a naughty kid. He made me feel like a third grader who was sent to the office. He's been pulling this kind of crap with me since he became principal. I knew him when he was just one of the teachers, but since he was promoted he's lost his friendly way, and he seems to be having difficulty knowing how to give leadership in the building. In fact, I've noticed he's been more this way since he got married. I don't know whether there's a connection there, but I do know he changed after becoming principal.

I got so mad after he chewed me out the other day that I called the union representative. I knew that what I was doing was legitimate under the contract, but I made an issue out of it just because he persists in handling me in this sarcastic way of his. I'm fed up with the whole damned situation, and I'd like to transfer to Sarah Blake next year. If I don't succeed, and I'm forced to stay, I'm going to screw him any way I can. He's not going to treat me like a kid any longer. When the union rep questioned him on the case, he finally had to back down, because according to the contract, a teacher can innovate with the curriculum as long as the requirements of the curriculum guide are met. During the conversation with me and the union representative, he charged it was an unprofessional practice and threatened to take it up the line with the director of elementary education. But that's just an idle threat, because the most he can do is recommend my transfer out of here, which is just what I'd like anyway.

You see, he's also bugged because I play the guitar during lunch period and the kids and teachers love it. He claims it's unprofessional, which of course is absurd. He hears people talk about my outside engagements—I play with a few of the local rock groups—and I think he resents it. I think he figures I can be so cocky because I have other ways of earning a living. Actually, the kids and teachers enjoy having me play and sing. You know, I think that's what bugs him—that I create a little bit of happiness around here. It's funny, but for some reason I think he's partial to the women teachers. He treats the other men the same way he does me, but with the women he's more decent. I don't know what his object is. Occasionally, I leave school a few minutes early, and sometimes some of the other teachers will leave with me, and so Mr. Dale thinks I'm the leader and usually picks me out to talk to about it.

So, you can see, I'm a marked man around here. He keeps watching me like a hawk. Naturally, this makes me very uncomfortable. That's why I'm sure a transfer would be the best thing. I've asked him for it, but he didn't give me any satisfaction at the time. While I remain here I'm going to keep my nose clean, but whenever I get the chance I'm going to slip it to him, but good.

Bob Knowlton (A)

Bob Knowlton was sitting alone in the conference room of the laboratory. The rest of the group had gone. One of the secretaries had stopped and talked for a while about her husband's coming induction into the army, and had finally left. Bob, alone in the laboratory, slid a little further down in his chair, looking with satisfaction at the results of the first test run of the new photon unit.

He liked to stay after the others had gone. His appointment as project head was still new enough to give him a deep sense of pleasure. His eyes were on the graphs before him, but in his mind he could hear Dr. Jerrold, the project head, saying again, "There's one thing about this place that you can bank on. The sky is the limit for a man who can produce!" Knowlton felt again the tingle of happiness and embarrassment. Well, dammit, he said to himself, he had produced! He wasn't kidding anybody. He had come to the Simmons Laboratories two years ago. During a routine testing of some rejected Clanson components, he had stumbled on the idea of the photon correlator, and the rest just happened. Jerrold had been enthusiastic; a separate project had been set up for further research and development of the device, and he had gotten the job of running it. The whole sequence of events still seemed a little miraculous to Knowlton.

He shrugged out of the reverie and bent determinedly over the sheets, when he heard someone come into the room behind him. He looked up expectantly; Jerrold often stayed late himself, and now and then dropped in for a chat. This always made the day's end especially pleasant for Bob. It wasn't Jerrold. The man who had come in was a stranger. He was tall, thin, and rather dark. He wore steel-rimmed glasses and had on a very wide leather belt with a large brass buckle.

This case was prepared by Alex Bavelas and is reproduced with permission.

The stranger smiled and introduced himself. "I'm Simon Fester. Are you Bob Knowlton?" Bob said yes, and they shook hands. "Doctor Jerrold said I might find you in. We were talking about your work, and I'm very much interested in what you are doing." Bob waved to a chair.

Fester didn't seem to belong in any of the standard categories of visitors: customer, visiting fireman, stockholder. Bob pointed to the sheets on the table. "There are the preliminary results of a test we're running. We've got a new gadget by the tail and we're trying to understand it. It's not finished, but I can show you the section that we're testing."

He stood up, but Fester was deep in the graphs. After a moment, he looked up with an odd grin. "These look like plots of a Jennings surface. I've been playing around with some autocorrelation functions of surfaces—you know that stuff." Bob, who had no idea what he was referring to, grinned back and nodded, and immediately felt uncomfortable. "Let me show you the monster," he said, and led the way to the workroom.

After Fester left, Knowlton slowly put the graphs away, feeling vaguely annoyed. Then, as if he had made a decision, he quickly locked up and took the long way out so that he would pass Jerrold's office. But the office was locked. Knowlton wondered whether Jerrold and Fester had left together.

The next morning, Knowlton dropped into Jerrold's office, mentioned that he had talked with Fester, and asked who he was.

"Sit down for a minute," Jerrold said. "I want to talk to you about him. What do you think of him?" Knowlton replied truthfully that he thought Fester was very bright and probably very competent. Jerrold looked pleased.

"We're taking him on," he said. "He's had a very good background in a number of laboratories, and he seems to have ideas about the problems we're tackling here." Knowlton nodded in agreement, instantly wishing that Fester would not be placed with him.

"I don't know yet where he will finally land," Jerrold continued, "but he seems interested in what you are doing. I thought he might spend a little time with you by way of getting started." Knowlton nodded thoughtfully. "If his interest in your work continues, you can add him to your group."

"Well, he seemed to have some good ideas even without knowing exactly what we are doing," Knowlton answered. "I hope he stays; we'd be glad to have him."

Knowlton walked back to the lab with mixed feelings. He told himself that Fester would be good for the group. He was no dunce, he'd produce. Knowlton thought again of Jerrold's promise when he had promoted him—"The man who produces gets ahead in this outfit." The words seemed to carry the overtones of a threat now.

The next day, Fester didn't appear until midafternoon. He explained that he had had a long lunch with Jerrold, discussing his place in the lab. "Yes," said Knowlton, "I talked with Jerry this morning about it, and we both thought you might work with us for awhile."

Fester smiled in the same knowing way that he had smiled when he mentioned the Jennings surfaces. "I'd like to," he said.

Knowlton introduced Fester to the other members of the lab. Fester and Link, the mathematician of the group, hit it off well together, and spent the rest of the afternoon discussing a method of analysis of patterns that Link had been worrying over for the last month.

It was 6:30 when Knowlton finally left the lab that night. He had waited almost eagerly for the end of the day to come, when they would all be gone and he could sit in the quiet rooms, relax, and think it over. "Think what over?" he asked himself. He didn't know. Shortly after 5:00 P.M. they had all gone except Fester, and what followed was almost a duel. Knowlton was annoyed that he was being cheated out of his quiet period, and finally resentfully determined that Fester should leave first.

Fester was sitting at the conference table reading, and Knowlton was sitting at his desk in the little glass-enclosed cubby that he used during the day when he needed to be undisturbed. Fester had gotten the last year's progress reports out and was studying them carefully. The time dragged. Knowlton doodled on a pad, the tension growing inside him. What the hell did Fester think he was going to find in the reports?

Knowlton finally gave up and they left the lab together. Fester took several of the reports with him to study in the evening. Knowlton asked him if he thought the reports gave a clear picture of the lab's activities.

"They're excellent," Fester answered with obvious sincerity. "They're not only good reports; what they report is damn good, too!" Knowlton was surprised at the relief he felt, and grew almost jovial as he said goodnight.

Driving home, Knowlton felt more optimistic about Fester's presence in the lab. He had never fully understood the analysis that Link was attempting. If there was anything wrong with Link's approach, Fester would probably spot it. "And if I'm any judge," he murmured, "he won't be especially diplomatic about it."

He described Fester to his wife, who was amused by the broad leather belt and the brass buckle.

"It's the kind of belt that Pilgrims must have worn," she laughed.

"I'm not worried about how he holds his pants up," he laughed with her. "I'm afraid that he's the kind that just has to make like a genius twice each day. And that can be pretty rough on the group."

Knowlton had been asleep for several hours when he was jerked awake by the telephone. He realized it had rung several times. He swung off the bed muttering about damn fools and telephones. It was Fester. Without any excuses, apparently oblivious of the time, he plunged into an excited recital of how Link's patterning problem could be solved.

Knowlton covered the mouthpiece to answer his wife's stage-whispered, "Who is it?" "It's the genius," replied Knowlton.

Fester, completely ignoring the fact that it was 2:00 in the morning, proceeded in a very excited way, starting in the middle of an explanation of a completely new approach to certain of the photon lab problems that he had stumbled on while analyzing past experiments. Knowlton managed to put some enthusiasm in his own voice and stood there, half-dazed and very uncomfortable, listening to Fester talk endlessly about what he had discovered. It was probably not only a new approach, but also an analysis that showed the inherent weakness of the previous experiment and how experimentation along that line would certainly have been inconclusive. The following day, Knowlton spent the entire morning with Fester and Link, the mathematician, the morning meeting having been called off so that Fester's work of the previous night could be gone over intensively. Fester was very anxious that this be done, and Knowlton was not too unhappy to call the meeting off for reasons of his own.

For the next several days, Fester sat in the back office that had been turned over to him and did nothing but read the progress reports of the work that had been done in the last six months. Knowlton caught himself feeling apprehensive about the reaction that Fester might have to some of his work. He was a little surprised at his own feelings. He had always been proud—although he had put on a convincingly modest face—of the way in which new ground in the study of photon measuring devices had been broken in his group. Now he wasn't sure, and it seemed to him that Fester might easily show that the line of research they had been following was unsound or even unimaginative.

The next morning, as was the custom in Bob's group, the members of the lab, including the secretaries, sat around the conference table. Bob always prided himself on the fact that the work of the lab was guided and evaluated by the group as a whole, and he was fond of repeating that it was not a waste of time to include secretaries in such meetings. Often, what started out as a boring recital of fundamental assumptions to a naive listener uncovered new ways of regarding these assumptions that would not have occurred to the researcher who had long ago accepted them as a necessary basis for his work.

These group meetings also served Bob in another sense. He admitted to himself that he would have felt far less secure if he had had to direct the work out of his own mind, so to speak. With the group meeting as the principle of leadership, it was always possible to justify the exploration of blind alleys because of the general educative effect on the team. Fester was there; Lucy and Martha were there; Link was sitting next to Fester, their conversation concerning Link's mathematical study apparently continuing from yesterday. The other members, Bob Davenport, George Thurlow, and Arthur Oliver, were waiting quietly.

Knowlton, for reasons that he didn't quite understand, proposed for discussion this morning a problem that all of them had spent a great deal of time on previously, with the conclusion that a solution was impossible, that there was no feasible way of treating it in an experimental fashion. When Knowlton proposed the problem, Davenport remarked that there was hardly any use going over it again, that he was satisfied that there was no way of approaching the problem with the equipment and the physical capacities of the lab.

This statement had the effect of a shot of adrenalin on Fester. He said he would like to know what the problem was in detail, and walking to the blackboard, began setting down the "factors" as various members of the group began discussing the problem and simultaneously listing the reasons it had been abandoned.

Very early in the description of the problem, it was evident that Fester was going to disagree about the impossibility of attacking it. The group realized this, and finally the descriptive materials and their recounting of the reasoning that had led to its abandonment dwindled away. Fester began his statement, which, as it proceeded, might well have been prepared the previous night, although Knowlton knew this was impossible. He couldn't help being impressed with the organized and logical way that Fester was presenting ideas that must have occurred to him only a few minutes before.

Fester had some things to say, however, that left Knowlton with a mixture of annoyance, irritation, and, at the same time, a rather smug feeling of superiority over Fester in at least one area. Fester was of the opinion that the way the problem had been analyzed was really typical of group thinking, and with an air of sophistication that made it difficult for a listener to dissent, he proceeded to comment on the American emphasis on team ideas, satirically describing the ways in which they led to a "high level of mediocrity."

During this time, Knowlton observed that Link stared studiously at the floor, and he was very conscious of George Thurlow's and Bob Davenport's glances toward him at several points in Fester's little speech. Inwardly, Knowlton couldn't help feeling that this was one point on which Fester was off on the wrong foot.

The whole lab, following Jerry's lead, talked, if not practiced, the theory of small research teams as the basic organization for effective research. Fester insisted that the problem could be approached and that he would like to study it for a while himself.

Knowlton ended the morning session by remarking that the meetings would continue—that the very fact that a supposedly insoluble experimental problem was now going to get another chance was another indication of the value of such meetings. Fester immediately remarked that he was not at all averse to meetings for the purpose of informing the group of the progress of its members—that the point he wanted to make was that creative advances were seldom accomplished in such meetings, that they were made by the individual "living with" the problem closely and continuously, a sort of personal relationship to it.

Knowlton went on to say to Fester that he was very glad that Fester had raised these points and that he was sure the group would profit by reexamining the basis on which they had been operating. He said he agreed that individual effort was probably the basis for making the major advances, but that he considered the group meetings useful primarily because of the effect they had on keeping the group together and on helping the weaker members of the group keep up with the ones who were able to advance more easily and quickly in the analysis of problems.

It was clear, as days went by and meetings continued as they had, that Fester came to enjoy them because of the pattern the meetings assumed. It became typical for Fester to hold forth, and it was unquestionably clear that he was more brilliant, better prepared on the various subjects that were germane to the problems being studied, and more capable of going ahead than anyone there. Knowlton grew increasingly disturbed as he realized that his leadership of the group had been, in fact, taken over.

Whenever the subject of Fester was mentioned in occasional meetings with Dr. Jerrold, Knowlton would comment only on the ability and obvious capacity for work that Fester had. Somehow he never felt that he could mention his own discomforts, not only because they revealed a weakness on his own part, but also because it was quite clear that Jerrold himself was considerably impressed with Fester's work and with the contacts he had with him outside the photon laboratory.

Knowlton now began to feel that perhaps the intellectual advantages that Fester had brought to the group did not quite compensate for what he felt were evidences of a breakdown in the cooperative spirit he had seen in the group before Fester's coming. More and more of the morning meetings were skipped. Fester's opinion concerning the abilities of others of the group, with the exception of Link, was obviously low. At times, during morning meetings or in smaller discussions, he had been on the point of rudeness, refusing to pursue an argument when he claimed it was based on the other person's ignorance of the facts involved. His impatience of others led him to also make similar remarks to Dr. Jerrold. Knowlton inferred this from a conversation with Jerrold in which Jerrold asked whether Davenport and Oliver were going to be continued on; and his failure to mention Link, the mathematician, led Knowlton to feel that this was the result of private conversations between Fester and Jerrold.

It was not difficult for Knowlton to make a quite convincing case on whether the brilliance of Fester was sufficient recompense for the beginning of this breaking up of the group. He took the opportunity to speak privately with Davenport and with Oliver, and it was quite clear that both of them were uncomfortable because of Fester. Knowlton didn't press the discussion beyond the point of hearing them say in one way or another that they did feel awkward and that it was sometimes difficult for them to understand the arguments he advanced, but often embarrassing to ask him to fill in the background on which his arguments were based. Knowlton did not interview Link in this manner.

About six months after Fester's coming into the photon lab, a meeting was scheduled at which the sponsors of the research would be present to get some idea of the work and its progress. It was customary at these meetings for project heads to present the research being conducted in their groups. The members of each group were invited to other meetings, which were held later in the day and open to all, but the special meetings were usually made up only of project heads, the head of the laboratory, and the sponsors.

As the time for the special meeting approached, it seemed to Knowlton that he must avoid the presentation at all costs; he could not trust himself to present the ideas and work that Fester had advanced, because of his apprehension as to whether he could do it in sufficient detail and answer such questions about them as might be asked. On the other hand, he did not feel he could ignore these newer lines of work and present only the material that he had done or that had been started before Fester's arrival. He felt also that it would not be beyond Fester at all, in his blunt and undiplomatic way (if he were present at the meeting, that is), to make comments on his own presentation and reveal the inadequacy Knowlton felt he had. It also seemed quite clear that it would not be easy to keep Fester from attending the meeting, even though he was not on the administrative level that was invited.

Knowlton found an opportunity to speak to Jerrold and raised the question. He remarked to Jerrold that, with Fester's interest in the work and with the contributions that he had been making, he would probably like to come to these meetings, but there was a question of the feelings of the others in the group if Fester alone were invited. Jerrold passed this over very lightly by saying that he didn't think the group would fail to understand Fester's rather different position and that he thought that Fester by all means should be invited. Knowlton then immediately said that he had thought so too, and that he felt that Fester should present the work because much of it was work that he had done; he added that this would be a nice way to recognize Fester's contributions and to reward him, since he was eager to be recognized as a productive member of the lab. Jerrold agreed, and so the matter was decided.

Fester's presentation was very successful; in some ways, in fact, it dominated the meeting. He attracted the interest and attention of many of those who had come, and a long discussion followed his presentation. Later in the evening, with the entire laboratory staff present, in the cocktail period before the dinner, a little circle of people formed about Fester. One of them was Jerrold himself, and a lively discussion took place concerning the application of Fester's theory. All this disturbed Knowlton, and his reaction and behavior were characteristic. He joined the circle, praised Fester to Jerrold and to others, and remarked on the brilliance of the work.

Knowlton, without consulting anyone, began at this time to take some interest in the possibility of a job elsewhere. After a few weeks, he found that a new laboratory of considerable size was being organized in a nearby city, and that the kind of training he had would enable him to get a project-head job equivalent to the one he had at the lab, with slightly more money.

Bob Knowlton (B)

Bob Knowlton applied for the new job and was immediately accepted; he notified Jerrold by letter, which he mailed on a Friday night to Jerrold's home. The letter was quite brief. It merely said that he had found a better position; that there were personal reasons why he didn't want to appear at the lab any more; that he would be glad to come back at a later time from where he would be, some 40 miles away, to assist if there was any mixup at all in the past work; that he felt sure that Fester could, however, supply any leadership that was required for the group; and that his decision to leave so suddenly was based on some personal problems—he hinted at problems of health in his family, his mother and father. All this was fictitious, of course. Jerrold was stunned; he took it at face value, but he still felt that this was very strange behavior and quite unaccountable, since he had always felt his relationship with Knowlton had been warm and that Knowlton was satisfied and, as a matter of fact, quite happy and productive.

Jerrold was considerably disturbed also because he had already decided to place Fester in charge of another project, to be set up very soon, and had been wondering how to explain this to Knowlton, in view of the obvious help and value Knowlton was getting from Fester and the high regard in which he held him. He had, as a matter of fact, considered the possibility that Knowlton could add to his staff another person with Fester's kind of background and training that had proved so valuable.

Jerrold made no attempt to meet Knowlton. In a way, he felt aggrieved about the whole thing. Fester, too, was surprised at the suddenness of Knowlton's departure, and when Jerrold, in talking to him, asked him whether he had reasons to prefer to stay with the photon group instead of the project for the air force that was being organized, he

This case was prepared by Alex Bavelas and is reproduced with permission.

chose the air force project and went on to that job that following week. The photon lab was hard hit. The leadership of the lab was given to Link, with the understanding that this would be temporary until someone could come in to take over.

The Road to Hell

John Baker, chief engineer of the Caribbean Bauxite Company of Barracania in the West Indies, was making his final preparations to leave the island. His promotion to production manager of Keso Mining Corporation near Winnipeg—one of Continental Ore's fast-expanding Canadian enterprises—had been announced a month before, and now everything had been tidied up except the last vital interview with his successor, the able young Barracanian, Matthew Rennalls. It was vital that this interview be a success and that Rennalls should leave his office uplifted and encouraged to face the challenge of his new job. A touch on the bell would have brought Rennalls into the room, but Baker delayed the moment and gazed thoughtfully through the window, considering just exactly what he was going to say and, more particularly, how he was going to say it.

This case was prepared by Mr. Gareth Evans for Shell-BP of Nigeria, Limited, as a basis for class discussion in an executive training program, and is used with permission.

John Baker, an English expatriate, was 45 years old and had served his 23 years with Continental Ore in many different places: in the Far East, several countries of Africa, Europe, and for the last two years, in the West Indies. He hadn't cared much for his previous assignment in Hamburg and was delighted when the West Indian appointment came through. Climate was not the only attraction. Baker had always preferred working overseas in what were termed the developing countries, because he felt he had an innate knack—better than most other expatriates working for Continental Ore—of knowing just how to get on with regional staff. Twenty-four hours in Barracania, however, had made him realize that he would need all this "innate knack" if he was to deal effectively with the problems in this field that awaited him.

At his first interview with Hutchins, the production manager, the whole problem of Rennalls and his future was discussed. There and then, it was made quite clear to Baker that one of his most

important tasks would be the grooming of Rennalls as his successor. Hutchins pointed out that not only was Rennalls one of the brightest Barracanian prospects on the staff of Caribbean Bauxite—at London University, he had taken first-class honours in the B.Sc. Engineering Degree—but, being the son of the Minister of Finance and Economic Planning, he also had no small political pull.

The company had been particularly pleased when Rennalls decided to work for them rather than for the government in which his father had such a prominent post. They ascribed his action to the effect of their vigorous and liberal regionalization program, which, since the Second World War, had placed 18 Barracanians at midmanagement level and given Caribbean Bauxite a good lead in this respect over all other international concerns operating in Barracania. The success of this timely regionalization policy had led to excellent relations with the government. And this relationship had been given an added importance when Barracania, three years later, became independent—an occasion that encouraged a critical and challenging attitude toward the role foreign interests would have to play in the new Barracania. Hutchins had therefore little difficulty in convincing Baker that the successful career development of Rennalls was of the first importance.

The interview with Hutchins was now two years past, and Baker, leaning back in his office chair, reviewed just how successful he had been in the "grooming" of Rennalls. What aspects of the latter's character had helped and what had hindered? What about his own personality? How had that helped or hindered? The first item to go on the credit side would, without question, be the ability of Rennalls to master the technical aspects of his job. From the start, he had shown keenness and enthusiasm and had often impressed Baker with his ability in tackling new assignments and the constructive comments he invariably made in departmental discussions. He was popular with all ranks of Barracanian staff and had an ease of manner that stood him in good stead when dealing with his expatriate seniors. These were all assets, but what about the debit side?

First and foremost, there was his racial consciousness. His four years at London University had accentuated this feeling and made him sensitive to any sign of condescension on the part of expatriates. It may have been to give expression to this sentiment that, as soon as he returned home from London, he threw himself into politics on behalf of the United Action Party, which was later to win the preindependence elections and provide the country with its first prime minister.

The ambitions of Rennalls—and he certainly was ambitious—did not, however, lie in politics, for, staunch nationalist that he was, he saw that he could serve himself and his country best—for was not bauxite responsible for nearly half the value of Barracania's export trade?—by putting his engineering talent to the best use possible. On this account, Hutchins found that he had an unexpectedly easy task in persuading Rennalls to give up his political work before entering the production department as an assistant engineer.

It was, Baker knew, Rennalls's well-repressed sense of race consciousness that had prevented their relationship from being as close as it should have been. On the surface, nothing could have seemed more agreeable. Formality between the two men was at a minimum; Baker was delighted to find that his assistant shared his own peculiar "shaggy dog" sense of humor, so that jokes were continually being exchanged; they entertained each other at their houses and often played tennis together—and yet the barrier remained invisible, indefinable, but ever present. The existence of this "screen" between them was a constant

source of frustration to Baker, since it indicated a weakness he was loath to accept. If he had been successful with all other nationalities, why not with Rennalls?

But at least he had managed to break through to Rennalls more successfully than any other expatriate had. In fact, it was the young Barracanian's attitude—sometimes overbearing, sometimes cynical—toward other company expatriates that had been one of the subjects Baker had raised last year when he discussed Rennalls's staff report with him. He knew, too, that he would have to raise the same subject again in the forthcoming interview, because Jackson, the senior draftsman, had complained only yesterday about Rennalls's rudeness. With this thought in mind, Baker leaned forward and spoke into the intercom. "Would you come in, Matt, please? I'd like a word with you," and later, "Do sit down." He offered the box, "Have a cigarette," paused while he held out his lighter, and then went on.

"As you know, Matt, I'll be off to Canada in a few days' time, and before I go, I thought it would be useful if we could have a final chat together. It is indeed with some deference that I suggest I can be of help. You will shortly be sitting in this chair doing the job I am now doing, but I, on the other hand, am ten years older, so perhaps you can accept the idea that I may be able to give you the benefit of my longer experience."

Baker saw Rennalls stiffen slightly in his chair as he made this point, so he added in explanation, "You and I have attended enough company courses to remember those repeated requests by the personnel manager to tell people how they are getting on as often as the convenient moment arises, and not just the automatic once a year when, by regulation, staff reports have to be discussed."

Rennalls nodded his agreement, so Baker went on. "I shall always remember the last job performance discussion I had with my previous boss back in Germany. He used what he called the 'plus and minus' technique. His firm belief was that when a senior, by discussion, seeks to improve the work performance of his staff, his prime objective should be to make sure that the latter leaves the interview encouraged and inspired to improve. Any criticism must, therefore, be constructive and helpful. He said that one very good way to encourage a man—and I fully agree with him—is to tell him about his good points—the plus factors—as well as his weak ones—the minus factors; so I thought, Matt, it would be a good idea to run our discussion along these lines."

Rennalls offered no comment, so Baker continued. "Let me say, therefore, right away, that as far as your own work performance is concerned, the plus far outweighs the minus. I have, for instance, been most impressed with the way you have adapted your considerable theoretical knowledge to master the practical techniques of your job—that ingenious method you used to get air down to the fifth-shaft level is a sufficient case in point—and at departmental meetings, I have invariably found your comments well taken and helpful. In fact, you will be interested to know that only last week I reported to Mr. Hutchins that, from the technical point of view, he could not wish for a more able man to succeed to the position of chief engineer."

"That's very good indeed of you, John," cut in Rennalls with a smile of thanks. "My only worry now is how to live up to such a high recommendation."

"Of that I am quite sure," returned Baker, "especially if you can overcome the minus factor, which I would like now to discuss with you. It is one that I have talked about before, so I'll come straight to the point. I have noticed that you are

more friendly and get on better with your fellow Barracanians than you do with Europeans. In point of fact, I had a complaint only yesterday from Mr. Jackson, who said you had been rude to him—and not for the first time either.

"There is, Matt, I am sure, no need for me to tell you how necessary it will be for you to get on well with expatriates, because until the company has trained up sufficient men of your caliber, Europeans are bound to occupy senior positions here in Barracania. All this is vital to your future interests, so can I help you in any way?"

While Baker was speaking on this theme, Rennalls had sat tensed in his chair, and it was some seconds before he replied. "It is quite extraordinary, isn't it, how one can convey an impression to others so at variance with what one intends? I can only assure you once again that my disputes with Jackson—and you may remember also Godson—have had nothing at all to do with the color of their skins. I promise you that if a Barracanian had behaved in an equally peremptory manner, I would have reacted in precisely the same way. And again, if I may say it within these four walls, I am sure I am not the only one who has found Jackson and Godson difficult. I could mention the names of several expatriates who have felt the same. However, I am really sorry to have created this impression of not being able to get on with Europeans; it is an entirely false one, and I quite realize that I must do all I can to correct it as quickly as possible. On your last point, regarding Europeans holding senior positions in the company for some time to come, I quite accept the situation. I know that Caribbean Bauxite—as they have been doing for many years now—will promote Barracanians as soon as their experience warrants it. And, finally, I would like to assure you, John—and my father thinks the same, too—that I am very happy in my work here and hope to stay with the company for many years to come."

Rennalls had spoken earnestly, and, although not convinced by what he had heard, Baker did not think he could pursue the matter further except to say, "All right, Matt, my impression *may* be wrong, but I would like to remind you about the truth of that old saying, 'What is important is not what is true but what is believed.' Let it rest at that."

But suddenly Baker knew that he didn't want to "let it rest at that." He was disappointed once again at not being able to break through to Rennalls and having yet again to listen to his bland denial that there was any racial prejudice in his makeup. Baker, who had intended ending the interview at this point, decided to try another tack.

"To return for a moment to the 'plus and minus technique' I was telling you about just now, there is another plus factor I forgot to mention. I would like to congratulate you not only on the caliber of your work but also on the ability you have shown in overcoming a challenge that I, as a European, have never had to meet.

"Continental Ore is, as you know, a typical commercial enterprise—admittedly a big one—which is a product of the economic and social environment of the United States and Western Europe. My ancestors have all been brought up in this environment for the past two or three hundred years, and I have, therefore, been able to live in a world in which commerce as we know it today has been part and parcel of my being. It has not been something revolutionary and new that has suddenly entered my life. In your case, the situation is different, because you and your forebears have had only some fifty or sixty years' experience of this commercial environment. You have had to face the challenge of bridging the gap between fifty and two or three hundred years. Again, Matt, let me congratulate you—and people like you—once again on having so successfully overcome this particular hurdle. It is for this very reason that I think the outlook for Barracania—and particularly Caribbean Bauxite—is so bright."

Rennalls had listened intently and when Baker finished, replied, "Well, once again, John, I have to thank you for what you have said, and for my part, I can only say that it is gratifying to know that my own personal effort has been so much appreciated. I hope that more people will soon come to think as you do."

There was a pause, and for a moment, Baker thought hopefully that he was about to achieve his long awaited "breakthrough," but Rennalls merely smiled back. The barrier remained unbreached. There remained some five minutes' cheerful conversation about the contrast between the Caribbean and Canadian climate and whether the West Indies had any hope of beating England in the Fifth Test, before Baker drew the interview to a close. Although he was as far as ever from knowing the real Rennalls, he was nevertheless glad that the interview had run along in this friendly manner and, particularly, that it had ended on such a cheerful note.

This feeling, however, lasted only until the following morning. Baker had some farewells to make, so he arrived at the office considerably later than usual. He had no sooner sat down at his desk than his secretary walked into the room with a worried frown on her face. Her words came fast. "When I arrived this morning I found Mr. Rennalls already waiting at my door. He seemed very angry and told me in quite a peremptory manner that he had a vital letter to dictate which must be sent off without any delay. He was so worked up that he couldn't keep still and kept pacing about the room, which is most unlike him. He wouldn't even wait to read what he had dictated. Just signed the page where he thought the letter would end. It has been distributed, and your copy is in your "in-tray."

Puzzled and feeling vaguely uneasy, Baker opened the "Confidential" envelope and read the following letter:

From: Assistant Engineer

To: The Chief Engineer, Caribbean Bauxite Limited

14th August

ASSESSMENT OF INTERVIEW BETWEEN MESSRS. BAKER AND RENNALLS

It has always been my practice to respect the advice given me by seniors, so after our interview, I decided to give careful thought once again to its main points and so make sure that I had understood all that had been said. As I promised you at the time, I had every intention of putting your advice to the best effect.

It was not, therefore, until I had sat down quietly in my home yesterday evening to consider the interview objectively that its main purport became clear. Only then did the full enormity of what you had said dawn on me. The more I thought about it, the more convinced I was that I had hit upon the real truth—and the more furious I became. With a facility in the English language which I—a poor Barracanian—cannot hope to match, you had the audacity to insult me (and through me, every Barracanian worth his salt) by claiming that our knowledge of modern living is only a paltry fifty years old whilst yours goes back 200-300 years. As if your materialistic commercial environment could possibly be compared with the spiritual values of our culture. I'll have you know that if much of what I saw in London is representative of your most boasted culture, I hope fervently that it will never come to Barracania. By what right do you have the effrontery to condescend to us? At heart, all you Europeans think us barbarians, or, as you say amongst yourselves, we are "just down from the trees."

Far into the night I discussed this matter

with my father, and he is as disgusted as I. He agrees with me that any company whose senior staff think as you do is no place for any Barracanian proud of his culture and race—so much for all the company "claptrap" and specious propaganda about regionalization and Barracania for the Barracanians.

I feel ashamed and betrayed. Please accept this letter as my resignation, which I wish to become effective immediately.

cc Production Manager
Managing Director

PART TWO

UNDERSTANDING ANOTHER PERSON

Introduction

The preceding section of this book focused on the process and problems of communication. It was also about the relationships between people and the problems people experience in working and living with each other. In exploring the topic of communication, we considered many factors: the languages through which people "talk"; the pervasive influence of setting and context on communication; the persistent possibility that the same words, actions, or events mean different things to different people; some commonly held attitudes and behaviors that impede communication; and finally, several ideas, concepts, and suggestions for improving the quality and effectiveness of communication, including a set of concepts for understanding how different people can experience the same situation differently and the importance of understanding the other person's point of view.

By now, it is probably apparent that of the many factors mentioned above, the one that has the greatest effect on the quality of communication is the degree to which two people in a relationship understand each other as persons. It is very difficult to correctly interpret another person's actions, words, and intentions without also, at some level, being able to understand that person. Similarly, the ability to prevent and anticipate misunderstandings or problems of communication is directly related to the capacity to understand another person and what is important in that person's world. The purpose of the chapters, readings, and cases in this section of the book is to develop, in greater depth, the ability to understand another person.

To a large extent, the chapter on "Problems of Communication" has already laid the groundwork for doing this by providing a language (assumptions, perceptions, and feelings) for making explicit the ways in which two people can experience the same situation differently. This *assumptive framework* provides a fairly direct and simple way for trying to understand another person. In the chapters that follow, we will elaborate on these ideas and introduce several additional concepts that go beyond the assumptive framework. The purpose of these chapters is to provide a way of thinking that will sharpen your capacity to understand another person. The reasons for trying to develop this ability are multiple. We have already mentioned how important this ability is to communicating effectively. A broader reason, however, is that the ability to understand others is basic to making relationships effective and mutually satisfying. It is also at the core of many managerial functions, including motivating, leading, working with, and helping others. Finally, a very important reason for understanding people as individuals is that this ability can help you understand yourself better: why you are the person you have become; what it means for your living and working with others; and what it means for your own development as a person as well as a manager.

The materials in this section of the book have been chosen with this double focus in mind and are intended to help you develop understanding, not only of others, but of yourself as well. Thus, this section has two agendas. The concepts in the chapters and the ideas in the readings are meant to help you develop better insight and understanding of others as people and the dilemmas they face, as well as to help you sharpen your own understanding of yourself and your own dilemmas. The cases will ask you to try to understand the problems of specific people as individuals and, we hope, also trigger questions about yourself that can lead to personal learning, growth, and understanding.

THE INDIVIDUAL FRAME OF REFERENCE

In doing this, we will use an approach whose purpose is understanding another person from that person's *own* point of view and from his or her own frame of reference. This approach is commonly referred to as "the individual frame of reference," and Chapter 5 will describe it in some detail. Chapter 5 will also introduce the idea of the self-concept as a means for understanding others. It will further elaborate on the ideas of assumptions, perceptions, and feelings as a way of operationalizing the individual frame of reference.

The ideas presented in Chapter 5 are useful not only in relationships where you know the other person quite well, but also in relationships of a less intense nature that are based on limited interactions of an everyday kind, such as those we commonly have with co-workers and others whom we do not know intimately. They are ideas that can be useful in a wide range of relationships.

Although Chapter 5 presents the individual frame of reference in a managerial context, you will find the ideas equally relevant to personal and intimate relationships. Indeed, several of the cases in this section of the book are not about managers, and we urge you not to confine your use of these ideas to people in managerial or organizational settings.

ASPECTS OF SELF-CONCEPT

Chapter 6 will introduce several aspects of the self-concept that are helpful in developing a deeper understanding of others (and yourself). The chapter will introduce the concepts of identification, expectations, and approval and their relationship to how a person's self-concept develops and how people behave. Unlike the ideas presented on the individual frame of reference, these ideas are about aspects of self-concept that are basic and persevering, and thus require greater familiarity with a person and his or her background and behavior.

You will find that the ideas described in these two chapters are relatively simple. Their usefulness is in providing a way of thinking about people that can help you organize your perceptions about others so as to improve understanding and trigger insight. You will also find that they are descriptive rather than normative, inasmuch as they do not present a theory about how people *ought to* behave or a formula for predicting how people *will* behave. They are simply meant to increase your awareness of how individuals *do* behave, what is important to them, and how they see themselves. We believe that if you are able to do this effectively, you will have accomplished a great deal.

THE READINGS AND CASES

The readings included in this section of the book have no central theme other than being about the dilemmas and questions that people face in understanding themselves and the world around them. Two of the readings deal with the "need to know." One, "The Need to Know and the Fear of Knowing," discusses the importance of the need to know in personal growth and some of the reasons why we are afraid to know. Another, "The Silence of the Sky," is about the frustration of not knowing enough and the need to make our own meanings in dealing with the incompleteness of our knowledge. The third, "Relativism in Organizations," describes the stages of intellectual and moral development through which people progress, and how a person's view of the world and the meanings he or she makes are related to these stages of development. None of these readings give easy answers, but all of them raise important questions.

The cases in this section are somewhat different from those included in the earlier section on communication. By and large, they are about people who are dealing with a personal problem or decision and include more information of a personal and biographical nature than earlier cases. They also lend themselves more easily to the purpose of this section, understanding another person, than earlier cases, and are less easily conducive to managerial action-taking. They were selected because they provide the kind of data necessary to develop skills in understanding another person. Our assumption is that this kind of understanding is a prior condition to effective action-taking in situations that call for it. For example, you would find these concepts very helpful in re-analyzing earlier cases that did require action; and you will find them necessary in later cases on interpersonal problems that will pose action questions.

Several of the cases involve problems of communication, differences in personal style, or misunderstandings. Several are cases about people who are faced with personal choices.

Chapter Five

The Individual Frame of Reference

In the course of a representative day, a man who is a manager of a good-sized consulting firm may meet with a junior consultant and a staff employee to review the progress of a cost-control project; discuss with another junior consultant the latter's seemingly avoidable and recurring errors; consider with the head of the San Francisco office the matter of the early retirement of a senior consultant whose effectiveness has been waning; have lunch with a client who is becoming anxious at the direction of a particular study; receive and make a dozen phone calls; dictate several letters; and attempt to close himself in his office to write a report on the implementation of a new time-sharing program for which he has firmwide responsibility.

The activities of this manager will range from using specific technical expertise to calling on his broader managerial judgment. Almost all these activities, however, have one element in common: interaction with people. It is inevitable that most of his day will be spent in the midst of relationships with peers and subordinates, colleagues and clients. In all these activities, he will be exercising sensitivity to the human problems that underlie the activities. Sometimes he will do this consciously, sometimes intuitively. His understanding of the behavior of the people he works with is important to the quality and effectiveness of these relationships. These relationships, in turn, are crucial to his effectiveness as a manager and, ultimately, to the success of his firm.

The purpose of this chapter is to introduce a way of thinking about individuals that can make it easier to understand them from their own point of view and thus enable you to become more effective in understanding and anticipating individual needs, wants, and problems. There are, however, two difficulties in using any set of ideas to understand another person. The first is that it is very difficult to separate one's own subjective view of another person from how that person is apt to see himself. The way the manager described above sees the people in his world, perceives them, is *his* way. Unless he is careful, his observations of others will tell him much more about himself than they will about the people he works with. Santayana said, "When Peter tells you about Paul, you learn more about Peter than you do about Paul." It is clear that you learn something about Paul, all right. It's just that you learn *more* about Peter. What one learns about either remains to be explored. You can never completely understand another person as that person understands himself or herself; nor can you ever completely remove your own biases and coloring from your perception of another person. However, with work, you can develop the ability to recognize when your own assumptions and biases are getting in the way. (Chapter 4 has already addressed this task.)

A second problem in trying to understand another person grows out of the difficulty above and is related to the familiar paradox, "You can't understand other people until you understand yourself; but you can't understand yourself until you understand others." Like all paradoxes, this one suggests a hopeless "either-or" that cannot be resolved unless you see the "and also" implicit in it. The paradox is a false one. The more capable you are of understanding others, the better able you become to understand your own dilemmas; and conversely, the more in touch you are with yourself and your own biases and assumptions, the more capable you become of understanding others. The way out of the paradox is to try to develop an understanding of yourself and also of others, both sequentially and simultaneously over time—sometimes focusing on "self," sometimes on "other," sometimes on both.

A WAY OF THINKING ABOUT INDIVIDUALS

Whose Point of View?

In this chapter, we will use an approach in which we will try to understand another person from *his or her own point of view, and his or her own frame of reference.* Psychologists call this a "phenomenological" or "perceptual" view of behavior. Combs and Snygg describe this view as follows:

> Human behavior may be observed from at least two very broad frames of reference: from the point of view of an outsider, or from the point of view of the behaver himself. Looking at behavior in the first way, we can

observe the behavior of others and the situations in which such behavior occurs. It is then possible to attempt the explanation of behavior in terms of the interaction of the individual and situations in which we have seen him operating. This is the "objective," or "external" frame of reference. The second approach seeks to understand behavior by making attempts to understand the behavior of the individual in terms of how things "seem" to him. This frame of reference has been called the "perceptual," "personal," or "phenomenological" frame of reference.

In the personal, or perceptual, frame of reference we attempt to observe behavior from the point of view of the individual himself. As a matter of fact, that is what almost all people, professional psychologists or laymen alike, do as soon as they confronted with the task of dealing with the behavior of an individual. "What does he want?"—"What is he thinking?"—"How does he feel about this?" are some of the questions they ask as they try to put themselves in his place to understand and anticipate his behavior.[1]

The Individual Frame of Reference

This approach to understanding another person requires that you try to imagine what the other person's individual frame of reference is—that is, how that person sees him- or herself and the situation from his or her own point of view. To do this, you have to temporarily suspend your own view of the other person, so that your ideas of how he ought to behave do not get in the way of understanding his frame of reference. Doing this requires careful attention to the other person's actions, words, and other behavior and inferring from these behaviors what the other's basic underlying assumptions, perceptions, and feelings are about self, the world as he or she sees it, and the particular situations he or she faces.[2] Doing this also requires developing a sense of empathy (not sympathy) for how and what the other person is experiencing.

The individual frame of reference assumes that each person sees the world uniquely, depending on his own past experience and his own personal meanings.[3] In a sense, it views each individual as stand-

[1] Arthur Combs and Donald Snygg, *Individual Behavior* (New York: Harper & Row, 1959), p. 16.

[2] One of the limitations of the phenomenological approach is that it does not take into account psychodynamics of an unconscious nature—e.g., drives or conflicts that are unconscious. However, since unconscious motives are, by definition, seldom understood by the individual himself, they are usually even less understandable or available to a manager working with that person. Furthermore, making correct inferences about unconscious motives requires substantial skill and training of a psychoanalytic nature, both of which exceed the scope of this book. The advantage of a phenomenological approach is that it can be used safely and effectively in everyday interactions based on the kinds of behavior that are generally observable to managers and people in work relationships.

[3] For grammatical simplicity, we have used masculine pronouns in many places; however, the comments apply to both women and men.

ing at the center of the world as he sees it. Each individual's view of the world may be very similar to how others see it in some ways, but it is also apt to be unique in other ways. This orientation also assumes that each person's view of the world is closely related to how the person sees himself in it, the roles he plays in it, what he should or shouldn't do, what is right and what is wrong, and so on. It further assumes that of central importance to how a person sees the world is how he sees himself as a person. In other words, a person's "self-concept" will have great bearing on that person's behavior.

If the manager cited above wishes to improve the performance of the junior consultant whose errors concern him, he might do well to seek to understand what in the man's world may be askew. If he can determine the meanings of retirement to his firm's aging senior consultant, he may be better able to sense how to approach this issue. Each of these situations involves the relationship between two adults in a particular business setting. Each has brought with him into the organization personal values, aspirations, problems. Each is in a different stage of the developmental life cycle. Each has some measure of influence on the other. Each has something at stake. In short, the situations this manager must deal with are complicated. How he attempts to deal with them will vary to the extent that he understands who these two men are and how they see themselves.

The Idea of Self-Concept

A very useful notion in understanding another person's frame of reference is the idea of self-concept. Self-concept is the internalized set of relatively stable perceptions that a person has of himself and of who he is. They are ideas the person has *about* himself, ideas that are stable, resistant to change, and of central importance.[4] It includes his conception of what is unique about himself, what distinguishes him from others, and what makes him similar to others. The self-concept includes all those perceptions that a person has of himself that are *important* to him and *relatively constant* over time.

For example, a person well acquainted with the manager in the consulting firm described above might conclude, based on observation and interaction with him, that an important part of this man's self-concept is that he is a highly skillful and effective administrator. This self-perception is perhaps one of the reasons why the manager is troubled by the junior consultant's recurring errors and the senior consultant's decreasing effectiveness. This manager's self-concept is also composed of many other important self-perceptions. Some of these may be more basic and central to him than being a skillful administrator, such as being an honest person, persevering, courageous, a strict but loving father, and a devoted husband.

A person's self-concept obviously changes over time, but slowly and

[4]Salvatore Maddi, *Personality Theories: A Comparative Analysis* (Homewood, Ill.: Dorsey, 1968), pp. 74-75.

selectively. For example, the self-perception "skillful and effective administrator" probably took the manager years to develop. When he first joined the firm as a junior consultant at age 28, "skillful administrator" was not a part of his self-concept. As he gained experience, he was given more administrative responsibility. First he was made an assignment leader, and then eventually an officer. He found that he enjoyed managing complex projects and other consultants. He also discovered that he was quite effective as a manager and that others came to admire and respect him for his administrative ability. Over time, he developed pride in his ability as a manager, and eventually it became an important part of his self-concept.

Two important points are illustrated by this brief example. The first point is that a person's self-concept develops in relation to past experiencing and the meanings a person makes from this experiencing. The second point is that once a self-perception has been firmly established as part of a person's self-concept, the self-perception will affect how the person experiences future situations. For example, it is likely that this manager now acts in ways that are consistent with his view of himself as a skillful administrator. Moreover, it is also likely that whenever possible, he will respond to problems in ways that will confirm and *enhance* his view of himself as being an exceptional administrator.

Indeed, the reason why understanding another person's self-concept is important is that central aspects of self-concept are usually acted upon in a person's behavior: in what matters to the individual; how he is likely to respond to a situation; and how he is apt to see himself in the situation.

To further illustrate what is meant by self-concept, ask a number of people to write down five nouns they would use to describe important aspects of who they are. The results are usually interesting. One such parlor game produced the following lists:

man	lover	entrepreneur	woman	professor
husband	singer	competitor	student	scholar
father	poet	father	cook	wife
banker	musician	husband	fiancee	author
citizen	artist	athlete	daughter	friend

Obviously, a person's self-concept is much more elaborate and complex than any of these lists would indicate. Also, not much can be made from such lists. But the lists do sound like very different people, and it is possible to infer that what each conceives of as "self" is significantly varied. Yet we don't know from such a game if what they said included all of what is important and relatively constant for them, or even if what they said was true. We can't see or hear a self-concept—it's an abstraction. However, we can hear and see things from which we can infer perceptions of self that are likely to be relatively constant and important to someone, and thus have a notion of how they see themselves. This notion can help us, as a kind of working hypothesis, to understand why people behave as they do.

For example, a customer whose self-concept includes being a very religious man is apt to be offended by an invitation from a salesman to join him for a weekend at a gambling casino with all expenses paid. In contrast, another customer, who sees himself as being a "real swinger," fast and free, would probably not be offended. A good salesman intuitively knows that each man's self-concept and his related values and attitudes affect how he would respond to the invitation. Each person's self-concept is an outgrowth not only of his life's experiences, but also of the particular meanings that he has created from these experiences. (For example, it is possible that both the customers in the illustration above were raised by strict and religious parents but that the second person rejected his parents' values for reasons having to do with the particular relationship he had with them.) Many aspects of self-concept (as the next chapter will show) grow out of a person's past relationships with people, groups, or institutions whose values he has internalized. Religious, cultural, ethnic, regional, class, and institutional identifications often become important aspects of a person's self-concept. To take a simple illustration, it is likely that a person raised in the South would be offended to hear a Northerner say that Southerners are "slow as molasses." Conversely, it is equally likely that a New Englander would be annoyed to hear a Southerner describe Yankees as "cold, unfriendly stuffed shirts."

If we wish to understand another person better, our task is not to observe him and his behavior from our point of view, but rather to try to get around and look at what is going on from the other's point of view. We can never do so completely, of course. But we can increase our capacity to "imagine the real" of another person, to use Martin Buber's phrase. With practice, most of us can increase our capacity to hear and see more of another person's world, and in so doing understand better what that person is experiencing.

Inferring Self-Concept in a Situational Context

Generally, a manager does not have access to information of a detailed nature on the self-concepts of people he or she works with. A manager seldom knows how their self-concepts have developed over time, nor is he or she likely to have much intimate knowledge of their personal histories. To have this kind of understanding, a manager would have to know each person fairly well—would have to be in relationship with each person long enough to know something about the expectations, sources of identification, and internalized needs for approval that each holds as important. In the next chapter, we will describe some ideas that are useful for gaining a deeper understanding of self-concept. But that deeper level is possible only in situations where one person is close enough to another, or has worked long enough with that person, to make such inferences. It takes a great deal of time to get to know a person that well, and often a manager does not have the opportunity to do so.

The question, then, becomes, How do you go about understanding another person's behavior and self-concept based on daily interactions of a situational nature in which a long-term prior acquaintance does not exist? As stated earlier, self-concept is an abstraction and not directly observable, so it must be inferred. Inferences about self-concept can be made based on what we observe about what matters to another person, as expressed in recurrent interactions, words, and actions.

For purposes of illustration, let's go back to the manager in the consulting firm described earlier, and the junior consultant whose performance currently concerns him.

If, for example, the manager recalls that the junior consultant has on several occasions expressed the importance of being "number one" in his endeavors, then the manager *may* be able to begin to piece together some of the reasons that the junior consultant has been ineffective. If the manager remembers the consultant's obvious pride at having graduated summa cum laude from college, and his disappointment at having been only third in his class at graduate school, then the manager may begin to infer that being "number one" and being a "competitor" are important aspects of the junior consultant's self-concept. If he further puts together these observations with the recollection that the junior consultant had expressed dissatisfaction that his billings were still relatively low compared to those of more experienced consultants, then the manager has a further observation to work with. If he also knows that the junior consultant had previously expressed disappointment at not being put in charge of a special project, then the manager may begin to tentatively infer that important aspects of this man's self-concept are being threatened and that these threats may be related to the consultant's increasingly poor performance. The manager does not yet have enough data on which to base conclusions or take actions; but he is certainly in a better position to develop some ideas or hypotheses about what is "off" with the man's performance. He is also in a better position to approach the individual and work with him to determine why the man's performance is poor and to help him improve.

Understanding Another Person's Frame of Reference

Certainly, understanding self-concept is useful in anticipating how a person will respond in a certain situation, or why a person has behaved in a certain way. However, self-concept alone is not a sufficiently broad idea to encompass all of an individual's frame of reference. A person's view of the world is contingent on many factors, only one of which is his view of himself. How a person behaves in one situation may be quite different from how he might behave in another. Furthermore, not all a person's actions are directly related to self-concept.

Let us probe more deeply into what constitutes an individual's frame of reference. Each of us engages and sees the world in ways that are similar to those of others and in ways that are different. An individual's view of the world and of how he ought to behave in different settings is based on "models" of reality that he carries around with him. Sometimes these models are in the person's conscious awareness; sometimes they are not. The models develop as a result of an accumulation of past experiences, and their formation begins with the first day of life. Jay Forrester describes such models as follows:

> Each of us uses models constantly. Every person in his private life and in his business life instinctively uses models for decision-making. The mental image of the world around you which you carry in your head is a model. . . . The mental model is fuzzy. It is incomplete. It is imprecisely stated. Furthermore, within one individual, a mental model changes with time and even during the flow of a single conversation. . . . As the subject shifts, so does the model.[5]

These models can be considered assumptive frameworks. They are related clusters of assumptions that are based on past perceptions, which then become, to some extent or other, "updated" by new perceptions and experiences. For example, a young child sees that all the objects she throws up into the air fall to the ground. From these perceptions, she forms the assumption that what goes up should come down. With further experience, she modifies that assumption with qualifiers such as, "Everything that goes up must come down, unless the object is caught by a person, a tree, a roof, etc." People could not negotiate the world without such assumptive frameworks. These assumptions include beliefs, values, and attitudes. Some of them are more important than others, and many of the assumptions that people make they are not even aware of, unless something occurs to challenge them. (For example, most people assume that the floor will not fall out from under them when they walk across a room.)

If self-concept must be inferred, so must an understanding of how another person views himself in a given situation. This is because each person's "world" is experienced in terms of important assumptions, perceptions, and feelings. These concepts were first introduced in the chapter on problems of communication because they enabled us to understand how different people could experience the same encounter differently. We will review these ideas again and elaborate on them in more detail, but this time with the explicit purpose of trying to understand another person's point of view.[6]

[5] Jay W. Forrester, "Counterintuitive Behavior of Social Systems," *Technology Review*, January 1971, pp. 53-68.

[6] As noted in Chapter 4, these ideas draw heavily from the concepts presented in Arthur Turner and George Lombard, *Interpersonal Behavior and Administration* (New York: Free Press, 1969).

ASSUMPTIONS, PERCEPTIONS, AND FEELINGS

Assumptions

In broadest terms, assumptions include all the beliefs, values, and attitudes that a person holds about how things are and how they ought to be. Almost all our assumptions are based on our own past perceptions and experiences, or on the perceptions or observations of others.

The assumptions that are most useful to identify in understanding another person's behavior are those that are charged with an imperative. These assumptions are not just about how people or things *are*, but rather how one *ought* to behave, or how things *ought* to be. These "charged" assumptions are all those "oughts," "shoulds," and "have to's" that an individual adopts from the world around him or her to such an extent that they become the basis for action. Assumptions are the beliefs, goals, and values that we incorporate into our conceptions of the world and into our conceptions of ourselves so that they become part of us. *To assume* means "to take to be with one." Assumptions are built-in beliefs, values, and attitudes by which we live our lives.

Beliefs are the most basic of assumptions. Beliefs are the relationships that people assume exist between two things or some one thing and a characteristic of it, such as that the world is round, or lemons are yellow. Collectively, a person's beliefs make up his basic underlying understanding of himself and his environment.[7] Ultimately, all beliefs can be traced back to the credibility of one's own sensory experience (that is, past perceptions) or to the credibility of some external authority. For example, until the space program provided the means to photograph the earth from outer space, few people had actually *perceived* the world as being round, even though most people *believed* that it was round. Their belief was based on what they had heard, read, reasoned, and learned about the earth, most of which was based on the reports of others.

Values also act as assumptions. However, unlike simple beliefs, values are beliefs that are evaluative in nature.[8] They are assumptions about *what is* or *what ought to be* that express a preference in a positive or negative way. Examples of values would include "Experience is desirable," "People ought to be honest," "People should be free," and so on.

Attitudes are also expressed as assumptions. Attitudes are more

[7] Daryl Bem, *Beliefs, Attitudes and Human Affairs* (Belmont, Calif.: Brooks/Cole Publishing Company, 1970), pp. 4-13; Edward Jones and Harold Gerard, *Foundations of Social Psychology* (New York: John Wiley, 1967), Chap. 5.

[8] *Ibid.* p. 17.

complex than simple beliefs or values, and although they are based on beliefs and values, they are more generalized in nature. For example, some people hold the attitude that the use of flouride in public water systems is dangerous and should be discouraged. This attitude can be thought of as an *assumption* based on the *belief* that flouride is a poison, and the *value* that poisons are bad.[9] Its implications, however, are more far-reaching and "loaded" than either the belief or the value on which the attitude is based. Thus, some assumptions, particularly those that express attitudes, are more charged, complex, and generalized than other assumptions.

At a general level of abstraction, the term *assumption* encompasses a great deal. It is obviously not necessary (or possible) to be aware of all of another person's assumptions to understand that person better. What is important, however, is to sense which assumptions are *salient* and *important* for a person in a given situation. By "salient," we mean the extent to which the person is preoccupied with a given assumption *in a given situation*, such as, "I ought to be the most technically competent person in my group." By "important," we mean the extent to which an assumption is *central* to other assumptions or beliefs. For example, the assumption, "I am a good manager and ought to be viewed by others as being good," is a very central assumption. Disconfirmation of this assumption is apt to call a number of assumptions into question as well, such as, "I ought to be a strong leader," or, "I ought to have influence within the company." *Important or highly charged assumptions are usually those that are most closely related to a person's self-concept.*

Because assumptions are so much a part of us, we tend to make many without even noticing. At other times, we may be very much aware of the particular assumptions on which we are basing our behavior. The more aware we are of the assumptions we make, the better we can understand what is going on inside us. Similarly, if we can identify the important assumptions of another individual, we will be better able to understand that person from his own point of view. Seeking out another's assumptions often helps us become more aware of our own, and vice versa. What may be most important in understanding another person is the ability to recognize and accept (if not approve of) the differences between our own assumptions and those of others.

Perceptions

Perceptions are what a person actually sees, hears, or otherwise perceives as taking place in a given situation. Whereas assumptions prescribe "the way *it ought to be*," perceptions describe "the way it is *currently* seen as being" for a particular person at a particular point in time. The verb *perceive* comes from the Latin *per* ("thoroughly") and

[9] Jones and Gerard, *Foundations of Social Psychology*, p. 17.

capere ("to lay hold of"), combining to mean "to take, receive, to become cognizant of." Thus, perceptions are the way in which we consciously take in what is going on in our lives.

The idea of perception is sometimes difficult to distinguish from the idea of assumption, because almost all assumptions are based on past perceptions. Another difficulty in distinguishing the two is that our assumptions about how things ought to be often influence our perceptions of what we think is taking place. The two folk sayings, "You believe what you see" and "You see what you believe," illustrate the close connection between assumptions and perceptions. Generally, a person's prior assumptions and past experience have a very large influence on what that person does or does not see in a given situation. It is, however, important to distinguish assumptions about how things ought to be from present perceptions of how things actually are, because most personal and interpersonal problems occur when a person's important assumptions are contradicted or challenged by what the person actually perceives as taking place. To go back to the example of the junior consultant, it is his perception that he is not doing as well as he ought to be doing that charges the situation with feeling for him.

Feelings

By "feelings," we mean the emotive and affective reactions of a person in response to a given situation. Feelings are the emotions a person experiences that are triggered by what he or she sees or otherwise perceives as taking place. Strong feelings of a negative nature (such as anger, fear, anxiety) are almost always an indication that assumptions of an important nature are in some way being threatened or violated. For example, the junior consultant's feelings of disappointment and dissatisfaction could be seen as signals that important assumptions and aspects of his self-concept were being disconfirmed. Usually, the disconfirmation of an important assumption will trigger feelings of at least surprise, if not anger, confusion, or other negative emotions. Conversely, confirmation of important personal assumptions will generally be associated with feelings of a positive nature, such as pleasure, joy, self-satisfaction, confidence, and so on.

SUMMARY

This chapter has presented several simple concepts for understanding another person's frame of reference. The ideas of self-concept and of assumptions, perceptions, and feelings do not provide a normative framework for how people ought to behave or for predicting behavior. Rather, these ideas are offered as tools for sharpening your awareness of how and why people (including yourself) see and experience situations as they do. Since the ideas of assumptions, perceptions, and feelings were first introduced in the chapter on "Problems of Communication," it may be useful to briefly review Exhibits I-2 and I-3 of Chapter 4 as an application of these concepts.

The cases and readings in this section of the book deal with problems of communication and interpersonal conflicts. The cases will raise questions about what actions a manager can take to improve interpersonal effectiveness. In most of these cases, as in real life, effective actions cannot be taken without an understanding first of the points of view of the individuals concerned and of why they see a situation the way they do. Thus, the concepts described in this chapter are basic to diagnosing interpersonal problems, including those that are more than simple misunderstandings. These concepts will also be applicable to subsequent material in the course, on motivating leadership and influence.

BIBLIOGRAPHY

ALLPORT, GORDON W., *Pattern and Growth in Personality.* New York: Holt, Rinehart & Winston, 1967.

BEM, DARYL J., *Beliefs, Attitudes and Human Affairs.* Belmont, Calif.: Brooks/Cole Publishing Company, 1970.

BENNIS, WARREN G., KENNETH D. BENNE, and ROBERT CHIN, *The Planning of Change.* New York: Holt, Rinehart & Winston, 1961.

BROWN, ROGER, *Social Psychology.* New York: Free Press, 1965.

COMBS, ARTHUR W., and DONALD SNYGG, *Individual Behavior*, rev. ed. New York: Harper & Row, 1959.

FORRESTER, JAY W., "Counterintuitive Behavior of Social Systems," *Technology Review*, January 1971.

HALL, CALVIN S., and GARDNER LINDZEY, *Theories of Personality.* New York: John Wiley, 1957.

JONES, EDWARD E., and HAROLD B. GERARD, *Foundations of Social Psychology.* New York: John Wiley, 1967.

LECKY, PRESCOTT, *Self-Consistency: A Theory of Personality.* New York: Island Press, 1945.

MADDI, SALVATORE R., *Personality Theories: A Comparative Analysis.* Homewood, Ill.: Dorsey, 1968.

ROKEACK, MILTON, *Beliefs, Attitudes and Values.* San Francisco: Jossey-Boss, 1968.

TAGIURI, RENATO, and LUIGI PETRULLO, *Person Perception and Interpersonal Behavior.* Stanford, Calif.: Stanford University Press, 1958.

TURNER, ARTHUR N., and GEORGE F.F. LOMBARD, *Interpersonal Behavior and Administration.* New York: Free Press, 1969.

Chapter Six

Some Aspects of Self-Concept

The preceding chapter described the idea of self-concept and elaborated on its importance in the understanding of the individual frame of reference. It also discussed the process of inferring aspects of self-concept based on everyday behavior. Most of that discussion was oriented toward understanding people and behavior (including one's own) in situational contexts. In this chapter, we will describe some aspects of self-concept that tend to be basic and persevering over time. Inferring these basic aspects of self-concept requires more familiarity with a person and with behavior than was required in the illustrations in the last chapter.

Combs and Snygg describe self-concept as being multifaceted and as continually developing over a person's lifetime.[1] In their view of human behavior, a person's most basic need is to develop and maintain a sense of *adequacy* in his or her life. Thus, a person's self-concept, and particularly "techniques" for mastering his or her world, will develop in ways that enhance or maintain feelings of adequacy.[2]

The ideas presented in this chapter have their roots in the perceptual approach to behavior developed by Arthur W. Combs and Donald Snygg, as well as earlier and subsequent writings of phenomenological psychologists. See Combs and Snygg, *Individual Behavior: A Perceptual Approach to Behavior* (New York: Harper & Row, 1959). The authors are especially indebted to Eileen Morley for her assistance in preparing earlier drafts of this chapter.

[1]See in particular "The Development of the Phenomenal Self," pp. 122-44 in Combs and Snygg, *Individual Behavior.*

[2]*Ibid.* p. 45

The most basic aspects of a person's self-concept are heavily influenced by early childhood and family experiences. In many respects, these early definitions of self provide the "basic stuff" from which a person's self-concept develops over the years.

A person's self-concept obviously does not develop in a vacuum; it is heavily influenced by people who have been important in that person's life. In particular, important others provide sources of identification, expectations, and approval that become internalized as part of a person's self-concept.

IDENTIFICATION

We identify with those people who are close to us and significant in our world; that is, we consciously and unconsciously adopt their ways of behaving and we become like them.[3] The initial influence comes from our parents. They are the people with whom we as children are most in contact, and on whom we most depend as a source of the knowledge and skills we need in order to survive. Later, as a child becomes old enough to interact with other children, a second level of identification develops—with siblings, if there are brothers and sisters, and with other peers. The importance of a child's need to be like other children can be very clear.

Identification with our parents has two aspects. We identify with their way of being effective adult people. We also identify with those aspects of their behavior that are specific to their sex. Such identification can be very strong, even when the behavior of that parent varies from what is generally accepted as appropriate male or female behavior. If a boy has a father who is very quiet and shy, he in turn may find it difficult to be outgoing and aggressive, or to express his feelings vigorously. If a girl has a mother who is unusually free in expressing feelings of anger, she may experience some conflict between what is appropriately "womanly" behavior inside the family and what is considered attractive outside. These stereotypes of male and female behavior are beginning to erode, so that a wider range of "people" behavior is gradually becoming available to both. But even where the behavior learned from parents is not directly sex-linked, our unconscious identification with the way our parents do things is likely to be strong.

It is important to note that not all identification with others is positive. Oftentimes, past relationships result in identifications that are negative—that is, strong desires *not* to be like a certain person or group of people, including one's parents. Thus, it is possible for a person to identify positively with certain aspects of a parent's be-

[3]Although the term *identification* has passed into everyday language, it is used here in the strict sense of consciously or unconsciously taking on another person's behavior and making it our own; of being like them. In this sense, one can identify with a person but not with an idea—only with other people who hold a particular idea.

havior, and negatively with other aspects. Several cases in this and the next section of the book provide illustrations of this, notably "James Edwards (A)," "Juanita Rodriguez," and "Dale Chapman."

The process of identification continues through life—sometimes with more deliberate effort than in childhood. Most of us choose a college or graduate school because we value the style of behavior it encourages in its students, as well as the knowledge it is likely to provide. We want to be like certain people, and like members of the occupations for which school will prepare us and to which we aspire. When we move into a work organization, we usually make substantial efforts to learn how things are done, and to adapt ourselves accordingly. Such identification is likely to influence certain aspects of our behavior very directly, such as the hours we work, the clothes we wear, and the way we talk. Research evidence is beginning to suggest that this process of "learning to be like . . ." continues throughout early adult life, but that in their 30s and 40s people go through a process of reformulating their sense of identity, affirming the behavior that seems most personally relevant, discarding that which does not.

EXPECTATIONS

If we are to survive[4] and succeed in any situation, we have to pay attention to the expectations of those more powerful people on whom our survival depends. Initially, these are parents; later, they are other people to whom our physical and psychological well-being is tied or whose approval we desire, such as a lover or spouse, a boss, professor, or major client.

The issues of identification and expectations are inseparable, because the people with whom we identify at all ages have ideas of what they *expect from us*—ideas of what is right and wrong, good and bad. They teach us by their behavior what they really believe (no matter what they say), so that over time we come to take many of their beliefs for our very own. Their "shoulds," "oughts," "musts," become our values, beliefs, and often goals. Parents have ideas about what a child should master—say, walking at a certain age, eating with a spoon, learning to read, getting good grades, being polite, or doing well at sports. Their expectations are experienced by us as the things we *must* do. Later, we are the object of other people's expectations.

Our perceptions of what other people expect of us are an important influence on our behavior. When these expectations become internalized as our own, they become important aspects of our self-concept and view of the world. In adult life, these internalized expectations form a complex interacting web of demands that we may not

[4]The word *survive* is used both in its concrete meaning of physical survival, for which we depend entirely on parents in our early life, and in its symbolic meaning of maintaining membership in a family, peer group, or other valued organization.

always be able to satisfy; and even if we can satisfy each separately, we may not be able to meet them simultaneously.

As we grow older, many important expectations have become internalized. We come to *expect of ourselves* the things we have previously experienced others demanding of us. And often we are not aware of how we got those expectations for ourselves, or indeed even what those expectations are. Thus, if for some reason it becomes impossible to behave in ways we expect of ourselves, we experience guilt and anxiety.

APPROVAL

When we are young, and trying to learn how to meet the expectations of those with whom we identify or depend upon, we wish for their *acceptance* of us as *us* as well as for their *approval* of our accomplishments. In other words, we want to be loved and valued even when we have not earned approval. Because we want that basic, unconditional acceptance, and at the same time wish for approval that is conditional upon our accomplishments, we often confuse the two. Some parents, of course, withhold acceptance and confer approval only when it is earned. Their children are likely to be rather more accomplishment-oriented than the children of parents who make it clear that they are accepted and loved even when they have not yet earned approval.

In any event, our search for mastery is undertaken not only because it feels good to increase our powers, but also because it earns approval. It is crucial for a child to experience approval and acceptance. But he can earn approval, and can only be *given* acceptance. As a result, children pay careful attention to what is necessary to get what they want. They quickly learn the clusters of attitudes, beliefs, goals, techniques, and skills that will secure approval for them, and these will become second nature to them.

These ways of gaining approval from parents expand as we grow older. The sources become more varied—neighbors, friends, teachers, bosses, and so on. Adult approval thus is multifaceted and requires complex sets of behaviors. If we fail to earn "enough" approval, we see ourselves as failing and inadequate, and suffer a loss of self-respect. In turn, if we are not given "enough" acceptance, we see ourselves as unloved and suffer a loss of self-esteem. This latter condition can lead to an even more intense search for approval via accomplishment, as a poor substitute for the missing acceptance. A person who earns much approval and is given (and can receive) great acceptance is rich indeed.

The need for adequacy and internalized sources of identification, expectations, and approval has been presented here in relatively simple terms. These ideas have also been described primarily in terms of the development of "self" in early childhood and adolescent years. As you study the cases that have been included in this section of the book, you will see the relatively rich and complex ways in which these aspects of self manifest themselves in adults and in their behavior. The cases will also serve the useful purpose of grounding the ideas presented in this and the preceding chapter.

TECHNIQUES FOR MASTERY AND SELF-CONCEPT

This chapter has thus far discussed the development of important aspects of self-concept. We have not yet discussed the process of how people actually go about behaving so that they gain a sense of adequacy and enhance their self-concepts. Much of what we know about individual behavior suggests that people develop highly individualistic sets of "techniques" of behavior that enable them to experience a sense of mastery and enhance important aspects of their self-concepts. Indeed, it is very difficult to think about self-concept without also considering the techniques that people develop for meeting their internalized goals, values, expectations, and needs for approval and identification.

The people we identify with present us with expectations we try to meet (and ultimately often make our own). Those expectations require of us that we develop certain skills, techniques, attitudes, and beliefs in order to meet them. Acquiring the ability to meet expectations gives us a sense of *mastery* in our world. Because the identifications we make and the expectations we receive vary so much from person to person, the *styles* of mastery we develop are also varied. One child, for instance, may rely predominantly upon sensitivity to others and abilities to relate to them—interpersonal skills. Another may depend largely on facility with factual or technical matters—cognitive skills. Still another may emphasize the use of the body in competitive sports—physical skills. And of course, overlaps are common. The point is not that one style of mastery is superior to others, but rather that great differences exist among people in the ways they attempt to meet the expectations of others with whom they identify.

Awareness of our own particular style of seeking mastery, and of its fit with the styles of those around us and the situations in which we find ourselves, can be a valuable insight. In any event, sensing that we are adequate to deal with the expectations of our relationships and our situations is to experience a sense of mastery. And that is a crucial foundation for a sense of adequacy as a person.

It is difficult to show the complex interrelationship of identification, expectations, approval, and mastery in a two-dimensional diagram. All we can do here is to indicate that important interrelations exist. Nor is it really useful to diagram the different ways in which these combine for each of us, to form a complex, yet unique, network that lends different personal meanings to our behavior in the world. One person, for instance, may have learned that doing carpentry is beneath his status; another that it is a high-status career goal. One person may have learned never to express anger because "it is bad"; another that anger is all right *if* expressed in certain ways; still another that *any* expression of anger is acceptable. One person may identify with father's ambition rather than mother's gentleness, and thus appear different from a sibling who does the reverse. Some may find they get only limited approval when they *perfectly* meet their father's expectations, others that they get enough approval even when they don't quite do so. And so it goes. And so we become.

THE BASIC CONDITIONS OF STABILITY, CHANGE, AND DIRECTION

The set of concepts just described provides some categories for thinking about who we are and who others are. Who we are is a function of what we want and need. And what we want and need is what we judge to be "good" for us. We adjust or try to change what is around us when the fit of us to the outer world is a bad one. Or we change ourselves to improve that fit. Often we do both. Always we are trying to get things organized so that we may feel good in our world and with those around us. What we judge to be "good" is largely a function of our need for a sense of adequacy. Combs and Snygg name our striving for *adequacy* as our most powerful need.[5]

Our search for adequacy is also characterized by three fundamental conditions. These are the conditions of stability, change, and direction. *Stability* is our sense of organization of our world and ourselves. We depend on certain things to remain constant, such as the physical world around us and basic aspects of our relationships with others. For example, once we determine the "best" route to and from work, we no longer actively think about the organization of streets. We travel along them almost automatically. We expect the street signs to remain the same and the drugstore on the corner to be there from one day to the next. Should a street along our usual route be closed for construction on a particular day, our sense of stability will be momentarily jolted until we go through the conscious process of reorienting ourselves in space and determining an alternate route. Likewise, we expect the relationships in our life to maintain certain elements of relative constancy. Culture, religion, family values, and roles provide a basis for relationships that remain stable over some period of time. A shift in one of these aspects may require adjustments in the overall pattern of a particular relationship. In order to accommodate such shifts, we have to reorganize our sense of our relationship with our world in some way. We have to do the same thing more extensively when the change involves the total loss of a relationship, as from death or divorce. A feeling of considerable insecurity and stress usually accompanies the sudden loss of any important stability in our world or our relationships.

[5]Combs and Snygg, *Individual Behavior.*

Of course, in our desire to grow and become more adequate, we, too, change internally. Generally, those changes are at a rate that we and others can handle without undue discomfort. But some changes can be so major that they have great impact. Adolescence, physical injury, an insight of great significance, and other such experiences can result in internal change that stresses our sense of our own inner stability.

It is this sense of stability, in fact, that glues us and our world together and allows us to deal effectively with the changes that do occur, provided they are not too overwhelming. As a child becomes adult, a fantastic amount of *change* occurs in the child's experiencing of the world. We respond to change by gradually reorganizing our perceptions of our world and ourselves so as to take account of it. When change is forced upon an individual faster than he or she can adjust perceptions to cope with it, the basic sense of stability is threatened. Those of you who have moved to another culture know how substantial the shock can be to your sense of what "you in the world" is like. When such change occurs too rapidly, our stable world is shaken, "we don't know what is going on" in our world, and we feel anxiety. Fortunately, change occurs most often in ways and at rates that an individual can handle, although recent books like *Future Shock* suggest that all of us are facing more rapid changes than we can handle without discomfort.

If you consider any person's evolution over time, you will probably also sense a *direction* that he or she seems to take. People tend to adapt to change in ways that are consistent with their particular needs and values and via their particular previous styles of dealing with the world. Thus, the personal change that occurs usually has a pattern that is consistent and meaningful to the individual, although this may be hard to describe in the case of any particular person.

How to Use These Ideas

Start with whatever you see most easily. Understand what you can of the other's assumptions, perceptions, and feelings. Ask yourself, What is the person's style of mastery, and over what? What do others expect of the person that he or she has internalized? What are the person's own expectations? With whom does the person identify, and in what terms (for instance, professionally, ethnically, ideologically, socially)? Look for relationships among sources of identification, expectations, internalized sources of approval, and techniques for mastery. Consider how a person's behavior reflects his or her needs and wants. Organize all that and then look again, this time using these ideas to direct you to the phenomena you missed the first time through. Keep moving back and forth between these ideas and the "data" until you sense that you are not finding much more. Pull your "data" together intellectually as best you can.

Then lean back and try to imagine yourself in the body, mind, and world of the other person. Try saying aloud what you think and feel he or she might say. Try to hold your body as you imagine the other might. See what you experience. Then combine your analysis *and* your experiencing of the other into a formulation of his view of himself—his self-concept. But gently here—it is not for grabbing or, as some say, "getting a handle on." It is for handling gently, turning around, becoming familiar with, all with the respect due another human being who has made personal data available to you.

Listen in class for *differences* between your sense of a person in a case and that of other students. Speculate on how the differences you notice between their views and yours are related to who you and they are. It is in those differences that much learning takes place. For they point back to the simple notion, "It may be silly to you, but it isn't silly to me." It is from those differences that you can gain insight about yourself as well as others.

BIBLIOGRAPHY

COMBS, ARTHUR W., and DONALD SNYGG, *Individual Behavior: A Perceptual Approach to Behavior.* New York: Harper & Row, 1959.

Readings

Relativism in Organizations

George F.F. Lombard

A central theme of student protests today concerns organizations and their administration. Some students protest the establishment as a whole. Others act against those in positions of authority. Still others protest inequities associated with the output of organizations, including profits and their distribution, faulty or unsafe products, and pollution of the environment.

There is substance to many of these criticisms. For the most part, organizations are not dealing successfully with today's problems, such as those concerning the cities, poverty, hunger, and race. This lack of success is apparent around the world. The difficulties are both geographically widespread and, in many kinds of institutions, pervasive. Thus:

- Business organizations, the most effective wealth-creating instruments yet devised by men, have not invented ways of distributing their products without leaving large areas of poverty in the regions where they have been most successful, to say nothing of whole continents of poverty where they have been less successful.

- The medical professions and the organizations associated with them do no better in the delivery of health care.

- Our religious organizations are bothered by schisms and a sense of purposelessness as perplexing as it is profound.

- Though governments perhaps can prevent at least some small wars from becoming large ones, they do not end them.

Widespread, radical, revolutionary change indeed seems necessary. At the same time, numerous observers of the world scene, while recognizing the seriousness of our unsolved problems, fear change in the processes and goals of organizations as we know them. According to one magazine:

> The single-minded pursuit of profit is the discipline that reconciles conflicting interests; it is the wind of reality that blows

Reproduced from the *Harvard Business Review*, March–April 1971, pp. 55–65.

> away executive cobwebs; it achieves renewal when businesses falter. . . . Change the discipline, introduce purposes linked with broad public responsibility, however praiseworthy they may be, blur the criterion of performance, and the result is likely to be confusion.[1]

The contrary views of revolutionists and defenders of the "establishment" frame the questions I wish to explore. Are today's ideas about organizations a source of our troubles? Are changes possible in them? If so, need the changes be disruptive changes, or can they be orderly? If the latter, to what agencies should we look to bring them about?

My thesis is that, especially during the last half century, an important change has taken place in the systems of knowledge and values which men use to guide their thoughts and actions. The direction of the change has been away from universals and simple, right-wrong, authoritarian formulations and toward multiple values and what I shall call *relativism.* This trend is clear in such areas as the sciences, art, music, literature, religion, and philosophy, but it has not affected men's ideas about organizations and administration, which typically are conceived in what might be called *dualistic* frameworks.

The tensions that result from these two differently structured systems of knowledge and values affect university students especially. Just when they are learning the ideas of relativism, they must live and choose careers in organizations that are bureaucratically conceived and administered. I think this situation helps explain why their protests are so intense.

Significant leads are available from recent research for the reconception of organizations and their administration in relativistic frameworks. The development of these leads calls for new programs of research and education on the part of the universities, and for new understanding and leadership on the part of businessmen.

[1]*Fortune,* September 1969, p. 95.

REVOLUTION IN OUTLOOK

I first became aware of the worldwide nature of the breakdown in universities at a conference I attended in Rotterdam more than three years ago. The conference concerned management education in Western Europe. The occasion provided an opportunity for impromptu discussions on topics of common interest to persons who otherwise do not often see each other. I was a participant in one such conversation which produced this thought-provoking question: What conditions in world affairs led to the crises of the 1960s being expressed in universities? After all, the world has seen many crises, but none has been expressed in universities to the extent that this one has. Moreover, the disturbances in universities are universal in scope and not to be explained by local and regional causes alone.

Attitudes toward Knowledge

Some valuable help in answering that question comes from a research report by William G. Perry, Jr.,[2] Director of the Bureau of Study Counsel at Harvard College, an office to which students go for help when they are having difficulty with their work. In the mid-1950s Perry and his staff, who have acquired a wealth of experience in working with student

[2]*Forms of Intellectual and Ethical Development in the College Years* (New York: Holt, Rinehart & Winston, 1968).

problems, undertook to document the experiences of students during their college years. The interviewers asked the students who volunteered to take part in the research to think and talk about the meaning to them of what they were learning. The quality of the resulting interviews is outstanding. It quickly becomes apparent to a reader that the students are answering the questions out of their own experiences.

The report begins with an inquiry into the changes that have occurred in the questions which professors ask on examinations in courses with large enrollments. Fifty years ago, Perry says, such questions as, "When was the battle of Hastings?" or, "Who wrote such and such a poem?" or, "What did so-and-so say about a particular experiment?" were typical. Today's questions are different. For instance:

- If the examination is about a poem, the student may be asked to state the significance of the poem to its author in the light of the knowledge and circumstances of his times and situation.
- A second question might well be, "What would Shakespeare, Freud, Dewey, Whitehead, and McLuhan each have said about the poem in the circumstances of his life and times?"

Perry infers from these changes in examination questions that professors' assumptions about knowledge and standards for knowledge have changed. Fifty years ago the questions showed that professors viewed knowledge as structured in ways that led to essentially simple, two-valued, right-or-wrong answers to questions and problems. Today's examinations show that professors hold knowledge to be relative, not absolute; not meaningful except in the context of the idea systems, times, and circumstances in which it was generated. Perry labels the first orientation "dualistic" and the second "relativistic." He calls the change revolutionary because it means that professors' views of knowledge as a source of authority do change.

In the first orientation, knowledge is a unidimensional source of authority, right or wrong, not to be questioned. In the latter, the authority of knowledge is relative to the situation. Perry points out that when professors add to their examination questions, as they frequently do, an additional one: "What does the poem mean to you, Mr. Sophomore?"—then the revolution in approach is indeed extensive. For the question tells a student that his professors expect him to commit himself to his view in order that they may compare it with those of authorities. To most undergraduates this is heady stuff.

Thought Processes

For the purposes of this article I do not need to go into Perry's careful analysis of the nine stages of student thought as it develops toward relativism, but I do need to comment on one intermediate stage between dualism and relativism, which Perry calls "multiplicity." I do this in an attempt to convey, albeit briefly, some sense of the significance of the changes of which Perry speaks. Even though we may not think about it consciously, changes we make in our assumptions about knowledge and in our ideas, values, and attitudes concerning knowledge affect deeply what we do in our everyday lives.

To characterize dualism, Perry uses the phrases, "we-right-friendly; others-wrong-hostile." He points out that such an orientation is characteristic of the knowledge with which primitives, whether aborigines or children, view the world. Dualism also characterizes many attitudes in modern adult cultures. For example, it is associated with much that we consider "good" about competition in our society, whether the competition is between football teams or brands of automobiles or other merchandise. It is also, of course, a major theme governing the relations between various other institutions of Western societies, including religious faiths and national states.

Perry uses the statement, "Every one has a right to his own view," to characterize a middle stage in the development from dualism to relativism. In this stage the student recognizes that others' knowledge, attitudes, and views about themselves and their world may differ from his. (The student must truly believe this; it is not enough that he accept the notion on the authority of his professors.) At this middle stage, however, the student is not aware, as he is at the more advanced stage of relativism, that his views of himself and the world have an internal structure, i.e., a consistency and self-reinforcing organization based on certain experiences. Other people's views and his own remain loosely organized in his thought processes, like a pile of sticks or a heap of sand.

At the stage of relativism a student *is* aware of the internal structure of his views, and he has the capacity to examine hitherto unstated basic assumptions in his thinking and thus to change them (and his behavior). Not only does he perceive events differently from the way he did earlier, but he can also perceive the same event *from different perspectives.* Thus he has choices in respect to his actions with others that he did not have at the stage of multiplicity.

A central characteristic of a student's thought processes at the stage of relativism is a capacity for independent study and decision. Perry says that when a student, as the result of an ordered process of observation and reasoning, can state what a poem or the data of an experiment mean to him or others, he is at the stage of relativism. The student recognizes the meanings that the poem or experiment has for others in the light of their lives, times, and ideas, just as he recognizes how his circumstances shape the meaning for him. Perry describes three themes as central to the discipline of independent study and action: (1) choice among alternatives; (2) awareness of choice; and, usually later, (3) commitment to a choice.

Perry does not fall into the trap of becoming absolute about relativism. Were he to do so, he would not have escaped from an "either-or" framework, for when relativism becomes a "must," it returns to dualism. Thus, Perry classifies as being at the stage of relativism a student who elects to conduct his life by absolute values, after considering alternatives, recognizing the limits of his own situation with its particular purposes, times, circumstances, and systems of ideas, and understanding that others may live equally intelligently by values different from his.

Universal Questions

The idea of relativism is not, of course, limited to the campus. It is basic to twentieth century culture. Its roots go back at least to the nineteenth century, perhaps to Darwin's theory of evolution. Einstein's theories of relativity and all that has followed are part of the same stream of ideas. Further reinforcements have come in the fields of literature, art, and music.

Recent technological advances, especially television and, in underdeveloped countries, the transistor radio, bring home to all of us that many other people live differently from the way we do. Modern decision techniques, too, abet the spread of relativism. Computers and Bayesian approaches to decision make it possible to study systematically a much greater number of alternatives for action,

EFFECT OF RELATIVISM

What difference does relativism make in decision making? Taking a relativistic approach rather than a dualistic one, a manager would be likely to:

- Recognize more different kinds of goals and needs for his organization, such as economic, individual, group, and social goals, always trying to keep them in some sort of workable balance.
- Consider more factors bearing on a decision, and attach different weights to them as circumstances change.
- Employ a wider variety of ways of making and carrying out decisions.
- Avoid following rules of thumb about administration (such as, "An employee should never report to more than one boss," or, "An executive's span of control should not exceed six subordinates").
- Evaluate decisions not one by one but in relation to each other and to other interests, knowing that the validity of a decision is dependent on other decisions, actions, and events about which he generally has imperfect knowledge.
- Appreciate the practical necessity for having certain policies and standards for employees to observe but recognize that such rules often come at a price (e.g., resentment or uncooperative behavior on the part of those who see the problem differently) and that their disadvantages must therefore be weighed against their advantages.

particularly in organizations, than ever before, thus pointing up the relativity of any particular course of action. Finally, in a still more personal sense, "the pill" raises questions about long-held moral and ethical standards and moves us in the direction of relativism.

Perry's research gives us data about the depth and extent to which this great idea of modern times is revolutionizing the outlook and decisions of college students. He reports that it is the commonplace of education in good liberal arts programs in U.S. colleges today.

If I were to seek data with which to answer the question asked at Rotterdam, I would use as a guide the hypothesis that student protest in the 1960s and early 1970s has been a function of the tension between conceptual relativism and bureaucratic behavior. That is to say, in organizations where relativism as a system of values is conceptually clear, and bureaucratic behavior is also clear, then protests will be both frequent and intense. A quick review of studies of protest at Berkeley, New York (Columbia), Cambridge (Harvard), Paris, Tokyo, New Delhi, and elsewhere indicates that systematic support for this hypothesis would not be difficult to find.[3] In these cases, relativism as a value important to students conflicted with dualism as a value important in the administration of universities.

Though Joseph W. Scott and Mohamed El-Assai formulated their variables differently in a study of 70 colleges and universities, their findings support the same point. They found that demonstrations were more frequent (most of the correlation coefficients fell between .70 and .90) in the large, complex, high-quality schools than in the small, simple, low-quality ones. They explained:

> Large, complex, high-quality schools, being more likely to use autocratic and bureaucratic means to redress student grievances ... encouraged and increased the

[3]See, for example, *The Cox Commission Report: Crisis at Columbia* (New York: Random House, 1968).

likelihood of student protest demonstrations.[4]

DUALISM IN MANAGEMENT

I have indicated that relativism is stimulated and reenforced by trends and practices in many aspects of life. Let us turn our attention now from the campus to business and other organizations.

Generally speaking, the theory and practice of formal organizations is still, I believe, essentially based on unidimensional, right-wrong, dualistic approaches. The principles of organization stated by such authors as Henri Fayol, Luther Gulick, Lyndall Urwick, James Mooney, Frederick Taylor, and their colleagues and successors rest on the primacy of technical and economic efficiency. Deviations, as they see them, represent inefficiencies and disruptions of organizational processes. An important aspect of executives' work is to provide standards, preferably written, for attaining efficiency. Any situation that is not so provided for is to be referred to the central authority for decision. Thus, the right-wrong, dualistic character of standards for action is clear. The sociological and psychological consequences of this model have been described by Weber and his followers.

In important ways, this model about how people in organizations are to behave characterizes today's actions and beliefs about management in large organizations in business, government, education, medicine, religion, the military, and almost every other branch of organized life. One unfortunate and unintended consequence is that undergraduates have to live and study in dualistically oriented organizations *as well as anticipate careers in them,* just when those we regard as the best among them have found the inner strength to commit themselves to relativism as a way of thinking. I believe this juxtaposition provides a source of dissonance and tension that underlies the current crisis in society.

Are organizations as we know them today doomed because of this conflict, or are there ways for executives to reduce the dissonance between value systems while keeping their organizations productive and viable? I believe that there are such ways and that we can learn to use them if we want to.

To elaborate on this belief, I shall turn now to a series of studies of organization and administration. I will limit myself to analyses of business operations because they are the ones most familiar to me. (The findings of comparable studies in other kinds of organizations are not essentially different, at least in the aspects we need to consider.)[5] My intent is a limited one: not to develop a new theory of organizations—to do this, much additional, difficult work would have to be done—but to show that such an understanding is feasible.

REVOLUTIONS IN IDEAS

To assist us in knowing what to look for, we need a way of thinking about what happens when new systems of values and ideas displace old ones. Such a process is not familiar to most of us, who usually assume that old ideas just disappear when they are replaced. For guidance on this question in his work, Perry turns to studies in the history of science.[6]

[4]"Multiuniversity, University Size, University Quality and Student Protest: An Empirical Study," *American Sociological Review,* October 1969, p. 702; see also *American Sociological Review,* June 1970, p. 525.

[5]See, for example, Peter M. Blau, *The Dynamics of Bureaucracy* (Chicago: The University of Chicago Press, 1955).

[6]Thomas S. Kuhn, *The Structure of Scientific Revolutions* (Chicago: The University of Chicago Press, 1962).

These studies make it clear that major changes in systems of ideas and values occur slowly over long periods of time and that, at least in some instances, it is not accurate to say that the old ideas disappear. Rather, they often continue to have validity in special and limited circumstances within the broad framework provided by the new ideas. To illustrate:

- Neither Newton's specific ideas about motion nor the broad views of the world associated with them have disappeared since Einstein suggested relativity.' Newton's ideas continue to be useful to all of us—for example, in understanding our motions and the motions of people and things around us.

- On an everyday level, I recall hearing the words of a careful radio announcer as he described the increasing speed of Apollo 8 returning from the moon and approaching our world at so many miles per hour "relative to the earth." That is, of course, accurate phrasing. Nevertheless, when I drive a car, I neglect to keep in mind that its speed as shown on the speedometer is relative to that of the earth through space. The older formulation serves me well enough for any actions I need to take when I am driving.

Thus, in reviewing studies of organizations and their administration, we need not necessarily discard older, dualistic values and ways of thinking. We can seek to find ways of reconceiving them within broader frameworks.

For the exploration that follows I choose three topics, formal organization, decision making, and productivity. I select the first because of its importance in the conventional wisdom about organizations, the second because the undeniably "go-no go" character of decisions seems to lead inescapably to dualism, and the third because it is frequently assumed that an organization's contributions to society are solely purposive.

New Organization Patterns

Many recent writers have commented on a trend away from simple, unitary concepts of formal organization and toward increasingly complex theories.[7] The trend has several dimensions and manifestations. For instance, aerospace firms have largely given up a form of organization based on simple concepts of unified command and narrow span control. Instead, their executives speak of matrix organizations, in which both project and functional supervisors and professional workers as a team have responsibility for the same project. Again, it is said that the artists and engineers who built Pepsi-Cola's pavilion for Expo '70 at Osaka "did what was required of them without supervision. There was no real chain of command."[8]

In addition, various studies suggest that there is no one best way to organize. In contrast to the bureaucratic theories referred to in a previous section, the findings of these recent studies suggest that the form of an organization depends on the context provided by its setting of individuals and purposes in society. This central theme of the conclusions is the more striking in that each researcher approached his study from a different perspective. Let me be more specific:

- Alfred Chandler's approach was historical. His conclusion, stated broadly, is that conditions in the environment of a firm demand different organizational structures. He says that "Different organizational forms result from different types of

[7]See, for example, W.G. Bennis, "Organizational Developments and the Fate of Bureaucracy," paper presented at the annual meeting of the American Psychological Association, Los Angeles, September 4, 1964; see also Peter F. Drucker, *The Age of Discontinuity* (New York: Harper & Row, 1969).

[8]Calvin Tomkins, "E.A.T." (Experiments in the Arts and Technology), "Onward and Upward With the Arts," *The New Yorker,* October 3, 1970.

growth . . ."[9] and that "Structure follows strategy."

• Lawrence E. Fouraker and John M. Stopford tested Chandler's broad hypothesis with data derived from modern, complex, and large multinational enterprises. They concluded that "the question of the characteristics of the organization is a question of management's choice between sets of problems."[10]

• Abraham Zaleznik's focus is on authority relationships within a firm. He finds "a formal structure in the final analysis represents one design of organization, among a number of options, in which the authority figure invests his confidence."[11]

• Paul R. Lawrence and Jay W. Lorsch suggest "a contingency theory of organization . . . the basic assumption . . . [of which] is that organizational variables are in complex interrelationship with one another and with conditions in the environment."[12]

These findings show how far modern concepts of formal organization have moved from dualistic, right-wrong approaches and toward concepts that are consistent with relativism.

Contingency in Decisions

In the study just referred to, Lawrence and Lorsch suggest the idea of contingency in relation to organizations and administration. I believe that this idea helps to delineate a relativistic framework for reconceiving the seemingly inescapable dualistic aspects of decision making. Let me illustrate in terms of some personal experiences and views,

• I have found it useful to classify organizational decisions into their internally and externally oriented aspects. In a large organization, particularly one with many functional line and staff departments, the internally oriented aspects are hardly ever simple and dualistic.

In my work in academic administration, I find that almost any decision I reach has not one but many consequences for action. A "single" decision suggesting, for example, a change in a professor's assignment may make it necessary for me to speak to two program chairmen and the administrative directors of their respective programs; to one or two area chairmen; to the registrar's office; and to the finance office. And that is fairly routine; a complicated decision requires even more implementation. Moreover, each interaction may produce information I had not taken into account at the time of the original decision, and I may have to extend or go back over and even reverse the communications I have already made.

Again and again this process has impressed me with the contingent and relativistic nature of the action I am taking. Though each step in the whole sequence is important in its place, it is the comprehension of the whole set of potentials, actualities, and interconnections that seems to make the difference between decisions well communicated and not well communicated.

• I had long thought of investment decisions and decisions to "make or buy" as two-valued. But a few minutes' reflection shows that carefully made decisions of these kinds are reached only after alternatives, perhaps many of them, have been considered. In many situations more than one of the alternatives would be equally good, were only one or two factors in the situation to be changed a little.

Thus, even a good decision of these types is actually based on contingencies. A slight change in one or more factors would

[9] *Strategy and Structure* (Cambridge, Mass.: M.I.T. Press, 1962).

[10] "Organizational Structure and the Multinational Strategy," *Administrative Science Quarterly,* June 1968, p. 47.

[11] Gene W. Dalton, Louis B. Barnes, and Abraham Zaleznik, *The Distribution of Authority in Formal Organizations* (Boston: Division of Research, Harvard Business School, 1968), p. 163.

[12] *Organization and Environment* (Boston, Division of Research, Harvard Business School, 1967), p. 157.

lead to other decisions than the one acted on.

In summary, a relativistic framework seems helpful in thinking of one's job as a decision maker. Whereas a dualistic framework describes only one step in the process, not necessarily even a final one, a relativistic viewpoint combines the outwardly oriented and visible steps of a decision with the internal thought processes that guide a manager. The apparent "go-no go" aspects of a decision become the limited, special instances of a broader, total, thought-and-action approach that includes alternatives considered as well as actions taken. Though the decision may appear dualistic in character, the total decision set, including both the obvious physical act and the inner subjective consideration of alternatives and contingencies, is appropriately conceived as a totality in a relativistic framework.

Complex Purposes

Companies no longer limit themselves to producing products and services sold in free private markets. The outputs of business today are varied and complex. For instance, hitherto private-sector organizations are moving rapidly in the direction of providing what in the past have been thought of as public-sector goods and services. Business firms contract to provide education, welfare, rehabilitation, and urban renewal programs and services, just as public-sector enterprises in many parts of the world perform what we would call private-sector activities. Everywhere the interconnections between the two sectors are on the increase.

What is more, companies think of their missions in complex ways. A manufacturing company's purpose is no longer conceived as making, let us say, toasters for the breakfast table and electric motors for industry. The General Electric Company says, "Progress is our most important product"—and this is not just an advertising slogan. Again, the conglomerate and the multinational corporation, with all of their complexities, are ever more frequent. Other events call to our attention that the products of organizations are not all benign. We are learning to think of industries' noxious effluents as outputs.

But this is only part of the story. The modern businessman is saying that his company is more than a producer of ever-changing goods and services. One executive puts it this way:

> I have never been particularly taken with the various single-thought definitions that have been offered to describe the role of as complex an institution as the American corporation.... Business discharges its true social responsibility by meeting individual and communal economic needs, to the profit of society and itself, while giving expression to the other, noneconomic values of society.[13]

Fritz J. Roethlisberger has suggested that an organization contributes to four needs or values: the norms of groups, the ideals of society, the personalities of individuals, and the purposes of the organization itself.[14] Many studies show how employee behavior serves individual needs and group norms as well as production and profit goals. The Hawthorne works study at Western Electric Company, the first to demonstrate this phenomenon, has now been confirmed in a wide variety of organizations.[15]

[13]Virgil B. Day, "The Social Relevance of Business," speech presented at the Annual College-Business Symposium, December 3, 1969, Providence, Rhode Island (reprinted by General Electric Company, Schenectady, New York), pp. 4–5.

[14]*Training for Human Relations* (Boston: Division of Research, Harvard Business School, 1954), p. 125.

[15]Fritz J. Roethlisberger and W.J. Dickson, *Management and the Worker* (Cambridge, Mass.: Harvard University Press, 1939).

Unfortunately, researchers have largely ignored questions about the contributions work groups make to the attainment of the broad ideals of society. I know of a few beginnings in this direction, but they were not followed up:

- In the course of the field work for his thesis a few years ago, a student at the Harvard Business School came across a situation involving the behavior of members of a work group in relation to questions of social justice. In one of these groups, the members had arranged their activities in ways that resolved their feelings and attitudes about differences in their backgrounds. (Their supervisors had paid no attention to this matter.)

  The 25 or so persons in the group represented at least 8 ethnic and racial backgrounds. Instead of showing covert hostility and aggression toward each other, the employees had arranged their work and a variety of other educational and recreational activities in ways that resolved individual fears about mistreatment and persecution at the hands of the others. They read books together and discussed them. They went to concerts together and organized their own picnics, golf tournaments, card games, and fishing trips. They and others referred to their group as "The United Nations." The student did not analyze the data in terms of relativism.

- In another Harvard Business School study, the researcher followed up similar leads with results that were so surprising we did not fully trust them.[16] The researcher was concerned with the pairs of individuals who "checked out" the purchases of customers in a supermarket. The tasks of the two persons in each pair were different; also, one was paid at a higher rate than the other. Moreover, there were differences among the workers with respect to sex, age, education, and ethnicity.

  The study showed the workers had decided views about what combinations of persons should work together. Some combinations they felt were fair and just, some unfair and unjust. Once expressed, their views on these matters turned out to be surprisingly clear and effective in terms of worker satisfaction and productivity achieved for the store. The study showed how much arrangements at work can contribute to the attainment of social values, and it demonstrated that behavior in organizations concerns goals other than productivity, efficiency, profitability, and similar corporate aims.

[16] J.V. Clark, *A Preliminary Investigation of Some Unconscious Assumptions Affecting Labor Efficiency in Eight Supermarkets,* DBA Thesis, Harvard Business School, 1958, unpublished; see also George C. Homans, *Social Behavior* (New York: Harcourt Brace Jovanovich, 1961), p. 255.

UNREALIZED POTENTIALS . . .

This brief review of studies of informal organization, decision making, and productivity suggests that the findings of modern research are consistent with ideas of relativism. Specific events may still be conceived in dualistic frameworks; supervisors still govern subordinates, subordinates still report to supervisors in a chain of command, a decision to do one thing is still a decision not to do another at that time, and purpose still continues as a dimension of productivity. But these matters can also appropriately be conceived in a wider framework of values and ideas that are structured relativistically.

This possibility is important, for it is sometimes argued that the inevitable consequence of the increasing size and scale of today's organizations is more bureaucracy. If this is so, we are in for difficult times indeed. We must not seek to deal with the conditions which produce disturbances and protests by repressing the ideas of relativism. Those ideas underlie too much of world society today for us to rid ourselves of them. Curbed in one area (e.g., business), they would thrive in others (e.g., science and the arts). Granted that the ideas have led to excesses in many phases of life, particularly and tragically among the young, they may still serve us well.

Today organizations are needed that can create greater equality in the distribution of wealth, more racial and social justice, and other social benefits. Civil rights associations, churches, universities, schools, and similar organizations seek to achieve such gains. Yet they typically are administered bureaucratically, like other organizations today, and in terms of dualistic values. Perhaps we need more of these kinds of organizations. If so, we are being well served, for new ones are formed every day. But perhaps what are being created are more failures.

We are not limited to creating organizations that, having single purposes such as the production of profit or power, must be managed in a dualistic manner. An alternative is available: we can reconceive our ideas about organizations and administration on a relativistic basis. The studies reviewed show that behavior in organizations can satisfy individual, group, and social needs as well as formal organizational objectives. Organizations and the leadership roles in them typically have not been conceived and designed to support such behavior—but they *could* be.

. . . and Some Problems

In the concluding chapter to an essay on social revolution, Brooks Adams wrote 50 years ago that administration is "possibly the highest faculty of the human mind." He went on to say:

> It is precisely in this preeminent requisite for success in government that I suspect the modern capitalist class to be weak. . . . Modern capitalists appear to have been evolved under the stress of an environment which demanded excessive specialization in the direction of a genius adapted to money-making under highly complex industrial decisions. . . .
>
> Advances in administration seem to presuppose the evolution of new governing classes, since, apparently, no established type of mind can adapt itself to changes in environment, even in slow-moving civilizations, as fast as environments change. Thus a moment arrives when the minds of any given dominant type fail to meet the demands made upon them and are superseded by a younger type, which in turn is set aside by another still younger, until the limit of the administrative genius of that particular race has been reached. Then disintegration sets in, the social momentum is gradually relaxed, and society sinks back to a level at which it can cohere.[17]

To avoid the disintegration of which Brooks Adams wrote, we need to comprehend, at a broad conceptual level, the depth and extent of the changes in the structure of knowledge, values, and approaches to life that the ideas of relativism have opened to us in the twentieth century. It will not be easy. If we fail, it will be a failure of the imagination, a failure to grasp the significance for administration of ideas already available in other fields.

When I have suggested to some executives what needs to be done, they have responded, "We don't want more relativism! There is too much now. If only someone would tell us what to do!" Others find the ideas I have described quite familiar. I can understand this latter reaction, for the ideas about which I have written are alive in the world today. At the same time, I do not know of an instance in which someone has designed a course for executives or has tried to run an organization with a relativistic framework explicitly in mind. In short, we have not yet tried to put these ideas to work. When we do, we will probably find ourselves wrestling with questions like these:

- Are ideals consistent with relativism? I have heard it argued—and vehemently—

[17]*The Theory of Social Revolutions* (New York: Macmillan, 1913), p. 205.

that if there are no absolutes, there are no ethics. The view is that an ethic must be an absolute. I do not know how tomorrow's students and practitioners will answer this question, though leads for further study of the problem are easily available.[18]

- How relative is relativism itself? In an interesting critique of his own research, Perry suggests the need for commitment to specific values within a framework of relativism, knowing that the values are not absolute for all times, circumstances, and systems of ideas.

- What about the impact on people at middle levels of organizations? It has been suggested that, while relativistic frameworks for action and decision may work very well at top levels of management, they lead to insecurity and uncertainty at middle levels. Perhaps Perry's suggestion would likewise be useful in handling this problem.

CONCLUSION

The implementation of these ideas calls for new effort on the part of universities. There must be new research to develop ways of teaching relativism to practitioners; administrators in many kinds of organizations must develop new competence in decision making. This in turn calls for strength in universities at a time when their internal problems make it difficult for them to attend to this work, and when others call for them to abandon the intellectual path to engage in direct action in society.

How will relativism affect management in the future? Its probable impact is not easy to describe; it is visible not in individual acts but in larger *patterns* of thought and action that give significance to what an administrator does. Although, as earlier suggested, the acts by themselves may seem to be two-valued—choices between alternatives—they can still be conceived as part of a relativistic thought-and-action approach. With this point in mind, let me outline some characteristics of administration under relativism as I think it will develop:

First, tomorrow's decision makers, more than their counterparts today, will need to be able to conceptualize the problems they face. They will need the ability to comprehend the appearance of the particular in the full complexity of its setting in society. To use an example to which I have already referred, the supermarket manager of the future will need to perceive the opportunity to take concrete action in respect to values regarding race, sex, education, and ethnicity when he orders boys and girls to work together to serve customers during rush hours at the check-out counters.

Second, executives of the future will need the capacity to examine problems from several different perspectives and along more than one value dimension. They will need to be able to think effectively about what differences will result from each of several diagnoses and actions in specific situations. To illustrate:

It will not be news, as it is today, when a company issues a plant location directive that stresses positive social criteria. This is what the Quaker Oats Company has done. On top of conventional economic yardsticks, Quaker Oats managers are asked to consider two other corporate goals: (a) decentralizing operations away from congested metropolitan areas, and (b) providing job opportunities for minorities. Management also recently decided to build a new frozen foods plant in Jackson, Tennessee, rather than in Memphis largely because of the availability of black labor "coming off the farms," an integrated school system, and the community's progressive attitude.

[18]Joseph F. Fletcher, *Situation Ethics* (Philadelphia: Westminster Press, 1966).

Earlier the company had refrained from committing a new factory to Danville, Illinois, until after the city fathers passed an open housing ordinance.[19]

Third, executives will evaluate situations on more than one basis. They will continue to use such scales of evaluation as productivity, sales, and profit—what might be called external, absolute scales because they are developed by top management for the organization as a whole. But they will also use scales of evaluation developed by members of a work group themselves—what might be called internal yardsticks. Examples of the latter are social codes and ideas about fair work standards. In short, just as physicists have used ideas about both mass and motion to improve their understanding of the behavior of matter, executives will use the two kinds of ideas I have mentioned to improve their understanding of behavior in organizations.

Fourth, leaders of organizations will use ideas without being bound by ideologies. Rather than acting in the situations they encounter according to stereotypes provided by their cultures (for instance, the white manager from an upper middle-class background who is repelled by what he considers the "laziness" of minority-group employees from poor homes), they will be able to work through different ideas and theories about situations to realistic and correctible diagnoses of them and of themselves. They will not be frightened by new problems and new solutions to them. More than now, they will be able to assess realistically the potentials of a situation, without distortion as a result of their personal involvement and values.

Fifth, the general manager's capacity for problem solving will be based more on his skills of *processing* information about a situation accurately than on his ability to contribute knowledge as an expert from a field such as engineering, law, or accounting. He will work in many roles—conceptualizer, negotiator, counselor, arbiter, teacher—to improve the capacity of individuals to affect their environment.

Sixth, to behave effectively in the many roles they will be called on to assume, executives will need a new capacity to assess the frameworks they use in evaluating situations. They will need an inner strength, the strength of knowing their convictions and the limits of them. Neither bound by their beliefs nor arrogant about them, they will try to know themselves and others with recognition, not denial, of the sources of their convictions. Thus they will work continually for new values and an open society.

The sooner such decision makers are trained to assume the direction of organizations in business, government, education, and other fields, the better off our society will be.

The profession of administration has been slow to develop conceptually during the twentieth century. This has contributed in no small way to the severe problems which we are experiencing in race relations, in schools, in the cities, and elsewhere. We must pay much more attention to the concepts and frameworks that we use in thinking about problems and events in our organizations. Relativism is an idea whose time has come—not only for young people but also for managers.

[19]*The Christian Science Monitor,* November 20, 1970, p. 21.

The Need to Know and The Fear of Knowing

Abraham H. Maslow

FEAR OF KNOWLEDGE: EVASION OF KNOWLEDGE: PAINS AND DANGERS OF KNOWING

From our point of view, Freud's greatest discovery is that *the* great cause of much of psychological illness is the fear of knowledge of oneself—of one's emotions, impulses, memories, capacities, potentialities, of one's destiny. We have discovered that fear of knowledge of oneself is very often isomorphic with, and parallel with, fear of the outside world. That is, inner problems and outer problems tend to be deeply similar and to be related to each other. Therefore we speak simply of fear of knowledge in general, without discriminating too sharply fear-of-the-inner from fear-of-the-outer.

In general this kind of fear is defensive, in the sense that it is a protection of our self-esteem, of our love and respect for ourselves. We tend to be afraid of any knowledge that could cause us to despise ourselves or to make us feel inferior, weak, worthless, evil, shameful. We protect ourselves and our ideal image of ourselves by repression and similar defenses, which are essentially techniques by which we avoid becoming conscious of unpleasant or dangerous truths. And in psychotherapy the maneuvers by which we continue avoiding this consciousness of painful truth, the ways in which we fight the efforts of the therapist to help us see the truth, we call "resistance." All the techniques of the therapist are in one way or another truth-revealing, or are ways of strengthening the patient so he can bear the truth. ("*To be completely honest with onself is the very best effort a human being can make*."—S. Freud)

But there is another kind of truth we tend to evade. Not only do we hang on to our psychopathology, but also we tend

Reprinted with permission.

to evade personal growth because this, too, can bring another kind of fear, of awe, of feelings of weakness and inadequacy.[1] And so we find another kind of resistance, a denying of our best side, of our talents, of our finest impulses, of our highest potentialities, of our creativeness. In brief, this is the struggle against our own greatness, the fear of *hubris.*

Here we are reminded that our own Adam and Eve myth, with its dangerous Tree of Knowledge that mustn't be touched, is paralleled in many other cultures which also feel that ultimate knowledge is something reserved for the gods. Most religions have had a thread of anti-intellectualism (along with other threads, of course), some trace of preference for faith or belief or piety rather than for knowledge, or the feeling that *some* forms of knowledge were too dangerous to meddle with and had best be forbidden or reserved to a few special people. In most cultures those revolutionaries who defied the gods by seeking out their secrets were punished heavily, like Adam and Eve, Prometheus and Oedipus, and have been remembered as warnings to all others not to try to be godlike.

And, if I may say it in a very condensed way, it is precisely the godlike in ourselves that we are ambivalent about, fascinated by and fearful of, motivated to and defensive against. This is one aspect of the basic human predicament, that we are simultaneously worms and gods. Every one of our great creators, our godlike people, has testified to the element of courage that is needed in the lonely moment of creation, affirming something new (contradictory to the old). This is a kind of daring, a going out in front all alone, a defiance, a challenge. The moment of fright is quite understandable but must nevertheless be overcome if creation is to be possible. Thus to discover in oneself a great talent can certainly bring exhilaration, but it also brings a fear of the dangers and responsibilities and duties of being a leader and of being all alone. Responsibility can be seen as a heavy burden and evaded as long as possible. Think of the mixture of feelings of awe, humility, even of fright that have been reported to us, let us say, by people who have been elected President.

A few standard clinical examples can teach us much. First is the fairly common phenomenon encountered in therapy with women.[2] Many brilliant women are caught up in the problem of making an unconscious identification between intelligence and masculinity. To probe, to search, to be curious, to affirm, to discover, all these she may feel as defeminizing, especially if her husband, in his uncertain masculinity, is threatened thereby. Many cultures and many religions have kept women from knowing and studying, and I feel that one dynamic root of this action is the desire to keep them "feminine" (in a sado-masochistic sense); for instance, women cannot be priests or rabbis.[3]

The timid man also may tend to identify probing curiosity as somehow challenging to others, as if somehow, by being intelligent and searching out the truth, he is being assertive and bold and manly in a way that he can't back up, and that such a pose will bring down upon him the wrath of the other, older, stronger men. So also may children identify curious probing as a trespass upon the prerogatives of their gods, the all-

[1]S. Cohen, "A Growth Theory of Neurotic Resistance to Psychotherapy," *Journal of Humanistic Psychology,* I (1961), 48–63.

[2]H.A. Overstreet, *The Mature Mind* (New York: W. W. Norton, 1949).

[3]A.H. Maslow, H. Rand, and S. Newman, "Some Parallels between the Dominance and Sexual Behavior of Monkeys and the Fantasies of Psychoanalytic Patients," *Journal of Nervous and Mental Disease,* CXXXI (1960), 202–12.

powerful adults. And of course it is even easier to find the complementary attitude in adults. For often they find the restless curiosity of their children at least a nuisance and sometimes even a threat and a danger, especially when it is about sexual matters. It is still the unusual parent who approves and enjoys curiosity in his children. Something similar can be seen in the exploited, the downtrodden, the weak minority or the slave. He may fear to know too much, to explore freely. This might arouse the wrath of his lords. A defensive attitude of pseudo-stupidity is common in such groups. In any case, the exploiter, or the tyrant, out of the dynamics of the situation, is not likely to encourage curiosity, learning, and knowledge in his underlings. People who know too much are likely to rebel. Both the exploited and the exploiter are impelled to regard knowledge as incompatible with being a good, nice, well-adjusted slave. In such a situation, knowledge is dangerous, quite dangerous. A status of weakness or subordination, or low self-esteem, inhibits the need to know. The direct, uninhibited staring gaze is the main technique that an overlord monkey uses to establish dominance.[4] The subordinate animal characteristically drops his gaze.

This dynamic can sometimes be seen, unhappily, even in the classroom. The really bright student, the eager questioner, the probing searcher, especially if he is brighter than his teacher, is too often seen as a "wise guy," a threat to discipline, a challenger of his teacher's authority.

That "knowing" can unconsciously mean domination, mastery, control, and perhaps even contempt, can be seen also from the scoptophiliac, who can feel some sense of power over the naked women he peeps at, as if his eyes were an instrument of domination that he could use for raping. In this sense, most men are Peeping Toms and stare boldly at women, undressing them with their eyes. The biblical use of the word "knowing" as identical with sexual "knowing" is another use of the metaphor.

At an unconscious level, knowing as an intrusive penetrating into, as a kind of masculine sexual equivalent, can help us to understand the archaic complex of conflicting emotions that may cluster around the child's peeping into secrets, into the unknown, some women's feeling of a contradiction between femininity and boldly knowing, of the underdog's feeling that knowing is a prerogative of the master, of the religious man's fear that knowing trespasses on the jurisdiction of the gods, is dangerous and will be resented. Knowing, like "knowing," can be an act of self-affirmation.

KNOWLEDGE FOR ANXIETY REDUCTION AND FOR GROWTH

So far I have been talking about the need to know for its own sake, for the sheer delight and primitive satisfaction of knowledge and understanding *per se.* It makes the person bigger, wiser, richer, stronger, more evolved, more mature. It represents the actualization of a human potentiality, the fulfillment of the human destiny foreshadowed by human possibilities. We then have a parallel to the unobstructed blooming of a flower or to the singing of birds. This is the way in which an apple tree bears apples, without striving or effort, simply as an expression of its own inherent nature.

But we know also that curiosity and exploration are "higher" needs than safety, which is to say that the need to feel safe, secure, unanxious, unafraid is prepotent, stronger than curiosity. Both in monkeys and in human children this can be openly observed. The young child

[4] *Ibid.*

in a strange environment will characteristically hang on to its mother and only then venture out little by little from her lap to probe into things, to explore and to probe. If she disappears and he becomes frightened, the curiosity disappears until safety is restored. He explores only out of a safe harbor. So also for Harlow's baby monkeys. Anything that frightens sends them fleeing back to the mother-surrogate. Clinging there, he can first observe and *then* venture out. If she is not there, he may simply curl up into a ball and whimper. Harlow's motion pictures show this very clearly.

The adult human being is far more subtle and concealed about his anxieties and fears. If they do not overwhelm him altogether, he is very apt to repress them, to deny even to himself that they exist. Frequently, he does not "know" that he is afraid.

There are many ways of coping with such anxieties, and some of these are cognitive. To such a person, the unfamiliar, vaguely perceived, the mysterious, the hidden, the unexpected are all apt to be threatening. One way of rendering them familiar, predictable, manageable, controllable, i.e., unfrightening and harmless, is to know them and to understand them. And so knowledge may have not only a growing-forward function, but also an anxiety-reducing function, a protective homeostatic function. The overt behavior may be very similar, but the motivations may be extremely different. And the subjective consequences are then also very different. On the one hand we have the sigh of relief and the feeling of lowered tension, let us say, of the worried householder exploring a mysterious and frightening noise downstairs in the middle of the night with a gun in his hand when he finds that it is nothing. This is quite different from the illumination and exhilaration, even the ecstasy, of a young student looking through a microscope who sees for the first time the minute structure of the kidney, or who suddenly understands the structure of a symphony or the meaning of an intricate poem or political theory. In the latter instances, one feels bigger, smarter, stronger, fuller, more capable, successful, more perceptive. Supposing our sense organs were to become more efficient, our eyes suddenly keener, our ears unstopped. This is how we would feel. This is what can happen in education and in psychotherapy—and does happen often enough.

This motivational dialectic can be seen on the largest human canvases, the great philosophies, the religious structures, the political and legal systems, the various sciences, even the culture as a whole. To put it very simply, too simply, they can represent simultaneously the outcome of the need to understand and the need for safety in varying proportions. Sometimes the safety needs can almost entirely bend the cognitive needs to their own anxiety-allaying purposes. The anxiety-free person can be more bold and more courageous and can explore and theorize for the sake of knowledge itself. It is certainly reasonable to assume that the latter is more likely to approach the truth, the real nature of things. A safety philosophy or religion or science is more apt to be blind than a growth philosophy, religion, or science.

THE AVOIDANCE OF KNOWLEDGE AS AVOIDANCE OF RESPONSIBILITY

Anxiety and timidity not only bend curiosity and knowing and understanding to their own ends, using them, so to speak, as tools for allaying anxiety, but also the lack of curiosity can be an active or a passive expression of anxiety and fear. (This is not the same as the atrophy of curiosity through disuse.) That is, we can seek knowledge in order to reduce anxiety and we can also avoid knowing in order to reduce anxiety. To use Freudian language, incuriosity, learning difficulties, pseudo-stupidity can be a defense. Knowledge and action are very closely bound together, all agree. I go much further, and am convinced that knowledge and action are frequently synonymous, even identical in the Socratic fashion. Where we know fully and completely, suitable action follows automatically and reflexly. Choices are then made without conflict and with full spontaneity.[5]

This we see at a high level in the healthy person who seems to know what is right and wrong, good and bad, and shows this in his easy, full functioning. But we see this at another level altogether in the young child (or in the child hidden in the adult) for whom thinking about an action can be the same as having acted—"the omnipotence of thought," the psychoanalysts call it. That is, if he has had a wish for the death of his father, he may react unconsciously as if he had actually killed him. In fact, one function of adult psychotherapy is to defuse this childish identity so that the person need not feel guilty about childish thoughts as if they had been deeds.

In any case, this close relation between knowing and doing can help us to interpret one cause of the fear of knowing as deeply a fear of doing, a fear of the consequences that flow from knowing, a fear of its dangerous responsibilities. Often it is better not to know, because if you did know, then you would have to act and stick your neck out. This is a little involved, a little like the man who said, "I'm so glad I don't like oysters. Because if I liked oysters, I'd eat them, and I hate the darn things."

[5]But see S. Cohen, "Neurotic Ambiguity and Neurotic Hiatus between Knowledge and Action," *Journal of Existential Psychiatry,* in press.

It was certainly safer for the Germans living near Dachau not to know what was going on, to be blind and pseudo-stupid. For if they knew, they would either have had to do something about it or else feel guilty about being cowards.

The child, too, can play this same trick, denying, refusing to see what is plain to anyone else: that his father is a contemptible weakling, or that his mother doesn't really love him. This kind of knowledge is a call for action which is impossible. Better not to know.

In any case, we now know enough about anxiety and cognition to reject the extreme position that many philosophers and psychological theorists have held for centuries, that *all* cognitive needs are instigated by anxiety and are *only* efforts to reduce anxiety. For many years, this seemed plausible, but now our animal and child experiments contradict this theory in its pure form, for they all show that, generally, anxiety kills curiosity and exploration, and that they are mutually incompatible, especially when anxiety is extreme. The cognitive needs show themselves most clearly in safe and nonanxious situations.

A recent book summarizes the situation nicely.

> The beautiful thing about a belief system is that it seems to be constructed to serve both masters at once: to understand the world insofar as possible, and to defend against it insofar as necessary. We do not agree with those who hold that people selectively distort their cognitive functioning so that they will see, remember and think only what they want to do. Instead, we hold to the view that people will do so only to the extent that they have to and no more. For we are all motivated by the desire, which is sometimes strong and sometimes weak, to see reality as it actually is, even if it hurts.[6]

[6]A. H. Maslow, *Toward a Psychology of Being* (Princeton, N.J.: D. Van Nostrand Co., Inc., 1962).

SUMMARY

It seems quite clear that the need to know, if we are to understand it well, must be integrated with fear of knowing, with anxiety, with needs for safety and security. We wind up with a dialectical back-and-forth relationship which is simultaneously a struggle between fear and courage. All those psychological and social factors that increase fear will cut our impulse to know; all factors that permit courage, freedom and boldness will thereby also free our need to know.

The Silence of the Sky

James F.T. Bugental

There is a kind of shuddery tension in me this morning as Jack talks to me. I take quick note of it and of the awarenesses that go with it, then I return the focus of my attention to what he is saying.

> And so I told her that she was expecting me to be God and take over her life. And I was pretty brutal about it, I'm afraid. But I really am getting fed up with the way she and so many people just won't take responsibility for their own lives and want to dump everything on me. And besides, it was for her own good, because . . .

Jack is reviewing a new instance of the conflict that is raging within him with increasing frequency. Indeed, it is this conflict, at least in part, which made him decide to come into psychotherapy with me. This conflict is between Jack's strong feelings of responsibility to the people who consult him and his feelings of being inadequate and guilty in helping these people. You see, Jack himself is a psychotherapist, and he is a good one. Because he is a good therapist and a responsible one, when he found this conflict growing in him, he took the responsible course and came back into treatment for himself.

Reprinted by permission of the author.

But listen to what Jack is saying now:

> I spent last night reading Grozet's new book—you know, *Modern Practice in Intensive Psychotherapy*. And it's a good book, but really, he's just saying the same old things, too. I finished about 2:30 in the morning with a headache and a flat feeling. Grozet talks like he's got it all worked out, but I wonder. What would he do with a really passive-dependent person like the one I was telling you about? I'll bet he wouldn't sound so confident then. . . .

> Maybe I ought to go back to the Post-Graduate Center and get some really top-notch training in group therapy. I often think I'm not making enough use of my groups. When I read what they're doing at the Center, it sounds like they may be onto something. You know the papers that have been coming out lately. . . .

Listening to Jack now, I can sense the almost desperate quality of his searching. The books and journals endlessly combed, the institutes and lectures faithfully attended. And still the incompleteness and frustration.

As a matter of fact, Jack is unusually well read in a field where the sheer bulk of professional literature coming out each year defies anything approaching comprehensive mastery. He is generally aware of the main views of the leading schools, is thoroughly conversant with the authorities in his own specialty, and is open-minded toward new approaches. Still, he is miserable at times as he thinks of the work for which he self-sacrificingly prepared himself over the years and which now takes most of his waking hours in one way or another. It's not surprising that late in the session he is telling me:

> And so I've been thinking of going into research or teaching or . . . [He pauses and switches the subject.] You know, there's such a shortage of teachers now that I ought to be able to get a good place at a nice university where I'd have a teaching load that left me some time for research and for thinking. And it would be pretty nice to work with students again and . . .

I decide to interrupt Jack here:

> Jack [I say], a few minutes ago you were telling me you'd been thinking of going into research or teaching or something else, but I noticed that you broke off and didn't talk about the something else. Did you find it something you were reluctant to mention?

Jack is silent for several long seconds before he says:

> Well, I really wasn't serious about it, and so it didn't seem worth mentioning. Besides, I'd really like to think about this idea of going into teaching and . . .

But his manner prompts me to cut in again:

> I have the impression, Jack, you're really quite uncomfortable with this idea that you don't want to talk about, even though you say you're not serious about it.

Now the pause is very long before Jack answers. He is obviously struggling with himself, and when he does talk, his words come out slowly and with much strain:

> All right. I'll level with you, but I want you to know this is just one of those fantasy-thoughts that everyone gets. I've just thought of stopping, that's all. There's nothing to it, really.

Again I interrupt:

> "Stopping," Jack?

There's an edge of irritation—or is it desperation?—in his voice when he replies:

> Yes, "stopping," you know. Just stopping. Stopping practice, stopping psychology, stopping—uh—anything.

I persist:

> "Anything?"

His voice is very faint this time. The fight seems gone as quickly as it flared up:

> Anything or everything—stopping living.

It is very quiet in my office.

Now what has brought this intelligent, well-educated, conscientious, and professionally successful man to this lonely brink where he thinks of ending his own life? An overly glib answer is that it is the product of almost exactly those qualities: his intelligence, his education, his sense of conscientiousness, and his professional success. But that is an overly glib answer, and I want now to try to trace out the matter in much more thoroughgoing fashion.

There is an old parable that goes something like this:

> Man shouts to the universe, "I exist!"
>
> "Nevertheless," replies the universe, "that fact arouses no feeling of obligation in me."

Perhaps if the universe did reply, even though so unrelentingly, the story might be different. I think the parable would be more accurate in a different version:

> Man shouts to the night sky, "What?" and "Why?" and the sky is silent.

It is the silence of the sky that plunges us into what Paul Tillich has termed the existential anxiety of emptiness and meaninglessness. We look out upon the world with questing eyes that search for meaning, and we are turned back upon our questions with no answers. We seek in vain for the value, the virtue, the cause that is ultimate. We propound our philosophies to paint the picture of the universe's significance, and we hear but our own words. Prophets and seers, messiahs and demagogues, teachers and politicians announce their interpretations, their solutions; but the interpretations and the solutions remain their speakers', and none converts all men; none answers all questions. We build our laboratories, launch our rockets, explore the depths and the heights, only to return again and again to the same questionings in ourselves. And still the sky is silent.

And what does it matter? Why is this important? It is important because we are alive and because we are aware. It is important because to be aware means we must act, and to act means we must make choices, and to make choices means we are responsible. To be responsible we want to know, and we do not know enough.

When we were small we looked out at the world, at other people, and even at ourselves with wonderment. Implicitly and explicitly we asked, "What kind of a place is this? What makes it this way? How does it go? What does it mean to be a person? Who am I? What am I?" In later years, the questions grew more implicit, more unconscious. We adopted our answers more by osmosis than by conscious selection; although education, religion, science, and every other form of communication each contributed its bit. And from all of these we built and have to build again and change and rebuild anew our views of the universe and of our places in that universe.

This picture—we might better call it a map—is crucial, is vital (and I mean both of those words very literally) to our lives. It is what we deem to be "reality." It is the map by which we steer our course in life, and right or wrong, good or bad, well prepared or carelessly assembled, this map will be the main basis on which we will live our lives. Just as with a road map that we get from the service station when driving in unfamiliar territory, so with this map, we are largely dependent on it and can be its victims if it gives us misinformation.

As children we thought that adults knew, if not everything, all that was needed to be people. We looked forward to being adults and having, at last, all the needed knowing. As we became adult and found we still did not know all we needed to know, we looked to further education, to experience, to some yet-to-be-achieved point when, we promised ourselves, we would know enough to be really ready to live. And then, we have come to realize, we will never get there. We will never know enough to be confident that our actions are all based on knowledge and reason.

When we have not known enough, we have turned to others to aid us; to the wise men, to the teachers, to the experts. And we are impatient with experts who do not give us the answers we seek. If I do not know, I want to consult someone who does know; I don't want to waste my time with someone who is also confronted by uncertainty.

This, of course, is part of Jack's fearful burden. As a psychotherapist, he is constantly being consulted by people who in great sincerity and with much of their lives hanging in the balance want answers to the questions which oppress them: "Is my wife right or am I when I say the husband should make the decisions about money?" "What can we do to help our son who has gotten mixed up with the wrong kind of kids?" "Should I marry this girl and break with my family or should I wait a while?" "How can I get myself to quit drinking when I know it's ruining my life and my family?" "What sort of career should our daughter prepare for?" "Why do I constantly fight with my husband when I really love him so dearly?"

The questions come unendingly. And behind these questions is the implicit message, "You are a doctor, a psychologist who has studied these things. Tell me, help me. I'm giving up things I want and need to pay you, help me. My life and the lives of those dear to me are being affected. Help me. Help me."

And Jack—and all of us—feel that appeal, respond to that responsibility. We want to help. Jack neglects his own living, his own family, his own needs to try to prepare himself to help more adequately. And yet he knows always the burden of uncertainty, of not knowing enough.

And so Jack feels the weight of guilt, feels the anxiety of his own limitedness, feels despairing and hopeless. He thinks of leaving the work for which he studied so long, of leaving the work which he really loves even as he hates it, thinks even of stopping, as he put it, stopping everything, including his own life.

Now let's back off from this situation and try to understand more about what it is that brings about the despair and confusion which accompanies our not knowing enough.

First of all, of course, is the expectation we have been developing from almost our earliest years: the expectation that eventually we will know enough. (For the present, let us just leave it in that somewhat vague fashion, "know enough," without trying to specify for what and so on.) Our parents, when we were quite small, acted as though they knew how things should be, and we looked to them for the answers, for guidance, for helping us to become sufficiently knowing like they were.

(As an aside, we should recognize that it is very hard for most parents to share genuinely and with open expression of feeling their uncertainties and anxieties with their children. Generally they argue that they don't want to make the child worry or feel insecure, so they "protect" him from these things. Thus the expectation that parents really know enough is unwittingly furthered even by the most loving parents.)

Nor is the converse necessarily the wisest policy. I certainly do not feel that one should suddenly start exposing a youngster to all of the uncertainties and anxieties of the adult world—especially when we have protected those children from such anxieties throughout their lives to this point.

As we grew a bit older, we were inducted into the main activity of childhood: getting educated. For 12, 16, 20 years, our lives—and indeed our families' lives—orbited around the all-important process of going to school. And why do we go to school? To prepare for life. To learn what we need to know to be adults.

To learn, it is obvious, the "enough" which adults by definition know. No matter that that education often gives more emphasis to how to parse a sentence than to how to choose a mate, more time to taking square roots than to how to make love, more skill to conjugating the verbs of a foreign language than to how to raise a child, and more encouragement to learning dates in history than to learning to cope with uncertainty. We went to school to prepare for life, to be sure we would know enough. So, from at least these two predominant authorities of childhood, our parents and our education, we were thoroughly indoctrinated with the idea that we were to learn and surely *would* learn enough to be adults.

Now the second influence that has been at work to bring about our confusion and Jack's despair is the emphasis in all our thinking on what is known and the general suppression of attention to what is not known. We honor the scholar for what he has learned, not for what he does not know. We look to the expert for his solid knowledge and prefer to ignore his areas of ignorance. So habitual is this attitude that we are not surprised when entertainment personalities make pronouncements about politics, political leaders speak on matters of artistic taste, or businessmen decide about educational policies. Nevertheless, this relation of the known to the unknown is so important that we should take a moment to think about it in greater detail.

Using very crude approximations, we may think about the whole of human knowledge at the time of Christ as being represented by the period at the end of this sentence. By the time that Columbus sailed to discover the Americas, that amount had multiplied several hundred percent, so that it might be represented by a nailhead. With the opening up of the geographic world, another hundred years saw that change to the area encompassed by a dime. By 1700 the pyramiding of knowledge meant that we would need a circle about the size of an automobile wheel to represent the sum. Now we are into the tremendous outpouring of new knowledge and new thinking which accompanied the Industrial Revolution and the great political and economic earthquakes of the eighteenth century. A circle with a 50-foot radius is needed to portray the expansion which must be represented for the year 1800. Again the more-than-geometric rate of progression as new sciences, new technologies, and new applications interact means that the year 1900 would best be represented by a circle with a radius of 850 yards; while the year 2000 probably would call for a circle with a radius of 36 miles.

So far the story is a familiar one. As knowledge grows, it breeds further invention and discovery and thus grows at an ever-increasing pace. What is not so familiar is that not-knowing or uncertainty is growing concurrently. Let me make that very clear: Whenever we add to the store of what we know—whether as individuals or as a science or as a culture—we are also adding to the sum of what we do not know, to the realm of uncertainty. To make this statement more understandable, we need to make two observations: First we must recognize that the general notion of a finite universe is no longer tenable scientifically. The universe (i.e., the sum of all potential knowledge) is infinite, limitless. Thus the acquisition of new knowledge does not reduce the sum of potential knowledge or the amount that is unknown. Heisenberg, in *Physics and Philosophy,* has said, ". . . one may say that the human ability to understand may be in a certain sense unlimited. But the existing scientific concepts cover always only a very limited part of reality, and the other part that has not yet been understood is infinite."

The second point that can help us understand the relation of knowledge and uncertainty may best be illustrated by returning to the circles with which we illustrated the expansion of knowledge. If we now make straight lines of their circumferences, they might range something like this:

1 A.D.	a point
1500	⅜ inch
1600	4⅓ inches (11×)
1700	100 inches (23×)
1800	314 feet (38×)
1900	3 miles (50×)
2000	225 miles (75×)

These lines are portrayed as rough measurements of the unknown or uncertain. That which is unknown is the border of that which is known. The unknown is always that which in some measure is adjacent to the known. That which is inconceivably distant from the known is just that, inconceivable. It may be the stuff of dreams or fantasy, but even these will be relatively close to the realm of the known.

Now the essential point is this: The unknown and the known are part of each other; each helps to define the other, and they are positively related: An increase in what is known means an increase in what is not known.[1] This means a very different state of affairs than what we are accustomed to assuming to be the case. When we implicitly believed that the total amount to be known was finite, was ultimately limited, then we could legitimately assume that the expert, the one who knew more than most people about some field, would have a much smaller area of not knowing or of uncertainty than most people also. While this may be so for fixed subunits of knowledge (such as how to repair an automobile engine), it is most definitely not so for knowledge at the level of science or in the area of human experience. In these realms, to have more knowledge is to know more uncertainty as well.

Now let me try to make it clear what it is I am saying here because it is an important point, but one at variance with our more usual way of thinking about this matter. In brief, the meaning is this: Being uncertain is a part of the experience of knowing. Or, to say it differently, knowledge about something always includes uncertainty—even though that uncertainty may be suppressed from the consciousness of the knower.

I need to pause to make explicit a distinction between knowledge and the accumulation of facts. One may know many facts about almost anything without having knowledge of that thing. Knowledge, at least as I am using the term, is the integration of the facts into a meaningful conceptual structure which makes possible the employment of those facts and their embracing structure in other than a rote-repetition way.

Thus a scientist may accumulate a great many facts, say, about the structure and functioning of the brain. The facts themselves are mute—e.g., the speed of transmission of the nerve impulse, the chemical composition of the synaptic environment—and indeed may be thought of as only the raw stuff with which science works. The genuine creative contribution of the scientist is his integration of these facts into a theory of brain function with explanatory potency. The theory then sets the facts in relation to each other and—often implicitly, and not infrequently unconsciously—articulates the realm of the unknown to the facts. This

[1]I am aware that some scientists argue that there may be an ultimate limit to what man can learn and that others insist we may be approaching a leveling off point where the astonishing progression in the rate of acquisition of new knowledge may decline. However these ideas may prove out ultimately for me as a person confronting the human situation today in my own life and with my patients, it is manifest that pragmatically the realm of potential knowledge is infinite, and—more important—the experience of not knowing ever grows with the attainment of more knowledge.

means that the embracing conceptual structure is always at least in some part a statement of the relation of the strictly known (the "facts") to the unknown, which includes the speculative.

When this structure of concepts, facts, and uncertainty is brought to bear on some problem—whether it be the diagnosis and treatment of a lesion of the brain, the planning of further research, or the teaching of students—then the scientist cannot work only with the facts but must use the concepts and the recognition of the uncertain and unknown as well. To put the matter most starkly: If facts are the essence of what is known, they are useless by themselves. The use of facts depends upon their incorporation with theory and with appreciation of uncertainty.

Inattention to what is uncertain may lead to foolish mistakes or tragic errors. Certain facts led pediatricians at one time to urge new parents to feed their babies strictly determined amounts only at 10:00, 2:00, and 6:00, 10:00, 2:00, and 6:00. Further facts where once there was uncertainty have now outmoded that guidance. Certain facts made parents anxious to have their children receive Salk vaccine as soon as it was available, but other unknown elements resulted in some of the first vaccine's being faulty, with the result that some of the loved children were crippled or died.

When Jack hears the questions addressed to him, he has much knowledge to which to relate the problems, but an intrinsic part of that knowledge is also uncertainty. And that uncertainty is crucial. To ignore it would be irresponsible. To use it as a part of his knowledge is to be unable to respond to the urgent seekings in the manner the seekers wish.

Nor is the answer, as Jack is painfully realizing, simply the accumulation of more facts or even of more knowledge. More knowledge will bring with it more uncertainty. Let me be clear. I do not say that more knowledge—and indeed, more facts—may not be helpful. I do say that simply accumulating more knowledge and facts is not the answer. The answer must lie in how Jack accepts and incorporates the always present uncertainty.

Well, what do people do with uncertainty? How do we react to the anxiety of emptiness and meaninglessness, to put it in more formal and existential terms? How do we cope with the eternal silence in the sky?

Some, as Jack has done, engage in a never-ending seeking for more knowledge. They cling to the ideal of "knowing enough" and endlessly pursue further learning, often postponing living in expectation of that culminatng day when they will "know enough." These are the perennial students, the people who take one degree after another, the ones who enroll for each new university extension course endlessly. (As one who has often conducted programs for university extension, I really must pause to make clear that I am not biting the hand that feeds me. One may continue with lifelong education for quite authentic reasons, valuing each learning experience for itself. I am here only characterizing those who look to such courses to provide them with the *final* answers so that they can *quit* getting educated and start living; that is, those who are sort of intellectual hypochondriacs, always finding a new course to remedy what ails them.)

Another way in which some people react to ever-present uncertainty is that of overrationality or scientism. In this way of handling anxiety, there is a complete repression of awareness of that which is not objective and specifiable.

Pete is a research physiologist. Technologically he is extremely brilliant. Everyone else in his department looks to him for aid in instrumentation. He is the holder of several patents for new measuring devices. He was long regarded by his professors and superiors as one of the most promising of the younger men. Yet his actual research production is very limited and is little valued in his field. Pete, you see, is vociferous and adamant in announcing that nothing exists except in some quantity, that emotions are only glandular changes, and that behavior is only muscle action. He is lonely, embittered, and has stomach ulcers.

I will skim fairly quickly over some other forms that the avoidance of uncertainty takes. Some react with a kind of nihilism, a denial of all meaning, an intellectual anarchy. They challenge all values, enunciate nothing positively, and proclaim the universe absurd. This is, of course, a perversion of the recognition of the emptiness of the universe. It says in effect, "Since the universe refused to supply its own meaning, it has no meaning." To be sure, some of the so-called "absurdist" artists—especially the playwrights—are demonstrating that much meaning can be brought out of the emptiness through their talents. Such a response is quite in contrast to that of some who hopelessly deny all meaning and give up on life.

Interestingly enough, the reverse sort of pattern may also arise from the terrible confrontation with the absence of universal meaning: This may take the form of zealotism in the service of some particular belief.

At forty-two, Grace had been divorced for three years and had seen the last of her children leave home. She was alone and lost until she became a convert to a minor, semireligious, mystical sect. Then Grace seemed to find a whole new role in life. She sought to convert everyone she contacted. She neglected her health and her friends as she worked tirelessly to spread the new gospel she had absorbed. She insisted on the divine meaning of certain occult signs, and she was impatient to the point of fury with any questioning of her arguments.

Let us pause now and look at these matters from another perspective. Existentialists, who concern themselves with this problem, are often accused of being gloomy fellows who think only of the unhappy, the tragic, and the disordered. I don't see it this way, and I hope to show that there are other and equally, if not more, important aspects to our confronting the silence of the sky.

We have said that when we hurl the question at the sky, no answer comes back. But let us fantasize for a minute that this was not so. Suppose a divine injunction came forth so clearly that none could question it. Suppose that one overriding value could be ultimately demonstrated. What then?

To me, it seems clear that man's condition would be utterly different. Were an ultimate meaning proven, we would be the creatures of that meaning. We would lose one of the most distinctive features of our lives, our autonomy.

The experience of emptiness and meaninglessness to the universe, which is of the same stuff with our personal experience of uncertainty, is also integral to our having choice. Where there is no uncertainty there is no choice. The confrontation of alternatives, of ambiguity, is inherent in having individual autonomy.

Now let me hasten to recognize that our autonomy is limited; let me recognize also that there are still classical determinists who insist that our choice is but a subjective illusion. This is not the place to debate those issues. It is sufficient for our present purpose that every one of us—determinist or not—in his own personal life experiences that he has choice. This is the existential and phenomenological fact, and no amount of rational argumentation will dissuade any of us on this point—so far as our own personal lives go.

Let us put this matter of choice in context and then comment on some further implications: In listening to my patients and in experiencing within myself and talking with those close to me, I find it helpful to think about what it means to be human, to be alive, to exist. And this thinking is furthered when I distinguish some aspects of the global fact of being. But please be clear what I mean by this: I am here talking about my thinking about being. I am not describing discoveries about the ultimate nature of life. Existence is, I think, ultimately a whole, but I have the need to separate out aspects to help my thinking. This is akin to identifying the constellations in the sky at night. The constellations are not truly in the sky, but they are handy ways we can use to point and to describe.

In this fashion, as we've seen, I have found it helpful to think that there are five aspects to being:

> We are embodied physically.
>
> We are finite: limited in what we can know, what we can do, and how long we will live.
>
> We can take or not take actions; we are not passive observers.
>
> We are able to choose among the actions we will and will not take.
>
> We are each related to and yet separate from all others.

I will not try to spell out here all the implications which this way of thinking about being has for me.[2] Suffice it to say, I think that there is to each of these an anxious or threatening aspect and an encouraging or growth-facilitating aspect. When one reacts solely in terms of the anxiety and retreats from accepting that part of his being—whether it be a denial of his death, a rejection of personal responsibility, an estrangement from others, or whatever—in that measure one is non-being, is—in more than a figurative sense—dead. Suicidal thoughts and suicidal acts are often but the expression of this subjective death or non-being which is their source. Jack is succumbing to this anxiety, which is so robbing him of authentic being that he is beginning to think of death as the expression of his plight.

But when one can confront the existential anxiety which his being brings with it, confront and incorporate that anxiety as a part of his being, then he is freed to experience his life more fully than ever before. This is the response of courage.

The existential anxiety of emptiness and meaninglessness can give rise to a retreat from life in which all seems absurd. But that same openness of our being to our choice can be taken as the empty canvas on which we may express our creativity. Creativity is the courageous response to the emptiness of the universe, to the silence of the sky. We will raise our song, will name the constellations, will fill the emptiness with the expressions of our courage.

Meaning, I am saying, is not found out there, is not the imposition of the universe on man. Meaning is the human contribution to the universe. Man is not separate from the universe. He is a part of all being, and he brings to all being the human creation: meaning. Just as clouds bring rain, as green growing things contribute to the air we breathe, as worms aerate soil, so man brings meaning into existence. This is Teilhard's "noosphere."

Erich Fromm has said that man is the animal who knows himself to be created, to be a creature, but that man must, if he is to remain sane, escape from being solely a creature. Man takes part in creation, becomes a creator through his creative response to the universe, to his being.

What is this creativity? It is the act of awareness in meeting, accepting, and going beyond the lack of externally given meaning. It is sometimes expressed in the various arts, although not all art is existentially creative as I am here con-

[2]See J.F.T. Bugental, *The Search for Authenticity* (New York: Holt, Rinehart & Winston, 1965).

ceiving this term. It is often found in the scientist's inventive weaving of fact, concept, and the unknown into pregnant structures, although much that may be labeled science is not creative but mechanical repetition (especially when it seeks to deny the ingredient of the unknown). It may be a characteristic of a very simple life and without visible outward product. Creativity exults rather than bemoans that there is no one right answer to any truly fundamental question, and creativity recognizes in that freedom to bring meaning into being the human part in the ongoing creation of what is actual.

This, then, is the glory of the human condition—that out of the anxiety of the emptiness, we can respond with the artistry to create meaning. Uncertainty and knowledge are both subjective experiences. Uncertainty and knowledge are ultimately but aspects of the same subjective experience, and in the creation of meaning we utilize both to make life possible and to express our being. This recognition does not deny or alleviate the fearful anxiety of emptiness and meaninglessness. It does not give us license to use our autonomy heedlessly. It does put the task squarely before us of how shall we fill the silence of the sky.

Cases

Julia Oakes

Julia Oakes is the director of personnel for Home Products, Inc., an international consumer-products company with annual sales well in excess of $100 million. The following interview took place in her apartment after work one evening in November 1975. Julia Oakes's conversation has not been edited to read better; rather, her remarks are presented in full, so you will know how she sounds in natural conversation. The interviewer's remarks have been shortened or, where possible, deleted.

Julia Oakes: Well, maybe I'll just start back at the beginning. I grew up in Missouri and went to a small college in Ohio. My senior year, we had to do a special project, and I gathered up the courage to ask this visiting personnel manager who was from the Globe Electronics plant in Cleveland if we could do our last year—the senior year project—with Globe Electronics. He was as amazed to have someone ask him as I was at myself for asking him. In that little college town, there was just nothing that I could see available to help us on this project. So in contacting Globe Electronics . . . I think our study was on recreation (at that time, in the personnel department they had recreational directors) and what they did and what that meant. It was in the days when they were first experiencing music in plants and things like that. So we did this project and I sort of had my heart set on going to Globe Electronics for work, but I didn't make it. We had numerous interviews, and he was transferred to Canada and then they sent me to the Akron plant. The personnel manager there was confused . . . so he was very nice and said, "I just have to send you home," which was back to Missouri. So I ended up being a receptionist in a . . . engineering . . . what do they call it . . . a consulting engineering organization—and it was field workers, too. The people were fairly crude—electricians and maintenance men and construction workers.

They were building a crude-alcohol plant (this was during the war years) in the Missouri bottoms, and this New York crew had come out to get this thing built and then had to work with all these construction people who had come from all over the country. So I really felt that I learned the facts of life [Laughter] in that office for six months where I was simply a telephone receptionist. And that's where I had to start.

But Globe Electronics called one day and said that they had a chance for an opening for a person to train women on an assembly line. They had a Navy plant in Akron, and they needed to see if they could train the women before they went down into these moving conveyors or into these secret rooms, because it was all a secret project. They had such turnover and poor quality that they wanted to set up what they called a vestibule school. If you could pass the vestibule school before you came into the plant, then they felt you'd make it. Well, they didn't want to *interview* me. They felt they already had known that much about me and I had to accept the job over the telephone.... My parents lived about 40 miles away from where I was working, and they said, "You always wanted to go there, so why not? You can always come home." So I went.

Casewriter: Were you a bit reluctant to leave at first?

J.O.: Oh, yes. Because I'd been terribly disappointed that I hadn't gotten Globe Electronics in the beginning, and to think that they were coming after me.... At that time, I'd sort of gotten involved with my first job; even though it really wasn't what I wanted. I learned to like the *people.* And I had gained a certain amount of recognition for understanding them and recognizing their voices on the telephone and knowing their individual situations.

Yet, I didn't know what I was getting into. I had asked the question specifically on the phone, "Will I have to be working with tools?" And they said, "Oh no, not really." Well, of course, when I got there, that's all we were working with were tools—oh, soldering irons and those screw things. They had talked about making things on a moving *conveyor* . . . and that I would be training girls to do assembly work. So I thought, "Well, how can you do that if you're not using tools?" *So,* I am not mechanically inclined and I thought, "My goodness, how will I ever get that?" The first job was training these people, ranging from very young to very old people just ahead of retirement. But we needed *anyone* who could work. We were bringing in *numbers* of people, because we had to fill these contracts. Well, I think I had bad dreams every single night that first year because I had to learn so much and I really didn't know what they were doing. The foremen were beating up on me every day, like, "We don't need you. [Laughter.] Unless you can do a better job training the people than we can do, go home." And . . . it was a part of being Personnel, maybe a part of being a woman, maybe a part of, "We don't know what you're going to do. You are keeping the girls, training them, and you come down here and you want to follow up and see how they are doing," and all this kind of thing. Mainly, I think there's just an *initiation* . . . into an organization and are you going to make it. I really hadn't experienced that. I was coming from college—there were probably a half dozen people in the plant from college—maybe some in the supervisory ranks, but certainly not in the working ranks or the lower levels of supervision.

So it was really tough, but I have found that usually there is always one person someplace who understands what you are trying to do and can give you a helping hand. That man was the superintendent of the plant. He was very helpful. I used to go down and talk to him about what I was trying to do and what suggestions and . . . he helped me over lots of rough spots. But I finally got the idea of simulations. And we found a man in the model shop who would build little things for me that we could practice on and use rejected material.

Then I discovered that I had to go down and sit on the lines and work. I'd go down after hours or I'd come early in the morning. I learned better by doing and experiencing and being with the people. So the people began to realize I was really trying and I was experimental . . . and . . . while they beat up on me [Laughter], I seemed to come back for more. We really developed a *model* training school, so that people in the Globe Electronics headquarters, Globe Electronics everyplace, they used to drag people out to see this *school.* That was a lot of fun in that we built something from nothing. The foremen then began to find that the girls they got could do better and that a lot of the initial training problems they had, they were *spared.* They could get somebody they could begin to work with, or at least the attitudes were better. We followed up very closely, so we began to know what our track record was. If we missed on people, then the next time we tried to find out why, because I had the *responsibility* to try to terminate people from the school. If I didn't think they were going to make it, then we terminated there, rather than have them go out into the plant. So I developed many fast friends in the organization along with the work—friends that I *still have.* I experienced being "brought up," if you will, by these people. They had a lot of ownership in helping me grow and develop.

I had a certain tenacity too. If I had a job, I had to keep trying. That doesn't mean that I wasn't a little discouraged. I cried myself to sleep many nights and had many bad dreams over trying to teach the people. I wrote a book—I can remember that very clearly—trying to write down what I had learned. I discovered Mondays were just terrible because that was when a whole class of 100 people came in. See, they turned over every week. So you had 100 new faces that you had to learn and get this thing all organized. At the end of the week you made a rating, and there were people that were happy and some were disappointed. So I began to really treat that as kind of a psychological challenge. What could I do to make my Mondays easier, in terms of getting my own self-perception ready—how I felt, how I dressed, what I did the day before, *everything* that would give me some kind of lift—and *then* really tried to document. I think this has been a style—I don't know where it came from—but I find that I do that still now. Any new experience, I'm trying to *document* what I learned (and document not in a real "researchy" sense, but just get down what happened). [Pause.]

Casewriter: What do those books look like? Are they notebooks, or . . . ?

J.O.: Oh, what?—that I write?

C: Yeah.

J.O.: Oh, yeah, notebooks, or just something I wrote back in the assembly on . . . it was how to run a vestibule school. Notes to the next instructor. I didn't know who that was going to be. And they were *me,* and that became a kind of a textbook. And that's what I try to give my people. It's called my legacy. That the people who come in shouldn't have to start from scratch. [Pause.] Because I learn from others a lot. Those people helped me a lot. And . . . the little toolmaker—I can see him yet—he was a little tiny German man, Werner Schmidt. He took great pride . . . he was *very* tough on me, *very* tough on me. I've always had demanding bosses, which, *again,* I shed my own private tears over that, but I really have respected them so much. I have had very clear-cut turning points or learning experiences in my working life. So Werner was one of those who helped me very *much* in thinking through, "Well, what could we do to make these models? How could we use the least costly materials? How could he get me old reject material?" and things like that.

I don't take new experiences easily. I really *feel* them all the way through. I feel the strangeness, but I have the tenacity to try to stick with it. I'm from Missouri, so whether that's a piece of "you have to hang in there" or what. . . . My parents are very Midwestern, very work-ethic, so that is very much a part of me. I will keep at it; and I make a lot of mistakes in the process. I don't like to. Mistakes bother me [Laughter], but I try. *Then* I usually develop friends in the process. And I can relate well to people down the line very easily. It was not hard for me to build relationships in the plant. I was back in Akron last year for the first time in probably 25 years, and I was surprised at the number of the people who remembered me. I really remembered incidents about them, and they remembered things we had done, and *that* was very gratifying. I was surprised, and it was *really* nice. . . . But they're very good solid people, and I think it was a unique experience because we had the *goal*—there was a clear-cut thrust—that we had to do something for the armed services. Then when that plant closed, when the war was over, we had the *very* unique experience of retraining every single person. The plant was *empty.* It was just like you had created a new building and then everybody had to come back through to learn how to do commercial work. That was a whole *'nother* thing, but that's a feeling of teamwork that you have to get against this common thrust which is very important.

So assembly-line training was helpful in having to manage a lot of things . . . get things going, assume responsibilities for people, and for dealing with lots of *feelings*—I saw almost every kind of feeling—people being frightened, or scared, or insecure, or glad, or disappointed—and I had to deal with those at a very early age . . . while I didn't have responsibility for them long-term. That week of training was a very important part in their lives. Then I would see them in the plant. Working with them that closely, I *really* did know most of the people in the plant.

C: What were some of the best ways you found to deal with the feelings?

J.O.: Oh . . . listening, talking, encouraging . . . trying to get them to develop some competency, I guess, and then . . . not being afraid of the feeling. It's all right for people to get angry or to be sad or to be depressed, so you don't have to . . . you might not *like* it at the moment, but you really don't have to be *afraid* of it. People are afraid of what's going to happen if the person gets angry or is in tears. Well, I don't know that I *like* those experiences . . . but then . . . you do realize that they're going to happen and they're going to happen again. So, not being surprised by them is one thing.

C: Then when someone does get angry . . . how . . .

J.O.: Well, I don't know—I sometimes holler back, probably. [Both laugh.] Other times, maybe I can be a little calmer about it. I've had some of those, too. I'm fairly intuitive, I think, as far as kind of reading where people are. I have a great deal of empathy. I'm *not good* on tackling people that may—what do I want to say?—give me a hard time. I don't seek out conflicts. I have learned better through the years how to deal with it, and if I'm really trying to get something done, I'll go after that. . . . My supervisors have all been good to deal with me on my weaknesses. Another time I was having a problem with my own boss. And the production superintendent said, "Hey, you know you've got to learn to go to Jake. If the two of you can't resolve it, *then* you can say all right, the two of you come and talk to me. But you've got to stay in there until the smoke comes out of the door." [Both laugh.] Well, it has taken a long while. I'm getting better, but it isn't easy. I don't like it—I probably cave in easier. . . . But it's *different* if we're really working on a program, there's a different kind of tenacity—there's something that I'm trying to get going and getting people to help get on board and getting it done. If I made a commitment to him, hardly anything would have gotten in the way of my meeting that commitment if it's at all possible.

Let me back into the next boss who really took me on, because that's an interesting experience. I had worked in this Akron plant five years, and as I said, I don't take new experiences that easily and I get very . . . ah . . . fond of where I'm at. So this man up in Cleveland who was the personnel manager at Globe Electronics had heard about what we were doing in Akron and he came to visit us. He liked what he saw and he thought, well, he had to get me up there to *analyze* their program and tell them what they should be doing in training. So I went and I told them. He liked it and so he said, "Well, come to work." I said, "No, I'm not going to come to work up here." Well, he couldn't *believe* it—that I was so dumb to turn down that job.

C: That was an obvious promotion to . . .

J.O.: Oh, it was a bigger plant and a bigger challenge, a bigger city—the whole works. But I didn't want to move. He figured, my gosh, she is dumb and a real *hick*.

So he went up to Newark, which was the headquarters for the appliance division. At that point, Globe Electronics was not yet a centralized company and it had these divisions. The appliance division was located in Newark, which is really a terrible place in New Jersey. So then Mark Wynn came back to my boss in Akron and said, "I'd like for Julia to come in for a summer. She can live here at the hotel (and that was a terrible place too). I just want her to take this summer and cruise around through the various plants in the appliance division and find out what we should be doing in training, write the policies, the plans, visit other companies—she's on her own. All I want is when she leaves at the end of the summer, she has to tell me what we should be doing in training." So I did that.

Well, I did have a lot of fun, because people were very interested and nice and I really was on a *learning* experience. They used to tease me, you know, this was my first time out of a little town and I was living it up and all this. So I went back and I had been back about two weeks when he came back to my boss and said, "Well, now I've got to talk to Julia about coming to work in Newark." He interviewed me in Cleveland and tears were streaming down my face, and he said, "You know *you are dumb.* [Laughter.] You won't take these opportunities. Now *come on.* You've been there, you know what it's like, you're going to have a ball. *But* . . . the way I want to set this thing up is—I have a man who doesn't know anything about training but he's a good salesman. And you're going to make the balls and he's going to fire them." Well, little did I know what I was getting into, but I went. I thought, well, he's right, I really have to take this opportunity in New Jersey. I never would go to Cleveland for him, but he finally convinced me I had to come to New Jersey.

So the day I arrived, this man who was a supersalesman—I always seem to get these little guys—and he was sitting at his desk and Mark Wynn brought me out to meet him. And his name was Hal. "Hal, this is Julia. You two are really going to do great things in training." Hal never turned around. He wouldn't look at me. So Wynn kept talking and Hal wouldn't acknowledge that I was there at all. . .

C: Did he sit with his back to you?

J.O.: Yeah. *So,* that was the beginning. Well, we had six months. I didn't cry, I just went home with headaches [Laughs] that were killing. That man, he wouldn't speak to me. He never called me by name for at least three months. *Or,* if he finally broke down, it was "Miss Oakes." Later, he'd remind me *daily* that it wasn't his idea to get me in there, that it was Wynn's idea and it was only because he liked Mark Wynn that he agreed to this thing at all. . . . We'd finally get into screaming matches. Speaking of resolving conflicts—he hollered, he never spoke below a roar. So I had to learn to speak that way in self-defense. I went in to Wynn one day when I had really had it and said, "I don't know what you got me into, and I don't think I like it." And he just said, "What's the matter, can't you take it?" . . . So I thought, "Well [Laughter], I guess I better go back and think about this a little more." And all these other people around there—as you see, I've known them for years . . . well, not years, *five* years . . . because they used to come and visit in Akron. They were from headquarters and they'd come out to see our personnel department and so we would visit. And I knew many of them personally. I had entertained them or been in their homes to be entertained. So Hal was the only one, and they used to think it was *funny.* They weren't [Laughter] taking this thing seriously at all, but *I was,* because I was the one getting beat up. That was it—"What's the matter, can't you take it?" Their expectations were that I *could* and *should.* I think it's those kinds of expectations that I've always responded to. You know, like maybe they're right. I didn't like the beating, but *what happened*—and it always does happen, which gives me a little nourishment now—is that we ended up the very best of friends. His family entertained me and I entertained them and I kept in touch with his widow for years after he died, until *she* died.

So we were finally beginning to develop a mutual respect. He was scared to death of me. He didn't know really what I could respect. He probably thought . . . I think he had all the stereotypes of women, because, oh, he assured me that we'd never travel together, we wouldn't do this or we wouldn't do that, and we ended up doing *all those things*. . . . He wasn't from Personnel. What I really didn't realize was that he was terribly insecure. And that was his way of dealing with insecurity. And it also was a kind of a style. His was a very rough-and-ready style—a little *bulldog* was really what he was. He was older than I, but he liked the stock market. Now, that was another thing. My father was interested in stocks, and so was Hal, so we began to get going on that and talk about that. *But*—talk about people teaching you, he was one who was very . . . he was a salesman, so he wanted to do things with a flair. He would insist that if were doing something, we had to *look* . . . at how we could make it unique. Like, today I can still hear him saying, "You fight for a position in a person's mailbox. There are a lot of papers in there, and there has to be something about what you're doing that will make them want to *read* or *pick up* your piece of mail." Or his writing, we fought for . . . for *weeks* over writing. He would make me rewrite and rewrite and rewrite, and I couldn't figure out what our problem was, because he couldn't really describe it. I think that it was, was many times I would be writing in the passive voice rather than an active voice, and he was a very action-oriented person, so his style was more that you start with verbs, things like this. My thing was more "it happened." So that was a point of conflict. I really am amazed, again, at how many times when I'm writing that I'll think of him; or, if we're trying to present something that has a chance for a little flair or style, of what he might have said.

A little later I had my surgery, and I had to be out of the office. When I came back, this Mark Wynn—who is now vice-president of a large industrial firm and was vice-president of Globe Electronics and also a large consumer-goods manufacturer—the first day I came back to work called me into his office and said, "Now sit down. I want to talk to you." Well, here I thought I was doing pretty well, having come back from surgery . . . after being out six weeks, which is the first time that I had been absent. And he said, "What comes *out* from you is always good, but people aren't remembering *you* . . . in terms of your impact on the organization now that you are working at higher levels. You can work down, but if you are going to begin to sell and work with managers, you have to learn how to package yourself. That means you have to do something about your Missouri accent, the way you dress, the way you present yourself, the way you organize your thoughts—and you just have to deal with different kinds of people. You tend to go with older people. You're not going out enough with different kinds of men. You need to be dealing with younger people. And so," he said, "get about it." Well, again I dissolved in tears that night, to think that here I came back, and instead of kind of being greeted with open arms [Both laugh], I was greeted with five things I had to go to work on. And *so*, . . . that led to speech training, and I went to modeling school, and help in dress, and weekends away. *Then* they were all good enough to come back and say, "Well, we didn't mean for you to kill yourself [Laughter] in the process," for I always attack with great vigor. But I have been very grateful always to him for that.

He was a big believer in "If you enter a room and people don't know you're there, then something is wrong. You have to have impact." So he worked with me. *He* had so much impact that he killed people in the process. But we always worked very well together because he could describe something that he wanted. Like that summer thing—he didn't tell me what he wanted other than the end product: "I want something that will tell me what training should be like." But he didn't have a clear picture of what it was, and he came out—which he often did—and gave me his gratuitous *comments.* Again, that was just a hint to get me going; it didn't mean that I had to do that. Many people feel that kind of a suggestion means that you have to really do that and they spend a lot of time on it. Then they get very frustrated if they went back to him and he said, "But that isn't what I meant." So . . . we always worked well together . . . because we could see the end product. He was *extremely* critical if something didn't meet his standards. He tore it to bits . . . which, again, I think is just excellent training. I seldom had a boss who said everything was great . . . but we always ended up being great friends [Laughter]. I think it was that mutual respect thing—and great friends with their families.

Every boss I've ever had, I knew their *families.* There may have been a couple or three in there in the process . . . after Hal Amanian—he got promoted onto something—and they brought in a man over me . . . two men over me . . . for whom I had *no* respect. They ultimately were . . . ah . . . let out of the organization, but that was just *all* wrong, and that happened to me a couple of times at Home Products. It was Mark Wynn, again, who put them there. He felt that at that particular time, they were apparently bringing something into the organization. Just like he took a chance on *me*—which I feel that he really did—he was willing to take chances on other people, and sometimes their qualifications might not be that good. I won't say that every boss—because I've had about four along the line—I really could develop a kind of respect for, although probably enough rapport that we could work together. But I have many lasting friendships—like with the man in the Missouri firm; I was in touch with his family until *he* died. The same way with Hal Amanian, Mark Wynn. Again, he and his family, his boys, the whole thing. . . . It develops . . . generally a relationship, a friendship.

Take Mark Wynn, he's very different. I mean there are a lot of people who can't . . . You either really liked him or you didn't, because he could get a lot of people upset because he was *brutally* frank and very critical of other people. So if he wanted to make a snide [Laughter] remark, he did. Some days it might hurt you worse than other days, so you learn to laugh at it or give it back to him. But if he noticed *progress*—for example, if I would have on maybe a new dress or something and he liked that—he might comment on that. During that period, and again at that period when I later hooked up with him at Home Products (which I'll talk about in a minute) . . . he understood me very well and he knew that I put in a lot of effort and energy. So that he was one of the first people to really realize that I wasn't well, and he became very concerned about that and knew I was going to a doctor. He was concerned that I wasn't going to do the surgery or whatever was necessary. But he *read* me extremely well and would know when I was tired or when I was enthusiastic. I won the merit award in Globe Electronics for the outstanding accomplishment of the year. They picked a dozen people throughout the company, and I was the second woman to get that. Well, he was very thrilled about that . . . and he was very nice about it. So he shared a lot of those things. He did give me encouragement, but also he never ceased to give you a kick either if he thought it was necessary. [Laughter.]

So, I had been at Globe Electronics

14 years, and, as I say, I get very comfortable at one place, and I never run out of getting ideas of what else needs to be done. I've never been bored, and never feel that we've accomplished everything. . . . But my brother was sort of giving me a hard time, and said that he wondered why I was staying on at Globe Electronics, what was my next step.

C: This was . . . after you had been in New Jersey for a time?

J.O.: Yes, I'd been there nine years. And he said, "Do you want to spend the rest of your life here? If you do, that's fine. But what's your next step?" And *really,* in the early fifties, Mark Wynn *did* get a great team together, and we *were* one of the outstanding personnel departments in the country, and there was a lot of movement and enthusiasm, and we traveled all over because we had plants throughout the country. We worked with Globe Communications, Globe International—so it was extremely interesting. And I knew lots of people, again, because most of the people that I started with had gotten promoted, and were either heads of a division or head of a staff department, so that I knew a *lot* of people. I did have many friends and I enjoyed it. But my brother was giving me the needle, saying, "Hey, there are other things to do, and is this really what you want to do?" So I thought, "Well, all right, he's right. I've been at Globe Electronics 14 years; if ever I'm going to make a move, I need to think about that now." So I started sending out résumés, and looking.

Wrote to many companies, and then when I started interviewing, found I had the unusual experience—when I got out of college I was too young and didn't have experience, and here I had 14 years experience with one of the top companies in the country, and one of the top jobs in personnel, and people couldn't believe that I wanted to leave. "Why do you want to leave?" and then they became very suspicious about why I was leaving. So I was very surprised at that, and got somewhat discouraged, but I did keep at it. And fortunately, again I ran into people in the interviewing process—there were enough people who encouraged me along the line that I didn't get completely discouraged, and would help me kind of understand the statistics of the process: how many interviews you have to have before you're likely to get even a *nibble* [Laughter], and then, if you get an offer, how many times you may be turned down.

So, that process went on, and dragged on, and one of the letters I wrote was to Home Products, Inc. And I couldn't *believe it* when here the person who called me up was Mark Wynn. Well, I had lost track of him because he had gone to the Overseas Division of Globe Electronics. And he was traveling around the world, whereas here I was circling the states in very mundane places. He said, "Well, *get up here*." Well I went up, and in his usual way he said, "Now look, I don't know what the job is, but we're going to need talent, and I'm going to take you, and I want you to talk to Mary O'Shay who is one of our vice-presidents."

Well, Mary, bless her heart, is *extremely* able in her field, but she's a little bit *stuffy.* And they hadn't treated her too well. Home Products was stuffier than . . . Globe Electronics is basically a manufacturing and research organization. And the people are very rough and ready, and, oh, you get bounced around a lot. And if you want to call people names, and swear, or all those kinds of things, or raise your voice, it's okay. Well, at Home Products, you see, that's an advertising, a

Madison Avenue background. And the halls are very quiet, and people were very well dressed. *Now,* they do allow a lot of different dress, and beards if you want, things like that. But they didn't then. And so, Mary, when I went to interview her, because at that point I must have been—let's see 22, 14—thirties, in my thirties, and she said, "Well, there are several things you have to understand about HP, and that is you'll never be invited to a meeting with men, and if you're traveling, you can *never* travel and live in the same hotel with them." And she filled me full of all these things that I'd been doing for years [Laughter] and with everyone knowing I'd been doing it for years. I'd been traveling with men all the time, going to meetings where I was the *only* woman always being included—if sometimes unwelcome. . . . And so I went back to Mark Wynn again and said, "What are you getting me into?" He just said, "Oh, for heaven's sakes, consider the source." So he wouldn't give me any time of day on *that.* Well, it wasn't long after I joined that he was giving a luncheon, and it was for one of the men in our department, the labor guy. And twenty-five, something really important, twenty-five years. And Wynn said to him, "Well, of course, we want to invite your secretary, Nancy Hanks, and Julia and so and so." And he said, "Oh, no, *you are not inviting those women.*" Well, Wynn was appalled, and he'd already invited us. [Laughter.] And so, and this had happened before too, so that was not a new experience, but it *did* sort of say that Mary was on the right track, that they were *much more concerned* about that than they . . .

I'm not trying to say that at Globe they had welcomed me with open arms. I had to *enter* and get in, but once I did, it was . . . oh my God, the fun we used to have on the train that went back and forth between Akron and New York. *All* the bigwigs were always there. So you'd get on in Akron and we had about five plants in Ohio, and that was the only way. . . . And those wild train rides—*oh,* my gosh, I wouldn't take anything for those days of growing up, and that *experience,* and meeting all these people, and . . . So it was just *accepted,* and then, to hit this *really Madison Avenue* here—oh, they shake your hand, very polite, but you never were invited to a home, or *no* friendly gesture at all. And, like when the Wynns would have me come up for a weekend or something, that was *very . . . not* the thing that Home Products people did. And they never raised their voice, and *he* hollered all the time [Laughter], so he didn't last too long at HP. But anyway, that's how I got there, and in a very unstructured job. It was sort of like, do this for awhile, and go out and find out all you can about college recruiting, or go out and do something or other.

C: Was Mary your boss at this time?

J.O.: Mary, my boss? No, no, she, she . . . I didn't go to her department, I stayed in Personnel, and Wynn again—some poor guy had to inherit me—he was always foisting me off on somebody [Laughter] who didn't want me. And so, that man wasn't any happier about the whole thing than Hal Amanian, although he was politer about it. He didn't have the *guts* to turn his back on me, not call me by name. So he . . . got poor old Stan Rule roped into taking me, and Stan didn't want me at *all,* but he didn't know how to handle it [Laughter] like Amanian did. So we rattled around and over time, you know, began to get different kinds of jobs, and then Wynn decided he wanted to get out of Personnel, and he went to a line organization, and they brought in a man from

Home Products who'd been around a *long* time. Had been president in Canada. And they were giving him this job in Personnel. He didn't know Personnel . . . and so when he walked in, because of the Wynn association, he said to me, "Ah, I really don't *want* you here, and you might as well know that. I don't know a thing about what you do. I'll try to find out . . . and we should know that there's a real possibility that you're not going to end up here." So he was all in hysterics. [Laughter.] So, you know, here you start all over again. This process of proving yourself *does* happen, *all* the time. And I guess that's something that maybe I almost take for granted now. I forgot about it. But I think I'm probably always doing it. I would hate to say it's because I'm a woman, or . . . It may bother me more in terms of the newness. I get attached to people, and a change requires a new adjustment. And sometimes I don't get my goal clear, like another time. . . .

Another man came in, and at this point, I had been reporting directly to Tony Giordano. And when the new man came in to replace Tony, he came to the line and said that he wanted this other man to come between us. Well this was a person for whom I had *very* little respect, and I was *very, very* disappointed, so I can remember talking to my father about that—who was always a big stabilizer, too. And he said, "Why don't you focus on trying to help Rick Streeter?" . . . He was our new boss, but he had inserted this new man in between. So my father said, "Why don't you focus on helping Rick? Find out what he needs. And *through* this other guy, make it happen. And focus on helping rather than trying to fight Ed or hurt him all the time . . . or finding out how you can get in his way." Because I really wasn't being too cooperative, I'm afraid. So I did that, and it wasn't too long till I really focused on trying to help or on what needed to get done, put my energy productively, rather than . . . ah . . . fighting. And the kind of *new* goal was not get rid of Ed, but help to Rick. It worked. And Ed vanished. [Laughter.] It just happened.

You know, mentioning my father reminds me. My parents are important in here too. Oh, I don't think they ever thought I'd work. My father was a self-made man, and he had never finished high school. My mother was a college graduate, and in music, so she had always brought the music and the arts into our home, and my father was very willing to have her do this. Well, he understood them over the years, but he didn't at this time. He was older than she was, and it was a second marriage for him. He'd lost a wife. So he was very adamant that my brother had to work his way through college, or *partially* work his way through college. *Both* of us had to work as we were growing up. I was to learn how to do all the household things, and my brother was to learn my father's business. So we both had music responsibilities, we were expected to get good grades, we had work responsibilities, but we had lots of good times and fun times, too. But it was always the sense-of-responsibility thing. And it was sort of all right for *me* to go to college because I was just supposed to get something there. [Laughter.] But most of the women in the family had been teachers, so if there was any background of expectation, it probably would have been that I was to be a teacher. His sisters were teachers, my mother's sisters were teachers, she was a teacher. And so when I ended up in business, he was the one who encouraged me. He said, "Why don't you do that, and if you don't like it you can always come home." But I didn't start out ever with the idea thinking I would work for a lifetime, or that I was against marriage, or anything like that. It just kind of happened, and there I was working, and I *have* been committed to whatever I'm doing, doing *well.* And that he insisted on. When I was very disappointed at the first job, which was a telephone receptionist, he said, "It really doesn't make any difference if you're scrubbing the floors. Whatever you're doing, just try to do it the best that you can. And if you can do it the best you can, why then probably it'll take care of itself." And in most cases it probably has.

I'm not sure that I was *aware* that I was learning from him or from Mother in the sense of developing your specialty. I believe that, and I try to work with the people that I'm with, and I guess they call that building on their strengths. And that was a funny thing in the telephone office, when the telephone operator came over to help me learn my job at the receptionist office. She said, as she was cracking her gum—I can see her to this day, very kind of crude person cracking her gum in my face, saying, "Honey, all you have to do is learn the *voices* on the telephone and they'll remember you." And there again I was a big nothing. Nobody knew my name. And one day the operations manager came running out, and he called me, "Julia!" I nearly fell out of my chair. "Julia, who was that person who was just on the phone, because you're the only person around here who knows people's names." Well, you know, it worked. And I thought, "Gee, it does, and it doesn't have to be big." But it was something that made me different, and I used to talk with people when they'd come in, and I did learn voices on the phone, and I talked to them on the phone.

I'm not terribly outgoing, although that was another thing along the way, too, that this first plant manager and his wife in Akron encouraged me on. She was very interested in me, and said, "You know you're very ill at ease socially. Now when you go into a room [Laughter], why don't you concentrate on somebody in the room who is as self-conscious as you are. . . . Or focus on a chair, and walk toward it, or have some purpose when you go in a room, and you'll stop feeling that way." So she *really* helped me.

And another couple, the Grabowskis, helped me in the social skills. So that way I've always done a lot of things, but in college . . . I'd probably be much happier in helping in the kitchen in the sorority house than out in the rush line. That's something I have learned a lot more about over the years. And I love to entertain. Oh, well, from the responsibility standpoint, mother had always thought I would have a family, be married, and all that kind of thing. She *really* trained me in the home, and I can remember oftentimes at work even now when I'm doing ten things at once [Laughter] that . . . she was always doing these simulations on you and you didn't know what was happening. One day I was at the stove, and suddenly she said, "The doorbell is ringing, your *husband's* coming home, the *baby* is crying, and *don't drop that pot*." [Laughter.] And here I am, and the thing is burning. She said, "you *learn* to hang on." Well, when the phone's ringing at the office and somebody is standing in the room with a problem, and I'm behind on ten letters to get out or something, I can hear her saying, *"Don't drop the pot."* [Laughter.]

So the responsibilities and handling lots of things at once, and planning and organizing, that is, has always really been a part of me. Probably to the extent . . . I think I was overprogrammed and overorganized—my brother is very anti all this. He won't, he won't make a plan if it *kills* him. Or if he knows he's going to be in your neighborhood, he wouldn't tell you. He will ring your doorbell. But he wouldn't let you know in advance. He . . . so that we reacted to those two situations very differently. I kind of, I think, I don't know . . . I kind of do what I'm told, a lot of times I . . . there's an expectation that I'm supposed to do what I'm told. He really was, he's *extremely* bright, very, very bright. And really didn't want to be told. And *didn't* ever want to get into this planning, organizing thing. Both of us grew up with a lot of older people. He and our family and our friends. I was taken out of high school a couple of years to live with an aunt who was a widow, and I lived with her in Topeka and in New York. So I was with her friends all the time, and I kind of missed high school. Not completely, but when I got back to being in my junior year as a stranger . . . to that age group, and I had a very hard time fitting back in. He . . . was *always* with his age group. We were in college . . . and again he got after me at college. He said, "You cross the street instead of speaking to somebody, and yet you wonder [Laughter] why you don't have friends." So that has been something that a number of people have helped me with over the years. I was probably more retiring.

C: I'm struck with how many people have given you very personal feedback.

J.O.: Yes. As I tell you, people have helped me a lot, and these are turning points. How many years has this been? I can almost remember the clothes I had on, the situations where we were sitting, the things where this happened. I must have *valued* it very much, or I wouldn't have remembered it. I think that I always trusted the people who gave it to me. Oh, I *often* dissolved in tears. I'm *very* . . . I can cry at the drop of a hat, I have . . . A friend's husband gets so disgusted with us because the two of us can be sitting in church and the first thing he knows we're weeping at the sermon. [Laughter.] And he gets *extremely* disgusted that it just takes one of us to get the other one going. So, I kind of am . . . very sensitive, but on the other hand, it's not . . . I'm not sensitive because you've hurt my feelings. Like at work, when the men get very upset about telling the secretary that she ought to do something because they're afraid she's going to be in tears. Most of the time I managed not to cry at *work.* I would cry at home. It's more, almost I think, a disappointment in myself, than somehow or other did I let them down, or . . . what should I be doing, but . . .

So, while it may have hurt at the moment, when Wynn told me the five things I had to work on—I was so *shocked* that he had to call this to my attention. But I knew that, kind of *instinctively,* that if he took the time to do that . . . I've thought about that so many times . . . it was the ideal time to do it. Because I hadn't gotten back into my routine. I had been *out of* that routine for *six weeks.* Everything I had done had been broken as a pattern. And it took a lot of guts for him to call me and say at that moment, which . . . he had to know me very well to know that I wasn't going to go to pieces on him, that it wasn't going to get me back in the hospital, and see, that's where I've always come out. Those people really had to care a lot . . . to do that. But it isn't easy when you're giving people feedback, nor is it easy to take, but . . . and I think . . . I also began to realize over the years, you see, there's been such a *pattern* of it . . . I've been so *fortunate,* because all those things have helped me and guided me, and the people have been right. It has all fit together, you know, and on some things I've made more progress than on others. But it was that they did care a lot, or they couldn't have done it. Or *wouldn't* have done it. They wouldn't have taken the time to do it. And so Wynn knew me well enough that either he thought, "Well, if she collapses, I can buck her up, or she'll go home and have a good cry." He probably had it all figured out—"She'll go home and have a good cry, come in and be as mad as hell at me tomorrow, and won't speak to me for a couple of days, and by Friday she'll be enrolled in six courses." [Laughter.] And that's what happened. [Laughter.] I have been extremely fortunate and I've *always* been glad that I've had tough bosses, demanding bosses, and I'm probably that way myself too. In my work now with my people, I'm very demanding, but I find that . . . most of them, not at the time but later on, *will* say that they learned a lot from it. And I'm not sure that they might put it together over the years, or that it has that kind of impact, but again I think that if they, if the person sees progress, well, if the person sees progress, then they feel good about it and it's not so hard.

I think most people can do more than they're currently doing, and some of them are a little lazy . . . and I generally . . . the thing I have to watch is oftentimes I care more about what they can become than they do. And so therefore, some of the standards are of my kind of wanting to say, "Hey, you can do more or do better"—until they can own that for themselves. It isn't fair for me to maybe want that for them. Now, that can get in the way of their performance. We have to be sure that, hey, if you're only going to perform this much, this is probably going to result in . . . you're not going to get compensation. But *for me* to want them to do more than that, unless they want to, is probably unfair. *That* I have to watch, because sometimes if they're bright, and I don't feel that they're operating up to their brightness, then I may ride them a little hard on that. I *do* have high standards but I believe many people think I'm fair. And that I would consider the elements. They will say that I have higher standards than most bosses. And I don't know whether I feel good or bad about that. [Laughter.]

There are a lot of people who have trouble keeping themselves wound. And I don't know what that motivation is, but my motivation *isn't* money. I certainly like to think that I will get regular increases . . . if I'm doing the job, that I haven't reached the top of my range. But I am motivated by expectations of others. If they *expect* that I will do something, or if I *commit* to do it, I will probably try to do it to the very best that I can. And it's more a self . . . I compete with myself, I really am not that good about competing with other people. If it really came to a showdown . . . we had this case not too long ago where we had some kind of competition on our own staff, for backstopping. My boss was in a tough spot, and the issue was, you know, you can only have so many backstops. There was a good deal of friction on the staff, and among . . . there were several other guys, I was the only woman, and I was still in a learning position and I knew that I still had a lot of room to go in my own salary range and a lot to learn. So I said to him, "Hey, I'm not eager to be put down as a backstop candidate." A *piece* of that reason was it made good sense for me, but a piece of the reason also was it kind of helped the staff, because it was very important for *those men* that they be equal in terms of the backstopping. Now that has changed, the lineup has changed some since then. And there was a timing standpoint, but *right then* it made more sense to try and keep harmony than it did to compete. Now, at other times I may compete more actively. But my natural tendency is to compete against my own standards or whatever the challenge is. If we're trying to get a job done, the challenge is, can we? And what are the odds on other things getting in the way?

C: Where do you find your most rewarding approval coming from?

J.O.: I really like a sense of accomplishment. I really do like and brag [Laughter] how I've handled a bunch of things when they come off and they've happened. I do get clear on what the thing ought to look like. I have a pretty good perspective of how I'm building the department, and what we're after. And as those pieces fall into place, that's fun to see. Or if we have a long-range project, or there've been a lot of people involved, or there's been a lot of skepticism about it or something . . . *and it happens.* There's a lot of reward and accomplishment. And it's nice to see people comment on what you were really trying to do. For example, on compensation, we were trying to really be *creative* in the mode of the communication, and . . . when people recognized that element as being the really distinct feature . . . that was fun, because our strategy was that if it worked, that's what would happen, and to *see* it work. . . . So it's sort of been the achievement. And I do like for my bosses, naturally, to say that we did a good job.

I'm not sure that there's a lot of that. I found a long time ago, and maybe that's why I count a lot on achievement, is that it's not very easy for people to say you've done a good job, or that this is outstanding or something else. Or they don't do it very frequently. So that to keep *myself* built up, accomplishment *is* important, because I can remember that I used to come home from the plant when I was first starting out and I was teaching people, and I really couldn't tell what was happening from those classes—I might come home and I'd scrub the same closet umpteen times, but it was a *physical* thing, and it was doing something. And I could say *I had done that.* Or it's like I'd try very hard to take long projects that are quite frustrating in the process, and carve out—well, we did this many letters, or we had this meeting, or we got these issues resolved, or *something* at the end of a week or at the end of a month that you can kind of wrap your hands around and say, "Hey, that got done as a piece toward the long-range thing." Then I do have to feel that sense of accomplishment. And I like very much when other people do comment on the work. That could be peers, it could be my subordinates. Sometimes young people come and visit my department. And if they find that it's a fun place to work, that's a very nice compliment. Or that they're challenged by what's happening.

Thom Sailer (A)

GIE Industries, Inc., was a large and profitable company that manufactured and marketed a diversified range of industrial and electrical products on a worldwide basis. The company was organized into four major operating groups, each of which concentrated on a different set of markets and technologies. As shown in Exhibit II-1, three of the four groups were headed by group presidents, and the fourth and smallest group by a group vice-president. The four groups operated relatively autonomously because of their dissimilar businesses.

John Hastings, 39 years old, had worked for GIE Industries for seven years. His most recent assignment was as director of planning for a large operating division in GIE's Industrial Equipment Group. In the spring of 1972, Hastings was sent by the company to a 15-week executive development program at a graduate business school. When he was about halfway through the executive development program (PED), Hastings was approached by his former boss about the possibility of his being assigned at the end of the program to GIE's Electronic Products Group as a special assistant to Thom Sailer, the group's controller and vice-president of finance.

Since all of Hastings's career at GIE had been within the Industrial Equipment Group, he was most interested in gaining added experience and exposure in a different part of the company. The assignment as Sailer's assistant was to be temporary—twelve to fifteen months—and to consist mainly of special-project work in the budgeting and planning area; it was presented to Hastings as a "stepping stone" to a line position within one of the Electronic Group's operating divisions. The main purpose of the assignment, in addition to working with Mr. Sailer, was to give Hastings a "home base" from which to learn about the op-

This case is a redisguised version of "Glen Taylor" and was prepared by Fred K. Foulkes with the assistance of John J. Gabarro.

Exhibit II-1 Thom Sailer

Corporate Organization, GIE Industries, Inc.

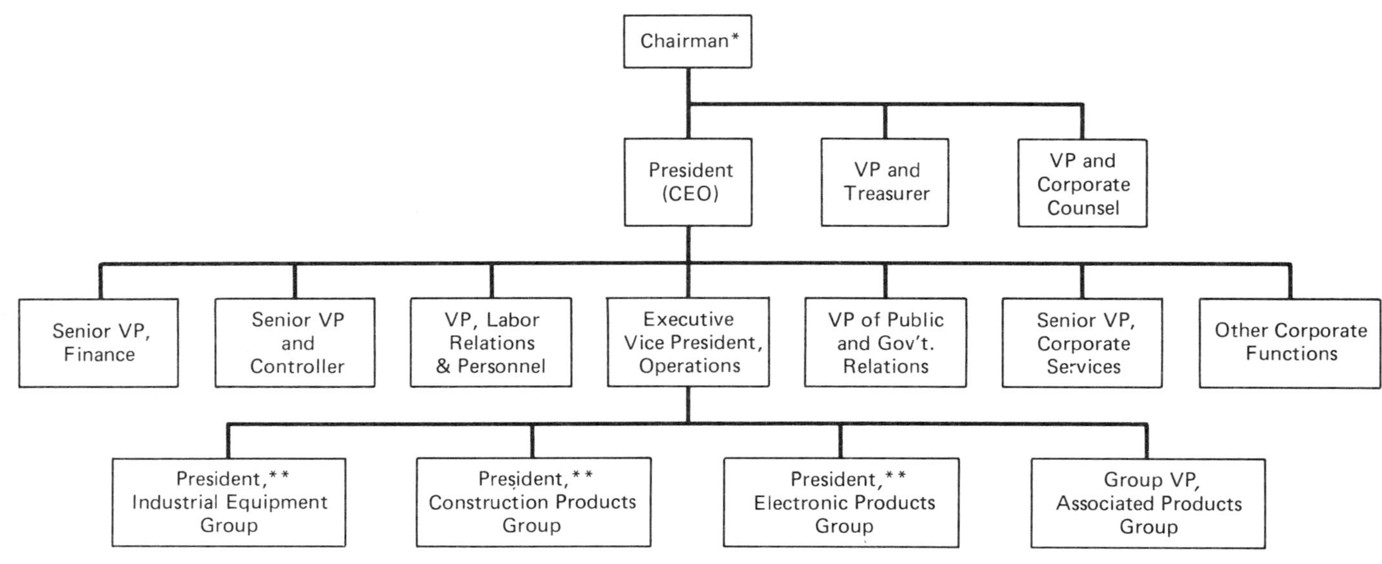

* The chairman of the board was also chairman of the finance committee

** All group presidents were also listed in the annual report as corporate senior vice presidents

erations of the Electronic Products Group.

When Hastings indicated interest in the assignment, Thom Sailer flew to New York to discuss it with him personally. At the conclusion of the day's discussion, both he and Sailer agreed that the assignment would be an interesting and useful learning experience.

Hastings genuinely liked Sailer and was very impressed by his obvious ability and enthusiasm. It was apparent that Sailer enjoyed talking with him. Sailer also seemed especially interested in Hastings's comments on the case method and the course he was taking in Human Behavior in Organizations. In fact, Sailer commented to the effect that the major problems in the Electronics Group were not technical or financial, but rather human and organizational. When Hastings accepted the job, Sailer said he would have a real "human behavior" problem for him when he started work and he would appreciate hearing his views on it. "In fact," Sailer said, "I'll write it out in case form on a confidential basis and give it to you on your first day of work." Without inquiring further about the specific nature of the problem, Hastings replied that he looked forward to tackling the "case problem" when he returned to GIE.

Thom Sailer was 50 years old and had joined GIE ten years earlier as assistant controller of the Electronic Products Group. Although Hastings had never met Sailer until his visit to New York, he had heard a great deal about him and knew that his work at GIE had been impressive. He understood that Chet Jamison, president of the Electronics Group, considered him one of the strongest men in top management. On several occasions, Jamison had credited Sailer with playing a valuable role in the rapid growth and success of the Electronic Products Group. In recent years, the group had made a number of acquisitions, and Sailer had played a key role in negotiating the purchase terms. In addition, Hastings knew that Sailer had almost singlehandedly introduced most of the planning and control systems that existed within the Electronic Products Group. These systems included a management-by-objectives program and both short- and long-term profit-planning systems. They involved budgeting of sales and expenses and were used for control purposes. Most of these systems had been introduced as part of a major reorganization of the Electronic Products Group implemented several years earlier. Sailer said that he had designed these systems for use by line managers at the request of Chet Jamison, who had originally hired him.

During their meeting in New York, Sailer had told Hastings that he was born and raised in the Presbyterian faith and tried to practice his religious principles in business. Business associates respected his high moral and ethical standards and his sense of fair play. Hastings remembered Sailer saying, "Central to the idea of controllership, it seems to me, are the ideas of responsibility, controls, and defining the rules of the game. The rules have to be administered fairly." Hastings was impressed by Sailer and was pleased that they had seemed to "hit it off" immediately.

After taking a two-week vacation at the end of PED, Hastings reported for work in his new assignment. Since Hastings's family had not yet moved to the new location, Sailer and Hastings had dinner together the evening he arrived. During the conversation over dinner, Sailer said he had prepared the "case problem" that he had mentioned and was ready to give it to him. He said that he had thought long and hard about the problem, because it had been bothering him for some time. Although he had talked about the problem with his wife and Jack Jamison, who was both the group's vice-president for domestic operations and a close friend, he had never talked about it to anyone else, inside or outside of GIE. He did say, however, that he had informed the group's president, Chet Jamison, "in general" about the situation.[1] (See Exhibit II-2 for an abbreviated organization chart of GIE's Electronic Products Group.)

Before giving his written case to Hastings, Sailer emphasized the confidential nature of the problem. "Confidentially," said Sailer, "the biggest damn problem I have is Tim Voigt. Sometimes I think I should say the hell with it and forget it, but I'm afraid that if I do, it will hurt the company too much." He suggested Hastings read the case that evening and they get together to discuss it the following day. Hastings thought this approach made sense, and was flattered that Sailer was willing to confide in him. Before departing for the evening, Sailer said, "Tim Voigt is the problem, and if you can solve this problem, you will go a long way in the Electronic Products Group." The written case that Sailer gave to Hastings appears in Exhibit II-3.

[1]Jack Jamison and Chet Jamison were brothers and major shareholders of GIE, since GIE had acquired a large electronics company that had formerly been controlled by the Jamison family. The two Jamison brothers had successfully expanded their family's business so that by the time GIE acquired it, it was already a major and profitable force in the industry. The old Jamison Company consisted of what was now GIE's Aircraft and Marine System Division, the Semiconductor Products Division, and the Electronic Devices Division. Chet Jamison was a member of the board of directors of GIE Industries.

Exhibit II-2 Thom Sailer

Abbreviated Organization Chart, GIE's Electronic Products Group

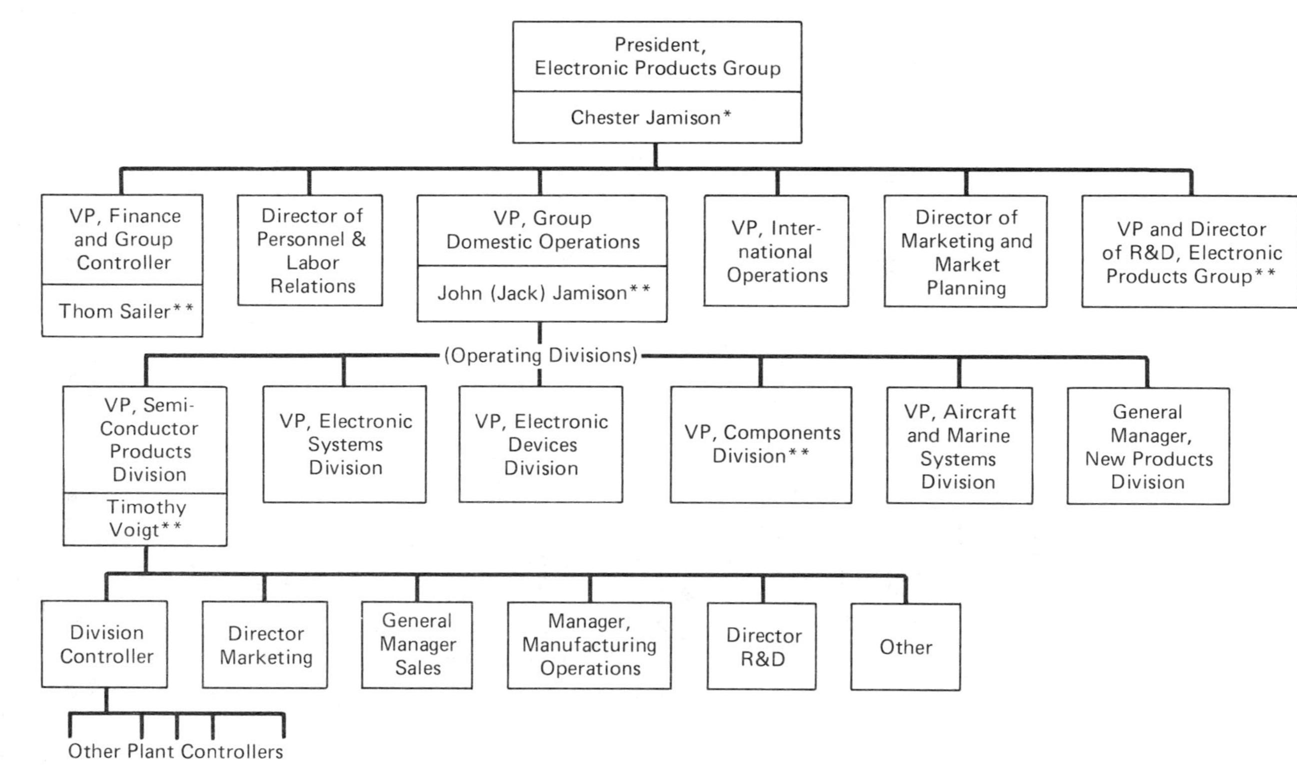

* Also a corporate senior vice president of GIE

** Also a corporate vice president of GIE (VP's in the Electronic Products Group, except as noted, were divisional vice presidents and were not listed as officers of GIE Industries, Inc.)

Exhibit II-3 Thom Sailer, Timothy Voigt

Mr. Timothy Voigt

Confidential

Timothy Voigt is one of the key executives in charge of operations for a significant business area of GIE's Electronic Products Group. He has been an employee for over 15 years, first in the role of a production supervisor then division production manager, and ensuing position changes to his present position as a divisional domestic vice president.

He has enjoyed a succession of promotions and is highly regarded by all those who have worked for him. In part, this is a reflection of his personality as the other side of the coin is being reflected in difficulties I am encountering with him.

First, Tim is a law unto himself and gives favorite treatment to those working for him. He freely disregards company personnel practices and procedures and administers to his people as he chooses. His secretary gets the highest salary of any secretary in the Electronic Products Group, works on a time schedule ignoring regular office hours, etc. This situation is widely recognized and resented by many others, but he has always gotten away with it and as a result he considers this his prerogative.

As he has progressed, this disregard for policy has become more noticeable on a higher level, even to the point of disregarding requests from the Group's president or responding to them in such a way that they have been disregarded for all practical purposes. For example, he has never chosen to completely comply with annual profit-plan requests. He will present location plans without review and personal commitment. Or at times he will submit data sufficiently different from standard forms to make collation and comparison difficult.

This has been accompanied by attempts to impose an iron curtain over the flow of information. This occurs with him personally and with operations under his supervision. When I request a meeting to discuss mutual problems, it rarely takes place unless forced by me.

Communications with others working under him become most troublesome and strong measures are sometimes required to keep avenues of communications open to operations. Relationships with an operating location become noticeably different when he becomes in charge of it or his responsibility no longer covers it.

This can be very unfortunate since many of our mutual areas of responsibility frequently overlap into areas with which he has no knowledge. To date we have been fortunate in preventing any serious losses, but solely by accident.

He works hard - long hours - travels a large part of his time - is unstinting as to his time on company affairs. He has a keen analytical mind, but tends to let small things prevent his deciding on major things.

Personally, away from the office we get along fine. He is affable, good company, and there is a free, open conversation without strain.

These relationships also appear to apply to others at his level and above.

Thom Sailer (B)

When John Hastings entered Thom Sailer's office the next morning, Sailer offered him a seat and then closed his office door. He told his secretary they were not to be disturbed.

Sailer: [Laughing] Well, John, I bet you didn't run into any cases like my case in your business school studies. Believe me, John, this guy is getting away with *murder* over there. I sure would like to know what to do about it next. . . .

Hastings: Thom, I don't know whether I can be of any help, but I would like to try. I wonder, though, if . . .

Sailer: [Excitedly] The whole trouble is this guy thinks he's a law unto himself. . . . He runs his damned division the way *he* wants to and says the *hell* with everybody else! I don't know, maybe the best thing for me to do is . . .

Hastings: Excuse me, Thom, but frankly, I'm still not clear on some of the facts here. For example, just what is the background history on this problem?

Sailer: Ever since Tim was promoted to vice-president several years ago, the relations between our people have become more and more difficult. It's gotten to the point now where my people come to me and say they can't get any information out of that division, and they're supposed to get reports as a matter of course. They're spending so much time trying to pry things loose there that other divisions and problems are suffering. When we finally do get stuff from him, it's likely to be scratched on the back of an envelope or something—absolutely no thought has gone into it, obviously. I tell you, he has no regard for the problems we're trying to deal with here.

Hastings: Thom, do you think a part of this problem may be explained by the image of your office? We had a lot of case studies about that at the school, and I found that to be the case in my

This case is a redisguised version of "Glen Taylor" and was prepared by Fred K. Foulkes with the assistance of John J. Gabarro.

last assignment in the Industrial Products Group.

Sailer: You've put your finger on something there. There can be no doubt about it. We're known as the checkers, the probers, and the spies. The office of the controller does not have a good image, and it is part of the problem. But we have a job to do, too, and I am responsible for developing full reports that go to the board of directors.

Hastings: I wonder what it's like working for a guy like Voigt. . . .

Sailer: Oh, I can tell you, he gets tremendous loyalty—his people just love him. He goes to bat for them, too. His secretary is the highest paid in the entire Electronic Products Group. And this is pretty well true of many of his people—they get more pay and benefits, and sometimes even faster promotions, than any other division. I tell you, after Tim's been in a slot for a while, it begins to close up to any kind of groupwide control. . . . The guy is really getting away with murder!

Hastings: What do you think Voigt himself thinks about all this?

Sailer: Well, he's convinced he's doing what he should. He's a real seat-of-the-pants manager—he just doesn't take any time for the systems we've introduced. He's been around a long time—he's 46 now—and he knows this business inside out. It's like pulling eyeteeth to get any information out of him. He doesn't pay any attention to routine requests of mine for meetings—and he certainly never takes the initiative to arrange one or ever try to find out what our procedures are. The only time we get together is when I *force* a meeting.

Hastings: He must be difficult to deal with.

Sailer: That's for sure. But it's funny, you know, he's not an angry type. Off the job, as I wrote in the case, we get together occasionally at a party at Chet or Jack Jamison's club and everything's fine—we get along fine. . . . I've only seen him mad about something once. That was when he was trying to protect another secretary of his after she had caused all kinds of trouble over in another division, getting information she had no business getting—those people wanted Voigt's head! Well, the personnel director and I put our foot down. Voigt got mad, I got mad, and I held firm. I said, "That woman has to go, and that's the way it's going to be!" He backed down at that point.

Hastings: What does Voigt's boss, Jack Jamison, know about all this?

Sailer: Oh, Jack is very aware of all this. He knows the whole story, but he says he has the same trouble with Tim as I do. He can't get any information either. He's wringing his hands over this guy running his division like it was his own company.

Hastings: Well, what about the president, Chet Jamison? Does he know about it? Can't he get action?

Sailer: Yeah, he knows about it too. . . . We've *had* to tell him why there are gaps in our reports, or where the unlikely estimates come from. . . .

Hastings: Why doesn't he crack down?

Sailer: Well, the trouble is, Voigt does turn in the results—he gets the profits. Last year he turned in the most profits of any division in GIE. It's been like that just about every job he has. He's always gotten the promotions, all along the line, since he came to GIE fifteen years ago.

Hastings: Oh, I see. . . .

Sailer: I'll tell you, though, something has got to be done. I think Chet is beginning to see more and more the problems Voigt is causing—and *could* cause. He told me last week he was going to look into this whole thing again.

Hastings: You mentioned there were problems he *could* cause. What kinds of things?

Sailer: Why, my God, he's writing contracts with suppliers and making sales agreements all the time, with nobody around here knowing about it. A year ago, he was about to sign a licensing agreement with another manufacturer that would have put us smack into a lot of trouble because of a new product being developed by another division! He just charges ahead, thinking only for himself. The key point is that Voigt could hurt the long-run profitability of the company in the area of trademarks, patents, and taxes. He almost gave away the company's patents in one horror case, and if he had changed one licensing agreement the way he wanted to, it would have cost the company $25,000 in taxes. There is a need for close cooperation between Voigt and me, otherwise there will be lost profits.

Hastings: Who runs his division while he's away? You say he travels a great deal, and he's away now on a long business trip.

Sailer: Jack Jamison is trying to run it, and he's asked me for help. As a matter of fact, I have a meeting with him tomorrow to see what we can do. Apparently, Voigt's people are tighter than ever since he's been away—Jack says they won't tell him any more than they ever did.

Hastings: What kinds of things have you thought of to do?

Sailer: I've beat my head on this one so much with so little results to show for it that I've just about decided to say "to hell with it." I don't know. . . . I suppose if I didn't care what happened to the company, I would just sit back and do my job and let the chips fall where they may, but I'm not like that, I couldn't do that after all the effort that's gone into building up the new organization.

[Thoughtfully] Voigt and I have never competed. He always gets promoted, yet he is a complete nonconformist who gets away with murder. He causes serious morale problems with his peers who try and follow our team-management concepts. Here is a good question for you: What do you do when a guy rejects management concepts (management by objectives, long-range planning, and budgets, for example) and still makes better-than-average profits? Top management in the Electronic Products Group has worked hard to develop what it considers the best available management and control techniques. To be honest, John, it may be that the best thing for me to do is to say the hell with it, but I find it hard to accept defeat and admit that "seat-of-the-pants" management is best after all.

As Sailer talked about his case, Hastings noted that he got red in the face on several occasions and appeared quite nervous. Hastings knew this was a serious matter for Thom Sailer, and he wanted to help to the extent he could.

Larry Baker (A)

Chuck Loring, a second-year student at a graduate business school, conducted the following interview with Larry Baker, a first-year student, as part of an assignment for a course Chuck was taking in interpersonal behavior. The purpose of the assignment was to practice understanding another person from the other person's point of view.

Larry Baker was slightly older than most business school students, was married, and had both military and business experience. The two men had first become acquainted the previous summer, while both of them were working for the same large manufacturing company in the Midwest. Although they had been in separate departments and buildings, their projects had overlapped to some extent, and there was some occasion to work together. The fact that Chuck had completed one year of business school and Larry was just starting had naturally carried their friendship beyond the work environment. However, their contacts were infrequent, and neither knew much about the other before the interview.

The interview time and the place—Chuck's dormitory room—were arranged by telephone. At that time, Chuck explained to Larry the nature of the assignment, that he could discuss anything he wanted, and that the object was merely that of understanding someone else's point of view; in this instance, he could talk about himself, a problem, or a particular subject. As an example, Chuck had suggested he talk about his future business goals.

The following interview was transcribed from over two hours of tape. (The numbers will be referred to in "Larry Baker (B)" in Part Four.)

Larry 1: One of our professors posed a question to us the other day, and that is, What is the businessman's responsibility to society? How should he act in relation to his personal goals and goals of society? It came up in connection with a case of a lobbyist. Of course, I knew that people took other people out to dinner and that favors were done. However, in this case, the fellow took them out to dinner, helped the legislators, and used grassroots pressures—but yet he took exception to giving them money or women, as some lobbyists seemed to do!

Chuck 1: This seemed to bother you.

Larry 2: Yeah, the thing that bothered me was, how do you draw the line? How do you say one thing is worse than the other? Of course, there is a difference of degree; I understand that, that according to society, to offer them money or to cater to their whims—to offer them women—is much worse in society's eyes than to offer them a business deal or the use of a car. Yet in my mind, I see these as the same things. A bribe is a bribe to me. If I take a man out to dinner, it is obvious that I am trying to get him to do something for me—that I am offering him the use of something I have control over in return for something he has; I'm bribing him same as if I handed him the money. And yet the class discussion says that favors are all right but we're to stop at money. But in relation to our employees, if I were a manager, I use money to get things, grant favors, give status symbols, and it is all right, but when I go to someone else, it isn't. I find it difficult to decide within myself which way I would go. I have the feeling I would go one way or another. At the present, I just don't believe in bribes, but I interpret being nice to people just to get something for myself as a bribe too.

Chuck 2: So you are taking this beyond mere monetary things and to your acting as a businessman, and saying, this is in effect a bribe and this bothers me.

Larry 3: Yeah, this bothers me. When I get out, I look upon the business world as part of a game, and there seems to be varying sets and degree of rules in the game, and I have to decide where I'm going to play. Uh, I have this drive—to make out, if that's the expression—I want something. If I didn't, I wouldn't be here. I wouldn't have gone to college in the first place. In the process of getting what I want, I have to decide how I'm going to play. And, uh, I've found that all the things I've done up to this point, I have had a very difficult time reconciling myself to stay in the middle; I either play on one end or the other. So I would just not do favors. I would have people act because they wanted to act in my favor. I would try to convince them, trying to use what I would call logical arguments, and if they could back me down—shoot holes in me—I have nothing else to stand on. I just couldn't say, you're right, I'm wrong, here's a few bucks and you'll do what I want you to. I would either do this or go to the other extreme—I would just buy my way along.

Chuck 3: So as you see it, there are two means—a means of logic to convince people, or just bribe them.

Larry 4: Yeah, I know I could build up a credit or debt from people. I don't know quite how I feel about this myself. If I do something for someone, I realize that they owe me a debt, and yet I don't want people to do something for me just to repay the debt because they feel they have to. I would rather have them want to. When I do get into a work situation, I would like to get in one that built up a team feeling—uh, a group feeling—so that they felt that what was good for the group was good for them. And the same with me—what is good for me is good for the group, rather than try to buy my way through the group or stepping on other people.

Chuck 4: So you are trying to find some way that you can be a success and attain the things you want in business by not going to either one of the extremes.

Larry 5: Yes! I'm trying to find a way—I suppose I'm predisposed to want to screw the system, is what it amounts to. To explain this, I feel that the system—and I define the system as IBM's way of doing it, the IBM look or you don't make it—you can't buck the system. Or some other places I worked, where the way to get ahead is to be nice to those people who are your supervisors and it does not make any difference what kind of work you do. I don't want people when they refer to me to say that he's a nice guy—he looks good. I want them to say he can do the job! The fact that his personal characteristics would enter in is incidental.

Chuck 5: So you might say that you would rather be judged on the basis of your work—your contribution to the organization—rather than on any outside factors, such as the image you project, the people that you know, the favors that you do for people, etc.

Larry 6: That's right, that's right! I would like to be able to say some day that I'm a success and that I don't owe anybody anything. Uh——

Chuck 6: You would like to be independent without knowing that your success was attributable to someone's knowing you or a favor you did for someone. You would like to achieve it on your own.

Larry 7: That's right. I want to feel that, and I suppose this goes to something deeper inside, that I want to feel that it was me who did it and not that it was through trickery or doing personal favors, or even being in the right place at the right time. I want to feel that I am where I am because I am what I am, that I've been judged on the type of work that I do and the benefit I am to whatever group I happen to be associated with, and not by the fact that I'm the boss's brother-in-law or because someone likes me. I don't appreciate that position. If I were in that type of position, I think I would feel that people talked among themselves and not to me that I was one of the chosen ones. "He isn't worth a damn but he is going to make out because of who he knows."

Chuck 7: So to go back, you think that this is what you would like, but yet what they seem to teach you here, and what society says, is just the opposite—that you are going to be judged on other things besides what you contribute to the organization.

Larry 8: Yes, uh, that is correct. This is, uh, one reason why I picked . . . or came to a business school, was that this would be the place, if any, that will give me the tools that I need, will give me the confidence that I need to go out and buck the system, maybe make my own system. I think I am predisposed to want to make something of my own with a small group of people, to build an empire, if you want to call it that, so that we can say we did this—we pulled each other up.

Chuck 8: But it doesn't seem to be that way now that you're here?

Larry 9: Well, uh, I don't know. Again, in one course we had a great deal of discussion of what legislators do and why they do what they do. It seems that in every case we've considered so far, that there has always been one legislator who is called unreliable, undependable, any number of derogatory names, yet he seems to be the only one in the entire group that we get to know from the case that operates according to his own convictions, who operates—at least it seems—in the manner in which he is supposed to. He takes the interest of an entire group—of the group he is supposed to represent—and considers their interests and does what he thinks he should do for them rather than casting his vote in favor of the particular pressure group or in any manner looking out for his own benefit. There seems that there is some sort of dichotomy here, that those who act like society says they should act, they don't get anywhere, and yet those that do the things that everyone thinks are underhanded, unacceptable, and what have you—get somewhere!

Chuck 9: And this is what bothers you!

Larry 10: Yes, this bothers me.

Chuck 10: You would like to be like the one you described, where he stood for his own convictions, yet you say that if you do this when you get out in the business world, you may be the one that won't be able to achieve the things that you want.

Larry 11: Yes, I'm afraid I'm going to dilute my character, to prostitute my ethics. I can see some inherent sort of danger that I feel, that if I give a little bit one time, that I'll do something a little worse the next time. I'm afraid I'll fall into some kind of a hole and maybe in effect be successful in the eyes of society or the eyes of the world but despise myself, destroy myself.

Chuck 11: Could we say that there is an aspect of manipulating people here that you don't like?

Larry 12: Yes! Even that word—I don't like the word "manipulating" people. I want to feel inside myself that people are doing something that I ask them to do because they want to, they want to do it for me, they want to do it for themselves, for the firm. In any case, they're not being tricked or handled or pushed or walked on, and yet it seems, to get ahead, this is the type of thing that is done.

Chuck 12: There doesn't seem to be any way to please both you and the people you work with at the same time. In other words, there has to be some dichotomy here, where the guy that gets ahead uses the people and the people don't get what they want, but the guy that manipulates them does get what he wants.

Larry 13: Yes, this seems to be exactly what happens. And this is the reality, but the reality is in direct opposition to what the schoolbooks say, to what people would like to believe what happens. They would like to believe that the red-blooded American boy goes out and makes good by being a Billy Budd type of character, a character who is truthful, who works hard and is sincere. And yet the people who are this way, and there's a saying that I've heard in industry that nice guys get squashed, they don't get along. Now, I'm not condoning that we let people do what they want to do. I understand that there are varying degrees of responsibility of intellect, and as such, some people are leaders and some are followers. But I would think that the leaders making decisions and getting people to do things would consider those that are underneath them as well as the goals that they would hope to attain. To say that the firm's goal is to make profit is all right, as long as it isn't at the expense of someone who could less afford it that we can. I suppose the best example is the exploiting of labor during the twenties. And today the exploitation of management by unions. I am directly opposed to union organizations, primarily because I think the officers of the union have their own self-interest in the face of more benevolent management. I think they taught management a lesson.

Chuck 13: So you would tend to avoid conflict and hurting people's goals and lives, is that it?

Larry 14: Yes, I would tend to avoid personal conflict. I've always tried to separate my being into two entities—the academic or logical side and my emotional side. I would avoid any conflict that I would be emotionally involved in simply because I would act according to my own feelings rather than what I logically thought I should do. As far as interfering in other people's lives, I feel that every individual has a chance to do whatever he wants to do. I realize it is more difficult for some than others because there are some who are given more opportunity. But this is up to the individual. Some people say you are lucky you go to business school. I say I am not lucky; I got here because I wanted to be here. If you want to go to a really good business school, all you have to do is want to and sit down and figure out how you are going to do it. I don't feel that I have had any special privileges.

Chuck 14: But yet when you push this thinking that a person has a chance to make what he wants out of life, it rubs against the fact that in reality, you almost have to manipulate people, etc.

Larry 15: Yes, I suppose that I must admit this. I must admit that in my own dealings with people, I'm not so much interested in what I do as much as how other people are affected by what I do, because how they are affected determines what will happen to me. Yet I don't expect them to make any concessions for me. I do my work to the best of my ability, and how this affects them is what interests me, and not really what I've done. I know what kind of work I do. I know what kind of person I am. I have had occasion when I've felt that people didn't understand me, didn't know who I was. This hurts, this bothers me. I've had people misconstrue the things I say. Sometimes they think that an academic argument is insight into my emotional self, and when I very coldly deny something that they think is a right of people, they think I am a callous person. This isn't true. This is only one side of me speaking. They only saw the academic side that looks at something and gives an evaluation, which has nothing to do with my personal emotions. Personally, I might feel just the opposite. A case in point is the fact that we have women students here. Two of them are in my study group. I've had numerous conversations with them, and I don't feel that women have any place in business. I have this feeling not because I feel they are inferior, but I feel that they have a distinct advantage to which they are not entitled, and that is just the fact that they're women. I confronted them with this and we argued about it. This is my logical self talking to them, but emotionally when I talk to them, I can see why they're here, why they want to be here. I can see why they want to get ahead. This is the Protestant ethic, that you must surge ahead. And I can see why they would be disgusted with the traditional role of a woman. Again, there is this dichotomy here. I can't resolve this.

Chuck 15: So there are really two sides here—the logical side and the emotional side—and you seem to think that your problem is resolving them, which one of you takes the front. Can they act separately, can you get them in agreement?

Larry 16: Yes, I think this problem with women, legislators, my business ethics—are all basically the same. As I gain experience, I see a two-standard system in operation, where people are saying something and doing something else. I can't, as you said, resolve this in my mind. I can't seem to approach a middle-of-the-ground attitude. I feel that to buck the system, to act at one extreme, I'm going to end up with nothing, and if I don't buck the system, I'm going to destroy some of myself, some of my feelings for people and human beings. I have had experience with people who I thought were hard and cold and had no respect for people. I didn't like these people; I didn't like what I saw. I don't want to see myself in that position; I don't want to do that to myself. Even at this school, the pressure of business contacts—I've talked to my wife and she can sense a change in my attitudes. I don't think this is bad, that I look at things from a profit-and-loss standpoint. I just see the inside of some things that I only saw the outside of before. This is the change she senses. We can see in some of the cases where people acted in a manner I don't approve of, in a manner which furthers their own interests and may well make them the most technically qualified individual in their particular area, but as a human being some of them are despicable. And I'm trying to resolve a center area for myself. I'm trying to develop some sort of attitudes so I can be firm but fair, so I can justify my moves to myself. If I had to fire someone who had worked for the company for 10–20 years, I could explain to them in logic, profit and loss, why, but in my emotional self, I can understand what this person feels. I'm trying to find the middle for these two things and I find it very difficult.

Chuck 16: So you can see where to be a success in business is going to require a firm and harsh logical approach, but yet this gets in the way of your feelings for people and——

Larry 17: Yeah.

Chuck 17: And how it affects them.

Larry 18: Yes. My family, my wife, and some of my friends think I'm foolish because I have a basic faith in people. I leave my key in my car or leave my personal things in places where people can pick them up if they wanted to. As far as I feel myself, I wouldn't touch something that didn't belong to me. If it's not mine, it's not mine. I realize that there are people that don't feel the way I feel. I know that I have to protect myself from people like this because they will take me for all I'm worth, but at the same time I don't feel any personal anger towards these people. If anything, I would just be further disillusioned with people. My business in the future should be an opportunity to push ahead and be perfectly honest and frank in all the dealings I have both above and below me. I am the type that can become very enthusiastic about a business development, and I hope that I can communicate this to the people below me. If I ever become a business executive, I hope that I can fight off the harmful attitudes of unions or the things that make a firm inefficient. I know I can be firm and hard when I have to, because I divorce my emotional self from the other part of my character. . . .

Chuck 18: But you don't like to do that.

Larry 19: But I don't like to do it, that's right, I don't like to do it. I like to feel at ease. I like to feel a serenity in both facets of my personality. Take my experience in the service as an instructor. I had occasions to fail students, and these were people of the same age as I but not with same backgrounds. I never failed anyone without first talking to them and at least first making them understand logically why I failed them, and I could feel some remorse on their part emotionally. I think my service experience reinforced my feelings about this reconciliation of this emotional versus the logical aspect of my personality. But I had some success with them.

Chuck 19: But you don't know whether you can do it in business.

Larry 20: I don't know whether I'll be

successful in business. For one thing, in the service I had an absolute authority and a captive audience, and in business people have the right to turn around and walk away when I try to logically explain things. They can turn me off, and I have my doubts that I can accomplish what I want to accomplish.

Chuck 20: So it won't be just the logical side that will be a success in business, but it will require something beyond just logically explaining——

Larry 21: I think so, I think so. People ask me what I'm looking for and who I consider successful. And invariably I consider people successful who have made a lot of money, people who are held in high esteem and who perhaps didn't make a lot of money. This is a personal thing. I do want to make a lot of money, although money is not my goal—my reason being simply because it has no inherent value. It's a means to an end, a way to get the things I would like to have. At the same time, I'm looking for the success that comes from being respected for who you are and what you are, and not just where you are.

Chuck 21: You don't think this will come from business?

Larry 22: I think it can come from business, but I have some doubts if it will come within the system. My exposure, until last summer, in business had all been very distasteful simply because every job opportunity I had taken advantage of, I found that unless I integrated myself into the system regardless of what I felt or thought inside—I had to outwardly appear that I was integrated into the system before I could get anywhere, and as a result was being judged not on what I did or how I handled myself, but on, I suppose, about what you would call my attitude.

Chuck 22: So it almost forces you to create a system of your own rather than adapt to a new system.

Larry 23: Yeah, this is close to being essentially true. I qualified my business experience because at the manufacturing company in the Midwest, I wasn't led by the hand or watched over, and I was given a free rein to do what I chose to do. I think they were satisfied, and I don't think I integrated into their system. You didn't see the organization man there, or the back-stabbers who would climb to the top over others. This is the closest I've seen of this group feeling I spoke of—what is good for me is good for the firm. They had this philosophy. For the first time in my life, I felt here is a monster, but I have a chance here. While in others that I worked in, I didn't even want to succeed, because they weren't ethical.

Chuck 23: So it is really a question of, do I create my own system, or do I find a large system that is compatible and allow me to keep my emotional values, etc., and operate successfully?

Larry 24: Yes, yes! This is exactly it. I have been out of high school over ten years and have had several work experiences and military, and I feel I'm perceptive. I have an inherent ability to find out what is going on so I can find out where I fit in. I have searched for the system that I would fit into, and at the same time thinking in the back of my mind, if that system doesn't exist, I'll create it. I have tried one business venture of my own, which went in the red, but that was because I lacked experience. I enjoyed it, though. I came to school because it should open new doors for me and I'll be able to examine new systems that I couldn't have before. Perhaps I will find this ethical situation—this logic-emotion tie I'm looking for. I think this will be available to me when I leave here. I expect to have at least three jobs after I leave here, because I will be able to inspect various systems. But then I get a little worried because, although I'm not old, I'm older than most graduates here. I realize my time is limited; I will have to pick something and do it soon. And if I can't find a system I can integrate into successfuly, or devise my own system, I'll have to settle for the next best thing and some way sort of adjust to fit. But yet I could never adjust to something like IBM, because it is so far from myself. So I would have to go outside the job to get my satisfactions of life.

Chuck 24: So when you add the time problem, it aggravates it—the fact that you have to find a system or create your own system and do it within a reasonable amount of time.

Larry 25: Yes! Yes, while I'm at business school I'm investigating at least two opportunities to create my own business. I may have grandiose ideas, but I couldn't be satisfied in IBM or with a corner grocery store. If I'm going to build something, I want to build it big, or at least to try to make it big. You couldn't give me something that was destined to be small.

Chuck 25: So you want something big. It would be nice to create something big that would have your own type of system, but this takes a lot of time and risk, so it would be easier to go into something that is already big, provided that the system was there that agreed with you.

Larry 26: Yeah, this is right. For this particular reason, then, even though I'm predisposed to look for a business opportunity of my own, I'm more seriously looking for an opportunity in industry. In any case, if I don't find exactly what I'm looking for, I will find something that will give me enough experience to make me more valuable to someone else someday who may have the system I'm looking for. Sorta, the added-value theory for each year I'm with someone. I'll always look at myself as ready to go on the open market given the opportunity, given something that more closely aligns itself with my feelings, ideas.

Chuck 26: So you don't think it does any good to adapt to a system?

Larry 27: I find it almost impossible—I can't adapt. I sometimes wish I could. Several of my friends have successfully integrated themselves into a system and are very happy. Some are machinists and are quite happy, and I'm a little envious of them because I know they are happy. And yet I know I couldn't do what they're doing and be happy, because I would want more—and not just dollars, but more prestige and more value to myself. I would feel wasted. So I keep pursuing my education because I know this adds value. Just like the two months I've been here. I've learned more than I ever thought I could. [Pause.] Perhaps it has something to do with Maslow's theory of needs. I guess I'm at the level of never being satisfied with oneself. I want to leave the world better than I started. I want to give my daughter things, more than I had. To not be as disillusioned with people as I have.

Chuck 27: So you still come back to this basic conflict, of sometimes you have certain aspirations and goals you want to achieve, but there is that logical versus emotional conflict.

Larry 28: Yes, I want to achieve these goals within my own context of values. And it seems sometimes as though it is almost impossible, and yet I have been reinforced by my constant belief that as I move within my values, I have progressed. I have been to college and through the service. Especially in the service, I saw many sets of values different than mine. I compared them and our statuses and decided I couldn't go back to working in a factory as I had before—I just wouldn't be satisfied. I found at college, the white tower, this clean competition I looked for. This evaluating a person on the drive, enthusiasm, etc., rather than who they know, etc. I found I could get ahead by pushing, and this is approved by society. Almost everyone approves of education, but I know there will be a difference when I get out. The system will be different.

Chuck 28: And this is what worries you.

Larry 29: This is a basic worry or problem. Maybe I have the whole thing colored, because my first business experiences were disappointing. But my summer job was encouraging, and this school I think opened that door. [At this point, the tape had to be changed, and he commented:] Boy, I sure am doing a lot of talking; I'm sure opening up. Don't let me down now.

Chuck 29: We were at the point where you were saying that you have your own system of values, your emotional and logical. You've had some experiences in business; your job last summer where this has worked out. But there is still that question that when you graduate from here, and you find that although it has been ideal for you in education because you can seem to operate successfully and be judged on your logical and not your side values, the people you know, etc., that you will really find it in business out of here. Someplace where you can operate within your own values but yet achieve the things you would like to.

Larry 30: Yes, yes, this is exactly it! I suppose some of my experiences in college and business have disillusioned me, that I couldn't reconcile in my mind. I had difficulty in fitting my values to what happened. A particular instance was in college. [He relates an incident where a student tried to sell him a final and he refused, and he was graded on a curve with those that had seen it and hence missed an A. He said he hurt himself because he did right. Then he goes on to tell about taking a job after telling himself he could do it. He found he couldn't, but rather than telling him, the company just delegated him less and less until he quit. He wished they had been frank with him and told him.]

Chuck 30: So you like to know how you stand.

Larry 31: That's right. I know who I am; I want to know what other people think I am. I want to know where I am all the time. I don't think I could run my life unless I did. [He then digresses regarding the school situation and how he stands.]

Chuck 31: So you work hardest when there is an objective end and not a subjective end.

Larry 32: Yes, yes, that's right. I wouldn't have come here if someone had told me that professors grade you on what they thought of you. I would rather have people judge me on how well I operate—do my work—rather than how well they like me. Some people just won't like me, because of the way I look or something. I wouldn't want to be judged on that basis, nor would I ever want to judge anyone else that way. Nevertheless, I realize that there are some people here at school that I like better than others, and some of those that I like are not as competent as those I don't like.

Chuck 32: So nevertheless, there is still this subjective side.

Larry 33: Oh, yes. There has to be; this is necessarily so. But I still would definitely prefer to look at things objectively, such as making decisions. To look at them as a cold entity. Since my emotional values are so closely connected to my logical values, I would prefer to detach my emotional values and keep them out of my business dealings.

Chuck 33: You would rather keep personal feelings out.

Larry 34: I feel that they don't have any place in business. I feel I have to disconnect my personal self from my business life; otherwise, I will tend to do that which will be unfair—that I wouldn't do objectively but I would do personally. I wish I could make an analogy. [Pause.] Take the women in our class. [He goes back over the women's situation, then expands to tests in school as not being a really adequate means of evaluation.] There are many things that enter in that tests can't do.

Chuck 34: So you can see where the emotional is important. In other words, tests would be a very objective means of looking at things, so there is a use for subjective evaluation.

Larry 35: Yes, in particular instances, because in the course of our conversation here, I have said that I do care for people and that I care for their feelings. But I don't like to have this color my judgment. In other words, I suppose—if you want to assign some rank order to these things—first comes my objective feeling, and second comes the modifying factor, my personal feelings. In regard to raising my daughter . . . [Goes on to relate an incident here]. I really like one of the courses here, because they discuss this very thing—values—and what you want to achieve and how you're going to get there.

Chuck 35: This again is your problem, then—what values do you set up, how do you achieve the things you're after, utilizing these values without bending them or losing them somewhere along the line?

Larry 36: That's right. I really think I could destroy myself in the process of becoming successful, I could get to a point where the world would say, "There is a self-made man," and inside of myself I would be saying, "This is a man who destroyed himself. I just chipped away at my foundation until it was gone." This is one of my fears about the business world. How do I compete with someone who doesn't feel as I do? How do I compete with someone who bribes, etc.? How am I going to cope with forces that oppose my foundation?

Chuck 36: So you realize there is going to be plenty of opportunity in the reality of the business world where this will become a conflict.

Larry 37: I think constantly. I think I'll be constantly challenged. I think my own personal measure of success will be how well I can withstand these things and still get ahead. I want to maintain a system and still be successful—of course, with some compromise, but only slight. If I can't, then my picture of disillusionment will be complete and I suppose I'll retreat or get out some way. I won't shovel sand against the tide—if it's impossible, I'll look for some way to escape.

Chuck 37: So you will try to find a system to match yours, but you will only go to the point where if it's impossible you will get away some way. . . .

Larry 38: Yes, yes.

Chuck 38: Changing jobs, careers, or something.

Larry 39: Yes, even though job changing is frowned upon and job changers are looked upon as misfits. I suppose that's what I'll be—a misfit—If I can't find the right system. But I'll always keep looking for my place when I say I'll escape.

Chuck 39: Always looking for the right system.

Larry 40: That's right.

Chuck 40: But you won't try to say, "This is my system, it doesn't seem to be getting me anywhere, so maybe I had better change it or look at it to see if it's right."

Larry 41: I've done that—I'm constantly evaluating my system. It would be ridiculous not to say it hasn't changed over the years. But it is a change of degree and not of kind—not direct changeover, but a modification from experience and learning.

Chuck 41: So you do recognize that your values will change over time.

Larry 42: Oh, yes. But some things to me are despicable and they always will be, but over the years I have been able to at least live with these things. [He recites an incident about a friend who changed.] Of course, his friendship meant a lot to me. It's like when I was a kid. You know how kids get the gang instinct. Well, I would often find myself faced with a decision of either dropping out of the gang or modifying my behavior. I usually dropped out and found another group to fit my system. [He cites an example from his service experience, where he sought out a group of friends.] So I've always managed to find some system somewhere. And even though I feel a little apprehensive about my business career, I do have the feeling it will work out, because it always has in the past. I didn't have to deviate. I could have; some things would have been easier, but I still got the same places without modifying. And I think I can in the business world. When I say modifying, I mean radically.

Chuck 42: So you think you can find that peace—that rationale—that you're looking for.

Larry 43: Yes, I think it's there! I think my system exists, but I'll just have to find it. But I am smart enough to realize I might not, so I think ahead as to what I would do. I know what I'll do. I refuse to force myself into mental slavery to appease anyone else, when I feel that, given time, I can find something that will be compatible to me.

Chuck 43: So there is really that question of whether you will find the system—whether you will be able to attain your goals without giving up your values. But yet you feel that in the past, you always found a group or someone with a system such as you have had, and you have been able to change from one group to another. So therefore, even though the possibility does exist, you feel you'll be able to work it out.

Larry 44: I think so, yes, I do think so. Some people may frown upon what I do. I have friends who don't approve of my going to college. But this is what I want to do. [Pause.] Some people feel they can get along without others. I can't; I'm gregarious. I realize I can't get along completely alone. [He relates an experience in California, where he had no friends, so he moved back to Ohio.]

Chuck 44: So on the one hand, you want to be independent, but yet you recognize that you have a definite need for association with other people, and that's what makes it hard.

Larry 45: Yes! Yes! I have to—uh——

Chuck 45: You have to have people around you that accept you and like you for what you are.

Larry 46: That's right. I want to be able to pick and choose the people I associate with. But I don't want to be forced into relationships like some companies do. For instance, in the service I loved my job, but I wanted to get out. My friends asked me why, and I told them it was because of the uniform. They couldn't understand this, but it was because I had to wear it. That's what bothered me.

Chuck 46: You don't like to have things forced on you.

Larry 47: That's right, that's right. They say that's not a big thing, but I say, maybe you can wear it but I can't. And in the same sense, I can't wear a blue suit for IBM. Here I suppose I look the same as any other business school student, but it's because I want to—I choose to be that way. I don't have to. If they said for everyone to wear ivy league clothes, I would probably seek some way to get away from it.

Chuck 47: "Just don't force me."

Larry 48: Yes, just don't force! Let me decide for myself; let me do what I want to do. And most times I'll conform. This is probably a basic reaction. If I am left alone, I work harder, if I'm not pushed or watched over. I guess I'm sorta like the workers on the assembly line, I restrict my output if I'm pushed. I do a much better job if I'm left to my own devices. I expect people to trust me and give me responsibility.

Chuck 48: So you're afraid that when you get out in business, you'll have things forced on you.

Larry 49: Well, I understand there are some things I must do. But there are things I couldn't live with without changing. I think change is basic to my nature. I couldn't just look forward to putting cards in an IBM machine all my life. Some men can do this and compensate by enjoying their leisure hours. I can't. I have to enjoy my job, because I can always control my leisure so I will enjoy it, but my job is more difficult. I realize I'll have duties, etc., to do. So I'll have to find something that fits into my system.

Chuck 49: All right. Well, this has been interesting. Ah, have you . . . throughout all of this discussion, has it clarified in your mind any of your own beliefs and resolved any of the conflicts? Or are you still in the same position that you started?

Larry 50: I think an extensive conversation like this where I could sit and talk for over an hour [It had been two hours] helps clarify things. I seldom get the chance. Yes, I think it has. It's crystallized a whole system for me, while before, I had just been considering these things. Through this monologue, I think I see more clearly how the whole thing fits into my previous experience and what I expect in the future. I think it's been a benefit to me, I really do.

Chuck 50: Do you see any new light now, that there is hope in this problem, that things will turn out?

Larry 51: Well, I always believed they would. Otherwise I would give up. I think I have seen throughout the monologue clearly how it will work out and have made it more evident to myself.

Chuck 51: Were you aware that it was becoming a monologue?

Larry 52: Yes, I suppose it's because I'm a vocal person. I tend to talk to myself even at times. At times, and I'm being quite frank, it was rather hard, but other times it just flowed, it just came out.

Chuck 52: Well, thanks a lot for helping me out this afternoon.

Juanita Rodriguez

Juanita Rodriguez, from Panama, was graduated from boarding school in the United States at the age of 16 and was admitted to Allegheny College at that time. Because of her age, on the advice of Allegheny, she did not enter college that fall but spent the year at home in Panama, where her father was a prominent surgeon and her mother taught Spanish literature at the University of Panama. She also visited her mother's sister's family in Spain and traveled in France and Italy with her parents. In September of that year, her mother brought her to college and remained in town most of the fall.

Early in November, Juanita telephoned Mr. Greene, the headmaster of her school, who had also been her teacher in chemistry for two years, and asked if he would talk to her about a problem. When she arrived in his office, Juanita chatted for a few minutes and then referred to her call.

Juanita 1: Well, Mr. Greene, here I am back for advice again. As you must remember, I was never a really good chemistry student, and my coasting along in chem at school has caught up with me. I'm flunking Chemistry A this year. I seem to understand it when I study it, and I get along all right in the laboratory. But I just don't seem to be able to do anything on the examinations. I'm too slow. I can't manipulate the expressions fast enough. It's worse than it was in school because I'm scared in this course, and I never was in yours.

Greene 1: What have your grades been so far?

Juanita 2: I got 30 on the first test and 4 on the midsemester examination. . . . I just couldn't seem to do anything on it. I couldn't get started. It was so long, and that frightened me. I couldn't decide what to do first. I think I can actually do every problem there [She handed him the examination question sheet] if I have time enough, but I can't solve the quantitative problems fast enough to do all that in one hour. Isn't that a mean exam? Nobody in the class got more than 60 except one girl who hasn't had a grade below 95 since we started. The instructor spends all his time lecturing to her, and the rest of us just pick up what we can.

Greene 2: Hmmm, it is rather a tough exam. You really have to have this stuff at your fingertips, don't you?

Juanita 3: I did what they said about not trying to remember equations, but learning how to balance them so thoroughly that I could reconstruct any reaction in my mind in a minute or two. I can do that, but not when I'm rushed in an examination—and of course not in a minute or two, either. I've studied hard, too, at least two hours on every assignment. I think I understand it until I get to class—and then he goes so fast I can't follow him.

Greene 3: You're pretty discouraged with the whole thing.

Juanita 4: Yes.

Greene 4: If I can help you with tutoring or extra explanations or anything like that, I'm only too glad to do it.

Juanita 5: I don't want to take up your time . . . It's very kind of you.

Greene 5: I feel a certain responsibility for your chemistry because you were my pupil. Besides, I'd really enjoy helping you. It would be fun to do inorganic again—you know I'm not teaching it this year—and it would be a relief from my own work. All you have to do is give me a ring, and we can get together for an hour almost any time.

Juanita 6: You shouldn't feel any responsibility for me; it's my own fault. If I had worked harder for speed when you tried to get me to, maybe I could solve the equations fast enough now. I didn't come to you for extra help on chemistry.

Greene 6: No?

Juanita 7: I want to drop chemistry. It just seems hopeless. I don't doubt that with your help I might get up to passing by the end of the semester, but just passing isn't enough. I'm so far behind now that I could never get a B.

Greene 7: You think you have to have a B, and you don't think you could improve that much?

Juanita 8: No. I have to have an honors record in my major if I'm to have a chance at all of getting a junior year abroad. If I follow my original plan to be a doctor, chemistry will count in my field—that's why I took it. But if I change my major to fine arts or romance languages, I won't need the chemistry and I can drop it.

Greene 8: You want to give up medicine so you can drop chemistry?

Juanita 9: Yes. Well, to tell the truth, I think I've been changing my mind about medicine all summer. I like the idea of helping people, and I do think I would enjoy figuring out what was the matter with someone—putting all the symptoms together to get a diagnosis—but I just can't see myself looking down people's throats or listening to their complaints day after day.

Greene 9: You don't think you would enjoy the actual practice of medicine.

Juanita 10: No. I don't think I'm the right type. Anyway, Dean White said it would be almost impossible for a premed major to get a junior year in Spain. Allegheny College doesn't have a regular arrangement for a junior year abroad, but a few girls who have special reasons, like language or fine arts majors, are sometimes granted one. In fine arts, I might get permission to go to Florence or Rome, but the only way I could be sure of going to Spain is to concentrate in romance languages with emphasis on Spanish.

Greene 10: A junior year in Spain is very important for you?

Juanita 11: Yes, it is. I want it very much.

Greene 11: Going to Spain means more to you than your medical ambitions?

Juanita 12: Yes. Well . . . lots of things seem different to me now than they did a year ago. . . . This spring my Spanish cousin introduced me to a . . . young law student . . . who lives near Madrid. . . . Even when I . . . had my moments . . . at school, as you may have observed, it was nothing like this. I never felt this way about anyone else. It makes me look at everything in a different way somehow. He's very handsome and brilliant. He's only nineteen, but he's fifth in the whole law school. My family likes him, too, very much. They all smile at him so. . . . I think Father and Mother and my aunt and uncle think José and I might make a good match. Of course, they don't dream, they would be shocked, that we are as serious as we are or have talked things over as far as we have. . . . My cousin was very helpful . . . and discreet.

Greene 12: You think they approve of the two of you?

Juanita 13: I think they wouldn't mind. . . . Maybe they'd even encourage us. I've almost talked Mother into going back next summer to be with my aunt and uncle and cousin. She could take the waters again—she didn't begin to get over her illness until we went to the resort near Madrid. That's how José and I really had a chance to get to know each other—his family lives near the hotel there where we stayed.

Greene 13: You feel that both you and your mother would benefit?

Juanita 14: Yes, she's almost given her consent. I've tried to explain to her about the junior year abroad, too, but she isn't so agreeable about that. I could live with my cousin at Madrid, and my aunt and uncle live only thirty-five miles from there. It would cost much less than a year at Allegheny, because prices are so low in American money. My aunt and uncle owe us a debt of hospitality from the time my aunt and cousin stayed with us in Panama for three years during the Civil War. I don't mean that I'd accept money from them, but my uncle is very well-to-do, and they want very much to have me.

Greene 14: You think it would be all right.

Juanita 15: It could all work out beautifully. . . . But it can't happen unless I get honor grades in my major, and I can't get an honor grade now in chemistry, so I want to drop it. Dean White said ordinarily a student can't drop a course just because she is failing it; otherwise, what is the use of having college rules? But in my case, where I am willing to give up the premed course, she said maybe I could drop chemistry if I could find any other course I could begin in place of it this late in the year. If I don't find a fourth course now, I'll have to take five next term, and that will make it still harder to get honor grades. The easiest thing for me to take would be Spanish, of course, and since a freshman ought to have a language, it fits in well. Dean White suggested that I talk to the people in the Spanish Department, and I went to Professor Alvaredo and Professor Cruz. I went in and spoke to them in my best Castilian style, and they were so delighted to have someone who could speak good Spanish, especially a girl, that Professor Cruz accepted me in his Spanish poetry course. That would be very easy for me. I love to read, and I think I've already read many of the works, and the others are things I intend to read anyway. There are only twenty men in the course, and I'd be the only girl. I've been going to the classes, and it's lots of fun.

Greene 15: You are very happy about the Spanish course.

Juanita 16: I was until I told Mother about it. She was terribly upset and made an awful fuss about coming all the way from Panama to the United States to study Spanish, and why didn't I stay in Panama if that was what I wanted, and what would people think at home. . . . We had a . . . well, a fight, frankly, and I left her in tears day before yesterday morning. I have to go see her again tomorrow, and . . . well, I don't know what to do. I don't know for sure if Dean White will let me drop chemistry and take Spanish, and even if she does, I don't know what to do about Mother, or what to do if I don't take Spanish. That's why I've come to you; maybe you can talk to her and get her to see it my way.

Greene 16: You think she doesn't pay as much heed to you as she would to me.

Juanita 17: Yes. If you talk to Mother, I know she will listen to you; she has great respect for your judgment. She hardly listens at all to me. I can't talk to her about things we disagree on. Whenever I do, I say things that hurt her, things that I don't mean, except for the argument, or that she takes in ways that I don't intend. When I argue with Father, he loses his temper too, and we have a row. But we understand each other, we get over it right away, without needing a lot of apologies and carrying hurt feelings for days afterward the way Mother does.

Greene 17: You feel that your mother attaches more importance to an angry word in an argument than your father does, and you can't talk to her freely.

Juanita 18: Yes. She tries to . . . to . . . not quite smother, but . . . maybe . . . hang on to me and is hurt if I don't want to do things her way. She . . . I can't be natural with her. Even when I agree to do what she wants, I don't have to like to do it that way.

Greene 18: She makes some sort of claim or demand on you. . . .

Juanita 19: That's it, she makes me feel guilty if I don't please her. She doesn't understand that I have trouble making up my mind, and when I have to argue it all over again with her, I get excited or angry, and I don't do it convincingly—or politely. . . . That's why I think, if you talk to her, she'll listen to you . . . or if you decide that I ought to do something else . . . I'll know it isn't just Mother upset because I don't speak to her sweetly enough.

Greene 19: You feel that if I made a decision for you, both your mother and you will accept it.

Juanita 20: Yes . . . no. Actually, I know that I have to make up my own mind—no one can do it for me. But [Long pause] actually, Mother ought to be glad, because it means I'm giving up being a doctor, which she never wanted anyway, and taking languages. That's what she's wanted all along, so I could be a language teacher.

Greene 20: You think she should be pleased with your new plan to study Spanish here.

Juanita 21: Um-m-m, well [Long pause], in a way, I suppose it does sound funny to come from Panama and Madrid to study Spanish literature in the United States. That's what Mother teaches at home, you know. . . . But Professor Alvaredo is from the University of Madrid. . . . Of course, he isn't Vasquez, that leading authority on Spanish literature, and I could work with him if I took my junior year in Spain. [Long pause, then laughs.] I suppose coming here from Panama and Spain for Spanish is like . . . carrying coals to Newcastle . . . only the opposite, somehow, I mean. [Pause.] When I think of all the people I've told about my ambition to be a doctor and my choosing Allegheny because it has such good science courses. [Long pause.] It might sound funny to some of Mother's students, too; for instance, the daughter of the cabinet minister. [Long pause.]

Greene 21: You think it might be embarrassing to her.

Juanita 22: Yes . . . I hadn't really thought of it that way. . . . No wonder she was upset. [Long pause.] But what else am I to do? If I don't take Spanish, I'll have to take five courses next term, and that will make it hard to get honor grades, and I might not even be able to drop chemistry. And the Spanish is only a one-semester course; I would be out of it at midyear.

Greene 22: You think there is no way out but for you to take Spanish.

Juanita 23: Yes. . . . I didn't tell you that when Dean White and I were talking about it first, I suggested Italian. I picked up quite a bit when we were in Italy this summer, and I am about as far along as the beginning class is now. I like Italian, and want to learn it. Mother wants me to learn Italian too. But there is a conflict. It comes at the same time as my Social Science 2. Mother suggested that I take French; I've had six years of it and passed the language requirement on my College Board. But when I was in France, I couldn't speak French freely; I was too much afraid of mispronouncing something. I knew too many rules, and the people I was with all expected me to be very good because I'd had so much French.

Greene 23: They made you self-conscious.

Juanita 24: Yes, I didn't want to make mistakes or mispronunciations in front of them. But with Italian, I was just learning, and I didn't mind making mistakes. None of our party knew any more Italian than I did anyway, except Father, who didn't care.

Greene 24: You feel that they expected so much of you that you didn't want to risk making a mistake in French, but you didn't mind making mistakes where they didn't expect anything more of you.

Juanita 25: That's right. I don't like people who expect things of you all the time. That's what Mother does; she acts like a teacher with a backward pupil. Father takes me as I am.

Greene 25: You like your father's way better than your mother's.

Juanita 26: I think maybe that's why I wanted to be a doctor rather than a teacher. . . . I thought it would be nice to work with Father. Going into Father's office sounded all right in Panama, and it seemed perfectly natural for me to want to be a doctor when I was in school here in the United States. But in Spain, when I said I wanted to be a doctor, they were all shocked. It wasn't a respectable occupation for a woman. The Spanish are still very strict and old-fashioned, you know. I'm afraid my American ways disturbed a good many of my uncle's friends. Even José thought it was funny I wanted to be a doctor. His mother thought it was too American.

Greene 26: They made you wonder what they thought about you.

Juanita 27: It frightened me a little to see how differently they thought about things. You wouldn't believe it, but my cousin, who is 21, had never worn a short-sleeved dress in her life until I lent her one of mine. She had never worn a low-necked evening dress until she borrowed one of Mother's, so that all of us could go to a party when we were in Paris. Everybody could tell right away that I had spent a lot of time in the United States. . . . I had to be terribly careful to observe Spanish proprieties and not embarrass my aunt and uncle. American ways are not very popular in Spain, you know, after the way the United States has treated the government. I was glad that I had my cousin with me most of the time. There are so many things nice girls don't do in Spain that can be done in Panama and the United States.

Greene 27: You weren't quite sure just where you were with them.

Juanita 28: I'm not used to deferring to men the way the Spanish women do. . . . The way my uncle ignored my aunt, and the way he treated my cousin! . . . They must have been surprised at Father and me. . . . José was very nice, but even he remarked how different I was.

Greene 28: You aren't accustomed to the Spanish attitudes toward women.

Juanita 29: No, I'm not, and I'm not sure I can get used to the way the women are restricted there. I don't know how I'd feel if José treated me the way other Spanish men treat their wives. I might get used to it if I lived there for a while; I might find that it didn't bother me.

Greene 29: But you worry about it just the same.

Juanita 30: Yes. Actually, I've spent so many years in the United States, I'm more American than Panamanian. And American girls are pretty much the equals of boys. Panama seems strict and old-fashioned when I go home, but Spain is much stricter than that; the women are really kept in a subordinate position. I'm so used to the freedom American girls have, and of course Father and Mother are very liberal, I'm not sure I'd fit in a Spanish family. José is very nice and treated me more politely than an American boy would. But after all, he's an only son and has been brought up in the atmosphere of "the man first."

Greene 30: No matter how polite he is, he may expect you to act like a Spanish woman.

Juanita 31: Yes; besides, he's never been out of Spain, and he doesn't know what it's really like outside, and he may not like my independent ways. He was really surprised to see how Father and I argued about things. Spanish daughters aren't supposed to argue; they say "Yes, papa," and try to get their way by coaxing. That's the way my cousin does it. She asks for something, her father says "No!" in a big voice, Maria says "Yes, papa," meekly and cheerfully. Then in a day or so her mother and father say to each other, "See how cheerfully the poor child is taking it. What an obedient child she is! She should have a reward," and generally they let her do what she asked in the first place. I could never work things like that; it makes me feel funny to see Maria have to do it.

Greene 31: You don't think you could manage to do things by indirection the way Maria does.

Juanita 32: I'm not sure I'd want to if I could. I don't like it. Oh, dear, I didn't realize it was so late. I'm afraid I'll have to hurry to get to class on time.

Mr. Greene assured Juanita he would be glad to talk to her any time, and she promised to get in touch with him within a few days.

Robin Scott

Robin Scott is a corporate attorney for a wholly owned subsidiary of a large Philadelphia corporation. As a long-standing, although not intimate, friend of the casewriter, Robin consented to what was described to her as a "free-wheeling" interview–actually more of a forum for allowing her to talk about some of her chief concerns, opinions, and experiences.

The following interview took place on a workday evening at Robin's suburban Philadelphia apartment.

Casewriter: OK, where I guess I'd like to start is, is there anything on your mind currently, any current issue or concern that you'd like to talk about?

Robin: Well, I guess the basic concerns that I have relate to my job and to the milieu that I live in, and at the moment I'm interested in three major things—my job, my personal life—probably I should reverse that order [Both laugh]—and the First Women's Bank of Philadelphia, which is sort of my major outside activity at the moment. I'm currently active in the bank's formation.

Maybe what I'd really be most interested in talking about is how my life interreacts with my job. Why don't we start with my actual job, and save my personal life for later! Maybe we'll never *get* to my personal life . . . if I'm lucky! [Both laugh.]

C: Sounds fine to me.

R: My job is really interesting. I love it. It's a very dynamic job, and it's not set into any pattern or any mold. It turns out differently every day. It's very *difficult,* because I'm the first woman there who has any kind of authority or any interaction with high-level management. Physically, my office is located with the president's office, the three senior vice-presidents, the assistant general counsel . . . and myself. We're the only people who are located there.

This case was prepared by Luise Cahill Dittrich under the direction of Michael B. McCaskey as a basis for class discussion. The names of people have been disguised.

There's one empty office, which rotates among the vice-presidents. It's a very interesting situation [Laughter], because here *I* am—twenty years younger than anybody else in the office, the only woman to work with them on a professional basis. They have four secretaries in the secretarial pool, and then all the upper-level muggglediwumps! . . . the big brass. The rest of the people in the company are located about eight miles away, in what has until recently been relatively very *poor* working conditions. Whereas I'm located in, you know, a large downtown office building . . . which is considered by some to be plush, and by others who know and love it [Laughter] to be hideous!

I report directly to a person who has been with the company for only two weeks, whom I have helped to bring into the company. Since I'm an attorney, he's also an attorney, but he had been practicing with a firm for five and a half years before he came, and brings with him some background in general corporate law, but not in our particular corporation, which is highly regulated and very different from a lot of other corporations. So I work a lot with one attorney in the holding company. And I also report sort of indirectly, because of the physical location of my office, to the senior vice-president, who is both chief legal and chief financial officer. And then, I often do work for our chief operations officer, which is really a *physical* operation, determining how we deal with our product. But it's a *really* interesting job.

C: So what does this kind of structure mean . . . with regard to you?

R: Maybe I should start out with how I entered this corporation, and what I felt on entry. I entered directly from law school. It was very strange, I had one interview with Bill, the senior vice-president, and then he called me back and asked me to meet with him for lunch with two of the attorneys from the holding company. And so I went, and it was at the Engineers' Club, and it was very nice. And about three-quarters of the way through the luncheon, one of them said to me, "What have you been doing since you graduated from law school?" And I said, "I'm still *in* law school, and this would be interviewing for my first job out of law school." And he said, "Oh, we didn't have a copy of your résumé." At the time, I guessed my résumé just hadn't been distributed. In fact, Bill had deliberately withheld my résumé from them, because he wanted to hire me and they had never hired anyone straight out of law school. That was difficult for the people in the holding company to grasp at first. He had wanted them to meet me first and judge me, and *then* judge what came behind me on my résumé. I really didn't grasp that until I had left that interview and tried to run through in my mind just *why* they hadn't been informed of what my background was, and *why* they had come to this meeting cold. It was a very strange . . . position for me to have been put in. At any rate, the interview went moderately well after that, after they got over their initial shock [Laughter] and didn't faint. Then about two days later, Bill called me and said, "We'd very much like to hire you. Will you come down and have lunch again?" and so I went down, and he told me about the whole thing. And there were several questions that I wanted to ask him, you know, like salaries and vacations and stuff like that. And although I'm not married, I said to him, "Just out of curiosity, what *is* the maternity-leave program of the company?" And he said, "To tell you the truth, I don't know, but I will find out for you." Now, at that point we were acquiring three other, smaller companies, so there was a long period of time when I didn't hear from him because he was very busy with this acquisition. So finally, it was before Christmas, and I was about ready to leave the state for a vacation, and I called him and said, "I've decided I'd like very much to come to work for you." And he said, "Well, thank you very much for calling, I really appreciate it. I'm sorry I haven't had a chance to write you about everything that we had said and put it all in writing for you as you had requested, but, you know, I've been on the go, and moreover, I haven't yet been able to find out what our maternity-leave policy is." [Laughter.]

So . . . I just . . . it was physically impossible for him to find out, apparently, which is hysterical. So I came to work for the company. I found out why he couldn't find out what the maternity-leave policy was, because it was in a state of transition at the time. And you'll be pleased to know that I am now on the third draft of the maternity-leave policy. [Laughter.] . . . It's sitting right on my desk to do again. Bill felt an obligation to keep me informed on what was happening on the maternity-leave policy, so it became an in-joke between us. And then I started to push some things. I said, "You know, really, this ought to change," and "Really, the law *is* moving in this direction, and we ought to start doing . . . some . . . first of all, we're obligated to give the time off, and don't you really think that we ought to put all these people into the sick plan, so that payment happens for maternity?" My boss had no trouble with that philosophically. And the senior vice-president of what we euphemistically call "Relations" [Laughter]—Customer Relations and Personnel and Industrial Relations, Labor Relations—*he* agrees with me philosophically.

The problem is the lower level. In my company, there is a real bureaucracy. It's the kind of company with people right out of high school, and maybe even not having finished high school . . . they go to work and sometimes they rise up through the ranks. And Personnel happens to be one of those areas. It's *very,* very difficult working with some of these people, who are, again, male, and, again, in their mid-50s. And they have, in fact, worked with some young women, but never in a professional relationship, and never where they have to, in effect, account to *me* on some of these things; you know, on, "Why haven't you instituted the policy that I wrote?" or "What are the problems? Let's see if we can deal with these intellectually, and not . . . and not emotionally, as they are sometimes dealt with." It's very difficult for them, and it takes an extreme amount of patience from me.

The kind of a thing that I do is, set a morning aside. They come in, and we go through the whole thing and get a new oral understanding of what the policy should be, or is. It's a give and take, and I make a conscious effort to *give* them some points—you know, to say, "That is a *very good point,* let's see how we can address that." And I *have* to work that way. It's much too much politicking for my way of doing things. But you know, eventually, some of the—well, "more intellectually" is a poor way of putting it . . . but some of them have an ability to grasp what I'm saying faster than others, and to grasp it on a theoretical basis and not on a practical basis. Anyway, we were talking about how I came to the company. Right, so that was fine. I had the job in December, and I graduated the following May. I took the bar exam in the last day of July and the first of August, and went to work September third. Great. Now, those of us who are in the major office building are on the 38th floor, and the only way to go between it and the holding company is to go down to the first and up to the 15th.

C: Oh, no!

R: And then if you want to leave, you go down to the bottom and up to the 38th—*or* you take the freight elevator [Laughter], which is a real trip in and of itself, because you get on the freight elevator and . . . well . . .

C: Good luck!

R: Oh, I don't mind! The workmen who are there are always very nice and very kind, and I always carry a sharp pencil with me and it's very evident, so I don't ever have any trouble. The only trouble I have is with the *executives* riding, who sit there and harangue me about why I shouldn't be riding in the freight elevator [Laughter]. I just get so annoyed. I was so embarrassed once—oh! . . .

C: What happened?

R: Oh, we were in—I guess we were on the 15th floor and we were going up to the eating club for lunch. So I was with three executives, when an executive from another company got on the freight elevator and spent the entire ride telling me why I should not be riding the elevator. And every time he said something, I would just say, "Thank you for your concern, I appreciate it." He'd say something else, and I'd say, "Thank you for your concern, I really appreciate it, but I'm fine." And I was just so embarrassed by the time I got to the eating club that . . . you know, to have done that was just ridiculous, and then to have done it in front of other people was silly. I was really embarrassed. And *mad.* [Laughter.] Maybe . . . I guess "embarrassment" *is* the right word. I was embarrassed to be singled out, I guess, and it happened because I was a young woman riding—*he* thought alone—on the freight elevator. He felt compelled to, I guess, take care of me, or to tell me that I was doing something wrong. He didn't think that I had the power to think myself, and to evaluate the situation, but he decided instead that he knew better, and that he would tell me so. And rather than tell him off, which I didn't feel like doing—and I generally would *not* do because that's just . . . the way I happen to be—I felt the best way to handle it was just to thank him for his concern and just to try and shut him up. But it didn't work. The man was just simply *stupid*! I was *so* annoyed.

Well, back to the 15th and 38th floors. All right, so . . . at first I was physically placed on the 15th floor, which if you remember is where the holding company is, and not where the company that I was working for is. And there was good reason for that. I was there for two weeks, and my boss Bill, who was the only other attorney who dealt with corporate matters, left for 13 weeks for an advanced management program [Laughter], which left me in a very unusual situation! I was the only attorney in the company who did corporate law. I had been there for two weeks. I had *no* background, *no* experience, and I was located 23 floors below the executives. It's called a little "trial by fire, see if you can survive." At the same time, we were making an offering, and so there were whole batches of SEC documents to be done . . . which required background information about the company . . . that was really hard to know! [Laughter.] And I also had to deal a lot with the holding-company attorneys, who were really—because my boss was gone—executing the SEC papers.

It was a very difficult situation, for two reasons. First of all, the two people who are attorneys in the holding company are relatively cold people . . . uh, you know, they wouldn't come in and volunteer anything. It was always, I had to go and find someone who I felt I could ask. When I was smart enough to think that there might be a problem and that I really should ask a question, and that's very difficult to know . . . you know, sometimes you go along the path and you think you've got all the corners covered, but in fact you don't, because there was a corner that you didn't even know existed . . . or there's a background history on a point, you know, that's four years in the making, and you've only been there a week! [Laughter.] You've no way of knowing even that that history exists. But as I was saying, the two attorneys are relatively cold people, and the kind of people who you don't want to go into their office and ask a question. First of all, they have physically imposing offices, they're big . . . and I'm little! [Laughter.] A lot of furniture . . . and you walk in the door—you know, how do you approach someone and ask them the kind of questions that obviously seem so rudimentary to them? But I just had no place to go to *ask* where I should go look for the answers. . . . You know, I'd say to them, "Is there a book on this subject that I can read?" and the answer in every case was, "No, there isn't."

But I *did* pick up the agency work as a sort of a specialty and they came to rely on me for the agency work. And that was very good for me because it gave me a relatively limited area to become proficient in, and with about two weeks of reading everything you can get your hands on, you can become moderately proficient in the way an agency operates. And therefore, I was able to provide the background information for the registrations that were going on at the time in that very limited area. But they *had* to come to me to ask me about those areas, because they didn't spend the time doing it. And the outside financial people who were involved with the registration had to come to me to ask me the questions, too. So I gained a *little* bit of credence during the period and a *little* bit of knowledge, and . . . that was very good.

The other thing they did to me was, they said, "Here are all the papers from the transaction that went on in December when we acquired the three small companies. Would you please go through them and see what is necessary and what should go where and what needs to be kept." And that was interesting because you got a background on *those* companies, as well as *some* dealing with some of the lower-level people in the company, which was frustrating [Laughter]. . . . "Interesting" is *not* a good word. Um, "frustrating" is a very good one. . . . I guess frustration at being ignored is the *real* problem, and I really haven't even yet been able to determine why. I *think* that it is *not* that I'm a woman, or *not* that I'm young . . . but rather that I am an authority figure from a different area of the company—from the *legal* area, which is like saying . . . well, when you have to go to the legal department—loosely speaking, "department" [Laughter]—it's just the worst thing that could ever happen.

C: So there you were, two weeks along.

R: And he leaves for 13 weeks! And here I am dealing with these people. I had two problems. First, I had the problem of the secretaries. And then I had the problem of the executives. The problems with the secretaries were relatively interesting. I am a very friendly-type person—you know, I'll go up and ask them a question, or make a comment, or try to speak to them every day that I saw them. But *they* never went out of their way to help me—never, ever, ever, ever. You know, I would always have to go and ask the question—like, finding the ladies' room . . . um, no one came in and said, "This is like this, and you ought to do this." And in the holding company at that point, there were maybe four other women who had jobs other than secretarial or bookkeeping or keypunching. You know, one of them was an assistant to the treasurer, and one of them was a librarian. . . . So there were maybe four of us—three of us in the same age category, mid-20s, and another about 38. It's . . . very difficult not to have a . . . not to have someone to confide in, not to have a role model—very, very difficult. I had a considerably different life-style from either the librarian or the other women my age. And as a professional woman, I felt that I should . . . I guess that's most noticeable in the clothing that I wear to work. They both wore whatever happened to jump out of the closet at them in the morning, whereas I always tried to look . . . what I term "professional." . . . That's a poor word, but I think maybe it conveys the idea. And the woman who was the assistant to the treasurer at that point almost did the same thing as the younger women . . . but . . . because of our relationship or happenstance of placement within this corporation, we have come to know each other a little bit better than . . . And it *is* true that I think the holding company needed to say they had a woman with a title, and she was handy. You know, it's the same reason that *I* was hired. My boss had a conviction to do it. They needed to have a woman *somewhere* who had some responsibility, which is why I was hired—which is why I was hired right out of law school, because they didn't have anyone in the ranks they could call on. . . . But I accept that, and . . . obviously in some ways it was good for me. You know, I got the job! As opposed to not getting the job. But on the other hand, you know, I do realize it, and sometimes more than others.

C: Robin, you were talking about having a difficult time with the secretaries and with the executives. Can you explain . . . *why* you had a hard time with the secretaries? What was going on there?

R: I spent some time at the time trying to analyze what was going on, and I'm not sure that it's clear in my brain now . . . but. . . . My office was physically located—again, rather unusually—with all the *big* guys! On the other three-quarters of the floor were people of considerably lesser rank. But here I was, physically located in this office, which was with all of these big people—you know, the president, the treasurer, the general counsel, and the executive vice-president. [Laughter.] Therefore, their secretaries had worked hard for the positions that they had and, within their bureaucracy, were very highly respected because they had higher jobs. And here I walk into this situation where I'm young, I'm a woman, and I have a better job than they do. But they have *achieved* in *their* profession. Very, very difficult for them to accept . . . and, you know, to look at me and to accept me. I even *look* younger than I am. And that's *very* difficult. I sensed at the time that that was one of the problems. Now there is a young guy in the office where I am now. I don't think he has the same problem. Another problem was that I didn't have my own secretary, so I didn't have someonc to work within *their* hierarchy for *me.* It had to be just me. The fact that I didn't have my own secretary also caused me to have to ask other people to do my work . . . and so there I'm in a problem again—you know, how do you go beg to have someone type for you? Now the people who handle the secretaries *thought* they knew where I was supposed to go, but obviously the people to whom I was supposed to hand my work, and ask them kindly if they would type it, had their own bosses that they had to work for, too! So on a priority schedule, mine had to be *way* down at the bottom, and I had to shop around for a secretary. So, there were all those problems rolled up into one, none of them making a very happy situation with the secretaries.

C: How'd you fix that?

R: I don't know if you can ever fix that situation, where there are whole batches of problems to deal with. What I *did* was, I put our relationships on a very familiar plane. You know, I'd ask them about how their families were doing, or something like that. I tried to be very personal with them, so that they *couldn't* treat me callously. And that was a conscious decision, and I'm sorry that it had to be, because that's the way I prefer to be normally, and that's the way I try to be. But I did have to make the conscious decision to go further than I normally would have gone. And I sort of confided in one or two key people among the secretaries and said, "Gee, I'm having a hard time getting my work done," and things like that. And I was therefore able to have them offer to help *me,* and by doing that get them on my side, or them *thinking* they were on my side, and that worked to some extent. And it was a tactic that I used when my office was moved up to the 38th floor—um, to put relationships with the secretaries on a very informal basis, which, as I say, is the way I would prefer to be anyway.

All right, now with the guys [Laughter], I dealt mainly with the two attorneys in the holding company. And, as I say, both of them are very impersonal people. One I dealt with a whole lot, and one I dealt with very little. The senior of the two, very little. But of the two, I judged him to be more personal, and so when I had a particular problem of whether or not an interview I had granted to someone would breach the attorneys' code of ethics, he was the one that I chose to go to to ask that question. And he did treat me . . . more humanely than I thought the other one would have on that topic. Some people are just that way, and I felt that, balancing the two, I was better off asking the general counsel. Even now—and I've been with the company more than one year, and I deal quite often with Paul, the assistant general counsel—but even now our relationship is mostly business . . . in fact, it's almost always *exclusively* business. Maybe just once or twice have we ever joked or laughed about something, or said something that wasn't totally business. We both happen to be very busy. On the other hand, he hasn't accepted me, even yet. And I don't know that he ever will. I can't yet analyze *why* he hasn't accepted me. I can't tell if he thinks that I have it too easy, coming straight into the corporation and not doing as he did, which is spend several years "apprenticing" with a large law firm. I don't know if it's a matter of proving myself or if it's just the way he is. I keep thinking that it must be a matter of proving myself, and that I just haven't done it yet. On the other hand, he has never criticized any of my work.

C: Why do you feel . . . why do you choose to take that view?

R: Because it gives me hope. You know, it makes me think that at some point he *will* accept everything that I do. And because of the glimmers of the joke every once in a while. Or the fact that he told me that it was his son who had done the linoleum block print, and I had said, "Oh, you know, that just brings back my youth, when *I* did those." And I said, "But, if you print that, the number on the sailboat is backwards." And he said, "Oh, yeah, that would be just like something *I* would do," and we both laughed at that kind of a comment. And that was as personal as I ever got, except once when I asked him where he got his belt buckle [Laughter], which is really handsome. But that kind of informal thing . . . rarely happens.

And then there's one other thing. We deal with the banks a lot, and in the course of that, I write a lot of opinions for people to sign, because they have to be in a very given form and very legalistic, and every comma has to be in the right place and that kind of thing, which is often what a lawyer's job is. And the substance of these documents that I prepare is attested to by different people. One of these documents Paul attests. And I have a thing, that women *are* in business and ought to be *recognized.* And so, on what is called the "greeting" of a business letter, I always put "Ladies and Gentlemen," rather than just "Gentlemen," which is the way our corporation had always started their letters. And I . . . I like to use humor in the way I deal with people. And it has become a joke among many people that letters from me always go out "Ladies and Gentlemen," and letters *to* me have almost always come *back,* "Ladies and Gentlemen." Sometimes, I'll go through this long legal analysis of a document, and I'll say, "Now the *most* important thing that's wrong is . . . this 'his' has to be changed to 'person,' " or, "this 'Gentlemen' has to be 'Ladies and Gentlemen.' " And I make a little joke out of it, but my feeling is there and they recognize my feeling is there. And I think they appreciate that I've done it with humor, rather than said, "This *has to be changed*!" At any rate, the people that I deal with on the outside, as well as on the inside, get a little chuckle out of this, so, you know, here I am with my little idiosyncrasy.

All right, now we're back to Paul, the assistant general counsel of the holding company, who attests to one of the documents. So I have it all typed up and it says "Ladies and Gentlemen" at the top. He gets it, has it retyped with "Gentlemen" at the top, signs it, and sends it up. This has been going on now for over a year. And it's a little thing that we have. And we both recognize it as a little thing, and I *clearly* have my principle and have so stated to him. And he is trying to have his principle, but he hasn't yet had the courage to state it to *me.* Now he has stated it to his secretary, and said, " 'Gentlemen' is the way business letters begin!" And I've said, "I don't care! If I'm preparing them, they're going to come out the way I'm preparing them, and that's 'Ladies and Gentlemen.' " So. The last time this happened, I sent down the draft to be signed. He had it typed over—now this is two documents together—going to two separate banks. He typed them over, and sent them back . . . signed. Right? So, it's the *last possible* day because of all sorts of other transactions, not my fault that we're on the last day of this particular deadline for filing. I read over the first one, and instead of "$500,000," the secretary has typed in "$5,000,000." So I call him up on the phone and say, "Paul, I have to take the document over to the bank, and you have two choices. Either you can sign the one I had originally typed for you, which says 'Ladies and Gentlemen,' or you can have your person retype it and wait to sign it." Now I knew that he had an appointment he had to go to. So he kind of groaned, "OHH, bring down the other one." Later, I got a phone call from the attorney from the bank on the *second* document, and he pointed out to me—now, he's a real nitpicker—that his punctuation changes hadn't been made. Paul had had it retyped from the original *draft,* which didn't have the final typing corrections which I had taken over the phone from this bank attorney. And when the document that the attorney gets did *not* have the corrections, he spent five minutes on the phone giving me grief. So I promptly hung up the phone, dialed Paul, and said, "I am giving you five minutes worth of grief, because I just *took* five minutes worth of grief! [Laughter.] Because of your stupid typing job . . . changing 'Ladies and Gentlemen' to 'Gentlemen.' And here's what's wrong with it!" [Laughter.] And he laughed at the end, and said, "Is my five minutes up?" And I said, "Not quite!" [Laughter.] I was so *annoyed*! So now we'll see what happens, because I have not had to do a filing for him since then. But you can bet, darn right, it's going to him "Ladies and Gentlemen," and I'm *dying* to see what he does, because I'm sure his secretary must be *super* annoyed at him at this point, having to retype everything that's perfectly done. And I keep telling her, "Now listen, Susan, you just tell him you're not going to do it, that it's a silly waste of time." [Laughter.] But they're not going to go out any differently. Anyway, that, as I say, has become a sort of a thing. On the other hand, I have a principle, and I'm not about ready to change it. All the secretaries who type for me know that. Liberation in the business world! [Laughter.] And, you know, the president of the company often has to sign the things that I have drafted and typed for him. And he always has a chuckle out of that, too.

C: But he agrees with it?

R: Well, he certainly doesn't have it retyped! [Laughter.] He just gets a chuckle, and sometimes he comments. I have also neutered everything, and people are really funny about how I do that, and they always laugh. I usually make a point of doing it, actually. It's sort of my statement in the business world, that things come out of my office in neuter form, rather than male or female form. They come out with the word "person" instead of "his," even if I have to change a whole sentence. I suppose it's a silly thing to be concerned about, but when you have a principle, you have a principle! I feel moderately strongly about it. I wouldn't say I feel exceedingly strongly about it. It's just the way it's going to be done. [Laughter.]

So, I was talking about dealing with these people. As I say, I don't know if I will *ever* be able to prove myself with Paul, but I like to think I *will* be able to. I don't know what the turning point is going to be, or if it's ever going to come, or how many years down the road it is, but maybe, just maybe. [Laughter.] I'm sure originally he thought I was probably incompetent. I don't know whether that was my lack of background or anything else, and as I say, he's never criticized anything I've done—other than "Ladies and Gentlemen" [Laughter]—in terms of substance. There's never any question that what I do isn't just right. On the other hand, I think anybody makes . . . or attempts to do that with their work. I don't know if I feel that more than anyone else, but I feel very *strongly* that in *everything* you do your best.

Now, after 13 weeks, my boss returns . . . from the dead! [Laughter.]

So he returns, and they physically move my office from the 15th floor to the 38th. I think in order to be with him, more than anything else. Secondarily, to be with other people in the same company! Which is a good way to start off! He had put me down on the 15th floor because there would be more people around, and because I'd be closer to the two attorneys in the holding company. Now I'm up on the real floor [Laughter]. As I say, there's the president, three senior vice-presidents, and myself for the next . . . over a year. The president is similar to the general counsel of the holding company. He's . . . well . . . very, very difficult to describe. A bit of a façade. I don't know if that's created in my mind because he's the president, or if that's just the way he is. I can't differentiate between those two, but he's a little difficult to approach, although quite personable when you *do* approach him.

Then the three senior vice-presidents are all very, very different. The one in charge of Relations is very, very personable, self-made, and has, because of his job, more women underneath him. But I am, *again,* the only one he's worked with on a professional basis. But he is very easy to deal with, there's no problem at all about that. Now the senior vice-president in charge of Operations is a very, very nice guy, and gets a *kick* out of me. He has a son who is a little older than I am, and he just gets a boot out of seeing me *there* in that corporation! [Laughter.] But it's sort of hard to articulate this . . . well, let me start this way. . . . I, as I say, use humor, and like to create a happy mood among people, and so I joke or, you know, just say funny-type things to people and keep it on a very friendly level. In return, he has felt free to kid me, and to joke a little bit about the fact that I'm a woman, and a professional, and how I don't fit his concept of what a woman should be doing. Now it's all well and good, but it's been over a year! [Laughter.] He jokes about the fact that I hail a cab when he's there. And he doesn't tell it once, he tells it *twenty-five times,* to twenty-five different people. He gets a great boot out of doing that. I take it with a grain of salt and sort of laugh, and I understand why he's having a good time telling the story. On the other hand, I'm a little tired! [Laughter.] We have done some traveling together, to Washington, where several of our regulatory agencies are, and obviously he'd *never* traveled with a woman who wasn't his wife before. And what's worse is that sometimes, the reservation will come in under "Mrs." Or in the Engineers' Club, where he happens to be a member, if a secretary makes a reservation in *my* name, it's often written as "Mrs." with *his* name after it. He and I just joke about it because it's just silly. But he just doesn't stop there, he keeps going, and again, it's very difficult to understand if that's his personality and he would do that to anyone in that situation, or if it's just my particular situation. And I really think of it as *my* particular situation because I am so different from anyone else that he deals with. Any time he sees someone, it's something new to talk about. . . . Maybe it's irrational for me to be reacting this way, but. . . . And I would *never* tell him, *never,* ever tell him, because he's too kind a person, and I would never want to tell him that kind of thing, but I also don't know how I'm going to stop it. An incident might have happened eight or nine months ago and he's still talking about it!

But you know, the reason I think that it's not just him is that the same thing has happened in another instance. I was traveling with an executive of another corporation in Washington. I happened to know the Washington restaurants better than he did, and so I chose the restaurant. We had a cocktail in the hotel first, and we walked into the lounge, and there was a table for four vacant, and a small couch, what they call a "love seat." The guy who was sitting on the love seat got up and moved to the table for four, and said, "Here, you two can have this." I didn't say a word, didn't say anything—what do you say? Just ignore it and sit down. A little later I left the room to call to make a reservation. I came back in on what amounted to the end of the conversation between the gentleman I was with and the gentleman who had left the love seat. And all I heard was, "No, *she's* the attorney and I'm the client." So they had been talking about the whole relationship, apparently. I later understood how this had happened, because we then left the cocktail lounge and walked to the restaurant. We got there, and I ordered the wine because he said, "Do you happen to know anything about wines?" and I said, "Yeah, I do." There was an excellent wine available, so I ordered it. And he ordered a very extravagant dessert, which caused the people next to us, who were maybe twelve inches away from us, to look over and ask him, "What *is* that?" They had been waiting, apparently, to try and find some entry into our conversation. It's very interesting to see this happen, because at that table and the table beyond it also, *and* the table on our right—we all sort of got talking about his dessert and what it was. It was a charlotte, with lots of whipped cream and berries—this huge mound in front of him! And someone asked, not what our relationship was . . . asked, I think, "What are you doing in Washington?" Somehow it had come out that we were from out of town or something. Which caused *him* to initiate the whole thing about, "Oh, no, *she's* the attorney and *I'm* the client. Oh, no, we're here on legal business." And he just got a big, huge laugh out of everybody's reaction to that. People two tables down had said to *me,* "What are you doing here in Washington?" And I said, "I'm on a business trip." They said, "Oh, really??!!" as if it was *inconceivable* to them that I was on a business trip with this man who was too young to be my father, but definitely was older than I was [Laughter] by, like, fifteen years. The whole thing was so strange!

I have an attitude about life that when something happens like that, I feel like laughing. At that point it was a bit *with* them, and a bit *at* them. Really, inside me, it was *at* them. At any rate, this is the same reaction I have to the senior vice-president of Operations.

C: They think it's cute or something?

R: Yes. I think if I were a young *man,* he would make jokes about my age. But . . . in fact, what he does do is make jokes about my not fitting into his concept of the role I should have, his concept of his wife's role. I think that's really what's accurate, you know, how he treats *her.* It's different from how he treats *me,* and it's also different from how he treats his secretary. But, as I say, he's a very affable person. It's very difficult to get annoyed at him. And he's too kind to ever get mad at, but it's nevertheless something that I sense. It's a little bit of, "You're different." In fact, it's a *lot* of, "You're different." [Laughter.]

All right, so there are these three senior vice-presidents and the president, and I deal mostly with them, and here I am physically *located* with them, and now, what are the people who are eight miles away, in slummy conditions, thinking about me? Well [Laughter], I can tell you! Not real pleased! You know, I'm in contact with them all the time. They're as much my clients as anyone else is. For instance, if it's a contract that one of them is working on, they have to come to me for approval of the contract. Their physical job location is just really, really poor. And here I am in the big building downtown, in what appears to be very nice conditions . . . with the big brass. I'm younger than most of them back there, and I certainly must *look* as if I have a very unique position. Now, couple that with the fact that attorneys are an anathema, and you really have a *great* combination, I must admit! [Laughter.] If ever a problem walked into a room, it's me! [Laughter.] I must say, it's very interesting to see how people react to this. Um . . . some of them do their best not to deal with me. I haven't found anyone intentionally zapping me, but I have found people *ignoring* me. Again, I'm not sure how much of that is "lawyer" problems, as opposed to "young woman executive" problems. But it's . . . it's very difficult. Part of the problem is that Bill is, to me, very personable, but he can be a little callous in the way he treats people. He doesn't couch his suggestions or criticisms very well . . . so that people react to what he says sort of negatively. And he's relatively new to the company—like, five years—and didn't come up through the hierarchy as the other two senior vice-presidents and the president did, and he does not have a very good reputation as a human being within the company. You know, he's sort of . . . "the great thing!" [Laughter.] And working for him doesn't help any! I'm doing the same kind of work, so I must be equally bad. Plus, what am I doing at that age, over there? Very difficult, *very,* very difficult. And it calls for a lot more politicking on my part than I should have to do. A lot more.

C: So, if you were going to sort of summarize your assimilation into the business world . . . what has it felt like, this first year?

R: OK, I think I have to differentiate between "within" the company and "without" the company. "Within" the company, it's been a very slow, pedantic . . . uh . . . march forward—I *hope,* forward [Laughter] . . . I keep *telling* myself forward—um . . . to have other people gain two things. First, confidence in my ability, which I feel I've had all along. Um, I made it to the position that I'm in, not through a lack of diligence . . . I worked *hard*! [Laughter.] And I feel that I'm capable of doing the job that I'm doing professionally. The other point is their acceptance of me in my position, and that is on a more human level. And I think that that is what I have found *most* difficult, because, in fact, I have no role model. Absolutely none. In either the holding company or my corporation . . . or *any other corporation* I *deal* with. Now, my corporation is such that there are a lot of engineers, and the engineering field has not been open to women for that long. Therefore, they haven't dealt with a lot of women. So they don't know how to react, and they think about it before they react, which is so totally different from spontaneous reaction, the way everyone *else* is treated. And I can see it happen. . . . Maybe I'm too sensitive to it, but nevertheless, I can see it happen. And it would be *so* much easier if there was a *role* model, but there's just none! Nowhere! [Laughter.] It's not . . . not to be!

OK. Now "without" the company is totally different. The people that I deal with outside the company are basically of two kinds. Either they're in a federal or state agency, or they're an attorney. And here, things are on a very professional level. Now, not to pat my profession on the back, but . . . [Laughter] there have been a few women around, and enough *young* women around . . . to have it still be a little bit unusual, but not *so* unusual to be dealing with me. And lawyers have *learned,* you know, they've been educated. *I* don't have to do the education of them. They have learned how to deal with people like me. Therefore, they don't have to *think* about dealing with me. They don't have to think about what their role model should be and make trials and errors along the way. . . . They've already made those errors. So they know how to deal with me on a professional basis. And, as I say, I do my job competently, so we never have any question about that. And we just *deal* on a professional basis. You don't have to go through the constant testing, or the constant initial testing of, "What should I do? What's this like? How will she react to this? If I use a swear word, what will happen? Will she faint? Will she drop through the chair?"

C: "Will she have a martini at lunch?"

R: Something like that, yeah! So outside, it *hasn't been* a march, a crusade. . . . It's just been more normal reaction and normal working conditions—at least, what *I* perceive as normal. *Now* I'm faced with the problem that I'm young, working in a professional community that is considerably older, because I often work with outside counsel to other corporations. And those are always the large downtown attorneys—not the people who are within ten years of my age category—because of my position, which is *very* unusual in the legal sense. I have more legal responsibility, as my boss says, then anyone within ten years of me, anywhere in Philadelphia. So this is a different problem, dealing with them. It's not really a *problem,* it's just that I think they look at me as being very strange to have this much—for lack of a better word—power. Maybe "authority" would be a better word. So I'm the youngest one in a room, but they have learned to deal with that, and I *think* it's because I've been able to act professionally and competently when I'm with them. But they've generally been just great, exceedingly *kind.* And interestingly, I was most fearful of them when I initially thought about going to my job, and tried to pick out the problems. As you go into *any* situation, I think you try and pick out where the problem areas will be. In fact, it hasn't turned out that way. It's much easier to deal on a professional basis with those people, but then I have an advantage because I have a profession, so I can fit in that "club" easily. Moderately easily, anyway. Again, the difficulty comes in dealing in the age gap, the authority gap . . . um, "How did you get where you are?" But *that* has basically stopped, because I deal perpetually with these people and I think they have seen that I'm competent, so we've gone through the trial on it. I hope. [Laughter.]

So you say, how has my first year been? It's been different in different areas. In some cases it's been a matter of having proven myself and now I can continue, and in other cases it's been a matter of continually proving myself. What I think is most interesting is that I've had the least problem with the *big* executives, and the *most* problems with the people who are in the bureaucracy. I don't know whether or not that's because the upper echelon is more highly educated and therefore can intellectualize what they're feeling and say, "Now that's a wrong thing to feel . . . I should feel *this* way." Whereas the bureaucracy-type person is not doing that stuff, he's just reacting . . . not thinking about how he's reacting. I'm really not sure, but it is clearly true that I have had the least problems with the bigwigs.

C: How does your professional life, and your professional growth, influence your personal life?

R: As I said, what I try and do is deal with people on a personal plane. I have found that that is the best way of doing things for *me,* for the way *I* am as a person, and for the things that I'm trying to achieve personally in my job. I'm single, and I'm young, and I'm a woman, and in today's sexual mores I think that means to *some* of these people I should be sleeping around the corporation, or doing something like that. This does not happen to be the way I am. So how do I *handle* this? First of all, I think they have a hard time thinking that of me as they look at me, because . . . um . . . personality-wise, I'm not the seductress by *any* manner or means. I'm much more gregarious than I am reserved or anything, which is what I think of as a seductress, which is my *own* hang-up. [Laughter.] At any rate, the problem is still there. I don't know whether all of it's in my brain, or in other people's brains, but sometimes I perceive it, and sometimes I just think that it *might* be there, and so I handle it always the same way. It's a conscious decision, and it's an easy decision for me, because I have a friend of very long standing, who I'm very close to. We do a lot of things together, and whenever I'm in a social context, I'm always with him. And I am very conscious of drawing our activities together into conversation at some point, so I say, "*We* did something," or "Kevin and I did something," and let them ask me, "Oh, who's that?" so that *they* find out there is a special person, which, I think, makes them think I'm not available. I think that's a protective mechanism on my part, but it's a very easy protective mechanism, and I'm lucky to have it. I have often thought, you know—for instance, when I've been in a social situation where he's not around—how lucky I am that he's there behind me, you know, to stand with me, so to speak. And how difficult it would be for someone trying to deal in my situation without having that protection.

C: You feel less vulnerable, essentially.

R: Yes, I do. But that, again, is in my own brain, and I presume that if he were not there, I would find some *other* defensive mechanism. I don't know what it would be. It's very easy for me to work him into a conversation, to—without "saying" so—say, "I am not available and please don't hassle me." And consequently, I've not been hassled. Because I've always made a point whenever a relationship with someone I'm working with goes into a social context, rather than a purely professional context—for instance, when I'm in Washington or elsewhere traveling, or I take someone out to dinner—when we start talking about anything social, I don't eliminate him from my conversation, because he's *there.* Again, that is probably because of the way I am. I could just as easily exclude him from the conversation, but . . .

C: You prefer not to.

R: Because he's part of it. It would be silly for me to exclude him, as far as *my* life is concerned. On the other hand, I could have made the decision *not* to include him in my conversation because it's none of their business. Which is also the case, but I have instead chosen to include him, as I say, partly for this defensive mechanism. And in some cases it was conscious. It's funny, you know, someone might say something about their personal life, or I'd ask them about their kids or something, and the fact that Kevin and I did something would come out, and they're very *interested* in him. They want to know what he does . . . everything like that, very, very interested in *him.* I haven't yet determined *why* that is—because he's a phenomenon? they haven't met him?—I really don't know why. But it happens, and it's very interesting indeed.

Now, how does my professional life influence my personal life? Not a whole lot! Kevin went to Wharton, and I went to law school, and our friends are mostly all professional people. And in the professions they're in, there are a lot of young women around, and they have all, like the attorneys, been able to establish their role, and so I never have any problem. But I *think* it's because the cross-section we deal with is . . . well, the people themselves are not homogeneous. I guess their *backgrounds* are somewhat homogeneous. But as our life patterns have developed—going to college, and then to a professional school after that—obviously, the friends we have made along the way have been in the paths that we have traveled, and therefore I don't have any problem at all. What is interesting is that there's a law firm downtown that we deal with a lot. And in several cases, two attorneys in the law firm have married. Men and women each time! [Laughter.] I once asked a friend why one of these women had left the law firm where she and her husband had worked. And my friend said something that was very interesting—that the woman felt that in the firm, she was being aggressive in her legal thinking, aggressive among her peers, and she found being married to one of them very hard. It was difficult to do that, because she was not as aggressive with *him* as she was to the rest of the world. And she, or they, were not able to handle this appropriately. I think she felt that it was easier to leave the firm and to find a different area of the profession to work in—teaching—and to do her own thing there, without coming in contact with him. He himself is a very aggressive person, and I think what happened is that they were clashing. Now, Kevin and I do not work in the same professions at all. And in many ways I think that's good, but among our peers, among the people we are friendly with, I have *no* problem maintaining a moderately aggressive stand, because that's the way I am, and I'm not going to change [Laughter] just because someone *thinks* I should be different. I *am* a relatively aggressive person. He has accepted that, and I have accepted *him,* and our friends accept us as we are. But we also choose our friends! [Laughter.] So that they *do* accept us. I think this idea about aggressiveness is very . . . I'm not sure that I *could* work in the same company as Kevin. I'm pretty sure I could, because we've got ourselves straightened out. I guess the place I see it most is playing bridge. [Laughter.] He always yells at me for taking the bid, and I always yell at him for something else, mostly because he hasn't gotten any good cards recently! [Laughter.] I guess I'd say that there's no difference between me at work and me among my friends. Whereas, this other woman who *left* the job found it necessary to change because of the difference within herself, the aggressive difference.

On the topic of aggressiveness. I've found that it has been useful. Again, I'm in a situation of having no role model, so I don't know whether or not it's uniquely my situation or everyone in my situation—or whether it's because I'm a *woman,* or I'm *young,* or I'm a *professional,* or where it stands

. . . or I'm unproven. But I have found that at some points it becomes necessary to just put my foot down and say "No" in a business deal, and gain a certain respect for standing up on the point.

C: Did you want to expand more on your personal life?

R: Well, I just don't want to leave you with the impression that my personal life is just in terms of Kevin. I have a family, and it's a very supportive family, which gives me a lot of . . . really . . . moral support more than anything else. My father's a professional. My mother's a housewife, so, again, I don't have a role model. But they're both very proud of what I am doing, and have done, with my life and are very supportive. I just didn't want to leave you with a unitary concept of my personal life. My mother *is* concerned with what I am doing. Once, several years ago, she asked, "What are you going to do if you have a child? Are you going to farm it out?" although those weren't the words she used. I have every intention of being an attorney as long and to the fullest extent that I can be. And I don't know what I'm going to do. I don't think there's any clear answer, and as I told her then, I don't *know* the answer and I want to wait until that situation happens. I'm not going to close a door now, or give myself only one path to follow, because I want to remain flexible, because I *have* to remain flexible in this world, and maybe the world or the society as we know it will change, or will give me an alternative that I feel is viable. If I had to do it today, I don't *know* the answer. I hope I would be able to find what I'm looking for. I don't know. All I can do is *hope,* at this point. But I didn't want to leave you with the concept [Laughter] that I don't have a family. I *do,* it's very important to me. It's a *group* that stands behind me, more than just one person. It's very, very important to me.

C: You've also mentioned another support group, which is the women attorneys.

R: Yes. We were talking about "within" the corporation and "without" it. And I want to sort of amend the "without" the corporation and explain that there are groups of people . . . I went to law school and to college in Philadelphia, and I have a lot of peers downtown—contemporaries I went to school with. And when I'm downtown during the day, I often see people I went to school with, as well as the fact that I belong to a professional organization, the Pennsylvania Association of Women Lawyers, which has been a mechanism for me to meet some very, very great women. And, it's very . . . well, few of them are in corporations, and certainly none of them are in corporations at the level that I am, with the responsibility that I have. But they're very supportive of me *in* my corporation and . . . just *morally* supportive of me as a young woman professional. Because we're all in that together, so to speak. And even though they're only a small portion of the people in the organization, they're very *good* people. And a moderately large group of us are in the process of forming the First Women's Bank of Philadelphia, which may or may not work. [Laughter.] It hasn't meant a tremendous amount of work for me yet, except for trying to interest other people in the bank. But it has meant a lot *to* me.

I think it's very exciting sometimes. I must admit, they're really fun to be with—*intellectually* fun to be with, because they're stimulating people and they almost all have very dynamic jobs. Currently, there are a lot of women in government, in relatively high positions, at relatively young ages, and I'm dealing with them all the time. And so, it's almost as if we who are the unusual have our own group. . . . "Outcasts" is the wrong word to use—"We who are outcasts." . . . We who are *unusual* have our own group, and a lot of them are in government. Lots of them are not attorneys. . . . I've dealt extensively with one new agency which had a woman as the head of its staff, four cabinet secretaries on the commission itself, two of whom are women. And I can understand more now the clubbiness of people than I could have before I became involved with these people, because there *is* a bit of, "We're all going through this together." I'm not sure that's what clubbiness is to other people, but to us, it is. For instance, the staff head of the new state agency once told me, when we were just shooting the breeze in her office, about what she had anticipated as the blocks along the way when she first looked at *her* job. One was that she would be the only woman she would ever work with, except for a secretary. And she said that when she first walked into the room, that first day, she almost died, because she couldn't believe there was another woman in the room, and that an eingineering-oriented corporation like mine had been with-it enough to have a woman who would actually be dealing with a governmental agency. And sometimes I think the reaction I get from dealing with this group of professional women . . . who are not always handling the same type of problems, but do have problems . . . and although we rarely articulate them, it's just sort of a comfortable feeling, that you don't have to go through everything with them, you know, they understand from the beginning. And maybe . . . that is my concept of what the clubbiness is. And it is my feeling with them.

James Edwards (A)

James Edwards was 33 years old and black. After graduation from college, he had joined a large consumer-products company and had worked his way up to a middle-management position. Then the company had sent him to Harvard Business School for his M.B.A., which he had earned with high distinction–in fact, he was one of the first blacks in the school's history to be named a Baker Scholar.

After completing his M.B.A., Jim rejoined his company and was made district manager of the Metropolitan Chicago Sales District, one of the largest districts in the company. (See Exhibit II-4.) Jim had held this position for over a year when this case was written, and had begun to experience increasing doubts about his future with the company. He had been particularly disturbed by top management's response to an article he had written for a national business magazine on the difficulties of being a black manager. He had based the article on his own personal experiences as a black man working his way up the management ladder. Jim suspected that the company's management had reacted negatively to the article (which they had seen prior to publication) and had misunderstood and resented what he was trying to say.

Knowing of these concerns, the casewriter asked Jim if he would be willing to discuss them and have his comments taped for possible use as a case. Jim agreed, and the following is a transcript of his remarks.

What it comes down to is, I will soon have to make a decision about which way to go. I've been running the district for well over a year now with no sign from anyone about what the next step is . . . what the future holds. They told me when I came back that it would be a short assignment—a year at the most. That period has come and gone, and I've met or exceeded every objective during the past year, and I'm beginning to wonder if performance is what counts. That's part of the frustration. The rest of . . . the other part of it is the reaction to the article. . . . They didn't understand it . . . they didn't understand what I was trying to say. I think they took it as a slap in the face. In fact, several people that I confide in have told me it was not a politically

Exhibit II-4 James Edwards (A)

Organization Chart, Metropolitan Chicago Sales District

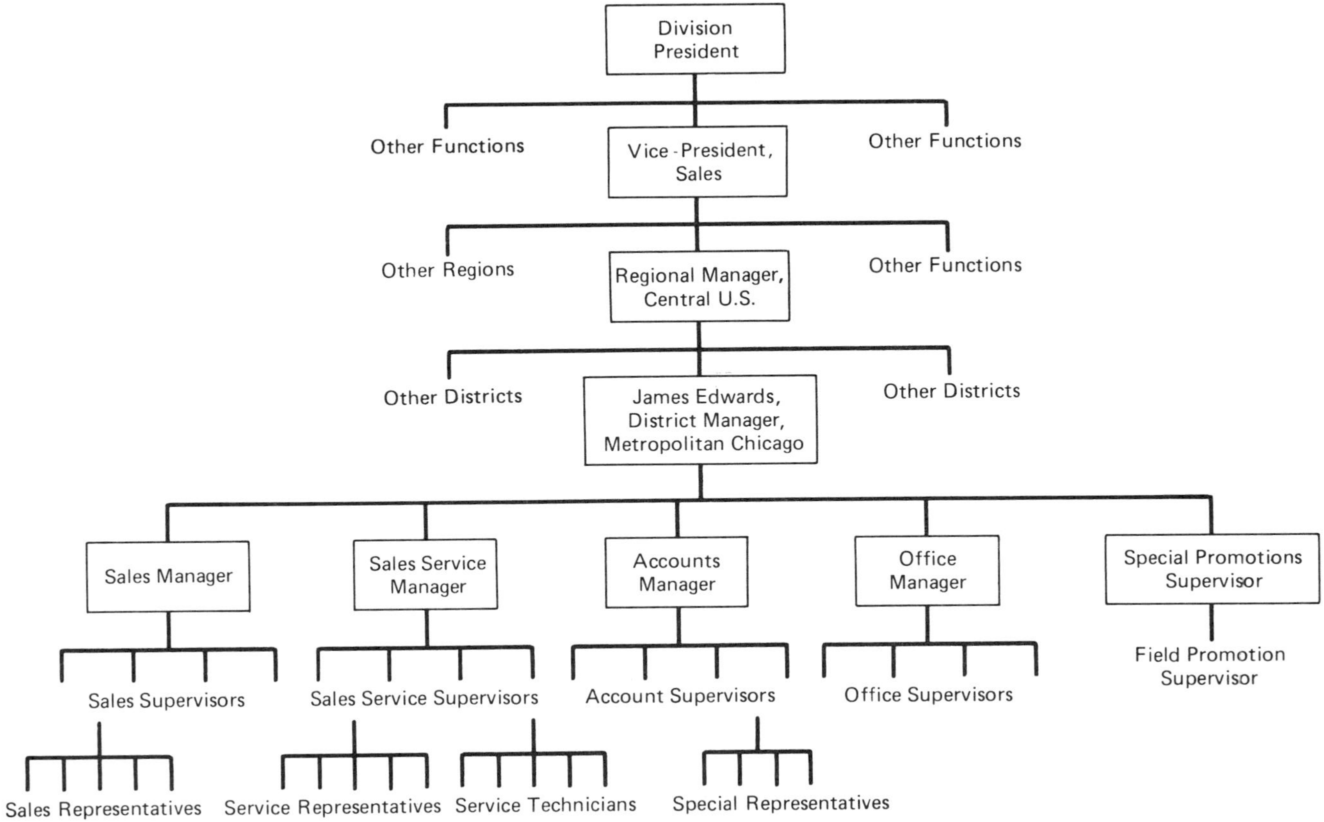

wise thing to do . . . to write that article. And this is what grates at me, because if I cannot speak the truth on something that is basic to me, then maybe I'm in the wrong company. Should I suppress what I have lived through and I know is important . . . suppress what I know can help make it less of a hell for other black guys . . . not tell what the experience is like, the built-in obstacles a black manager faces? Suppress that? I don't know that it's worth the price.

I guess I'm really wrestling with a more basic question, which is, what can I do to make a maximum contribution? I can stay here and show them that I can withstand whatever they give me, and become a proven performer so that there can be no doubt. . . . That's the obvious option. I could go back to school and get a Ph.D. or something, which would allow me to focus on the whole problem of black managers and write about it. Or I could switch . . . I could go to another company, which is not a solution but is at least a change. . . .

Which is why . . . I guess I am coming to realize that there are some things that are bigger than me as a person. It's been a trauma for the last two months, since I first sent the rough draft of the article around the company. I didn't get any response for weeks—and when it finally came, it was noncommittal as hell. I guess I am learning that with some things, you can't go right through the middle. I am having to develop the graciousness to accept that Jim Edwards cannot necessarily go out and change the world. I have to suppress the temptation to stand up and scream, "Can't you see what you're doing? Don't you understand?" I'm fighting to get myself geared up after this vacation—to reinstill my pride that says, damn it, if there's an objective, I'll meet or exceed it—I won't fall prey to disappointment or disillusionment.

But I have had . . . great disappointment . . . in terms of my ideals as a black thinking of all blacks. There's also disappointment as a person thinking of his own career. On the other hand, I'm caught with the fact that if *I* can't do it here, then, goddamn it, I look behind me and I don't see anyone else who I judge is able to really do it, and there's a danger in thinking of yourself as omnipotent—which I'm not . . . which I damn well . . . I found that out these last few months, when I found that I couldn't sleep at night. But I think I came damn close to the breaking point—in fact, one of my men, one of the sales service supervisors, told me yesterday, "You seem much more relaxed now. Some of us were starting to notice that you were getting tense beyond compare." And they were recognizing it, and that's one of the things that started me to fight it, because one thing I am not willing to sacrifice is my personal effectiveness.

I've been feeling so tense these last couple of months, it's unreal, and that's due to the article, basically, and the inability of some people to look upon the article in terms of its purpose and message, as opposed to Jim Edwards, the guy who wrote the article. I think that I will have to accept a slightly longer horizon about influencing the company. I have other options. I could go out and get another job, and probably make more money if I wanted to sell my blackness. But the fact of the matter is that I don't want to sell my blackness for more money to get in a showcase position where I'm as useless as a tit on a bull. In which I have no authority, no responsibility, no decision-making power, and where I cannot influence the direction of an organization. As a person, it grates against me, because I would not be a performer—if I am not a performer and I don't . . . I want the chance to prove myself.

The last two months, I have been trying to decide my course of action, because I find it very difficult to be a passive entity in life. To just sit here and wait. And I've considered all the options. I could leave the company, and find some way of devoting full time to raising people's awareness of the problems facing black managers and what companies can do to give them a fair chance. I could go back to school and do that, get a Ph.D. and make that my research specialty. That would be a way which could allow me to do that directly—use leverage on business as a whole. But the other alternative is to stay here and prove that I can go to the top and become the first black VP in the company. And this is also direct, but in a different way—by showing it can be done.

And this company matters to me; it's an important part of me. I want to shape my own direction, and I guess the part I have been wrestling with is whether to mount an offensive or dig in for a moral issue, on which I know I'm right. It's very frustrating, because I can't get other people to see that it's not Jim Edwards, the person, looking for selfish ambitions—at least, not necessarily ambitions by themselves—but what I'm trying to say is something that's far more general and far broader . . . and I have received some satisfaction from the letters I have gotten from outside the company. But those who know me as an individual in the company refuse to look beyond their nose for what I'm trying to say—and they don't evaluate the statement; they evaluate the person making the statement, and then it comes down to missing the whole point.

They say that I am ungrateful for what the company has done for me. The fact of the matter is, I am doing as well or better than any guy who came into the company when I did. And that's frustrating, it's frustrating; and when I say it's frustrating, I mean frustrating to have to back off, to accept the fact that maybe it's not wise to consume oneself in trying to idealistically plow straight through, no matter what the odds are. The reason is, you see, I'm playing in someone else's ballgame and they are allowing me to play, and I'd better damn sure recognize that. It's funny, I've become especially aware of that limitation now that I've got a daughter. This has changed perhaps my motivations—which were almost all self-centered—to now include someone else.

Having a baby has suddenly made a big difference, because, you know, a marriage is a type of thing where, if two people get married, let's say, in their late thirties or forties instead of in their twenties, they are looking for different things out of marriage, because they have spent a long time alone, they have had a chance to do things. But when people get married in their early twenties, they haven't really fulfilled themselves, and in that case there's a tendency and a desire, after being together for, let's say, seven, eight, nine years, as in my case, to say, "Well, damn it, if I don't achieve self-realization now, I never will," and that sort of makes you a little selfish. There is a tendency to say, "Well, I know what my wife wants, but on the other hand, I want this, and hell, my needs are just as good as hers. I have as much of a right as she has," so you become a little selfish. But the inclusion of a child, where both of your goals and desires and ambitions are totally coincident, changes that. So my daughter's arrival has started to shift my thinking, and all of a sudden I have to start to suppress myself in many ways.

So the baby certainly has made me more cautious, and it's funny, because I was talking to a fellow who is a friend of mine, no more than two weeks ago, and he's followed this whole thing about the article. He's one of the few guys who really appreciates what I am saying. Being a white guy, it's rather difficult for him, and he has found that many of his peers have turned him off when he tries to explain that I'm trying to make a general statement about what it's like to be a black manager—not just about me. And in sharing these things, we have become pretty friendly. A couple of weeks ago, I made the statement to him that I was quite capable of going after a *pure* victory if that's the only victory I could score, and I'd be damned if I'd admit defeat in making my point, because I don't want other black guys to go through the grief I went through. And I want them, the company, to get the message one way or another. And he said, "Well, Jim, you know, what about your family?" And I said, "Well, some things are more important than family," and it's funny, looking back, I have to smile, because a couple of weeks later, after the baby was born, I can see exactly what he meant. And it's only been three weeks since she was born. He's on vacation now, and I've been waiting to see him, because I'm dying to tell him that very thing. Because I can really understand what he meant now. Other things are more important to me now than just *my own goals.*

And choices that I have been struggling with in the sense that . . . I think that the thing that frustrates me most is my inability to get an acceptance within the company about the article, and I was really trying to say something to the company, not just to business in general. There's no doubt in my mind that it's more important for me to communicate this to the company than to business as a whole. I'm glad that the article got a favorable acceptance nationally, but on the other hand, my pride in working for my company and wanting the company to be ahead of the others and for the company to be right in what it does, to be successful, frustrates me in not getting the message across to them, or at least, in their not acknowledging it. And I guess that frustration has increased even more with the receipt of each positive letter from outside companies.

In fact, I received a letter from Honeywell which said, "Jim Edwards is probably a pen name—he could have been one of *our* black managers, and we have noticed the same things he describes." And GE is going to use that article as a training vehicle for increasing awareness of its white managers. On the other hand, in my company, the reaction—from at least one of the people who has been most important to me in my career and whose opinion matters to me—was, "That goddamned ingrate." And I put that together by tapping my various—well, my grapevine. The other source of frustration is that I, as a person, as an M.B.A. and as a business man, I guess I've always met or exceeded all objectives prior to going to Harvard Business School. I also met or exceeded all objectives while *at* the Harvard Business School, and I broke everyone's expectations at the B-School. I have never acknowledged the fact that certain limitations were on me because I was black. But the fact of the matter also is that at one time I didn't think it would be possible for me to go farther than what my present level is. But when the company sent me to the B-School, that changed. I became totally dedicated to the books and made what some people considered ridiculous sacrifices, and at this point I'm not sure they weren't right. I was determined to be a Baker Scholar, and somehow, by God, it came about—through determination because I'm not . . . while I think I'm of above-average intelligence, I don't think I'm of exceptional intelligence. Most of the guys up there are above average, you know, and I think I'm comparative with them, but certainly not the genius that outshined everyone else. I have to get mine from sweat and determination. But I made it there—in that field of competition—and I determined to become a Baker Scholar, and I made it.

But having been there, and then coming back with broader horizons—with raised horizons—I became very frustrated when I got here. It was like, when all of a sudden, say, I'm out there playing basketball and they start playing football, and I'm out dribbling on the court and they've changed the backboard to a goalpost and they didn't tell me the new name of the game. What happened was very similar to Mr. Moynihan's "benign neglect." I came back, and I was told by the VP of sales, "You don't have to do anything, Jim, you've proven how smart you are. All you have to do now is show you can get along with people, and I wouldn't be surprised if in three or four months . . ." Well, hell, I heard him, and, of course, this didn't depress my horizons, this confirmed that my evaluation was correct. I had a reputation for being a hard charger before I went to Harvard, and for getting results—but not necessarily for being a Mr. Nice Guy. But then, my pride said, "I'll be damned. I've never been a cake eater and I don't intend to start now." So I figure there's got to be a way to prevent blowing this place to hell as far as getting along with people is concerned. On the other hand, I've gotta meet or exceed my objectives, and there's no way that I'm gonna let someone say, if I do get a promotion, that I got it because I was black. So that old determination went into play again, and after getting back from exams and graduation, I shifted into high gear. And we had an awful lot of problems and a long way to go, and there were questions of sales and services and receivables, and with the economy going bad in the particular area that I'm responsible for, and we geared up—in fact, my boss told me that I could not achieve a top rating at that time.

And it's not because the district was in such bad shape. They don't assign guys that they don't think highly of to a district like Chicago Metro. It's probably one of the most difficult in the division, or in the whole company for that matter. But my boss didn't think that I could get a top rating for the simple reason that I was relatively new and untried. Well, I pointed out a few other cases where fellows had gotten top ratings who, in effect, had had less field experience than me, because I had, in effect, run a district without the title before going to the B-School. In fact, before I went to B-School, when I was a level lower, I was assigned to a district sales manager south of Chicago, and was told to turn his district around without upsetting the applecart; which I did in five months. I brought him from number twelve out of thirteen in the region to number two out of thirteen. And of course, I didn't have the title. And I did his job. I retrained his entire district. I got things understood and I got them clicking. . . . Well, ah well, but my current boss didn't think I had the experience, and I gave him a few examples of other guys who didn't have much field experience but who I guessed were top rated, and I challenged him to tell me what he wanted and to evaluate me based on performance, not seniority.

So he came up with objectives—and it wasn't the mutual goal setting that we're taught at the B-School. He told me what he wanted, and I said, "Well, gee, that's pretty rough—in this area and that area, etc.," and he said, "That's what it's got to be." And the objectives were set down even though I wasn't able to change his mind in lots of areas. But when the year was finished, all the objectives had been met or exceeded in every category. And he had no choice but to give me the rating that I told him I was determined to get.

So I had come back to the company, and after a year the district hadn't blown apart, but that's another frustration, in that I don't think the company realizes the internal chaos and additional problems I faced in preventing the district from blowing apart. First of all, I am the only guy who is black in a field job. There are a couple of guys in public relations and other BS jobs, but that isn't the same. I walked into that district, and I anticipated many problems, and unfortunately, my anticipation was correct. When I went into that district, I made myself promise that I was going to act like any other manager who would go into a district. But I had been there all of three days before the tension and the tightness that I saw all around me made me back up. And quite frankly, I saw that I had a problem which, if I didn't deal with, was going to result in an explosion and in failure. And my honest evaluation was that if there was an explosion for whatever reason—whether I was right or wrong—I would have, in fact, lost the game. So while I wanted to approach it as any other manager, I had no choice but to deal with what I saw was creating the tension—which, of course, was me and the response that people had to me, because their response would preclude me from being effective. What I felt was tension everywhere—among the nonmanagement employees, among the first-level supervisors, and among my managers—everywhere. And I had four white managers working for me, and all college graduates—two of whom had come into the business the same time I did, all of whom had heard that I was coming from the Harvard Business School. And my grapevine had confirmed that there had been rumors flying all about the place when it was announced that I was being assigned to that district.

The assignment to that district was . . . the significance of the assignment to that district was evident—it's one of those districts designated as *the* most difficult and designated as being a stepping stone to a promotion. It's historical that certain assignments such as that one are the steps prior to moving up. When I went in, I met everyone, and I smiled and I shook hands and I was polite and courteous. In fact, I tried to observe and keep my mouth shut and just see what was going on. But, after three days, the tension was . . . and I don't think I'll ever know whether it was something that only I felt or that was really present. But I think that some of the things that I found out since then verify that it was real, and still is, to some degree, present. I felt at that time that all they saw was a black district manager—they never saw Jim Edwards, the man.

And it's funny. This wasn't a problem of just the whites who worked for me, but it was a universal problem within the district. From both sides, both ends. For example, blacks would say, "Any guy who can get to this level is an Uncle Tom." Or, blacks . . . I remember when I was a kid, you know, you used to get mad at someone, and the worst thing you could say to them was, "You black so-and-so," and then you'd stop and you'd think about that. In effect, you were dealing in self-deprecation just as the white guy who saw you and didn't like you would give a remark such as that and you would make a remark such as that, too, to your own friends, or buddies, or sisters when *you* got mad—which says a lot about the psychological damage that's been done to all of our minds, both black and white. The tendency is for whites to think that maybe blacks don't feel that way, but I don't think that's true. Black pride and years and years of processed minds being exposed to newspaper headlines that say, "Black Man Kills So-and-So," or "Black Man Rapes Someone," or, "Black Man Robs Bank," and everything that a black man did wrong, it was mentioned that it was a *black* man, and on the other hand, when it was a white man, it just said, "Man." Or the exposure to blacks on TV, which is a recent phenomenon, but when you did see them in the past, they were maids or janitors or Step'n'Fetchits or Amos'n'Andys, or the lack of an ability to get a job, or the total . . . the total association of blacks with everything low, or the lower status, or lesser importance. Ah, this has to have an effect on people's minds. Around 1968-69, black pride got to be fashionable—people began saying black is beautiful. Well, that's really great, but that's just a phrase, and blacks and whites don't realize what's been done to their minds in this shaping that's been taking place from birth to the place where they can say black is beautiful. And just saying black is beautiful doesn't erase ten, fifteen, twenty years of, say, having a processed mind. We develop natural hairdos now because black is beautiful; yet, and still—remember when Sugar Ray Robinson was fighting, he used to have a process? He used to go out and get a comb and grease to get his hair to look long and straight. That's called a process, and, in effect, blacks' minds were also being processed when they got their hair straightened. But psychologically, internally, they weren't aware that they had been processed, that they had been programmed by everything they had been exposed to since they were a child—that black was inferior. Did you ever see the cowboy-and-Indian shows? You know that if the good guy's on a white horse, the guys on the black horses are bad guys. It's black and white—very seldom do you see a pinto in those movies. And you think about that, it's frightening. Everything good is white, everything bad is black—and it has affected people.

And that's why, getting back to the district and what I was saying before, I have thought about these things, and my experience has taught me that blacks were not yet where it was all "right on, brother" and total pride. They themselves have their prejudices against blacks, which, in many cases, is built-in just like white prejudice is. For example, I have observed that it is very difficult for one black to be second best to another black. But when blacks are in a competitive situation with whites, it is not as damaging to their ego to come out second. It's almost as if blacks have said to themselves, "OK, I gotta be second best when it comes to whites, but I'll be damned if I'm not the best when it comes to blacks." And I've read about some studies that I think verify those observations. Some tests taken at Lincoln University show that blacks, when they are in mixed groups, tend to be nonaggressive and more political and more tactful, and when they're pitted against blacks, they are more competitive. It's as if they have learned to back off, and it's more of a blow to be second best to another black. It's as if they can no longer rationalize—that they can't do something because of the color of their skin—which is a damaging thing to you as a person, to have to say, "I didn't reach a certain level because I just didn't do it." When, maybe for thirty years, you have said to yourself, "I never got that promotion because they're prejudiced and they don't like blacks." But if another black gets it, I anticipated some of these reactions.

The blacks were saying, "He's gotta be an Uncle Tom. If he's an Uncle Tom, he's gonna play favorites with them. At least we had a chance with his white predecessor." Well, on the other hand, I saw whites who were uptight, and I perceived them to be thinking, "Well, we're gonna swing the other way, now. Black is in charge, and black is beautiful, and all of a sudden, you know, we have gotta change our whole stance." It seemed to me necessary to call it for what it was, because if I ever started to let subjective factors change my evaluations, then I would become inconsistent. So I have tried to develop a knack for removing all feelings, all emotions from making decisions, because if ever I veer from the line—if I veer toward the blacks, then I have become a militant to my white staff—I'll have part of my force that doesn't want to work with me or cooperate with me. If I veer toward the whites, then I'm an Uncle Tom to the blacks, and that's a cause for double dissension, because there are always going to be some whites who are going to side with the blacks simply because they think it's a moral thing to do [Laughs]. These are some of our liberal friends who feel guilty or something [Laughs].

That's the situation I saw. So after—well, it was as if everyone was sitting there like turtles with their heads pulled back in their shells, expecting me to come in like the Grim Reaper, changing things, doing things different, or, "Oh, my God, what's about to fall on us?" like there was a great scythe about to come down and decapitate them, and this tightness was something that I had to deal with one way or another. First of all, I recognized that no matter what I did, it was going to be a losing proposition, because someone would be able to find fault with it no matter what. What I finally decided was to take a low-key approach, but be very candid about my recognition of the problem. I decided to work through my managers, so after that day, I called my managers in. And I told them that if I were in their position and I had heard there was a black district manager who had just left Harvard Business School, I would have some serious problems. These problems would be enhanced in my mind if I had come into the company about the same time as him, because, after all, why does this guy go to Harvard and I not go to Harvard? So I said, "I want to assure you of several things. Number one, I do not leap tall buildings with a single bound. Number two, I expect from you total honesty, and I expect you to be totally candid," and I said, "I recognize that some of you don't know me well enough to just take my word and give me that trust." I said, "However, I am going to *demand that trust* until you have reason to tell me to my face that this should not exist. And my reason for saying this is simple—that none of us are going to achieve our objectives unless we understand the extent of the problems."

And I told them that while I knew that I was very strong-minded and opinionated, and had a tendency to be forceful at times, that I did not expect anybody to back off. If they disagreed with me, I expected them to say so, because I did not want a yes-man. Well, that was the tenet that I approached them on. And so, what I then did was sit back for three months, and thank goodness, things generally went OK. I did not go out and talk to the folks, or become buddy-buddy with the supervisors or the sales people or office people. I tried to run that operation through the managers, and at the end of about three months, I thought I detected some people's heads coming out and saying, "Hey, the sky hasn't fallen down on us. This isn't so different than what it was before." Now, doing this was very difficult for me, though, from a personal point of view, because my style is basically one of putting my nose in every corner and talking to everyone so that I understand exactly what the problem is.

You see, my style is to be with the people—eyeball to eyeball, and in close to the problems. And one of the things I learned about myself during that period was that I don't like being out of the action. But, you see, it was important in those first few months to keep a low profile—to avoid that explosion.

Then the audit came, and that's when I found I couldn't hold back any longer. The district was audited by the overall company. Not the division headquarters, but the company headquarters, and there's only one audit in each division a year. There are roughly fifty districts in my division and, unfortunately, mine was the one that was chosen, which, I must admit, I wonder about. Because I thought that was one hell of a chance—a district run by a black man, the only district of 50 to be run by a black man, and it gets audited. But be that neither here nor there, I had only been there about three and a half months. It was early enough so that my predecessor, who had a good reputation, could not totally disclaim any responsibility, and I hoped they couldn't hit me all the way. But what I did after that audit was rather embarrassing in many ways. I reaudited the audit. I took almost a solid month of my personal time out of my nights and weekends, and I turned into a doer in addition to an administrator, because I was determined to find out the truth, whether the audit reflected the operations properly. I tore into the audit. I audited every part of it, and I found out where it had been distorted. And, in a 25- or 35-page epistle, which was probably the best report I have ever done, I put egg all over the auditor's face, and dared them to come back and reaudit and disprove my claims and my statements. And we came out smelling like a rose.

And at this point, my basic nature said, "This is the time to stop letting the managers run the show totally." My nature, which had been grated by my acting in a way which was basically uncomfortable for me—it took over. All of that time being passive—of working through others—where, instead of driving the car, I was in the shotgun seat, saying, "OK, fellers . . . now, driver, make a right turn here at the corner," or worse yet, "What do you think about making a right turn at the corner?" Ah, that's a little uncomfortable when things get hot and heavy! I don't like to miss objectives, and now I was faced with the need to take charge. There hadn't been the trauma or explosion that I had to avoid earlier, and if I was ever going to take charge, I had to do it then. So I did. I put together—I told the managers that I wanted to talk to all of the supervisors in the district, all 25 supervisory people—I put together a one-hour course which I gave to all the supervisors. And it was amazing. I had given out copies of the audit and my report to all the management, and they were absolutely befuddled to see that I walked, and talked, and thought and wrote, and that I was vicious with the pen! And they grinned from ear to ear and said, "Wow!" And some of them thought the words I used were a little big, but they were impressed [Chuckle]. Now—so I guess they were pleasantly surprised, so I guessed that now they knew what it was all about to be a district manager.

All of a sudden, without any trauma, the black district manager had become *the* district manager! And there was no doubt in anyone's mind that I was in charge when I stood in front of the management people and I took on their questions one by one, telling them what direction we were going to take, and why we were gonna go that way, what the alternatives were and the rest of it—all off the cuff. There was no doubt in anyone's mind who was running that district. And I think I was rather proud of myself that there was such a smooth transition from "that black district manager" to seeing Jim Edwards *as* the district manager! No one could say, "He took charge this day," or "He took charge that day." They just didn't know; all of a sudden, this thing happened. They looked in the driver's seat, and I was winking in the rear-view mirror, saying, "Leave the driving to me now. Everything's gonna be OK."

So I began to be on top of things—on all fronts. For instance, several incidents sort of confirm . . . here. So after a while, I started to . . . we have a black union steward, and I started talking to him as a person, because I was fighting this Uncle Tom thing, and I wanted somehow to spread the word without my going out and hanging around every black's neck telling him that I wasn't an Uncle Tom. On the other hand, I wasn't going to play favorites either, but I wanted to let them know I was a regular guy, so a couple of little things—like, for example, one night they were having a little going-away party for someone who was leaving the district, and people were playing cards in the lounge. Now, there's a black game that's called bid whist—almost all blacks know how to play bid whist. Well, I went by, and—you know, I'm a nut about bid whist. I happen to think I'm *the* best that ever played bid whist, as all blacks do [Laugh]. It's an ethnic game that . . . it's part of the rap that if you can't play bid whist, then you just can't make it among the ethnic—you just can't, but you gotta be good at it. So, I . . . they were looking for a fourth as I went by, so I said, "I'll play a couple of hands." And I sat down, and sure enough, we played bid whist—you have to talk bad and loud, and deliver. I played bad, loud, and delivered, and got up and left a winner! [Laughs.] And I think that helped set the stage. And then I went over to the whites and I talked with them. So I wasn't just saying, "Brother, right on," and the rest of it, but, on the other hand, I wanted them all to see that I was a normal black guy and that I wasn't an Uncle Tom—that I could write, and I could talk, and I could walk, and I could think. And—and I could play bid whist, and damn well, too! [Laughs.]

But then the black guy, the union steward, confirmed that I wasn't being paranoid when I first took over the district. That all kinds of rumors had been going around, that people had heard I was a hard nose, etc., or an Uncle Tom. Everyone, both black and white, had diverse opinions about me, but I think the consensus was generally negative. They had me indicted, tried, and judged before I could prove who I was. I had to prove that I wasn't any of those things—that's a form of prejudice, you know, that's what prejudice means, prejudgment.

I guess that it was a very tough period, it's still tough. I'm still in the process of mentally and emotionally trying to adjust to the fact that I—that it's not necessarily pure performance that counts. I guess I can be a well-oiled performance machine, but I now have to recognize realistically that it's not my actual performance that counts so much as . . . that's not really what will move me ahead. And that's disappointing to me at this point, 'cause I'd like to think that's what the system is all about—that performance *is* what counts.

But it seems as if the guys who really get ahead are those who have "rabbis." A "rabbi" is like a patron, a godfather, he looks after you from up higher in the organization. Those guys who have rabbis don't have to have good performance behind them, and seem to move out of tight spots just before they explode, and move into good spots and then leave them before they explode. And I've seen several guys who are top-rated but have never met an objective, and they are still top-rated and they keep on moving. It's as if someone up above has deemed that they had the ability from the day they came into the company, and they are going to make it. So they've been moving them along. On the other hand, it's sort of . . . when, say, OK—if a man proves himself, then he can determine his own destiny. When that's the case, it's entirely up to you, but it may be a real fact of life that it may not be what you do but who you know that's important. And I'm caught between these two things, because my personal pride says that I *should* perform, *be number one,* no matter how difficult it is. And I've got to achieve no matter how difficult, because that gives me the feedback that says, "*You are able, you are capable,* you *can* do it." If I ever fail to get that type of feedback from my own performance, then I'm in trouble. I need to be in a situation where I can prove myself, because if I'm not, I would not be a performer—and if I am not a performer and I don't . . . there's nothing for me to test, then how the hell am I going to have the assurance that I am still capable as a person? Because I have had to accept the reality that I may never be able to rely on accurate feedback from my boss or my peers because of their own prejudices. So if I lose my ability to perform, or if I ever fail to meet or exceed my objectives and begin to have self-doubts, or am in an environment in which I cannot totally trust the quality of the feedback, then I've got problems. I've got serious problems.

Serious problems, and that's part of what bothers me now, because I am starting to realize that . . . I don't know . . . accept that I am no more than a pawn on a board, that I am being moved around and my success is being determined by the judgments of others more than my own individual performance. In fact, my boss perhaps accepted that same idea when he said to me when I came in, "You don't have to prove how smart you are. All you have to do is get along with people." That's a hell of a contradiction. Well, he is in effect saying we've got one thing in theory and another thing in actuality. And I guess it worries me from the point of view that if we are ever going to have real equal opportunity in this country, it's going to have to be based upon performance. And if we don't now have real equal opportunity among whites based on performance, damned if we haven't got one hell of a problem when we mix blacks in there! And if you don't have the chance to prove that you can do it before you move ahead, then how the hell do you ever get the reassurance that you can do it? Now, I know that's not true in one hundred percent of the cases, but it's true in far too many cases, more than I'd like to accept.

And this bothers me; it worries me at times. I feel that if there are blacks who are going to do well in my company, and on a larger scale in the system in this country, then they have to be guys who *can* perform, and these guys have got to take the extra burden of the crap that comes along because they're black, and be able to handle that *as well as* be a performer. And if necessary, then, they have got to be . . . they've got to be the meanest son-of-a-bitch in the valley. And, I . . . maybe . . . I don't know whether I ever told you my motto—I have to admit that I have to smile when I say my motto is that, "Yea, though I walk through the valley of the shadow of death, I will fear no evil, for I shall be the meanest son-of-a-bitch in the valley." I have to smile for the simple reason that this motto is an admission that I have survived when there was little possibility of surviving. The cards were not stacked for my survival. There was certainly no one planning for my survival. And I don't want it to sound as if I had a plan for survival, because there wasn't any. There was more or less benign neglect, and there were no steps taken to ensure my survival, and therefore, I was subjected to everyone's prejudices—which they weren't even aware of, but which I had to deal with. Like my going into that office—that district—I'll be willing to bet you that nobody above my level, none of my supervisors other than my boss Frank, recognizes what I went through. [Pause.] The crossroads I'm at now, I'm fighting to get myself geared up after this vacation to reinstill that pride that says, damn it, if there is an objective I'll meet it or exceed it. [Long pause.]

It's important to me to prove myself as a performer. . . . I guess part of it has to do with the way I grew up, because I moved so many times, and you know you have to reestablish yourself every time you move. Kids being kids, they always want to try the new guy, and if you couldn't fight—man, I got sucker-punched so many times, it was unreal. And so I had to learn how to fight. I had to prove myself every time we moved.

I think also that a lot of it probably comes from my old man. My father comes from a large family in the South. He was the oldest boy, and after his real father died—he was about 12—well, I guess his stepfather kicked him out because he wouldn't work in the cotton fields to help support the family. Dad wanted to stay in school and become a Pullman porter. That was hot stuff for a black guy in those days. And two old maids who were schoolteachers in North Carolina had seen how bright Dad was, and they took him in, and they said, "No, son, you deserve to be more than a Pullman car porter." Well, they gave him a place to live and guidance, and he shined shoes, and he told me how he ate peanut butter sandwiches to save money, but somehow he got to school. He got a scholarship, and he also worked as a waiter, and he boxed, and he did just about everything under the sun to get through. He came out salutatorian or valedictorian—I forget which—in his class. He then went on to a theological seminary and got to be an ordained Presbyterian minister, and I think that's one of the things that carried him through. He has a very deep faith and a religious outlook on life. But he was still not satisfied, he wanted to achieve more, and he went on to the University of Pittsburgh and worked on his Ph.D. in physics, which was his undergraduate major. And he completed everything, except he was failed on his orals. The reason for this was that he had made it known that he wanted to go into business rather than teach in some black school when he finished his Ph.D., and that was against their values. So he had his master's and he'd completed his requirements for the Ph.D., with an A average in class work, but I remember that even with all that, my Dad still had to work as a dishwasher to keep his family fed and sheltered, even with his master's in physics, and that was about 1947.

But we moved some twenty times. He was determined, however, that we would make it, and that he would make it for us, and boy, some of the things he's done—I would never have had the guts. He moved from company to company, which was par in the defense industry, twenty-some times before I got out of high school, back and forth. His calling was to the ministry, but his obligation was to succeed, and his—his calling was torn, really. He had a personal inquisitiveness that could not be satiated, but combined with a very strong idealism. He is very intelligent. He'll whip a word on me today and I'll have to go look it up. I will never . . . though I will never admit it to his face now—pride—but he'll use a term I've never heard of before, and I'll have to look it up. [Laugh.] He's very articulate. And he's got to be *the* most forceful person I've ever met, although I gotta say that he has been too forceful at times.

That's also a trait of mine, which I am sure I take after him—that forcefulness. I also look at his other weakness, which is political naiveté. And I try not to make the same mistake. Dad went on and worked in engineering and physics. He helped design guidance systems for missiles, and has written a lot of articles on guidance and space. But my father could never really get into the big stuff. As bright as he was, he never made it big, he never played the game quite right. He finally got hung up from his own doing. There were little shenanigans going on in the company he worked for—missiles were blowing up after launch, and the company knew they had a mistake but wouldn't correct it, and millions of tax dollars were going down the drain. They asked him to analyze the problem and he said, "OK. Here's your problem—nose-cone stress—you underdeveloped your nose cone." And, then he was told, "OK.

Thanks a lot, but we're going to shoot off the rest of them anyway." And he said, "But that's dishonest." And he threatened to write the president. And, of course, that was not too smart a thing to say, because that meant he was being disloyal to the company. At any rate, he wound up in a jam. He was also getting older, so he went over to the government civil service to work, and then was let go when Nixon had his big layoff. Dad is really giving himself away, in the sense that he's got a hell of a lot more ability, potential, and capability. He has been forced to teach high school in order to make it these days. And that's a long drop for a guy who was once an assistant dean and head of a physics department and who helped design guidance for missiles.

But even to this day, I see my old man sit there and dig into his books, and he's determined. He never, never, never says die, and I have to admire that in him, and I guess I get that from Dad, that I'll never say die—I don't want to back off, just like Dad does. Although I want to use more prudence and judgment than he has—I don't want to make the same mistakes Dad has made.

You know, we were very, very close, and he is such a dominant guy that there has to be a certain—well, if you're going to grow up, you run into conflict, and when I look back and analyze it, that's exactly what happened. We got into a physical conflict that was unreal. I got my head banged a few times, and I always had the utmost respect, but one time, the first time he . . . I said my Dad boxed in college, and I had always respected my Dad, because I've seen him a lift a block of an engine out of a car—a sight which was overwhelming to me. Well, I'll never forget when I was 16, and one time I was sassing Mom about something—kid stuff, I didn't want to wash the floor, it was my sister's turn to wash the floor—and Dad got mad, and he ran into the living room and backed me into the corner. And all of a sudden, he did something he'd never done before—he always hit me with a belt—all of a sudden, Dad swung, and when Dad swung on me—and as I said, you learn the hard way when you get sucker-punched—my reflexes took over and I knocked him across the chair. Well, that was the beginning of three or four years of knock-down, drag-out fights. He was kicking me in and out of the house all the time. Of course, at that time I was determined that I was going to be my own man, and it was about the time I went to college. Looking back on it, it's so funny. It teaches me certain things which I don't want to repeat as far as my own kids go. But I've always respected him.

And a lot of my competitiveness also comes from him. In fact, all of us—my sister and my younger brother are very competitive. My older sister is one of the most determined people you ever want to meet. She won't back off for anybody. *Man,* she is a competitor all the way. *I'm* a competitor, and my youngest brother is a competitor. It's funny. My middle brother was always the baby. Dad always thought he was small and puny. So he always sort of sheltered the middle one, and he never developed the aggressiveness that the rest of us did. But my sister, I look at her, and she has three kids and went back to get a master's degree after her second. She won't be counted out. And my brother was a leader in the demonstrations at Cornell—when the takeover occurred. There were certain things he would not accept. He doesn't know how to back off either. He and I are the closest, even though we've taken very different paths. His has been confrontation while mine has been working through the system. But we can talk to each other about anything. There isn't anything we can't say to each other. It's funny, I could respect what he was doing and the reasons he was doing it, and he could respect what I was doing and the reasons I was doing it. And one thing that we both respect about each other is we are damned good at what we do. For example, he was called on to testify before Senator Kennedy's Committee on Health Care while he was teaching at Cornell.

It's interesting what I used to talk to my brother about—about the system. About how you do develop power and get into a position to change the system. He has accepted it, and he's playing the game beautifully. He has come one hundred and eighty degrees, and he's basically going in the same field, the consulting field, as I am. He's just changed jobs, and the president of his company didn't want him to leave and promised him a vice-president's job to stay. My brother, at the age of 23, was making 24 grand as a consultant, and he had already taught at Cornell.

And here again, it's that thing about being competitive. Because he and I *are* competitive. I root for him all the way, but I want him to be just a half step behind me. It's more a matter of family pride, you know. Just for that. Neither one of us knows which one is really the best. I think I am and he thinks he is. As far as my other brother, my Dad still worries about him, and I tell him, "You've got to let him stand up and be his own man—that's the only way, or he'll never develop responsibility." That's a rough spot for him, being the middle guy of three knockdown competitors, the only one without a college degree. In fact, the only one without at least a master's. And it's a rough situation, one in which I happen to be sensitive, at least as far as his feelings are concerned. So, that's basically my family except for my mother. Mom was dominated by Dad, although I'm very fortunate in having had a very good mother. A very good housewife, a very good mother, very dedicated and very loyal. Mom used to teach school, and after we grew older she went back, and she just stopped teaching school about two years ago.

We lived in so many places that the family was very important because it was constant. We lived all over, lived in so many places. If I had to select two cities, they were Philadelphia and Pittsburgh, where we spent most time. But we have lived in Minneapolis, North Carolina, upstate New York, Jersey, Queens—hardly anywhere over a year. So, it's a situation which, I guess, helps explain why in some ways I might appear to be cold to some people, because I think it is difficult for me to develop close relationships. I can think back about certain relationships which I have developed, but as you get older, it's more and more difficult. Then, you put your nose to the grindstone and you don't worry about that any more. And, as I say, there's no in-between with me. So if something worries me, I give my energies to it, and it's full speed ahead, come hell or high water. In fact, have I ever told you what Frank told one of the VPs who came up to visit me while I was up at Harvard? You know who Frank is, don't you? He is the one I refer to in the article, who really squared with me—the one who helped me get moving. Well, he's a good friend of one of our VPs who came to visit me in Boston to see the Harvard-Yale game, and this VP was asking me how it was going, and I explained how it was rather difficult, and that it was one of the most difficult things I had ever done. And he went back after his visit, and he told this to Frank, my old boss, and Frank's remark was, "Well, if it can be done, he'll do it. In fact, if they make it too rough, that bastard will find a way to steal their exams if he has to, but he'll get it." [Laughs.] So there was no doubt—he said that facetiously—but there was no doubt in his mind that one way or another, I would find a way to prevail. Frank's an excellent manager who did a lot for my development. He really helped me come into my own. His is one of the relationships that I really value in the company, and as you can imagine, leaving the company would not be an easy choice.

James Edwards (B)

Several weeks after his conversation with the casewriter, Jim Edwards was surprised to receive a phone call from Robert McIntosh, one of the company's three executive vice-presidents.[1] McIntosh began the conversation by saying that he had read Jim's article and thought it was very interesting, but that it had left him with several questions that he wanted to discuss personally. McIntosh continued by saying that he had arranged to be in Chicago the following week and wondered whether Jim could meet him for lunch. Jim immediately agreed, and a date was set for the following Wednesday.

[1]The company Edwards worked for had sales of about $2.5 billion and employed nearly 80,000 people. The company's corporate offices were located in Los Angeles, while its divisional headquarters were scattered throughout the country. See "James Edwards (A)" for other background details. Jim reported to a regional sales manager, who in turn reported to the sales vice-president of one of the company's several consumer-product divisions. The division's president reported to a group vice-president, who in turn reported to McIntosh. See Exhibit II-5 for a simplified organization chart of the company.

Jim's grapevine had told him that several of the company's top management had been "put off" by his article, and he wondered if this was why McIntosh wanted to talk with him. McIntosh was widely respected within the company, and from what Jim knew of the man, he found it hard to imagine that McIntosh would have reacted negatively to it. On the other hand, Jim really could not be sure. The only area he felt certain about was his district's performance: He had met or exceeded every sales, service, and collection objective, and the record spoke for itself. Nonetheless, Jim's curiosity began to grow. In many ways, the lunch meeting would provide an ideal opportunity to explain to a key member of top management what he was trying to say in the article.

Jim arrived for the appointment several minutes early and was surprised to see McIntosh enter with Wayne DeVoto, another executive vice-president of the company (see Exhibit II-5). After the preliminary introductions were made, DeVoto explained that he had been in

Exhibit II-5 James Edwards (B)

Company Organization (Simplified)

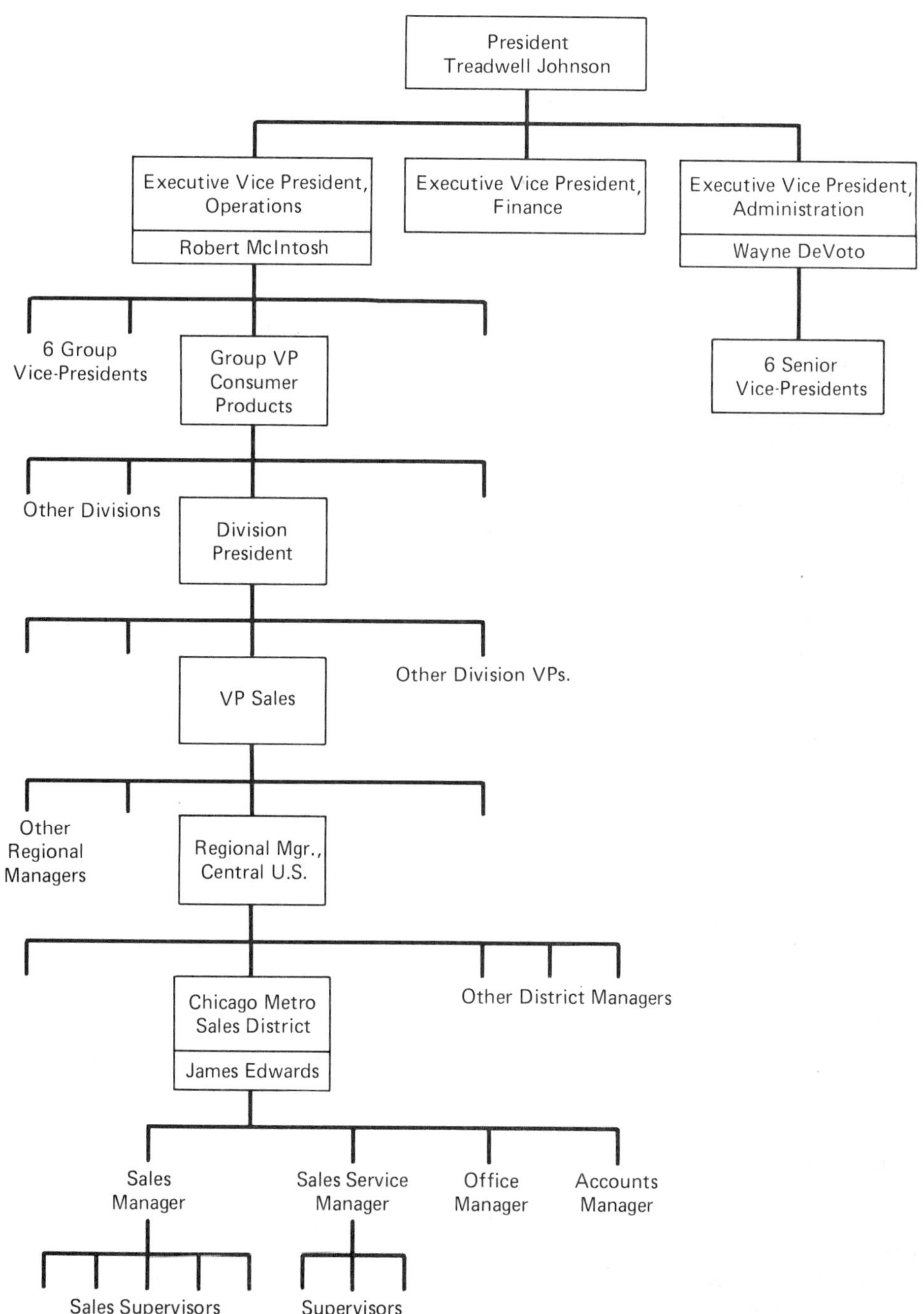

New York earlier in the week and had flown to Chicago to join them for the meeting before returning to Los Angeles. During lunch, the two men discussed the article in considerable detail with Jim, asking him why he felt as he did about certain issues and probing him on others. Jim attempted to answer their questions and to explain as well as he could the points he had tried to make.

After about 45 minutes, McIntosh concluded the discussion by saying that the points that Jim was trying to make in the article were valid and made sense. He added that there were several officers of the company who did not agree with Jim's perceptions, but that that did not necessarily mean they were right.

After a brief pause, McIntosh told Jim that there was a second reason why the two men had come to talk with him. They had come to offer him the job of special assistant to the president of the company. If Jim accepted the job, he would be in charge of a special project and would report directly to the president. The assignment would require that he move to the corporate headquarters in Los Angeles. McIntosh explained that the assignment would be to serve as director of the Job Action Coalition of Los Angeles (JACLA), of which the company's president, Treadwell Johnson, was chairman. JACLA was a coalition of business organizations, social action groups, labor unions, and local, state, and federal agencies. The organization had as its purpose the creation of jobs for members of disadvantaged groups, Vietnam veterans, ex-convicts, and youth. If Edwards accepted the job, he would have to work directly with many different organizations, and especially with representatives of local black and Chicano groups. In addition, he would have to work with Southern California businessmen, the mayors of major cities in the area, boards of education, and state and federal departments of labor.

McIntosh pointed out that Johnson, the company's president, had been chairman of the coalition for over a year and had become very dissatisfied with its lack of progress. Johnson was particularly disappointed with JACLA's unsuccessful attempt to create jobs for youth the preceding summer. McIntosh added that JACLA's initial lack of success had been a source of growing personal embarrassment to Johnson and that Johnson intended to do everything he possibly could to make the program work. Johnson had made a special trip to Washington to tell the secretary of labor that he did not wish to be associated with a failure and, unless he could "turn the program around," he would resign as chairman.

McIntosh continued by saying that Johnson felt that the present director of JACLA had not been effective in working with businesses and, as a result, had not gained their support. Johnson wanted to replace him with someone who would be more effective in working with them. The situation was further complicated by the fact that the current director was a black whose salary had been paid by an important black social action organization in Los Angeles. McIntosh added that the program was far behind its targets and was becoming politically unpopular as well as ineffective. Straightening out the program would be a very difficult job, but they would ask him to do it for a year only.

McIntosh said he felt that Jim was ideal for the job, but that after reading Jim's article, he wanted to offer it to him in person. He was afraid Jim might think it was a "showcase" job, and for that reason, he wanted to explain the context of the offer. He finished by saying that he hoped Jim would accept the job, but that it definitely would not be held against him if he chose not to take it. At this point, Jim asked McIntosh if he thought the position really had the potential for effecting change, to which McIntosh replied he thought it did but it would be "damn tough," and that was the reason why they were asking Jim to do it. DeVoto added that unless JACLA began to deliver on some of its promises, both Johnson and the company would be publicly embarrassed. McIntosh concurred with DeVoto's observation and then asked Jim if he would accept the offer.

PART THREE

Understanding Persons in Relationship

Introduction

Almost all the material introduced thus far has been about people in relationships. Even though Part One focused on languages and problems of communication and Part Two focused on understanding another person, most of the cases, readings, and chapters have dealt with people and their relationships. Thus, much of what we have already covered has been about the topic of this section of the book, understanding persons in relationship. You will find the ideas presented in earlier sections useful in working with the issues raised by the materials that follow. This section is meant to build on those learnings.

However, in contrast to preceding chapters, the materials in this section focus explicitly on the relationships that people develop. Our purpose in doing this is to increase awareness and understanding of how people form relationships, and what some of the problems are that occur as relationships develop over time. Again, the issues and problems we will be discussing are not specific to either work or personal relationships; they are applicable to interpersonal relationships in general.

Chapter 7, "Some Further Aspects of Two-Person Relationships," introduces several ideas that build on and go beyond the concepts presented in earlier chapters. In particular, Chapter 7 describes how relationships develop between people and why some previously strong relationships often run into trouble. It will begin by addressing the basic question of why relationships form in the first place. The chapter will cover a number of aspects of two-person relationships, including interpersonal attraction and how the initial sources of attraction sometimes become, for better or worse, central to the relationship.

The chapter will also describe the *unstated,* yet powerful "contracts" that develop between people in a relationship, and how these contracts influence the people involved: some of the problems that occur when these contracts are violated, and what happens when one or more people in a relationship change in ways that make these contracts obsolete. In addition, the chapter will describe some ways in which these contracts can prevent people from growing, personally and professionally. Finally, Chapter 7 will present some ideas that can be helpful in making relationships more adaptive and vital.

The two readings in this section of the book elaborate on some of the ideas presented in Chapter 7. "Games Managers Play" by R. Jack Weber describes some destructive games people play in which they unconsciously act out roles of persecutor, rescuer, or victim. Weber discusses the structure of these games, their underlying agendas and how to identify and break them. The second reading, "Development of Expectations, Trust, and Influence," describes the evolution of working relationships, how they differ from personal relationships and how they can be developed more fully and effectively.

The cases in this section of the book are about people in a variety of relationships: boss and subordinate, peers, partners, and spouses. The "Acting Out of Character" case is about an intensely felt conflict between two peers, and the events leading up to this conflict. The Frank Mason cases are about the evolution of a relationship between a new manager and the president of his company, and describe the interpersonal problems facing the manager after six months on the job.

The Neely and Chapman cases are perhaps the richest, most interesting, and most comprehensive cases in this book. They chronicle the development, growth, and eventual dissolution of a successful business partnership. However, these cases are about much more than just the events that led to the breaking up of this partnership. The four cases respectively present the views of each of the two partners and of their wives. Taken together, these cases are a chronology of the relationships that developed between the two couples over the years, as well as the individual relationships that developed among all four people. Understanding and fully appreciating the lives and experiences of each of these four will require the skills and sensitivity that the previous section on "understanding another person" attempted to develop. Understanding the evolution and changes in their relationships over time and why things turned out as they did will require that you use the ideas introduced in Chapter 7. These cases also raise a number of more personal issues and questions, which go beyond the scope of the readings but are at the core of living and working in relationships with others.

As in preceding sections of the book, we ask you to use these materials not only to strengthen your conceptual understanding of what occurs in relationships but, more imporant, to help you in understanding your own relationships. Our hope is that these materials will raise questions and trigger personal insights that will be of value to you in your own life.

Chapter Seven

Some Further Aspects of Two-Person Relationships

What kind of relationships work out? Why do two people become business partners, friends, or lovers? What about each other do people find sufficiently attractive to form a relationship in the first place? Why do some relationships flourish, grow richer, and endure, while others die in acrimony or sorrow, and still others creep along, almost monotonously, without growth or deterioration?

These questions come to mind over and over again as I experience my own relationships and observe those of others. I find that I am repeatedly surprised and fascinated by the ways in which relationships come into being, change, grow, or fail. For example, I know two men who have been business partners and close friends for years. Together they created a thriving and, by any standard, successful business. They are also each other's closest friends. Yet they are so different in personality and life-style that when they started in business, few people thought their venture would last longer than a year, let alone result in a strong personal friendship. One of them is outgoing, brash, a wheeler-dealer, an outdoorsman who is bored by music and the theatre, and is aggressive and expansive in his business style. The other is reserved, conservative, likes music and the arts, is not interested in sports, and is cautious and compulsive in his business life.

In contrast, I also know a firm in which the partners and associates are so similar in personal style, skills, and attitudes that they are virtually interchangeable. Their similarities are not just accidental.

We are particularly indebted to Eileen Morley, who assisted in the preparation of an earlier draft of this chapter.

They work hard at courting and recruiting people who are like themselves—socially as well as professionally. They unabashedly admit that a candidate for a position with their firm must be not only professionally compatible, but also socially compatible. The partners and their spouses spend much of their time entertaining each other and key clients. It comes as no surprise, then, that they invite both the candidate *and* spouse for a three-day interview. Perhaps this sounds a bit oppressive to you. It would to many people, yet they appear to enjoy their work and social relationships more than most people I know, and the firm is very profitable.

It seems that for every satisfying relationship with one set of characteristics, we can find another relationship that appears equally satisfying yet has an opposite set of characteristics. The variety of ways in which our relationships grow or fail, satisfy or frustrate, is so diverse that it seems impossible to give firm answers to the questions at the beginning of this chapter. Yet it would be inaccurate to say that we do not know anything about two-person relationships. Each of us has been inevitably involved in human relationships from the moment he was born. Our folklore and literature have long savored the mystery, comedy, and tragedy of human relationships, while their logic is the central focus of contemporary psychology and sociology. Undoubtedly, the reason our relationships with others fascinate us so much is that they form a core part of our very being.

Each of us has had to learn a great deal about how relationships work just to have become who we are. It is not a lack of human experiencing of relationships that makes it difficult to generalize about them, but rather their variety, subtlety, and complexity. It would be naive to think that we can cover as large a topic as two-person relationships in any total sense in this chapter, in class discussions, or in a course in interpersonal relations. But we can focus on some aspects of relationships that can sharpen our insights into them and, in the process, into ourselves.

WHY ARE TWO PEOPLE ATTRACTED TO EACH OTHER?

Let us begin by asking a basic question: Why are two people attracted to each other in the first place? If you consider your own experience, you will probably realize that there are both important similarities and differences in what attracts you to the people with whom you are in relationship. What attracts you about a lover is in some ways quite different from what attracts you about a friend, yet both may share certain qualities or attitudes. Moreover, in some nonpersonal relationships, such as in business, the sources of attraction may have nothing at all to do with your liking of the other person, but rather with economic or other benefits that come from the relationship.

Types of interpersonal attraction have been studied extensively by social psychologists, with the conclusion that the sources of attraction vary widely with the situation and, obviously, with the people involved; but that at a fairly high level of abstraction, all relationships—even those that are neurotic and self-destructive—have a common basis. One person is attracted to another when he or she finds that being with that other is in some way satisfying or has the potential of being so. A relationship comes into existence when two people find that it is more satisfying and meaningful than other alternatives; or when being out of the relationship is more painful than being in it. Conversely, a relationship fails when being in it becomes more painful than being out of it.

Exactly what it is that people find rewarding is varied and complex, ranging from the love and affection that satisfy profound needs for acceptance and affiliation, to economic rewards that satisfy needs for survival or mastery (in people who measure their achievement in dollars). The cost of being in relationship can also vary, from the amount of time required to keep it alive to more severe costs, such as the pain suffered in it, or the abuse to which another might subject us.

We seldom experience the satisfying and dissatisfying aspects of relationships in unidimensional terms. More often, what we experience is a range of simultaneous feelings that come together as being more or less rewarding. Often we are not even aware of the particular sources of these feelings; only that a relationship feels comfortable, or somehow a little "off"; especially good, or rather painful. Almost everyone has left an evening with friends, or a meeting, sensing that something did not feel quite right, but not knowing specifically what or why. It is not impossible to sort out what is particularly rewarding or dissatisfying in a relationship, but it cannot be done unless we attend to what is going on between ourselves and important others, and give thought to the nature of the interaction and of what each party experiences as inviting about the other.

In doing this, it may be useful to start by considering two broad sets of conditions that are sources of interpersonal attraction and can therefore lead to the development of relationships. The first occurs when two people see each other as being similar in ways they value highly. The second occurs when two people experience each other as being different in ways that are complementary.

Similarities That Attract

Generally speaking, people are attracted to and like being with people who are like themselves, who have similar attitudes, values, and interests.[1] We can sometimes sense this from the personal appearance of complete strangers. If we look around a theatre lobby or an airport, we seldom see a person who looks very "hip" with a date

[1]The ideas presented in this and the following section draw heavily from Ellen Berscheid and Elaine Walster, *Interpersonal Attraction* (Reading, Mass.: Addison-Wesley, 1969). This highly readable, yet exhaustive review of interpersonal attraction is strongly recommended to the interested reader.

or friend who is "straight" or is conventionally dressed. Usually the young, long-haired men will be with even longer-haired young women, while men with relatively short hair and wearing suits will more often than not be with women wearing dresses, even though all of them may be waiting in the same area. Seldom will dissimilar-looking people of the same generation be found in the same couple.

Similarities in clothing are, of course, pretty superficial. But there is considerable evidence that suggests that people prefer to be with others who have similar rather than dissimilar attitudes, and that the greater the agreement about matters that are considered important, the greater the mutual attraction.

One explanation for our tendency to be attracted to people who are similar to ourselves is that we experience such relationships as satisfying because they affirm important aspects of our self-concept and create for us a more stable and predictable world. Our important assumptions, perceptions, and feelings, as well as our expectations and sources of identification, are reassured and validated when the other person holds or expresses similar attitudes. Being with someone who is unlike us means that our assumptions may not hold, acceptance may be withheld, and our sense of mastery of the situation may be challenged—all of which cause us to experience undesirable anxiety.

Since we know from experience that another person's past attitudes and behavior are usually indicative of future behavior, we can expect continued rewarding interactions in the future, and the attraction is sustained. We also expect that since our attitudes and convictions are similar, the other person will tend to experience *us* as rewarding, and be likely to offer us even more acceptance and approval. The importance of similarity to interpersonal attraction is so great, social psychologists have shown, that in situations where people are uncertain of their own likability, or feel that it is especially important to be liked, they are particularly anxious to associate with people whom they perceive as being similar to themselves.[2]

Opposites That Complement

Similarities between people are only one source of attraction. Birds of a feather may flock together, but the other old adage, "Opposites attract," is also true. Certain similarities along some personal dimensions are not sources of attraction, but of repulsion or conflict—for example, in a relationship where two people have high dominance needs and both wish to be boss.

There is in reality no contradiction between these two folk sayings

[2]The importance of self-affirmation in relationships is so pervasive that social psychologists have found that people are not only attracted to those who are similar to them, but they tend to be attracted to people they perceive as *liking* them, even when they are dissimilar (unless the liking is seen as insincere). Relationships with people who like us are intrinsically rewarding because they tend to affirm our self-concepts and meet our needs for acceptance and adequacy.

when we consider that both rest on the more fundamental basis of attraction—mutual need fulfillment, in terms of each person's self-concept, individual needs, and the way each sees and experiences the world. Opposites do attract when each person's differences are complementary to the other's, so that each offers what the other needs. Examples of such complementary differences abound, some of them very basic to the nature of human relationships. Consider for example the complementary nature of these relationships: male and female in sexual relations; buyer and seller in economic exchange; performer and audience in entertainment.

Fulfillment of Complementary Needs. Complementary differences can be sources of attraction and a basis for a relationship under a number of circumstances. The most common of these is when two people find in each other what each lacks but needs for some aspect of living. Such complementary differences are often found in traditional marriages, for example, where in the past the wife has taken care of the social and emotional aspects of life (which she enjoys and does well and which he may not), while the husband has taken care of the instrumental aspects of living, such as paying bills and negotiating other practical affairs (which he enjoys and does well while she may not).

Examples of complementary attraction can also be found among people starting new ventures, especially small businesses. In forming these ventures, people often choose as partners others who offer what they lack in skills, experiences, or orientations that are needed to make the business go. It's not uncommon to find an "operations man" choosing a "finance man" as a partner, or two engineers with a new product idea picking out a person with a marketing background as a third partner. If the necessary complementarity is not developed, the business may well run into trouble. I think, for instance, of a new venture that was founded by a team of R&D people who had a low opinion of business administration. After three years of trying unsuccessfully to fill the role themselves, they finally admitted the importance of a business orientation, and they hired a business manager.

Differences along more basic dimensions of personality can also be a basis for attraction, either consciously or unconsciously—for example, as where a man who needs large doses of attention chooses as his wife a woman who is basically nurturing and has a great need to look after, comfort, and take care of others. Similarly, it's not uncommon to find a daring, risk-prone, and aggressive manager, whose natural tendency is to start more things than he or she can finish and to overextend the business, choosing a partner who is careful and compulsive and will tie up (or pick up) the pieces. In a sense, these people are attracted to each other because both of them together make a complete person by making up for each other's inadequacies.

Complementarity of Interpersonal Styles. A second type of attraction can occur between people when their interpersonal styles complement each other, so that one person's preferred way of relating to others allows the other person to also behave in his or her preferred way.[3] For example, a person whose preferred way of interacting is to take charge, assume responsibility, and dominate will tend to form a number of relationships with people whose preferred modes of interacting are to be submissive and dependent. Similarly, a person whose preferred mode is to be benevolent and sympathetic will tend over time to form relationships with a number of people who are docile and in need of support. In a sense, these forms of behavior "invite" each other and provide a source of attraction between two people even though neither may be aware of what is taking place.

There is, in fact, some basis for saying that all our behavior toward others invites or "bids" certain kinds of responses. Submissive behavior bids dominant behavior on the part of the other; dependent behavior bids controlling responses; supportive behavior bids cooperation; oppressive behavior bids rebellion; and so on. In a very real sense, the person who goes around behaving as if he or she were a "poor little thing" who cannot make decisions is asking for others to respond with advice, protection, and direction.

Complementary patterns of interpersonal style have been studied by a number of social psychologists. Their work suggests that several recurring patterns of complementarity exist in both bidding behavior and relationship formation that are generally predictable. These patterns of complementary behavior are usually described in terms of two dimensions, such as love-hate (that is, affection-hostility), and dominance-submission. Generally speaking, complementarity exists in terms of *reciprocity* along the dominance-submission dimension, so that dominance on the part of one person tends to invite submissiveness on the part of the other, or vice versa. This does not mean that a dominant bid will get a submissive response, only that the bid invites it. In contrast, complementarity tends to exist in terms of *correspondence* along a love-hate dimension, so that loving or supportive behavior on the part of one person generally invites a loving or supportive response from the other, while hate or hostility tends to invite reciprocal hate or hostility. Using these two dimensions, some social psychologists have developed a number of patterns of complementarity that exist between various types of interpersonal styles.

For example, a person with an interpersonal style characterized by strong elements of caring and supportiveness combined with strong elements of dominance will tend to bid responses from others that are cooperative and dependent. Over the long run, this type of person will tend to form a number of relationships in which the other person's style will be friendly and docile, with overtones of dependence and help-seeking behavior. Conversely, this type of person will tend *not* to be attracted to people whose preferred style is to be hostile, attacking, and dominant, and it is unlikely that this person

[3]This section on complementarity of interpersonal styles is an elaboration of ideas developed in Robert C. Carson, *Interaction Concepts of Personality* (Chicago: Aldine, 1969). Although the book is somewhat technical, it offers a very complete and exciting discussion of complementarity in personal interactions and is recommended to the interested reader.

would enter into any long-term relationships with such people unless forced to do so.

Although the research and theory on complementarity of interpersonal styles are quite specific in their delineation of possible patterns of behavior and their complements, few people can be characterized by a *single* specific preferred style, as the example above might suggest. Usually, a person will have a broad range of preferred interpersonal styles, some of which may be more typical than others, based on past observation or knowledge. People vary in the range of styles with which they can naturally relate to others. Some people have a very narrow range, and others are capable of genuinely responding in many different ways.

Most people are capable of a great variety of ways of being in relation to others and have a broad repertoire of interpersonal styles. In most "normal" relationships, a person will vary his or her behavior so that he or she may ask for help on some occasions, give advice on others, be supportive sometimes and critical other times, be the leader in some situations and the follower in others. This kind of flexibility is characteristic of an adaptive personality, and when two people each show and allow the other this versatility, it is usually a sign of a healthy relationship.

Preferred styles are rooted in people's upbringing and are related to their present conception of self and to the way they have learned to deal with the anxiety provoked by past interpersonal relationships. In some cases of pathological behavior, the person is so dependent on a single preferred style that he or she cannot behave otherwise in relationships with others.

The notion that interpersonal style can be a basis for complementary attraction and that our behavior can bid for certain responses from the other can be very useful in exploring and understanding our own behavior and relationships. Just the awareness that we have many ways of responding to another, and that our actions have an influence on how the other responds in turn, can increase insight into how and why we form relationships. The bosses who complain that all their subordinates become hostile, untrustworthy, and unable to make decisions might look at the extent to which their own behavior asks for it. And conversely, people who complain that they have never had a decent boss might wonder what role they have played in creating the bosses for whom they have worked.

I have often been amused by the influence that a person stopped for speeding can have on the way he or she is treated by a police officer. It often depends on how the person behaves toward the officer. Invariably, if the person begins with a hostile attack on the unreasonableness of being stopped (which, in terms of the two dimensions described above, is hostile behavior from a dependent position), the police officer will usually respond in a firmly authoritarian fashion (behavior that is also hostile but dominant). On the other hand, if the person responds with a cooperative or inquiring attitude (cooperative, from a dependent position), the police officer is more apt to give him or her the benefit of the doubt (behavior that is also cooperative although dominant). It is even more interesting to speculate on how parents, co-workers, or spouses help "create" the people they are in relationship with by the way they behave in those roles.

UNSTATED "CONTRACTS" IN RELATIONSHIPS

Although our relationships change and develop over time, we tend to develop a set of assumptions and expectations in each of them about what our behavior and that of the other "should" be like. Most of these assumptions are not in our awareness, but nonetheless they provide important expectations about how we should "be" in the relationship. It is almost as if an unstated contract develops between us and the other, which we are often not aware of until one of us breaks it. The feelings of surprise or hurt that we sometimes experience over another's behavior when he or she does something or behaves in ways we did not expect is often a signal that some part of an unarticulated contract has been violated. The existence of these contracts does not have to be in our awareness to influence our behavior. In fact, the power of contracts that are out of our awareness can be seen by the emphasis that some proponents of the feminist movement have placed on the process of discovering and then questioning the traditional assumptions people have about the role of women in marriage.[4] Some proponents of "liberated" marriages go so far as to advocate the creation of "marriage contracts," which specify how marriage roles such as child rearing, household chores, and breadwinning are to be shared or allocated within the marriage. Their emphasis on making explicit these new contracts is vivid testimony of the power of the more traditional, although *unstated,* contracts about how each person ought to behave in a marriage.

In many of our relationships, some of the initial bases of attraction become an important part of the unstated contract that develops, so that each person is expected to continue behaving in ways that made the person initially attractive to the other. In many cases, these expectations are central to the growth of a relationship and enable each person to derive satisfaction from it. This may often be the case in relationships between people who complement each other in their personalities and abilities so that the relationship provides a major source of mutual enhancement. By complementing each other through their differences, each person is able to increase his or her sense of mastery and acceptance, because the relationship enables each to concentrate on those aspects of living that he or she does well, while the other takes care of those aspects that the person does not do well. In these situations, the relationship may enable each person to experience a heightened sense of adequacy, mastery, and acceptance

[4]See, for example, Nena O'Neill and George O'Neill, *Open Marriage* (New York: M. Evans & Co., 1972).

by doing for the other and for himself what he does best or most enjoys.

However, such relationships can also become traps that keep people from growing. This can happen in complementary relationships if the unstated contract is that one partner shall continue to behave inadequately in certain ways, so that the other has a basis for taking care of him or her. The danger is that the unstated contract may include assumptions out of awareness either suggesting or requiring that each remain inadequate in a particular way, so that the other can draw self-esteem and satisfaction by being the one who takes care of things. In a case of this kind, the relationship is in part based on a mutual reinforcement of incompetence. Such nicely complementary relationships may be a means by which each person can behave in ways that are easiest while avoiding those things he or she finds hardest and yet might benefit most from learning. If we stick closely to a contract of this kind, it not only binds us into the relationship, but does so in a way that prevents us from becoming a richer, more effective person.

Often, when a change in circumstances or a crisis alters the configuration of such a relationship, it is surprising to discover how well one person can learn to do the very thing for which he or she had previously relied on the other partner. I have been impressed by the married men I have known in graduate programs who were forced because of work pressures to give up chores they had previously felt their wives could not take care of, such as paying bills, keeping the checkbook, or taking the car to the garage. Sometimes they discover that their wives not only learned quickly how to do these things, but do them better than they did. Similarly, a number of married professional women I know are now discovering how much more capable their husbands are at looking after children and preparing meals than they had dared or wanted to assume. I can also think of examples of similar situations in work settings, where the enforced absence of one partner or associate required that the other take over functions that he or she might have felt incapable of performing until the work actually had to be done.

In cases like this, it is possible that neither person ends up feeling a sense of loss or experiencing less adequacy in the relationship if they both value the increased competence of the formerly dependent person, or if the capabilities of both people have been expanded by the enforced change. The situation is potentially most difficult if, when the crisis period comes to an end, the question arises, "Do we go back to our formerly complementary roles?" This sometimes happens with wives whose husbands finish a tour of duty overseas, or with husbands whose wives recover from a lengthy illness, or in the business setting when the absent partner returns to find that his or her associate has learned to handle the absent partner's part of the operations. In such cases, the successful continuation of the relationship may require some subtle renegotiation of their former contract. Sometimes both partners acknowledge and accept the newfound competence that the formerly dependent partner has acquired. Other times, the relationship lacks enough resilience for this to happen, because the absent partner wants to reestablish the former role, and the other person complies by reverting to the old patterns and forfeits what he has discovered he could do or become. Sometimes one or both refuse to resume their old roles, and the relationship fails.

We have just focused on complementary relationships that can serve to mutually reinforce inadequacies. Relationships based on similarities can be just as confining if the contract that grew out of the initial attraction remains unchanged over time. Such unstated contracts can preclude either party from deviating in thought or action from the original, acknowledged commonality of the relationship. This can sometimes occur even when the relationship has grown far beyond the similarities that each person originally found attractive in the other, and encompasses so many other, more profound sources of satisfaction that the original similarities are a trivial part of the relationship.

The purpose of this discussion of how unarticulated contracts can become constraints to personal growth is not meant to suggest that such contracts are bad, nor that relationships based on strong elements of similarity or complementarity are necessarily constraining. Rather, the point is that it is important, if we value our potentiality for growth, to be aware of the unstated elements that bind people together and to question what the consequences are for both persons in the relationship. Otherwise, assumptions that may not even be in our awareness can be constraints that keep us from growing.

STAYING IN RELATIONSHIP

We have just looked at how the unarticulated "contracts" implicit in relationships can affect the people involved and can influence behavior. Equally interesting is the question of what happens in a relationship when one or both of the people involved are changing in ways that make an old set of assumptions and unarticulated contracts obsolete. People do not usually "stay put" in terms of who they are or what they want out of life, especially in relation to the people who are important to them. Many of the misunderstandings and strains that occur in ongoing relationships come about because at least one of the persons in the relationship is in the process of changing while the other may not be aware of that change—or if aware, may not like it or fully understand it. In such cases, their expectations and assumptions are based on who the other person *used to be.*

The fact that people do change and develop over time has important implications for developing awareness about relationships that we value and want to last. First is a need for awareness that the other person may be changing in ways that mean that our assumptions about them and about the relationship are out of date. Second, we ourselves may be undergoing changes of which the other person is not aware, so that our present behavior is inconsistent with the other's expectations and creates problems for him or her in the relationship.

Sometimes we are aware that we have changed in ways that the other has not perceived, and feel that we cannot acknowledge this because we do not want to disturb or change the other person's assumptions or hurt his or her feelings. To take a small but illustrative example, I have a friend whose mother always serves him lima beans when he goes home for a visit. He hates lima beans, and has disliked them for some time. As a boy, however, he loved them, and he knows that his mother is still using the assumption that was appropriate when he was little. He can't bring himself to tell his mother that he has changed, because she would feel hurt to discover that she had been serving him a dish he does not like, so he continues to eat the lima beans.

Many times, however, we are not aware of the ways in which we are changing. I am often surprised to discover that I have undergone subtle changes in needs, directions, and behavior when another person points them out to me because he or she finds my behavior inconsistent with former expectations. I also find that the converse is true; that misunderstandings or annoyances develop in my personal relationships because the other person has been undergoing subtle changes in his or her needs or expectations, and that these changes have taken place out of my awareness, and sometimes out of the other person's awareness as well. I do not find the process of becoming aware of such shifts an easy one, even in close relationships that matter very much to me.

For example, my wife and I have shared the same workroom in our house for some time. She uses it as a studio and has her drawing board and equipment on one side. I use it as a study and have my desk on the other side. My wife is a free-lance graphic designer and works at home several mornings a week. Since our daughter is at nursery school during those hours, the mornings are important times for her. Although most of the work she does during these mornings is for commercial clients, she occasionally works on personal projects as well, such as prints, constructions, or sculptures. During the past year, I have occasionally worked at home on Friday mornings, one of the days she also works in the room. On these occasions, we have shared the room and things went smoothly—that is, until late last summer, when, after a lapse of three months or so, I stayed home one Friday morning to work. To my surprise, I found that she was being especially critical of my presence in the room and annoyed at the things I normally did when I worked at home, such as my rustling pages, the number of trips I made to get coffee, the noise I made in the kitchen, and so on. Since I felt that I was behaving normally, I was annoyed at her criticisms. Before long, the room became tight with tension as her sense of annoyance increased and my sense of indignation over the unreasonableness of her comments escalated. Finally, when she complained that I was stirring my coffee too loudly, I became outraged, packed my papers, and left for the office, brimming with anger.

After I got to the office, I tried to figure out what had happened. We had been sharing the work space for over a year, and my behavior had been no different from what it had been in the past. Could it be that she was really angry about something else, something I had done earlier, yesterday, last week? When I returned home that evening, we talked about what had happened, and she said that she felt I was crowding her personal time and space. It was not until we had talked for some time that it became clear that several changes had occurred in her needs and life that made the old contract about our sharing that time and space inappropriate. One very important change was the nature of the work she was now doing. During the spring and summer, the focus of her work had shifted from design for commercial accounts to more personal and creative work that she was doing for herself. Since I had used the room very infrequently over the summer, I wasn't aware that this shift had taken place. The concentration required by her more creative and intense work made my mere presence in the room a distraction. Her work, and her need for privacy, had changed in ways that made my assumptions and expectations about our sharing inappropriate.

Once we both became aware of how her needs had changed, we rearranged our morning use of the room, and it ceased to be a problem. Although this whole sequence of events now seems humorous to me, it was not a funny matter when it occurred, and it could conceivably have gone on for some time, with both of us getting angrier about the situation.

This little example is not about a situation in which profound personal changes had taken place, but it still captures the difficulty of staying in touch with another person as he or she develops in a relationship. It also illustrates how difficult it is to understand what is going on when our expectations of what *should* take place in a relationship are disconfirmed. There are, unfortunately, no formal techniques or easy answers for staying in relation with another. But several aspects of attending to the question of staying in relation do seem to be important. The first is an awareness of the possibility that you and the other may be changing in ways that make past assumptions obsolete. The second is that the experiencing of strong feelings is the most frequent and powerful signal that something is wrong, especially when they are feelings of surprise, betrayal, or resentment at the other person's behavior. Strong negative feelings, more than perceptions, are the symptoms that someone is changing in ways that make old working assumptions obsolete, and as such, are something to be consciously explored. When feelings are suppressed or denied under the assumption that it is just another "off" day, the assumptions underlying those feelings are never checked out. The signal is especially strong when the feelings of anger or hostility seem out of proportion to the magnitude of the event, as happens when one person "explodes" over a trivial matter. When the feelings are especially powerful, it is very often a sign that the outburst is related to more than the specific events that triggered the reaction.

Exploring what underlies our feelings requires more than mutual awareness. It requires that both people develop enough openness to express their feelings and to explore underlying assumptions. It also takes an inquiring, nonjudgmental, and accepting openness to what the other person is expressing.

The level of openness possible within a relationship varies with the people involved and, of course, with the nature of the relationship itself. The type of relationship we are talking about here is one that is of some duration, or that at least has the potential of lasting over time; one that both parties value and are committed to making last; and one in which both people desire to communicate with each other. If these conditions exist, both the need for and the appropriateness of openness is great.

It may also be useful (and realistic) to point out that although greater awareness and openness can increase the likelihood that understanding will take place as each person changes, there is no guarantee that it will preserve a relationship or keep it from ending. In fact, there is the very real possibility that greater awareness of how each person is changing could accelerate the ending. On balance, however, the potential for greater understanding that more open behavior can offer far outweighs the risks involved in exposing a truth that both people may wish to avoid. Greater mutual awareness of how each person has changed holds the promise that some conscious accommodation or change might take place that could strengthen or reestablish the relationship. This seems far better than perpetuating a precarious relationship that can only offer the possibility that things could become worse, for reasons that are not understood. The passive acceptance of such a situation can promise only continued anger, frustration, and the anxiety accompanying the realization that what is wrong is either unknown or must be denied. In most cases, efforts to be open will result in making relationships more adaptive, vital, and fulfilling to the people involved, and will allow for the growth of the relationship as well as that of the people in the relationship.

BIBLIOGRAPHY

ARGYLE, MICHAEL, *The Psychology of Interpersonal Behavior.* Baltimore: Penguin, 1970.

BENNIS, WARREN, "Interpersonal Communication," in Warren D. Bennis, Kenneth D. Benne, and Robert Chan, *The Planning of Change.* New York: Holt, Rinehart & Winston, 1961.

———, EDGAR H. SCHEIN, DAVID BERLEW, and FRED STEELE, *Interpersonal Dynamics.* Homewood, Ill.: Dorsey, 1964.

BERNE, ERIC, *Games People Play.* New York: Grove Press, 1964.

BERSCHEID, ELLEN, and ELAINE WALSTER, *Interpersonal Attraction.* Reading, Mass.: Addison-Wesley, 1969.

CARSON, ROBERT C., *Interaction Concepts of Personality.* Chicago: Aldine-Atherton, 1969.

MCCALL, GEORGE J., and J.L. SIMMONS, *Identities and Interactions.* New York: Free Press, 1966.

O'NEILL, NENA, and GEORGE O'NEILL, *Open Marriage.* New York: M. Evans, 1972.

ROGERS, CARL R., *Becoming Partners.* New York: Delacorte Press, 1971.

———, *On Becoming a Person.* Boston: Houghton Mifflin, 1961.

SCHUTZ, WILLIAM C., "Interaction: Interaction and Personality," in David L. Sills, ed., *The International Encyclopedia of the Social Sciences,* Vol. 7. New York: Macmillan, and Free Press, 1968.

Readings

Games Managers Play

R. Jack Weber

Do you sometimes blame other people or departments for your own mistakes? Do you know someone who takes on more responsibilities than he or she can handle or who feels and looks harried? Do you know people who repeatedly procrastinate on important projects or arrive late to meetings and invite criticism from superiors? If these situations sound familiar, then you or others may have been engaging in a recurring pattern of dysfunctional behavior colloquially known as a "game."[1]

As with Monopoly or checkers, people start playing psychological games in childhood. Children learn to manipulate their parents to elicit the attention they can't get by asking directly. Thus, the boy who asks his father to play baseball and is refused may moments later provoke his sister to fight. Dad then breaks up the quarrel with unnecessary force and the little boy cries. Mom intervenes, criticizes the father, and provides the children with a snack. Each time the pattern recurs, reinforcement takes place, and through a process of social learning, the child unconsciously learns to pick fights or break rules when he feels neglected.

Indeed, it is asserted that the patterns of behavior developed in the context of dependency during childhood become archetypes for subsequent authority relationships such as those between managers and subordinates in organizations. Learning to identify games and their underlying hidden agendas can provide the basis for more productive, satisfying, and growthful relationships.

GAME ROLES

When people engage in games, they unconsciously act out roles of Persecutor,

[1]The original statement on interpersonal games, such as those described in this paper, is found in Eric Berne's *Games People Play: The Psychology of Human Relationships* (New York: Grove Press, 1964).

Rescuer, or Victim.[2] In the situation described above, the boy's invitation to his father is apparently direct, nonmanipulative, and free of games. Having failed, however, he initiates a game by Persecuting his sister who plays Victim by exaggerating the actual transgression. Father rushes to Rescue his daughter (who could handle her own problems) and ends up Persecuting his son by slapping him. Shifting to the Victim role, the little boy screams for his mother who Persecutes the father and Rescues her son by fixing him chocolate milk.

As the boy grows up and becomes the general manager of a subsidiary and his achievements go unrecognized by the home office, he unconsciously repeats his childhood scenario by missing targets and turning in reports late, and is finally reprimanded by his boss. The boy-turned-manager angrily leaves the office early and complains about his superior to his wife who agrees with him and fixes him a drink. And although the actors have changed since childhood and he gets a double martini rather than chocolate milk, the game roles and dynamics are essentially unchanged.

It is important to note that game role behavior is nonproblem-solving, avoids responsibility, and results in bad feelings or otherwise fails to satisfy the underlying need. Thus, the boy's attack on his sister does nothing to identify other alternatives for playing ball or for getting his father's attention. Similarly, the manager's poor performance, criticism of his superior, and double martini do nothing to solve the original problem of inadequate recognition.

The three roles and their dynamic relationship may be represented in the form of the Game Triangle[3] as shown below. The Persecutor (P), Rescuer (R), and Victim (V) roles are connected in the diagram to indicate that games involve two or more roles and that people frequently switch roles during the course of one game or may play different roles in different games. However, most people have a favorite game role and tend to favor associates that behave in ways that permit them to play that role.

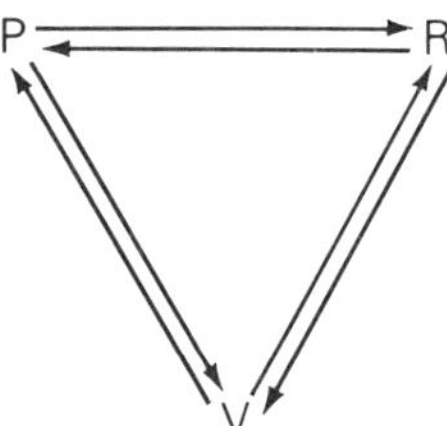

The Game Triangle

Each of these roles is described in greater detail below together with some of the principal games associated with each role.

PERSECUTOR GAMES

The person in the role of Persecutor manipulates others to feel badly through blaming, shaming, ridiculing, bullying, threatening, criticizing, nitpicking, belittling, mocking, and so on. People playing Persecutor use one-up language laced with imperatives and judgments such as "you ought to know better!," "how could you be so stupid?," "you'll never learn!," and so on. The verbal statements may be accompanied by an accusing or threaten-

[2]The psychodynamics underlying these roles is clearly described in Claude Steiner's *Scripts People Live: Transactional Analysis of Life Scripts* (New York: Grove Press, 1974).

[3]The Game Triangle is also known variously as the Drama Triangle or the Karpman Triangle after its originator. See S.B. Karpman, "Fairy Tales and Script Drama Analysis," *Transactional Analysis Bulletin,* Vol. 7, No. 26 (April 1968), 39.

ing pointed finger, arms folded across one's chest, eyes rolled upward, a furrowed brow or frown, and loud, punitive, or condescending voice tones. The underlying feeling is anger or contempt and the underlying assumption is that others ought to be perfect or otherwise behave in ways consistent with the Persecutor's grandiose expectations. Specific examples include NIGYSOB and Blemish, two games that are described below.

Now I've Got You, You SOB (NIGYSOB). The "NIGYSOB" player tries to make other people feel bad to cover up his own negative feelings. He criticizes others excessively when they violate his standards or expectations, . . . frequently unrealistic or ambiguous. The psychological "payoff" for the Persecutor is a justification for feeling self-righteous and angry, an avoidance of intimate or authentic relationships with others, and an escape from his own underlying low self-esteem.

Case Example

Professor Corsini teaches finance in a major M.B.A. program. One day, in the middle of a case discussion that Corsini felt was not going very well, he noticed that Susan Morris was covertly whispering and smiling to her neighbor. Corsini imagined that the students were laughing about how poorly his class was going and he punitively snapped: "Miss Morris, what are *your* thoughts?" Miss Morris apologetically admitted that she hadn't followed the prior discussion. Rather than giving her enough information to respond, Corsini gave her an icy stare and turned to another student.

"NIGYSOB" can be avoided by negotiating clear, mutual expectations and achievable goals, by providing or acquiring the information and resources necessary to succeed, and by ongoing problem-solving.

Blemish. The "Blemish" game player criticizes insignificant flaws in performance rather than rewarding major successes. The "Blemish" player also Persecutes by constantly looking for minor gaps in logic rather than trying to understand the bigger picture. "Blemish" players experience an uncontrollable need to correct and find fault with others.

Case Example

Sydney Rogers asked a young marketing manager to evaluate his company's marketing strategy on their major product lines. When the subordinate submitted his detailed report, Rogers circled a couple of minor substantive and typographical errors in red pencil and wrote in red on the cover sheet: "Rewrite!"

Managers who play "Blemish" covertly invite their subordinates to concentrate on the inconsequential aspects of their jobs and to try to do everything perfectly without regard to priority. Subordinates also tend to develop feelings of inadequacy and resentment.

VICTIM GAMES

People in the role of Victim feel helpless or inadequate to solve their own problems or achieve their own goals when in fact they are not. The person playing Victim manipulates others to Rescue or Persecute by complaining, whining, bitching, agitating, getting sick, procrastinating, making mistakes, apologizing, and so on. The person playing Victim differs from a real victim (such as someone who is drowning) in that the Victim's helplessness is imaginary. The Victim also frequently does not ask for the help or support he or she needs, rejects advice or help when others offer it, and does not work at identifying and solving his or her problems.

People in the role of Victim use language such as "I don't know" (when they really do), "I can't do it" (when they really could), "I can't stand it" (when they are), "I've tried everything" (when they have lots of other options), "It wasn't my responsibility" (when it was), "I didn't do it" (when they did), and so on. Frequently this kind of verbal behavior is accompanied by slumped or dejected postures, depressive voice tones, pouting or helpless facial expressions, and downcast eyes.

Kick Me. "Kick Me" players unconsciously provoke potential persecutors to criticize, condemn, punish, or otherwise put them down. They always seem to be getting into trouble and ask themselves "Why does this always happen to me?" The payoff to the game is a feeling of inadequacy and an opportunity to ask someone for sympathy.

Case Example

Karl Glasser is an account executive at a New York bank. Karl always seems to have more than he can get done. But while Karl efficiently processes paper work concerning his clients and other departments in the bank, he always seems to put off reports requested by his immediate superior. In fact, his boss frequently has to ask Karl a second time for important reports, which irritates Karl's boss and leaves Karl feeling guilty. Karl also plays "Kick Me" by frequently arriving late to meetings.

The game can be stopped by negotiating clear contracts with the potential player, by providing recognition or positive "strokes" for achieving commitments, and by withholding negative strokes or criticism for his or her mistakes.

If It Weren't for You. The basic theme of this game is that "there is someone else who keeps me from doing what I really want to do." The payoff of the game is to avoid doing something that one deeply fears.

Case Example

Earl Watson worked for a major public accounting firm in New York City. He hated the bureaucracy of the large organization almost as much as the two hours a day he spent in commuting from Westchester. He griped about his situation constantly to friends on the train and talked repeatedly about his desire to return to the midwest to start his own firm. When asked why he didn't leave, he said that his wife was afraid that they wouldn't make it. Over time he became increasingly bitter towards his wife and complained to a broader circle of people that "If it weren't for Nancy, I would get out of New York."

The game can be broken up by granting the player permission to do what he or she claims to want to do. In the example above, if the wife would have said, "Go ahead and make a crack at your own business," the husband's underlying fears would be revealed and he could no longer hold his wife responsible.

Ain't It Awful. As the name suggests, "Ain't It Awful" involves protracted complaining about some aspects of one's life or work. The covert message is a plea for sympathy that the Victim usually rejects on the grounds that the situation is hopeless. The payoff is a feeling of hopelessness or despair.

Case Example

John Wickenden was in the first year of a demanding two-year M.B.A. program, and every few days John would wile away two or three hours with a classmate at a local coffee house bitching about the work load and various professors. When they had finished, both would feel even worse than when they started.

The problems that are the source of the material for "Ain't It Awful" are frequently exaggerated or imaginary. But even when they are serious and authentic, the situation is a game because it does not lead to problem-solving nor to an improvement in the player's life or work situation.

The game can be stopped by shifting the topic, by asking the person what has been going well in his or her life, or by engaging the person in an exploration of ways that they might improve their situation.

Why Don't You? Yes, But. In this game the initiator solicits advice from another on a decision or problem and then rejects any suggestions offered.

Case Example

Dick Pfeiffer, a first-year M.B.A. student, had recently flunked his accounting midterm exam and had gone to talk to his faculty advisor, a professor of marketing. Dick asked his advisor's advice, but when the professor suggested that he ask his accounting professor for help, Dick replied, "Yeh, but he is awfully busy and I really don't want him to know how much trouble I'm having." The advisor then suggested that Dick ask one of his classmates to help, to which Dick replied, "Yes, but they already have enough of their own work to do."

The professor next suggested that Dick hire a part-time tutor from the student tutoring agency, to which Dick replied, "Yes, but I don't really have the money." The professor quickly informed the student that there were long-term, low-interest loans available for such purposes and the student responded that "Yes, but I already have a lot of loans and I wouldn't want to get into any more debt." By this time the advisor was experiencing a lot of frustration and politely told the student that he had an important meeting to go to.

In organizational life a "Yes, But" player presents a personal or work-related problem in such a way that his superior or other potential Rescuer is induced to offer advice. When the superior offers a possible solution to the problem, the subordinate responds by saying "Yes, but . . ." and adds information that renders the advice redundant, gratuitous, or presumably unworkable. On the surface, the situation appears to be a direct and straightforward request: "Here is a problem. Do you have any ideas on how I can solve it?" However, if the person is playing "Yes, But" there is also a covert message that belies that "If you try to give me advice, I'll find fault with every suggestion."

The game ends in an exasperated silence that ensues after the superior has offered several solutions and has run out of ideas or is frustrated. This tells the subordinate that he has won the game. It also demonstrates that the boss is inadequate and reinforces an early childhood decision that "parents are dumb."

If the superior above had suspected the beginning of a game, his first response to the request for information above might have been to say: "Sounds like a tough problem. What ideas have you thought about?" This approach also has the advantage of strengthening the subordinate's capacity to solve his or her own problems. Even if the subordinate did accept the superior's advice or solution it is still the superior's solution and he or she is responsible for its success or failure. As such, solving other people's problems is also a set-up for "See What You Made Me Do." Finally, it is important to understand that bosses can initiate the game by inviting "participation" in decisions when they have strong feelings about the preferred outcome.

RESCUER GAMES

A manager Rescues when he helps someone who does not want help, someone who does not need help, or someone who is not helping himself. A manager Rescues when he meddles in other's decisions, underestimates other's abilities, or fails to require people to carry their share of the work load.

A manager who Rescues may deny his own needs, delegate too little, work too hard, and become a Victim when others take advantage of his generosity and concern. Or he may shift to Persecutor when others whom he "helped" do not respond by helping themselves.

A manager who Rescues secretly believes that others cannot solve their own problems and that others will grow through his making decisions for them or through his giving them advice. He may also believe that others will be destroyed if confronted with their inadequacies or otherwise given straight information. The Rescuer perpetuates dependence.

People playing the Rescuer role appear helpful and use language such as "Sure. I'd love to do it" (when he really hates to do it), "Let me do it for you" (when the other person hasn't asked for help), "If I were you, I . . ." (When the other person is capable of making the decision), and so on. Nonverbally, Rescuing behavior is frequently accompanied by sympathetic or supportive voice tones, encouraging head nodding, or consoling pats on the back.

Harried. The "Harried" player in his effort to be loved and approved by everyone takes on everything that comes down the pike, agrees to do things he really doesn't want to do, and seeks out more things to do even when he is already grossly overloaded. He agrees with all of his superior's criticisms and accepts all of his subordinates' demands. Eventually his performance suffers and he blames it on having too much to do, feigning that he had no control over his decisions to accept each new responsibility.

I'm Only Trying To Help You. In this game the player offers advice to someone who hasn't asked for it or who really doesn't want to change. The "client" takes the advice but returns and reports that the suggestion did not have the desired effect. The player who offered the unwanted advice feels inadequate, privately thinks "Nobody ever does what I tell them," and offers new advice.

Case Example

A first-year M.B.A. student went to one of his instructors, Professor Patsy, and confided that another first-year student, David Maxey, was not speaking in any of his classes and might "flunk out" due to poor participation. While Professor Patsy knew that Maxey wasn't speaking in his own class, he was unaware that it was a broader problem for Maxey.

Professor Patsy sought out David Maxey and invited him to his office. Patsy told Maxey that he had a problem, and after listening to Maxey's somewhat unrelated personal problems for two hours, advised Maxey to change seats and prepare a few "key points" to make in each class.

Two weeks later Maxey still hadn't opened his mouth and Patsy called Maxey in again for more coaching. Another week passed and Maxey quit school, informing the Dean's Office that there was "unreasonable pressure" to participate and that the emphasis on quantity of participation was "sophomoric."

People who receive unsolicited and unwanted advice or help in making decisions can stop this game by telling the player that they will ask for help when they need it. Likewise, people who initiate this game and other Rescuing games can learn to say no without feeling guilty, can reserve their help and advice for people who take the initiative to ask for it, and can contract with the people with whom they live and work to take responsibility for asking for help when they need it.

BEYOND GAMES

Why do people play games? After all, why would someone repeatedly show up late to class or to meetings when they know their superior values punctuality? While the complete explanation for the self-defeating quality of games is beyond the scope of this paper, the simple explanation is that "people need strokes to survive" and that "negative strokes are better than no strokes." To a child, to be yelled at may be preferable to being ignored. And unfortunately, the patterns developed in childhood tend to persist in organizational life even when they fail to produce satisfying outcomes.

Eric Berne once observed that the question is not "*Do* I play games?" but "*What* games do I play?" The challenge then is to learn to identify and stop your own games, to refuse to buy into others' games, and to find honest and assertive ways to get the strokes you need.

The Development of Trust, Influence, and Expectations

John J. Gabarro

The broad topic of interpersonal relationships, how they are formed and how they develop, has been studied extensively by social scientists. Much of this research is relevant to managers in organizations. However, relatively few studies have focused on the development of working relationships *per se,* and even fewer on how managers, in particular, develop working relationships with their subordinates.[1]

The purpose of this paper is to describe some characteristics of how managerial relationships form and develop over time. In particular, we will focus on how trust, interpersonal influence, and mutual expectations are created. In doing this we will draw on the findings of a study we have completed of newly appointed company presidents and the process they went through in developing working relationships with their key subordinates. This research was an exploratory field study that followed the development of these relationships over a three-year period of time.[2]

In doing this study our primary purpose was to understand how these new presidents and their subordinates went about developing working relationships and what problems they faced in doing so. We had no prior hypothesis to test nor theories to validate. We simply wanted to understand, as well as we could, how they experienced these relationships over time and why some relationships we observed seemed to be more effective than others in terms of how well

The ideas presented here are based in part on a working paper prepared for the 1976 Organizational Behavior Research Conference sponsored by the Division of Research of the Harvard Business School, Concord, Massachusetts, February 28, 1976. The author is particularly indebted to Renato Tagiuri for his suggestions and to Richard Walton and Jay Lorsch for their comments on an earlier draft.

[1]Some notable exceptions include Hodgson, Levinson and Zaleznik (1965) and Dalton (1959)

[2]The study was clinical in nature and involved four days of observation at each site before interviews were begun. Interviews were conducted at the three month, six month, twelve month, and eighteen month time periods both with a new president and his subordinates. Follow up interviews were conducted with the new presidents in the second year of the study and with the new presidents and their subordinates in the third year of the study.

people were able to work together in performing their jobs. We were especially interested in seeing if there were any common patterns that could be found across the thirty-three superior-subordinate pairings we studied.

The research was conducted in four companies, each of which had named a new president prior to the beginning of our field work. In all four cases the president had been selected from outside the company and previously had established a "track record" of success in prior assignments. All were judged "seasoned" and successful executives before assuming their new posts. By the end of the study, all four had also proved successful in these assignments as evidenced by their companies' economic performance.[3]

The number of key subordinates with whom each new president worked varied, ranging from seven to eleven. Most of the president's subordinates were vice presidents and all of the presidents and their subordinates were men. As one might expect, some of these subordinates left, were fired, or were reassigned during the three years of the study.

In discussing these relationships we will first describe their evolution over time and how this process appears to differ from the formation of social and intimate relationships. Then we will discuss separately some bases upon which expectations, trust, and influence developed.

THE EVOLUTION OF THESE RELATIONSHIPS

Our interviews and observations suggested that the evolution of these working relationships differed in some important respects from those of an intimate or social nature. For example, interpersonal attraction appeared to play a relatively less important role in the development of these relationships than it does in purely social relationships. Similarly, self-disclosure (in terms of information of a personal or private nature) was generally described as being relatively unimportant to either the development of trust or influence. However, openness about task problems or task related issues was seen by both superiors and subordinates as being *very* important to developing trust.

Why initial liking and attraction were less important in these relationships can be explained by a variety of factors. Some of these include the strong performance orientations of the new presidents, the asymmetry in formal power between the presidents and their subordinates, the specific cultures of the companies studied, and the fact that all four companies (and therefore their top management groups) were under pressure to increase profits. Whatever the reasons, it was clear from our interviews with both the new presidents and their subordinates (as well as subsequent interviews with executives in other companies) that the dominant motive for developing a "good" working relationship was to enable both parties to be more effective. Initial liking was, at best, a secondary motive.[4]

For this reason, a subordinate's competence, reliability, and openness more than compensated for a lack of initial liking or attraction. Many personal attributes that could be troublesome in a purely social relationship (e.g., personal style, interest outside of work, mannerisms, etc.) were

[3]In two of these cases the new presidents had been faced with "turn-around" situations because their companies were initially in serious economic difficulty. In the other two cases, the companies had been judged relatively successful in terms of economic performance.

[4]By way of qualification, there are obviously many managerial settings in which this generalization would not apply, as for example, where a superior does not have a strong performance orientation or where an organization's culture is highly political. Also, we would expect that personal liking would be particularly important in situations where a superior and subordinate had to spend a major portion of their time physically working together.

often overlooked or discounted in these relationships.

An excerpt from an interview with a subordinate in which he describes his relationship with his new president makes this point succinctly:

> He's not an easy man to like. He's very closed about his personal life and doesn't mince any words. But he knows what he's doing and he listens. You know where you stand with him and everybody appreciates that. He's the best boss I've ever had and I respect him immensely. So if you ask me if it's a good working relationship, I have to say yes, a very good one.

The comments of one of the new presidents (in another company) express the same sentiment:

> I don't know where I'll come out with him [one of his subordinates]. I've cut back his influence on sales and production and we'll see how he does with [new product development]. I could have been a hero if I'd fired him the first week I was here. Everybody would have loved me for that. Nobody likes him. He's abrasive and obnoxious. But I think he's very good at [product development]. I suspect he's the best in the industry. I don't like him personally; he's not the kind of guy I'd like to have over to dinner. But I think there's potential there, and if I can focus him on what he does well, I think he will work out.

The important, although not surprising, characteristic of these relationships is that task accomplishment was a central, and often dominant, aspect of their evolution. If anything, the experience of working effectively together led to eventual mutual liking rather than initial liking leading to an effective relationship.[5]

Interviews and observations over the three year period indicate that these working relationships did develop in an evolutionary manner. This evolution occurred in terms of learning about the other person, the working-out of mutual expectations, and the development of trust and mutual influence. A comparison of our interview data over time suggests that this evolution occurred in several sequential stages beginning with a period of initial impression-making and culminating in a stage in which both parties had worked out a relatively stable set of mutual expectations. Progression through these stages occurred in *all* relationships (including those which were seen as ineffective) except for those in which the subordinate quit or was fired.

Indeed, this process can be characterized as an evolutionary development of an "interpersonal contract."[6] By interpersonal contract we mean an agreed upon set of mutual expectations concerning performance, roles, trust, and influence. This interpersonal contract developed over time with some aspects of it evolving tacitly and others being negotiated more or less explicitly. In those cases where one or both parties were unable or unwilling to accommodate to the other's minimal expectations, the relationships terminated with the subordinate either quitting, being fired, or being reassigned. Since the issues worked out at these stages involved principally the development of expectations, trust, and influence, we will describe these processes in more detail before proceeding to a discussion of the stages in the relationship building process.

DEVELOPMENT OF EXPECTATIONS

The expectations with which these new executives and their subordinates were

[5]Wortman and Linsenmeier (1977) essentially arrive at the same conclusion in their review of experimental studies on interpersonal attraction in task settings.

[6]The notion of a psychological contract between two people or a person and an organization (as personified by his superior) has been articulated by several students of organizational behavior including Thomas (1976), Levinson (1966), and Lawless (1972).

concerned spanned a broad area of issues. One of the most important of these issues was, of course, performance, including business goals, how they should be achieved, priorities, and standards of performance. Expectations about roles, i.e., what each person should do in his job, and issues of autonomy and influence were also very important as were expectations about the relationship itself in terms of openness, support, and how conflict should be worked out.

When our interviews were compared over time, it became apparent that as expectations were worked out, they became more concrete and specific in nature. (There were several exceptions to this generalization and they will be discussed below.) The development of these expectations typically progressed from the general to the concrete. In somewhat over-simplified terms, this progression occurred in the following sequence: (1) an initial "trading" of individual expectations of a relatively general nature; (2) exploration of more specific expectations of an individual nature; and (3) finally attempts to work out or negotiate differences in individual expectations. Obviously it was necessary to first discover the other's expectations and articulate one's own expectations before differences could be worked out.

Indeed, one of the patterns that emerged was that the process of going beyond general and superficial expectations was very important to developing an effective relationship. In most of the cases where one or both parties perceived the relationship as being less than effective or satisfying, there had been a failure to clarify, test, or work through expectations. An example would be a subordinate who, after six months, was still not clear on what the new president expected, or a superior who had not yet been able to work out specific priorities with a subordinate.

All of the subordinates we interviewed were very interested in trying to learn what the new president's expectations were of them as individuals and of the company as a whole. "What does he want?" "What are his concerns?" "What are his motives?" These were all questions they wanted answered. The new presidents were equally curious, but about a somewhat different set of questions concerning subordinates, such as "how good is he?" "can I rely on him?" "will he talk straight to me?" "what does he see as the problems?"

Expectations were communicated and worked out by both parties in many different ways. Often they were communicated formally and explicitly in meetings of the entire top management group or between the new president and individual subordinates. (All of the new presidents had met initially with their key executives for this purpose, and all of them continued to meet individually with key subordinates during the life of the study.) Preparation and review of budgets, operating reports and five year plans were also occasions on which expectations were communicated and worked through.

More often, however, expectations were communicated and worked out in the process of day-to-day interactions of a routine nature such as *ad hoc* meetings on specific problems. In interviews with both superiors and subordinates these spontaneous situations were cited as being the most frequent and important settings in which expectations were communicated and worked out. "On-the-spot feedback" was viewed as the most effective way of clarifying them.

Expectations were also communicated symbolically. For example, in two of the companies we studied we were surprised by how many subordinates made mention of the new superior's working hours as an example of how he had signaled his expectations.

> He was the first one in the office. His car was in the lot by 7:00 a.m. every morning

and he never left before 6:00 p.m. That told people a lot about what he expected from us.

An excerpt from an interview in another company illustrates the same point.

> I knew immediately, the first day, he was going to be different from [his predecessor]. Everyone knew he was going to be more demanding. A lot of little things—he spends no time on small talk, and whenever someone else does, he changes the subject back to business. He sat behind his desk while [his predecessor] always sat in the easy chair. [His predecessor] was very informal, vague, kind of a "good Joe," seat-of-the pants, type guy. [The new president] was prepared to the teeth. We all knew it was the start of a new era.

Both of these excerpts concern initial impressions about expectations of a general nature but similar examples also were found of symbolic behavior communicating more specific expectations as well. For instance, in another company every member of the top management group (without exception) and several people in middle management referred to an incident that occurred in the fourth month of the new president's tenure when the company had again missed its shipments quota. The new president called together the executives involved and suggested that every member of that group physically remain in the plant until the quota had been met. By four in the morning of the next day, the quota had been shipped and as one person put it "there was no question of our being late on shipments again." This request was perceived by several of his subordinates as extreme, by others as appropriate, but all agreed it had made its point.

DEVELOPMENT OF TRUST

Trust has been defined or operationalized in the literature in many different ways including the level of openness that exists between two people, the degree to which one person feels assured that another will not take malevolent or arbitrary actions, and the extent to which one person can expect predictability in the other's behavior in terms of what is "normally" expected of a person acting in good faith.[7]

To some degree it is artificial to discuss the development of trust, mutual expectations, and influence as separate processes because in reality they are so closely interrelated. For example, many interviews suggested that the development of trust in a subordinate or superior was very much a function of how clearly mutual expectations had been worked out with that person and how well that person had met those expectations. The comments of one subordinate make this point succinctly.

> Why do I have so much trust in him? Well, he's very clear on what he wants done and what he'll do. When we agree on something, I *know* he'll stay to his word. He's very predictable; he never surprises you . . . you know what he expects and what he will do.

Similarly, the degree of influence one person had on another appeared to be very much dependent on how much that person was trusted by the other. For example, in the excerpt that follows the interviewer had just asked a president why one subordinate had developed so much influence over him during his first three months in the company.

> Why does he influence me? Because I trust him implictly—on every count. He doesn't distort the facts. He's a "pro" and he knows the business better than anyone else.

[7]Perhaps the best review of research and theory on trust, particularly as related to expectations and power, is included in Walton (1968). An excellent discussion of the characteristics of trust in interpersonal relationships is given in Altman and Taylor (1973) and a comprehensive review is given by Berscheid and Walster (1969).

I can rely on him to have thought through a recommendation pretty thoroughly before he makes it.

Implicit in this executive's response are several of his own personal definitions of trust. Given the exploratory nature of our study and our desire to understand what the presidents and their subordinates saw as important in their relationships, we wanted to discover how they themselves defined and operationalized trust. We intentionally ignored various definitions given in the literature and instead we probed in our interviews for the person's own conceptions of trust and how he thought it had developed.[8] Although this process was tedious at times, it resulted in a relatively concrete set of bases and criteria on which managers assessed trust.

It became clear from our interviews that neither the presidents nor their subordinates viewed trust as a unidimensional or undifferentiated characteristic of a relationship, i.e., that there were several bases of trust, although some were more important than others. Our interviews also suggested that trust, like mutual expectations, developed over time and the nature of this trust became more concrete and differentiated as people came to know each other better. In other words, they became clearer on which areas they could trust in each other's judgment and behavior and which areas they could not. We also found considerable convergence in what our interviewees described as bases of trust.

Bases of Trust

Of the many criteria for trust described in interviews several were mentioned repeatedly. At the most general level, these bases can be grouped in terms of each person's perceptions of the other's character, competence, and judgment. These bases are briefly summarized below but we will discuss each individually.

[8]To a large degree our approach was ethnomethodological in nature. We intentionally used systematic observation and codification of everyday events in an attempt to identify the underlying bases and procedures upon which our respondents made certain judgments. See Psathas (1972) and Garfinkel (1969).

BASES OF TRUST

Character:

- Trust in the other's integrity
- Trust in the other's motives and intentions
- Trust in the other's consistency of behavior
- Trust in the other's openness and discreetness

Competence:

- Trust in the other's functional or specific competence
- Trust in the other's interpersonal competence
- Trust in the other's general business sense

Judgment:

- Trust in the other's ability to make good judgments in his work and behavior

Character-Based Sources of Trust

Integrity. By integrity these managers meant the other's honesty in the relationship. They used this term in the personal and moral sense of the word. Both superiors and subordinates used such expressions as "moral character" and "basic honesty," as well as integrity.

Motives. Next to integrity, the most frequently mentioned basis for developing trust was what one perceived as the other's intentions. Words used to describe this included "commitment," "posture," "agenda," etc. In all of the cases we studied, subordinates found it difficult to trust the new president until they had first made a favorable assessment of his motives, e.g., "it was hard to trust him until we knew that his purpose was not to conduct a witch hunt and that he was willing to let us prove ourselves."

Consistency of Behavior. It was surprising how much consistency mattered to both the new presidents and their executives. They used such terms as reliability, predictability, and so forth to describe this trait. As one president put it, "How can I rely on someone if I can't count on him consistently?" One executive made a similar comment regarding his new president, "he was so consistent in what he said and did, it was easy to trust him." Compare this with the comments of an executive in another company: "The one area in which it was hard to trust him was his lack of predictability; he's impulsive and I'm never sure when he'll change signals on me."

Openness. We use the term here in its conventional meaning, i.e., leveling with another and being honest in discussing problems related to the business and the relationship. Our managers used such phrases as "I can count on his being straight with me," "he doesn't hide problems," or "he's not afraid to speak his piece."

Discreetness. Discreetness was the perception that the other person would not violate confidences or carelessly divulge to others potentially harmful information, e.g., "he has a big mouth so it's hard to trust him with sensitive information."

Competence-Based Sources of Trust

Thus far the bases of trust we have described would pertain to purely social relationships as well as working relationships. However, in the working relationships we studied, competence was also seen as a very important basis of trust. In our interviews three different areas of competence emerged as being important: trust in the other's specific area of functional competence (e.g., marketing, finance, etc.); trust in the other's ability to work with people; and trust in the other's overall business sense.

Specific Competence. We are using this term to mean competence in the specialized knowledge and skills required to do a particular job. As mentioned earlier, the new presidents had to rely on their key executives to run different parts of the business, and thus assessing their level of competence was a very important concern in the early stages of these relationships. Take, for example, the following comment about a vice-president of marketing:

> Not only could we not agree on what had to be done to improve our marketing but I also discovered he didn't even know the basics. It was impossible for me to trust his judgment on anything.

Interpersonal Competence. At this level of the organization "getting the job done" also required competence at working with people. We are using the term interpersonal competence here to describe these "people skills" (although none of our interviewees used the term). All of the presidents we studied emphasized this as an important basis of trust in subordinates, easily recalling specific incidents to make their point.

> I can trust him. He knows the business and he knows how to work with people. He understands organizations. That's why I want him here as soon as possible and in charge of that operation.

Business Sense. By business sense we mean a more generalized competence than expertise in a given specific area. In our interviews, people used many different expressions to describe this type of competence including "experience base," "good head for business," "sharp common sense," "wisdom," etc. One president described one of his most trusted executives in this way:

> He sits there and listens and has the ability to get to the heart of the problem. He thinks beyond just marketing. Did you notice the questions he asked [in a meeting the researcher had observed]? They cut to the marrow. It's not just that he knows his own area well—it's more than that. It's superb common sense and an understanding of how a business works.

Judgment

To a large degree judgment transcends all of the above bases of trust. For example, judgment and competence are hard to distinguish although managers often did so in interviews ("he's a first rate marketing man, better than anyone around, but I can't trust his judgment on forecasts"). Similarly, discreetness and openness are also, to a large extent, manifestations of a person's judgment as well as his character. Also, the bases of trust overlap. A person's openness and discreetness are to some degree sources of interpersonal competence.

So far we have discussed in some detail the bases upon which trust developed in these relationships but not *how* it developed. Not surprisingly, our interviews suggest that trust develops in much the same way as mutual expectations do; that it grows (or fails to grow) along the dimensions described above as a result of two people working together. Appraisals of how much and in what ways one could trust another were based on an accumulation of interactions, specific incidents, problems, and events. Some of these were critical incidents and dramatic events (such as the discovery that one party had intentionally withheld important information) that created a discontinuity in a relationship by calling into question whatever trust had already developed. Most, however, were routine interactions of an everyday nature. In an important sense, these everyday incidents provided opportunities in which each person tacitly or explicitly tested and explored the ways and limits in which he could trust the other. Indeed, when this kind of learning and tacit testing had *not* occurred, the relationship tended to evolve somewhat superficially and became one in which no real basis for trust existed.

It was also apparent that as this process of mutual testing and learning took place that the nature of trust became more differentiated (in terms of the various bases of trust described above). By the end of twelve months, both the presidents and their executives could give fairly detailed descriptions of those areas in which they trusted the other and those in which they did not. For example, "his sense of the market is excellent, but he's consistently too optimistic," or "his technical knowledge is superior but he has real blind spots in dealing with people."

In the realities of running a business, the question seemed not to be "how much I trust him," as it was "in what areas and in what ways can I trust him." This differentiation took time to develop.

When pressed to justify why they trusted one person more than another, people inevitably responded by referring to specific prior events, discussions, or reports. The following reconstructed example illustrates this:

> It became obvious to me that I just couldn't trust his judgment about equipment decisions or his honesty either. A couple of years ago he recommended we not purchase the [X] machines because of [Y] problems with them and that they had been a failure in our overseas operation. Well, it turns out they have been very effective in Italy, Sweden, and that we have had six of them in Spain for three years—which he didn't even know about! Now, when I combine that with the problems we're having with the [Z] machines that we have in our domestic operations I can't help but question his judgment. Then I later find out that he now wants to order [X] type machines to replace the [Z] machines. I conclude he's a man I just can't trust. He also claims that the production data on the European machines was misrepresented to him. I know he's lying because those production reports are in manufacturing's files. He either didn't bother to look, or he saw them and disregarded them.

The president then went to his file cabinet and pulled out a copy of the five-year plan and read sections of it that were written by the man in question, pointing out errors or omissions. The subordinate was subsequently demoted.

The point of this vignette is threefold. First, it shows the accumulation of relatively routine events on which these assessments are made; and second, it is an example of both the tacit and explicit testing on which judgments about trust are made. Finally, it also illustrates the differentiation along which the president's judgments were made in terms of his trust in this executive, i.e., his subordinate's specific competence, integrity, and consistency of behavior.

Our interviews also suggested that some bases of trust were more critical than others. Integrity, competence, and consistency of behavior were most important to a president's ability to develop trust in a subordinate, while integrity, motives, and openness were most important to subordinates.

DEVELOPMENT OF INFLUENCE

A large literature exists on the topic of influence in social and organizational settings. (We are using the term influence to include also power and authority.) This literature contains many different definitions and typologies of influence, each of which focuses somewhat differently on the sources and processes of influence.[9]

For all practical purposes, our observations would support most of the more widely used definitions of influence. However, our purpose was not to validate any of these definitions or theories but rather to understand how the managers we interviewed (both the new presidents and their subordinates) perceived influence and the bases upon which it developed in their relationships. Hence our own working definition of influence was intentionally broad and simple: one person's ability to affect the behavior and thinking of another. When we inter-

[9]For example, some definitions are given in terms of personal and positional resources (e.g., Weber, 1947; Barnard, 1938; French and Raven, 1959; etc.); some in terms of social exchange (e.g., Thibaut and Kelly, 1959; Homans, 1961; Blau, 1967); some in terms of dependency relationships (e.g., Emerson, 1962; Kotter, 1977); others in terms of control over scarce resources (e.g., March and Simon, 1958; Thompson, 1967; Crozier, 1964); and still others in terms of the psychodynamics of individuals as related to all of the above (e.g., Zaleznik and Kets de Vries, 1975; Levinson, 1968; May, 1972, etc.).

viewed these managers, this was the definition we used.

As with trust, we found that both the new presidents and their subordinates described interpersonal influence in multidimensional terms. An analysis of our interviews yielded several recurrent themes about sources of influence that are listed below. We have called them bases of influence and have grouped them into two categories: (1) those that are positional in nature (i.e., influence associated with the formal authority of an individual), and (2) those that are personal in nature (i.e., influence attributed to particular personal resources, personality traits, or abilities of an individual).

BASES OF INFLUENCE

Positional Bases of Influence

- Power to structure tasks of others or formal organizational relationships
- Power to reward and punish
- Power to allocate or control scarce resources
- Power to direct another person based on one's legitimate authority

Personal Bases of Influence

- Ability to create common goals (i.e., define, articulate, and get others to subscribe to shared goals and priorities)
- Personal credibility
- Charisma or force of personality
- Decisiveness
- Willingness to use available power if necessary

Although these bases of influence were derived from interviews with both presidents and their subordinates, it is important to point out that many of them were available only to the president in the context of the relationships we studied. It should also be clear that these bases of influence are neither mutually exclusive nor of the same type, but are descriptions of what both superiors and subordinates perceived as important sources of their own or the other's influence in the relationship.

The bases of positional influence are fairly straightforward and need little elaboration.[10] Similarly, many of the personal bases of influence are easily recognizable and not unlike definitions given by other writers but several are different in important ways.[11] To a large extent these differences reflect the fact that the managers we interviewed conceptualized influence in descriptive everyday terms. For example, both superiors and subordinates often used the term "credibility" or "confidence" in trying to explain why they were influenced by someone (e.g., he has a lot of credibility with me, or I have a lot of confidence in him). When pressed to elaborate on what they meant by these terms, their responses were surprisingly similar to the answers given to our questions about trust. They responded in terms of what they perceived as being the other's judgment, "track record," competence, openness, and their

[10]They are indeed very similar to typologies developed by Weber (1947), Barnard (1938), and French and Raven (1959).

[11]For example, French and Raven's definition of "referent power" would subsume some of what we have called charisma, force of personality, and ability to create common goals, and their definition of "expert power" includes in part what we have referred to as personal credibility. Zaleznik has treated from a psychoanalytic point of view (but in more depth and complexity) several aspects of personal power related to what we have called charisma, force of personality, decisiveness, and willingness to use power.

ability to trust the other's recommendations and motives.[12]

The construct of one's ability to create commonly shared goals as a basis of interpersonal and organizational influence seems at first a cumbersome and inelegant definition. Yet it was mentioned repeatedly in our interviews as an important source of influence, especially in regard to the new president's success in affecting the behavior of key subordinates.[13]

The relative importance that both the new presidents and their executives assigned to these bases of influence was somewhat surprising. At the end of the study, we asked our respondents to rank the bases of influence listed above in terms of their importance. Subordinates ranked a superior's ability to define common goals and his personal credibility as the two most important sources of the superior's influence. In contrast, they ranked a superior's power to reward and punish, the legitimate authority of his office, and his power to allocate scarce resources as the *least* important. The presidents' rankings of their own bases of influence were very similar. They ranked their own credibility and ability to define common goals (along with decisiveness) as their most important sources of influence. Their rank orderings of their least important bases of influence were also similar to those of their subordinates: power to reward and punish, legitimate authority of the office, and power to control scarce resources.

The importance of credibility as a basis of influence is even more striking when we look at how the presidents perceived their subordinates' sources of influence. When presidents were queried about this they identified a subordinate's credibility (i.e., how much trust they had in a subordinate's judgment, recommendations, and performance) as the single most determining factor on how much influence a subordinate had over them.

If we are to believe our interviews and final rank orderings, interpersonal influence appears to be largely (though not exclusively) a consequence of one person's credibility in the eyes of the other. And since credibility has been described in interviews principally in terms of one's trust in the other, then the development of influence is largely a function of the development of trust.

Thus the concept of credibility provides a link between trust and influence just as the creation of common goals is a link between expectations and influence. The more credible (i.e., trustworthy) one person becomes to another, the more influence he will have within those areas in which he is trusted. So that in matters where either positional influence or control over scarce resources are not determining factors, one's influence over another is very much a function of how much he or she is trusted in the broadest sense of the word.

This relation between trust and influence is not surprising when we consider that superior-subordinate relationships are by their very nature mutual dependencies [as Dalton, Barnes and Zaleznik (1968) and Kotter (1977) have pointed out]. To the extent that either party allows himself to become more influenced by the other, he also allows himself to become more dependent on the other. To the degree that this dependence is discretionary and not dictated by circum-

[12]To some degree, credibility includes what French and Raven have described as "expertise," but to the managers we interviewed the construct of credibility meant more than just expertise. Credibility is a much broader and more holistic concept than expertise in that it refers to trustworthiness in a more multifaceted manner than expertise alone does.

[13]This construct could alternatively be conceived of in terms of referrent power or persuasion. However, as experienced by people actually working together the relevant gestalt compromised and transcended both persuasion and referrent power.

stances, it is based on the perception that the other can be trusted in that dependency.

Before concluding this discussion, we should point out that the relative importance of credibility as a basis of influence might be very different in managerial relationships that involved less inherent dependency than the superior-subordinate relationships we have studied. An immediate example that comes to mind would be a working relationship between two managers who are peers and only occasionally dependent upon each other. In such a relationship, control over scarce resources or one's ability to persuade the other would conceivably be more important.

STAGES IN THE DEVELOPMENT OF WORKING RELATIONSHIPS

As the preceding discussion has pointed out, influence, trust, and expectations emerge as a result of a process of mutual learning, exploration, testing, and some negotiation. We have described this process as one in which both parties tacitly work out an "interpersonal contract" that at some point becomes relatively stable. Implied in what we have said about this process is the notion that the way in which expectations, trust, and influence develop has a bearing on the resulting quality and effectiveness of a relationship.

A comparison of the themes raised in our interviews over the three years of the study also suggests that this process develops in stages, beginning with an initial period of impression making and mutual orientation, followed by a period of more intense exploration and learning.[14] This exploration stage naturally evolves into a third stage that is characterized by tacit testing of the limits of trust and influence and attempts to arrive at a mutual set of expectations. After this period of mutual testing and definition, most relationships that lasted for longer than eighteen months became "stable" and underwent relatively little change thereafter in terms of trust, influence, or expectations. Some of the relationships we studied did not progress through all of these stages because one or both parties were unable or unwilling to reach a mutual accommodation in the testing and definition stage. When this occurred, the subordinate either quit, was fired, or was demoted. In some cases both people had worked through all of the stages, but superficially, so that the resulting relationship was not a very effective one. Most of the relationships that persisted were ones that became stabilized and were viewed by both parties as effective and satisfying.

The point, however, is that it was the way in which two people worked through these stages that determined whether they developed an effective relationship; not simply that they had progressed through them. Those relationships described by both parties as being effective and satisfying tended to be ones in which general expectations had been clarified early on, specific expectations were explored in detail, differences were surfaced and negotiated, and the bases and limits of trust and influence had been tested and worked through.

Several examples existed of relationships that had reached relatively early stabilization, but in which important issues of a business or personal nature had not been worked through thoroughly in the prior exploration and testing stages. In all of these cases the relationships subsequently became destabilized or created problems for the people involved and the organization as a whole. In one instance a president and his executive vice presi-

[14]The problems and dilemmas that characterize each stage and the interpersonal tasks posed by each stage are described in more detail in Gabarro (1977).

dent had gone through a rapid and cursory orientation, exploration, and definition of their relationship. The consequence was that a number of important issues (such as influence and expectations) had not been worked out. Key subordinates were receiving mixed signals from both of them, creating considerable strain within the organization. Nonetheless, it was a stabilized relationship, though a highly ineffective and dissatisfying one.

In another case the same occurred with a president and vice president. The president's testing had been cursory and their mutually defined expectations were sufficiently vague that they had not taken into account a number of important differences in each man's underlying assumptions of what needed to be done to improve the company's performance. Although the relationship was relatively stabilized for over twelve months, the individual's performance ultimately became evident in the end of year financial results. The poor results provided an impetus for destabilizing the relationship. Subsequent exploration and attempts at redefinition of expectations failed, and the VP was demoted. This is the danger of working through these issues superficially. It is possible to attain a "pseudo" stabilization in a relationship in which important underlying issues have not been sufficiently dealt with. The two situations cited above provide examples of this. It is not that the two managers had not worked through the four stages; rather it is that they had not worked through them well enough.

BIBLIOGRAPHY

ALTMAN, IRWIN and DALMES A. TAYLOR, *Social Penetration: The Development of Interpersonal Relations.* New York: Holt, Rinehart and Winston, 1973.

BARNARD, CHESTER I., *The Functions of the Executive.* Cambridge, Mass.: Harvard University Press, 1938.

BERSCHEID, ELLEN and ELAINE WALSTER, *Interpersonal Attraction.* Reading: Addison-Wesley, 1969.

BLAU, PETER M., *Exchange and Power in Social Life.* New York: John Wiley and Sons, 1967.

BLAU, PETER and J. RICHARD SCOTT, *Formal Organizations.* San Francisco: Chandler Publishing Company, 1962.

CROZIER, MICHEL, *The Bureaucratic Phenomenon.* Chicago: University of Chicago Press, 1964.

DALTON, GENE, LOUIS BARNES, and ABRAHAM ZALEZNIK, *The Distribution of Authority in Formal Organizations.* Boston: Harvard University, Division of Research, Graduate School of Business Administration, 1968.

DALTON, MELVILLE, *Men Who Manage.* New York: John Wiley and Sons, 1959.

DAVIS, MURRAY, *Intimate Relations.* New York: Free Press, 1973.

EMERSON, RICHARD M., "Power-Dependence Relationships," *American Sociological Review,* 27, no. 1 (1962), 31-41.

FRENCH, J.R.P. and BERTRAM RAVEN, "The Bases of Social Power" in *Studies in Social Power,* Dorwin Cartwright and Alvin Zander, eds. Ann Arbor: Research Center for Group Dynamics and Institute for Social Research, 1959.

GABARRO, JOHN J., "Stages in the Development of Working Relationships." Unpublished working paper, Harvard University Graduate School of Business Administration, June 1977.

GARFINKEL, HAROLD, *Studies in Ethnomethodology*. Englewood Cliffs: Prentice-Hall, 1969.

HODGSON, R.C., D.J. LEVINSON, and ABRAHAM ZALEZNIK, *The Executive Role Constellation*. Boston: Harvard University, Division of Research, Graduate School of Business Administration, 1965.

HOMANS, GEORGE, *Social Behavior: Its Elementary Forms*. New York: Harcourt, Brace and World, 1961.

KOTTER, JOHN P., "Power, Dependence, and Managerial Success," *Harvard Business Review*, July-August, 1977.

LAWLESS, DAVID J., *Effective Management: Social Psychological Approach*. Englewood Cliffs: Prentice-Hall, 1972.

LEVINSON, HARRY, *The Exceptional Executive*. Cambridge, Mass.: Harvard University Press, 1968.

——, *Men, Management and Mental Health*. Cambridge, Mass.: Harvard University Press, 1966.

MARCH, JAMES G. and HERBERT A. SIMON, *Organizations*. New York: John Wiley and Sons, 1958.

MAY, ROLLO, *Power and Innocence: A Search for the Sources of Violence*. New York: Norton and Company, 1972.

PSATHAS, GEORGE, "Ethnomethods and Phenomenology," in *Symbolic Interaction*, eds. Jereme G. Manis and Bernard M. Meltzer. Boston: Allyn and Bacon, 1972.

THIBAUT, J. and H.H. KELLY, *The Social Psychology of Groups*. New York: John Wiley and Sons, 1959.

THOMAS, ROOSEVELT, "Managing the Psychological Contract," in *Organizational Behavior and Administration*, eds. Paul Lawrence, Louis Barnes, and Jay Lorsch. Homewood, Illinois: Richard D. Irwin, 1976.

THOMPSON, JAMES D., *Organizations in Action*. New York: McGraw-Hill, 1967.

WALTON, RICHARD E., *Social and Psychological Aspects of Verification, Inspection, and International Assurance*. Lafayette: Purdue University, 1968.

WEBER, MAX, *The Theory of Social and Economic Organization*, ed. Talcott Parson. New York: Free Press, 1947.

WORTMAN, CAMILLE B. and JOAN A.W. LINSENMEUR, "Interpersonal Attraction and Techniques of Ingratiation in Organizational Settings" in *New Directions in Organizational Behavior*, eds. Gerald Salancik and Barry M. Stow. Chicago: St. Clau Press, 1977.

ZALEZNIK, ABRAHAM and MANFRED F.R. KETS DE VRIES, *Power and the Corporate Mind*. Boston: Houghton Mifflin Company, 1975.

Cases

Acting Out of Character

"We've just had a real fight in my group. I think I've got things straightened out now. But for a time, I was worried."

The speaker was Mike Mayo, a section head in the Sounds System Laboratory of Rolands, Horn & Oliver, a medium-sized producer of electronic signaling systems. Mike went on to explain to the casewriter how the conflict had arisen.

My group got this project. Potentially, it had a huge pay-off—$20 million or more. My boss, Dr. Spoke, considered it top priority, and it looked to both of us like an outstanding opportunity to make a breakthrough. We put three of our senior associates on the project, and right away they were fighting.

I won't confuse you with technical details, but we were working with transducers that had to have very low breakdown voltages. I called together the three associates, Don Steiger, Jo Arnes, and Kurt Kalcheck. Almost right away, Don Steiger objected to the project on grounds that it was theoretically doubtful, if not impossible. Don is only about 26. He received his Ph.D. last year and demonstrated his first device three years ago. Frankly, I think he's brilliant. He's going to shoot up in this organization.

The rest of us were rather taken aback by the speed and certainty with which Don responded. I'm not sure what Jo Arnes would have said if Don hadn't been so positive. At any rate, Jo was lukewarm at best. However, I received immediate support from Kurt Kalcheck. Kurt is much older than the other two, who are close friends. Kurt must be in his fifties. He has very little advanced math and a background in engineering. He's one of the very few senior associates without a doctoral degree. But Kurt is very loyal, diligent, practical, and reliable, and he'll work tremendously hard. We get along very well. Kurt said he would set up an experiment and see what happened.

It was agreed that the three of them should get together and plan a preliminary investigation to decide whether the project should proceed. I remember thinking at the time that Don Steiger wasn't going to do any collaborating with anyone, and I was right.

At 9:30 the next morning, Dr. Spoke received an elaborate theoretical report, which demonstrated the mathematical impossibility of the project's objective. There was a forceful summary to the effect that we would be wasting our time proceeding any further. Don must have stayed up half the night to complete it. Both Dr. Spoke and I were impressed by Don's speed and thoroughness. It was typical of him.

It was going to take time for us to evaluate the report, and Dr. Spoke was very busy that week. I was wondering whether to call Kurt Kalcheck off the project when, some five days after Don's report had been submitted, Kurt came to see me. He had assembled the transducers and they worked. He'd done it! I was tremendously excited and so was Dr. Spoke. Many people were congratulating Kurt. Don and Jo were called in and told the news. Don said nothing about having been wrong but began to examine Kurt's setup minutely.

A couple of hours later, I received a call from Dr. Spoke. Don was in his office complaining that Kurt refused to share information with him. I said I would handle it, and I called Don, Jo, and Kurt into my office. I said that this was Kurt's discovery and that no one must deprive him of the full credit for it. Probably Don could write a better article for the professional journals, but Kurt must be permitted to exploit his work. I sympathized with Kurt's fear that his ideas would be taken over.

Don shrugged this off. He denied that he had the smallest intention of depriving Kurt of any credit. He merely wished to build on Kurt's work, for which he required information. Shared information was the basis of science.

That fight was two weeks ago, and I think I resolved it. In a way, Kurt was acting out of character. He isn't *expected* to discover new things. In fact, Jo has announced that Kurt was only following my orders, which isn't true. Kurt is expected to be the practical one.

But you know something, I think Kurt has a lot of talent, if only he and others would start to believe it.

The casewriter asked to speak to Kurt Kalcheck. Kurt was a thin, balding man with glasses. He had a polite but earnest style of speaking and a distinct Polish accent. He was asked about his background and his life up to the present.

Kurt Kalcheck: I was born in Poland and educated in Munich, Germany. In 1939 I won a scholarship in engineering to Michigan University, where I studied for my master's. A few years later, America entered the war and I came to work here at Rolands. It didn't seem so important to have a doctor's degree in those days. I had only been here a few months when I was fired as a security risk. It was my Munich background and the fact that Poland was occupied.

It was a pretty bad time to be a security risk or to speak with any sort of mid-European accent. I couldn't afford to return to the university and had to take temporary jobs. In 1945, Rolands took me back again, and I did some really important work on vacuum tubes. Thousands of systems used the miniature tubes I developed. Then, quite suddenly, the technology changed over to solid-state devices, and I was given only routine assignments on tubes. The creative work was no longer coming my way, and hundreds of young Ph.D.s fresh out of the university were way ahead of me.

Have you ever stopped to think what happens to people in these technical upheavals? I often wonder what it must have been like to be an expert on propeller-driven airplanes and then suddenly find oneself at the bottom, nobody wanting all your knowledge. Industry makes these studies on how to use waste products, and it never stops to think of the human beings it consigns to the scrap heap. Management says it's "up to the individual." There's all these orientation programs for newcomers, but what about *reorientation* for some of us?

Sometimes I think of all the brilliant people we have here, and yet most of us are alone. Just a few yards away, behind a wall, there are probably a dozen men from whom we could learn so much. And yet there are high walls everywhere, with many noncommunicating people duplicating each other's efforts. Oh we *emphasize* teamwork, but our individual noses are so close to our individual grindstones that we just don't notice each other. People here are strongly opinionated and individualistic. They like to work by themselves. Maybe they fear others will steal their ideas.

I'll give an example of the quite needless rivalry that goes on here. One of the production division's development groups has been sent over here—to the research laboratory. The idea is to "facilitate" the production of our ideas. They'll come in and seize your idea, and five days later they'll be developing it in a half-cocked state before we've even evaluated it ourselves. And since this new pressure on us to do application work is intensifying, we are converging with this fiercely competitive, marketing-oriented group, who seem intent on hustling everything through. This is duplication, and it's hurting the company. Why doesn't management give us clearer assignments, which don't overlap? We're doing some work on missile defense systems, as you may know. Now, what happens when the government gets competitive bids from different parts of this company? Because that's going to happen any day now.

I've complained several times about this. The other day, the marketing manager of this manufacturing division that has invaded us was in here. He told me, "Don't cry about it. Get in quickly—that's life!" He wants all our information. I must confess I've always found it difficult to push in front of people. We spend hours laying down a list of priorities, then all of a sudden it turns into a game of how to get around them. It seems so destructive to me. Beyond a certain point, competition becomes detrimental to the organization. While I'm waiting my turn—as I promised to do—someone else comes barging in and grabs the needed equipment. It gets so that my civilized behavior is just exploited. There has to be a better way!

It's bad enough when this fighting goes on between departments, but when its *inside* the very group you are working with, when you cannot even trust your closest associates, then things are really falling apart.

Casewriter: I understand that there has recently been a dispute between you and Don Steiger. Is that what you were referring to?

Kurt Kalcheck: Well, that was typical, although more unpleasant than usual because it was so close to us all. We were called into Dr. Spoke's office to discuss the development of very low frequency transducers. There was a definite application in mind. We all agreed to explore it, but after the meeting, Don walked off by himself and began writing a paper. He likes to show how quickly he can respond. He didn't consult us, of course, and the memo virtually told us, "That's my conclusion, and that settles it."

Well, Don's got a good brain—but it doesn't matter how brilliant you are, it's always dangerous to say that something can't be done, and even more dangerous to put it into writing. I couldn't follow Don's theoretical arguments very closely, and he didn't seem inclined to explain them to me. Mike Mayo had told me to go ahead, and so I did.

I went to the manufacturing division and succeeded in getting some low-frequency devices from them, which they had recently developed. It was difficult getting them, and they made me promise not to let anyone else use them. That's the sort of suspicion we have around here! I set up some experiments, and within eight days I'd achieved 20 percent efficiency, which Don had argued couldn't be done.

Well, you never saw a faster change of attitude from anyone than Don's. Instead of offering to work with me, he began taking notes, and a couple of hours after my first demonstration, he was setting up a duplicate experiment on his own. Every few minutes he would come down from his lab and look at what I had done. It was quite clear that he was imitating my setup.

I didn't protest until his lab technician came into the room, went over to my setup, and, without asking me, picked up a couple of filters. I said, "Hey—I'm using those!" He said, "You're not. They were on the table." I explained that I borrowed the equipment from many different people. I'd waited my turn until it was ready, and I would need all the filters I had. "Why can't you wait your turn," I said, "and why duplicate this setup? Aren't we supposed to be working together?" "That's what *I* thought," he said. "All right, keep your filters!" and he threw them down hard onto the table and walked out. Why did he have to do that? We've been friends for ten years. We used to sit together at lunch—now he won't speak to me. And it's all so silly and unnecessary. I'm really ashamed to discuss it.

Well, a few moments later, Don comes into the room. He says, "I understand you obtained some special devices from the product division. Can I have some of them, or at least their specifications?" I said I was sorry but the information was confidential. If he went to the product division they might help him, but I had been made to promise that I would keep the devices to myself. He didn't argue but went straight to Mike Mayo, who followed him back into this room. He said, "Mike, tell Kurt that he must share information or I'll go straight to Dr. Spoke." I said, "The information is confidential." As Mike hesitated for a moment, Don left the room, heading straight for Dr. Spoke's office.

I repeated my story to Dr. Spoke, who said that if the information was confidential, that was that. A promise was a promise. I told Don he could have all my measurements but not the product division's specifications. I said, "Don, we can go on fighting, but people get hurt in these fights. No one really comes out ahead."

He said he could do nothing without the specifications, and I knew it. Last I heard, he was trying to order a duplicate set of devices from the division. And I've got all we need already!

People like Don don't realize that one *has* to work with other people. The equipment we use is expensive, and we have to borrow back and forth all the time. No one can afford to be an island in this place. If you don't cooperate with other people, then they are not going to help you when you're in a jam and need equipment. There's no point appealing upstairs to Dr. Spoke. He can't tell us how to cooperate. We have to learn.

The casewriter next tried to meet Don Steiger. After a series of delays, he eventually managed to speak to him. Don was very cautious, would pause some time before answering, and chose his words carefully. Of the many persons interviewed in this company, he expressed the most concern that his opinions could get him into trouble.

Don Steiger: Yes, I'd say I was satisfied with my job. Very satisfied, on the whole, although there are always exceptions. I've sought employment elsewhere from time to time. Complaints? Well, it's a loose organization—too loose, in my opinion. We don't always get cooperation from the other divisions and from each other. I feel we should be apprised of what other people are doing and have access to their work. People upstairs should take the reins more firmly in their hands, ensure better cooperation and that we get the equipment we need. It's a false economy, being as short of equipment as we are. My technician takes a week to get equipment together. It shouldn't take that long. There isn't enough attention to doing what is best for the company. That has been my chief objective.

Casewriter: I've been talking with Kurt Kalcheck. That's his chief objective too.

Don Steiger: Well, of course, you have to have some trust of people, and he hasn't. It is in his makeup, his personality. He thinks someone is going to take something away from him. He's an extreme case, as far as I'm concerned. I've never come across such distrust. . . . But I don't see how you're going to disguise all this I'm saying. It's bound to get out, isn't it? As far as I'm concerned, this incident is closed. Who's going to read this case?

Casewriter: Well I'm not sure how to reassure you. My experience has been that by the time these cases are typed, disguised, and presented to the company for clearance, the incidents described are all water under the bridge. I've talked to about a dozen people. They have all expressed several opinions, which were more negative than any expressed by you.

Don Steiger: Hmm . . . all right. Well, I assured Kurt that my motives were entirely honorable. I had no intention at all of depriving him of credit. All I wanted was to set up some more advanced experiments. There was a good opportunity for collaboration between us. He had made an interesting discovery. I could have come up with a model and proposed a further series of experiments.

Of course, I do move a great deal faster than most other people. I realize, even if they don't, that a relatively small laboratory like this has some running to do. I attend professional conferences and I know what's going on. RCA has ten people on a project similar to ours. I suspect that Bell has thirty. We have the advantage of flexibility and concentration on one area, provided we react fast. Kurt doesn't realize that I chose him to work with us. I'm all for cooperation. When you're working by yourself, just one small mistake can put you weeks behind. Kurt is thorough and he checks things. I've been a loner here for five years, and I felt the need for collaboration. That's the only way we're going to beat RCA. Every time I work on a project, I think, will they beat me to it? We're up against keen competition, make no mistake about it.

I've got a good record so far. A number of awards from the company and a couple from the industry. I'm after a reputation as an inventor and an original theorist. Most of my friends are professionals, and the people I want to impress are fellow theoreticians and people at home. There was an article about me in the local paper last week.

Casewriter: Mike Mayo feels that he helped to resolve the dispute between you and Kurt.

Don Steiger: Mike didn't solve anything. I solved it. I solved it by keeping right away from Kurt. It's the only thing to do. I can work with Jo Arnes but not with Kurt. He wants to keep everything under wraps. Mike gets very enthusiastic and so does Kurt, but we need to inject some realism into our work. But I'd rather not say anything more. . . .

Frank Mason (A)

"It was like stepping out of a steam bath into a cold shower," Frank Mason reflected, as he recalled the day he left Great Pacific Paper Company. He now wondered if he would have left had he known what awaited him at the Abbot Business Supply Company.

Frank sat in his office on Monday morning, September 14, and glanced out his door, noting that Ed Nolan, president of Abbot, had not yet arrived. In recent months, working for Nolan had been the most difficult experience of his otherwise successful career. When Frank had joined the company in March as vice-president for marketing and sales, Nolan seemed to be a delightful, charming, almost charismatic gentleman. He had given Frank a free hand in reorganizing the marketing area and practically guaranteed that Frank would be president of Abbot within two years. But then, things began to go wrong. He and Nolan no longer got along, his autonomy had been severely limited, company sales were again declining, and things in general were rapidly deteriorating. To make things worse, Daryl Eismann, president of Houston Electronics, Abbot's parent company, would be flying in the following week to review the company's current situation.

The previous week, Frank had decided to take some action before Eismann arrived. It seemed that it was time to have a candid talk with Nolan and try to resolve their differences. Frank had thought that Nolan would surely want to talk these things out before Eismann's impending visit, but even after working for Nolan for six months, Frank still found him unpredictable. On Tuesday, Frank had asked Nolan to have drinks with him that afternoon, but Nolan declined. He also declined, without explanation, Frank's invitations for lunch on Wednesday and Thursday. However, Frank noted that Nolan continued to have lunch with some of the other managers in the firm. Frank still felt that a candid discussion about their relationship and the problems at Abbot could no longer be delayed, and he was determined to see Nolan as soon as he arrived. Nolan usually arrived at 9:00 A.M., which gave Frank almost half an hour to review the situation and gather his thoughts.

FRANK MASON

Frank was 35 years old, single, and a native of Peoria, Illinois. Before going to business school, he had received his B.A. in economics from Antioch College and served four years in the navy. Upon completion of his M.B.A., he joined the Great Pacific Paper Company in Spokane, one of the country's largest and most profitable manufacturers and marketers of consumer paper products. The company sold nationally advertised facial tissue, bathroom tissue, paper towels, paper napkins, and other paper products. It was primarily Great Pacific's good reputation in the consumer-products field that had appealed to Frank. His success in the marketing division had been spectacular—product manager in two and a half years (a company record), and senior product manager in only six more months. His salary had more than doubled by the end of his fifth year at Great Pacific.

But Frank also recalled the sense of personal stagnation that was growing on him during his last months there. Establishing new products had lost its charm, it was the same procedures again and again, and he felt that there was simply nothing new to learn there. Moreover, because of Great Pacific's strong hierarchical control, ever-present committee work, and endless rounds of required approval, he felt that he had not really tested himself. In fact, with such strong control and competent staff support, it seemed almost as difficult to fail as to succeed. He also recalled Great Pacific's disastrous acquisition of a regional chemical company, which forced them into austerity measures and restriction of expansion and advancement.

For these reasons, Frank left Great Pacific and went to Gleason Pro Shops, a retail sporting-goods chain based in Seattle, as VP for planning and marketing, receiving a 15 percent salary increase over his Great Pacific pay plus a bonus. The autonomy he had there was indeed like an exhilarating cold shower. But corporate financial problems seemed to follow him from Great Pacific, for Gleason fell into a severe cash-flow bind a few months after his arrival. Being unable to afford Frank's salary, the company sent him on his second search for employment in less than 18 months.

As he thought back on the experience, there were two things about his 15 months at Gleason Pro Shops that still concerned Frank. Although he did not consider himself a "job hopper," he found himself beginning to fit this unattractive mold. Second, none of his coworkers there were college graduates, and they all used strong profanity, which seemed crude and unsophisticated to Frank. In retrospect, however, he suspected that he may have been too severe in his assessment of them, which may in turn have caused some of the personal animosities that had developed there.

After he left Gleason, Frank was contacted by an executive search agent, whose firm had been engaged by Houston Electronics to find a vice-president of marketing and sales for its Abbot subsidiary. Abbot had been a family-owned company with a very paternalistic style of management prior to its acquisition a year earlier by Houston Electronics, a producer of military avionics and space-tracking radar systems. Abbot was a regional manufacturer of stationery and other paper products, as well as a distributor of related business-supply items. The company sold over 2,000 products, with annual sales of about $10 million. In addition to stationery and business forms, the product line included envelopes, typewriter paper, machine rolls, folders, loose-leaf sheets, pens, pencils, duplicating supplies, staplers, blotters, and steno supplies. Stationery and business forms were Abbot's largest items, accounting for 45 percent of sales, and were produced and printed on Abbot presses. About 50 percent of their orders were received from stationery and business-supply stores, 30 percent from businesses, and 20 percent from school systems and colleges. Abbot was located in San Francisco, with 70 percent of company sales in the Bay Area, 20 percent in Los Angeles, and the remainder in Sacramento. School systems, colleges, and businesses were contacted by company salesmen on a regular basis, while stationery and business-supply stores sent their orders directly to the sales department. The company had been urgently in need of a vice-president of marketing and sales, and the agent offered Frank a salary 20 percent higher than his salary at Gleason Pro Shops, plus a 25 percent bonus at the end of the year. Although not initially interested, Frank eventually agreed to a luncheon interview later that month with Ed Nolan, president of Abbot Business Supply Company.

INTERVIEWS WITH ED NOLAN

After a discouraging interview for an unattractive job in Burbank, Frank arrived in San Francisco on a beautiful, clear day in late February. It was at the Top of the Mark restaurant in the Mark Hopkins Hotel that Frank first met Ed Nolan.

Nolan appeared to be in his mid-fifties, about medium height, and slightly overweight, with large, heavy jowls, and a full head of grey hair. He had initially reminded Frank of Laurence Olivier. Nolan was originally an engineer and had spent much of his career in high-technology companies. He had impressed Frank with his excellent mind, which could accumulate, sort, and evaluate a large amount of information and reach a conclusion in a very short time. Frank was also impressed with Nolan's personal charm, good sense of humor, and attentive interest, which made him seem almost benevolent. But the one thing that Frank remembered most strongly about the meeting was that it seemed strangely unnecessary to "score points" with Nolan. It was as if Nolan was selling him on the job, rather than the other way around.

Frank also remembered his surprise when Nolan told him that he was also president of another division within Houston Electronics, with $300 million in sales, and that he was only acting as steward of Abbot until he could find an aggressive, intelligent young manager to take his place there. It soon became apparent to Frank that the next VP for marketing and sales was very likely to become the next president of Abbot within two years. Frank expressed interest in the job, and, without making any firm commitments, they left the restaurant and Frank took a cab back to the airport.

Ten days later, Nolan called Frank at his parents' home in San Diego and asked him if he was still interested. Since he was, they agreed on a date for Frank to fly to San Francisco for a visit to the company plant and offices. Nolan told Frank he would pick him up at San Francisco International Airport on Monday morning, March 6. In thinking back to that March morning, Frank was a little amused at the comedy of errors that had occurred. Nolan had not shown up as expected, so Frank called his apartment. Nolan's wife explained that Ed had already left for the office, and a second call to Nolan's secretary revealed that he was not yet in, but he was expected shortly. Frank felt it would be a waste of time to wait at the airport, so he took a cab to the Abbot offices. Nolan greeted Frank warmly upon his arrival and seemed genuinely sorry for the mixup. They discussed company operations for the rest of the morning. Frank had researched the company thoroughly and was able to conduct an intelligent, knowledgeable discussion. In fact, it had seemed to Frank that he was more prepared to discuss specifics than Nolan was.

However, Nolan seemed to have some strong general opinions on how to run a business. He was a strong believer in management by objectives and stressed the importance of good communication among top management. But he was equally convinced that each manager should run his own area completely and without help from other functions. Nolan emphasized the importance of the controller as guardian of the company's assets, and he stressed the need for efficiency and tight inventory control in production. Then he added, "But in this business, control and marketing are the most important functions." Frank got the impression that Nolan saw people as either competent or incompetent, and had great contempt and distrust for the latter. Nolan also talked for quite some time about his experience at Houston Electronics and the importance of accurate cost estimates in calculating required margins for their government contracts. According to Nolan, there were no serious pressures from the parent company, even though Abbot's sales had been declining. Until things were turned around, Houston Electronics could make up any Abbot losses. Frank talked with Nolan until midafternoon and then flew back to San Diego.

Two things bothered Frank about his prospects at Abbot. First, Nolan had failed to introduce him to any of the other people in the company (see Exhibit III-1), explaining that they were busy with the quarterly report. Second, the job was in industrial marketing, which lacked the excitement of surveys, mass advertis-

Exhibit III-1 Frank Mason (A)

Partial Organization Chart, Abbot Business Supply Company, March 1

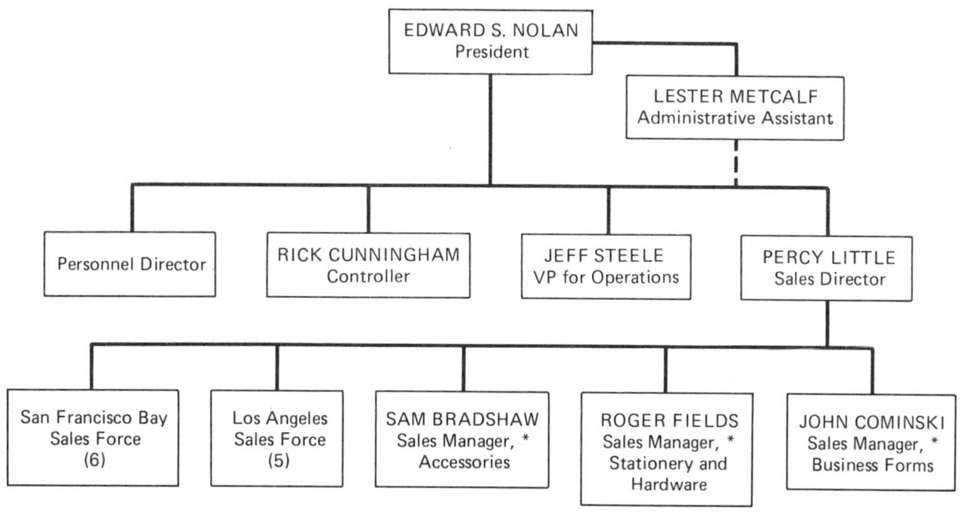

*The company was divided into three product groups, each with its own product manager:
- The Accessories Group included bulletin boards, rubber bands, paper clips, maps, and art supplies (18% of sales).
- The Stationery and Hardware Group included stationery and envelopes, appointment books, scratch pads, calendars, card indexes, steno supplies, fasteners, and paper punchers (39% of sales).
- The Business Forms Group included business forms, business envelopes, machine rolls, typewriter paper, indexes, folders, and expanding envelopes (43% of sales).

ing, packaging, and so on. However, Nolan had promised the autonomy Frank wanted, and there seemed to be a very good chance that he might be president within two years. To Frank, the autonomy and challenge of making major marketing decisions seemed to greatly outweigh the less exciting marketing problems of a small, nonconsumer company such as Abbot. Additionally, he could live in the San Francisco area, which he had always liked. When Nolan offered him the job the following week, Frank accepted with no hesitation.

A TALK WITH ST. CLAIR

On March 22, Frank began his job as vice-president for marketing and sales of Abbot Business Supply Company. He soon met Bob St. Clair, a consultant to Abbot, who had been a consultant to Great Pacific Paper Company. They quickly became good friends, and Frank asked St. Clair to talk with him about the company's background. They met for lunch, and St. Clair explained that Nolan was apparently the protégé of Art Lincoln, executive vice-president of Houston Electronics (see Exhibit III-2). St. Clair was on good terms with Lincoln, since they had been roommates in college. Nolan had been the only high-level manager in Houston Electronics who was in favor of acquiring Abbot. His influence with Lincoln and his record as a high performer had apparently outweighed any objections to acquiring a company in such a different industry. Nolan was made president of Abbot and put under heavy pressure from Eismann to improve its performance. St. Clair confided to Frank that Nolan had just told Lincoln that Abbot was in serious trouble. Lincoln had recommended that Nolan spend all his time in San Francisco and leave his division in Houston in the hands of his capable deputies. However, Nolan was still spending half his time in Houston.

St. Clair also told Frank that, while most people seemed to have difficulty in getting along with Nolan, Rick Cunningham, the controller, and Lester Metcalf, the administrative assistant, were on good terms with him. They usually had lunch with Nolan three or four times a

Exhibit III-2 Frank Mason (A)

Partial Organization Chart, Houston Electronics Corporation, March 1

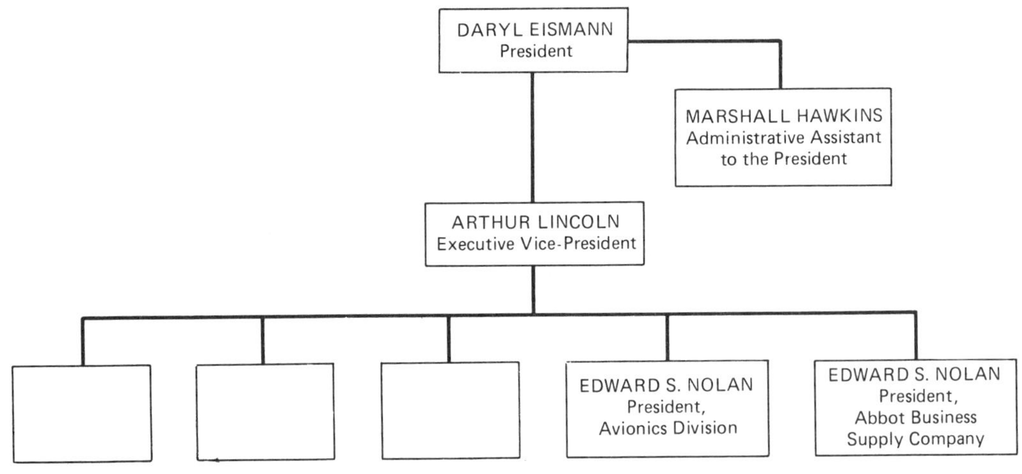

week. Both men had worked for Nolan at Houston Electronics. Metcalf was very loyal to Nolan; rumor had it that several years earlier, Metcalf had been near personal bankruptcy and Nolan had saved his career. Cunningham was an accountant who strongly emphasized cost control but reportedly had no sympathy for salesmen's problems. He, too, was very loyal to Nolan, and they occasionally attended Warrior games during the basketball season. As far as St. Clair knew, these basketball games with Cunningham were Nolan's only social life.

St. Clair knew that Nolan considered Frank a possible candidate for the president's job. However, he warned Frank that Jeff Steele, VP for operations, also wanted to be president of the firm, so Frank could be in for a difficult time with him. As a final word of advice, St. Clair urged Frank to move into the vacant office next to Nolan's office, "before someone else tries to gain the favored position." Frank thanked St. Clair for the information and advice, and he returned to his office. The next day, he moved into the room next to Nolan's office, as St. Clair had suggested. At first, Frank had been very apprehensive over St. Clair's warning about Jeff Steele. Later on, however, Steele became one of Frank's best friends, while his relationship with Nolan became worse over the summer.

THE FIRST THREE MONTHS AT ABBOT

Initially, Nolan seemed to have absolute confidence in Frank's ability. Frank's recommendations on marketing strategy met no resistance, and he seemed to be the commanding influence on Nolan for his first few months at Abbot. Nolan had given Frank full autonomy over pricing, even though St. Clair had recommended that Nolan retain pricing control over very large orders. Although St. Clair had also recommended that Frank be allowed at least two months to gain a foothold in marketing before taking over sales as well, Nolan wanted Frank to take responsibility for sales in early April. Frank was reluctant to take on too much too soon, but he hesitated for other reasons also.

When Frank had first joined the company, Percy Little was in charge of sales. Frank saw Little as a highly regimented person who paid careful attention to detail but often could not see the forest for the trees. He thought that if Little had a personal motto, it would be, "Everything to please the customer." Although Little had excellent relationships with the men in the field, he seemed to have little administrative ability. Nolan would often ask detailed, probing questions of Little, which he could rarely answer without checking his books or asking one of his salesmen. Little's failure to have the answers at his fingertips invariably angered Nolan, who made it clear to Frank that he thought Little was incompetent and should be fired immediately. Frank also recalled the attitude of the sales force at that time. They were mostly "old-timers," many of them having over 25 years of service with the company. In his initial contacts with them, Frank found them to be shy, very responsive to his questions or requests, and seemingly frightened of him. This appeared to be a situation in which he did not wish to become involved at that time.

But Nolan was persistent, and Frank finally yielded and took charge of sales. He felt that he would have to manage the salesmen as best he could, dealing with them primarily through Little. Even though he, too, was one of the company "old-timers," Little proved to be loyal to Frank, and seemed to be relieved when Frank took charge of sales. After this change, the organizational chart for Abbot Business Supply was redrawn as shown in Exhibit III-3.

Exhibit III-3 Frank Mason (A)

Partial Organization Chart, Abbot Business Supply Company, May 1

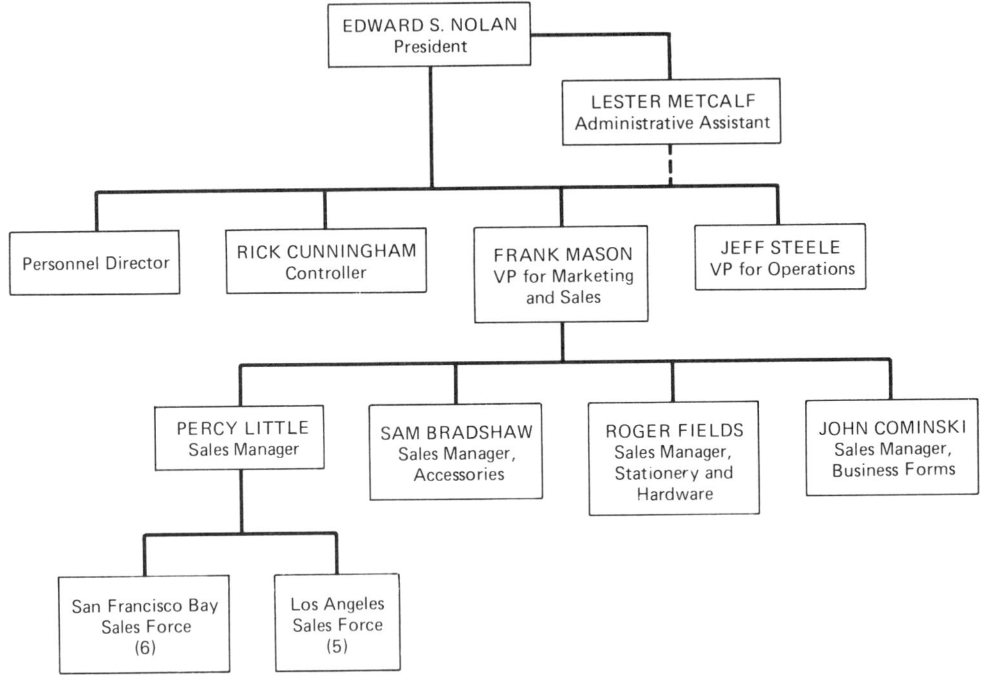

In early May, the company had a visit from Art Lincoln, executive vice-president of Houston Electronics. The main purpose of his visit was to hear Frank present Abbot's business plan. When Nolan introduced Frank to him, Lincoln remarked, "So this is the guy who walks on water." Frank was somewhat surprised, but replied, "It depends on how deep it is." The presentation for Lincoln was a one-man show, and Frank was the star performer. Much of his presentation concerned a reorganization of the marketing function and its communication needs. He recalled that after his presentation, everyone had been happy except him, because he knew that now he had to deliver.

In his first three months at Abbot, Frank had been faced with several difficult decisions. In late May, he found it necessary to release the entire Los Angeles sales force, since the volume for that region was not large enough to justify the operating costs involved. He contacted four large stationery stores and three distributors in the Los Angeles area, which agreed to order exclusively from Abbot. Frank felt that this action would retain most of the volume in Los Angeles without the high operating costs of the salesmen. He appointed James Au, the Los Angeles warehouse manager, to be watchdog over these accounts and to call on them at regular intervals. Although the salesmen were released because of financial considerations and not age, Frank still had mixed feelings about firing them. One salesman was 69 years old, even though the company had a policy of retirement at 65. He reportedly had a private agreement with Nolan to remain in his job past the normal retirement age. Frank felt a great sense of relief when he later learned that all of them had obtained jobs within two weeks of their severance from Abbot Business Supply. Another thing he found necessary to do was to fire Sam Bradshaw, one of the sales managers. Sam was 57 years old, with 32 years of service with the company, and was afflicted with Parkinson's disease. Frank had discussed firing Bradshaw with Percy Little, and after a long and labored discussion, Little grudgingly admitted that it probably wasn't necessary to keep Bradshaw. Although he did not find it easy, Frank eventually gave Bradshaw his notice.

As he began to get the feel of his new job, Frank also made friends with Roger Fields and John Cominski, his two sales managers, who seemed quite happy for Frank to be taking the lead role in the company. Both of them also seemed to have considerable difficulty in dealing with Nolan. But Frank had dismissed any concerns he might have had about Nolan, believing that these men were simply too unsophisticated to deal with him effectively.

In mid-May, Frank added Steve Lewis to his staff as a product manager. When Frank first met him, Lewis was working for Cunningham in the controller's office. Frank and Lewis were both bachelors in their mid-thirties, and they soon discovered that they were very similar in their life-styles and senses of humor. One evening over drinks, Lewis expressed an interest in working for Frank. Frank had been impressed with Lewis's ability, and he remembered Cunningham commenting favorably on Lewis's competence. When Cunningham later returned from a meeting in Los Angeles, Frank indicated his interest in having Lewis transferred to the marketing division. While he could understand Cunningham's reluctance to let Lewis go, Frank was nevertheless persistent, and Cunningham eventually agreed to the transfer.

Frank had also hired Tony Buccini as a product manager in May. Although Buccini often appeared abrupt and stubborn, his enormous energy and strong ability with numbers made him a good product manager. Frank thought back to the day in mid-May when both Lewis and Buccini were officially assigned to marketing. He had remembered how Nolan had emphasized that each manager should be able to run his own area without help from other functions. Therefore, he told Lewis and Buccini that, although their official functions were in marketing, they should keep themselves informed of other aspects of the company as well. The following week, Buccini approached Frank with what he saw as an impending problem in the company's cash position. They discussed it with Cunningham, who assured them that there was no problem with the projected cash flow. Neither Frank nor Buccini were convinced, and later that afternoon they met with Nolan to explain the problem. Nolan could see no problem either and, over their objections, dismissed the issue as unimportant. Frank remembered the staff meeting two days later in which Nolan had emphasized the soundness of the company's cash position and how it was not a subject of concern. In retrospect, Frank felt that this incident may have strained Buccini's relationship with Cunningham. Now that Lewis and Buccini were working for Frank, the company organizational chart was again redrawn, as shown in Exhibit III-4.

After a short time, Frank began to have mixed feelings about his job at Abbot. After having searched for greater and greater autonomy, he suddenly found himself thinking that he had almost too much autonomy. Whereas the Great Pacific Paper Company approach had been tight control, supplemented with strong staff support, the approach within Houston Electronics could be summed up as self-sufficiency, or, as Frank often put it, "parochial functionalism."

Exhibit III-4 Frank Mason (A)

Partial Organization Chart, Abbot Business Supply Company, May 25

EDWARD S. NOLAN
President

LESTER METCALF
Administrative Assistant

Personnel Director

RICK CUNNINGHAM
Controller

FRANK MASON
VP for Marketing
and Sales

JEFF STEELE
VP for Operations

PERCY LITTLE
San Francisco Bay
Sales Manager

San Francisco Bay
Sales Force
(6)

JAMES AU
Los Angeles Area
Representative

Los Angeles
Stationery Stores (4)
& Distributors (3)

ROGER FIELDS
Sales Manager,
Stationery &
Hardware*

STEVE LEWIS
Product Manager,
Stationery &
Hardware*

JOHN COMINSKI
Sales Manager,
Business Forms*

TONY BUCCINI
Product Manager,
Business Forms*

* The products in the Accessories Group were absorbed by the other two product groups. The Stationery and Hardware Group (49% of sales) now includes rubber bands, paper clips, and bulletin boards, and the Business Forms Group (51% of sales) now includes maps and art supplies.

For Frank, this meant doing his own control, budgeting, planning, and so on. Also, it seemed to Frank that he, not Nolan, was supplying the leadership for the company. This seemed to him like so much autonomy that it was a little frightening.

PROBLEMS WITH NOLAN

During May and June, Frank began to see unexpected and unpleasant aspects of Nolan's personality. Nolan began to appear volatile and unpredictable, particularly in the way he treated other people, such as Percy Little. Frank's tour in the navy had taught him that when dealing with subordinates, the rule was, "Praise in public, censure in private." Nolan seemed to take exactly the opposite view. It seemed to Frank that Nolan was a "Theory X" manager—"If something goes wrong, raise hell!" Also, during his frequent outbursts, Nolan would liberally use strong profanity, even during staff meetings, which Frank personally found distasteful and at times upsetting. At Great Pacific Paper, he had never heard an oath stronger than "S.O.B.," and even that was seldom used. He was shocked that a man of Nolan's stature would use such language at any time, but especially when conducting company business. At first, Frank had attributed such behavior to the other managers' ineptness in dealing with Nolàn, but even so, he felt that Nolan's methods and language were unnecessary.

One particular incident stood out in Frank's memory. At a staff meeting in May, Nolan had wanted Jeff Steele to set up the warehouse like a supermarket, to get away from the computer printouts they were using at that time in inventory control. "When I want to know what we have in inventory," he shouted, "I want to walk through the warehouse and see it with my own eyes!" Steele had argued that the computerized location system was efficient and reliable, and that there was no need to group and display their products in the warehouse like supermarket merchandise. Nolan became furious; he apparently disliked computer printouts and believed that a good manager should have the relevant information in his head. What seemed quite strange to Frank was that Nolan seemed to look to him for assurance as he argued with Steele. Nolan even interrupted the meeting to ask Frank for advice on the matter. Frank responded that from his own perspective there would probably be no problems, but the real issue was whether or not the company would incur incremental costs by changing to the supermarket-type arrangement. The company changed over to Nolan's system within a month.

In June, Frank began to notice that his relationship with Nolan was growing more tense. Nolan had become very concerned about Abbot's recent financial performance, especially the firm's low margin. The low margin was primarily the result of Frank's price-cutting strategy, aimed at reversing Abbot's declining sales. Also, the price of paper had sharply increased shortly after Frank took over pricing, which further hurt performance. Although the company's performance was not good when compared to the business plan, Frank pointed out to Nolan that it was still an improvement over the February figures. But his reasoning had little impact on Nolan, who continued to complain about the poor margin.

Frank's relationship with Nolan grew more strained in July, and early in the month they had their first major argument. Frank had approved the sale of an order at below the breakeven point. Since he believed that the customer would not pay a higher price, and since the firm was experiencing high inventory levels, he approved a price that at least covered variable costs and provided some contribution, rather than lose the order. Cunningham informed Nolan of Frank's decision, and Nolan became very upset with Frank, since his decision would further reduce the margin. After expressing his anger at Frank for several minutes, Nolan suddenly demanded to know the margin on a small order for desk pens. Since Frank regarded his role in the company as strategist, he left details such as this to his subordinates. When he told Nolan that he would have to check, Nolan became furious. During the next few minutes, Nolan also expressed his displeasure that the former owner of Abbot had somehow obtained some sensitive information about their operations in Los Angeles. He was sure that one of the marketing people had leaked this information, and he demanded to know what Frank was going to do about it. The entire discussion left Frank feeling very disturbed, confused, and angry, but he managed to tell Nolan that he would bring it up at his next staff meeting.

A few days later, Frank opened his staff meeting with a few words on the sensitivity of company information. He later informed Nolan of this action, but Nolan demanded to be present at the next meeting to see for himself. A week later, Frank presented the same information to his staff, as Nolan had instructed, while Nolan sat by the wall near the head of the table. When Frank finished his opening remarks, Nolan abruptly left the room, slammed the door, and did not return.

At Nolan's next staff meeting, he told Frank that he should send Percy Little to Los Angeles on Mondays to visit the major stationery stores there. Frank protested that there was no need to send Little to Los Angeles, and that he could be of more help in the home office. Nolan became visibly angry at Frank's response and instructed Frank that he wanted Little in Los Angeles on Mondays "even if all he does is sit there!" Then, without looking directly at Frank, he said, "When I tell someone to do something, I expect them to do it!"

Shortly after the incident over the breakeven sale, Frank felt the need to talk with Nolan about how things were going. He spoke to Nolan one morning and expressed his frustration and confusion over what was expected of him. Nolan, however, responded that things were going fine and there was nothing to be greatly concerned about. This discussion left Frank feeling very unsatisfied. It seemed to him that such a discussion should have had a more powerful impact on Nolan, but instead, Nolan had been very calm and approving. He decided that it would be better to discuss the matter with Nolan during their trip to Los Angeles the following week.

Frank and Nolan arrived in Los Angeles on a hot, smoggy afternoon in late July. During the ride from the airport in their rented car, Frank began to tell Nolan about the problems he saw at Abbot Business Supply. He said that since Nolan spent much of his time in Houston, there were communication problems, a lack of central focus, and a power vacuum in the company. Also, since Lester Metcalf, the administrative assistant, also went to Houston fairly often, no one was in charge of the company for fairly long periods of time. Frank felt that Nolan needed to be at Abbot either all the time or not at all, and if he could not be there at all, then he should make some sort of power arrangement. After expressing these thoughts to Nolan, Frank suggested that a conference-phone hookup from Houston might be feasible. Nolan listened to Frank and seemed to be very understanding of the problems and frustrations Frank was experiencing. He agreed with Frank's analysis and seemed appreciative of his candor, and Frank began to feel optimistic, since Nolan seemed ready to make some needed changes.

THE CONSTRUCTION PAPER INCIDENT

After their conversation, Nolan casually mentioned to Frank that the company ought to sell more school construction paper. Frank agreed and, upon his return to San Francisco, began to gear up for increased construction paper sales. One week later, Frank was surprised to discover that there was no more construction paper remaining in inventory. For an explanation, he went to Jeff Steele, who told him that Nolan had ordered him to stop purchasing construction paper a few days earlier. Frank then went to Nolan and expressed his distress that he had not been informed of this decision. Nolan remarked, "This is a small company. When I tell one guy something, he should tell the others." He had little else to say, so Frank returned to Steele's office and they discussed the matter for over an hour.

The following Tuesday, a salesman from a major paper producer offered to sell 40,000 reams of construction paper to the company at a very good price. Frank talked to Steele and then to Nolan, explaining that the supplier would guarantee the order to the company's specifications and would allow Abbot to inspect the shipment before delivery. Although 40,000 reams is a small amount of construction paper, Nolan said no, stating, "I don't want to go into it. I've talked to paper experts and they say we're too small to be hedging in the paper market." The next day, Steele asked Frank about the order, and Frank told him of Nolan's decision. Steele responded, "I want to talk to Nolan," and went straight to the president's office. Twenty minutes later, Steele returned to say that Nolan had changed his mind and had decided to buy the 40,000 reams of construction paper. When Frank confronted Nolan about this reversal, Nolan explained, "For that amount, we can sell it. Besides, Frank," he continued, "you didn't give me all the facts about this deal. You never told me that we could reject the order at no cost to us if it wasn't prepared to our specifications." When Frank pressed him, Nolan simply dismissed the issue, saying that Frank needn't be concerned about it. Frank left Nolan's office feeling very angry and frustrated.

THE NEW PRICING SCHEME

In early August, Nolan took control of all pricing. The margin for July was as poor as that for May and June, and Nolan decided to remedy this problem with his own pricing scheme for Abbot's products. His pricing scheme was based on a required overall company margin of 24 percent.[1] Since the cost of each item was known, Nolan could calculate a price for each of the company's products that would produce a margin within two or three percentage points of the required figure.

However, Frank felt that this scheme was far too simple. It treated every product the same, regardless of differences in demand, competitive situation, or unique qualities of each item. Also, it had the effect of lowering the price on high-margin, low-volume goods and raising the price on low-margin, high-volume goods. Since stationery stores often carried thousands of items, they could not absorb large orders and, therefore, would be unable to take immediate advantage of a

[1]Margin, in percent, was calculated by dividing gross margin (sales revenue minus cost of goods sold) by sales revenue.

lower price on the high-margin, low-volume items. Furthermore, if prices were raised on high-volume, low-margin items, which were typically price competitive, the company might lose those sales to lower-priced competitors. Although Frank voiced these objections, Nolan insisted on going ahead with his plan. When Frank saw the new price list, he protested that he couldn't possibly generate the volume at these prices. Nolan replied, "When did I expect you to worry about volume?"

As Frank had expected, Nolan's pricing scheme proved to be a complete failure, and the company's performance for August was even worse than it had been for May, June, and July. Nolan had received the August performance results on September 4, and since that time he had spoken to no one except Cunningham and Metcalf. Since Frank's autonomy was now very limited, and since Nolan was no longer speaking to most of his managers, it seemed to Frank that there was no longer any leadership in the company.

RICK CUNNINGHAM

It occurred to Frank that his deteriorating relationship with Nolan was paralleled by his deteriorating relationship with Cunningham. During April and May, he and Cunningham had got to know each other fairly well, and they would occasionally have drinks and dinner. Although they got along well after working hours, it seemed to Frank that Cunningham was a completely different person at the office. Frank felt that "apple-polisher" would be too kind a word for Cunningham, who blamed everyone else for any problems and always answered Nolan with "Yes, sir," "No, sir," and "Right away, sir." Cunningham also saw Percy Little as a major problem in the company, because he was "giving the products away" with low prices and easy credit terms.

It seemed to Frank that Cunningham and Nolan were always on the same side of every issue. After Nolan's reprimand over the breakeven sale, Frank had discovered that Cunningham had informed Nolan of Frank's decision to approve the order. That afternoon, Frank had found Cunningham in the hall, and asked him why he had gone directly to Nolan and not seen him first. Frank made it clear that if Cunningham didn't have the decency to deal with him directly instead of running to Nolan, then he too could play that game. In response, Cunningham demanded that Buccini mind his own business and accused Frank of letting Percy Little operate in his usual way, which was causing the company to lose money. After a short time, both men calmed down and returned to their offices.

After this incident, it seemed to Frank that his relationship with Cunningham became more openly hostile. A few days later, Buccini drove to Sacramento and returned via San Rafael on company business but neglected to acquire receipts for the bridge tolls. The controller's office had recently established a new policy that specifically prohibited reimbursement of expenses for company business without a receipt, and Buccini's request for $2.35 was refused. Buccini explained the situation to Frank, who was amazed at the pettiness of the refusal. Frank was so angered by it that he went directly to the company clerk and complained. However, the clerk argued that he could not make the payment under the company's policy, and Buccini never received payment for this expense. A few days after this incident, Frank received a memo from Cunningham that said, essentially, "If you have a complaint, don't talk to my people, talk to me." To Frank, the note seemed to be the last straw. By the time he reached Cunningham's office, Frank was so angry that he simply crumpled up the note, dropped it in Cunningham's waste basket, and told him, "I got your note."

THE CURRENT SITUATION

The most recent problem facing Frank involved Nolan's insistence that he dismiss James Au, the Los Angeles area representative. Frank had put Au in charge of the Los Angeles accounts after he had released the sales force there. He had felt that the volume of business there was large enough to warrant a company representative to service these accounts. It seemed to him that, without a local representative in Los Angeles, the company would probably lose these accounts to competitors. Nolan, however, felt that these accounts could be serviced equally well from San Francisco, and that Frank should dismiss Au to cut costs. Although Frank had recommended that no raises be given to himself, his product managers, or his sales managers in an effort to reduce costs, Nolan still insisted that Au be fired. Frank felt that this problem, as well as the pricing problem, had to be settled before Daryl Eismann arrived. The impending visit of the parent company's president gave him an added sense of urgency in resolving these and other problems that had developed over the last few months.

Over the weekend, Frank had even considered resigning from Abbot. At first, the idea seemed appealing under the circumstances, but the more he thought of it, the more distasteful it became. A resignation, to Frank, would be an admission of failure, and if he took another job, it would be his third in less than two years. Additionally, he had recently purchased a house overlooking the bay, and the prospect of being without income again for an undetermined period of time would strain his resources. Frank had invested most of his savings in the property, and he did not have enough cash to sustain a prolonged job search. Also, he liked the Bay Area and did not look forward to leaving it, if he could not find a job nearby.

Frank leaned back in his chair and tried to put the last six months into perspective. He had taken a job with substantial autonomy, a good chance for advancement, and a very good relationship with the company president. But the relationship had deteriorated, his autonomy had been severely curtailed, and his chances for advancement looked dim. Nevertheless, he felt that he could not continue much longer with things as they were, and believed that he had to take some immediate action to improve the situation with Nolan and Cunningham. Frank became lost in his thoughts for a few minutes, until he heard the familiar sound of heavy, purposeful footsteps down the hall. Frank looked up and stared at the president's door, waiting expectantly.

Frank Mason (B)

Nolan walked into his office and closed the door behind him. Frank entered Nolan's office and began to tell him of his frustrations. As he was becoming more excited, Frank heard himself saying, "What do you expect from me? I don't understand my role in the company. If Cunningham is your 'chief of staff,' let me know." For each of these statements, Frank provided examples. Nolan was very quiet and nodded slowly as Frank reeled off point after point. Nolan finally broke his silence while Frank was discussing Cunningham. "I feel comfortable with Rick," he interrupted. "I know him from our days in Houston Electronics, I communicate with him very often, and I probably shouldn't." Frank continued to complain that, as VP for marketing and sales, he should be involved in pricing. Nolan countered by stating that the new scheme was his own idea and he would run it himself. "Besides, Frank," he continued, "you let me down before. Try it my way now." Then Nolan became more active, complaining that Buccini was interfering with other areas. Frank defended him, stating that he believed Buccini was doing a fine job. Nolan suddenly demanded, "Why haven't you fired Little?" Frank explained that Little was his link to the salesmen, and firing him would be a mistake. They continued their discussion for about twenty minutes and, as Frank was about to leave, Nolan said, "Frank, you shouldn't feel that we have to get away from the office for us to talk. My door is always open, you can come in anytime."

Frank left Nolan's office feeling somewhat relieved. What had begun as a difficult, emotional argument had ended surprisingly well. Nolan seemed to understand the problem Frank was facing and indicated that he would try to be more reasonable. On the whole, it had gone better than Frank had expected, and he was looking forward to a better relationship with Nolan and a gradual return of his autonomy.

The next morning, it was as if they had not talked at all. Nolan began his staff meeting by criticizing Cunningham, but looking at Frank as he did so. Then Nolan began to complain loudly about the poor margin for the last four months. Although he was very active during the staff meeting, Nolan was aloof the rest of the week except for lunch with Cunningham and Metcalf.

The following Monday, Daryl Eismann arrived and met with Nolan and his managers all day. Eismann asked many difficult and pointed questions, and Frank got the impression that Nolan and Cunningham were attempting to smooth over the problems at Abbot. After Eismann left, Frank drafted a letter to him on yellow paper, but did not mail it. (See Exhibit III-5.) Later in the week, Nolan had another staff meeting and announced that Marshall Hawkins, Eismann's administrative assistant, would arrive at Abbot on Monday for additional meetings. Nolan's opening words were, "Eismann is sending his sleuth for a visit."

Hawkins arrived on Monday and talked with each of the top managers in Abbot. Frank also showed Hawkins the letter to Eismann he had drafted a week earlier. When Hawkins read it, he remarked, "It's a good thing you didn't send it." It seemed to Frank that Hawkins was sympathetic to his problems. Hawkins thanked him for his time and candor and left his office. Frank noted that Nolan and Cunningham were again attempting to smooth over the company's problems. The next day, Hawkins issued a list of six actions that

Exhibit III-5 Frank Mason (B)

Frank's Unsent Letter to Daryl Eismann

Dear Daryl,

I enjoyed meeting you and found your comments helpful in moving the business ahead.

While you were exposed to many of our problems during your visit, there are others of which you may not be aware. I would like to speak with you further about these problems at your convenience.

Sincerely,

Frank Mason

he designated as high priority, three of which involved marketing. Hawkins left on the afternoon plane for Houston, and Nolan left for Houston the following morning.

One of the priorities on Hawkins's list was to increase the prices on Abbot's line of desk calendars and appointment books. However, when Frank showed Metcalf the new price list, Metcalf refused to approve it. Frank reminded him of Hawkins's instructions, but Metcalf replied, "Hawkins is staff, not line. As long as Ed Nolan is president of this company, we sell these items at the lower price." Frank asked for a memo of his decision, but Metcalf remarked, "I'm sending a letter straight to Hawkins!"

Two weeks later, Steele received a call from Hawkins, who asked for his observations on the company's progress since his visit, expressing a particular interest in Frank's area. Steele informed Frank of the call, explaining that he had said a few encouraging words in general but had declined to discuss Frank, stating that he felt it inappropriate to evaluate a peer.

A few weeks after Hawkins called Steele, Metcalf invited Frank to lunch and explained that "some things were going on" that he could not divulge. After making sure that Frank was doing all he could to comply with Hawkins's instructions, Metcalf added, "If you have any problems, call me. I'll be in Palm Springs." A week later, Metcalf called Frank to see what progress he was making on Hawkins's instructions. Frank made a favorable report, adding that he had also completed James Au's severance papers as Nolan had wanted. During most of the following month, Frank worked to implement the priorities on Hawkins's list, as did most of the other managers at Abbot. Nolan was beginning to play a conspicuously small role in the management of the firm. Since Eismann's visit, Nolan had spent only about one day a week at Abbot and the rest in Houston.

Two months after his initial visit, Daryl Eismann returned to Abbot and informed the top-management group that Nolan had been relieved of his duties. He went on to add that in his opinion, Abbot was in serious trouble and every member of top management was suspect. He also pointed out that an "internal person" would not be chosen to replace Nolan. Eismann concluded by promising each of them an answer as to their future in the company as soon as circumstances permitted.

A week later, Hawkins arrived at Abbot and informed Frank that he was fired. Hawkins explained that the only reason they were dismissing him was because Houston Electronics had a policy of "cleaning house" whenever a division president was fired. "It's nothing against you," he added, "it's just company policy." In a strange way, Frank felt relieved and vindicated by his statement. Two weeks later, Frank called Buccini to inquire about the situation at Abbot. Buccini replied that Hawkins had taken over as acting president, but that no one else had been fired at that time.

Neely and Chapman Company

The Neely and Chapman Company, an electrical contracting organization, is located in San Diego, California. It was founded by Richard Neely, who subsequently took on Dale Chapman as a partner. After successfully building the business for thirteen years, Neely and Chapman decided in late 1968 to dissolve their partnership.

A casewriter from Harvard Business School asked in late 1969 if he might talk individually with Neely and his wife Peggy, and with Chapman and his wife Jennifer, about their respective views of the partnership of the men and the reasons for its dissolution. The conversations were tape-recorded and are reproduced in the four cases that follow.

Richard Neely

The following interview with Richard Neely, in November 1969, began at 5 P.M. in the master bedroom on the second floor of his home. Neely sat in an old rocking chair smoking a cigar, and both he and the casewriter had a drink at hand. Both could hear the sounds of children going up and down the stairs, a telephone ringing, and dinner being prepared by Mrs. Neely in the kitchen below. Neely was occasionally called Dick, but more often, people who knew him well called him Elmer, which was also his father's given name. The casewriter had been a friend of Mr. and Mrs. Neely for about six years prior to the following conversation, and had discussed the events of recent years with Mr. Neely a number of times prior to this interview.

Casewriter: One of the things I want to address is—and ask you to talk about, Elmer, is—here you are, you know—*were*—in a partnership that proceeded over a period of thirteen years to the point where it dissolves. And what is interesting to me is how did it get started, how in your view did it proceed, and how did roles change, within the business. What were the relationships between you and Dale, and then as time went on, between you and Dale and Peggy and Jennifer,[1] and all the way up to very recently, the last two or three years? But maybe if we start at the early days, you can take it——

Elmer: Yuh, yuh. Okay. I have . . . had a driving urge to be in business for myself, and did so, for about three years. And during the course of that, I started an embryonic business which had a cash flow. But it was very small. And I intermingled *socially* with Dale, who worked for U.S. Steel, and he attract— — He was a very easy guy for me to get along with—emotionally, and personally. And we used to *talk* to each other, a great deal, at parties. In fact, for probably the first five years of the partnership, where the two of us would end up at a large party, the two of us would end up *talking* to each other, a whole lot—because we enjoyed

[1]Dale Chapman was Mr. Neely's partner. Peggy is Mr. Neely's wife; Jennifer is Mrs. Chapman.

each other's company more than we would somebody else, even though we more or less spent the day together.

The idea of his coming into partners with me, at the time . . . I guess I almost didn't really believe that he'd *want* to, or something. He was working for a large corporation, and it was a pretty risky thing for him to do, in my eyes. But on the other hand, the two of us set off as—— Let's see. I had two things, this kind of—— I *really had* something. I had a tangible thing. I had a going concern. Which is a difficult thing—even in my mind—but I flopped back and forth all the time, and I said it wasn't very big, and hence it wasn't worth much. But . . . at other times I went around and I'd take a lot of credit unto myself for the fact that I created initial *life*—or some damn thing like that. I get all . . . and God . . . I guess I think I'm *God* or some darn thing, right in that area. I *caused* this thing to happen! And then, *I brought you in*. But on the other hand—and I'd flip-flop—and the other way I'd have of looking at it is that, what in the hell value is there to a small electrical contracting company? There are nine thousand of them in the United Sta—— in the San Diego area, and who cares?

And, in fact, continuing through the partnership are those—is that ambivalent situation, where one minute I'm saying, you know, *I caused it to happen,* and also *I am the driver* of the goddam thing, or the soul force—s-o-u-l. And the next minute I'm saying—and this is the way I think I viewed Dale then, and probably did through the whole thing—is that he's a *powerful engine*. And he comes in with this . . . this . . . powerful force that he has. And he says, for reasons that I'm not quite clear, but he was somehow attracted to me, and to the idea, and he said, "Let's do this." He said, "Okay." I remember the stuff about when we were fooling with putting the partnership togoda—— together. At first you can't believe. It's kind of like saying . . . "Let's screw," or something like that. At first you think it's kind of kidding, but all of a sudden—well, finally, you know, it's about to go in! [Laughter.] Or some darn thing like that.

But . . . And even there, this back and forth. And we got down to the point of, well, what should the split be? Well, literally, when the partnership was put together, we each contributed assets worth $7,500, which, at the time, was all I had. And Dale had to borrow money from his father to produce the $7,500. So it was a pretty big personal commitment on both of our parts that we tossed into a pot. And then, what's the sharing? Well, at the time, I said fifty-fifty—which seemed right to him, too, in that the basis of the partnership was kind of a marriage thing. It wasn't a business partnership. It was a marriage partnership, where you—— What else would it be? It turns out in retrospect it might have been better if I'd kept sixty and given him forty, and maintained a dominant father role, or some damn thing. But basically, this is a couple of guys, and we're going to be married. And we're scared to death of the world. And we're out attacking it. And the basis of the partnership, up until probably the last two years, *was* the two of us against the world.

We got into a thing on whose name got to be first. And I remember I got my back up on that one. And Dale kind of horsed around, and he suggested alphabetical order, you know. In other words, we were both a little bit "that" way. And I said—— Oh, and we handled each other very gently, there. This was all about——

Casewriter: By "very gently," you mean competitive?

Elmer: Yes. Yuh.

Casewriter: I'm not sure I understood it.

Elmer: No, it's a little different than competitive. It's the—— I want—— I don't know. I wanted my name first. I'm not *proud* of it. I'm just saying that's what I *wanted*.

Casewriter: And he did too?

Elmer: And he did too. He gently tried it. But at that point, the thing was very . . . very tender, and I guess we both wanted it, but somehow I didn't hang in tough for it, and I think I probably could have been pushed out of it. But on the other hand, I hung in tough for that.

Then we got down to the point of who gets to be the president of the thing. And literally, we flipped a coin for it. And I won. And that—— But then I never gave it up. But the subject never came up. I—— I—— The subject never came up, and I never offered it up. And also, as the thing evolved—at least in my opinion—it became . . . not obvious . . . but it became increasingly difficult to change that situation. Although there again, I suppose, under some kind of pressure I would have changed it. . . . I don't know. And especially—there you get into the last couple of years—I think I was making plans to change it. I was preparing to abdicate, practically, I think. "Take the power."

I'm jumping into the tail end of the thing. I think part of what I did was to start to push this . . . something I call spiritual responsibility—trying to—— trying to—— tried to unload it onto him. And I think one of the things that was going on at the end of the darn partnership was that I was trying to unload the spiritual responsibility on him, and he figured he didn't want it, and he was trading that off against the idea of his letting me have my jollies by being president, and stuff, as long as I wouldn't horse with him on the—— on the—— thing.

We got the thing started. It was very tender. I remember he brought a desk . . . he *bought* a desk, for $26, and brought it in, and—— to a little shanty office that we had. And one of the first few days, I remember, I went and bought a vase with some flowers in it, and put it on his desk, and just *bombed* him. He really thought it was a kind of a neat deal. And . . . so did I. And it was that way.

There were competitive jealousies from the very beginning, in that Dale is an extremely hard worker, which makes me anxious. I can't stand to be around hard workers. And I end up saying to Peggy a bunch of times, I said, "Hell, I do not want to go into comp—— into working competition with anybody, because I won't work that hard." And I'm saying, "Hell, let him do all of the work!" or some darn thing. I was trying to feel better myself. But gradually the partnersh— And going in, we didn't even define our roles, in the partnership. We were both just *there*.

And as time went on, I, who knew at that time how to do everything that we knew how to do, and Dale knew how to sell big jobs to big contractors, and he had an extremely well organized mind. And he started jumping in with large estimating concepts, and stuff. And he tended to move in on the estimating thing. And it just evolved. And he became damn good at it. And soon learned how to do the estimating. And over probably a period of the first five or seven years, he virtually took it over, and was so good, and worked so much harder than I did at it, that I just quit doing it. And engineering, too. I initially showed him how to do the engineering that I knew how to do. And he liked engineering and estimating, and all that stuff, and I gradu—— Let's see. I was the mechanical man, going in. I had to be, because that's all there was. And as time went on, he felt so good with it, and *was* so good, and worked so hard at it, that I gradually atrophied, in those areas. And moved out of it. And it allowed me this kind of a humanistic life that you see going on here now! God knows what would have happened if I'd had some different kind of a job, or something like that, where some guy was guiding me, and telling me, "Here is your 'mechanic' that you're supposed to be doing."

But what happened was that Dale liked to do this mechanical thing so well that I ended up holding the personnel together. More and more. And there got to be more and more personnel. And——

Casewriter: This was what you'd call operations? In the sense of getting the jobs done after the——

Elmer: Right.

Casewriter: ——everything else is——

Elmer: That's just about it. And Dale had the hard-edge thing going in of—of getting the jobs, and being correct on estimates. Those are the hard-cutting edge. You've got to be *right.* And you've got to go convince somebody that they've got to give you a contract. And that's the cutting edge of a contracting organization. But meanwhile, in order to *have* a cutting edge, you've got to have a back man—backing. And I kind of drifted into providing this backing, and kind of pushing Dale from behind to be the cutting edge, and trying to supply him the coolant to cool off the cutting edge, and making him strong.

After probably three or four years, we still had not divided our roles, and we started getting anxious. And I remember, I went in one Sunday and sat there and just fooled with the whole thing. And it was—— It's a technique that I continue to use with myself. And that is: "I don't feel good. I'm very anxious. And I'm getting mad at Dale. And we're—— and it isn't—— it's all messed up." And I sat and created a division of duties. In that we'd—— been interplay . . . I was doing sales, and he was doing sales. And we were all out running the men, and the whole thing.

And I came in the next Monday. And I was scared to death. And it wasn't exactly an ultimatum, or anything else, but I said something to the effect, "You know, we're screwed up. I propose *you* take care of sales, and I'll take care of production, and bookkeeping, finance." And I think it was one of those kind of things where my fears were—— well, anything that's kind of *neat*—well, a lot of times you're afraid while it's going on. But Dale thought that was great! It'd just fit right in. He had to sacrifice his—um—participating in the control of the books. But on the other hand, he got full bore to go do what he wanted to do in the sales end of the thing. And he was absolutely free in any sales things that came in. I *had* to, by this agreement, shuffle over into him. And the production thing was pretty much mine, going in. That wasn't too serious.

Dale considered himself knowledgeable in the—um—bookkeeping manipu—— accounting manipulation, and I didn't, and don't. As of right now. Even though that's the basis of the very *job* he has, right at this stage of the game. I still don't think he's any good at it. But——

Casewriter: You took on the finance?

Elmer: Yup.

Casewriter: But you separated that from accounting?

Elmer: Well, finance and accounting. I

did all that. The banking—anything of that. And basically, it put Dale in a selling and estimating business, which, if you were ever to talk about a contracting company, and say what's the soul of the contracting business, I'd say it's selling and estimating. If your estimates are right, and you're able to sell 'em, with a profit in it, well, all it is, then, is all you have to do is do it. And collect for it.

This thing worked for a long time. And I think it caused the flourishing of the enterprise. I really think that was a good thing—that separation thing . . . the division. . . . And God, all of a sudden we were clean again. And we started going, and God, it was very happy, and plugging stuff in, and Dale was getting all kinds of kicks out of the—— what he was doing, and successes. And his successes were isolated to the point where he—— I mean, he knew *he* was personally responsible for what was happening, and getting his return—his——

Casewriter: He could see the outcome of his own work?

Elmer: Yuh, he could see the outcome, and he—— And I think that's what made that good, for awhile. And I seemed to see the outcome. I was getting this over, and the outcome that I was getting was, no matter what happens, that balance sheet is bigger every year. And Dale was saying, "And I'm selling all this stuff, and basically, when that sales figure increases every year, I caused it." And I think, somehow, I was saying, "I caused the profit figure."

Casewriter: So each got . . .

Elmer: Some darn thing. And then we both shared in the profit figures. So that was great.

Casewriter: That takes you in—what? Five, six, seven years?

Elmer: That takes—— yuh, uh—— okay, what's happening to us then? There's a kind of a blackout, almost, in my mind, in there, then. We were just grinding it out, and it's in that area that—that we're still *pushing,* and—— And by the way, there was great kind of esprit de corps. We'd have a Christmas party, and the employees would take up a collection, and give Dale and me *gifts*—briefcases, and crap like that. And everyone was—— kind of high on this thing . . .

And from about the eight- to ten-year period on it, I don't know what happened. There's a couple of missing years in there, somehow. I never—— And then we—— And then Dale and I started to sort of drift ap—— Not apa—— Yeh, I guess it adds up to drifting apart. And he—— I guess a polarization kind of started. And he became very—— as an example, very active in the Founders Club. And for about four years, the last four years of our partnership, he was on the road to becoming president of the Founders Club. He became anxious about my—uh, let's see—*unsocial* acts. And I started getting—— I started kissing off people in the—— in the—— the soci—— in the social world. In not returning invitations, and a whole bunch of junk. And Dale was going hard the other way, where he was joining new things. And I know something in there, and that is that I was considering that Dale was taking care of that end, and I was relying on him to take care of the social end. And this is ramified by, the minute he's gone, I instantly joined two clubs, to kind of run over—fill in that damn thing. For what, I don't know, but partly I mean to fill it in for me. See, he was filling it in for me, at the time. Not just the business, but for me. And I'm saying, you know, I may not be much, but Dale Chapman will take me anywhere. I can go to the Founders Club, or the so and so—and I'm even better, I don't have to joi—— I'm superior to joining the damn thing. I can go, but I don't ever have to—or some damn thing like that.

And I got a hunch—I was probably starting to get to be a dra—— I—— I think he was starting to feel the drag. He was saying, "You enjoy my social prestige, but you're not contributing. In fact, you're making it difficult. I go somewhere and they say——" I don't know whether this really happened, but it certainly sounds like, as if, "How are you getting along with Dick? Because he's acting like a real nut, or some darn thing, going to body awareness classes, and all that kind of stuff."

Casewriter: Well, that takes you up to three or four years ago. Can you go back and look again at the personal relationships that were building while the business was growing, and you and Dale were working out ways of dividing up the work by function, and then getting to the point where you were successful enough that you could—you know, Dale could get into clubs, and you could go to outside classes; and you both could get away. Before that, earlier on, you and Dale, and Peggy and Jennifer, were getting to know each other too. As that built, does that feed into the—— I mean, is there a cycle there?

Elmer: Let's see. Yuh, there is some kind of a cycle, where we—— God, we had a kind of a—— a—— *very warm* love between the two families. I mean, a family to a family. And I know in my own mind I ended up kind of thinking that—really, almost, it was one of those deals where everything he has is mine, and every—— I—— I—— wouldn't—— The feelings were, I—— I'd walk into his house, or expect him to walk into my house. Just as . . . there was no particular dividing line—*property* dividing line. And I remember when the beach house they have, the parents were going to—they didn't quite know what to do. And basically, I was kind of thinking, that'd be great. I'll contribute with Dale, and we'll buy Dale's beach house, and we'll all have a beach house together, and we'll all live our whole life out, together. And stuff. And we'll just almost *pool* our financial interests in all pursuits. And the thought then was that this was kind of forever. I—— I think I'd be—— would have been *astounded* at that time if I'd seen what—— where we are right now. Because it was a very close thing. And I don't think Dale was particularly doing anything to prevent—— prevent that. I think we both were given into the thing pretty damn well.

Dale and I would fight, and come home . . . I mean . . . we usually fought underground. . . . But we'd get feeling badly, and we'd come home, and Peggy would always take Dale's side. So I was able to fight with Dale by arguing with Peggy. And there was a long period, of probably four or five years of that business, where I'd come home and tell Peggy what a dumb shit Dale was, and she'd then objectively point out how he could possibly have arrived at the position he did, and I'd attack it, and in a way it relieved me, because I could go back the next day and be pretty well calmed down, and also felt secu—— I was allowed to take pretty big risks in fighting with Dale, because I knew I could patch it up by going back to Peggy, who would go to Jennifer, who would go to Dale. And I had a kind of a round-around there.

Casewriter: You found it—— you know, that—— it's interesting that you'd have a fray with Dale, but not really have it.

Elmer: Never let it out.

Casewriter: So you'd come home and—— do it with Peggy.

Elmer: That's right. Our real arguing—— Dale and I to this day have never really had at each other.

Casewriter: Well, why is that, do you suppose?

Elmer: I think we're both scared to death of each other, I suppose. I—— I—— I don't know. I don't want to fight. . . . Let's see. . . . For one thing, I know he's very hard to fight with. In that it doesn't get to be a regular old fight. It gets to be—I don't know how to say it—it gets to be a—— a debate, and I personally feel that I'll lose a debate. And I don't want to lo—— I don't—— Let's see. I don't want to lose a debate. In that Dale is really almost a *super*-businessman, in a way, and the debate's going to end up in some kind of an agreement, and every time I end up in one of these things, I end up having made some kind of an agreement with him. Which I don't want to live with. So I'll do all kinds of stuff to avoid—— to avoid leading up to the point where I'll say, well, okay, then you agree . . . and I really think I—— I won't get anywhere close to an agreeing commitment with him, because in my opinion he's lying there *waiting* for a commitment, of some kind. It adds up to a contractual obligation.

Casewriter: So you found you didn't really have to, because if you could talk to Peggy, and presumably she'd talk to Jennifer—and you must have assumed that——

Elmer: Um——

Casewriter: Or did you? Because the two gals——

Elmer: *She* would talk to him. I assumed probably 20 percent of this arrived back, but I also—— Let's see. I assumed that the combination of Peggy-Jennifer had some kind of control over Dale which would stop him from withdrawing, from a real major—— I—— I knew I could push him around, and keep him from withdrawing. But I still had him on the backside. Because he's afraid of Jennifer. He's—— you know, or some damn thing. . . . Something like that, I think.

And—— well, *hell,* it's still going, right now. Jennifer can still get him to—— uh—— I don't know—— somehow or other I have a goofy feeling that he *has* to mind. I don't know . . . he has to *mind* . . . and it ends up minding Jennifer. And if Jennifer makes up her mind that he should or shouldn't do something, she—— he almost has to do it. I don't know . . . I don't even know about this myself. . . . I kind of think I—— I guess I had a pipeline to Jennifer through Peggy, or some darn thing like that. . . . This may be a little harsher than it really is. But, uh. . . .

Casewriter: Well, the gals had a role, in helping the two of you to overcome—

Elmer: Extremely, yuh. Extremely strong role.

Casewriter: And the four of you saw a lot of each other. In the early years, and on through, I guess. . . .

Elmer: Right. Right.

Casewriter: So that you didn't know each other just as couples, then. I mean you knew Dale as a person, and as a partner, and you know Peggy as your wife, and you knew Jennifer as a person too.

Elmer: Yuh.

Casewriter: How did your relationship develop individually with Jennifer in the social context that you found yourself in?

Elmer: Well, Jennifer and I . . . Let's see. Jennifer *interpreted* Dale to me, and I started ending up a *confessor* to Jennifer where Jen—— and I don't know what stage of this, but probably about five years ago, or something like that, where Jennifer decided that I was wise in these things, and also she ended up dissatisfied with Dale—I think she's—— with Dale's humanness, or some damn thing, I don't know. Sensitivity! There's some damn word in there. And she—— and Jennifer started talking to me. And she started talking to me about Dale. And I listened. And we'd go round and round. And we'd end up with this—with a quote—— We were one time in San Francisco, Jennifer's saying—— shaking her head and saying—— We were talking about Dale and she ended up saying, "Well golly, Dale thinks you're a *god*," or some darn thing. She's telling me how *admiring* Dale is of whatever the hell I have, or something. And this is a little double, or some darn thing, cause I'm also kind of halfway seeing Jennifer saying, "I really wish you'd talk to *me*," or something, and "Dale thinks you're really something, in this thing." And it isn't *sexual* attraction, but—— but literally, through a period of time, Jennifer kind of half-assed fell in love with me—or something. . . . That may be too strong, but—— She *really* likes to talk to me. And I don't even know *what* my reverse role is, but I like to talk to her a hell of a lot, too. So we have a swell relationship. A swell relationship to the point that right at this instant in time, Dale won't bring her around. It's a—— it spooks him. And so that is one of the—— I mean, *that* was growing.

You say, "What's going on, in the last three years?" But there is a—— there was a threat there, to Dale's . . . domestic security. And I'd say—— you know, and that kind of evolved out of the—— of her——

Casewriter: Of her enjoyment of talking with you, and vice versa. And she was also getting close to Peggy in that period, so that——

Elmer: Right. And I'd say—— oddly enough, I'd say she was starting to become in love with me, but I think she is equally in love with Peggy, or more so. She's *allowed* her love with Peggy, and she is not allowed her love with me. And as a consequence, I think she really has a deep relationship with Peggy, and I think if we weren't—— if there weren't a sexual problem, or a marriage problem, she'd be very deeply involved with me, too. We have a *good* relationship. I like her a lot, and she likes me a lot.

Casewriter: Well, then, this all was going on, and these forces were building, over a period of time, and the differences in the explorations that you and Dale took on when the business got successful enough that you could, when the adventure had accomplished some of its goals, in the sense that you had made some money, and you had some time. You found you had more time, and you didn't want to work that hard. You say Dale really enjoyed working hard, and he wanted to, and wanted the clubs and the social things. And you went after sensitivity training and I don't know what else during that period.

Elmer: Politics and Youth Foundation. And I went out after—— oh, yeh, and the President's Forum, which is just about the same. Even though it sounds different, it's the same speed. It's kind of what do you *do*—what *else* do you do, and so I started to fool around with exterior things. And also I started traveling, and I started in going to San Francisco on a regular basis, which pulls a big chunk of time out. Going to South America. And, uh—— By the way, the South American thing—you can start a thread *way back,* in about the fourth—the third or fourth year of the partnership—and my idealism was running at the time, in that even though our financial security was not by any means established—— In fact, it was at that time that Dale panicked and went under, and he said, "We're going broke." Because there was a job, and he was running the job, and he collapsed. And said, "I can't make it. We're going to go broke." And at the time I—— Let's see, *why*? . . . Anyway,

I said, "No, we're not going to go broke. It's going to be okay." And right in the face of this I went to South America, which some—— based on an overall look at life, or something or other like that, it's important that I start the South American thing now, and—— that was 1959, and we were partners in '56, so that was three years into the thing. And started the damn thing, which was also extracurricular, compared to our survival. Although I think I assumed that it was partly survival. So you see we had—— We didn't quite know where we were going anyway. It turns out that we grew a company. But it—— I don't know, I thought maybe South America could make us all rich. Or . . . something. Basically, we just wanted to make a lot of money.

But as the thing—— The balance sheet increased every year, and we had our eye on that damn thing, and it got to be a certain point where I think it became obvious to both of us that we were making more money than we could use. And it was *easy* to do. And then Dale went off into his pursuits. . . . By the way, he worked very hard. But also he put an awful lot of time in on *his* things. And I put a lot of time in on *my* things.

Casewriter: And they were quite different.

Elmer: They were absolutely. And they got to be sort of liberal and conservative things. Mine were T-group hippy stuff, and his was Founders Club stuff. And Dale has . . . has . . . what?—given me credit for literally liberalizing his life. I think he may—— probably still does that. And that he learned a little bit of that, and I learned—— what I did, was relax my terrible need for a conservative side of the damn thing. Um. Where the hell were we?

Casewriter: Well, let me take this up to a couple of years ago. Two or three—two years ago, I guess, or so. You were going up to San Francisco a lot. And it must have been about that time that you—you got involved with Virginia. Was it—— Is it about right in time?

Elmer: Well, of course—— But there is another foursome deal, growing, alongside the business, the whole time. And it is in *that* foursome that my *real living was.* I really *loved* that—— Virginia—— P.J. thing. And God, somehow it seemed to explain life to me. Or—— I mean, it—— it—— And when we were together, it was rather ordinary, but when we were apart, I kept thinking that we've got—— that things were only *real* when I'm mixed up with the Whitmans somehow. And quite frankly, I didn't really analyze it in terms of just Virginia. I really kind of thought it was the both of them. And that thing's growing up alongside, and Lord knows what kind of jealousy games I was playing, where I was explaining the Whi—— I held the—— for instance, I'd hold the Whitmans over Dale's head. In a way. And it was very easy, because Dale would end up kind of beaten in the thing, and says, "Shit, I don't understand the Whitmans," and—you know—"They're too much."

That's another feature through this whole thing. I'm always telling people, "I like you, *and* the Whitmans," and all this kind of junk, and he allows himself to be crushed by it. I—— Lord knows why he does. But he did. And so I'd help him with it, a little bit. And—so then you bring the Whitmans along. And—let's see. This is odd—— P.J. ends up growing almost over kind of like Dale. P.J. ends up rather logical, needs money or . . . needs public position. And I ended up separating from P.J. in much the same way I was separating from Dale. And P.J. ends up having to take more and more conservative positions, and I end up saying, "Let's swing. Let's smoke pot," and he saying, "God, I hate pot, and it's a felony." And stuff. And each one of us taking extreme posi—— I'm not too sure I really want to smoke pot, but I *got* him, so I'm saying, "Oh, I can hardly wait," and he's saying . . . the other. And that's—— I mean, I'm in about the same boat with Dale. But that really did happen with P.J., and we'd have an argument with P.J. over—— P.J. makes crude statements of, "If there's a war on I'll have my son go to war, in the honorable way," and I'm saying, "My God, being a conscientious objector is the only way to be." And that kind of jazz.

During the course of this—— God, I met—— let's see. I end up more—— more and addicted—addicted? Huh!—to Virginia, and the period for seeing the Whitmans started to increase. And I think it started to increase—— and we'd play games. And basically, in retrospect, I know—I know now, it was Virginia and me playing games. But I didn't even know it, at the time. And that is, I'd get my feelings hurt, during a—— one of the times when the four of us, the Whitmans, were all together. And that was—— I know now—that Virginia hadn't treated me right. She'd pull the . . . rug out, in some damn way or another, and I'd say, "Okay, we'll quit." Well, then, all of a sudden an invitation from the Whitmans would come *through Peggy,* and all of a sudden we were going to see the Whitmans—for dinner, or some damn thing. And then it'd go dead for awhile. And then *I'd* concoct a complex scheme, such as we'll all go to New York, or we'll all meet at Hearst's castle. And all this junk. And uh . . . um . . . let's see—— A key thing in the Whitman thing was where we sat out on our patio here one day, and P.J. says, "I've got—— been given access to a house at Squaw Valley. I don't know what to do." I've never been to Squaw Valley, and it doesn't mean a damn thing to me. And I say, "Well"—— and it's also he has to pay his boss $1,500 a month for it. And I say, "Well, God, Squaw Valley really turns me on, P.J. And we'll split it. And we'll go to Squaw Valley." This is very subtle. And the next thing that happens is that pretty soon we get an invitation to the Whitmans'—"Come up and spend a week with us at Squaw Valley." No mention of the fact that I'd offered to back half of it, or anything like that.

So, okay. What about my offering to share it? He says, "Well, hell, we're renting the place for three weeks or a month," or some darn thing, "and you're only coming—— you're only invited for a week, and it all gets kind of confusing," and also, "you're not invited to pay for part of the thing." And I got—— That's how *my* feelings work out. My *feelings* were hurt in there somehow. I kind of said, "You know, I backed you in the thing. I wish you'd told me you weren't accepting my backing. And that you were going on your own. But you're on your own. But somehow I think . . . I got a sneaky feeling you're riding on me." . . . Anyway. And I got kind of sore at P.J. on that thing, and boy, I can't explain it in business terms, but somehow he *used* me to support himself to go do something he wouldn't ordinarily have done. And I complained about it, openly, to him. And he contends he doesn't know what I'm complaining about. And that—— that was not a separation, by any manner of means. But on the other hand, we went to Squaw Valley, and we had all these great times. And Virginia and I'd end up playing *way-out* games, and probably about four years ago, or something, we—— one day, Virginia initiates the thing, and she says, "You know, you have a lot of feelings about me." And I think it's my change of life, right there. You know, I kind of said, "I *do*?" [Laughter.]

And I kind of mull the whole thing over, and I think it was about one of my first ideas that maybe I had feelings about anything, or some damn thing. And so we fool with that. Then we fool with—— um—— Well, basically she's right. It was merely . . . it was a kind of an *objective* observation of *me* that never occurred. . . . I didn't think anybody could ever *see* my feelings. And she says, you know, what the hell, you have a whole bunch of feelings! And I said, okay. So we finally figure out those feelings. And then I get—— in all of this—— *Then* I started *allowing* the feelings a little bit more, and then I get in this terrible bind, which ultimately led to going into therapy three years ago.

Um. Saying, you know, what the hell, I hurt all over. I'm getting all—uh—torn up, and you know I'm married. And I'm in love with Virginia—I think. Or I mean, I don't know what it is. I'm unhappy with how I am. I'm not unhappy with Peggy and I'm not something, but I'm kind of clawing up the wall, or some damn thing. And I said, "Calm me down." And the therapist, a big humanist, he just says, "Well, what's inside you? Come on, keep coming. What do you want to do? What do you want? What do you want—you want the business? You want Dale? Or——" And then the way you end up in therapy sessions, you end up with him saying, "Well, what would you like to be doing? I mean, what do you want right now?" And I'd say, "Well, hell, I'd like to be in San Francisco with Virginia." And he says, "Well, why aren't you?" "Well, because—— [Laughs.] Because of an enormous number of things! And that is the business, and I'm married, the kids, and the whole goddam thing."

And we'd play that out. And . . . in the meanwhile, the Whitmans are probably playing something similar out in their own world. And for reasons beyond my comprehension—although they were all explained at the time—P.J. *chooses* to go off to New York to work for three months. And Virginia felt *left*. No matter what was going on with him, she felt left. And at a certain stage of the game, Virginia went "click." And said, "Okay, you did it." And Virginia dropped the bars down, and says, "Go for it." . . . And so Peggy and I end up arguing about it. Peggy says Virginia *caused* it by dropping the bars down. Virginia says—— Peggy says Virginia dropped the bars down, and that's caused it. And I say, hell, I've been pushing just like anybody else. The fact that Virginia has to drop the bars down to make it work, I—— I don't feel consid—— Am I lured in, or do I push into the lure? I don't know. What the hell. I wanted what was going on. I recognized all the dangers, and the whole goddam thing. It just is a fabulous thing, and at this stage of the game, if I had all those choices to make, I'd make 'em in spades. So.

Casewriter: So you got involved with Virginia, really importantly, then.

Elmer: Um hm.

Casewriter: That went on—what? For some time before you found yourself needing to do something about it?

Elmer: Yuh, probably six months, or some darn thing. Or something like that.

Casewriter: What'd you do?

Elmer: God, we ended up with screwy things, where I really can't read my own mind. But some key points are where I'm sitting in a bar in San Francisco—— No, what I *did*, was I told Peggy. And then the roof fell in. And Peggy called P.J. the next day. To—— Peggy's—— The direction of Peggy's things are backfire operations. She'd keep saying to everybody else, "I want to *stop* this whole goddam progress of this thing." And to me she'd keep saying, "Hang on. Now we'll hold the marriage together. And it's going to be all right, as we—— This is a very bad situation, but we'll work it on through." One of her techniques . . . this is too tough . . . but anyway, one of the things she did was to call P.J. and said, "You dumb shit. Go take care of Virginia. Get her the hell off the—— Get her away." And also, Peggy was pretty overwrought and she wanted some *comfort* from P.J. In fact, she was kind of *hanging* on him. While meanwhile, P.J. is a drowning man himself, and he said, "My God——" P.J. is really very much involved with Virginia and this thing is collaps—— And Peggy was bombing the whole thing, and he's kind of going under, and . . . uh . . . P.J. ultimately—— or not—— and it didn't take him too long—he said to Peggy, "Leave me alone." Very harshly. "Go away," he said. "There's only one thing I want, and that's Virginia. And I don't want *you* around, . . . acting like another female." And also P.J. said to me, "Thanks a lot for pointing out the value of my wife to me. And the intensity of some feelings that I never really understood were going on. And I owe that *to* you. And I admire you." And a whole bunch of nice things. "But on the other hand, under the conditions, I *really* hope I don't ever see you again." Which even to me seemed like, from his point of view, the very logical point of view absolutely. Don't—— Go away. *Do* go away.

Um . . . The thing having been exposed, and that—— So now it's all over the place. And this led to, among other things, a meeting between Virginia and me, and Virginia saying, "What'll we do?" I mean—— "*Do* you want to marry me?" And I'm saying, "Yes. I do. Therefore I have to get a divorce." "Are you going to?" Or something—anyway, it all comes to that. "Yeh." And . . . and I leave San Francisco with a completed situation: "This is okay. I'm going to marry you. And I'm going to go put this—— put a divorce together."

And the strong issue there to me—I mean the thing I'm stuck with—is that I made a commitment to Virginia, right at that stage of the game, which I'm not very pleased about. I mean I didn't have any idea when I said oka—— I mean this is how strongly I feel, and this is, at that instant, what I want to do. And it also put a whole bunch of wheels in motion.

Oh, also. I also thought I was *rich.* The—the euphoria of the constantly increasing balance sheet, and all the—— and the success, and being able to deviate from the business, in the way we were. . . . And I don't think I really analyzed the thing very carefully. And I said, okay, I'm—— I'm at the point now of *doing* it.

Casewriter: Mm.

Elmer: And in my—— and what really happened is that I got around to absolutely analyzing the various costs, to implement the thing that I'd committed to, and the costs are in two realms. One is financial, and one is emotional—family. And the financial thing—well, I got a—— you know, I talked to a lawyer, and the whole damn thing, and got the whole thing spread out, and I looked very cleareyed, here, right now, what a divorce involves. And—— And I believe this is to be true, anyway—basically, a divorce involves being able to split what you have in half, more or less. It can be adjusted. But the half you have to give to the wife is more the liquid half. And the half you end up remaining is the nonliquid half of it. And of—— from the nonliquid half, you have to make your own living and produce enough *more* liquid to keep other things—child support and alimony and other stuff. So even the liquid you can produce out of a nonliquid situation—some of that's drained off, too.

And in my position, even though I think I'm rich, it turns out I'm not rich—in fact, I'm dead . . . I'm *minus,* when it comes—— when it's all laid out, on those—— on those terms. And all of a sudden I went through the experience of finding—— of . . . of *thinking* I was rich, but under these conditions, finding out I was worse than *broke*! And that brought me up to the position of finding out how dear survival and material and stuff were for me. And we argu—— I had a discussion with Virginia in the course of this, and Virginia's very passionate right in—— she's very passionate, period. She says, "I don't care! The money's not the big deal. No money." And I got kind of cool in there, and I said, "Do you know what? I know it *is.* And the idea of being broke, you don't really know about. And the idea of being in your late *forties* and not being able to produce money—and really, the odds are not going to improve as far as this point—it's got to be a life situation. You know, if I end up broke now, with you, and in love with you, and all that kind of stuff, I'm not—— I do not have the confidence that I can bounce out of a broke situation, at least—especially—to *my* satisfaction, and probably to your satisfaction. And I have a terrific doubt in my mind whether even the world's greatest love can survive that kind of a—— the handicap of poverty." Poverty scares the pee out of me. It really *does.* And I think it's a real thing even for a *real* smart-ass like me.

And then the other aspect of it—I think that's the over—— I'm sorry to say, but I think the financial is really the more *profound* of the two. But the other thing has to do with some sort of a guess at what my relationship with the kids would be. And I really enjoy the development of the kids, and my relationship with them. I've got a sneaking hunch that were I to become divorced, and marry Virginia, I could still keep some sort of a kid relationship going, and I don't think that is an overbearing factor. And a kind of an equal to the kid thing is . . . is that . . . Peggy's a damned important—— Here you come up with a funny thing. She *really is* my wife! And I really *think* she is. This gets . . . to the . . . you get to be the—— what the hell is a wife, and what the hell—— and who are you in love with? Or who—— what the hell is love? And all this kind of junk. 'Cause Peggy's . . . great. And I en—— In fact, the very things that allow the spread of thinking that I come into the—— is, um . . . the idea of divorce is the idea of giving up all for the *pearl* of—— and all that kind of junk. And I—— And it's in that thinking . . . and then, okay, I'll sacrifice everything because I've really found the deepest love, and that's the time, and that's the go-for-it, in the good old hippy fashion. And literally, I don't know. But I chickened out in the middle of the hippy fashion. And——

Casewriter: Can we chase that? Because you must have spoken to Dale somewhere in there, too. About your intentions.

Elmer: Okay. Soon thereafter—while talking to Virginia and saying, okay, we're going to do it . . . and I'd make a concrete plan, in my head. And I rode in Dale's Jaguar, down to the Founders Club, and had lunch, and I just laid it on him crude. And I said—— We were riding along, and Dale thinks everything's all right, and we're going into the next job, and I said, "Dale, tell you what. I'm going to divorce Peggy."

And God, he flinched about an inch. He said, "That's *terrible.*" I don't think it had ever occurred to him, because all we'd do is run around together, and it really was a very nice-looking operation, and it *really* is. It is to this day.

And after a thirty-second pause, I say, "And also I'm going to go marry Virginia." And it was an *equal* shock. Those were two situations with Dale. One is that he could probably stand a divorce, if somebody wasn't getting along at home. But the idea of running off and marrying somebody else's wife was really—— I think that was the really . . . the jolt, to him. And what the hell.

We managed it through lunch, but he was very shook by the whole thing. And I know on the way home I'm saying, "Well, Dale, I really appreciate your—— your"—let's see—"sort of noncritical attitude about the whole thing. You've absorbed it," and all that kind of stuff. And Dale said, "*In no way.*" He says, "I haven't absorbed it. I don't approve of anything you're doing," and, "I'm just trying to *live* with it." On the other hand, he said, "If there's anything I can do *for* you—if you want to hide your assets, or screw the business around in some such way that makes a divorce more palatable, I'm with you." And he was very dear, at that—in that.

A-a-and that—— Where are we now, 1969? So that's in 1967, late. And we fooled around in that state for about a year. And that was where I'm chickening out, for really causing the thing to happen, and Peggy's saying, "Postpone it, postpone it, postpone it. I hear what you're saying, but let's get the kids through one school, and then another——" and all this kind of stuff. And it got to be kind of a day-to-day basis, and I'm communicating constantly with Virginia, and this and that. And—— Oh, also, Virginia, in the midst of this, went to P.J. and said, "I'm going to go marry Elmer." And then P.J. is big about it, the way Peggy is, and he says, "Okay, fine, how does it all work?" And we had a couple of meetings, you know—all this kind of junk. A-a-and P.J.—God, he's saying, you know, "Go ahead," and all that, and, "Hopefully it won't work out, and then in a year or so, why we'll all straighten the damn thing out."

And after a year of *that* kind of stuff—— And also, Dale's . . . Dale's *successes* started dropping off, in the business end. A whole year went by, and nothing really *great* came out of him. And he'd have ever-increasing greatness, some days, of selling bigger and bigger and more complex things. And he was well on his way to being the president of the Founders Club, and a whole bunch of junk. But he kind of pooped out, and really wasn't doing much, for about a year. And he was starting to make . . . literally, *mistakes,* in the stuff during this year, where he should have followed up on a potential thing, but he just said, "I'm not interested," and *not* follow up on it. And he started paying more attention to—— *he,* that started putting more of his attention into golf, and some other kind of junk. And, you know, obviously, I think he kind of got broke, broke in himself, at the whole damn thing. And then we ended up, on a night in October of 1968, where we were sitting around and we were really neither one of us particularly pleased with ourselves—each other, I mean. And—although not mad. And my daughter had gotten in—— her gang, some of them got busted for pot.

And it was a sort of an ordinary night, and I was starting to go home, and it was six o'clock, and I s—— and I sarcastically said to Dale, "Well, I'm going home to my wayward daughter." And Dale had been critical of her for not kissing off a whole bunch of friends because they were involved in . . . uh, narcotic—— in marijuana, or some damn thing. And he said, "Well, don't——" After a certain amount of discussion he said, "Look, I really don't want to discuss domestic affairs with you. Or your kids. I don't agree with you. I think your kids should be pulled out of—— If they were my kids, I would disallow them from associating with other kids who were in the process of getting in trouble." And I took another position, and that is that, hell, the kids that are getting in trouble I know, and I like 'em, and the trouble isn't all that serious, and I really don't want to dictate to my kids.

And then he said, "Well, that's fine, but I don't want to . . . I just don't want to . . . get into—— All right, let's not discuss domestic things. Let's just talk *business* with each other." And his proposal then was, you—— "We'll just be businesslike." And, with anger, I said, "That's great! We'll just talk business, and . . . um . . . we won't relate, domestically." And we made it through that, and of course I'm kind of ho—— I'm mad, about that. And we walked . . . started to walk out, and—— uh . . . somehow we evolved from there, and in a we—— Um, I was mad, and I'm sure Dale was too, and then I said, "Well, maybe——" Somehow it came out as if, "Maybe you'd just as soon not have the partnership continue too?" And Dale says, "I've done some thinking about it." And I said, "Well, maybe we'd better go back into the office and sit down and talk about it." And he says, "Okay." And of course it had pretty well *happened,* by the time we got to that point.

And then I said, "All right, what's the deal?" And he said, "Well, do you wa——" No! I . . . I was pretty pushy then, *I* said, "Do you want to buy or sell?" And he said, "I don't know," he says, "but I've got a feeling you probably want to buy more than I want to sell." And I said, "Well, that's really true. I'm more dependent on the operation of the business than you are."

A-a-and, uh . . . I noticed . . . I was looking through a Country Club roster, and this all happened about a year—— this happened back in '68—I mean '67. They made this thing up, and they got all—— And it says, "What is my occupation?" And under *my* occupation I say, "Electrical contractor." And under Dale's occupation it says, "Engineer." And this is a year earlier. I just saw this the other day. And so I'm kind of arguing now that I think . . . I think Dale had a problem with being an electrical contractor. A social problem. In addition to a problem with . . . I think he started—— I think his idea—his social aspiration, and his blueblood thing was starting—that was on the rise too. And with that, I really think the association with me and my divorcing and all this . . . adultery, and all that kind of junk, I think really got him down.

A-a-and, uh. . . . To go back to the narrative. We decided, right then and there, and we did it in a rather peaceful way. And it's okay. We—— It made me very ho—— Uh . . . uh . . . it—— I came home and told Peggy, and I says, "Well"—kind of calmly—"Dale and I have decided to not be partners any more." She was a little shocked, but not too bad. And, "What's going to happen?" I said, "I don't know, but we're going to try to separate the assets of the business, and he'll take his and I'll take mine. And one of us is going to buy and one of us is going to sell. And the—— And um, frankly, I want to buy, let's see, and he . . . I think he wants to sell. But we'll have to negotiate it for awhile."

And we did negotiate it for probably a month, and the thing actually came together. Started then in October, and kind of came together in November, and it closed in December.

A-a-and, uh. . . . And then—— A terrible air of unreality on my part, through that whole thing. I can't really believe it, and I . . . and I didn't . . . I kind of threw up my hands, in there. And his brother, our lawyer, started preparing the possibilities. And Dale was talking to his brother a hell of a lot right in there, and they came up with the proposal, which is somewhat the one they finally did. And I'm kind of analyzing it, and not very carefully, and all of a su—— And let's see. The closing date where we all signed the papers—the wives and everything—was on the sixteenth of December. And I remember that day, because I'm asking the lawyer, the one I had, finally, who was our tax attorney, and I literally was all set to cop out on the thing, that morning. If the lawyer had gotten there a half hour earlier, and I'd had a chance to talk to him, I was really going to ask him if we've gotten in this far, can we still get out? Because during the course of that the business started to f—— not f—— well, to fail. I *thought* it was starting to fail. And big contracts that we had were starting to go bad. The purchase price was based on a very euphoric situation. God, we thought we were going to make nothing but money, and the future was really bright. And during the time between October and December, the . . . the, um . . . bloom came off of the whole thing, and all of a sudden *I* was sitting there in the position of taking the *bad* end of a deal, and Dale was going to get a whole bunch of cash and real estate and securities. And I was really *sick* about the whole thing. But on the other hand, I was into it, and also I was kind of out of my head, and I just kind of let the whole thing ride. And it went—— And we all signed, and we all walked out into the sunshine, and . . . and . . . it was all done.

And I remember—— And also during the course of this, in order to have flexibility in operating the company, part of the agreement was I'd signed a thing which . . . I guaranteed everything that happened—so I had all my . . . *all* my assets on the line, on the success of this business.

And then for the next two months, the business just continued to fail, and fail. And it rained all through February. Which caused a tremendous loss. And a tremendous depression, on my part. And—— uh . . . um . . . and I really got pissed off. And thought we were—— and thought, whether actually or not, I'd kind of gotten screwed. But I can in no way think that Dale *understood* this. I don't think he could *plan* what's happening. But the fact remains is that several months earlier I thought I was rich, and a couple of months later I think I'm absolutely dead broke, and Dale's still rich. And I really feel *terrible* about the goddam thing, and I go to Dale and say, "Jesus, how about letting me out of the . . . the commitment on my house. And some of the stocks that I own." And he says, "No." Which was the . . . and that's the ultimate end of the partnership. That and the—— The partnership finished in December, but Dale says, "Tough shit. You signed a thing, and it's cold turkey from here on in." And, um . . . *goddamn,* that was a pretty tough one. And that was an . . . um . . . I guess that's the nadir of our relationship, as far as I was concerned. I was really, uh, insanely mad, about—— I mean I really kind of said I'd been dropped in the grease, as far as I was concerned, by not being able—— And there was not . . . by—— And I was out of control. I mean I couldn't *do* anything except say okay. And . . . and . . . then I went to a lawyer, and went through all of the hard stuff about saying I didn't—you know, I think I'm going broke. What do you do when you're going broke? How do you hide what you have? And he looked at the whole thing, and he says, "There's nothing you can do." Just, "You're stuck with whatever you got."

And somehow that was the bottom of the whole situation.

Casewriter: It was really make it go, or else.

Elmer: That's what he said. "If you fail, you fail. There's no way you can hide assets. There's nothing in the world you can do. And if you fail, just get ready to fail. You've lost your house, and your whole goddam thing. And so whatever course you take is up to you, but of course the most obvious one is to take the goddam business and . . . and use what you've got, and try to make it go."

For some reason, from then on, more and more, *better* things started happening. And the—— the—— uh . . . the rain stopped! Contracts started coming in. The biggest contract changed from a cost-plus to a fixed fee. It's produced a pretty good profit. It produced enough profit so that at the end of the year the business, rather than lose it, we drew a statement in February which showed the business as losing $400,000. And in the end, on June 30th, the business showed a net profit of $100,000. That was between February and June 30th, it——

Casewriter: It turned right around——

Elmer: It turned right around. As a consequence, my attitude toward Dale is swell. Dale now starts talking about maybe buying part of the business, or buying the business on behalf of his new employer. And I—— I don't—— I treat him kindly, but in a way I say, "In *no way* would I . . . would I really basically have any damn thing to do with you whatsoever."

Casewriter: You say that—or you imply that your deep feelings are still . . . that you don't *want* anything to do with him.

Elmer: Unh-unh.

Casewriter: Something about that house thing? Is that where that . . . you said, boy, that's where it ended?

Elmer: Well, I assumed—— It sort of starts where I say, way back earlier, when I kind of think I could walk back and forth into his house. Talk about what's my relationship with Jennifer. Or some darn thing. Do *I* feel that I have access to . . . to his wife, or something like that? *No way*—nothing like that. But I do think that what he own—— Something. I can walk into the beach house, if I want to—— And that's kind of the *high* point of the relationship, whether we really have a total commune going. And we get down to the point where, in a very friendly way, we separate the partnership. It's okay. I don't really mind. I'll get half. And I'll get the operating half and you get the other half. But, we're still—— you're st—— I *know* that you still aspire for my best interest. Which he always has, in a—— You know, when we separate the partnership, I say, well Dale, now *I* want to join the Founders Club, so go—— because we can't use your membership. God, he goes out of his way, and does a whole bunch of fancy stuff, and gets me in the Founders Club.

And he continues to do that—*that level* of stuff. But he kind of—— um—— but, um . . . um . . . And then I got used to assuming that we were in partners, and that if I were . . . if I were to start to go broke—which is basically what I said: I'm going to go broke, and you're going to have an ex-broke partner on your han—— conscience, or some damn thing like that. And he says, "No, I'm not." It just—— The mech—— He let—— relied completely on the mechanics. "We have separated the partnership, and it's all done." And I'm still saying, "Yuh, but we're still kind of partners. And we're still working out the thing. . . ."

Casewriter: And he said, "No, we're not."

Elmer: And he said, "No, we're not. It's all done." And that was a terr—— That was a shock, to me. In that I assumed—you know, I'm thinking, Jesus, if I went broke, and had no money, Dale would come over and give me part of what he has.

Casewriter: Um-hm.

Elmer: And all of a sudden it dawned on me, he wou—— I mean it didn't dawn on me, he said he wouldn't. And . . . um . . . I think I have a natural propensity for thinking somebody will *do* something for me. For . . . Why? . . . and I don't know why. . . .

Casewriter: Well, at that point he made it clear that the partnership was ended . . . when you talked about the house. But what you seemed to hear was that the *relationship* was ended. You know, is it—— You had those two things all of a piece.

Elmer: A *type* of a relationship *was* ended, as far as I'm concerned. That was the end of my thinking that we were interrelated. And now, although we still have the nostalgia, and there's a kind of a warmth that goes back and forth, I can't depend . . . I—— I don't know, let's see. . . . He clearly doesn't *owe* me anything. I think, up to that point, I think I thought he, in effect, *owed* me something, and I owed him something. But there was an absolute account in each other's bank account, somehow. And that there would be some sort of a—— uh, he *would* do something for me. Not only—— But almost because he *had* to. It's an emotional *have* to. You just . . . yuh, you *have* to. And he's saying he doesn't have to.

At this stage of the game, I still have that relationship with Virginia. I think Virginia *has* to do something for me, and I *have* to do something for her. Obviously, I have that relationship with Peggy—I *have* to do something for her. I *have* to do it. But now, I don't know what this thing is. I'm just inventing it right now. But there are certain people that I expect under almost any conditions—even when I'm a *bad guy*—they still have to do something for me. I mean the word "have to" shows my understanding of the level of the relationship.

Casewriter: Yuh. . . . And now it's, what—nine months after, ten months after the end of the partnership. Is that right?

Elmer: Right.

Casewriter: Yuh.

Elmer: It's December '68 to November '69.

Casewriter: And how—— Do you see Dale at all now? Under these new conditions?

Elmer: Yuh, I see him monthly, probably. And he still wants my approval. He wants to tell me about his business. He subtly, but not openly, draws me out for my opinion on what he's . . . not only on what he's doing, but how he's . . . how he's *being*—— although he doesn't want to hear it too clearly, and he won't allow me to get too close to the thing, and I can also see that he is . . . that when it's right in there, he doesn't *want* to become too dependent on my opinion, but he still wants it.

Dale Chapman

The following interview with Dale Chapman took place in the afternoon of a day in late November 1969. Chapman was at home, coming down with a cold, but feeling well enough to talk. Mrs. Chapman made coffee, and the casewriter and Mr. Chapman sat in the living room, while Mrs. Chapman remained in the kitchen talking with a friend who had come by.

The casewriter had met Chapman once, several years before the interview, at a lunch with Neely and the head of the Politics and Youth Foundation. Since that lunch, the two had not had any contact, and the casewriter met Mrs. Chapman for the first time just before interviewing her husband.

Casewriter: I don't know where you grew up, and I don't know——

Dale: Well, I grew up right here in San Diego. All my life. Went to public schools. Went through the Depression. Didn't have any money. It was tough. And then I . . . graduated from high school, young. And was able to get a year and a half at college, before I went into the army. And I spent three and a half years in the army. Got out of the army. And finished college.

Casewriter: How old were you when you finished college?

Dale: Well, I finished college in '47. I was 21.

Casewriter: 21?

Dale: Mm-hm.

Casewriter: After—— And you'd had how much time in the army?

Dale: Three and a half years in the army. I finished high school young.

Casewriter: Boy! . . .

Dale: And I had planned really to go on through college, to Harvard Business School.

Casewriter: Oh, really?

Dale: I had an application in there and was accepted. And I guess the experience of military life, and growing up more rapidly in that environment than you do otherwise, I just sat down and created an earning curve. I started from the day I graduated from college, and projected my earnings against starting two years later at a higher rate, and the damned curves crossed so far out—46, 47 years—that I said, I'll take my chances without it.

Casewriter: Mm.

Dale: And then I went to work for an engineering firm. Traveled all over the country, and——

Casewriter: Where did you go to college, then?

Dale: Cal Tech.

Casewriter: Cal Tech?

Dale: Mm. Took engineering.

Casewriter: And what was the engineering firm, then?

Dale: Oh, it was called Morgan Corporation. They manufactured sophisticated process equipment. Process equipment for which you have to design a kind of a state-of-the-art. It was really quite interesting, because the design of the equipment was creative. Art work. Each application was different. There was never a duplication. It was collecting dust out of smokestacks, primarily.

Casewriter: Hm.

Dale: But there really aren't any two identical situations anywhere in the world. . . . And that was fun, and I traveled with them. And then I got married. Since then, I lived in Quebec for a year or so. The first year of our marriage. And then I came back. And there really wasn't an opportunity for me in this company. After four years. Because the action was in the East—the big plants, and everything. So I was offered a job with U.S. Steel, and I went to work for them. And I worked with them for four years. And I had a degree of success—no, truly, I really did have some pretty *good* degree of success. I sold a damn big job—the biggest job they'd ever sold—the price to be determined on a later basis, cost-plus basis—and I thought I was the greatest salesman in the world! So I went and asked for a raise. And the boss was in Pittsburgh. And he came out and said, "Sure you can have the raise." I was quite surprised. "But," he says, "you've got to go to Pittsburgh." And I said, "For how long?" And he said—[Laughs] you know, here again—"That's where the action is."

So I was in that company forced to fish or cut bait, so I gave notice right then. And I didn't have the vaguest idea of what I was going to do. Really, that's a very awkward position.

Casewriter: How old were you then? Do you remember?

Dale: Well, I'd be eight years over——29, I guess.

Casewriter: 29. . . . You were married then——

Dale: Yes, married, and I had——

Casewriter: ——for five years——

Dale: ——at least two kids. No . . . no separate account. I had made enough money to—— We owned this hou—— We lived in this house, here. Which we bought very cheaply, a long time ago, 1951 I think. We owned the house, and I owned a car. And every dime that I made went to meet the overhead. We were expanding our family all the time, so I left U.S. Steel with a great deal of confidence in myself that no matter what I did, I could do *something,* and protect the family. So—that's where I stood. No, I had no specific ability to do anything. I didn't know anything, you know, specific. I didn't have a trade. I was an electrical engineer, but that . . . you know, that doesn't mean anything.

Casewriter: Mm-hm.

Dale: So I just thrust myself out in the world.

Casewriter: That must have been a scary time——

Dale: Oh, not really.

Casewriter: No?

Dale: I had a lot of confidence in myself.

Casewriter: Boy, you must . . . yuh, I guess . . . just to, you know, walk out on—what? A promotion, is what it is. And, you know——

Dale: Well——

Casewriter: ——to say, "No."

Dale: But I have since learned that as you get older, I guess you get—— I found out that I wasn't quite as good as I thought I was. Because of my recent experience with—— Things have been pretty tough. Prior to that time, of leaving U.S. Steel, and launching myself out into space, I met Elmer and Peggy. We met them socially at a cocktail party. I don't think we'd ever—— My father knew his father. My father went to Stanford and his father went to Stanford. My mother knew his mother, at the Women's League. They were just occasional acquaintances—old-time kind of San Diego mid—— middle-class people and everything, you know, like we were. But I went to a party, somewhere, and Jennifer was going to the Junior League thing, and we—maybe a year before this U.S. Steel thing—we met the Neelys, socially. And every now and then in life something really *wonderful* happens. You meet somebody. *You make a friend.* And . . . you don't really have any . . . [Laugh] And he was a real friend. We just related beautifully to each other. We—— Can't remember now, because it's been so long ago, but we . . . we'd visit, we'd have dinner with them—fascinating conversations. And at parties—large parties—we'd always gravitate to each other. And occasionally I think we spent a couple of weekends together, at the beach or somewhere. They were just very—— We weren't long-time friends—friends for maybe a year or so—but we were really *close* friends. And it happened quickly. It's a very rare thing.

Casewriter: Yuh.

Dale: So I don't know what . . . I don't what caused our going together. I remember vividly the moment that it happened, but Elmer, prior to my leaving the steel company, had gone . . . had gone out into business on his own. Became an electrical contractor. And he worked his tail off. God, he worked hard. Crawling under houses, and making—— doing $200 jobs, and just struggling. Working out of his home, and his backyard and everything. And I guess in this period of time—and I'm speaking for him—but I guess he recognized that he just couldn't make it. Alone. He was undercapitalized. He didn't have any contacts. It was a tough, tight business. Highly controlled at the top by the major contractors. Really tough.

And so he probably thought about—he's a very good thinker—he probably thought about a way to break out of this thing into the big time. So—— And I'm an electrical engineer, and I've been in contracting, basically—had been. Knew a lot of the general contractors, and everything. And so it seemed to him, I guess, a natural thing. It never occurred to me. So one day, one evening, the Neelys asked us to their summer house. It's since slid down into the sea. And we were driving in the car—Jennifer and I were in the back seat of the station wagon, and Elmer and Peggy were in the front seat of the station wagon. And Elmer said—about halfway there, apropos of nothing—"How about coming into business with me? As partners?" And without even taking a breath, I said, "Great!" It was just like that! I mean, normally, a decision of that magnitude, you'd think about it. I'd never thought about it ahead of that time.

Whether he had or not, I don't know. We never really talked about that. But I said, "Great!" And then we kind of talked around about, a little bit, went down to the beach, sat around, and—— I was much more dominant than he, so I started saying, "Well, I'll put up some cash, and you put up——" . . . started telling him what to do. He was in business, bringing me in, but I was trying to tell him—— I know this now, but I didn't know it then. Started telling *him* what I would do. Just because that was my way. I wasn't very sensitive. And he's extremely sensitive. . . . I'm much *more* sensitive now than I was then, but——

So I started telling him, "Well, I'll put up $7,500 cash, and you put up the inventory, and you keep those jobs that are in progress as your own, and we'll go into business together. And we'll have two businesses until you finish out your jobs, and when they're finished, we'll have one business. And I'll keep the books, and all that kind of stuff."

So at the end of that weekend, I went back to my office, where I'd given notice—and I still had some work to do—and I started thinking about the deal, then, for the first time seriously. And I went and borrowed the money from my father—— Didn't have the money, had to borrow. And Dick and I sat down, probably two or three days later, and just created a . . . on a piece of paper, my $7,500 input, and his input, in material things mostly, which would equal the $7,500. And then we incorporated. We felt that was the right thing to do. And it was. And we were in business! [Laugh.]

Casewriter: When was that? That was in 19——

Dale: That was in May 1956.

Casewriter: '56. . . .

Dale: May 5th, or something like that. May 5th, 1956.

Casewriter: And you would have been how old then?

Dale: Well, I was . . . 20 . . . let's see . . . 30.

Casewriter: 30 or so.

Dale: 30 years old. Born in '26. I was 30 years old. And I launched into the business with fantastic enthusiasm. Knew nothing about anything. And so did Dick. And I remember the very first thing I did was—Dick gave me a set of plans. Dick's a good boss. He gives you something and expects you to go and do it, and come back with it done, or with a *lot* of questions instead of just a whole bunch of nitpicking questions while you're trying to do it. He gave me a set of plans, and said, "Go make an estimate on this." So I came over here, and sat at the dining room table, and made an estimate for this job, and we bid it. Our technique of bidding in a construction job was as a subcontractor. And we got the job. From a very good friend of mine. He gave us the job. We were . . . had no money. It was really a big deal for him to do it. Within two weeks we got another one. For a hundred thousand dollars.

So here we're sittin' in our little stinking $125-per-month-rent office, with *two* good jobs. Within a week! And . . . Dick had his hands full, running and finishing the jobs that he had contracted prior to our going together, and he was pretty much full-time engaged on getting that stuff done. It was a big job—a couple of big jobs had to get finished. Which meant a lot to him, from an income point of view, because when we went in business together—and as I was dictating to Dick how it was going to be—I said, "Let's not take any salary out of this thing for six months. We'll accrue salary, from a tax point of view, so that if we have any money, we can't pay it, legally. But——"

So Dick was dependent upon these

jobs he had to make out. I had just told Jennifer, and said, "We're just going to have to tighten up our belts and see if we can get along." . . . I think you're more interested in interpersonal relationships.

Casewriter: Well, that's . . . that's just on matters of interest to you. And this is the setting in which, you know, the—

Dale: Yes. . . .

Casewriter: How did you, at the beginning—— You know, you must have had some ideas, as you say, about how you would set things up—how did you determine between the two of you who would do what? I mean here were two guys who . . . you know, how did you decide what your special competences were, that you would lean on——

Dale: We didn't. At the beginning, Dick was most fully occupied in doing his jobs. And I didn't have anything to do. So I took on all the bookkeeping for our comp—— for our partnership, and company. And did all the work associated with the two jobs that we had. So that what I did is, he ran his end of the business for three months, and I ran everything else—our joint business. Leaning on him heavily for advice, and what-do-I-do-next sort of thing. And I kept the books. And I bought the materials. And I hired the labor. And I told them what to do next. Under Dick's guidance, of course. But I ended up doing everything. Dick at the same time was doing everything.

And then after three months—God, we were young!—after three months, Dick kind of finished out his private business. We came in together. Why, we'd estimate jointly. And we would buy—— And we'd do everything as a tea—— just together. Just like one person. But we'd do it all together. And it seemed to work pretty good, because we were full of enthusiasm, and loved each other, and we had no problems. And economically, we didn't have any money, so there was nothing to be jealous about. And we were just two guys on a great big exciting adventure, and a big business possibility, and everything.

That first year we got along famously. And every job we bid was an adventure. An exciting adventure! And we shared it. We'd work until ten o'clock at night. Bring our estimate right up to the final price that we were going to bid. A lot of money for us! A big risk! And after that we'd run across the street and have a beer, and then come home at eleven o'clock at night. Or we'd work Saturday, and Sunday, and do all of this same stuff. We did it together as a team.

Well, that worked pretty good for about the first year. And then we got a job, which really was a change—the major change that took place. . . . This was the first major change that took place in our business, in the way we did things with each other. It was a big job. It was a tough job. It was a big wind tunnel, and buildings associated with it, and all the equipment, and wiring, and so forth. And we didn't have any really qualified field people. And at that particular stage of the game, Dick was taking some jobs as a project manager, and I was taking some jobs as a project manager. And I ran this job. This was a big job, as I said. That job could make or break us. And the industry—the electrical construction industry in this area—recognized that we were beginning to come along, and they began to see that we were a threat. So they took that job and tried to put us out of business—through their relationships with the unions, suppliers, and all the rest of 'em.

And so I spent from six in the morning till six at night, every day, on this darn job. And I didn't use myself effectively. The job . . . I was able to keep the job going, and we managed to survive, and we made some money—not much—on the job. But we survived that job. But as a result of my efforts on that job, it became apparent to Dick—but not to me, then—but it became apparent to Dick that my long suit wasn't in managing these jobs, that I was better in sales, getting orders, buying material. . . . But when it came to action, bossing the men on the job, I wasn't very good at that. And Dick also at that period of time—which was about 1959, I guess, or '60—wasn't about to communicate too well with me.

Probably because I couldn't communicate with him. We were very good friends, and we did everything together. But he couldn't sit down and say, "Lookit, Dale, you have no business going down and running those men. You take over estimating and bidding all the jobs"—which I was doing—"and I'll take over *running* all the jobs." Which would have been the proper thing for us to do at the time. He couldn't say that. He couldn't say it, probably, because I wouldn't accept it, or he was afraid that he would injure me, or—— He was too sensitive about my feelings. And he would sit back in a funk and do nothing. And right at that stage—and I remember it very well—we would share—— sit in the same room, and I'd have a desk, and he'd have a desk, in the same room, and everything that was said, on the phone or anything else, we knew about. There's pros and cons to *that* idea.

But I would get a phone call, and the job would panic, and I'd run out and get in my car and rush down there. And we really didn't have anybody in the organization to do it except Dick and me, and Dick would sit there and say to himself, "That isn't the right way to do that thing." But he wouldn't say it to me. So he'd sit in a funk. Because I was either—well, probably both—I was unwilling to accept criticism from him, and he was unwilling to give it to me. Because I was very . . . I would react very violently to criticism. And he knew it. And I thought I was doing a great job, making money, and all that kind of stuff. And then he'd criticize me—and I'd get sore.

So as a result of that particular experience, I think within a year we decided to reorganize ourselves. And we decided that we would take me out of the field operations—which really wasn't my best suit—and put me into pure selling, estimating the jobs, and bidding them, and going and getting them, and buying the materials, and managing the jobs from a contractual point of view. And Dick would do the operations in the field—supervise all field operations.

I'm trying to look back on it and see if there's any interpersonal relationships, about at this stage of the game—

Casewriter: How did that decision get made? You mention that you had this big job, and that was where it became clear that you ought to not—— you ought to break down by function, how you were organized on that, and you say yet he couldn't raise it, and you didn't see it. How did that come about that you guys——

Dale: There are certain things in this whole fifteen-year business that stand out with enormous clarity. I can see, magnificently, certain things. Other things, I just can't remember. And all of a sudden—not all of a sudden, but as a result of that job, that turning point, it became obvious that if we were going to grow—and we had to grow—that if we were going to grow, we could no longer be project managers. We'd have to hire project managers. We could no longer estimate all the jobs ourselves—we had to hire an estimator. We could no longer buy all the material ourselves—we had to buy a material expediter, a purchasing guy. It was just obvious, that we can't do everything ourselves. So we hired an estimator, at great expense. So we hired a superintendent, at great expense. And we hired some people. Then the question, I guess, came up, for whom are they going to work? Who is going to be responsible? And I think that probably over a period of six months, we rearranged ourselves, where Dick took on field activities, and I took on selling activities.

The—— There was no emotion, no problems. Everything worked out beautifully, in this transition, that I can remember. It worked out just beautifully. And it was clear in my mind what I had to do, and very clear in his mind what he had to do.

So. We continued to be successful. We continued to get good jobs. We continued to make money. With an occasional setdown—setback. We borrowed money on a job here or there, but we were fortunate to have such good jobs that we could absorb the losses. And by and large, we just went right along, doing pretty well, and at the same time we made more and more money. We made more salary. We made more expenses. We joined clubs. And we bought buildings, and bought property, and built buildings. We just started making more money. And our relationships were still pretty darn good.

There were a couple of little incidents, which, as I say, stand out clearly, and which illustrate the fact that underneath all this thing there was still a little bit of explosive potential, a little bit. I remember, Dick had been in the traffic signal business, selling equipment, before he became an electrical contractor. And he knew the traffic signal business quite well. Dick also had a very good friend in Los Angeles who was a paving contractor. And the paving contractor in Los Angeles got the job which required the installation of some traffic signals. And he phoned Dick up at the office, and said, "I want you to do the job." I didn't know anything about this. It was a fantastic market. Fantastic opportunity. But I was so damn busy doing what I was doing, I didn't even think about it. I didn't see far enough ahead. But he saw it—saw how great it was. But he said nothing to me. This is just an anecdote. So we were driving to a party, at Pasadena . . . there was a lot of this going on at this period of time, we went everywhere together, women and . . . couples. We were always together. Too much so. But we were driving to Pasadena, and about halfway out the Pasadena freeway, I remember clearly Dick saying, "We've got an opportunity with this Los Angeles paving contractor, to take this job. Traffic signal job." And I don't remember what I said. What I said, I know, was something . . . "Oh! Well, that's interesting." Or something like that, rather than, "Oh God, there's the greatest opportunity in the world!" Though he had one up on me. He'd been thinking about it, for a week. I hadn't heard a thing about it. And immediately, when I said, "Oh," or "Gee," or "That's interesting," he said, "If you don't want to do it, I'll do it on my own." And boy, that was just like hitting me—you know—in the face! With a glove! So I just shut up.

But that happened, maybe, after three years of our partnership. But we'd been . . . everything had been going fine. Beautiful. And for all of a sudden to have him hit me like that—

Casewriter: Yeh. . . .

Dale: Uh. . . . And I remember Jennifer talking about it later. And she said, "What in the world is wrong with him? Saying a thing like that." I said, "*I* don't know."

So underlying all of this there was . . . there were a few little explosive things, a little bit of jealousy. I think our relationships for the first ten years were that I tried my damnedest to do more than he did. And he tried *his* best to do more than I did. If something had to be done, we'd run, and try to do it first. And this whole attitude prevailed throughout the first ten or fifteen . . . the first ten or eleven years of our business. And we really did have a wonderful working relationship. And a feeling between the two of us, of trying to help the other, trying to feel that as a partner he was pulling his oar stronger than you were—that kind of a thing. Except underneath it, there were a few little explosive things. And I wasn't able to cope with them. I wasn't able to cope with criticism. I wasn't able to cope with these neurotic outbursts. That took place occasionally. But I couldn't handle them.

Casewriter: You mentioned one of those. Can you think of others?

Dale: Oh, yeh, lots of them. Oodles of them.

Casewriter: Because they're interesting to me. The, uh——

Dale: This, of course, is a personality thing. I mean, I've—— I'm half nuts myself, but I think I have more control of my—— self. Which is not necessarily good or bad. I'm not saying it's either one. I think I control myself better than he, and then when I get madder than heck, which I can do, I hold it in. Where he doesn't—he lashes out. He became—— There were—— These were not very serious, the first ten years. But I would spend six or eight months very, very carefully cultivating a customer. . . . God, I worked hard. And then we'd get a contract, a job. And then we'd go out to the job and have a communication with this customer, to be sure that the job was going well, and he would read out his problems, and I'd tell him ours, and so forth. And every now and then jobs get pretty hairy. When the owner wants the building, and we apparently don't have enough men or something, you know, the contractor gets sore, and he starts treating us like we're . . . riffraff. Which they do. And Dick came out to one of these meetings at which the president of this company, the one we were doing business with, was there, and Dick just rode him—tore right into this guy! Irrationally! And verbally beat him up. Would hit him, I think. And the president of this company looked at me, and grabbed me, and said, "I don't want to talk to that guy again." Sort of things. This was a neurotic explosion, which took place and was very costly to the business. I had to go out, patch up things, and he wouldn't give us the next job that we were low on, and all. He just said, "I don't want you guys running it."

There were others of these blowups. We had another job to do, a very fine contract. . . . I was telling you about a couple of these jobs. . . . I'm sure Dick feels the same way about me, too—you know. I'm just telling you the way I see it.

Casewriter: Sure.

Dale: But, uh. . . . I'm not apologizing for it. I'm just saying these things because they were very large in my life. But—we had this job, with Mark Jones Construction Company, probably the finest contractor out here. And I've known him since I was a baby. And it was hard getting a job with them. You had to be proven. You had to be the Tiffany, to get a job with them. But I finally got a job. Well—it is a simple building, and it was three stories, and it had phone plugs and everything, all around the place, and all of a sudden Jones Company said they wanted another telephone outlet, on the third floor, at the end of the hall, for the kids—it's a dormitory—for the kids to talk on the telephone. I wasn't there. I was . . . they would call me and say, "I want another plug." And I would say, "Who's going to pay for it?" and they'd say, "Put it in. And if we can't do it we'll put it on the next change order. Don't worry about it." And we'd have done it. But they got Dick. And Dick said, "Send us an order." And Jones Company were used to doing business with *other kinds* of people, and they said, uh, "I'm not going to send you an order. I haven't got an order to give you. The owners want it. We'll make it up to you. Put it in, don't worry about it." And Dick said, "Screw you." . . . And we didn't get another job out of Jones Company for five years.

These are little anecdotes. They happened maybe every six months, something like that would come along. And I guess it was those kind of explosive things, and Dick's criticism of me when I felt that I was doing such a magnificent job, and all that kind of stuff. . . .

Casewriter: And during that time, then it would make you feel damned uneasy. I mean you wouldn't know when what was going to happen.

Dale: I didn't know how I stood.

Casewriter: Did these things get more frequent, Dale, as you remember back? I mean, at first——

Dale: First ten years, no. First ten years . . . no.

Casewriter: No. . . .

Dale: No problem. There were these underlying neurotic outbursts. Occasionally. But he was happily married. Socially, we were moving up into . . . socially, but I—— *You know* what I mean by that——

Casewriter: Mm.

Dale: I think he was having more time for lunch, he would go out to dinners, and nicer restaurants, and made a lot more money. And everything was okay. Except Dick would have ideas about doing something. He's really got *rights* to be a lot sore at me, too. But . . . He wanted to go into South America, to do business. And going into South America to do business—my side of the thing was, it would require the investment of $25,000. It would require the investment of at least half of his time. We would go down there and make things—which were totally unrelated with our business. And I'd gone into partnership with him as an electrical contractor, with the avowed purpose of making money. But not to see where we could go in oddball areas. If we had $25,000, and he had half his time, we could easily have opened an office in San Francisco. And been tremendously successful. But he got this idea about going to San Francisco . . . going to . . . going to South America. And he researched it. And he and Peggy went down three or four times. They met a lot of people, and it was fun to talk about things, and Dick liked to be able to talk about kind of different things. And all that stuff. And uh . . . I never, ever, accepted that South America deal.

Casewriter: That just didn't feel right in terms of the options you had otherwise?

Dale: Oh, yuh! It was just totally unrelated. Totally unrelated. And Dick resented my failure to give him full blessing and everything else. Resented it deeply. And he would spend money, and do things, and use talent, and bring Mexicans up here and put 'em on the payroll, and then we would have to pay for them. They were pure deadweight. And I wanted to see that money . . . doing something . . . something else done with the money. But we didn't—— he—— I was scared of him. Right about this time, perhaps, after six or seven years, I guess I became scared of him, frightened of him. And I wouldn't—— I told him. I said, "Dick, I'm not interested in the

South American deal." He says, "Well, we're going to do it anyway." So I tolerated it. Just tolerated it.

And he wanted to—— Then another thing came along. And I mean, Dick has some wonderful ideas, magnificent ideas, and a lot of 'em *were* good, and a lot of 'em were *bad,* but we got into a smoke detector, and I couldn't see how a smoke detector in any way, shape, or form fit into our business. But he wanted to make the smoke detector. So we made the smoke detector. And I think when we were off—we would have lost about $40,000 on the smoke detector. But it had no reason to do it, at the beginning.

So I guess after about . . . I keep using numbers of ten years, or eight years, or something—but after about eight years, my failure to bless his, what I called, way-out ideas, my failure to understand his . . . his feelings better, which I really should have done—and I didn't know how—we began to . . . there began to be created a little tension. Also, a lot of this time there was . . . we had quite a bit more money—a lot of money. We started to have money in the kitty.

Casewriter: Mm.

Dale: And he took it onto himself to invest all the money. He handled all our money, in all our firms. And I didn't know what the hell he was doing with it, half the time. But I trusted . . . and I do trust him. Absolutely. Implicitly. With my last dime. I did then, and I do now. But I just felt that it would be better to talk about, "What are we going to do with these . . . this fifty thousand dollars?" Well, we bought a piece of land, and we put some buildings on it. But—that was his idea. Not mine.

Well, we opened an office in San Francisco. Which was a good idea. I liked that idea. Jennifer always gives me credit for it being my idea, not that it makes a damn bit of difference. But this fit—in my mind, structurally, this made sense. We were electrical contractors, damn good ones. San Francisco—there was a big vacuum there. We needed to go there. We took the best man in our organization and put him up there. . . . Just the whole thing made sense, and the San Francisco office eventually became a success. And that was a smart thing to do. We went into Orange County. Which was a sensible thing to do.

But as we started doing these things, I retained my authority over all the bidding aciivities, all the selling activities, all the contracting functions, and all the purchasing, regardless of whether it was San Diego or San Francisco or Orange County, or where it was. I was in charge of selling. Elmer was in charge of jobs.

And this worked out pretty good. My God, San Francisco, we went up, we got some great jobs. Made a lot of money. And Dick did a great job of running them, and I got a . . . did a damn good job of getting 'em. Estimating them and getting them.

About ten years after we started, for some strange reason—and I was never able to fathom this—Dick started elbowing me out of San Francisco. He took it upon himself to go up there once a week. And his going up there once a week, naturally he was involved with the day-to-day operations, and so forth, and I gradually began to be excluded. When we bid a job, Dick would say, "Well, there's no sense in your bidding it, we'll bid it up here" sort of thing. Well, this kind of hurt my feelings. Because I had helped create the thing, and founded it, started it, and gotten the jobs that made the money, that he ran, then made the money to support it. It was a heck of a—— And then all of a sudden I started getting eased out. And I just couldn't understand why.

About the only rationale that I can come up with was, that there were interpersonal relationships between the office personnel and the office managers and me, and that Dick thought that I was not a very good executive at managing people, and therefore it would be wise if I just kept my nose out of there and stayed down here. As a result I began getting a terrible inferiority complex. But I continued to keep getting jobs. I say "I." *We* did. Good jobs. We were offered good jobs here, and I could get 'em up there, but he wouldn't let me in. He'd push me out. But he didn't push me out at Orange County. So I says, geez, there's something funny going on here. And then I'd say, well, when things come up, I'd always try to communicate openly, and I'd say, well, gosh, this is a problem in San Diego, and Dick's in San Francisco—I'd better phone up there. And he's nowhere around! And nobody knows where he is. And this is from ten in the morning till four in the afternoon! And I said, "This is absurd!"

And then his trips began to take two days. And I'm working hard down here, and getting used up, and in his absence I have to absorb his problems. It got down to something like three days a week. This was the last three years of our business—we were together a total of fifteen years. And I think these things . . . although there was this little underlying possibility of problems . . . I think at the ten-year period—from ten to fifteen—it began to boil up. To where I just knew that he was—he was up to no good in San Francisco! [Laugh.] But I didn't have any . . . this was just my feeling. He hadn't told me anything. Had told me nothing about it. Hadn't told me a thing about it.

So here our interpersonal relationships were really put to the test. I was working five days a week, hard. He was working two days a week, that I could identify—not hard. True, he was doing a great job, financially. Our financial affairs were—well, I shouldn't say a great job. He was doing the job. And we had been able to train some pretty good field superintendents, so the jobs in the field were going pretty good. And he was tending to 'em when he was here. But Jesus, I had to pick up—drop a lot of things I was doing, and go rush out and—— We lost a feeling that as partners he was doing more and I was doing less. All of a sudden, for the first time, I woke up and said, "My God, I'm beginning to think that I'm working harder than he." And that's an unholy relationship. It really is bad.

You'd probably ask did I ever talk to him about it. I don't think I really did. I'm not a very direct person in that. I probably alluded to it. I probably . . . suggested, "What do you *do* in San Francisco, Elmer?" And of course he became defensive, and, "Gee, Elmer I tried to call you three times yesterday, I couldn't get you. Very important." And he became defensive. I'm attacking what he's doing. And he thinks what he's doing is right. He thinks what he's doing is absolutely right. And, uh. . . . So he'd clam up with me. So we didn't really ever, ever, ever sit down and freely discuss, talk out, this new feeling that I had. And I know he had, too. And on top of that, I had a terrible inferiority complex. Right about then. Because he had kicked me out of all these things that I was doing pretty well in San Francisco. We weren't getting any jobs in San Francisco. The jobs we were getting, we were losing money. And uh. . . .

Well, that's the feeling I had.

Casewriter: There were really two things

there. One was, you . . . the only explanation you could come up with, originally, for his elbowing you out of San Francisco was that you must be doing a bad job.

Dale: Yuh. This was the rationale that I——

Casewriter: And so that made you wonder about yourself.

Dale: Yuh! I'm screwed up! I said, "What am I doing wrong?"

Casewriter: But, given your relationship, then, you weren't able to talk about that. And then when you tried to get him, and he wasn't in the office, and he'd be gone for two days, you'd wonder what the hell he was doing. So two things: one—— There're really three, aren't there? One, you began to feel—

Dale: Unwanted!

Casewriter: ——doubts about your own competence. Unwanted. And unloved. [Both laugh.] Two, you wondered what the hell he was doing.

Dale: Sure!

Casewriter: And then that funny business about each making sure you gave all you could.

Dale: Yeah.

Casewriter: You know. . . . So that there was no problem about . . . who was carrying the load. You began to feel like you were carrying a bigger share——

Dale: I began to feel that way. And Dick started . . . in addition to these days that he was taking off, he started taking these lessons, these psychiatric lessons, and he was gone—I never audited his time, but I would observe that when he *was* in San Diego, two or three days a week, at least two hours of each of those days was spent in psychiatric treatment. And then he would go, in the afternoon, to a think session once a week. And then he was taking a course in brain waves. And when I audited a whole week, it turned out that he was there about four days a week. So I began to say, what in the heck is this all about? It's ridiculous. . . . And yet we were still making money! Hand over fist. All kinds of money.

Casewriter: So it wasn't the money that—

Dale: Well, the money probably brought on a lot of it. Having the money, and a lot of money——

Casewriter: Made it possible——

Dale: Made it possible for Dick to do the things. I st—— stayed at the ship. . . . How effective I was, I don't know. But I—I checked in at eight in the morning, I left at five in the afternoon. And even if I did go play a half a day's golf or something, it was a big deal. And I'd announce that fact to everybody. They knew where the heck I was. And uh . . . so I began to get this feeling of, My God, what's this all about? I *needed* Dick. Badly. I *wanted* him. I wanted him from a person—I wanted his help. I wanted him to start pulling his oar harder. And a lot of things were going down the tubes, too.

Well, he was in charge of finances. This maybe is kind of a dirty trick, and I really shouldn't . . . Maybe it's important. Maybe it's relative. But it affected me strongly. He came along, and his job was to run the financial aspects, run the cash flows in the business. How much money are we going to make. And he came along and created a cash flow, about a year and a half before we broke up. And the cash flow indicated that we were going to make a million dollars that one year. And I was pretty much in touch with the business. And I said to Dick, "There's just no way. I know the jobs we have. I made the estimates on all——" I say "I." I was responsible. We had a—eight or ten people estimating. "I know the gross margins that were there. They're just—— If you add everything up, and make everything go perfectly," I said, "you can't make it. And he says, "There it is: a million dollars." [Sigh.]

So with a million dollars, he goes out and he creates . . . he *dominates* our personnel, and creates a profit-sharing and a pension program. I didn't want it. Our people didn't want it. We sat around in rooms, and our people said they would rather have the money on the barrelhead than invest in some long-term—— True, there were tax advantages, and all the rest of it. But they didn't want it. And Dick's a very strong person. And he went to each one individually. And he told 'em this and that, and the advantages, and all that. And he got 'em in a room, and he's the boss, and owner of the company, and he said, "Goddamn it, we're going to have it. Right?" "Right!" So he shoved it down their throats. It cost about $200,000.

Then we remodeled our offices. Huh! I'm—— You know that's not—not a big deal for me. Sitting around in a fancy office, with a big desk. But we spend twenty-five or thirty thousand dollars on the offices. And what else did we do? God! [Laugh.] We started throwing money around like it was crazy. Irreversible commitments! And I can't rightly say, but I think we probably blew about $400,000 in a month. In order to take it out of earnings as tax deductible expenses of that year. And when the year was done, and the financial reports showed it, we'd make only $600,000. And the $400,000 would be all expense. So we did it.

Well, about two months after . . . about a month and a half after the year had closed, and these irreversible reactions had taken place, we discovered that Dick had made an error, in his forecast of—— Would you believe $600,000? And we had blown $400,000. So we end up with zero. Plus we'd used the money, and shoved it down their throats on pensions and profits and all these kind of . . . all these kind of things.

So I was pretty upset. The way I figured it out was, had Dick toed the mark, and had he been at the store, and had he done his job, and had he used some check and balance, and had he communicated with me, or just in general had his good senses about him, this would never have happened. And I was really . . . sore. I mean you can't go—— And it was an error. Outright error. And I went and told Dick. I said, "I'm sorry. I'm sorry as heck this happened. It's too bad. How in the hell did it happen! I told you we weren't going to make a million bucks, but you're doin' that, and I should have checked it. We didn't, anyway."

But to me, this was an obvious byproduct of his psychiatry, and his—— And by then I think I knew about his love life—his love affair, *or affairs.* His constant absences. And tremendous emotional problems. This was getting close to the thing that I . . . about that period of time said, "My God, I just can't go on. The guy's kooky." He—well, I don't think he is any more. I think he's come out of it.

So that's about . . . up to about a year, or half a year, or something, before we . . . pulled the plug.

Now. At the same time all this was going on down at the office, Jennifer and Elmer were having kind of a halfway romance going, halfway intellectual romance, or something. And I guess I'm naturally jealous, which is a very damaging thing. But I was extremely jealous. But, as I say, we'd go to parties with them *constantly.* We'd go to dinner with them *constantly.* And we would go to . . . We were with them all the time. And we'd drink a lot. And after drinking a lot, there'd be a lot of *real deep talk.* Sure your mind's all befuddled, and it's all screwed up, but it's big, deep talk. Why, one time, I remember, I think we ended up looking at the test pattern on a TV, you know—real exciting thing to do.

But I became quite concerned about the interrelationship between Peggy . . . Oh, I never got involved with Peggy. [Laugh.] I kept telling myself. Maybe I did. I don't know. Jennifer probably felt I did. But in any event, I'd see *this* thing going on. Maybe four or five years before the events that I'm talking about, where we lost all the money—or where we *should've* made a million dol—— a lot of money, we didn't, because of these bad investment ideas. . . . I saw what was happening, that we were becoming so dependent on 'em. We'd say Tuesday night, and they'd come over here for dinner, Thursday night we'd go over there for dinner. Pretty soon you run out of things to talk about. And you get too close. And I don't like to get too close to people. Not that I don't like their feelings, but there's a lot of temptations happening. And I saw it, and I told Jennifer, I said, "Cut it out. We will not go out with the Neelys. Period. Chop it off. Poom." Well, you just don't go, you know, poom, like that. And she didn't want to. And I kept telling her, I said, "You're destroying our relationships. I'm *affected* by these parties, and these things that happen, in the office." And about one out of every two times, Elmer and Peggy would have a big fight. An *enormous* fight! And they'd get up and go home. And so we were sitting there with our bare face hanging out. So I'd go to the office, and I've got to either acknowledge the fight, or forget it—it's none of my business. And this is going on for five years. So you see I had these two thi—— Outside of the business, terrible relationships. Inside the business, screwy things happening.

And all of these things are beginning about a year before I . . . we pulled the plug—beginning to really injure me, and destroy me. Anxieties. Tremendous anxieties, which affect my . . . which made me very ineffective. My lack of confidence. Every now and then I'd turn on, and get kind of an excitement going on something, but by and large I'd just lost interest. The last year of our business I went—I audited it—I went to twelve weeks off. The last 52 weeks that we were in business together. Which I'd never done before. But I just said the hell with it. Just completely said the hell with it.

Also, Elmer told me that he wanted to get a divorce. It screwed Jennifer up something terrible. She was crying for a full month. Peggy Neely was over here every single day, completely unloading herself on Jennifer. Jennifer would unload herself on me. And so I would have all of these personal—interpersonal—things churn on me, as well as the di—— the problems of the business.

So this is about what happened. More or less. The thing that caused us to break up. It could have been any one of a hundred things. You can't blame it on them. But we . . . Elmer was much more liberal, and much more—exciting. He had much better ideas than I ever did. *Interesting! Fun! Creative!* Great idea guy. And he had very liberal ideas—way-out ideas. He thought marijuana was slick, and walking around the beach without any clothes on was fun—you know, and all that kind of stuff. And I'm very conservative and stuffy, and I don't think that is.

And he has a charming daughter—do you know her? Yes, she's the sweetest little thing that ever lived. And she was running around—I mean, school was about to get out, summer, and everything, and she had been running around with a couple of pretty bad characters. So I went to Elmer and I told him, I said, "Don't, whatever you do, let her get too thick with these guys, cause they're just bad news. They're terrible bad news." And I knew it. And everybody in town knew it. Well, he says, you're an old stuff-butt. . . . He didn't say it, but—he sort of nodded. And that was the end of it. Well Goddamn, she spent the whole summer with these bad characters. One of the boys is going to be tried next week for killing a girl. Maybe weekend after next. The other boy has been put up for marijuana, and mainlining, and all that stuff. And this is really a bad association. And we love that little girl. We love—we love the whole family. And we've supported the whole family. I mean, I put Dick up for the Founders Club, and I'm *proud* of it. And I'd put him up anywhere. With pride. But we're worried about the daughter.

Well, I told Elmer that. That this is what's happening. And you're screwing up her reputation. And—"Aaah," you know, "I don't really think so. That's . . ." Well, by God, Jennifer was out somewhere, socially, around the pool, or some darn thing this summer, and she heard that everybody in town, all the squares in town—who gives a damn—but anyway, all the squares in town were talking about that little girl. And how she's a dope addict, and this and that. . . . Well, she wasn't. And she isn't. And the people that were saying that were trashy people—not important to us, really. The Neelys are important to us, but they weren't. But it was reflecting on the reputation of this little girl.

And so Jennifer . . . Peggy Neely didn't know anything about this. So Jennifer thought about it a day or so, talked to me about it—and I'm getting all churned up again on something else, you know, here we go again—so Jennifer went to Peggy and leveled with her. Told her what was going on. And Peggy was horrified. And started to cry. And oh, God, it was terrible. Wouldn't accept it! The facts of the matter were, that little girl *was* going with these people. These people are bad. That doesn't syllogistically mean that the girl's bad. We don't think she was. But everybody in town was saying it, and she's—she's got friends at school, and she's got to go out socially and everything, and you know, when you want to preserve your reputation, you can.

Anyway, it was terrible blow to Jennifer—emotional blow. Enormous emotional problem. And in effect, it affected me. So—I go to work. And Elmer's there that day, I guess. And we talk about it, a little bit. And I said, "Elmer," I said, "God, I told you at the beginning of the summer not to have her run with those guys. You *wouldn't* take my advice. And now you want to sit here and unload on me about how terrible everybody in San Diego is." So I said, "Sure they're terrible. But I don't want to talk to you about it any more." "Well," he says, "*I* want to talk about it." And I says, "Well, I *don't* want to talk about it." . . . You know. So what.

Casewriter: Mm.

Dale: And he said, "What do you want to do about it?" And I said, "Let's bite the bullet. You know, either you buy me or I'll buy you." Sort of thing. Just that simple.

Casewriter: That was the trigger, anyway.

Dale: That was the trigger. But it could have been anything else that triggered it. I had already—I know *he* had, and I already had—spent three or four months figuring out some way that I could break our partnership off without hurting his feelings. And I think he had done the same. . . . How could we break our partnership off without hurting our feelings.

And part of the whole thing was, too—I mean, I really had a conscious thought about it, seriously, but—if I pulled myself out of the business, there'd be a financial strain. But it would make Dick go back to work. And if he went back to work——

Casewriter: Things might——

Dale: ——he would give up this girl, and he would become a father, and a wife, and all the rest of it. I really did. I was making a hundred thousand dollars. Growing, had an equity interest in a million dollars down there, and—a lot of money and everything. And I went from that to *zilch.* Absolutely nothing. And that's a hell of a—huh!—a change. But it was that important to me. To get away from his—his hysterics, his Rasputin-like influence—that's the way I felt towards the end. And get away from the tremendous emotional stirring-up that goes on. My God, there was enough problems right here in this house without having to absorb all *their* problems too.

And that was a—— [Sigh]. We managed to make it through that thing in about a month. And that wasn't too bad. From the time we pulled the plug until the time we closed. And then Dick went into a real funk because he thought he was going to go busted, and I had a note, and security to buy his home, and all, and he thought I was going to attack his home, and all that kind of stuff. And he was really pretty screwed up.

But by God, after three months, about April, this year, all of a sudden he began—— I used to go down to see him once a week, and talk to him and everything, after about a week, after about April, all of a sudden he saw the light. Said, "My gosh! Things aren't quite as bad as I thought. I'm going to *make* some money. And I've got some good guys. And things are straightening themselves out." . . . And he ended up last year with a profit, and he's going to end up this year with a big one. So. It's worked out pretty well.

Casewriter: And then—what did you do after, you know, when you say you pulled the plug on it, and then it took a month to negotiate the deal, you know, to leave—you went back to work at some pla——

Dale: I did not.

Casewriter: You did not.

Dale: I went looking for a job! [Laugh.] And I had one hell of a time finding a job. Let me testify to one more point.

Casewriter: Yeh. What point?

Dale: That after this enormous, emotional, traumatic, divorcement from the whole man, and the consequent separation of Jennifer and me from Elmer and Peggy, as a couple, we went through a period of tremendous strain and—uh—almost as if it would be—never come back together again. But I'm happy to say that things *are* better now. That he and I have a very close relationship. I don't think it'll ever be as close as it was in the first ten years of our business. But it's . . . we now call each other freely. And Jennifer continues to see Peggy, and we have seen them socially three or four times in six months. So although we'll never get back to the tremendous closeness, we're at least back to the point of where we have salvaged our friendship. However, he still owes me money. And whenever one person owes somebody else money, you've got a hangup. I've got a hangup, and he's got a hangup, and as long as that goes on, for another five or ten years, why, things'll never be quite like they were. . . . That's the end of that.

Okay. What did I do with myself when I left—pulled the plug? Our closing was actually the 15th of December, and I stayed on until the first of January. When I say "closing," I mean I resigned as a director, resigned as an officer, went off the payroll——

Casewriter: Made all the——

Dale: Everything was finished, financially, between us. Everything was defined—how I'd get my money, and how he'd get his, and the whole works—property transfers. And I stayed on for a while. And then after the first of January, I tried to phase myself out—you got to make the break sometime. It was hard to do. You know, after you've spent fifteen years creating this really very profitable, exciting, wonderful business and everything, it was a little tough to all of a sudden say, "That's all there is to it, gentlemen."

So I set about looking for a job! At the age of 42. And I didn't have a single job offered for six months. And I tried. I went to every accounting placement firm; I went to every management consultant; I went to every executive placement, professional flesh-merchant kind of guy; I wrote letters, responded to ads in the *Wall Street Journal,* talked to everybody I could talk to, about my wanting a job. And I had some interviews. But nobody wanted me. . . . Then, I'll tell you, I really got feeling kind of low.

And then finally, I was blessed by having an offer from this guy Robert Doolan. I met with him a couple of times, and he offered me a job. And I accepted it, and I'm now working for him. And I'm enjoying it very much. And Doolan had surrounded himself with a whole lot of merchandisers—advertising guys, merchandising guys, promotional guys, and all that stuff—and he had really practically no one in the—in the so-called nitty-gritty business area, that knew how to hire people, and fire people, and make cash flows, and just run a sensible business. Had nobody, literally nobody. So. I hired on as . . . I got a salary of $30,000 a year, and a couple of clubs, and some stuff like that. Which isn't a tremendously large salary. But it's a . . . better'n being a teacher!

Casewriter: [Laughs.]

Dale: And—he's, um, he's got me various titles and things, now. But I'm really basically responsible for the operation of most of the businesses there. I'm a director of one company, and a vice-president of a couple of others. And what I do now is not . . . is very meaningful, and exciting, and fun, and there's an opportunity in the future, to make some dough.

Casewriter: And your responsibilities are very much not on the promotion side, but on the——

Dale: The other way. Management.

Casewriter: ——the hard-nosed part of it, what you called operations in——

Dale: Yeh. Inventory relationships to sales. And whether or not to buy certain machinery to save labor. And should we raise the price in cost estimating. And should we fire the people, and are the people in the right slot. And how much money are we going to make at the end of 1970—you know, just so-called forecasting. And—it's a regular, ordinary business, and there's a lot of guys around that can do it. Oodles of guys. But Doolan doesn't have any. With all of his—— I shouldn't say he doesn't have any, but he doesn't have many. With all of his organizations and everything, he doesn't have many, and he needs 'em.

So that's what I've been doing. But I'll tell you, I was in pretty much of a funk come about June. Nobody loved me. Nobody wanted me. And——

Casewriter: You know, it interests me—that. Because you did that once before. You know, you mentioned that at 28 or 29, when the steel company said go to Pittsburgh and you said "Nope." You didn't know where the hell the next thing was——

Dale: Well, I was 29 and I knew *everything* then!

Casewriter: [Laughs.] I see!

Dale: I think I said at that time that I found out later that I really didn't know quite as much as I thought I knew.

Casewriter: Right.

Dale: And I think I learned that. In the first six months of this year. I learned that I wasn't quite as valuable as I thought I was. In that people wouldn't come racing up to my door and hire me. I didn't have a single viable job offer, in six months. And boy, I worked at it. [Exhales.] So that brings me about up to here. [Pause.]

Casewriter: And let's see. As you project into the future, the . . . the . . . I gather the legal arrangements that were made are such that Elmer has to pay you money each year, interest for so many years. . . .

Dale: Yeah, when we settled . . . our thing . . . is a unique thing. Probably. I've talked to several of the large accounting firms, and a lot of lawyers, about how we did it, and it's extremely unique. That he and I, after deciding to separate, he went in *his* office, and listed the value of all the things we owned. Of which there were quite a few things. Different things. There were seven buildings, and property, and trucks, and companies—four companies—bonds, cash—inside of the company and outside of the company—all kinds of things. And he made a list. And at the same time, in my office, on a yellow sheet of paper, I made a list. And we ran our total. And we agreed, between us, that we would . . . we didn't know who was going to buy who, at that time. I could buy him, or he could buy me. So we agreed that we would arrive at a value for the . . . all the assets, the whole lock, stock, and barrel. And that whatever value we arrived at, we'd split it in two. And one would get one half, and one would get the other half. And when we ran our list out . . . and then he—— I don't know, we'd got together, and we turned our papers over—we weren't but a few thousand . . . we're talking about two million dollars, a little over two million dollars' worth of business assets—we were within a few thousand dollars apart. That in itself is unique.

And then we took the assets, and some of the assets could easily be transferred—to an individual. Such as property owned by the corporation. Such as buildings owned by, say, Dick and I individually, could be transferred over. Some of the assets couldn't be transferred over, like the electrical contracting corporation, which had a net worth of a million dollars. We couldn't very well take the million dollars and transfer it—I mean you just can't do it, taxwise. So we took all the assets that were easily separable, and put 'em over in one column, and then that totaled about a quarter, perhaps, of the whole, or half of a half. So whomever was going to get the separable assets would not get the corporation. But the corporation would have to agree to pay——

Casewriter: The remaining quarter——

Dale: ——the remaining quarter. So

that's what we did. We took the assets here, plus a note, and the sum of that represented a million bucks. And the company, then, and a few other things, represented the other million. And then we decided who was going to get . . . decided Dick was going to buy me out.

Casewriter: How'd you do that?

Dale: I don't know. . . . [Pause.] I don't know—I think that I just kind of thought about it philosophically. Dick had started the business. He was in business a year, or something like that, before I came along. So he'd conceived it. He'd had the baby. And his name was first. And—that was important. I thought about it seriously—and I really did—that he's older than I. And for him to get another job would be damn difficult. Much more difficult than me. I am much more flexible and pliable, and I can get along with people a lot better than he can. Not selected people, but I mean in general. Just in general. I'm a WASP, you know, more or less, and he's a . . . reactionary, more or less. He's looked at that way. And I also saw that in order for him to preserve his sanity—which he was about to lose—he had to do something strong, hard, fast. So it just seemed to make sense that he—— We really didn't know, right up until the—my gosh, until we signed the papers—who was going to do it.

I remember sitting in Dick's office and . . . with a couple of the lawyers and everything, and we were negotiating interest on a note, or something like . . . some inconsequential thing, and he said, "Five," and I said, "Six," and he said—uh. . . . By then we'd decided that he was going to buy me out. But we were right to the end, right there to the end. And he said, "Aw, the heck with it. You buy me out. And we'll make it six." I says, "Okay." And he knew I wasn't bluffing. I *would* have bought him out. But then he backed down. I mean he tries to run a bluff all the time. We all do, I guess. But he was trying to bluff me into a better deal at that stage of the game, and I says the hell with it. Right up until the closing, the final document signing, it could have gone either way. However, about a week before the closing, we had more or less discussed that he should buy me out. And for those three reasons that I mentioned.

Casewriter: You had a law firm help you do this?

Dale: Well, yeh. My brother is an attorney, my natural brother, a year younger than I am. And a darn good attorney. And he'd been our attorney. And when we decided to do this thing, I had kind of touched base with him on the tax impact. I wanted to be sure that it minimized the tax for everybody, downstream, and so I pulled him in, and then said, "Dick, we'll have—— Do whatever you want to do, but I'd like my brother to take care of writing up the papers, and all that stuff." And I said, "I want it clear to you that if there's any objections, you do what you want to do." Well, he had run into a young Jewish attorney. He'd met him some place, in one of these therapy groups or something, and was quite impressed with him. And he brought him in to help him, and to advise us on some of these profit-sharing pension things, which I wasn't turned on about.

Casewriter: Mm.

Dale: And I wasn't impressed by him at all. Well, as it developed, Dick said, "Well, I'll retain this guy to represent my interests. Your brother is retained by you. And the law fees, when we're all finished, your brother puts in his bill, and my lawyer puts in his, and we'll just divide it by two. You know, your brother can do all the work." So he did all the work. He drew up all . . . a massive set of papers, all the documents, and policies, and everything. And a buy/sell agreement, which set forth precisely every detail. A covenant not to compete. I agreed not to go into the electrical contracting business for ten years, in return for a salary. Not a salary, but a payment.

Casewriter: Yuh.

Dale: That's legal. A lot of things like that. Well, my brother drew those all up. And then he gave the pro forma copies to Dick, and Dick gave them to his lawyer. And his lawyer came back with a bunch of . . . of objections, which we immediately agreed to. There was no . . . it didn't take any time at all. We were very flexible. Both sides were flexible. And then we had the actual closing. And—I don't know why I mention this, but it was just almost like "I told you so," I think I feel that way—that this guy of Dick's completely overlooked some things that perhaps Dick could have negotiated, to improve his advantage. Like, I have a note from Dick, and the corporation both, and it's secured by him and the corporation, *and* his house. I don't want his house! If Dick went busted, I wouldn't *take* his house. *Never!* I've told him so. I'm going to free the whole thing up here, one of these days, if I get around to it. Although in my mind, it don't make any difference. I'm not going to do it. All he had to do was have his lawyer say, "Why don't you take the house out?" I'd have done it in a minute!

So we ended up, the lawyer charged him as much as my brother charged. My brother did all the work. And I had to pay half of his lawyer's fee too. And the guy gave Dick bad advice. And Dick curses, now, using him. But he used a lot of people like that! He'd go to a session and meet some guy that's exciting, and use him. Public relations guy. Got to a public relations—— We hired a public guy that was kind of that way. . . . I'm being very critical, here, of little things, and they're not important. They're not important at all.

That's . . . That's pretty much the whole . . . the whole story. I think. I—learned a lot. It's the most valuable relationship I ever had. I learned an *enormous* amount from Dick. My life is much richer because of it. I think I'm sensitized—nowhere near as much as I would like to—but much, much better with people. And I really *do* like to sit down and talk to people. And I hate to stand at a cocktail party and yell at people. I dislike to do those things. And that's . . . Dick taught me that. He taught me all . . . a whole lot of wonderful, rewarding, meaningful things. I don't know whether Dick's any richer from experience with me, but he does know a lot more now than he did before about certain parts of the business. I think we both enriched each other.

My marriage is much happier now.

Casewriter: It is. . . .

Dale: Oh boy, is it. *Much* happier. I've relieved myself of all these anxieties—

Casewriter: Yuh——

Dale: ——that were destroying me. Completely destroying me. My effectiveness. And my anxieties produced all these guilt complexes, and they produced a feeling of incompetence. They produced all sorts of neurotic type things that . . . I'm still neurotic, but maybe I mean like nowhere near as much. Nowhere near as much. I would fly off the handle. I say crazy things. I would . . . anonymously go to a party and get drunk.

Casewriter: Mm.

Dale: Until I was incoherent. Not always, but occasionally. No reason for it. Now if I'm mad at somebody, or I'm depressed or something, I might go drink too much. But—I'd do this for no reason! The only reason was that I was filled with these nutty anxieties.

Casewriter: How does Jennifer feel now? About that? I mean, your——

Dale: Oh, she's—— Well, you'll have to ask her.

Casewriter: Yuh. I wondered how you saw her view, at this point.

Dale: I'm much happier with her. And when I'm happy, she's much happier with me.

Casewriter: Yuh.

Dale: She sees Peggy a lot. Which is great. They're great friends. And that's good. But she sees them on a different level now. During our business, Peggy Neely would probe Jennifer to find out what I was thinking or doing, and then tell Dick. I'd catch 'em at it a lot of times. Where Dick would say, "I understand that you don't want to do this thing." "Well, where do you understand that?" "Oh!" . . . I'd catch 'em, you see. Like reading somebody else's mail and then remarking about it, an anecdote in the mail, and then you get caught. But now they have a wonderful relationship. They love each other. And they're friends, for being just pure friends, and all that. . . .

Casewriter: You know one thing in this that really intrigues me—you've touched on it a couple of times—is that early on, uh . . . way back, when you first got to know Elmer and Peggy, and you found that first year so exciting. I guess you'd found a couple that you really connected to. . . .

Dale: Yes. . . .

Casewriter: ——and made a quick, deep friendship——

Dale: Yeah.

Casewriter: ——which was very exciting. After that, something happened where the . . . you and Elmer, anyway . . . began not to be able to talk to each other about things that really mattered.

Dale: Um-hm.

Casewriter: And several times, on the way through, you found that . . . you said he couldn't say some things to you that needed saying, because you were—tough to take—you know, you found it hard to take criticism. And so he couldn't say something. On the other hand, you felt there were some things you couldn't say to Elmer.

Dale: Um-hm.

Casewriter: Or didn't. And, so then Peggy was helping—or not helping, or doing whatever she was doing by checking out with Jennifer——

Dale: Bridging the gap.

Casewriter: ——where you were—you know. And that intrigued me about . . . during the—— enough time came along that . . . well, and you could *not* communicate about some things that really were important. At a time when things were going on that——

Dale: Mind you, I wasn't conscious of it then.

Casewriter: Yuh.

Dale: I *wasn't*. . . . I didn't have this rich experience with Elmer, where I learned this—to become more sensitive, and *listen* to other people. And it's only now, looking back, that I'm able to see this, now, that I didn't recognize it then. Like when we first decided to go into business, I was telling him—Dick always accused me of oneupsmanship. He'd go to the Bohemian Club in San Francisco for luncheon, and come back and tell me that he'd been to the Bohemian Club for lunch in San Francisco. And I'd say, "Gee, isn't that a great spot?" He'd never heard of it. Because he thought he was telling me something. That I hadn't—— He thought he would be able to do something that I'd never done. And I had to level, I had to equalize the thing by saying, I've been there too. And I did that a lot to him. And finally he told me. He says, "You're playing games with me." And I became aware of what I was doing, and I quit doing it.

At first, a conscious effort. And then later just a—— And I don't think I do it now. I'm much more . . . I stayed at the Yale Club in New York last week, and there probably isn't a more elegant place to stay. It's just magnificent. And five years ago, I'd have gone around and told everybody that I stayed at the Yale Club. But while I was in San Francisco, I didn't tell a soul. I met a lot of people. Finally, the lawyer—one of the lawyers—said, "Dale, I've got to send you something." And then he says, "Where are we going to send it?" And I says, "Well, you'll have to send it to my hotel, unless I can pick it up." He said, "Where is it?" And I told him. Five years ago I would have bragged. And now—because of Elmer—I didn't.

But there was a lot of that. You know, I really, philosophically, I've thought about partnerships, and you talk about—in your course that you give at Harvard—you talk about, say, a law partnership. Law partnerships are *nothing* compared to what we had. Nothing. A law partnership, if you want, you can count for everything that partner one and partner number two does, during the year. You have so many hours you bill in. There it is. At the end of the year, you got a kitty. You split the kitty up in accordance with a predetermined percentage. There is no accumulation of a large amount of funds, which *you* might use in a way that Partner Z didn't want to use. So you relieve yourself of an awful lot of economic interrelationships. You relieve yourself of that, in most law partnerships, I *think*. Whereas with us, there was no really absolute way to measure it—relative contributions. Yet we built these large—relatively large—amount of funds up. And there was no way of splitting them, taxwise. They had to be joint funds. And if he'd use them one way that I didn't approve it, it created a jealousy, or something.

Casewriter: Hm.

Dale: So our kind of a partnership was different as night and day to the other kinds——

Casewriter: Right.

Dale: ——that are pretty well . . . you can audit them, and at least remove the economics—or *define* the economics. I billed twice as much as you billed. Therefore I should get twice as much of the kitty.

Casewriter: It's nice and clean.

Dale: Sort of thing. It's clean! . . . The other thing is, in the partners that I know, that wives—they get too darn close. Can destroy them. Can contribute to the destruction. And I've seen it happen. Quite a few times. And I've seen some partnerships that lasted a *long* time where the partners make a conscious effort to live, one in La Jolla and one in La Mesa, and to keep their social lives separate. And of course there's exceptions in all the fields——

Casewriter: Sure——

Dale: But. The thoughts that I've given to it seem to me that if you can remove your wives from influencing your business, in everything that goes on, well, you're better off. It's a generalization.

Casewriter: Yuh, and it's a very intriguing one. Because in a sense what you're saying is you and Jennifer and Elmer and Peggy became so close as persons——

Dale: *Tremendous.*

Casewriter: ——that there was some imaginary line that got crossed——

Dale: Yuh!

Casewriter: ——that affected the business in a whole bunch of ways, because it affected you as a person——

Dale: Um-hm.

Casewriter: ——in a whole bunch of ways.

Dale: Mm-hm. And him as a person.

Casewriter: Sure.

Dale: And Elmer speaks his mind. He'd come right out, and he'd say, "There's only three women in the world I love." And he'd mention the three, and he'd include Jennifer in the three. And he'd say, "There's only three women in the world I'd go to bed with; bang, bang, bang." And I'd say—I'd get sore at him—"For Chrissake"—and I'd want to get up and hit him.

Casewriter: Yuh.

Dale: But I knew he was just talking off the top of his head. But these—— And then coupled with that would be some of their peculiar activities at parties, and . . . I remember at a lovely formal ball out at the Harbor Hotel, Jennifer and Elmer were dancing, and they started to talk. And they were talking almost like they were hypnotized, to each other. And everybody left the dance floor. And for twenty minutes they stood out there—completely oblivious of anybody else in the world. Jennifer's normally very shy, to do a thing like that. And Elmer was just talking to her, like this . . . and most everybody in the whole place was looking at them, and saying what in the hell's going on. It was a very screwy thing. It made *me* mad.

Casewriter: Sure.

Dale: A threat—you know. [Pause.] But it seems to me like I've talked more about the problems than I have about the *excitement,* and the *thrill,* and the *fun* of building and creating and working together. And for ten years, really, with the exception of one or two little isolated incidents—maybe one a year or two a year at the most—everything was just peaches and cream. We were building together. [Pause.]

Casewriter: You know, during that ten years, one of the things that occurs to me is that I was trying to get dates related to ages, in my own mind. You mentioned earlier that Elmer's older than you. You're now 42.

Dale: Now I think of it, I might be 43.

Casewriter: [Laughs.] Elmer's—what? Do you know?

Dale: I think Elmer's about 48 or 9.

Casewriter: Forty-eight or nine. . . .

Dale: Something like that. He's older than I. I'm the same age I think exactly as Peggy. Almost exactly. However, the age difference *never* affected us. At all. Maybe we'd mention it. Very rarely—just as a joke. But it didn't affect us at all. *Then* the ten years were just wonderful, great, exciting, fun years. We got great satisfaction out of creating, and doing, and succeeding. There were a lot of problems. We solved the problems. Made a lot of money—and that's important. We got foundations. And we became members of the community. By our own efforts. It was just *wonderful.*

Casewriter: It's sort of like when you've got—you know—maybe I'm wrong on this, but it's as if when you arrived, at sufficient income and stature in the community, and you were established—the things that you'd wanted—that the problems started to come.

Dale: Yeh! That's exactly when they started to come! We were able to hire more people. And not work as hard. And then take the time that we weren't working so hard, and do something else. And . . . this is when I—— Of course I blame this . . . or do I? . . . both sides. You know. But this is when Dick started getting enamored, up in San Francisco, with Quakers, and girls, and . . . right at that instant of time. And it took . . . gradually increased over a period of five years—the dates I'm not sure about, but the time is just exactly within the realm of . . . to my recollection. But by God, he just went head over heels—kooky, in my opinion. And he knew it. And it scared him. And so he took—the next thing, he went out and took very *expensive* psychiatry. He kept it a secret from me, for a long time. But Jennifer told me, after awhile. "Don't tell Dick you know, but he's taking psychiatric——"

Casewriter: Yeh. . . .

Dale: And I says, "Well he must have been doing something, because he leaves at nine every morning and doesn't get back till eleven-thirty every afternoon." I mean, "every morning."

Casewriter: Mm.

Dale: And—when he's in the office. So I knew he was doing something like that. And you could see the product of this treatment come out. I don't know whether it's good or bad—I really don't. And . . . then he would go to these T-group things, and—that he's talked to you about, I'm sure——

Casewriter: Yuh——

Dale: ——and all that crew. And he'd come back and tell the wildest ideas. As I say, I'm a WASP. So they're wild ideas to me. "It was a wonderful, rewarding experience, to sit, and never say anything for four hours, and look into somebody's eye." You know. Or the wonderful feeling of being able to *touch* somebody. And all this kind of thing. . . . Well, it is wonderful I guess. But—it isn't too much for me!

Casewriter: There's one thing I'd like to go back to, if we have a little more time. It's the . . . when you were talking, at the very beginning, about where you grew up. I wonder if we could go back and get a little more of that. You mentioned that you grew up in the Depression, and——

Dale: Having just read *Portnoy,* I'm all aware about . . . talk about mothers and all that stuff.

Casewriter: [Laughs.]

Dale: I grew up in a very secure household, extremely secure. I was born in the house. And lived in the house all the time until I went into the service. And then my family moved away—it's just down the street here. And my father was . . . I was one of four children. And my mother was a very strong, *very* dominating, and very smart woman. And my father is a college graduate—pretty smart, too, but he worked for his father, never had to really work too hard. And I guess my mother—and my father, too, really—set goals for me, that I had to reach. I had to be the best. I had to—I sold *Saturday Evening Posts*, and then I became a district manager, and I reached the point where I was selling more *Posts* in San Diego than anybody else was selling *Posts*. And I got recognition. And I won the yo-yo contest. And those type of things. . . . Trying to think about it—you know, when you lay on the couch and think about it—I'm trying to figure out whether or not . . . why I had those goals; and I just can't help but think that my mother—and my father, too—must have set them for me.

We had the ROTC over here in San

Diego High, and I became the head of the ROTC. Not only did I become the head of the ROTC—which is pretty good in itself, I thought at the time—I was so good, and did so many unique things as the head, that they made me the head of the city—all the ROTCs in the whole city, the student cadet ROTC——

Casewriter: Yuh.

Dale: They'd never done it before, or since. And these are crazy goals. You know, when you drive yourself to achieve these perfections. And maybe that's the reason I can't stand criticism. Possibly. Because you want to get to the number one, to the best, the absolute top. Of course, as I get older I find out that—that's not real important any more. [Laugh.]

I don't know what to tell you about my childhood. It was a lovely childhood, normal. We went through the Depression, like everybody else, and . . . around here. We didn't have much to eat, and we couldn't go anywhere. But we were well fed at all times, simply. We went to public schools. And always had clothes. Had a lot of friends. It was really a very nice childhood.

Casewriter: Were you the oldest of the kids, or——?

Dale: No. That was a little screwed up. I had a sister, and she was older by about eight years. There was enough difference between my older sister and me to where we had absolutely no relationship, almost none. She had her life, and her friends, and her room, and I had my life, and my friends, and my room. My brother was a year away. And although we had, I think, a very normal brother—— you know, sibling relationship, we fought and all that kind of silly stuff—but we really got along pretty well. Today our relationships are perfect. He leans on me and I lean on him, and—we just can't do enough for each other.

Casewriter: This is the brother who became a lawyer?

Dale: Yes. He's a lawyer.

Casewriter: He's younger—a little younger——

Dale: So I had that funny deal—an older sister, so much older that we had no relationship, and then between her and me, my mother and dad had a daughter who at birth was mentally deformed. I guess there's a lot of medical terms for it, nowadays. In those days they didn't know what it was. And it was terrible. She was a blithering idiot. Still is. She's still alive. And Mom and Dad, during the bleakest part of the Depression, went around to every doctor they could find, and most of 'em told them there was nothing to do. But you'd find a couple every now and then who'd say, "Well if you'll put her under my treatment for six months, I'll take care of her," something like that. . . . Well, that went on. . . . And that must have affected our childhood tremendously, although I don't see how it relates here. In any event, my mother and dad both took the very—I'm proud of them—took the alternative, and transferred her to an institution. Hopeless. She didn't recognize them, or anybody. Physically she appears all right. But mentally she has no brain.

Casewriter: Retarded, unh?

Dale: Terribly retarded. And there's no history in the family of it. It's just one of these aberrations of life, as near as we can tell. . . . But in any event, they took her out of their life. So it wouldn't affect us.

Casewriter: She was just a little older than you then?

Dale: Yuh. Well, she was about half—I'd say four years older. Something like that. But this all happened . . . maybe she was removed from my life when I was two years . . . I just barely remember her. And occasionally, the first couple of years, Mom and Dad would bring her back. I really don't think she was much of an influence. Although I've since—having children, and everything—I respect what they did.

Casewriter: Yuh.

Dale: It was pretty tough. And I guess the only other thing which happened in my life that was kind of traumatic is that my grandfather came to live with us. And I was forced to share a bathroom with him. And he was an elderly gentleman, and had all kinds of operations, and he was a complete slob. And I didn't get along with him. And he didn't get along with me. And so for the terminal years of his life—five or six of them—he invaded my life, to the point where I resented it. And fought with him all the time.

Casewriter: What kind of business did your grandfather have, that your dad worked in?

Dale: Well, my *father's* father—my paternal grandfather—was in the land business in California—land and oil well drilling, and all that kind of stuff. And he'd been here a long time, you know, and everything. And then he had two sons—my father and my uncle. And when the boys got out of college, they went to work for him, in this land business, drilling oil wells, and all that stuff. And I guess he tried to thrust 'em onto their own, because they did go to Texas and drill some oil wells, very successfully, and then . . . but they still worked for the old man. Just before the Depression, they went out and leased a lot of buildings downtown. Bought 'em on a 99-year payout basis. And then the Depression came along, and nobody could pay the rent, and they just left! And Dad was . . . the family was sitting there holding these buildings, and didn't have any money to pay the taxes on them. So they went . . . they didn't go busted—they eventually worked out of it. But they had to give back all the property.

So it was main—— basically, land, and oil drilling and all that kind of stuff. I think my brother and I were influenced quite a bit, *there,* in that we decided we'd go on our own. And do something other than be dependent upon him. Break away. Be free. And we've done it, I think, rather successfully. I hope, anyway.

Casewriter: And you—I don't know how many kids you have.

Dale: Four.

Casewriter: Four. And how old are they now?

Dale: Well, our oldest boy's in Redlands University. And he's 19, I reckon, or 18—18 or 19. And Mark, the second boy, is in the tenth grade. And he's about 15. And then we have two girls, one of whom is 9, and one was 7 yesterday, and they go to a little Lutheran school. A little church school over here. And that's all. But that's two families—the boys are quite a bit older than the two girls.

And Jennifer—her parents are very much alive, right down the street. My parents are very much alive, right down the street. My brother has four children, and he lives right over here. We're all close together, geographically. And I think we're pretty close family-wise. It's kind of nice, really.

Casewriter: Yuh.

Dale: Christmas, and Thanksgiving—it all means a lot. To the kids. . . . I've never really been—I've never had any psychiatry, or any opportunity to really think what happened in my early childhood, which makes me do what I do now. I don't think I'm afraid to look at it. I just haven't ever done it. [Laugh.]

Casewriter: Well, there has to be a need.

Dale: Well——

Casewriter: I mean, you know——

Dale: ——plenty of need here. I just—take that thirty thousand dollars and invest it in the boat, and sail on it, and probably have a better time.

Casewriter: You mentioned, too, that you think that at this stage now, as of today—I've forgotten the date now—at some point, Elmer began to catch on, and realize that he did have a viable business, where he was afraid he was going to go bust——

Dale: In April.

Casewriter: In April. That's right.

Dale: Three months, or four months after the—the schism.

Casewriter: And then you say he seems to be making better sense——

Dale: Well, he had his fiscal year—his financial year ended in January—on June the 30th. And he made a profit. That's the year I left at the halfway mark. And he made a *good* profit. And the business that he has now, which we had booked mostly prior to my leaving, has turned into just a very, very fantastically successful and profitable business. And that will go into this year, and he's making a big profit this year, which will end June 30th. The fiscal year. He'll make a lot of money then. I think. I hope. And I told Dick, I said, "Yuh, I hope you make a—— ten million dollars. And if you do, I'm not going to be jealous of you. And I'm always going to be emotionally involved with something we helped—I helped create and build and everything." I'll always hurt about that. But the very fact that he gets rich isn't going to bother me. I hope he does. I'm not hung up there.

But I think he just came back down to earth. It takes awhile you know, when you're out on . . . Planet 9, to—

Casewriter: Yuh. This affair in San Francisco is a . . . a . . . well, you mentioned that that's when you really began to be aware that things were coming apart. And that the difficulties you'd had you'd been able to live with. Even, for example, his outburst at a customer or something. As irritating or painful as that was, you were able to live with it. . . .

Dale: Get over it.

Casewriter: ——But then, that the affair came at the same time you said as he was getting into . . . with the Quakers, or this—— He was searching at something——

Dale: Yeh.

Casewriter: ——and——

Dale: The ends of life: Do what you want to do.

Casewriter: Yuh.

Dale: "Do your thing." Whatever they say. And I don't know—I guess, when you get to be a certain age, your sex begins to leave you, your masculinity begins to leave you, and most, perhaps, you get scared. You say, I'm not going to be able to have good sexual fun any more. And so you run around and try to prove your virility. Maybe that was part of it. But it hurt me, because he was horsing with his very best friend—or our best friend's wife—and screwed him all up. It was an unholy relationship from the outset, and I said, ten years ago, I said to Jennifer, I said, if they don't quit—they were with them two times a week. Well, you know that . . . the kids would stay here. Stay with them up there. It was almost like their home. Walk in unannounced in the middle of the night. Had their own key. Same thing here. And those things aren't healthy relationships! In my way of thinking. They just led—and lead into—real trouble. And it did.

It culminated one day. . . . We said, "I want to have lunch with you." Dick has ways of saying things. He'd say, "I want to have lunch with you." And I could say back to him, "I can't today, because I've got to go to lunch with this other guy." Or, "You're welcome to come with us." But he walked in and said, "I want to have lunch with you." Probably if you recorded the voice, you wouldn't be able to detect any difference between the two occasions, but this time he really did. So we were driving downtown for luncheon. He said, "I want to divorce Peggy." And I damn near ran into a truck. And we sat there at lunch, and he *wanted* me to tell him—he told me the story, and the whole thing, and everything—he wanted me to tell him how right he was. And he, in his own mind, thought he was right. And I couldn't! And I guess I must have made him sore. I said, "You're out of your mind." I said, "You're crazy. It's *wrong.* You don't want to divorce Peggy. It would screw up your whole life, and your kids' life, and everything else." And I didn't come on and defend him, and say, do it. His psychiatrist did! His psychiatrist said, "Go do it! It's great!" But not me. I don't think I made him very happy. [Laugh.] In that situation.

Isn't it funny how all these things kind of boiled up, in the last year or so. All at once.

Casewriter: They all came and reached some sort of peak——

Dale: Yeh . . . He'd made a lot of money. He wanted to use the money in screwball ways—taking the psychiatry, leaving the office, falling in love. All of this happened just about . . . you know, you take cream and whip it and it becomes whipped cream all of a sudden. Well, the same thing happened. It became whipped cream all of a sudden. It just changed from—litmus, you know——

Casewriter: Yeh. . . .

Dale: Red to blue! Instantly. [Long Pause.] So, I guess I've criticized him more than I should.

There were things which were present, for which you can criticize. It's so much easier to talk about those things than it is about all the good things.

Casewriter: Yuh.

Dale: Because, really, there were fantastically good things. God! Hikes in the hills, and . . . sailing trips, and . . . all that stuff. So I'm kind of looking back on what I've said, what you've recorded, and it seems that I've pooped out a lot of—of *his* irrational things, or the things that I couldn't accept with him. And haven't said about how wonderful it was. [Laugh.] Huh. . . . But it was! A lot of it. . . .

Casewriter: I sense somehow in the way you talk about it, too, that some of those—those marvelous things, especially earlier, and then even on for ten years—and the way you talked about, you know, you helped create this damn thing—that the sense of loss is——

Dale: Oh! It's *terrible*——

Casewriter: ——is high, and——

Dale: Oh, *it's terrible.* [Sigh.] And, I get a lot of hangups. I go out and I belong to a golf . . . kind of a group of guys, and every single one of them has—*is*—successful, and they're all on their own. And I'm the twelfth one, and I'm working for a guy. I'm on a salary. Whereas I wasn't, before. And this affects me. And I'm too old to go out and do it again. It takes a lot out of you. So maybe you do it once or twice in a lifetime.

Another funny thing—and I don't know whether it had anything to do with this at all, but my boss is Robert Doolan. Robert Doolan is a man who's 46 years old. And is probably one of the worst paranoids that I've ever seen in my life. Unbelievable. I went from one situation to another situation.

Peggy Neely

The following excerpts are from an interview with Mrs. Peggy Neely. The interview took place on an afternoon in late November 1969, in her daughter's bedroom.

Casewriter: I'm interested in your best understanding of what led to the dissolution of the partnership. . . . I don't know where you want to pick it up. Whatever interests you.

Peggy: Well, it started socially when a mutual friend of ours was getting married, and we went to lots of parties, and met Dale during that time. And I'd known Jennifer as a little girl—she was five years younger than I was—but when I was at college, I . . . she lived two doors down, at the beach, in Balboa, from where . . . the people I stayed with. And she was a little girl. This always impressed me, because I mean, she was 14, and I was in college. And 14 was a little girl, at that time. And . . . So then I didn't see her again until this party series. . . . And I never knew her then, she was a little girl that lived down the beach. And at the parties, um—I don't quite know how Elmer and Dale got together. But anyway, they began to talk. And Dale was 20 and light, and they got along very well. And then Dale was offered a job in New York, and he had to transfer to New York, on this job. And he was talking a great deal to Elmer about this job.

And Elmer, on impulse—we'd just finished building a house at the beach—Elmer said, "Why don't you come visit? Why don't you and Jennifer come and spend the weekend with us?" Um. So they came. And they were out weeding—which I don't think either one of them have ever done since—but anyway, they were out weeding in the garden, down at the beach house, and I heard one of them say, "Well, I don't think that . . . I think that'd be a great idea. Why not?" And they at that time had been discussing the partnership. Which surprised me greatly, because Elmer, knowing how I felt about it, that he was a man that had to be . . . work for himself, he couldn't work in an organization, and that's why he started the business for himself—um, it surprised me, that he . . . that this happened. It was really quite startling to me. Um. But I liked it. It seemed to be a relief, to m—— to . . . in that business wouldn't be so much encompassing for him. It would give us more time, and we could take vacations. . . . You know, it just sounded great! And I liked . . . probably also a little bit, I liked Jennifer, what little I knew of her at that point, and I was more socially conscious in those days, too. I liked the position they had in the community. And having come from a small town, that was—— It looked kind of good. I mean—I had nothing to do with it, but I mean, but . . . all those things, all those things, are kind of parts of the whole. But I was nervous. Because Elmer, in a close relationship, *always* makes me nervous. You know. In the way he acts. . . . Let me see. So that's how the partnership started.

Casewriter: So that, that all was going for you, but you had a nervousness about whether Elmer . . . what Elmer . . . you said the way Elmer acts when he is working closely, or being closely——

Peggy: Yes. Because I always——

Casewriter: ——and that was a worry.

Peggy: That was a worry, and I think in our marriage situation that I was always the protector, of him, with close relationships, in the sense that—um—I made all the social contacts. Or this is my impression of it anyway, that I . . . most of the people that came to . . . were friends of ours—were people I brought into the friendship. And I——

Let's see. I just couldn't picture him. It was . . . seemed like working in a corporation again. I can't picture him in that close relationship exactly.

Elmer always discussed—he'd been in business alone for I can't remember how many years, five, seven, something like that, before this happened—and he'd always discussed a lot of these business things. And in *that* sense, he discussed it with me. But not any opinions, of what I had——

Casewriter: Right. . . . You would——

Peggy: Contractual things, or anything like that.

Casewriter: Yup.

Peggy: So I had nothing to with the business.

Casewriter: Well, then, how did your relationship develop with . . . Jennifer, and yours to Dale, and then yours to *them?*

Peggy: Uh. . . . Well, I suppose it grew mostly, I think, through Jennifer. I mean, Jennifer and I slowly became better and better friends. And Jennifer was such a kind of straight, clean person, and . . . that she—— When she was nervous, she said it. And when they would have little hoo-hoos, and maybe he would—— Elmer would come home and complain about Dale, somehow there was some sort of *filtering,* that went on that way. Jennifer and I did kind of communicating, vis-à-vis the men. But we never had any part in *business* things.

Casewriter: But if the men had a problem, and they each went home and talked to their wives, the wives would then talk to each other? And then would you go back to Elmer, on behalf of what Jennifer had said had been going on——

Peggy: Sometimes. And . . . I mean, it . . . there was a lot of—*sorting,* I think, in my mind. You know, it's even hard to go back. But I think there was a lot of sorting that went on in my mind. What I brought back to Elmer and what I *didn't* bring back to Elmer. But, um—[Sigh] for quite a few years, it didn't have many . . . it was just kind of a growing—a little bit rough relationship. But it also developed they had very different talents, that worked together very, very well. As far as mechanics were concerned. And personality, they had a good time with each other, for a lot of years.

Um. He always felt Dale stood in his way, in some ways. This is where the complaints came from. Rather—I mean, this is what he complained about. They were almost hurt-feelings type things. Not mechanical things. Not things to do——

Casewriter: Elmer'd be hurt——

Peggy: ——by some way that Dale talked to him, or some way that——They'd communicate with each other with . . . as two *men,* rather—and not in the business sense.

Casewriter: Not as partners.

Peggy: Not as partners. And they never had any conflict—like the *trust* between the two of them, financially, was fantastic. They never had any——

Casewriter: ——any problems——

Peggy: ——*any* problems, that I ever felt, that way.

Casewriter: Do you remember any . . . any things that—um—how Elmer felt he was . . . you said, held back, by Dale

Peggy: Um. When he had a business contact—somebody he felt was good, or he discovered a job, or he thought Dale should bid a job—those contacts never panned out, in Elmer's mind, because Dale—again, in Elmer's mind—never pursued *his* contacts. He really . . . Elmer's point was that Dale wanted that priority. *He* was doing the bidding. He was making the contacts.

Casewriter: Wanted to keep that . . . his territory——

Peggy: And that was a complaint. And whether it was true or not, I have no idea. But that was——

Casewriter: That was the sort of thing. . . .

Peggy: That was the sort of thing. That he would complain about. As it developed—you know, I'm thinking more in the later years—it was some of the ways that Dale led his social life. I mean, belonged to the Gourmet Club and to the Hunting Club, and all the things that Elmer wasn't interested in. I think he had trouble understanding Dale's interest in those things. And I repeat, all this seemed to be in their personal . . . not business-wise—where they hung up, and——

Casewriter: Yuh.

Peggy. It—— When it finally got involved in the person—in the business thing—was when he felt he wanted to set up a structure, for Dale to go into the field, which was organized, where he would cover all the bases, and sort it out, and have an organization behind Dale that would do these things. And Dale never liked that. He almost liked to deal out of whim, and—uh—intuition.

Casewriter: He didn't want a structure—

Peggy: He didn't want a structure.

Casewriter: And Elmer did.

Peggy: And Elmer did want a structure. But that really wasn't—I mean in the dividing of jobs, that really wasn't——

Casewriter: Right, right. Well, the firm grew, from the time those guys got together, and then you really came to know both Dale and Jennifer pretty well. For about ten years.

Peggy: Yes. Especially in the—— We would go out to dinner, the four of us, together, quite a bit. We went on the Chapmans' boat, over the weekend. And I can remember Jennifer's mother . . . waving goodbye, and saying, "Well your partnership will either be broken at the end of the weekend, or it will be all right," or something. I mean there were lots of—— And again, Jennifer always kept this very clean. 'Cause as—— Sometimes when there'd be tension, I'd say, "Why don't you come over for dinner," and she'd say, "I don't think Dale feels right about that. Right now." Or, "Dale is ready for it." And so *we* could always talk, and be very straight with each other, about what we felt would be okay, as far as the men were concerned.

Casewriter: So it kind of put you in the personal realm of that relationship—two women in charge of managing activities so that they'd fit the feelings that you knew your men were having.

Peggy: That's right. That's right.

Casewriter: You were very much wrapped up in your own husbands, and very close to each other, and could talk straight about those feelings. Did the relationships grow, or change, or——? Can you get at that, in any way?

Peggy: Uh. I think it . . . grew. I'm sure *it grew* in relationship to Jennifer and me. It just got stronger, and stronger. And I think we became more and more confident, so to speak, all the time. There came times when we wouldn't see each other for a while—the four of us—because things would be tense. And, he—— I always think of it mostly Dale was the one that kept . . . he would get upset with Elmer and feel uncomfortable with the three of us. It was like the three of us talked, and he was an outsider. I always felt he was an outside—— I mean, I always felt *he* felt he was an outsider.

Jennifer's very interested in a lot of the same kind of conversations that Elmer and I are—how people work, and what they think about, and that sort of thing—that made Dale nervous. It was always like those conversations were *intruding*. They were not things people should talk about.

Casewriter: So Dale was kind of left out of . . . that.

Peggy: Yuh, he was left out of that. *Felt* left out of that.

Casewriter: So, the three of you were . . . sounds in some ways closer than anybody was to Dale.

Peggy: That's right. That's right. I—— In the early part of the relationship, I always felt Dale had a great deal of *trust* in me. He *could* trust me. And although he found it hard to open up—if I can use that term—he . . . every once in a while, we would have very straight conversations. I can remember maybe four. I mean that's not terribly many, in the years that we were together, but they were very, very clear, and straight. But they were always when he and I were alone, at a large dinner party, or something like that. When he would—the *two* of us would talk.

Casewriter: Well, the business was growing, Elmer and Dale were achieving their goals as businessmen, in many ways. When did this thing begin to unravel? I mean, when did the partnership start to go down, to the point where they'd dissolve it. Can you account for that?

Peggy: Well, I think it—— You know, I'm sure it began to unravel before . . . um. It began to unravel before, uh . . . I'm sure the tensions between the two men were building up before, um, Elmer had this affair with Virginia. But, uh, I can't really talk about it on specifics. I mean *that* was such a specific thing, but——

Casewriter: Well, how did the affair come up as important in the business?

Peggy: Dale—— It felt to me as if Dale *couldn't work* with a man that handled his private life in that way. He literally couldn't work with a man like that. Um. Meanwhile, I was thinking about the tensions between them would get quite intense, and we wouldn't see them for a period of time. Together. I *always* saw Jennifer. All of this time. But we wouldn't see them together, very much. And then it would kind of . . . the air would clear. And we'd see them, together, again. And feel comfortable with them. As a matter of fact, I think we feel quite comfortable with them, now. Again. But, uh . . . that . . . you know, I can't think of anything specific up until the affair came. And along with the affair was—— Of course, when *we* were having troubles—Elmer and I were having troubles—the children began to be tense, and our daughter was going around with a boy that—that wasn't all acceptable in the social swim, and Dale recommended, often, that she not see him any more. And that always bothered Elmer a great deal. That he got into that, at all. Or worried about that. It said something to Elmer very significant about who Dale was. I can't tell you exactly what he said to him, but what those meanings are, but—it bothered him, a lot. Bothered Elmer a lot. And those all came up during this very tense year, period.

Elmer—— I think the tenseness between them personally was that Elmer felt Dale was putting him down, or ignoring him, in some sort of ways. Also, as the business grew, and got stronger, Elmer worked himself out of a job within the business. I mean that was his goal, and that was kind of what he wanted to do. And so as he developed South America—and that enveloped him for awhile—and then he developed San Francisco, and that kept him busy. It's like he was very restless. Yet as long as he was developing something, their relationship was good. Or workable enough. Quite good, as a matter of fact. But when he would work himself out of a job, and his projects would get going, and he had all of his projects going, he got his own administrative source working fine, he had worked himself out of a job. And he literally, I felt, didn't have much to do. This is before—but in my opinion had something to do with the affair too. But he literally didn't have that much responsibility. I think Dale *felt* a lot of resentment, like *he* felt that he was carrying the business, and Elmer was not interested, and really wasn't a part of the business. So that was probably the buildup, that's where things began to—— And he talked a lot. Elmer talked a lot about breaking up the partnership. But it was really—it got, in my mind, to be just talk. Because he was always saying he was going to leave the partnership, but he really never did.

Something happened to Elmer. I—— You know, when he was very, very busy, and when he was, as I say, building this organization, he didn't worry about meaninglessness, and where was it all going, and all of this kind of thought. Partly age, partly the business getting organized. When he began to really get preoccupied with meaninglessness, he became hostile. More hostile than he'd ever been before. And had fights with everybody. . . . This is how I *felt* about it, that he was really, literally, at odds. And the conversations in the home that used to be—with friends that came in, which used to be just discussions—always seemed to end up heated. And people were always . . . really, he was very harsh. And very, um, upset. And hard on people. And at the time, *I* became very upset. And this is quite a few years ago. Like four years ago. And that time he had talked vaguely about going into therapy, and I really wanted him to go into therapy. I suppose it's the old classic case of, if my husband would be all right, then I would be all right. And I felt that if he went into therapy, this would kind of clear up. And at this particular time, um—I—we knew a therapist that Elmer had asked if he would take him. And he did. And he took Elmer as a patient.

And that seemed . . . as long as he was going to do something about how . . . his hostilities . . . that—— I'm talking about, much more now, about my own personal relationship with Elmer. I felt as long as he would try to do something, that that made me feel better, about us, and made *our* relationship worth working on.

Casewriter: So that he did then start into treatment himself. And that must have gone on a couple of years——

Peggy: That went on two years.

Casewriter: Two years——

Peggy: Up to the——

Casewriter: The break.

Peggy: The break.

Casewriter: Right.

Peggy: Where he . . . wanted to leave me and marry Virginia.

Casewriter: Right, and uh . . . so that he—he told you that he was, you know, having this affair, and wanted to leave, and wanted to marry Virginia. How did that get into the Chapmans' life? Do you know how that——

Peggy: Well—I was terribly upset, naturally, at this time. And I didn't want it to get into the Chapmans' life. But meanwhile, Jennifer and I had developed this relationship where we didn't lie to each other, about anything. And she called and said, "How are you?" And I burst into tears. And I . . . although I . . . you know, my better judgment said, don't tell her, there wasn't any way out. Because I really wasn't in control of myself at that time. And so I told her. And very soon—like a matter of a few days—Elmer told Dale about this. And Dale was very, very upset.

Casewriter: And how about Jennifer?

Peggy: Jennifer was extremely upset. It was shattering, upsetting to her. She felt a lot of anger toward Elmer. Very sympathetic toward me. Meanwhile, my feelings were that she really loved Elmer very deeply, as a human being. And she had a lot of close feelings about him. But this . . . she . . . you know, she would say things like, "I don't know how I'm even going to be nice to him when I see him." And, "How am I going to handle this?" and, uh. . . . But she could say all these things to me. And we talked a great deal. And she was extremely supporting to me, during this period. That was in June, and it was in about October or November, I don't remember exactly which month, the following October or November, that Dale announced that he would not continue the partnership.

Casewriter: I see. How did you feel about Dale's not continuing the partnership?

Peggy: I think I felt it was a hope for our marriage. I also—I felt lots of things. I felt it was a hope for our marriage, because it was going to make him totally . . . well, at the time when he . . . the partnership was announced as a . . . they were going to dissolve it, there was quite a period in there, say of several weeks, where it was who was going to buy and who was going to sell. And during that time I thought it was terribly important that I said nothing. I had strong feelings of what I wanted. I wanted Elmer to buy. Because I felt if he sold, then that was . . . then we were all through, kind of. Because then he would have his money, and do . . . he would have no responsibilities, and he would have the wherewithal to do what he wanted to do. And that would almost automatically . . . I felt the decision was almost a decision for our marriage.

And I had another feeling that—— One of my conversations that I had, again with Jennifer, always with Jennifer, was that if Dale is doing this for my marriage, I appreciate it. But that's a hell of a dumb way to make a decision. And I . . . you know, I think you, Jennifer, should make this very clear, as far as Dale is concerned. And their feelings. Because I—I guess I didn't want the responsibility of feeling that Dale was selling his life away, if that's what it felt like to him, to sell the business.

Casewriter: And it occurred to you that he cared enough about you that he might do that?

Peggy: It occurred to me that he did care enough about me to do that.

Casewriter: Uh-hm. . . . Well, then, the decision was made that Elmer would buy, and Dale left the business. Then what happened? As you saw Elmer deal with this, and your relationship with Elmer?

Peggy: During the business negotiation period, Dale's brother was the lawyer, and he made a very tough contractual agreement—again, my information comes from Elmer. But from other men whom I talked to during that time felt it was a tough contractual relationship—er, business deal, too. But Elmer's feelings along that line were that if it were a good going business, the difference in the prices weren't worth haggling about, because he could make it up in the earnings of the business. So he . . . there was no arguing. There was no fighting. There were no disagreements during that time. He offered more money for things that I thought were kind of silly to do. But anyway. And that Dale didn't even ask for—like a company they had just bought for $25,000. And Elmer gave Dale $100,000—or offered Dale $100,000, for that business. Which was not really a going businss yet. But, anyway, this is the kind of thing, and there was no bickering or arguing at all. At the time of the negotiation. But then when the contract was drawn up, Elmer felt it was tough. And he was very bitter about Dale, right at that time. But he'd never . . . did anything. The contracts were signed, and it was all legal.

And then there was the period, I would say, of extreme bitterness on Elmer's part toward Dale. He felt that Dale had screwed him, and he felt that he was incapable. He felt that he couldn't handle it. And that Dale maybe *had* in reality run the whole business, and Elmer had just not been there at all. And he went into a period where he was *sure* he was going to go broke. And as he became sure that he was going broke, he got madder and madder at Dale. He . . . and the business contract, even our house would go. And so he went to Dale and asked him if he would let the house not be part of the business.

I was never there when there were any of these discussions that Dale held in tough, and said no. Elmer would *panic,* and say, "Dale, come help me." And Dale wouldn't. I think Dale was very wise in these things. But—the first two months of that panic I felt it was all right, and that Elmer was just in panic, but by the third month, *I* began to get in panic, and feel that maybe in truth it was going to become a fact.

Casewriter: That the whole thing would go down the drain——

Peggy: Yes.

Casewriter: And then—what happened, I mean . . . that was . . . for three months it looked pretty black. And Elmer was pretty angry at Dale. And feeling incapable, and threatened, and——

Peggy: And didn't want to see Dale during that period. And I think Dale sensed all that. And probably was feeling a lot of the same things himself.

Casewriter: Yuh. . . .

Peggy: He'd had to make a whole life

change, and Elmer had *caused* it, and—you know, I'm sure Dale must have had a lot of these same feelings. Jennifer and I kept . . . then Jennifer and I just kept our relationship clean. It had probably been some time since we had worried about the men. There was some point, maybe two or three years ago, when we finally decided, screw it. Yuh, this is dumb, what are we even fretting about? They're either going to make it or not, and that *still* is not going to have anything to do with our relationship. And we'd had that kind of discussion on many occasions. And that was one of my great fears—one of the *bad* things about the dissolution of the partnership that I worried about—that I would lose my relationship with them. It did not work out that way. I mean, I don't feel that I have.

Casewriter: That you still see Jennifer and Dale——

Peggy: And the other *good* thing I felt, about the dissolution of the partnership, was that both Dale and Elmer had gotten to a spot in their life where they had the ability to stand on their own two feet, and they didn't need to hide behind each other. Whatever their needs were in the original partnership, they'd outgrown in reality. And it was time for each of them to be their own man. Whatever that means. But to stand . . . to stand up there alone—I particularly felt this for Elmer, naturally—to stand up there as a man committed to something . . . and in this case, his business.

Casewriter: Well, where would you say the relationship now is among the four of you? This is, what, six months after the partner—— no.

Peggy: Yes . . . well, January . . . yuh, more'n six months.

Casewriter: Nine months——

Peggy: Nine months. Um [Pause.] I would say my feelings for Jennifer—particularly right now—feel almost unshakable. Like, we have been through so much hell together, and she's never left me in any of this—and I never felt Dale left me, either. But I mean, my closeness was with Jennifer. That nothing can . . . she may outgrow me, or other things may happen, but there is never going to be something that comes up that could dissolve our relationship. My trust in her is very, very deep. As a human being.

Casewriter: And how about Dale?

Peggy: I don't suppose my feelings about Dale are that pure, because I never—uh—*had* much of a relationship with him in reality. He was very hard to open up, to me. And on the rare occasions he did, I *liked* it. Um . . . I don't—I think it's so much harder for Dale to express himself, and to be . . . feel close to anybody, I mean, let alone me, but anybody. So I don't think there is much change there. But I think I feel very easy with him. And I feel no . . . I feel very . . . you know, I feel his support. It's on a . . . not as deep a level—although I shouldn't even say that. It's a—it's a non-talked-about support that I just plain feel.

Casewriter: And how about now you and Elmer?

Peggy: You mean *our* relationship, our marriage?

Casewriter: Yuh, how is that?

Peggy: Um. [Laughs.] It's a funny expression. I feel our marriage has had a curettage. And we're both feeling better, because of it. And if the marriage is going to continue, it's going to be a much clearer relationship between the two of us. *Is* a much clearer relationship. There are still a lot of things to work out. But I think we're having more fun together again. Feeling—*I* am feeling, maybe, more relaxed with him than I've ever felt in our entire marriage. Partly because I've been in therapy for two years, and partly because, after being that frightened, I can't really go—I can't be any *more frightened,* and therefore being straight with him seems more important and necessary.

Casewriter: One other thing. When Elmer got involved with this other woman to such an extent that he—you know, it occurred to him, anyway—that he might want to get divorced and marry this gal, you *knew* her, I gather, before this affair developed.

Peggy: *Very* intimately.

Casewriter: What was the nature of that relationship?

Peggy: Virginia and I were sorority sisters at college, and although we weren't close at college, when *we* were early married and *they* were early married, they were *my* friends. And we began to go to basketball games, and see each other out socially, a little bit. And Elmer really liked them. And so did I. And the four of us—it was the first time four of us, or two couples, ever really meshed, in our married life, to that extent.

One of the very closening events of our relationships were that Virginia called me one day and said that her daughter had died. Her little girl, who was three and a half. And we went immediately that night—although we didn't feel very close to them—to their home, to be with them. And nobody else was there. So it was—— And from that time on, there was tremendous intimacy between Virginia and me. And we kept the relationship—again, Virginia and I kept the relationship going. I would say—and during that time, I always knew, particularly in the last few years—that Virginia and Elmer were very, very close, as friends. And I liked that. P.J. and I were close as friends, too. And I liked the fact that—I had this fantastic trust in Virginia. She was very perceptive, I thought, as a human being, and saw the way relationships worked, and understood Elmer, and understood his . . . the way *he* operated. And I never—I just thought of them as very good friends. It really never . . . entered my mind until, maybe *vaguely,* in the last six months, or four months, of their relationship—I mean before it all came out in the open—we spent a few weekends together. We were always together, a *lot* on weekends. And we spent a few weekends where I began to get funny feelings. But kept them evidently so downed that I never . . . um. Now that I look back on it, there were lots of hints. But I evidently wouldn't let them in, or whatever. And I never *challenged* anybody on them. I suppose I was too frightened to.

But there were times where she began to make fun of me. Put me down. And that—she had never done that, in all of our relating. We'd been these close confidantes, where we talked a lot about our children, or a lot about our husbands, a lot about our relationship with our husbands. And she'd call me long distance, and she could tell me things that—you know, how furious she was at P.J. And I wouldn't take it that they were getting along badly. It was just a moment in time, and we had a lot of understanding, was my feeling.

Casewriter: Did Dale and Jennifer know Virginia and her husband?

Peggy: They had met them through . . . and Jennifer and Virginia had liked each other. Dale was always nervous with our friends, somehow. But Jennifer had liked Virginia, particularly.

Casewriter: So they were aware of the . . . Virginia's relationship to you as old——

Peggy: Oh, yes! They were very, very conscious of that. And we *talked* about it a lot. I mean we talked about . . . what we did, and where we went, and—I suppose Virginia and Jennifer were my two friends. But at that time, I was closer to Virginia. We had a lot of life experiences together, and lots of . . . families. Our families had spent weekends together. And the children had grown up with each other.

Casewriter: I see. Is there something that I haven't thought to ask, that you'd like to talk to? about? . . . that might throw some light on how a relationship between two men, in this instance, gets to the point where they need to stop it . . . uh——

Peggy: Well, part of it I suppose are the dynamics of how Elmer worked. I don't really understand Dale's dynamics. But part, as I see Elmer's dynamics work, that when there were troubles, or things that didn't go well, he always . . . it seemed to me he had a propensity for saying it was the other person. And he always talked . . . he never talked about his own *responsibility* very much, I would say, in their partnership. It was always that Dale was doing wrong, or how he didn't relate, or things of that kind. And I was always very conscious that I would think . . . I was just very . . . I always knew how Dale *felt.* Because I felt that our marriages were similar.

Casewriter: Similar to the partnership?

Peggy: Yes. That Dale was—had the same spot in *his* marriage as I had in our marriage, and we were both married to the same man, and therefore I had a lot of sympathy for Dale, over these years.

Dale and I are the kind of people who I suppose are . . . [Sigh] well, we had enough similarities that we were the kind of people that Elmer could tolerate. To be with, or whatever. I'm trying to think what some of the similarities are. One is we're not very confronting. And we're not very hostile. Either one of us. But somehow the relationship to Elmer—I think Dale was scared of Elmer. *I* was scared of Elmer. That was more in that area, that I tuned in with Dale. Not in our personalities, and the way we . . . what we wanted for ourselves. I think we are quite different, our value systems are different. I'd say my value systems are really quite similar to Elmer's.

Casewriter: Would that have been true thirteen years ago? When the partnership started?

Peggy: N-n-no. I think there's been change. Because I would say my value system . . . I was very, as I mentioned earlier, interested in the social scene. And Dale *is* interested in the social scene, always has been. Um. I had a lot of images of how I wanted to live. And I think Dale did, too. We were both very strong image-people. I think Elmer and Jennifer were more direct, more confronting, more *straight.* And—maybe not as big a phoney. I don't like to say that, but I think that's true.

[Both laugh.]

Jennifer Chapman

The following interview with Mrs. Chapman took place in the living room of her home the morning after the casewriter had interviewed Mr. Chapman and first met Mrs. Chapman. The casewriter arrived at 9 A.M. and found Mrs. Chapman doubtful about going ahead with a tape-recorded conversation. After some time talking over coffee, she indicated reluctantly that she might be willing to begin.

Casewriter: . . . Well, you know, one of the things that we did, of course, was start talking, and one of the things that you mentioned was way back, you said you were—27? When you and Dale met the Neelys, you found them very exciting, in some ways. You said they had ideas, and they . . . talked about them and—you . . . you found that exciting, because you wished a lot of people did that. How did the relationship go, then? You saw an awful lot of them after you . . . the business got put together.

Jennifer: Yeah. Then we, of course, saw more of them. We saw each other often. And they were, I would say, therefore, they probably came in—they probably saved our lives.

Casewriter: Really? How? What do you mean?

Jennifer: Um. Our marriage was probably a *very* squeaky one. We'd been married young. And—rather quickly. And moved away, when we were first married. Lived in Quebec. And, uh—Dale was working for some company there. And we kind of got our bearings together. We were pretty happy there. We were completely alone, and . . . and we had some nice friends, just a couple of 'em, but people we liked. And then we came back here and were thrust into the sort of social environment of San Diego, which was Momma and Daddy telling us—telling *me*—what to do every minute, and his family telling *him* what to do every minute. And [Sigh] we just really didn't have any good friends. I mean, we had all of our *old* friends. Dale had an old friend that he was terribly close to, but . . . he has since died of . . . killed himself, as a matter of fact. And that was his closest friend. We saw him every Friday night. And his wife. That was *darling.* Finally, *that* got so bad that . . . you see, I was just . . . as I was thinking last night, it was only seven years we'd been married. And so that's not very long! Considering now, we've been married twenty years.

Casewriter: Well, and you'd moved——

Jennifer: And we'd moved.

Casewriter: ——to different places, and so you'd cut off——

Jennifer: And we'd had two babies. In the seven years. So our life was a kind of hodgepodge mess, of no real, meaningful—I hate that word, but you know! No real relationships, of . . . I have friends that I still see, that I saw *then,* you know, not in a . . . excluding them from my life, just because they not . . . because they don't think exactly the way I think, and vice versa. But anyhow, the Neelys came into our life. I was 27 and Dale was 30.

Casewriter: Let's see. I'm a little confused about . . . You got married. And how old were you then?

Jennifer: Barely 20.

Casewriter: Barely 20.

Jennifer: Mm-hm. I'd had two years of college.

Casewriter: Where was that?

Jennifer: Oh . . . [Laughs.] Socially, you know—Briarcliff.

Casewriter: Briarcliff. And you went two years, and then you married——

Jennifer: Yuh.

Casewriter: And where did you get married, here in San Diego?

Jennifer: We were married here in San Diego. *Large* wedding. Nothing really was real, from the very beginning. So. When the Neelys came into our lives, it was very great. Because it meant more to me than anything else had, up until that time. And it also did to Dale. Because we could sit and talk to them, and they were *real.* They were not—not—I can't explain it. And the people—— We've grown an awful lot, and I think we've grown *because* of the Neelys. I mean, that's why we'd hate to see them—our relationship—just go by the wayside, because . . . we've grown, I *feel,* because of them. And that's why I feel that they—they always meant more to us than we meant to them. And . . . so.

Casewriter: It sounds at that time you were young, and kind of lonely, and some very exciting people showed up. And . . . and so, whammo! It really kind of took off, as a relationship. And then Elmer invited Dale to get in the business.

Jennifer: Yuh.

Casewriter: And so—Dale says okay.

Jennifer: And so he did. And this was terribly exciting, and at first said to Elmer, "Well, for heavens sake, no! [Laughs.] That's the dumbest thing I've every heard of!" And then as soon as Dale made up his mind about . . . which he made up in one night—that was perfect. And they started off in a little tiny office, and it was all very happy, and cozy, and *we* saw each other—but not every second, you know. They had their own friends and we had our friends, but we would see each other a lot, because of the business, and they were just getting started. And—I was never a real part of the business, in any way. I was not that interested in the mechanics of the business. And probably—I don't know whether that's good or bad, but I wasn't. And that's just the way it was.

Peggy, I think, was more interested. She . . . we would always talk about it. I mean, Peggy and I probably talked about the business more than Dale and

I talked about it. Although when I would ask Dale about what happened during the day, or something, it would always be on a personal level. And I think he resented that. I think sometimes he wanted me to ask about a particular job. Or——

Casewriter: That is, did they *get* the job, which was a big deal for the company?

Jennifer: Yes, some huge, marvelous job, that Dale had worked his tail off on. And then here I would just say, well, how was *Elmer* today? [Laughs.] How did he *feel,* to you, today? . . . Well, and that'd make Dale furious. It didn't make him mad for ten years. [Laughs.] I think he went through that for ten years and . . . or longer! Possibly.

Casewriter: But you feel then that Dale would have appreciated it had you been more interested in the business as a business, rather than the persons as persons.

Jennifer: I . . . That's what he tells me. And Peggy and I would talk, probably every day, and then—then Dale would come home, and we'd have a drink, and we'd talk a little bit about . . . I'd say, "How did your day go?" But always in a more or less personal vein rather than in a . . . being completely interested in some specific thing in the business. And I think—well, I don't *know* what Peggy did. But it is—I'm sure—different than the way I handled things.

Casewriter: Well, then, things went along so well in the business for ten years or so, and they were building it, and it was a big adventure, they were going from that shack to . . . becoming the large enterprise. And during all that time you were having children?

Jennifer: Yes, we had two more children.

Casewriter: Two more kids. While that was going . . . The relationship, then, was developing, of course, between you and Dale, and then *your* relationship to Peggy, and yours to Elmer. And then you were all getting to know each other, I assume, much more . . . better.

Jennifer: Much, much better. And—we just . . . we kept seeing each other the same, and—— And as you say, it just got deeper and deeper, and closer and closer. I—I suppose that's just the way it happened, you know. [Pause.]

Casewriter: Well, what do you think caused their . . . in the last several years of the partnership, things must have—some things, *different* things—must have come up, to a head, that finally made it necessary for these two guys to stop being partners.

Jennifer: Well, I do think Dale was basically jealous of my relationship with the Neelys. Because it was a personal thing—love. And—this bugged him. That's just one of the things. And I'm sure there are many. And, uh . . . and let's see what else. Everything became . . . everything was really just perfect! I don't—— You know, it's so hard to go back, because it was damn near perfect. It was perfect until three years ago. I mean perfect. We had a Christmas party, and we all sat around here, after everybody had left, and we said life couldn't get any better, could it? And we just were happy, together. We'd go out together and we'd *laugh,* hysterically. And we'd just . . . really . . . just great fondness, you know. And I don't know what in Sam Hill happened. It was just this very intenseness that *must* have been building up, through the years, although it—— Even if I try to think about it, intellectually, it doesn't seem possible that it . . . that there must be some reason for it, in the last three years, even though

I'm sure things built up, and—you know, I guess it's 13 years, they were to—— And there's . . . well . . . [Pause.]

Casewriter: Well, you say that Dale was a little uneasy or jealous, or . . . that your relationship with Elmer and Peggy was so close, and so personal. And earlier I think you mentioned something about, you talked to them about some things, at times, that were important to you as a person——

Jennifer: Yes, right——

Casewriter: And——

Jennifer: They were the only people on this earth that I could ever go and talk to. I'd talk to them about me, how *I* really felt. If I felt really *low,* suicidal, what have you, I could talk to them. I couldn't talk to my mother. I felt for some reason that Dale didn't understand me. And they did. They were just great that way! They still are. I mean I'd go to them in a minute, you know, if there were any real . . . tragedy. I would go to the Neelys.

Casewriter: And Dale resented this?

Jennifer: Yes. And he unfortun—— I won't say fortunately or unfortunately, but he resented it, and probably had good reason to.

Casewriter: Good reason——

Jennifer: Well, good . . . good reason being that—— I *don't* think, it's good reasoning, no! [They both laugh.] I don't think it's good reasoning. I think he—that's the way he felt, and he can't help the way he felt. But . . . the real uneasiness in the relationship, I would say . . . for about . . . started about three years ago. And *not before that time.*

Casewriter: Now what . . . can you see any . . . what . . . what was going on then, that, looking back, you might say——

Jennifer: Well, of course they'd *made* it. As far as the business——

Casewriter: Financially——

Jennifer: Financially, they were in good shape. Elmer didn't have any great *goals.* And Dale liked it the way it was. It was just fine, you know.

Casewriter: That's fine.

Jennifer: That's *great!* I love this. I'm having fun. And I think, in a sense—now this comes from . . . from Dale—but I think Elmer lost interest in the business. And I—I can't say that for sure, because I don't know that much about the business. I really and truly don't. And that's why I don't know how valuable talking to me is going to be, because I . . . it's just *all* on a personal vein. Gee, I just can't s—— It's hard to say. Well, he . . . Elmer was always looking for something. You know, there was always something out in left field that looked—— But that's . . . you know. And Dale understood that. And he always sort of backed him, because he thought he *had* some marvelous ideas. And there one—— Some of the ideas that Dale thought were the screwiest were the ones that turned out to be the most productive. And he was kind of the brain of the business. And after all, it was his *idea,* it was his baby, and he—he was the creative force behind it. Dale was the plodder who was—you know—trying to get the jobs, and fighting with the people. But, uh . . . it's just hard to say now.

Casewriter: Were you aware in recent years that things were getting tighter, before the decision was made to end the partnership?

Jennifer: Oh yes. For a year. And they were really sticky. And because of . . . of . . . Elmer, who act—— I think as far as the business has turned out, also he was . . . very, you know, intense about everything. You'd go out to dinner with them, and they'd . . . we'd have these fights, and it wasn't the same at all. It was upsetting, and it would make me *sick. Physically* sick.

Casewriter: Were there other events that——?

Jennifer: Well, *events* are hard to know. . . . I can't say any *events.* It's just that—it just happened. Whether it was—— It was certainly not one specific event. I think it was probably Dale's buildup of this jealousy, which reached a peak, and he just absolutely said, "Now, lay off." We had about three of these dandy fights. In their living room, or our living room, or some restaurant, and one night Dale broke into tears, and . . . which was amazing in itself. That was at least three years ago. So possibly it's been longer. And, uh——

Casewriter: But Dale began then, to set some limits, or something. He said—what? We won't——

Jennifer: We won't *see* them very much.

Casewriter: And what did that mean to you?

Jennifer: Well, *it just seemed terrible.* Because I . . . *wanted* it. I mean, Peggy and I certainly kept our relationship growing. We still have. And I'm very . . . I think it's great, you know. Close, friends, and . . . well, anyhow. The buildup. And I seem to think it possibly . . . it probably was Dale's resentment of m—— of me probably caring more for them than he liked. And the depth of in—— of the friendship had gone beyond his limits, as an individual. I don't unders—— you know, I don't agree with that, because I think you can have—— Although, as you know, things *did* get a little *bizarre!* [Laughs.] This was very hard to take, for both of us, when Elmer—you know, things that——

Casewriter: This was when Elmer started going to San Francisco?

Jennifer: Absolutely. Absolutely. And then there was really no . . . he had no interest in the business. And Dale came home and would say, "There is just nothing I can . . . he's not *with* me. He's not interested." And, of course, this was bound to affect him. And he—— And then when we went to Europe, the first time—[Laughs]—the Grand Tour . . . little bit . . . trying to hang on to all this. Thought maybe the trip would do us some good, and we hadn't taken a vacation for . . . it was a three-week jobby. We hadn't done anything like that, *ever.* So we went, and thought, well, this will do us good, and we'll get away, and——

Casewriter: Was this you and——

Jennifer: Dale. Just the two of us. And we had the trip, and it was fine. Had a . . . received a lovely letter from Elmer. In fact, I wish I'd saved it. Because this was at the time when he was probably going through the worst of his . . . worries. Which we knew nothing about. Except Dale had surmised that something was going on. And either Elmer was having a complete nervous breakdown [Laughs] or he was in love with somebody else. And he had not said that to me, but——

Casewriter: He had felt it——

Jennifer: Dale had definitely felt it. And I—I've always felt that they sort of had these dear people that they held very close to them, and they . . . and we were *two* of the dear people—but they wouldn't share the other people with us. They finally shared the Whitmans with us. About five, six years ago. But not often. Only very select times. And they were straining those evenings, that we spent. The four of us—the six of us.

Um. Anyhow, the trip didn't do the

trick. [Laughs.] And we came back, and Peggy arrived one morning and—it was the day we'd . . . the day I'd returned home from Europe, I think. Dale had gone back to work. And she burst into tears, and she said, uh, "Jennifer, Elmer wants to leave me. He's in love with Virginia." And I almost fainted! I mean I didn't know what. . . I . . . I . . . physically was sick for three months. You know, it's all so crazy, that I don't remember it? I can't remember it when . . . well, it was in May, obviously. That's when we got home, late April. And we went away that summer . . . *I* went away. Dale commuted to the beach.

And I was hoping that it would all go away. And so was Dale. He told Dale in a car. And Dale's only reaction was, I'm going to hit you in the face!

Casewriter: It made Dale angry?

Jennifer: Yes. But a *funny* angry. He wanted to *kill* him, kind of. He . . . and that just—— Dale said to me later, he said right at that moment, "When he told me in the automobile, I knew that was the end. That was it." Now, that is . . . that is *it.*

Casewriter: Something about that Elmer could leave Peggy did something to *your* relationship, yours personally, and Dale's too.

Jennifer: Well, of course I was madder than hell. I mean, I was furious! I mean, I got sick, and furious, and how could he do such a thing, and—you know, as time passes, you realize that *any*body can do such a thing. For heaven's sakes—it isn't so odd, after all. But now I think back on it, now that I've lived with it . . . but at the moment, it . . . from the old Victorian upbringing, it was a real shocker. And as far as Dale was concerned, and as far as he still is concerned, I think that was—that was the severing point.

Casewriter: Triggered, right then.

Jennifer: And I think from that moment, until they broke the partnership, which was about six months later, he was thinking—of doing so. . . . I'm trying to think now . . . summer . . . and then fall. . . . [Laughs.] Fall came. And Dale was thinking all this time—I'm *sure* he was thinking. He didn't talk about it much, until about November.

Casewriter: Yuh.

Jennifer: And he said, "Jennifer, I'm going to——" He came home one night to me and said, "I'm just go—— We're . . . I'm just going to leave them." And I said, "Dale, well, if that's your decision, fine." I . . . I'd really had it, by that time. With everything.

Casewriter: You were worn, too?

Jennifer: I was kind of sick—and everything else. And I'd just had it. And I said, "Fine, if that's your decision, you just . . . have had it. You know. You've tried, and if this is the way it's going to be, that's the way it's going to be." So he made up his mind, and tried to write things down, tried to read books about . . . psychology! and people! How . . . why things happened to people. And he did delve into life a little—and was thinking, probably in a confused manner—as I *usually* do—but at least he had . . . he had *compassion,* by then. I mean this is . . . time had passed. And——

Casewriter: He wanted to understand it?

Jennifer: *He* wanted to understand it, and I—I think any man understands that, for heaven's sake. Even if they don't admit it, they understand it. Um. And when he ca—— Nothing was ever really resolved, about . . . that he was ever going to do it. I just said, you have my blessing, if that's the way it's going to be, that's the way it's going to be. And so—I . . . I've forgotten just when they decided to dissolve the partnership. Some small thing triggered it. And—something about the children. And—that was that. And that was just an easy way to—— And in a funny way, I feel probably Elmer was thinking the same way—I don't know why I feel that, because I have no basis for thinking that. But it was so *easy,* the way it happened. And so *fast.* It was scary. And—— So Christmas went by, and they had decided to dissolve the partnership. Uuergh! It was about eight weeks in there that was . . . hell, for everybody. And then I had an operation. And it's all a big blob in my mind. And, it's just so—— It's *still* a big blob. All very upsetting to me, even right now [Laughs]. And I'm not articulate, and I'm so sorry.

Casewriter: I get the feeling, you know, that——

Jennifer: There's a lot more to it. You know you can't go through thir—— You can't have two people in your life mean so much to you, and you can't just *say* it . . . I—— There's just so much more to it than——

I—I don't know how happy Dale's going to be. I certainly . . . I . . . I *hope* it's going to work out all right.

Casewriter: Since the . . . well, when Dale and Elmer dissolved the partnership, Dale must have been around awhile then, because he didn't have a job, at that stage.

Jennifer: He was home for six months. But I was recuperating for almost that long, from this silly operation, which put me down, and I was really sick, for about . . . *really* sick, for three months, in the sack. So, that's one reason why it's all a little hazy. 'Cause——

Casewriter: You were having physical troubles?

Jennifer: I really was physically sick, then. And, uh, probably Dale was too! [Laughs.] And we both sort of brought ourselves back to life again. He . . . found this job, and it seemed the right thing for him, and—here he is. But there's still a great tie, as far as I'm concerned——

Casewriter: Yes. . . .

Jennifer: With the Neelys, I mean.

Casewriter: There must have been a period there where it was hard to deal with the Neelys. Or was that not so for you?

Jennifer: There have been ups and downs. It's a funny thing. I—I for a time was so mad at Elmer I couldn't look at him. So I didn't see him. And then I got over that. Isn't that si—— It's so strange, a—— react. And I didn't, uh . . . I didn't mind any more! And—in fact, was even *more* crazy about him. And he—you know, God bless him, the old Rasputin, here he is. [Laughs.] Working at you, all the time. So—you know. I just practically accepted what he had done as just being *nifty;* you know. And I think this has been resented, by Dale. The complete acceptance. As a matter of fact, I wanted . . . uh . . . oh——

Casewriter: You what?

Jennifer: [Sigh.] I've even wanted to talk to Virginia. But——

Casewriter: But you haven't.

Jennifer: But I haven't.

Casewriter: Well, you and Peggy have maintained a relationship all during this kind of—— For awhile you excluded Elmer——

Jennifer: I——

Casewriter: ——I guess.

Jennifer: Well, that wasn't very long. I haven't *seen* Elmer a lot, and—Dale hasn't seen him either. Maybe for lunch once in awhile. But I think when they have, they've gotten along very well, and Elmer seems now—— He went through a very terrific panic situation. I mean it was just—despair, I *guess.* I mean I did not experience it, because I wasn't near him, and didn't see him. But I guess it was just absolute utter despair. And I think now he seems fine. People have so many problems. People problems. I don't have one friend that doesn't have a . . . just a terrible [Laughs] problem. I don't have anybody who's just . . . as Dale says, "You don't have one friend, going back from the kindergarten age, that has not had some terrible problem." I mean really bad. Divorced. And—in the nut house. All kinds of things. But they're all . . . these people, that I gravitate to, people like that. I just lo—— I must like 'em! I find them more interesting. And they *happen* to be all my—it's a funny thing, but they happen to be all my *oldest* friends, too. And they're all kind of crazy. And they all have so many problems that they don't know what to do with them. And I seem to——

Casewriter: You enjoy them?

Jennifer: I must! Yes, I obviously must or I wouldn't have them. There are a lot of Pollyannas running around. but—maybe that's *my* problem. I don't—— That's probably my . . . hangup. I don't know. I—I'm beginning to think I'd damn well better find something else, rather than people with problems. They do involve me so. Like the Neely thing involved me so that I was practically sick, over the whole thing. And I *did* take it to heart. And I took every ounce of it to heart. Another friend, this last summer, when I was away from Peggy, had a tragedy in her life. And I absorbed that, so that I couldn't sleep or eat, or——

Casewriter: You feel the problem as if it was yours?

Jennifer: I feel like they're mine. And I must like it. And I don't know why I like it.

Another thing. Peggy and Elmer obviously understand themselves an awful lot better than Dale and I understand ourselves. Due to the therapy. And this is an interesting point—that since . . . that they're getting to . . . obviously to see the difference between a—— the two couples.

I've *always* seen a difference! The *difference* has always been there. Peggy said it was because of my fear of her. I said the hell it is. She's just always been a different person. So that—— But you're basically interested in what caused the split——

Casewriter: Well, yes. I guess that when Elmer announced he wanted a divorce, you got upset and everything. It's as if he's leaving, not just Peggy, but you and Dale.

Jennifer: Well, I think so, absolutely. I thought of that. We were . . . we were abandoned . . . babies. That takes a pretty powerful person.

Casewriter: Yup.

Jennifer: To be able to make you that upset.

Casewriter: You know, that takes an awful lot of caring, to get that upset.

Jennifer: And we *cared.* Every one of us cared. Tremendously. Still care.

Casewriter: Still do. . . .

Jennifer: And Dale may try to fool you, but he still cares. I don't—I doubt very much if there'll ever be a person in Dale's life that will mean as much to him as Elmer. Ever. Because he usually tries to avoid them.

Casewriter: Friends . . .?

Jennifer: Uh . . . just . . . well, strong relationships.

Casewriter: And Dale prefers a little more distance.

Jennifer: Um-hm. As he says, the "normal" relationship. I—— [Pause.] It's funny. Life goes on, and you do find friends that . . . new ones. And we have. New friends that are . . . great! We've met them in just the last couple of months. So—you know. After all, we—— For awhile I just didn't think we ever would *date* [Laughs] anybody else, that would—— But this was my fault, I think, for—— Because, as I say, I think that I . . . the power that possibly the Neelys had over me, and probably Dale too, was much greater than we ever had for them. Maybe that's wrong, but I don't think so. It's just how it seemed to be.

Casewriter: So in a sense, you really were abandoned, then, at that moment. That word really makes sense, then, by the way that you're saying that you were so influenced by them, that his cutting out on everybody really sets everybody afloat.

Jennifer: Yuh. And in a funny way I think Dale still is afloat. You know. He hasn't really found the niche. At all. He may be trying to chalk up a few points, but . . . it's not . . . well, it's certainly not what *I* think of him doing. I felt that it was . . . wrong. And I still do. But also, he feels there's something to do in the interim——

Casewriter: Yeh . . . until he finds something that he really wants——

Jennifer: But, time's *passing*. [Laughs.] He's 43.

PART FOUR

DEVELOPING SKILLS IN UNDERSTANDING AND HELPING ANOTHER PERSON

Introduction

In previous sections of this book, even though several chapters and readings have described ways of behaving for improving communications, giving and receiving feedback, and making relationships adaptive, most of the text has focused on developing analytic ability in understanding the nature of interpersonal relations and the problems that arise in them. In this section, however, our focus will shift from developing *analytic understanding* about relationships to developing *behavioral skills* in relationships.

The purpose of the material in this section is to describe an approach, and a way of listening and responding to another person, that can improve your ability to understand that person and what he or she is experiencing. The particular skills we will describe can also make you more effective in helping others, especially in helping them think through personal problems, dilemmas, or conflicts. Thus, our focus in the following chapters will shift from the process of thinking about another person to the process of actually engaging and talking with another person. We will be concerned with specific attitudes and ways of behaving in an encounter that are useful for gaining understanding and/or helping another person.

The orientation we will use in doing this is based on the work of Carl Rogers and is commonly called the "client-centered" approach. It is an approach that has been widely used by managers as well as by people in traditional helping professions such as consulting, interviewing, counseling, and psychotherapy.

The chapters in this section of the book are arranged so that they progress from a general description of the client-centered approach to the specifics of the technique associated with it. Chapter 8, "Understanding and Helping Another Person," will describe the history of the client-centered approach and the basic orientation and assumptions on which it is based. It will also describe how the client-centered approach is relevant to many interactions of an everyday nature, and why it is particularly useful to managers. This is an especially important chapter, because it explicates the basic philosophy and premises of the client-centered approach. We believe that the underlying orientation is more fundamental than the specific techniques associated with it, because the techniques derive important meaning only within the context of the orientation.

Chapter 9, "Listening for and Responding to Another Person's Meanings," describes what psychologists have come to call the "reflective technique." The reflective technique grows out of the client-centered approach and is a particular way of listening for and responding to another person that facilitates exploration and understanding. This chapter describes some basic guidelines of the reflective technique and why these guidelines are conducive to developing openness and understanding. Chapter 10, "Degrees and Kinds of Reflective Responses," goes into the reflective technique in greater detail; it describes several different kinds of responses and the degree to which they can facilitate exploration in an encounter in which one person is trying to help or understand another.

Finally, Chapter 11, "The Reflective Technique in Broader Perspective," discusses the conditions under which the reflective technique is appropriate and effective, and the conditions under which it is not. Chapter 11 also discusses responses that are not reflective in nature, such as "challenges" and "confrontations," and some circumstances under which they too can be helpful.

The readings in this section of the book were selected to complement the text. "A Therapists' Perception of the Good Life," by Carl Rogers, provides a much fuller view of personal growth and development than that offered in the text. In this reading, Rogers elaborates on the implications of his philosophy for becoming a fuller and more effective person. "Interpersonal Skills and Helping Relationships," by Eileen Morley, discusses the process of developing interpersonal skills. It also describes the process of associative thinking and how people make conscious and unconscious associations as they explore their thoughts and feelings.

The cases we have included in this section are about the process of listening and responding to another person. The Ashok Rajguru case is a transcript of a conversation between two people, one of whom is trying to use a client-centered approach to understand and help the other. Chuck Lorring's interview with Larry Baker is an analysis of the conversation that makes up the Larry Baker (A) case, which is included in Part II of the book. We urge you to review the Larry Baker case and also the Juanita Rodriguez case (also included in Part II), as examples of client-centered interviews.

Before you begin reading the chapters that follow, we feel it necessary to make more explicit our own view of the client-centered approach. We believe that if you are able to develop skills in focused listening and responding reflectively, you will significantly enhance your capacity to understand and help others. We also believe that if you are able to internalize and develop these skills, you will find them very useful in a number of different situations and settings, ranging from counseling others and working through misunderstandings and conflicts, to helping others understand and work through their own problems. In specific managerial situations, a client-centered approach can be very effective in problem solving and exploration, performance appraisal, career-development counseling, and in surfacing and understanding interpersonal conflicts. The client-centered approach is especially helpful in personal relationships and the problems that arise between friends, spouses and intimates.

We do not believe, however, that the client-centered approach (or the reflective technique) is "the answer" to interpersonal interactions or problems. Also, we do not believe that it should be used as a managerial style or as *the* way of responding to or working with others. Nor do we believe that it is appropriate in all encounters between people. We *do* believe, however, that the ability to respond in a client-centered way is a skill that can be enormously useful in a wide variety of situations that have understanding or helping as their purpose. In a given conversation, you may feel it appropriate to be client-centered for only a short period of the exchange, whereas in another encounter, you may want to be client-centered and reflective for most of it. These are contingencies that occur at the moment, and judgments that only you can make based on your skills at being client-centered, your own intentions, and the other's expectations. However, the ability to engage another person intensely and helpfully when these occasions arise is a very useful skill to have. We also believe that developing this skill will leave you with the ability to simply hear more of what others say to you in normal conversations and with much more awareness of what others are feeling and thinking in virtually all interactions.

Developing this or any other skill requires practice. In several chapters, we will urge you try out and practice listening and responding in a client-centered way. Some of the chapters will offer suggestions for how to do this in your normal interactions and conversations with others. We also urge you to ask someone to allow you to have a practice interview with him or her in which your expressed purpose is to use the client-centered approach to understand that person better. These practice sessions are very important in internalizing the skills described in the chapters and readings. Although you may experience your initial attempts at being client-centered as somewhat awkward or uncomfortable, these skills develop quickly with a little practice, and they soon become a natural part of your own unique personal style. We think that you will not only find these skills useful, but also find the process of developing them exciting and rewarding.

A bibliography covering all the chapters in this section will be found at the end of Chapter 11.

Chapter Eight

Understanding and Helping Another Person

In preceding chapters of this book, our attention has been devoted to developing some ways of thinking about people as individuals so that we can better understand how they think, feel, and behave, and most important, how they see themselves and their situation. The self-concept model and other ideas we have discussed have served as tools for organizing our thoughts and perceptions so that we can more richly imagine the other's reality. They are deceptively simple ideas that enable us to be more aware of ourselves and others and of the meanings we make from our different frames of reference. In applying these concepts, you have probably used written cases, readings, and of course your own experiencing. These cases have provided the kind of information we needed to develop skills in using these concepts, and the concepts themselves have been effective for making sense of these cases.

However, in all the materials we have used, whether case histories or transcribed interviews, the data had already been gathered for us and neatly presented in written form. Thus, you may have experienced a certain *ex post facto* flavor while analyzing these cases, because you were working from materials in which the data had already been acquired and organized for you.

In some of these materials, the data were made explicit in a way that seldom occurs in daily relations with others. The subtle feelings and nuances in perceptions that were made available to us in these cases are precisely the kinds of insights that are not usually accessible to us as we try to understand another person. Furthermore, these materials were about situations that did not personally involve *us* as actors. We were not part of the drama, nor were we faced with the need to intervene or take action. We were not part of the problem we perceived.

What do we do when we are in a real, living relationship, and it is up to us to gather the data? To put the question in more concrete terms, what could *you* have done had you been either Dale Chapman or Elmer Neely a year before their partnership finally broke up? For example, had you been in Dale's place and wanted to help Elmer as well as yourself, what could you have done to understand what Elmer was going through? What could you have done to gain a better sense of the conflicts and ambivalences that he was experiencing? How could you have listened and responded so that he might have shared more of his thoughts and feelings with you? How could you have responded to help him better express and explore his feelings? And, perhaps most important of all, how could you have helped him understand *himself* and his conflicting feelings better, so that he could have been more consciously aware of them and thus more effective in working them out?

The purpose of this chapter is to begin to answer some of these questions. Beginning with this and subsequent chapters, we will shift our focus from analysis and thinking about another person to the process of actually encountering another person in ways that increase our understanding of that person and also help him understand himself better.[1] In a sense, we will begin to shift our emphasis from looking at a person "out there" to focusing on two of us "right here."

Our reason for wanting to develop skills in understanding and helping is that, potentially, these skills can be of major value in enriching our relationships in our personal lives, as well as increasing our personal effectiveness as managers. It is in large part upon human relationships that enterprises rise and fall; and it is upon mutual help and understanding that human relationships persist or die. Men and women who choose management as a career will live their lives working with and through others. The ability to understand and help in relationships is central to the process of management.

Given these purposes, this chapter will begin to address the following question: *How can I listen to and respond to another person so that I am able to gain a better understanding of how that person sees himself and his situation, and also help him better understand himself?*

You notice that the question above has two facets to it—understanding *and* helping. It is important to make explicit the underlying relationship between understanding and helping, because much of the discussion that follows in this chapter will show that any successful attempt to better understand another person will also result in that person's understanding himself better. Conversely, any attempt that succeeds in helping another person understand himself better will also result in our gaining a deeper and richer understanding of him as a person. This interrelatedness between helping and understanding will

[1]For grammatical simplicity, we have used masculine pronouns; however, the comments apply to both men and women.

emerge more clearly as we explore these two processes in greater depth.

You may also have noticed that the question as stated above emphasizes two aspects of the process: How we *listen to* and *respond to* another person. Both research and commonsense observation suggest that these two aspects of how we relate to another person affect *directly* the quality of the understanding that takes place between us. Almost everyone has had the experience of being consistently understood by some people and consistently misunderstood by others. Most of us know people who are described by others as being "a hard person to talk with," or "a little bit thick" when it comes to understanding. Conversely, almost everyone can think of people whom others view as "an easy person to talk with," or "a person who can really understand what you're trying to say." We tend to attribute these characteristics to personality factors, and sometimes quite correctly so. But more often than not, a person's ability to understand another person has more to do with *how* he goes about doing it than with some deep-rooted personality trait. It usually has to do with how he broaches a question; how he listens to the other (if indeed he does listen); and how he responds to what the other has said.

For example, everyone at one time or another has had the experience of sitting through a meeting or overhearing a conversation in which what was actually communicated could have occurred in half the time, and often with half the frustration and anger, if only one of the persons had stopped talking long enough to listen to what the other was trying to say. Such conversations sometimes appear slightly comical, because both people may be trying so hard to communicate that their efforts border on desperation. It is not that they do not want to understand each other. They usually do. Rather, it is that they do not know how. And that is the point: *How* we respond and listen to another person influences our ability to understand or help that person.

Although this point may be stating the obvious, how we can go about improving our ability to understand and help is not quite so obvious. This is because many of our commonsense reflexes actually impede the process of understanding or helping. For instance, a common reaction when another person does not understand or agree with what we have said is to restate our position even more emphatically instead of trying to listen for *why* the person does not understand. Similarly, a common reaction when someone comes to talk out a problem, especially if it is a painful one, is to immediately assure him that "everything will be all right"; or to give a quick solution from our own experience before we have even heard enough to really understand what the person is experiencing. None of the responses above facilitates communication, and in most cases they tend to impair or cut off further exploration of the other's point of view. Yet these are very common responses, which we hear others and ourselves making much of the time.

The general question, then, is, What skills and ways of behaving can we learn that can make us more effective in understanding or helping others?

IMPORTANCE OF THESE SKILLS TO MANAGERS

Before we address this question, let us try to be more explicit in answering another question: "Why should I *as a manager* want to develop an ability to understand or help another person?" (Except, perhaps, for reasons of sheer altruism.) Reference has already been made to the importance of these skills as they affect the relationships through which organizations function. But the more concrete reason that these skills are important lies in the human realities and complexities that fill a manager's life. A manager needs these skills, not just in situations where the human and economic stakes are high (such as with Neely and Chapman), but also in the wider range of interactions required to lead, motivate, and develop people.

For instance, a common problem, which nearly every experienced manager that I know has faced, is a situation in which two subordinates have such difficulty working with each other that the quality of their work as well as their relationship suffers. The work may suffer because the two subordinates need to collaborate to perform their tasks but cannot do so effectively. Or it may be that their mutual misunderstanding has escalated to the point of an ongoing feud so psychologically disabling that neither person can work well, even independently of each other. Whichever the case, the manager must be able to intervene in some useful way or accept the costs of work poorly done in an environment of misunderstanding. The manager's ability to understand and help both people work out their problems is crucial to a successful resolution of this problem. Even more important, however, is the situation in which the manager is himself part of the problem—that is, where *he* is having difficulty working with another person, and at least his own effectiveness or satisfaction is impaired.

Nearly everyone who chooses management as a career will be faced with situations such as these. Some will be essentially business-related, some personal. Most will have aspects of both, such as a situation in which a subordinate or co-worker needs to talk out an impending career decision.

For the sake of illustration, let us look at a specific situation where a problem has both business and personal components: A senior partner of an accounting firm, who manages one of her firm's large Midwest offices, is approached by one of her most promising junior associates. The associate wishes to discuss a "personal but also business" problem with the manager. The problem the man describes is that his wife's father has recently died, and his wife wants to return to the East Coast to be near her mother. Yet the associate feels that he has just begun an exciting phase of what the manager knows is a promising career in the firm's growing Midwest office. Clearly, the manager would like to keep him.

Indeed, the preference of most people in the manager's situation would be to ask the man to stay in the Midwest office, or, at worst, lose him to one of the firm's East Coast offices rather than to a competitor. But the manager cannot even begin to usefully advise this man from either the company's or the man's point of view until she first understands the complexity of what the man is experiencing. And the problem is that the man is ambivalent. He himself does not know what he wants to do, or at least what he wants most. Before the manager can give any useful counsel, she must first be able to listen and gain a better understanding, while helping her subordinate explore his own inner feelings, assumptions, goals, fears, and ambitions.

If the man stays in the Midwest, what effect will his wife's discomfort (and the resulting guilt he may feel) have on his work? If he moves to the East Coast, what effect will his resentment over lost opportunities have on his relationship with his wife, or on his work in the company's East Coast branch? A manager would be foolhardy to recommend that the man either stay in the Midwest or move to the East Coast without first understanding the conflicts the associate is feeling, and what the man's tacit assumptions, hopes, and fears are about his present and future. The process of both understanding the man and helping him understand himself is crucial to any resolution that would make sense to either party. It is important to note that both processes, understanding and helping, are interrelated in this case. The manager's understanding will progress *only* to the extent that she is able to help her subordinate understand himself better.

Although this type of situation is triggered mainly by personal considerations, it is important to add that the ability to understand and help is also relevant to issues that are principally nonpersonal in nature. Understanding alone is never a substitute for professional or technical competence in matters of substance. But the capacity to understand why others stand where they do on a substantive question, and the ability to help others explore what they do not fully understand about their position, are at the very core of effective decision making. For this reason, the ability to understand and help another person is especially important to people who manage. It might even be argued that these skills are as essential for managers as they are for counselors or consultants whose profession it is to understand and help.

AN APPROACH TO UNDERSTANDING AND HELPING ANOTHER PERSON

Let us now go back to our original question of how we can effectively listen to and respond to another person. The remainder of this chapter will describe a general approach to understanding and helping others that has been extensively used and found to be effective in a wide variety of situations. In particular, we will focus on several conditions that have been shown to facilitate understanding and helping in relationships.

In doing this, we will draw heavily on the work of counseling psychology and psychotherapy and, in particular, on the work of Carl Rogers. This is not because we want to become counselors or therapists, since this is clearly not our intention. Rather, we do this because much of this work has important implications for the kinds of everyday relationships managers face in both their personal and professional lives. It should not come as a surprise that the learnings of psychotherapy and counseling are useful for our purposes, because the principal objectives of these professions are to understand others and help others understand themselves.

The Client-Centered Approach

The approach we will take has its roots in Rogers's "client-centered" therapy.[2] Like any approach that requires developing skills, the client-centered approach includes both a general orientation and a particular set of techniques. We will begin by first looking at Rogers's underlying philosophy and theory, because we believe (as does Rogers) that *the orientation of the approach is more important than its technique,* and because the technique derives important meaning only within the context of the orientation.

The term *client* in "client-centered" has its origin in the setting that Rogers first studied: a therapist working with a client to help the client understand himself better. For simplicity's sake, we will also use the term *client,* but to mean "a person we are trying to help or understand," rather than a "patient" or "counselee." There are two reasons why we are using the same term even though our purposes are different. One is simply that it will make the language less cumbersome in places. The other, more important reason is that the term *client* captures some of the attentiveness and sense of concern that we want to develop for the other person as we try to understand him and help him understand himself. As the expression "client-centered" suggests, it is an approach in which the person in the helping role focuses his attention on the client's frame of reference rather than his own. This point will be elaborated on in greater detail later in this chapter.

Why This Approach?

We have chosen to focus primarily on the learnings of Rogers's "client-centered" approach for several reasons. First, it is the approach that in our experience has proved to be most applicable to everyday

[2]This discussion draws heavily on the work of Carl Rogers, Brammer and Shostrom, Shertzer and Stone, Benjamin, and Arbuckle. The interested reader can find a bibliography of their work (as well as that of several others) at the end of Chapter 11.

living, and especially to the kind of human problems managers face. The client-centered approach has been successfully used by many managers and administrators in the course of their work and has direct applicability beyond the traditional helping professions of psychotherapy and counseling, as, for example, in managerial situations like the one described earlier. It is also of considerable value in personal, more intimate relationships, such as with spouses, friends, or acquaintances. Second, it is an approach that most people, once they have acquired certain skills, find powerfully effective in understanding and helping others, especially in terms of simply being able to hear and understand more of what another person is saying and feeling. Finally, it is an orientation and a set of skills that can be acquired without extensive prior training of a specialized psychological nature. Related to this is the factor that the client-centered approach is one that leaves the initiative of "how far to go" to the person being helped. Unlike other approaches, it is not one in which we will try to probe or rearrange another's psyche, activities that are dangerous in the hands of laymen, and especially inappropriate in the realm of everyday work relationships.

Our purpose in the next several chapters will be to describe some ways of responding to another person that are effective and helpful rather than obstructive or hindering. This will take considerable work and some questioning of old assumptions, because many of the responses we have been taught to use in the past actually impede free and open communication, and hinder rather than help.

Some General Assumptions Underlying the Approach

Implicit in a client-centered approach are two assumptions concerning the importance of the client. The first is that open communication between us and the person we are trying to understand or help will occur only if we are able to create a relationship in which the other person finds us trustworthy and accepting. This sense of trust and acceptance is essential in order that the other person can take the risk of exploring personal meanings with us without fear of being judged negatively or being betrayed.

The second assumption is that the person we are trying to understand is the best guide to what issues, thoughts, and feelings should be explored. You notice that we phrased this so that it is the client, and *not the person in the helping role,* who is the best guide of what to pursue. This is an important premise—that the client has the best sense of what matters to him from *his* frame of reference. Also, this premise is counterintuitive. For most of us, our natural tendency in trying to help another person is to tell him what *we* think he should do. Similarly, when we are trying to understand another person's point of view, our tendency is often to direct the other by asking questions, especially questions that we think will probe deeply, or highlight aspects of what we think he does not yet see about his situation. Although these responses are sometimes useful, they are usually helpful only *after* we have gained some sense of how the other person sees and experiences his situation.

One of the reasons why the client is the best guide is that he knows himself, his needs, and his situation better than we do. Furthermore, only he has the capacity to develop thoughts and feelings that are only partially in his awareness. If we really want to understand his frame of reference, we need to help him develop his thoughts rather than direct them ourselves. As counterintuitive as some people find this premise, it has been borne out by the experience of counselors and therapists of many different orientations and persuasions. Although different theories of helping relationships may vary in many of their specific assumptions, this premise is one that most theories share. Some of the reasons for this will become clearer in subsequent chapters and readings, and also from your own attempts to actually practice understanding another person. However, until you have had the opportunity of testing out this assumption, we will ask you to temporarily accept it as an important premise that is supported by much theory and practice.

CHARACTERISTICS OF A HELPING RELATIONSHIP

Rogers first began to formulate the ideas that underlie the client-centered approach when he found that certain patterns of behavior seemed to recur consistently in successful therapeutic relationships, as compared to those that were not successful. Subsequent and more detailed research by him and others showed that several conditions distinguished effective from ineffective therapeutic relationships, regardless of the individual therapist's particular theoretical orientation, "school of thought," or training and background. The consistency with which these conditions occurred in successful therapeutic and other helping relationships led Rogers to postulate a theory of helping relationships. Later work by him and others showed that these conditions also applied to many other kinds of relationships that had growth and understanding as their goal, including those of a normal, day-to-day nature. For our purposes, we will think of these conditions as applying to any encounter in which our intention is to understand or help another person, whether that encounter is as brief as five minutes or as long as several hours.

The essence of Rogers's theory can be fairly easily stated. It is that constructive understanding, personal growth, and help occur only if the person we are trying to help and understand perceives a certain psychological climate in our encounter. The conditions that compose this climate do not consist of specialized knowledge, techniques, or intellectual quickness. Rather, they are certain feelings and attitudes that the person in the helping/understanding role must genuinely experience as he tries to help and understand the other, and that the other must actually perceive if the encounter is to be effective. The conditions Rogers has identified as essential to this climate are the following: a sensitive and empathic understanding of the client's feelings and personal meanings; a warm acceptance of the client as a person; and a realness and genuineness on the part of the person in the helping or understanding role.

To gain a fuller sense of what these conditions mean, let us look at them in greater detail.

Empathy

One of the most important conditions identified by Rogers as essential to helping and understanding another person is empathy. By empathy, he means our capacity (and willingness) to understand the inner experience of the other person—to understand, through his eyes and from his frame of reference, what the other person is saying. Developing this sense of empathy means trying to understand thoughts and feelings as if we were the other person, and trying especially to capture the quality of the *feeling* that the other is expressing, be it fear, anger, anxiety, frustration, or excitement. Empathic understanding of this kind requires that we temporarily let go of our own frame of reference as an evaluative outsider and try to get into the other's inner world as he experiences it.

The value of empathic understanding in our ability to understand another's point of view is fairly obvious. If we have succeeded in listening and responding empathically, we have, almost by definition, succeeded in understanding the other's point of view. This does not necessarily mean that we agree with what the other person has said; only that we genuinely understand what his point of view is and how he feels about it. Less obvious, however, is the importance of empathy in helping the other person understand himself better. Rogers hypothesizes that the more empathic our understanding (and the better our ability to reflect that understanding to the other person), the more able and willing the other person will be to explore his own inner meanings in further depth, whether these meanings be feelings, assumptions, perceptions, or insights. If the other person feels that his meanings have been accurately understood, he will begin to trust us and the process enough to explore those meanings in greater depth—perhaps to the point where he can bring into his awareness meanings that he may not have fully understood in the past. Another way of saying this is that when a person feels truly "heard" by another, he becomes more willing to listen to himself, and therefore more willing to explore his own underlying assumptions and conflicts.

Unfortunately, empathic understanding of this nature is seldom given or received. More often, the type of understanding we give and receive is from an external, analytic, and evaluative point of view—such as, "I understand what's wrong with you, let me tell you how to fix it," or, "If I were you, this is what I'd do," or, "Let me tell you what you've overlooked; where you've been unrealistic," and so on.

This type of understanding usually invites a defensive response, which inhibits further exploration and openness because the other person subconsciously (or consciously) fears our negative judgment and also feels unaccepted at the outset.

If we respond to the other with this kind of evaluative and external understanding, the other person will, quite naturally, shun topics about which he is not certain, for fear that our evaluative responses will leave him feeling incompetent or misunderstood. He will also be less willing to explore topics about which he feels vulnerable, or meanings that he only partially understands, if he senses that we will view them judgmentally from our own external frame of reference. Yet it is precisely those areas—those in which the other person feels most confused, puzzled, or tentative—that he needs the most help exploring. For this reason, empathic understanding facilitates exploration and openness, while responses reflecting our own frame of reference, particularly when it is critical, get in the way of further exploration.

A second reason why attempts on our part to "set the record straight" inhibit exploration is that many people experience these attempts as intrusions on their autonomy and on their right to pursue their own meanings. Also, this type of evaluative understanding often misses the point that the other person is trying to make. Or worse, it misses that which is truly central to what the other is experiencing, because what he is trying to say to us gets filtered out by our own screen of assumptions about what we think ought to be important. This is not to say that we should not have our own point of view, or that we should not at some later stage in the conversation share it with the other person. Rather, it is to say that while we are trying to help the other person, empathic understanding facilitates exploration, whereas responses that reflect our own point of view impede it.

One of the reasons we tend not to listen empathically is the fear that if we are truly open to how another person experiences a situation, we run the risk of having our own view changed. And to keep our view from being changed, we may distance ourselves from the other's inner world by making sure that what he says or feels is screened through our own set of assumptions. But really sensing another's world is one way to change our own world and allow ourselves to grow richer in meanings. Thus, an additional advantage of understanding with empathy is that it provides the possibility that we ourselves may be enriched by the encounter.

Empathic understanding may at first sound like a very tough condition to meet, and perhaps, for some, even a bit bizarre. However, I think that if you look at your own past experiences when you were in a "client" role, you will find that you have been most open with people who offered you empathic understanding. My guess is, you will also find that they are the same people who were most helpful when you were trying to work through an important dilemma or problem. Empathic understanding is so powerful that even when a person tries, but only partially succeeds, in being empathic, the mere attempt is often enough to free up communication. Perhaps this is because the attempt is in itself an expression of respect for the other person's view, a statement of caring for him and his situation, and, most important, a desire to truly understand him.

Acceptance

This sense of caring is related to a second condition postulated by Rogers, which can be described as "acceptance." Another term often used to describe this is "unconditional positive regard." The more able we are to accept the other as a person and accept what he says about himself and his situation, the better able he is to accept himself, good and bad, and the freer he becomes to explore his meanings in greater depth. Acceptance can be thought of as having two interrelated aspects to it. One has to do with genuinely caring for the other person and his situation and having this caring in the encounter. Rogers has used the term "prizing" to describe this caring, saying that it has "somewhat the same quality of feeling that a parent has for his child, prizing him as a person regardless of his particular behavior at the moment."[3]

The second aspect of acceptance is that the caring is as unconditional as we are capable of providing—that is, that we allow the other to explore his thoughts and feelings without our passing judgment on what he says or feels during the process. Acceptance is an expression of a basic underlying caring for the other that is not contingent on what he happens to be saying at the moment. This sense of caring is an important part of why the other can trust the relationship as a means for exploring his own thoughts and feelings. It is part of a climate of "safety" enabling him to take the risk of exploring feelings that he may not be fully aware of himself, or that he may find difficult to admit having. In this regard, acceptance is related to empathy, because it means allowing the other to express himself freely without fear of being contradicted or punished. It means neither approving nor disapproving of what the other person is saying at the moment he says it, but instead, deeply respecting his right to feel and think as he does even when his feelings are different from our own. This is a *very* important distinction, because offering a person acceptance is not the same as agreeing with him or telling him he is correct. It is simply accepting him and what he expresses in the present as having value and relevance to him.

What Acceptance Is Not. In this vein, it is useful to talk about what acceptance is not. If acceptance is not approval, *acceptance is not neutrality* either, in the sense of having a neutral attitude toward the other. We are neutral only in terms of not taking a position on the other's values, as we try to understand what they are. But we are *not* neutral in terms of our concern and caring for him as a person.

[3]Carl Rogers, "The Interpersonal Relationship," *Harvard Educational Review,* Special Issue 1962.

Similarly, *acceptance is not tolerance,* or simply putting up with what the other says. Acceptance involves actively trying to understand what the other person is trying to say. Finally, *acceptance is not sympathy* in the sense of feeling sorry for or pitying someone. Acceptance is responding nonjudgmentally while showing caring in a way that tells the other that it is all right for him to express his ideas and feelings, even when you (and even he) may wish they were different or less painful.

One of the reasons acceptance is so important in a helping relationship is that it enables the person in the client role to reduce his defenses. The acceptance he is given frees him of the fear of being judged negatively for what he might say and enables him to relax his defenses and overcome his own blocks around self-judgment. When he has experienced us as accepting his thoughts and feelings, he becomes more able to accept them himself, including those parts of himself that he sees as good *and* bad. Having accepted these feelings and thoughts as real, he will begin to accept other aspects of himself that he may previously have only partially allowed into his awareness. The more he is able to accept these aspects of himself, the deeper he can explore his needs, conflicts, and feelings, and the greater will be his insight and understanding into himself and his situation.

Congruence

A third and very important condition identified by Rogers as essential for understanding and personal growth is what he calls "congruence" or "realness." Rogers hypothesizes that we can help another person explore and develop his own thoughts more freely if we are "real and who we truly are" with that person. Being genuine is another way of describing this condition, not hiding behind a "front" or façade, or "putting on" a role. Congruence occurs when what we overtly express to the other person (verbally and nonverbally) is consonant with what we are actually experiencing internally at that moment, and when we are aware of what we are feeling. In a sense, it means allowing the other person to "see" into us. When the other person experiences us as being congruent, he knows who we are in that moment and senses that we are not intentionally hiding anything. As a result, he feels that he too can be congruent in exploring himself and that we can be trusted as a companion in that process.

Although this notion of congruence may at first seem radical, all of us have in one way or another sensed its quality in our everyday life. Most of us know people with whom we are seldom open because they always seem to be operating from behind a role or façade, or because they say things we know they do not really feel or believe. We cannot trust them, because we do not know who they really are or where they truly stand. Because of their lack of genuineness, we intuitively respond by being guarded and seldom seeking them out on personal matters.

The importance of congruence extends to the expression of negative as well as positive feelings. Being congruent means not only expressing feelings of warmth or concern, but also owning up to feelings of anger, puzzlement, or boredom. Incongruence is especially apparent when a person feigns interest or caring that he does not really feel. I have had the experience of hearing a person tell me how interested he was in understanding my point of view or in helping me with a problem, and then seeing his words betrayed by his nonverbal behavior as he scanned the papers on his desk in distraction or stifled a yawn. My impulse under those circumstances is either to say something dramatic to capture his attention or to withdraw and take my concerns elsewhere. I have also had the experience of sensing another person as real in the moment and trusting him because I knew where he stood and sensed that he was not "playing games" with me.

It is not simple to achieve congruence in our behavior. Nor is it desirable to blurt out every impulsive feeling or judgment that crosses our mind under the guise of being congruent. *Congruence occurs within the context of what is taking place and what we are aware of.* It is a condition that is seldom totally achieved, and it is especially difficult to attain when we disagree with the other or when what the other is saying threatens us or raises our defenses. This is why being congruent with another person requires that we be in touch with our own feelings and assumptions and recognize when they become barriers to our ability to really hear the other.

As later readings will discuss, it is neither possible nor desirable to be fully congruent with all people, at all times, in all situations. However, congruence is a condition that is very important in situations where two people wish to understand or help each other, and when both want the relationship to persist over time and be a source of personal growth.

Rogers has stated that congruence may be the most important of the conditions he describes as necessary for a helping relationship. He has described it as being so important that when we cannot achieve the other conditions and also be congruent, it is better to be genuinely ourselves than to pretend these other conditions. For instance, in personal life, this may mean that there are some people whose point of view we find virtually impossible to understand because of the negative feelings we experience in their presence. It is important to be aware of these feelings and the limitations they place on our capacity to empathize and accept the other person. The dilemma, of course, is that it is often under these circumstances that mutual understanding is most needed. Oftentimes, an attempt to simply hear out the other person and refrain from negative judgment is a way of beginning a process in which acceptance, empathic understanding, and congruence can develop over time.

On several occasions, I have had the experience as a consultant of trying to initiate such a process between managers. These were situations in which the people involved held such strong negative feelings about each other that it was almost impossible for either party to be fully congruent except in a destructive way. However, they agreed to make an attempt to try to improve the situation by simply hearing each other out while refraining from making negative judgments of each other. Over time, as each person's understanding of the other's point of view grew, their negative feelings receded to the point where they were eventually able to work effectively with each other. However, there are also situations in which the legacy of past animosities is so deep and painful that even a process as gradual as the one just described is insufficient. But even in cases this extreme, an attempt to initiate such a process is useful and often leads to personal growth as well as increased interpersonal effectiveness.

The importance that Rogers attributes to congruence should not be interpreted as suggesting that empathic understanding and acceptance can be dismissed as peripheral conditions. Indeed, the extent to which we *truly want to* and attempt to display them often affects how congruent we can be with another person. If the desire to try to empathize and accept is real enough, the resulting behavior is usually experienced as congruent.

SOME ADDITIONAL POINTS

We have discussed Rogers's conditions for a helping relationship and some of the premises that underlie a client-centered approach to understanding another person. At this point, let us consider some of the ramifications of what we have covered thus far.

First, it is important to point out that the conditions we have just reviewed have pertained to us as the person in the understanding/helping role, or in terms of the attitudes we should attempt to develop if we are trying to understand or help another person. We have referred to the other person only insofar as these conditions are apt to influence his self-understanding, exploration, and growth. One condition, however, *must* exist in the other person. The other must *perceive* the conditions we have described as being present in us and in the relationship. In other words, he must *actually experience* us as being relatively congruent, empathic, and accepting in our encounter with him.

This is an important condition to add, because it means that it is possible for the other not to perceive these conditions in us even when we experience them as real and our intentions as genuine. Given this possibility, it is especially necessary to be aware of the other's meanings and how he is experiencing the interaction. For example, it is possible that the other person may perceive our attempt to be accepting and empathic as a lack of involvement or interest, because we are not actively challenging what he is saying; or he may very much want to be told what to do and may resent that we are not giving him direction. Or conversely, he may experience our attempt to be empathic and warmly accepting as being too close and threatening.

Another real possibility is that our attempts at being empathic or nonjudgmental may be perceived as incongruent because these characteristics may be inconsistent with our normal style of behavior. This is especially possible if our general tendency is to be highly judgmental, argumentative, or critical. I might add, however, that in my own experience, when I genuinely feel accepting and empathic, I am rarely experienced as being incongruent by the other person, regardless of how aggressive or judgmental I might normally be in the relationship.

This last possibility has a second implication, which is the importance of being able to create these conditions in ways that not only make sense to us, but also fit with who we really are. This means finding out how *we,* and not some vague copy of Carl Rogers, can listen and respond with empathic understanding, congruence, and acceptance. The process of developing, personalizing, and internalizing these skills will not be without some initial awkwardness. For some, this will be a new way of "being" in a relationship. It should not, therefore, be surprising if your first attempts at it feel artificial, or are experienced by the other person as incongruent behavior on your part. The process of learning any new skill or pattern of behavior is almost always difficult initially, whether it be learning to ski, to play tennis, or to respond differently in an encounter. Only after trying it out, working at it, "playing around with it," and learning these skills will they feel comfortable enough to fit into your natural way of being. In a sense, this initial awkwardness, and perhaps even incongruence, is often a first step before these skills can be internalized in a way that feels personally "right."

This initial difficulty may be further complicated if the orientation described in this chapter requires behaviors and attitudes that are not rewarded by the world in which you live. This is particularly the case in a graduate business school in which verbal aggressiveness and quickness at judging are systematically reinforced, while responsive listening and the simple acceptance of another's point of view are systematically ignored or punished. Unfortunately, graduate schools are sometimes places in which "points are scored" by winning arguments from one's own point of view rather than understanding another's point of view.

Your very ability to be quick-witted, aggressive, critical, and competitive may have been the source of much of your past success and undoubtedly the source of future success as well. Furthermore, it is also likely that the same skills and traits are important (if unconscious) determinants of why many of you went into management in the first place. Yet the ability to listen, understand, and help others is also essential to the quality of living and one's effectiveness as a person and manager. The process of acquiring this second set of skills may require that some of us develop an additional set of assumptions, which may often fly in the face of what we have been taught in the past and also what we have become good at doing. Although these two sets of skills and ways of "being" are not necessarily mutually exclusive (and most people are capable of incorporating both sets within their natural range of behavior), the process of learning them may well be a source of some initial discomfort and difficulty. It will require considerable practice, and some initial awkwardness, in trying out and developing these skills before they can become "yours" and fit into your own distinct way of being in the world.

Chapter Nine

Listing for and Responding to Another Person's Meanings

The preceding chapter described the basic orientation and assumptions of what we have called a client-centered approach. The purpose of this chapter is to help "operationalize" this approach and make it more concrete. We will do this by describing some specific ways of listening and responding to another person that can help the other person explore and develop his meanings more deeply.[1] In a sense, what we will cover can be considered the "technique" that is associated with a client-centered orientation.

The basic technique we will discuss is what counselors and therapists have come to call *reflection*. Reflection is a process whereby one person attempts to reflect back and clarify what he understands another person to be saying. This type of response has the double advantage of providing a way of checking out our understanding of what the other person has said and of helping him clarify what his own thoughts and feelings are, especially those he himself only partially understands.

As you may have already guessed, this type of response also lends itself to developing acceptance of the other person, since good reflection captures the other's meanings and feelings as he is expressing them. It also lends itself to developing empathic understanding, by helping us move into the other person's frame of reference because that is what we are trying to reflect. You may have noticed that we said reflection "lends itself" to developing conditions of empathy and acceptance, not that it necessarily will. Empathy and acceptance (as

[1]For grammatical simplicity, we have used masculine pronouns; however, the comments apply to both men and women.

well as congruence) are attitudes and feelings that no technique alone can create; they exist only if we and the other person experience them. However, because of their nature, reflective responses tend to make it easier for these conditions to develop, and therefore they serve to facilitate communication and exploration.

Before proceeding, it may be useful to point out again that we will be drawing heavily on the learnings of client-centered therapy and on the broader and more recent work of counseling and interviewing psychology. Our purpose in doing this is not to become counselors or therapists, but rather to develop some skills and awareness that can increase our effectiveness in living and working with others.

Our major goal in doing this is *not* to learn the reflective technique, per se. Indeed, it is unlikely that we will use the reflective technique in its "pure" form in most of our normal interactions. Our purpose in focusing on the reflective technique is to use it as a *means* for developing personal skills in listening responsively and responding more effectively. Before we can acquire this sensitivity and skill, however, we must first learn the technique in a more intense way and at a much greater depth than is usually necessary in everyday interactions. Only by our first learning and internalizing reflective responses in a concentrated way will they become a *natural* part of our ways of responding to another person. And only when they have become a part of what we are competently capable of doing can we use these skills in a normal and less intense way in daily interactions. In addition, in-depth knowledge and skill in the reflective technique will enable us to engage others more deeply and effectively on those occasions when it *is* important for us to be able to understand and help in a concentrated and focused way. Thus, our purpose is to master these skills in enough depth so that we can use them to a greater or lesser degree, or with greater or less intensity, as the occasion requires.

It is also important to add that we have intentionally used the term *technique* even though the word evokes a number of connotations that are negative in nature, such as "putting on" behavior that may be unnatural, artificial, or mechanistic. As offensive as these connotations may be, it would be dishonest to use another term. At this stage, that is all that reflection can be to you—a technique. It is not yet part of your natural way of being; you haven't yet made it yours. In fact, your first attempts at being reflective may very well be artificial and awkward. However, after you feel your way into it and learn to be reflective in ways that fit into your own natural style, it should cease to be merely a technique and truly become a personal skill that fits naturally into your repertoire of being with others.

THE SETTING

To put our purpose in further perspective, it is important to add that the kind of situation we are talking about is one in which one person is trying to understand or help another person about a problem, question, or issue that is *essentially personal or human in nature.* This might include work-related problems (such as people having difficulties working together, or a person making a difficult career decision) or purely personal situations (such as those that occur between friends, spouses, or intimates). The kinds of situations we are *not* talking about are those in which the issues are purely technical or intellectual in nature—for example, a situation in which a person is trying to understand how a budget has been put together, or the details of a marketing plan, or when one person is helping another prepare a financial forecast; that is, *if* the issues are purely technical. We emphasize the *if* because even problems we initially see as technical or intellectual are often, on further exploration, found to be rooted in misunderstanding or personal conflict. But much of our day-to-day business of living and working is conducted at a straightforward technical or intellectual level. Purely technical problems are not the kinds of situations in which a reflective technique is useful.

In making these comments, we do not mean to imply that the conditions of a helping relationship (described in the preceding chapter) are not relevant to misunderstandings about matters of substance; only that they do not pertain to them as directly as they do to matters that are mainly personal in nature. However, the *specific types of responses* that we will discuss in this chapter seem in our experience to apply most usefully to interactions in which personal understanding is the major problem, and less so to matters of an objective or nonpersonal nature. Since most of our interpersonal interactions cover a broad spectrum (and mixture) of issues, ranging from the purely technical to the purely personal, one of the abilities we will also need to develop is a sense of when reflective responses are appropriate and when they are not.[2]

We will come back to the applicability and usefulness of reflective responses in a later chapter, after we have gained a better sense of what these responses are and why they are effective. However, before we can do this, we will first have to learn the technique itself and how it "feels" to us. This requires not just learning *about* it but developing skills *in* it as well, which in turn means trying out reflective responses in everyday situations where we are trying to help or understand another person. We cannot know whether a reflective response will "feel" right to us or the other person until we have actually developed and internalized the capacity to respond reflectively. When we have made these skills ours, we will be in a better position to intuitively choose when to respond reflectively and when not to. For the moment, however, let us focus on the first task, that of learning about the technique and practicing it enough so that it does become a part of our own range of natural behavior.

[2]We should note that our view of the applicability of reflective responses differs markedly from that of many others who share a "Rogerian" or "client-centered" orientation, in that we do *not* believe that reflection is appropriate (or even helpful) in all situations.

SOME GUIDES TO LISTENING AND RESPONDING REFLECTIVELY

Perhaps the most direct way of describing the reflective technique is to outline some guides that generally help us listen for the other person's point of view and help us respond to him in ways that facilitate his exploration of those meanings. These guides grow out of a client-centered orientation in that they help us focus on the other person's inner meanings and help us accept and empathize with what he is saying. Although these guides are rooted in considerable research and practice, they are still *only guides.* They are not rules. *These guides should always be considered within the context of what is taking place.*

At the most general level, we can describe reflective responses by several simple characteristics:

- A greater emphasis on listening than on talking
- Responding to that which is personal rather than abstract
- Following the other in his exploration rather than leading him into areas we think he should be exploring
- Clarifying what the other person has said about his own thoughts and feelings rather than asking questions or telling him what we believe he should be thinking, seeing, or feeling
- Responding to the *feelings* implicit in what the other has said rather than the assumptions or "content" that he has talked about
- Trying to get into the other person's inner frame of reference rather than listening and responding from our own frame of reference
- Responding with empathic understanding and acceptance rather than with disconcern, distanced objectivity, or overidentification (i.e., internalizing his problem so that it also becomes our own)

Although these brief generalizations may appear to suggest that reflection requires passive and generally inactive behavior on the part of the person who is trying to help or understand, quite the opposite is true. The reflective technique requires *very careful* and focused listening. It also requires *a high degree of selectivity* in choosing what to respond to in what the other person has said. The importance of this selectivity will become more apparent as we get into the specifics of responding reflectively.

In order to make the language simpler and less cumbersome, we will borrow two conventions from counseling psychology. First, we will refer to the person who is trying to understand or help another person as the "interviewer," regardless of what his real role or relationship might be. In fact, in all the situations and examples described in this chapter, the person designated as interviewer is either a friend, peer, or manager of the person he is trying to understand, and in no case is he an interviewer in the formal sense of the word. Second, we will refer to the person that the interviewer is trying to understand or help as the "client." Again, "client" is used as a convention, and we do not mean to imply that a formal client relationship exists.

With this brief overview as an introduction, let us look at several specific guides to listening and responding reflectively.

Respond to What Is Personal Rather Than Impersonal

The most basic of these guides is to respond to that which is personal rather than impersonal. "Personal" refers to material the other person has covered that is about him as a person rather than about others in his life, or about abstractions, or distant events or situations, or theories. The assumption underlying this guide is that we help the other person explore personal meanings more easily if we respond to what is most central to his self-concept and most directly related to what he is experiencing, rather than what is impersonal or peripherally part of his experience. The difficulty in trying to do this is that often, all of what a person says has at least *some* personal meaning to him, and choosing what to respond to becomes a matter of degree rather than kind.

The following example from a taped conversation may help illustrate what we mean. The interviewer is trying to understand some personal but work-related problems that a woman manager is experiencing in a large bank. The woman has just begun to discuss her situation:

> On the banking floor itself, there are no females that are in officers' positions. Now, in other banks in the country, there are, but not here. And, uh, and it's very difficult for me because the concept they have of me is so . . . well, there just is no concept in most of those men's minds that a woman could actually be on the banking floor, because women aren't supposed to do those things.

All of what this woman has said has personal meaning to her. But some of it is more personal, and some of it is less personal. The most personal aspect of what she has said is that *she* is finding it difficult on *her* bank's floor because the men *she* works with cannot conceive of a woman being in her role. The least personal thing she has said is that there are women in officers' positions in other banks, a statement that obviously also has strong personal meaning to her but is not as immediately personal in her experience as what she says about herself and her own situation.

Responding to that which is *most* personal, her own difficulties in her own bank, is more apt to trigger personal associations about why she feels the way she does than would be responding to the more general problem of sexism in banks, or the situation in banks across the country. An example of a response to the more personal aspects of what she has said might be, "You're finding it difficult working on the bank floor because the men there think that a woman shouldn't be holding a job like yours." In contrast, an example of a response to the less personal aspects of her situation might be, "There are no women officers in your bank," or, "Some banks have women in officers' positions, but not your bank."

In this particular case, the interviewer *did not* respond to her personal situation, and the discussion that evolved went to the more general topic. The woman went on to discuss career paths for women within her bank and banks in general, as well as the larger problems of sex discrimination. She did not, until much later in the interview, come back to discussing herself or her own particular situation in depth. Not surprisingly, she returned to her own dilemma when the interviewer responded to a very personal aspect of what she said later in the interview: She thought that because of her ability, she threatened one of the men on the floor. The interviewer responded to this statement by saying, "So you see him as feeling threatened by your presence there." This more personal response enabled her to focus on her personal situation, triggering important associations about her aspirations, her values about not being too competitive, and a more central issue in her life, the difficulties of having high career aspirations while also having strong needs to establish a satisfactory home life and marriage.

Not until she had begun to explore these more personal aspects of her situation was she able to surface some of her own crucial underlying assumptions about what she had thought she "ought" to do. Once she had surfaced these apparently conflicting assumptions, she was able to discover, on further exploration, that these needs were not necessarily mutually exclusive.

The point here is that when the interviewer responded to impersonal topics, the client stayed at the impersonal level. But when the interviewer responded to personal material, the client explored the personal aspects of her own situation and eventually surfaced some very important ambivalences and assumptions that she was not even aware of having.

Respond Rather Than Lead

A second guide is to respond rather than to lead—that is, respond to the other person's associations and train of thought rather than leading him in other directions.[3] By responding, we mean reacting to what the other person has said from his frame of reference, so that we help him build on his own thoughts and feelings. By leading, we mean reacting to what the other person has said by directing him into areas that we think he should explore. When I respond to what someone has said, I speak to him in terms of whatever thoughts and

[3]This discussion of responses and leads draws heavily on the distinctions made by Benjamin and Rogers. See Alfred Benjamin, *The Helping Interview* (Boston: Houghton Mifflin, 1969), Chap. 7, "Responses and Leads"; and Carl Rogers, "Releasing Expression," in *Counseling and Psychotherapy* (Boston: Houghton Mifflin, 1942).

feelings he is currently exploring or discussing, rather than in terms of my own ideas on the subject. When I lead, I take charge by directing him to areas that *I* think he should explore. To illustrate the difference between leading and responding, let us look at an exchange between two managers. The two men are peers, and one of them wishes to understand why the other is contemplating a transfer. The man in the understanding/helping role we have called "Interviewer," and the one contemplating the transfer we have called "Client."

Client: . . . and so I feel caught in the middle between [the sales vice-president], who wants me to work on next month's problems, and [the marketing vice-president], who wants us working on a new format for a five-year market plan and on a new [product] line. So a transfer to corporate planning would get me out of this mess. . . . But if I did that, I wouldn't be doing what I originally came here to do [Interviewer: "I see."], which was to develop a first-rate market planning group. So that's not a satisfactory solution either. And in a way, I'd be abandoning ship.

Interviewer: Well, how does Tim [the company's executive vice-president] feel about it? He must have some ideas about it.

Client: I don't know. I doubt if he's even aware of it.

Interviewer: Maybe you should talk to him about it.

Client: Yeah, I suppose I could, if I approached it the right way.

Interviewer: How about your group? They must also feel pretty [angry] about it. At least, George must.

Client: Yeah, he does, but he doesn't really understand all the var— — all the factors in it. The other guys see it as, uh, harassment from the sales division.

Interviewer: Hmmm. Maybe you should talk to them about it. It might help you get a better idea of . . .

Client: [Interrupts.] They're not a problem, they'll work well whatever the conditions. They're good people. I'm the one who doesn't like it.

Interviewer: I see. Yeah, I see. It's really a problem, isn't it? [Pauses.]

Client: Have you got any other ideas?

Interviewer: Well, let's go back to what you were saying about the transfer. Do you think you'd like it in corporate planning? I mean, you know, you wouldn't be running your own group. . . .

Although the material above is only a brief excerpt from this conversation and is not a verbatim transcript, it captures some of the quality of what happens when the interviewer leads during the early stages of an exploratory session. Notice that the interviewer's leads increasingly move the client away from what he was originally exploring—his own personal feelings of being in a bind and the unsatisfactory nature of a transfer to corporate planning. Notice also that after several exchanges, the client has put the initiative for further exploration on the interviewer, by saying, "Have you got any other ideas?"

The ball is now in the interviewer's hands. And in a sense, the interviewer asked for it by leading the conversation. Finally, the interviewer (perhaps realizing that his digressions did not help) goes back to what the client was originally talking about—the transfer. But even here, the question is framed from the interviewer's point of view: "I mean, you know, you wouldn't be running your own group." In phrasing the question this way, the interviewer is implicitly making a value judgment about "being in charge of your own group" that is in itself a lead. It implies that the client ought to view "being in charge" as desirable.

During this entire exchange, all the interviewer's leads miss the opportunity to explore in greater depth why the client feels in a bind and what his deeper feelings and assumptions might be about himself and his situation. The reason is that the leads were from the interviewer's frame of reference, and they directed the conversation to what the interviewer was interested in, rather than the thoughts and feelings the client was in the process of developing.

A more useful response on the part of the interviewer might have been simply, "So neither alternative feels good. You feel in a bind in your current job, but being in corporate planning is not what you really wanted to do when you came here." This simple reflective response would have enabled the client to build on and further explore his own thoughts and feelings. It would also have helped the interviewer get a better idea of what was actually bothering the client. (Why did he feel in a bind? Why did he see a transfer as "abandoning ship"?) The session between these two men did not last very long; it ended once the person in the interviewer's role ran out of ideas to explore. Neither of the two people found the session very helpful or satisfying.

Questions and Answers

As the discussion above about responding rather than leading suggests, the use of questions can actually impede the process of understanding and exploring.[4] Questions are usually direct leads and can be damaging to the process if they point to specific areas, diverting the client's attention from his own thoughts and feelings. Usually these questions lead the client into areas that the interviewer is interested in but that may not be relevant from the client's point of view. Questions from the interviewer's frame of reference can be especially hindering when the client is trying to develop or clarify his own thoughts and feelings.

I have often sat through meetings in which the interviewer's questions actively prevented the other person from giving the relevant

[4]This discussion on the use and misuse of questions draws heavily on the work of Bruce Shertzer and Shelly Stone, "Counseling Techniques and Practices," in *Fundamentals of Counseling* (Boston: Houghton Mifflin, 1974), and also Benjamin, *The Helping Interview*.

answers. This was because all the questions were from the "asker's" frame of reference, and the "asker" did not know enough about the other person's situation to ask relevant questions. In most of these situations, the questioner would have received his answers more quickly and with less frustration if he had just shut up and listened long enough to hear how the other person described his situation. Questions can be particularly troublesome in the early stages, when the person trying to understand or help has not yet gained a sense of how the other person sees his situation or problem. The conversation referred to above is an excellent example of this.

Second, questions also put the initiative on the person in the interviewer's role. Again, the preceding conversation is an excellent example of this. If enough questions are asked in succession, the client will begin to sit back and simply wait for the next question rather than take the initiative of exploring his own thoughts and feelings. The exchange then often develops a rhythm of question-answer, question-answer, question-answer, somewhat like a Ping-Pong match. Once this tempo has been established, it is usually difficult for either the interviewer or the client to break. Since only the client has access to his own inner meanings and associations, such question-and-answer sessions usually stay at a superficial level and deal with only what is obvious. They are also often characterized by a certain sense of randomness and a "hit-or-miss" flavor.

A third problem with questions is that if they are asked suspiciously (or are perceived to be), they arouse defensiveness in the client. Questions, by their very nature, seem to require that the other person not only give an answer but also justify it. Thus, questions can subtly act to introduce an element of evaluativeness and defensiveness that detracts from empathy and acceptance and impedes open communication and exploration.

A particularly troublesome question is the simplest one of all: "Why?" Given our backgrounds and cultural conditioning, the question "why?" begs for justification. It invites defensiveness, since the client assumes that his answer must appear rational and clear to the interviewer. And it is particularly in those areas that the client needs most help that he is least able to give rational answers without deeper exploration. The problem is that once this defensiveness develops, it gets in the way of the client's ability to explore the very issues about which he is unclear or troubled.

Related to this is the difficulty that some questions are simply unanswerable. Or at least, they are not easily answered, because the important factors are too complicated or ambiguous in the client's mind. Thus the question "why?" (which implies a rational reply) raises defenses that impede the other person's ability to explore these very factors. This is especially the case when the "why?" has to do not with rational factors but rather with feelings or events that are emotionally charged. This is why, for example, children, when asked why they act a certain way or why they like a certain thing, sometimes reply, "Because." Their reasons cannot be expressed in rational terms.

As a general guide, it is safer to avoid asking questions when trying to understand or help another person, especially when we do not yet have a full sense of how the other sees his situation. Under some conditions, a question can be very useful, and we will return to the use and misuse of questions in greater detail in a later chapter ("The Reflective Technique in Broader Perspective"). But for the moment, let us consider the use of questions a type of lead that often impairs understanding.

Respond to Feelings Rather Than Content

Perhaps the most important guide in responding reflectively is to *respond to feelings rather than content.* By feelings, we mean emotions such as anger, fear, puzzlement, anxiety, confusion, ambivalence, tension, joy, elation, and so on. By content, we mean ideas, thoughts, assumptions, philosophies, theories, descriptions of events or places, and the like. Rogers has described the process of responding to feelings as being a central aspect of understanding another person and helping that person understand himself.[5] Like the tenet, "The client is the best guide," the importance of responding to feelings rather than content is borne out by much research and practice by psychologists of many different orientations. In this regard, it is not a tenet (like "Respond rather than lead"), espoused only by a client-centered approach. It is an assumption implicit in almost every major theory of therapy, counseling, or helping relationships, including the classically Freudian, psychoanalytic, Gestalt, and "directive" approaches. The fact that it is held by so many different approaches is evidence of the universality of its power in facilitating the exploration of personal meanings.

Furthermore, responding to feelings is a more direct route to uncovering *relevant* underlying assumptions than is the seemingly more direct approach of asking questions about assumptions. There are many reasons for this apparently paradoxical situation. Perhaps the clearest explanation has been offered by Rogers: that responding to expressed feelings is the most direct way of triggering associations about material that is *emotionally relevant* to the client. And if the problem is personal and emotional in nature, then these are the associations that matter. Emotionally charged assumptions or conflicts are more apt to surface in the client's awareness by a response to the feeling tone of what the client says than by a response to his content and ideas. It allows the client to acknowledge the power of his feelings, thereby enabling him to move on to those factors in his life that are most closely associated with his feelings, be they assumptions, perceptions, or other feelings. The point is that when we respond to feelings, the client's explorations develop in directions that are *emotionally relevant* to him, often surfacing assumptions, needs, or other thoughts of which he may be only partially aware.

An example. For purposes of illustration, let us go back to the conver-

[5]Rogers, "Releasing Expression."

sation between the woman banker and the person she was talking with (a man who was a friend of hers but not employed by her bank). Later in this conversation, the woman begins to explore some of the conflicts between the roles of wife and banker as traditionally defined by our culture, and how they affect her life:

Client: . . . and you just wonder what the value is of doing this bang-up job and being this great banker [Chuckle], you know, and then a year, five years later, having children and all of a sudden leaving it completely. And I really wonder if I'm pursuing the right thing or putting my time into the right places. [Interviewer: "Um-huh."] And I don't know how much of a change it is. I don't know if it's so important to me or the way I would be fulfilled to have a housekeeper or governess or something like that, and go to work every day. I don't know if this is part of the way I can satisfy myself, or if I should do it to feel fulfilled.

Interviewer: But right now, your work is important to you 'cause you don't have any children, you don't have home responsibilities during the day.

Client: Right. [Pause.]

Interviewer: So your work is very important to you now, and this is the way you approach it.

In this exchange, the client first expresses feelings of ambivalence about the importance of being "this great banker" in the context of what it will mean to her if she later has children. She further expresses a sense of ambivalence, or at least concern, about whether she would find it fulfilling to have a housekeeper take care of her children. The interviewer's response, however, fails to recognize either her feelings of ambivalence or those of concern and internal conflict. Instead he responds to content—her current responsibilities. Indeed, he does so in a way that subtly implies, "Yes, but don't worry about these feelings; they're not an immediate problem." Then, with his second response, he virtually denies her feelings of ambivalence by concluding (from his point of view), "So your work is important to you now, and this is the way you approach it." By responding to this rather than her feelings of ambivalence, he has cut off the opportunity for her to explore what underlies these feelings. Furthermore, he tacitly suggests that she should not feel bad about her ambivalences, as if to say, "That's OK, they'll go away."

Not surprisingly, the client does not explore what underlies these partially expressed ambivalences, because they were never acknowledged (and were in fact denied) by the interviewer. Immediately after the interviewer's last response above, the client and interviewer went into a long and detailed discussion of the woman's boss, her relationship with him, and again back to the general situation in the bank.

Not until later in the interview does the woman return to her ambivalence.[6]

Let us compare the exchange above with one that took place later in the interview, in which the interviewer *does* respond to feelings. The client has again begun to discuss the ambivalence she had started to express earlier:

Client: [She has been talking about her boss, strategies for dealing with him, the bank, etc.] And that is more complicated as well. The whole idea of me having a little home life is not something I dreamed up by myself. That was dreamed up by society. And so I'm sort of encumbered by the idea of what I think I should be doing. I don't know if I should really be doing it, and Bill's [her husband] really good, 'cause he helps me with everything, and we really do share things pretty evenly. But I sort of feel I'm neglecting him. I don't feel like I'm really doing my part if I'm not here to make dinner on most nights or that kind of thing, which is not right. I should feel that I can do pretty much what I want to do, but you have the fine line of where you decide. [She goes on to describe a specific situation where she felt like a wife who was simply "tagging along."]

Interviewer: You feel a dilemma here not only at work, but you're also questioning how much you support your home life with Bill.

Client: Right! But I think that's something that you just have to work out—what you two expect from your marriage. I don't think it will become really a problem until I decide to have a family, and then I'm going to have to really make . . .

Interviewer: You feel a conflict between a career and family.

Client: Yes, and that's when I'll have to really make some big decisions, because I feel that if you're going to have children, you really have to give them your all; and if you're going to have children, you ought to do a good job with them, and they're not just little nothings. They're human beings, and they require an awful lot of time and love and care. And I don't know if they can get really what they need in a few hours when you come home at night, not seeing you all day long. And if both the husband and wife are that way, I don't know if they are being brought up as best as they could be. But when it's your child, I think you are inclined to give them the love and attention they need, as opposed to a housekeeper, who I don't think would have quite the amount of con-

[6]It may be worth noting that central issues usually resurface over and over again in an encounter of this kind, even when the interviewer does not respond to them. The reason for this continued resurfacing is that these feelings are important enough to the client to have multiple associations, and thus the client keeps coming back to them. The value of responding to feelings rather than content is that these feelings can be explored much more directly and, in a sense, effectively.

cern. . . . But I just think, at least at this stage, it would be a real drag to have kids. [Both laugh.] It's a big step when I decide to do that, because of how I really feel about children.

Interviewer: You want to do a good job in both areas.

Client: Um-hum.

Interviewer: Both your job or career goal and also your children.

This exchange provides an example of where the interviewer *did* respond to the client's feelings, thereby helping her explore them and their underlying causes. After this exchange, the client went on to explore in greater detail the fact that she did hold conflicting assumptions about raising children and having a successful career. She then went on to realize that she is more introspective about these matters than she thought. She more carefully questioned her assumptions about having to spend all her time with her children and realized that being a full-time housewife would be so stifling to her that she could not do it with fulfillment (further challenging what she had earlier expressed as an important assumption). Having reached this point in her exploration, she was able to recognize the importance of banking and success to her self-concept, and the need to think about having children as less of an "either-or" proposition. Eventually, she concluded that preparing herself to do both could be an evolutionary process in which banking did not necessarily preclude satisfaction in both areas.

In the context of the total interview, her initially unexpressed ambivalence about banker versus mother/wife roles emerges as being of far greater importance and a far deeper source of anxiety than her work-related problems, although both problems were related to the common theme of sexism in the traditional definition of male-female roles. But once she had been able to explore and tentatively resolve this underlying ambivalence, the work problems receded in importance and became more manageable in her eyes. One reason for this might be that much of her anxiety (and perhaps even guilt) over the more basic issue (banker versus mother) had been confused in her mind with some of the real aspects of her problems at work. Once these were acknowledged and explored, it was possible for her to sort them out and deal with them separately.

We can learn several things from this exchange. One is that the client could not have dealt with the underlying causes of her ambivalence until her feelings of internal conflict had been expressed and responded to. When the interviewer failed to respond to these feelings earlier in the interview, the client did not feel free to explore them. When the interviewer was able to recognize and respond to them later in the interview, his responses enabled her to explore her underlying assumptions and expectations in depth, eventually allowing her to recognize the sources of her conflict, and finally allowing her to arrive at a resolution.

Second, neither she nor the interviewer had any conscious awareness that this ambivalence even existed when they began the interview. It was only through a process of associative thinking, in which important feelings were acknowledged, that the ambivalence emerged into its full (and central) importance. Had the interviewer stayed at the content level, it is unlikely that these feelings and their underlying sources would ever have surfaced. It is also important to add that although this conversation was less than 45 minutes in length and that the interviewer was, like us, a layman and not a professional counselor, he was able to help her significantly. He was also able to increase his own understanding of her as a person. For example, he had assumed that she was a fully liberated woman who had already worked through conflicts about professional versus mother roles. Perhaps this assumption was one of the reasons that he was unable to respond to her early expressions of ambivalence—because they were so inconsistent with his prior conception of her. It is also important to add that the interviewer's eventual responses to feelings were sufficiently effective to make the total session very helpful even though he had in several other places directed the client, responded to content, and missed feelings.

Difficulties in Responding to Feelings. There are several difficulties to be overcome in responding to feelings. The first is that most of us are trained to listen for ideas and thoughts rather than feelings. Thus we are, in simplest terms, not cognitively as good at recognizing feelings as we are at hearing content. In addition, feelings tend to be viewed in our culture as "untouchable." We associate them with embarrassment, either to ourselves or to the other person, or as something that should be dealt with only in private. This is particularly the case with negative feelings, such as shame, guilt, fear, or anger. Thus, in normal conversations we try to smooth over negative feelings that someone has expressed. They make most of us uneasy. Similarly, we correctly associate feelings with what is emotional rather than rational, and we are, for obvious reasons, more comfortable with what is rational. The catch is that most problems in interpersonal relations are emotional. They become rational only when we have understood the sources of the feelings. But our tendency to avoid feelings often prevents us from getting to the underlying causes.

A second difficulty with responding to feelings is that they are seldom expressed explicitly; they are almost always expressed in the context of content—a situation, other people, and so on. For that reason, it is necessary to listen for the *feeling tone* of what is being expressed. For example, in the excerpt above (where the banker expresses her ambivalence over career versus family), she never explicitly says, "I'm ambivalent," or "puzzled," or "conflicted." But a reading of the excerpt suggests clearly that she is. We sense the feelings of ambivalence from what she has said and how she has phrased it. A more obvious example where feelings are not explicitly expressed but can be clearly inferred is the following excerpt from a different conversation:

> . . . And after the meeting, the bastard told [the boss] about the problems we were having, even though he promised he would do everything he possibly could to help relieve the pressures on us. Especially the pressures

we're getting from the brokers, which he knows the boss is really sensitive to. . . .

It does not require great insight or perceptiveness to recognize that implicit in the feeling tone of the passage above are two loud feelings: anger and a sense of betrayal. Usually, the feeling tone of what another person is saying is not as easily discernible as in this example. Hearing and capturing the feeling tone of what a person has said requires very careful listening and the ability to keep track of both ideas and expressed feelings.

In a later chapter, we will describe in more detail some of the problems of "over-" and "underreaching" in responding to another person's feelings and their effect on the process. For the moment, let us conclude by saying that responding to feelings rather than content is a *very* important aspect of a reflective technique. Responses to negative feelings or feelings of ambivalence are especially effective, because they help the client focus on sources of underlying internal conflict. Since positive feelings are not usually related to problem areas, responding to them is generally less effective in helping the other person explore problems.

Other Functions of Responding to Feelings. The discussion above has tried to show how and why responding to feelings is a more direct route to exploring important assumptions than is responding to content. There are several other reasons why responding to feelings rather than content facilitates exploration and understanding. One is that feelings simply *are.* Feelings, once acknowledged, are nondebatable. If a person feels ambivalent or angry or anxious, the fact that he feels that emotion is not subject to question in the same way that a thought or idea might be. The person is simply feeling what he feels. The reasons he feels this way may be debatable, in that his interpretation of the cause may or may not be correct. But because the feelings themselves simply *are,* the client does not feel required to justify or defend what he has said, as he might if the interviewer responds to an assumption.

Another function of the acceptance of feelings is that it enables the client to express and acknowledge the feelings and therefore to proceed to explore why he experiences them. Oftentimes, the acceptance of feelings is experienced by the client as "freeing." Once he has owned up to a feeling, he no longer has to defend against it. The accompanying release of expression (sometimes referred to as catharsis) does not occur because the client has solved a problem or fixed anything. Rather, it occurs because he has unburdened himself of the need to defend against the feeling. No longer needing to suppress the feeling, he experiences a release of tension. The psychological energy that went into keeping the feeling in check now becomes available for exploring the internal and external sources of that feeling. In this sense, the expression of feeling often acts to reduce barriers in the way of deeper and freer self-understanding.

THE SELECTIVITY OF CLIENT-CENTERED RESPONSES

As the discussion above of reflection as a technique suggests, responding to a client's meanings is a highly selective process.[7] It is by no means a passive, nondirective, or uninvolved process on the part of the person who is trying to help or understand. Responding reflectively requires *very careful and intense listening* and attention to what the other person is trying to express, and an *equally careful selection of what to respond to.* In order to provide a systematic review of this selection process, we have summarized the guidelines to reflective responding and listening in Exhibit IV-1.

Although we believe that this simplified diagram is a good summary of the selectivity required to facilitate understanding, we want to emphasize again that these are guides and not rules. These guides have emerged over time, based on considerable experience, but their power lies only in the service of understanding another person's meanings. They should always be considered in the *total context* of what is important to the other person as he describes his situation. There may be times, for example, when what the client says about a situation or about another person is of central importance to him—more important than what he is saying about himself. Such meanings should be responded to and should not be ignored. Similarly, there are also occasions when it is very important to the other person that we understand the content of a particular situation (although this is usually because the content is associated with strong underlying feelings). In these cases, an attempt should be made to capture a sense of both the content and the feeling of what he has said, and where possible, to clarify the relationships between what he has said and why it is important to him.

BEGINNING THE PROCESS OF PRACTICE

Exhibit IV-1 summarizes several of the most important guides to listening and responding reflectively. The purpose of these guides (and therefore this chapter) is to provide a starting point from which to actually begin to practice reflection as a technique. Only through practice and experience will these guides really come alive, and the reasons for their effectiveness become apparent.

All first attempts at anything new tend to be somewhat awkward or unnatural, and it is likely that your initial attempts to use these guides may also feel (and may be perceived as being) a little artificial. For some of us, this initial awkwardness may be enough to leave us feeling

[7]We are particularly indebted here to the ideas presented by Arthur N. Turner and George F.F. Lombard, in *Interpersonal Behavior and Administration* (New York: Free Press, 1969), Chap. 7, pp. 305–6.

EXHIBIT IV-1

The Selective Process of Listening and Responding to the Reflective Technique

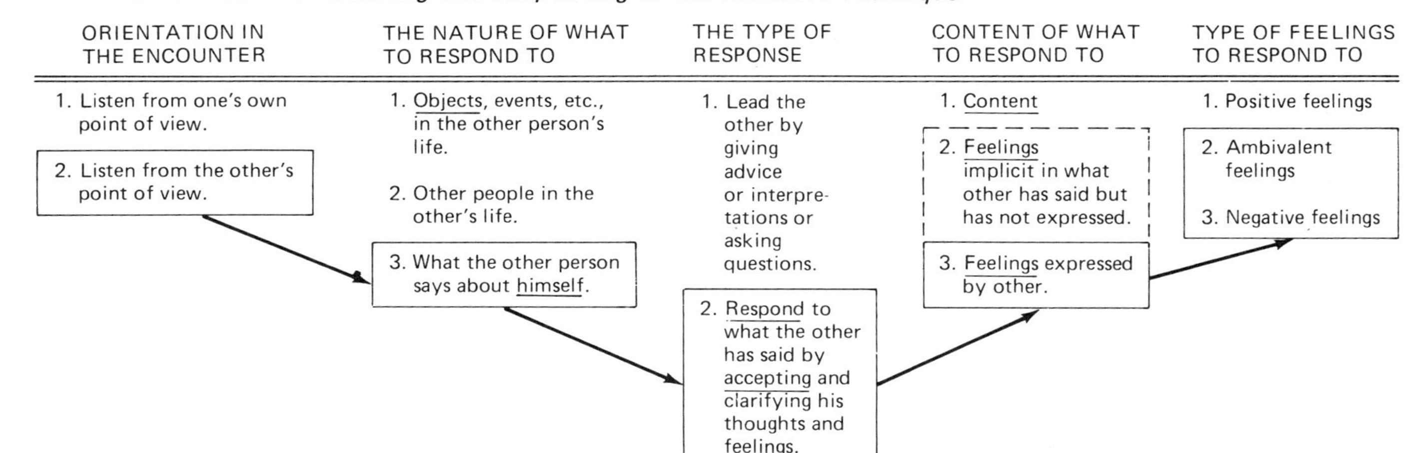

ORIENTATION IN THE ENCOUNTER
THE NATURE OF WHAT TO RESPOND TO
THE TYPE OF RESPONSE
CONTENT OF WHAT TO RESPOND TO
TYPE OF FEELINGS TO RESPOND TO
1. Listen from one's own point of view.
2. Listen from the other's point of view.
1. Objects, events, etc., in the other person's life.
2. Other people in the other's life.
3. What the other person says about himself.
1. Lead the other by giving advice or interpre-tations or asking questions.
2. Respond to what the other has said by accepting and clarifying his thoughts and feelings.
1. Content
2. Feelings implicit in what other has said but has not expressed.
3. Feelings expressed by other.
1. Positive feelings
2. Ambivalent feelings
3. Negative feelings

This is a modified adaptation of schemes presented in Arthur N. Turner and George F. F. Lombard, *Interpersonal Behavior and Administration* (New York: Free Press, 1969), "The Counseling Process," p. 306; Bruce Shertzer and Shelley Stone, *Fundamentals of Counseling* (Boston: Houghton Mifflin, 1974), Chapter 7, "Counseling Techniques and Practices," p. 277; and Lawrence Brammer and Everett L. Shostrum, *Therapeutic Psychology* (Englewood Cliffs, N.J.: Prentice-Hall, 1968), "Reflective Relationship Techniques," pp. 194-98; and of course, Carl Rogers, *Counseling and Psychotherapy* (Boston: Houghton Mifflin, 1942), "Releasing Expression."

(or appearing) slightly incongruent. Thus, a paradox: Our initial attempts at beginning to respond in a client-centered way may violate one of the conditions described by Rogers as essential to a client-centered approach—congruence. But again, this is part of the learning process. As you become more skilled at hearing and responding reflectively, these responses will become better integrated with your natural style, and as this integration develops, your initial feelings of incongruence will recede.

You may find it useful to begin by responding reflectively during a normal social conversation for only a couple of minutes, to get a sense of the technique and how it feels to you. Then, as you gain comfort and ease, try increasing your ability to be reflective in normal conversations until you build enough confidence to ask some people if they will allow you to practice this technique with them, with the intention of trying to understand them or their situation better from their point of view. Try several such practice interviews in which your expressed purpose is to develop skills in listening and responding reflectively. The more experienced and practiced you become, the more natural and appropriate your use of reflective responses will be in normal, everyday encounters.

Chapter Ten

Degrees and Kinds of Reflective Responses

The two preceding chapters concentrated on describing and making more concrete some ways for improving our ability to understand or help another person. In particular, the chapter on "Listening for and Responding to Another Person's Meanings" outlined several guides for listening and responding reflectively and described in some detail the selectivity implicit in the reflective technique. We have not as yet, however, said anything about the specific types of responses that fall under the general headings of "reflective technique," or the degree to which different types of responses can vary in their depth of clarification or reflection.

The purpose of this chapter is to describe several different kinds of reflective responses and how they vary in their intensity and depth. After we have reviewed these various responses, and their limitations and strengths, we will then look at several problems that people often encounter when they first begin to use a reflective technique. Finally, we will discuss some ways of dealing with these problems.

KINDS OF REFLECTIVE RESPONSES AND THEIR DEGREES

Responses generally categorized as reflective can vary considerably in their depth of response and in their ability to clarify or surface underlying meanings and feelings. The most direct way of describing the range of possibilities is to review several types of reflective responses in terms of the depth to which they respond to what the other person has said. You will probably realize that you have already been using most of these responses in your attempts to practice reflection.

Simple Phrases That Affirm Contact

These are simply responses that tell the other person that we are listening and that we understand what he is saying.[1] Examples of such responses might be simply, "Uh-huh," or, "I see," or, "Yeah," or, "Yes, I see what you mean." Their purpose is to affirm contact and can often, depending on the accompanying nonverbal behavior, express empathy, acceptance, caring, and interest. They are especially useful when the other person has begun to explore his thoughts and has not yet framed them for himself or for us.

Paraphrasing Expressed Thoughts and Feelings

These are responses that capture in our own words what we understand the other person to be expressing. Paraphrasing is most useful when we want to check out our understanding of what the other is saying, especially when he is having difficulty putting his meanings into words or when he is expressing partially developed thoughts or feelings. Paraphrases also serve the purpose of affirming contact and telling the other that we are trying to understand. Again, depending on our tone of voice, facial expression, and other nonverbal behavior, paraphrases can also help build a sense of empathy, acceptance, and especially caring and interest. One of the characteristics distinguishing a paraphrase from other reflective responses is that it reflects only what the other person has said *explicitly*.

Clarifying Implicit Thoughts and Feelings

This type of response, in contrast to paraphrased reflection, goes beyond what the other person has explicitly said; it tries to clarify thoughts and especially feelings that are implicit, not explicitly stated. Clarification takes place when what is implicit has been responded to in a way that makes it clearer to both the other person and to ourselves. However, when we use a clarifying response, we work off of what we think is *in the other person's awareness,* even though he may not have made his thoughts or feelings explicit.

Responses that clarify can be much more powerful than those that simply paraphrase, because clarification helps the other person focus his awareness on what he is saying in a way that sharpens his own understanding of underlying thoughts and feelings. Clarification is also more effective than paraphrasing in helping the other person

[1]For grammatical simplicity, we have used masculine pronouns; however, the comments apply to both men and women.

because it triggers important associations related to what he is trying to explore. Clarification is especially effective because it gives the other person the sense that he is truly being heard and understood; that we are paying attention to what he is saying, and trying to understand what he is experiencing.

Clarification can also be of value when we as the interviewer are confused or unclear about what the other person is trying to say. Clarification provides a way for us to gain a clearer understanding without directing or threatening the other person through the use of specific questions.

Reflecting "Core" Feelings Not Completely Expressed

This type of response goes beyond clarification (which responds only to what is in the other person's awareness). When we reflect core feelings, we respond to feelings that we think are at the core of what the other person is expressing, even though they may be *only partially in his awareness.* Such responses can be especially helpful to the other person in surfacing feelings and assumptions of which he is only dimly aware, thereby enabling him to understand more clearly aspects of his situation. They can also facilitate exploration of new areas, or facilitate insight. They are often experienced by the other person as a "breakthrough" that helps him recognize some aspect of his experience that may previously have been unclear to him. Such responses can also help the other person pull together conflicting thoughts in a new way, so that he can make new meanings and explore them more deeply.

Problems of "Overreaching." There are, however, several potential problems with responses that attempt to reflect "core" feelings. Such responses should be used with great care and only when a strong sense of empathy, acceptance, and congruence has already developed in the encounter. One problem with reflecting core feelings is that although *we* may be certain that these feelings exist, the other person may not be able to recognize them as real because they are not in his awareness. Sometimes this occurs because important defenses (which should be respected) prevent him from allowing these feelings into his awareness. When this is the case, there are two dangers. The first is that the other person will feel misunderstood and begin to question our capacity to understand his meanings as *he* sees them. Second, he may experience our response as going too far, or to use Rogers's term, as "overreaching." If this is the case, he is apt to feel that we are taking undue liberties in making our own meanings from what he has said.

Also, it is possible that even if the core feeling *is* in his awareness, he is not yet ready to confront it or explore it. This may occur when the other person is threatened by the core feeling, or when he needs further exploration before he is able to accept it himself. When this is the case, a typical reaction is for him to become defensive and withdraw, or go to a content level and distance himself from the feeling.

When this has occurred, we have overreached in a way that, at least for the moment, impedes further exploration or openness. For example, the following exchange.

Client: . . . So if Mary [the client's wife] takes this job [as a consultant], it will require a lot of, uh, readjustments. And I'm not so sure how they'll work out. Like, for example, we'll both be traveling, and a lot of times we won't see each other for a week at a time. And then there's always the possibility that, uh, you know, she'll have an opportunity for a better assignment in another office. Like Chicago, for example, where they tried to hire her in the first place because they don't have any women with her kind of experience there. And also, what if *I* get a chance to go to Los Angeles, which any promotion in the company is bound to lead to, then, what does it mean for me? Do I turn it down? You know, it could be a real disaster.

Interviewer: It sounds like her taking the job is, uh, really threatening to you.

Client: What do you mean, threatening? No, I don't think it's threatening. It has problems for both of us, but threatening, no. There are some things we could do to work it out. [Pause.] Like, uh, you know, well, there are things that can be done. It wouldn't threaten me.

Notice that in this exchange, the client quickly backed off from the idea that his wife's job offer threatened him. *If* the client was, in fact, threatened by his wife's job offer, he was certainly not yet ready to deal with it. Under these circumstances, the client will react to the overreaching by denying the feeling and defending himself. If, on the other hand, he is *not* feeling threatened (or at least not at a conscious level), then his response would be one of surprise and defensiveness.

Often, a direct and honest way to deal with a situation in which we have overreached, as in the excerpt above, is to acknowledge that we may have gone too far in stating our understanding of what we thought the other person was expressing, and try to recapture what he was saying prior to our overreaching.

A final danger with reaching too deeply is that it may be a subtle way for the interviewer to lead under the guise of being reflective. Again, another example from the preceding conversation may help:

Client: . . . Well, two people traveling, that's bound to . . . just has to create some strains on a marriage. Mary will be gone three or four days at a time, and, uh, everything will depend on those times when we're both in New York at the same time.

Interviewer: Yeah, I see. Sounds like maybe you're wondering about what she'll be doing when she's traveling.

Client: What do you mean by that?

Interviewer: Well, you know, she'll be on her own. . . . She'll have to spend a lot of time working with other men, and after hours talking with them—things like that.

Client: That doesn't bother me.

Interviewer: Oh, I see, that doesn't . . . that wouldn't bother you.

Client: No, it wouldn.'t.

Here is an example where the person in the interviewer's role is actually leading, although what he says is phrased as a response. He is leading into an area that perhaps he feels is bothering the client, based on his intuition and knowledge of the other person. But in doing this, the interviewer goes far beyond what the person in the client's role has actually expressed. Often, this kind of overreaching occurs because the interviewer is leading the client into an area that the interviewer is interested in exploring. Clearly, the effect of the interviewer's responses in both the excerpts above was to impair further openness or exploration on the part of the client, unless a very great deal of trust, empathy, and acceptance already existed in the relationship.

For these reasons, it is especially important to be careful in reflecting what we perceive to be core feelings that are not fully in the other's awareness. Although the potential usefulness of reflecting core feelings can be great, the dangers and risks involved in overreaching can be equally damaging.

Problems of "Underreaching." Not so clear as the problems of overreaching, but almost as important, are the problems created by underreaching. By underreaching, we mean consistently missing expressed or implicit feelings, or responding in a way that understates the feeling. Underreaching also occurs when we respond to the content of what the other has said rather than its feeling tone. Continued underreaching usually results in a situation in which the material being explored stays at a superficial or obvious level, unless the person in the client's role is especially open or insightful.

A process of sustained underreaching can also result in a certain amount of circularity in what the client talks about, so that the exploration seems to be going nowhere, or in circles. We will discuss this problem of "looping" later in this chapter, but the following may give a sense of how underreaching causes "looping" and superficiality in the exploration. (The responses in this excerpt are numbered because we will refer to them later.)

Client 1: Every time he comes into the office, I can't help it, but it makes me anxious. Anxious as hell. . . . Maybe it's because of what happened at Palm Springs last May, I don't know, but I get all tight.

Interviewer 1: It bothers you when he visits the office.

Client 2: Yeah, it does, damn it. I get fidgety, and when I do, so do the analysts—they can tell it. Last Tuesday is a case in point. By the time we finished, I needed a drink. I was so anxious by the time I got home that Sue asked me what was wrong.

Interviewer 2: Hmm. Makes you feel uneasy.

Client 3: Yeah. . . . I can never tell what he's thinking. He looks around but never says anything. He only asks questions. It leaves me really uptight.

Interviewer 3: He just asks questions.

Client 4: Yeah, just questions. No way of knowing what's on his mind.

Interviewer 4: No feedback, no nothing. . . . Just nosing around.

Client 5: Right, no feedback. [Pause.] Thing is, I wish I knew why he gets to me that way. . . . It's not just lack of feedback.

Interviewer 5: It really bothers you.

Client 6: Yeah, it really bothers me.

Interviewer 6: Makes you feel uneasy.

Client 7: Very uneasy.

Interviewer 7: Probably makes other people feel that way.

Client 8: I don't know. Maybe. Chris doesn't seem to be bothered by his visits . . . but then they're involved mainly with lending. Lending is more straightforward.

Interviewer 8: Yeah, more straightforward than analysis.

Client 9: Hmm. Maybe that's it.

Interviewer 9: The way he comes around makes you feel uneasy.

Client 10: It's more than that. It rips my gut. I begin to wonder about where I stand. Where is it all going? I knew [the firm's] style is different from [where he worked before], and that there would be, uh, risks in coming here despite all the assurances that [the firm's president] gave me. So sometimes it's like, well, driving in a fog. . . . You can barely see the road. . . . Like I ask myself, am I playing a different game from everyone else? Are they all playing tennis while I'm playing squash? It gets scary as hell. I wonder if . . . well . . . it's too late, anyway.

Interviewer 10: No feedback then, he gives you no feedback.

Client 11: That's part of it. People want to know where they stand.

Interviewer 11: That makes you uneasy.

Client 12: Yes, it does, very uneasy.

Interviewer 12: Hm, sounds like it bothers you a lot.

Client 13: Yeah, it does.

Interviewer 13: Not comfortable.

Client 14: Right, not comfortable.

Although this exchange can hardly be called unproductive, since it has raised a number of issues for the client, one cannot help but sense a certain amount of redundancy and incompleteness in it. A more detailed examination of this exchange may help to explain why.

Throughout all of it, the interviewer systematically underreaches or misses feelings.

For example, even in I1, which is perhaps the interviewer's best response, he understates the client's expressed feeling of "anxiety" in C1, by responding with the words, "bothers you," which are much lower in feeling tone than the word "anxious." Nonetheless, the response was reflective enough for the client to reexpress in C2 his feelings of anxiety, which he again explicitly labels as such. However, in I2, the interviewer again responds with the understatement, "uneasy." Had he reflected the full sense of the client's anxiety, the client might have been able to explore the sources of his anxiety more deeply. However, even with the interviewer's low-tone response, the client proceeds to explore lack of feedback and expresses feelings of being "uptight" in C3. However, in I3 the interviewer responds to the content of "he just asks questions" and again misses the client's feelings of anxiety. The next several responses (through I5) focus on lack of feedback, again missing the feeling tone. In C5, the client suggests that the problem is more than just lack of feedback. But in I5, the interviewer goes back to "bothers you," again underreaching the client's sense of puzzlement. Again, in I5 through C7, the exchange is stuck at the now-obvious sense of "uneasiness." This circling continues until C10, when the client finally corrects the interviewer by saying, "It's more than that. It rips my gut." Then the client explores feelings of not only uncertainty about where he stands but also implicitly expresses doubt about whether he made the right decision in joining the firm.

In fact, the client goes so far in C10 as to describe his feelings as "scary." But the possibility of helping the client explore these feelings and their underlying sources is missed entirely when the interviewer responds to content in I10, "no feedback." I10 misses not only the feelings of anxiety and fear but also those about uncertainty and inner conflict. None of these feelings or their underlying causes are explored, as the interview goes back to the more superficial discussion of feeling "uneasy," "bothered," and so on, which is where the exchange began. Subsequent to this exchange, the conversation moved on to a prolonged discussion of a content nature about how the firm is organized. The opportunity for the client to explore the sources of his anxiety and conflict in greater depth was lost.

We should point out, however, that even though this interview did not go as far as it could have in either helping or understanding the client's situation, it *did* help the client raise a number of issues in his own mind. Although the interviewer's underreaching helped create a situation in which the client's exploration became "stuck," the effects of his underreaching were not as damaging as those cited in the earlier examples, where the interviewer overreached and led. The reason is that even though the interviewer may have missed expressed feelings, his responses did not threaten the client. It is very likely that the material that surfaced in the client's mind during this session stayed with him, and that he was able to explore it further on his own.

Silence as a Response

The one response we have not yet discussed is silence—not saying anything at all.[2] The absence of a verbal reply is in itself a response, and one that can be powerfully effective when the other person needs to *stay with* his own developing meanings or feelings and fathom them more deeply. The effective use of silence as a response depends very much on the context of what the other person is experiencing at the moment and what has preceded in the encounter.[3] Silences can be experienced by the other person in many different ways, depending on the context, movement, and feeling tone of the conversation. For example, a silence can be experienced by the other person as a form of acceptance if our facial expression and other nonverbal behavior suggests that we understand that he needs to pause to think for a moment or to simply "sit" in his feelings. Conversely, a silence can also be experienced by the other person as negative and rejecting. This type of silence can communicate to the other person such feelings as, "OK, go ahead, try to get out of that one," or, "What you've said is so stupid that I can't even comment on it." Note, for example, the use in everyday language of the expression, "the silent treatment." Again, the way in which a silence is experienced by the other person depends on the nonverbal cues we give, the amount of trust that has developed in the encounter, and the context of what has preceded in the conversation.

For example, silence can be experienced as either a *sign of embarrassment* or as a *source of embarrassment.* This may be especially so when a silence occurs early in a conversation and the other person has only just begun to explore his meanings. Under these conditions, a silence may be felt as conveying the message, "Well, what else do you have to say?" or, "I have no way of responding to what you have just said." Experienced in these terms, a silence will be a source of embarrassment to the other person and perhaps even a source of anger.

Silence as a response is most useful when we sense that the other person has stopped because he needs to think about what he has just said, or when he has difficulty expressing what he is thinking and needs to explore it further in his mind because it is too powerfully loaded. Under these conditions, responding with silence, or with a simple phrase that affirms contact, tells the other, "It's OK, go ahead and take the time you need to think (or feel) it out." It allows him the psychological space he needs to stay with his own thoughts and feelings and explore them more deeply, or to simply feel a powerful feeling.

When Silence Is Useful. There are many different ways of being silent, and silence can be useful for many different purposes. As we have

[2]This discussion draws heavily on Benjamin's work on the stages of an interview, and Shertzer and Stone's work on techniques and practices. The interested reader can find a more detailed and especially useful discussion of the use of silence as a technique in Alfred Benjamin, *The Helping Interview* (Boston: Houghton Mifflin, 1969).

[3]Benjamin, *The Helping Interview.*

just said, silence is most helpful when the other person needs to sort out his thoughts and feelings. This type of silence needs to be respected; it is more beneficial than many words we might be able to conjure up.[4] Or a silence can be useful when the other person simply needs to be quiet and absorb what he has just said, and silently explore its implications for him. This is especially so when he has surfaced an important feeling that he had not previously allowed into his awareness, such as a sense of fear, despair, anger, confusion, or tragedy. And silence can also be a useful response when the other person finds himself really confused and needs the time to untangle his thoughts.

Responding to a Silence. All our remarks have thus far discussed silence as a response, noting that it is most helpful when we sense that the other person needs to stay with what he has just said. Usually, it is a silence on the *other person's part* that tells us we too should remain silent and not interfere with his train of thought. There are of course other ways of responding to silence on the client's part, such as trying to clarify what he has said, responding to its feeling tone, or reflecting what we think are his core feelings.

In general, however, when the other person suddenly becomes quiet and introspective, it is safest to respond with a silence or some simple phrase or expression that affirms contact. *After* the other person has had a chance to stay with these feelings and mentally explore them, there are several responses that can help him verbalize what he needed to sort out. One is a response to the implicit feelings that we think are the reason he became quiet and introspective. An example of such a response might be, "It must have been a really painful experience," or, "It's really a tough problem, isn't it?" When the source of the other person's silence is confusion, a helpful response may be to help structure the situation for him by trying to clarify what we have understood him to be saying.

There are, however, other reasons why the other person may become silent. Silence can also be a sign of resistance. The other person may stop talking because he is resisting exploration of further feelings, or he may feel that we are probing beyond what he thinks is appropriate. Silence can often be a client's reaction to overreaching on the part of the interviewer. When this is the case, the best response is to back off to a point that restates what the client had explicitly expressed before we overreached. This will often serve to reinitiate the process.

In summary, silences occur for many different reasons and should be responded to in the context of what we think the other person is experiencing. As a response, silence tends to be most helpful when the other person needs time to consider what he has just said, and it tends to be least useful during early stages of an encounter, when it may be a source of mutual embarrassment. We might add that silence is not an easy response for most of us, especially given the premium

[4]Benjamin, *The Helping Interview.*

that most educational institutions place on being verbally active. Our natural tendency is to jump in and fill the silence with something that "fixes" it, makes it better, or provides an answer. It is especially difficult to remain silent when the other person is experiencing or quietly exploring *powerful* feelings. The other person's discomfort tends to make us feel uncomfortable, and our reflex action is to say something that soothes the other person or, even worse, denies him his feeling.

Nonverbal Responses

The discussion above of silence highlights the importance of nonverbal behavior when we are trying to understand or help another person. Nonverbal behavior, such as facial expression, posture, and tone of voice, is far more powerful in communicating acceptance, empathy, and congruence than verbal behavior is, and also much less easy to fake. Our "presence as a person" is very important to a reflective technique. Some would argue that it is more important than specific verbal responses in facilitating openness and exploration. That is why initial attempts at a reflective technique often look very awkward on a written transcript, but turn out to be very productive in their reality. Despite our awkwardness with the verbal aspects of the technique, the other person experiences our intentions as genuine and takes the risk of exploring personal meanings with us. I have had the experience of observing managers whose actual verbal response patterns defy all the guides to verbal responses that we have outlined in this chapter, but whose "person" and nonverbal behavior create a sense of trust, congruence, empathy, and acceptance that transcends their verbal responses. When this type of nonverbal behavior is combined with a reflective response pattern, then the growth and exploration that take place can be especially effective.

PROBLEMS IN USING THE REFLECTIVE TECHNIQUE

Before leaving our discussion of reflective responses, let us cover several problems that are often encountered when people first attempt to use a reflective technique.

Looping

One of the most common of these problems is what we will refer to as "looping." Looping occurs when the other person keeps coming back to the same theme, or seems to be "stuck" in his exploration. We have already discussed one of the causes of looping under the topic of underreaching. We will not go over this dynamic again, except to say that consistent underreaching inhibits the other person from exploring his meanings more deeply, and thus the exploration stays at a superficial or content level. The frequent use of simple affirmatory phrases, such as "um-hum" and "yes," also contributes to looping unless they are accompanied by responses that clarify or reflect core feelings. One of the ways to break out of this kind of looping is to reach deeper in responding to feeling, or to attempt to reflect and clarify rather than simply paraphrase.

Paradoxically, looping also occurs for just the opposite reason: because the interviewer consistently overreaches in his responses. Under these circumstances, looping occurs because the other person is not ready to accept our overreaching and keeps moving back to a lower feeling tone that he may find more acceptable, or diverts the discussion to a safer, content level.

Finally, a third reason for looping is that the person may not feel satisfied that he has finished with the topic around which he is looping, yet he is unable to explore it further. In this case, it is not just the process that is stuck, but also the client himself. Under these circumstances, it is sometimes helpful to reach deeper in attempting to reflect and clarify the meanings the person is "stuck" on; or conversely, to simply stay with him.

Depth of Response

Directly related to looping is the problem of responding to the other in such a way that what he has said is clarified, not simply repeated.[5] Reflection of feeling is an attempt by the person in the interviewer's role to express *in fresh words* the essential *attitudes and feelings* expressed by the client.[6] The use of the word *fresh* is important, because it is our ability to capture in a different way what the other person has expressed that allows him to not only accept it but also to move beyond it and trigger new associations. This is why simply repeating what the other has said or using simple paraphrases often contributes to looping. Repetition of what the other has said usually does not help him clarify his thoughts further, and it may be greeted with a reply such as, "Isn't that what I just said?" or, "What's wrong with the way I said it?"

Using Stereotyped Responses

Another problem that sometimes occurs when one first attempts to use a reflective technique is "stereotypy," or using stereotyped responses over and over again, such as, "You feel that . . .," or, "I hear you saying that . . .," or, "What you're saying is. . . ."[7] The repeated

[5]We are heavily indebted to Brammer and Shostrum's clarification of this as a classic problem in the reflective technique.

[6]Lawrence M. Brammer and Everett L. Shostrum, *Therapeutic Psychology* (Englewood Cliffs, N.J.: Prentice-Hall, 1968), Chap. 7, "Reflective Techniques."

[7]Brammer and Shostrum, "Reflective Techniques."

use of the same phrase often arouses feelings of resentment on the part of the other person and the suspicion that we are "playing a game" with him, or are "head-shrinking" him. It can also be experienced by the other person as being "mechanistic," so that he ends up feeling that we are not really interested in what he is saying, but are just going through the motions of hearing him out.

Selection of Feeling

A very difficult problem in responding to feelings is selecting the feeling to respond to. There are two difficulties associated with this: First, most of us are not accustomed to listening for feelings or feeling tone, and it takes some practice before we are even able to "hear" feelings. Second, when we do become good at hearing feelings, we discover that the other person may be expressing several different feelings in what he is saying. The question then becomes which of the expressed or implied feelings to respond to. We have already said that it is usually more effective to respond to and to surface negative and ambivalent feelings. However, oftentimes the other person is expressing several negative feelings simultaneously, such as anxiety and anger, or pain and fear. The best guide under these circumstances is to respond to the feeling we think the other person is experiencing most powerfully. We should try to choose, from among the feelings and ideas that the other person expresses, those that have the strongest quality of feeling and are in greatest need of clarification.

Again, effective use of the reflective technique is not a passive or inactive exercise. To use the technique effectively, we must be able to listen hard and select from among the many possible meanings those that will further the process most effectively. It is, of course, not always possible to do this, especially in the context of a quickly moving flow of ideas and feelings. But the ability to hear and quickly respond effectively develops with practice.

Timing

Another problem associated with our initial difficulty in hearing feelings is the timing of our responses. Since we are slow at hearing feelings, we may initially lag behind the other person in responding to them simply because it takes us a while before the feelings finally "register" inside us. This sometimes results in our being out of phase with the other person. We may realize that we have missed an important element of what the other person has said only *after* we have already responded to something else. When this occurs, our tendency is to ignore what the other person goes on to express and then, at our first opportunity, go back to the feeling we had previously missed. This makes the exchange disjointed and can leave the other person wondering if we are really listening to him.

A second problem associated with timing is that when we first attempt to respond and listen reflectively, we are often afraid to interrupt the client to capture his feelings. We assume that we must wait for him to stop or pause before we can respond. The problem here, of course, is being able to discriminate between occasions when our response will interrupt unproductively because it disrupts the other person's flow of thought, and those when our response intervenes in a useful way so that it clarifies what he is saying. When in doubt, it is generally safest not to interrupt, but instead to continue to listen.

Telling a Response From a Lead

Another problem in first attempting to use a reflective technique is discriminating between a response and a lead. This is more difficult than it may sound at first. Part of the difficulty lies in our natural tendency to lead rather than respond, a tendency that is reinforced by the fact that most normal conversation is an exchange of initiations between people. In our early attempts to respond rather than lead, we may discover that what began as response ends up as a lead. But, again, that is part of the learning process.

Second, it is impossible to sharply define the difference between a lead and a response.[8] A lead may have been meant as a response and interpreted as such by the other person. We may also lead in response to what another person has said by asking a question that helps clarify an issue. The important point is not whether our reaction is technically a lead or a response, but rather whether it responds to the other person's meanings, relates to his frame of reference, and helps clarify his thoughts and feelings. Although it is important to know when we are responding and when we are leading, there is little need to be pristine in the purity of our wording. It is far more important that our reaction capture, reflect, and clarify the other person's thoughts and feelings and contribute to a climate of empathy, acceptance, and congruence.

Responding within the Context of the Other Person's Expectations

In using reflective responses in everyday interactions, an important problem is that they need to fit within the context of the other person's expectations. If a person approaches us and clearly expects a direct answer to a question, then his expectation that the question be answered is a part of the reality that cannot be ignored. If we feel that we do not know enough about how he sees his situation to answer his question, then we should say so, and ask him to talk about his situation further. A reflective response that would clearly *not* be appropriate under these circumstances would be, "You want me to tell

[8]Benjamin, *The Helping Interview,* Chap. 7, "Leads and Responses."

you what I think about? . . ." The other person's reaction would be, "Of course, that's what I just asked you."

It is likely that once the other person begins to talk about how he sees his situation and what is important to him, we can begin to respond reflectively in a manner that is not out of context with what would typically be normal behavior.

"Head Scraping" and "Head Shrinking"

Another fear (and possibility) is that our attempt to respond reflectively will be experienced by the other person as a "head scrape" or a "head shrink," so that the person feels he is being "psychologized." This is a real possibility if our responses are highly stereotyped, or if we are overreaching beyond the material the person feels comfortable in sharing. It is also apt to occur if we don't really care about what the other person is thinking and feeling, so we are giving all "technique" and no caring.

My own experience has been that when we do care and listen carefully, the other person seldom feels he is being "head-scraped" or manipulated. Instead he feels heard, helped, and understood.

The Uneven Exchange

Related to this is a fear that when we respond reflectively, we are not holding up our end of the conversation—that the other person is doing most of the talking and that we are only responding. We tend to think that we are not contributing our fair share, that the other is doing all the giving and we are only taking.

This can sometimes become a real issue in a situation where our main purpose is to gain a better understanding of the other person's point of view. Under such circumstances, it can be helpful and also make us more congruent if we share our own feelings with the other person. However, what usually occurs when we really listen hard and respond reflectively is that the other person *does not* experience a sense of "uneven exchange." Indeed, he usually feels that we are giving quite a lot. People are so seldom truly "heard" by others in our culture that when we do listen responsively to another person, we are giving him something that he rarely enjoys: undivided attention, caring, and understanding. Students are often surprised at the end of a practice interview to have the other person thank them for the experience (when, in fact, the student should be thanking the other person for allowing him to practice the technique). The student is being thanked for what he has given: careful listening, understanding, and oftentimes help.

This aspect of the "exchange" extends far beyond practice interviews. In most real-life situations, especially those in which another person is seeking help, our ability to hear and respond to the other's meanings is a large enough contribution to more than equalize the exchange. From my own experience as a consultant, I have come to believe that one of the reasons managers hire consultants is not so much to get answers as it is to have someone to talk to who will listen carefully and with whom they can safely explore their own doubts and problems.

When we succeed in listening and responding to another person's meanings in a way that helps clarify them in his or her own mind, we are giving a very rare gift. There is no need to feel guilty about an "uneven exchange."

Chapter Eleven

The Reflective Technique in Broader Perspective: Directive as Well as Reflective Leads and Responses

All the chapters in this section of the book have focused on the client-centered approach as a way of understanding and helping others. If you have tried practicing a client-centered approach, you have probably begun to master the reflective technique and have developed some skills in listening and responding to others. For most of you, the acquisition of these skills has been accompanied by a growing intuitive sense of when reflective responses are appropriate and when they are not, particularly in the realm of normal conversations or encounters. By now, you have probably also begun to develop a feel for the power and limitations of this approach, as these skills become better integrated into your own personal style and way of being with others.

The purpose of this chapter is to address more explicitly the question of appropriateness. Specifically, we want to explore in greater depth two questions:

1. When is a reflective mode of responding and listening useful and appropriate, and when is it less so?

2. What are some alternative ways of responding that are not reflective but that may also be useful; and under what circumstances are these more directive responses appropriate?

In addressing these questions, we will broaden our focus from the kinds of encounters that have understanding or helping as their *expressed* purpose (such as your practice interviews), to include also those in which the possibility for deeper understanding or helping occurs within the context of a normal interaction or conversation. We will also begin to think less in terms of specific responses and more in terms of "modes of responding." By a mode of responding, we mean the *general tendency* that characterizes a sequence of responses as we talk to another person, whether or not all the specific responses in that sequence are "purely" reflective or "purely" directive. Normal conversations evolve and develop over time; we may wish to respond directively at a certain point in a conversation and then later shift into a more reflective way of responding. For example, we might respond in a reflective mode in the middle of a normal conversation for as short a time as five minutes, or engage another person reflectively for as long as an hour.

Let us begin by outlining some of the conditions under which responding in a reflective mode is apt to be more appropriate and useful.

WHEN ARE REFLECTIVE RESPONSES MOST APPROPRIATE?

We have already learned that listening and responding reflectively are most useful when the expressed purpose of an encounter is to understand another person as he sees himself or his situation; or when our purpose is to help another person understand himself, his problem, or an internal conflict more deeply.[1] But what about conversations that do not begin with this as an explicit purpose?

In our experience, there are two useful questions that can be asked in deciding whether or not to move into a reflective mode of listening and responding.

Whose Point of View? The first of these questions is, "From whose point of view do I want to understand what is going on in this conversation?" If the answer to this question is, "I'd like to understand the other person (or what he is saying) better as *he* sees it," then moving into a reflective mode is not only appropriate but also the most effective way of responding. However, this answer begs the more basic question, How do we know when it is important to better understand the other person's point of view, especially in the context of a normal social or business exchange? There are several circumstances under which it is important to gain a better understanding of the other person's point of view:

- When we sense that we do not fully understand why the other person feels or thinks the way he does, and we would like to learn more about how he experiences his situation.
- When we sense that there is more to what the other person is saying than what he is expressing or has been able to surface; or when we sense that what is *not* being said is more important than what *is* being said.

[1]For grammatical simplicity, we have used masculine pronouns; however, the comments apply to both men and women.

- When the other person appears to be so confused or conflicted that we cannot understand his situation or the problem he is describing without first helping him sort it out.

We might add that these conditions apply not only to conversations as they evolve and develop; they are also useful as guides in an ongoing relationship. For example, think back to the Neely and Chapman cases; all these conditions would have applied to the relationship between these two men. Had one of them been able to respond and listen reflectively during their difficulties, it is likely that at least one if not both of them would have gained a better understanding of the complexities of the problems in their relationship. Even if this understanding had not been enough to save their partnership, it would at least have enabled them to know why they were having problems working together.

Who Owns the Choice? A second question to ask, especially in a situation where another person has come to us for personal help, is, "Who owns the choice?"[2] By this we mean, Whose problem is it, and who has to make the decision? Is it the other person's, or is it ours? If the other person is seeking help on a personal decision that only he can make, then responding in a reflective mode is not only appropriate but also most likely to be effective in helping. This is because reflection will help him better explore his situation, and will give us a better understanding on which to base any advice we may subsequently wish to give.

A good example of this kind of situation is the vignette described in an early chapter about the senior partner and her junior associate. Only the junior associate can make the decision of whether or not to move to an East Coast office or stay in the Midwest. And only he must face the personal and professional consequences of that choice. All that the senior partner can do is help her subordinate make the best choice possible. This requires self-exploration on the part of the associate and in-depth understanding on the part of the senior partner. Both these processes are facilitated by listening and responding reflectively.

Other Circumstances in Which Reflective Responses Are Appropriate

In addition to those above, there are several other conditions in which responding in a reflective mode can be helpful. These circumstances go beyond the simpler situation in which the other person clearly "owns" the problem or choice.

When both you and the other person share the "choice" or problem, and

[2]We are especially indebted to Eileen Morley for making this distinction in determining whether a reflective mode of responding is appropriate in a helping relationship.

you cannot give useful advice or take reasonable action without first understanding how the other person sees the situation. An example of this would be two peers or partners making a joint decision that will influence both of them personally. Another example is a situation in which a boss is helping a subordinate explore possible alternatives for his next assignment.

When the "choice" or problem of concern is yours, but your decision is likely to affect the other person. In this type of situation, it is often important to understand how the other person sees himself in the context of the current situation, so that you can anticipate how your decision might affect him. An example of this would be a manager contemplating an organizational change that would affect the satisfaction of his peers or subordinates and thereby the effectiveness of the change. In this case, the manager would do well to ensure that he understands how "important others" see the situation. Listening and responding reflectively would be very useful even though the final decision rests with the manager, and in that sense, the "choice" is the manager's and not the other person's.

WHEN ARE REFLECTIVE RESPONSES NOT APPROPRIATE?

There are many circumstances in which moving into a reflective mode in the middle of a normal conversation would not be appropriate.[3] We will cover only some of the more obvious ones, with the assumption that a person's intuition in a given context is generally better than a detailed list of guides. The following are several circumstances in which responding in a reflective mode would *not* be appropriate:

- When it is our role and the other person's expectation that we give direction, and not doing so would be an abdication of personal responsibility. An example of this is when a person comes to us to get advice on a straightforward substantive matter and we have the information to give him. An extreme example would be someone's asking for data that we have and that he needs to make a third-quarter forecast. A reflective response to this request, such as, "So, you're concerned with the third-quarter forecast," would be experienced by the other as ludicrous.

- When another person has come to seek personal advice and we have reached sufficient depth in our understanding of how the other person sees his situation to give reasonable counsel or direction. The roles and responsibilities of managers are such that a manager must often be able to respond with clear and sound advice on these occasions. The other person may choose not to take the advice we offer, but the expectation that a friend, colleague, or senior should be willing to offer advice (if he can) is realistic and appropriate. This is especially the case for managers who are asked for counsel by peers or subordinates on problems that are both

[3]We feel the need to point out again that, unlike many others who share a client-centered orientation, we do *not* believe that reflective or client-centered responses are appropriate, or even helpful, under *all* circumstances.

personal and professional in nature. A manager's ability (and willingness) to give good direction is part of what makes him effective. It is also one of the reasons that others have seen fit to invest him with influence and status.

• When the purpose of an exchange is to openly debate an issue, so that each person's views must withstand the test of his adversaries. (But even here, reflection is often useful in clarifying what the other person's point of view actually is.)

• When our own views on what emerges in a conversation are so strong that they prevent us from hearing what the other person is saying because we are so distracted by our own thoughts and feelings on what he has already said.

• When our feelings on what the other person has said are so powerful that an attempt to respond in a reflective mode would greatly exceed our capacity to be congruent, and the other person would experience our behavior as deceitful, fraudulent, or greatly out of character.

THE FULL RANGE OF RESPONSES AND LEADS

We have just focused on the appropriateness of *reflective* modes of responding. Let us now broaden our perspective to also include *non-reflective* responses and leads, and address the question of when they can be useful in helping or understanding another person.

Exhibit IV-2 lists several general types of responses and leads that we use in everyday life, ranging from the most client-centered to those that are most directive and most nearly from the interviewer's frame of reference.

More specifically, the responses and leads of Exhibit IV-2 have been ranked in terms of the degree to which they are from the client's frame of reference rather than the interviewer's, the extent to which they follow rather than lead, and the degree to which they are accepting rather than judgmental. (We will again be using the terms *client* and *interviewer,* according to the convention used in earlier chapters. In the following discussion we will also use the term *client* interchangeably with *the other person,* since we will be looking at leads and responses from the perspective of the person in the interviewer's role.)

With the exception of the two extremes, "Silence" and "Commands or threats," Exhibit IV-2 includes most of the responses and leads we commonly use in interacting with the people we work and live with. These responses and leads have been broadly classified into ranges of "Reflective responses" and "Directive responses," with an overlapping "Middle range" that can be classified as either directive, reflective, or both, depending on how they are used. The category "Question" has been used to mark the transition point in the range, because questions can be asked either in response to what the client has said or as a lead from the interviewer's frame of reference.

Exhibit IV-2

Responses and Leads

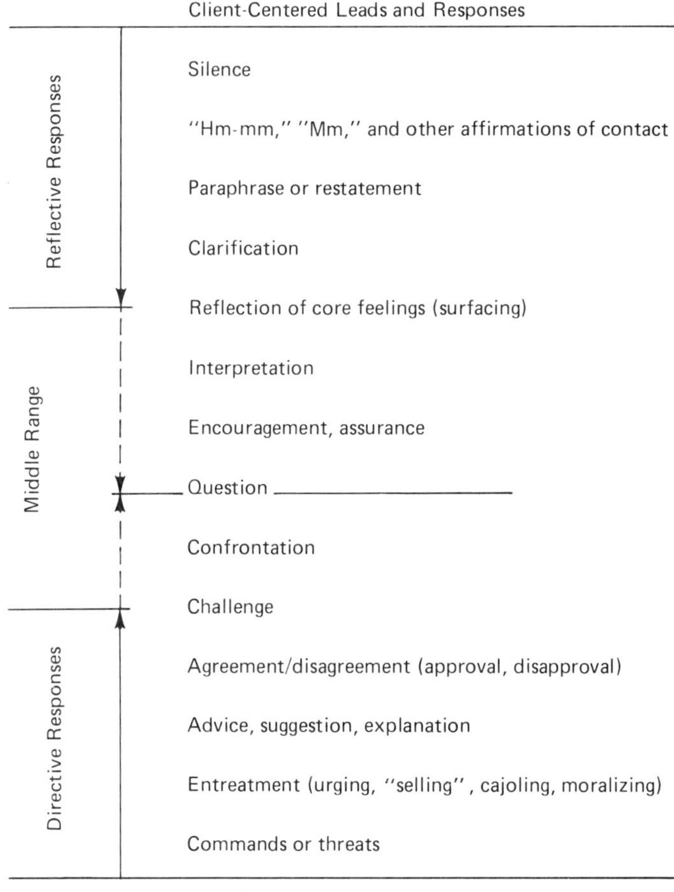

Although this scheme for categorizing responses and leads is simpler than those developed by counseling psychologists and is different from theirs in several important respects, it draws on aspects of categories developed by Benjamin, Shertzer and Stone, and Robinson.

To gain a broader perspective on the functions of these various responses and leads, let us briefly discuss them in terms of where they fall within the ranges outlined in the figure.

Reflective or Client-Centered Responses

These responses include all those we have thus far described as reflective, whether they respond to feeling or to content. The functions of these responses will be alluded to only briefly, since we have already covered them in depth in earlier chapters.

Silence. Simply not saying anything; allowing the other to stay with his thoughts or feelings. This can be considered an extreme, in that it is the least interviewer-centered of all responses.

Its value as a response is in allowing the other person to stay with his feelings. Appropriate use of silence as a response depends on the context of the conversation, since a silence can be experienced as embarrassing or punishing by the client. Silences are generally more useful once the client has begun to explore his meanings in depth, and generally less useful in the initial stages of an encounter.

"Mm-hm," "Mm," "Yes," etc. Expressions that affirm contact, but do not build on what the client has said. Again, the interviewer's role (at the verbal level) is minimal.

Paraphrase or Restatement. Simply reflects what has been explicitly expressed by the other person. Paraphrases are useful for "checking out" our understanding of what the other has said and for affirming contact.

Clarification Reflects what is *in the other person's awareness* but only *implicitly expressed;* attempts to make clearer the client's thoughts and feelings.

This response is particularly useful in helping the client clarify and develop his own thoughts and feelings, and is generally more effective than simple paraphrases. It tends to be most useful in early, exploratory stages of an encounter, but is broadly applicable in almost all conversations or settings that involve either focused understanding or a more mutual dialogue.

Reflection of Core Feelings. Reflects what the interviewer thinks is at the core of what the other person is experiencing, even though it has been *only implicitly expressed* and is *only partially in the other person's awareness.*

This response can be especially effective in helping the client surface underlying assumptions and feelings. The danger is that this response may also overreach and create either defensiveness or a sense of being misunderstood on the part of the client. Reflection of core feelings is apt to be most effective in later stages of an encounter, when a sense of empathy, trust, and acceptance has already developed and when we have gained a fuller understanding of the other person's meanings.

Middle-Range Responses and Leads That Are Essentially Reflective in Nature

These responses, although essentially reflective in nature, go beyond what the client may be aware of and involve some intrepretation on the part of the interviewer. All these leads and responses, however, are in reaction to what the client has expressed and are principally directed to the client's, rather than from the interviewer's, frame of reference.

Interpretation. Reflects what we (as the interviewer) think is at the core of what the other person is expressing, but in a way that reconfigures it so that it is presented to the client in a new light. Usually, interpretation responds to aspects of what the client is experiencing that are *not* in his awareness.

Because it involves the interviewer's reconfiguration of what the client has expressed but may not be aware of, interpretation runs the risk of overreaching and may leave the client feeling defensive or misunderstood.

It is usually most effective when a good relationship has already developed, when we have a fairly complete sense of what the other is experiencing, and when we feel fairly certain that the interpretation will be helpful to the other person and that he is "ready" to hear it. Thus, interpretation tends to be more appropriate during later stages of an encounter, when these conditions have developed, than in earlier stages. Its greatest usefulness is in helping the client see the connections or aspects of his situation that he was not aware of, thereby facilitating better self-understanding.

Encouragement and Assurance. Openly encourages the other person to pursue a line of thought that he may be hesitant to explore but that we think would be fruitful. Here, as in interpretation, the interviewer's own thoughts and feelings become more important, although his reaction is in response to what the client has expressed.

Again, this response is most appropriate when conditions of trust, empathy, and acceptance have already developed. It can be a useful response when the other person appears slightly reluctant or ambivalent about pursuing a topic but his behavior also suggests that he would like to explore it further.

Encouragement can also be useful if we think that the other person is reluctant to go on because he is afraid that we might not approve of what he is about to say. When this is the case, encouragement or assurance can be a way of verbally affirming that we are willing to accept his thoughts and feelings, regardless of what they might be. When encouragement is given with warmth and genuine caring, it can be a very powerful response in enabling the other person to explore a conflict or problem more deeply.

Question (from the Client's Frame of Reference). Asks the client a direct question, but the question is in response to what the client has previously expressed and attempts to clarify the client's own thoughts and feelings.

When a question is asked in response to the client's meanings, it can be especially helpful if it is asked in the true interest of understanding the other person, and when our interest and lack of suspicion are conveyed by our phrasing, "person," or tone of voice.[4] When asked in this way, questions can be very useful in helping a client clarify his own thoughts by directing him to an aspect of what he has said that needs further exploration.

Middle-Range Responses and Leads That Are Essentially Directive in Nature

These responses are essentially directive in nature but still work off material the client has expressed. They direct or confront the client in his exploration but stay within the general bounds of the client's meanings, as opposed to introducing new information, passing judgment on what the client has said, or offering him advice or opinions.

Question (from the Interviewer's Frame of Reference). Asks the client a question from the interviewer's frame of reference that leads the client to an area the interviewer wants to explore and away from what the client has been previously expressing.

This type of question can be useful for obtaining specifically needed information (which may be necessary for understanding what the client is saying). It can also be useful for directing the client's attention to more fruitful areas of exploration, especially where the going may be difficult.[5] Again, the appropriateness of such a question depends very much on the trust, empathy, and acceptance that have already developed in the encounter and, obviously, on the way in which the question is asked. Because the danger exists that the interviewer's question may be irrelevant or overreaching from the client's point of view, questions of this nature are usually best asked in the middle or later stages of an encounter. Questions directed to content inevitably result in disrupting the flow of the client's exploration.

Confrontation. Confronts the client with inconsistencies or contradictions in what the client has expressed (at least as the interviwer sees it), or confronts the client with gaps in what he has said. Although this is clearly a directive response and from the interviewer's frame of reference, it is directed to and works off material the client has already expressed.

Confrontation can be especially effective in helping the other person recognize inconsistencies in his assumptions or when he is evading an important aspect of what he is experiencing. However, great risks are involved in using confrontation as a response, and it should *not* be used unless a great deal of trust, empathy, and feelings of acceptance have already developed. It should not be used unless we are fairly

[4]Lawrence M. Brammer and Everett L. Shostrom, *Therapeutic Psychology* (Englewood Cliffs, N.J.: Prentice-Hall, 1968), Chapter 13, "Counseling Techniques and Practices."

[5]Brammer and Shostrom, *op. cit.*

certain that the confrontation will be beneficial in helping the client better understand himself, rather than destructive in the sense that it will put him on the defensive or make him feel attacked. Again, the context and the way in which we confront the other person is pivotal to whether it will help rather than hinder.

Interviewer-Centered Responses and Leads

These responses are essentially directive in nature and come from the interviewer's frame of reference. In all these responses or leads, the interviewer is reacting from his own point of view to what the client has said and is implicitly or explicitly passing judgment on the truth, usefulness, or importance of what the client has expressed.

Challenge. Regarding a statement, idea, or feeling that the client has expressed, the interviewer challenges its veracity or the degree to which it is consistent with the interviewer's view of the situation.

This type of lead can be useful in questioning assumptions the client holds that may impair his ability to fully understand the situation. They can also enable the client to see where important assumptions or feelings do not check with reality (or at least with the interviewer's view of reality). A challenge can also help the other person gain a broader perspective on his situation, and therefore give him a better understanding of it. It can also be useful, as a last resort, to get the client out of what Perls has called a "bullshit" level of discussion in which he is avoiding important aspects of his problem.[6] However, this kind of response or lead is risky, in that it is implicitly judgmental and from an external frame of reference, and it may leave the client feeling threatened and attacked. Any of these outcomes will certainly impede further exploration, growth, or openness. It should be used only when a great deal of understanding already exists on our part, and when we feel that the challenge will be useful. It should not be used unless a great deal of trust, empathy, and acceptance has already developed in the relationship; otherwise, the client's reaction will surely be defensive. It tends to be more appropriate and useful in later stages of an encounter, or when the other person's clear expectation is that we will react to what he says from our own point of view.

Agreement or Disagreement. Similar to a challenge in that the interviewer is passing judgment, except that approval or disapproval is explicitly expressed by the interviewer.

This response is most useful in the later stages of an encounter, in which the client has asked us for our own reaction and we know enough about his situation to react. In earlier stages, it usually introduces an element of evaluation that undermines the climate of empathy and acceptance needed to facilitate exploration and openness. It

[6]Frederick S. Perls, *Gestalt Therapy Verbatim* (Lafayette, Calif.: Real People Press, 1969).

can, however, be necessary in earlier stages of an encounter if the client's need for an evaluative reaction is so great that his ability to proceed fruitfully is impaired unless he receives it.

Advice or Suggestion. The interviewer gives advice or counsel from the interviewer's point of view on the client's problem or situation.

This lead or response (depending on the context) is most useful toward the end of an encounter in which the other person has asked us for our advice. It is least useful in the early exploratory stages of an encounter and can actively impede further exploration. It is especially appropriate when the client has explicitly sought advice and we feel we know enough about him and his situation to give it.

Any explanation from our point of view of why a client is experiencing difficulties can be also considered part of this category, since we are telling him how and why we think he is having a problem or conflict.

Entreatment (Urging, "Selling," Cajoling, Moralizing, etc.). Entreatment is stronger than advice, in that the interviewer truly wishes to convince the client of what the interviewer thinks the client ought to do. Entreatment includes attempts to convince the client to take a certain course of action or to think a certain way, based on the interviewer's own interpretation of the situation. (This also includes, of course, situations in which the interviewer feels his suggestion is in the client's best interest.)

Entreatment is appropriate (at least as the interviewer would see it) when the interviewer feels that the consequences are serious if the client does not act on the recommended advice. Although skillful "selling," cajoling, and moralizing can often get a client to change his behavior for the moment (and perhaps even change his mind temporarily), they are seldom effective responses in helping the client surface the underlying reasons for his initial resistance to the advice.

Usually, entreatment is effective only in dealing with surface attitudes or issues that are not central to the other person's self-concept. Where the issues or conflicts are deeper, it is seldom of help to the other person, nor does it increase self-understanding. It is, in a phrase, close to the last resort. The most entreatment can do in effecting deeper or longer-term understanding is "buy time" in the hopes that the other person will subsequently gain enough insight into himself and his situation to change his view (assuming, of course, that his view is not as good as the interviewer's, an assumption that the interviewer should question).

Commands or Threats. These are implied or expressed threats on the part of the interviewer to punish the client unless the client acts as the interviewer wishes him to act.

This *is* the last resort. When commands or threats are needed among adults, it is a sign that all attempts at communicating, helping, and understanding have failed. Its use is obvious: to prevent another person from acting in a way that we see as highly undesirable or self-destructive. Its appropriateness is limited to those situations in which all else has failed and we believe it is so important to impose our will on the other person that we are willing to deny him his freedom and autonomy.

Given my own values, this is an extreme, punitive, and inappropriate response among adults in personal settings. In a business or organizational setting, it is also an extreme reaction that can be justified only in terms of the organization's goals, the needs of the organization as a whole, or the needs of others within the organization.

APPROPRIATENESS OF RESPONSES IN TERMS OF THE EVOLUTION OF AN ENCOUNTER

As the discussion above of leads and responses suggests, the appropriateness of these various modes of responding depends first of all on the purpose of the encounter. Given that our purpose is to understand or help, then the appropriateness of these responses depends on how much empathy, acceptance, and trust have developed, the depth of our understanding, and how far the exploration has gone. Generally, all these factors move together, so that as a successful helping relationship develops, so do the trust, empathy, acceptance, understanding, and exploration in the relationship.

If we are to draw any generalizations about helping and understanding from the review above of leads and responses, it would be that reflective responses tend to be most useful in the early and middle stages of an encounter, whereas middle-range responses tend to be most useful in later stages. Directive responses in which we challenge, agree, or give advice tend to be most useful in the late or final stages of an encounter, assuming they are needed at all.

It is important to note that different people will move through the stages of an encounter at different rates, and that in normal conversations, an evolution as neat as the one just described does not usually occur. Thus, the generalization above is only a guide. It is not a prediction, a rule, or the optimal pattern for any given encounter. As stated earlier, the appropriateness or usefulness of any mode of responding depends on the context of what is taking place and awareness of what the other person is experiencing. As your skill increases in both hearing the other person's meanings and responding in these different modes, you will find that your ability to respond appropriately will also improve.

BIBLIOGRAPHY

ARBUCKLE, DUGLAD S., *Counseling: Philosophy, Theory and Practice.* Boston: Allyn & Bacon, 1969.

ARD, BEN N., Jr., ed., *Counseling and Psychotherapy: Classics on Theories and Issues.* Palo Alto, Calif.: Science & Behavior Books, Inc., 1966.

AVILA, DONALD L., ARTHUR W. COMBS and WILLIAM W. PURKEY, *The Helping Relationship Sourcebook.* Boston: Allyn & Bacon, 1972.

BENJAMIN, ALFRED, *The Helping Interview.* Boston: Houghton Mifflin, 1969.

BORDIN, EDWARD S., *Psychological Counseling.* New York: Appleton-Century-Crofts, 1955.

BRAMMER, LAWRENCE M., and EVERETT L. SHOSTROM, *Therapeutic Psychology: Fundamentals of Actualization Counseling and Psychotherapy.* Englewood Cliffs, N.J.: Prentice-Hall, 1968.

BRAYFIELD, A.H., *Readings in Modern Methods of Counseling.* New York: Appleton-Century-Crofts, 1950.

CALLIS, R.A., "Toward an Integrated Theory of Counseling," in *Counseling: Readings in Theory and Practice,* eds. John F. McGowan and Lyle D. Schmidt. New York: Holt, Rinehart & Winston, 1962.

DANSKIN, DAVID G., "Roles Played by Counselors in Their Interviews," *Journal of Counseling Psychology,* Vol. 2 (1955), 22–27.

DICKSON, WILLIAM J., and F.J. ROETHLISBERGER, *Counseling in an Organization.* Boston: Harvard Business School, Division of Research, 1956.

DIPBOYE, W.J., "Analyses of Counselor Style by Discussion Units," *Journal of Counseling Psychology,* Vol. 1 (1954), 21–26.

FIELDER, F.E., "The Concept of an Ideal Therapeutic Relationship," in *Counseling: Readings in Theory and Practice,* eds. John F. McGowan and Lyle D. Schmidt. New York: Holt, Rinehart & Winston, 1962.

GIBB, JACK R., "Defensive Communication," in *Organizational Psychology,* eds. David A. Kolb, Irwin M. Rubin and James M. McIntyre. Englewood Cliffs, N.J.: Prentice-Hall, 1971.

HAMACHEK, DON E., ed., *The SELF in Growth, Teaching, and Learning.* Englewood Cliffs, N.J.: Prentice-Hall, 1965.

LOWE, C. MARSHALL, *Value Orientations in Counseling and Psychotherapy: The Meanings of Mental Health.* San Francisco: Chandler, 1969.

MCGOWAN, JOHN F., and LYLE D. SCHMIDT, *Counseling: Readings in Theory and Practice.* New York: Holt, Rinehart & Winston, 1962.

MOSHER, RALPH L., RICHARD F. CARLE, and CHRIS D. KEHAS, *Guidance: An Examination.* New York: Harcourt Brace Jovanovich, 1965.

PERLS, FREDERICK S., *Gestalt Therapy Verbatim.* Lafayette, Calif.: Real People Press, 1969.

ROBINSON, FRANCIS P., "Are 'Nondirective' Techniques Sometimes too Directive?" in *Readings in Modern Methods of Counseling,* ed. A.H. Brayfield. New York: Appleton-Century-Crofts, 1950.

———, "The Dynamics of Communication in Counseling," in *Counseling: Readings in Theory and Practice,* eds. John F. McGowan and Lyle D. Schmidt. New York: Holt, Rinehart & Winston, 1962.

ROETHLISBERGER, F.J., GEORGE F.F. LOMBARD, and HARRIET O. RONKEN, *Training for Human Relations.* Boston: Division of Research, Harvard Business School, 1954.

ROGERS, CARL R., *On Becoming a Person.* Boston: Houghton Mifflin, 1961.

———, *Client-Centered Therapy.* Boston: Houghton Mifflin, 1965.

———, *Counseling and Psychotherapy.* Boston: Houghton Mifflin, 1942.

———, "The Development of Insight in a Counseling Relationship," in *Readings in Modern Methods of Counseling,* ed. A.H. Brayfield. New York: Appleton-Century-Crofts, 1950.

———, "The Interpersonal Relationship in the Facilitation of Learning," in *The Helping Relationship Sourcebook,* eds. Donald L. Avila, Arthur W. Combs and William W. Purkey. Boston: Allyn & Bacon, 1972.

———, "The Interpersonal Relationship: The Core of Guidance," in *Guidance: An Examination,* eds. Ralph L. Mosher, Richard F. Carle and Chris D. Kehas. New York: Harcourt Brace Jovanovich, 1965.

———, "My Philosophy of Interpersonal Relationships and How It Grew," *Journal of Humanistic Psychology:* San Francisco, 1973.

———, "A Theory of Therapy as Developed in the Client-Centered Framework," in *Counseling and Psychotherapy: Classics on Theories and Issues,* ed. Ben N. Ard, Jr. Palo Alto, Calif.: Science & Behavior Books, Inc., 1966.

———, and F.J. ROETHLISBERGER, "Barriers and Gateways to Communication," in *Organizational Psychology,* eds. David A. Kolb, Irwin M. Rubin and James M. McIntyre. Englewood Cliffs, N.J.: Prentice-Hall, 1971.

SHERTZER, BRUCE, and SHELLEY C. STONE, *Fundamentals of Counseling.* Boston: Houghton Mifflin, 1974.

SNYDER, WILLIAM U., "An Investigation of the Nature of Nondirective Psychotherapy," in *Readings in Modern Methods of Counseling,* ed. A.H. Brayfield. New York: Appleton-Century-Crofts, 1950.

THORNE, FREDERICK C., "Directive Psychotherapy: III. The Psychology of Simple Maladjustment," and "VII. Imparting Psychological Information," in *Readings in Modern Methods of Counseling,* ed. A.H. Brayfield. New York: Appleton-Century-Crofts, 1950.

———, "Principles of Directive Counseling and Psychotherapy," in *Counseling and Psychotherapy: Classics on Theories and Issues,* ed. Ben N. Ard, Jr. Palo Alto, Calif.: Science & Behavior Books, Inc., 1966.

TURNER, ARTHUR N., and GEORGE F.F. LOMBARD, *Interpersonal Behavior and Administration.* New York: Free Press, 1969.

Readings

A Therapist's View of the Good Life: The Fully Functioning Person

Carl Rogers

About 1952 or 1953 I wrote, during one of my winter escapes to warmer climes, a paper I entitled, "The Concept of the Fully Functioning Person." It was an attempt to spell out the picture of the person who would emerge if therapy were maximally successful. I was somewhat frightened by the fluid, relativistic, individualistic person who seemed to be the logical outcome of the processes of therapy. I felt two questions. Was my logic correct? If correct, was this the sort of person I valued? To give myself opportunity to mull over these ideas, I had the paper duplicated, and in the ensuing years have distributed hundreds of copies to interested inquirers. As I became more sure of the ideas it contained, I submitted it to one of the major psychological journals. The editor wrote that he would publish it, but felt that it needed to be cast in a much more conventional psychological framework. He suggested many fundamental changes. This made me feel that it was probably not acceptable to psychologists in the form in which I had written it, and I dropped the idea of publication. Since then it has continued to be a focus of interest for a wide diversity of people, and Dr. Hayakawa has written an article about the concept in the journal of the semanticists, ETC. *Consequently this was one of the papers which came first to my mind when I contemplated the present book.*

When I reread it, however, I found that in the intervening years many of its most central themes and ideas had been absorbed, and perhaps better expressed, in other papers I have included. So, with some reluctance I have again put it aside, and present here instead a paper on my view of the good life, a paper which was based upon "The Fully Functioning Person," and which expresses, I believe, the essential aspects of that paper in briefer and more readable form. My only concession to the past is to give the chapter heading a subtitle.

Reprinted from Carl Rogers, *On Becoming a Person* (Boston: Houghton Mifflin, 1961). Reprinted by permission of the author and publishers.

My views regarding the meaning of the good life are largely based upon my experience in working with people in the very close and intimate relationship which is called psychotherapy. These views thus have an empirical or experiential foundation, as contrasted perhaps with a scholarly or philosophical foundation. I have learned what the good life seems to be by observing and participating in the struggle of disturbed and troubled people to achieve that life.

I should make it clear from the outset that this experience I have gained comes from the vantage point of a particular orientation to psychotherapy which has developed over the years. Quite possibly all psychotherapy is basically similar, but since I am less sure of that than I once was, I wish to make it clear that my therapeutic experience has been along the lines that seem to me most effective, the type of therapy termed "client-centered."

Let me attempt to give a very brief description of what this therapy would be like if it were in every respect optimal, since I feel I have learned most about the good life from therapeutic experiences in which a great deal of movement occurred. If the therapy were optimal, intensive as well as extensive, then it would mean that the therapist has been able to enter into an intensely personal and subjective relationship with the client—relating not as a scientist to an object of study, not as a physician expecting to diagnose and cure, but as a person to a person. It would mean that the therapist feels this client to be a person of unconditional self-worth: of value no matter what his condition, his behavior, or his feelings. It would mean that the therapist is genuine, hiding behind no defensive façade, but meeting the client with the feelings which organically he is experiencing. It would mean that the therapist is able to let himself go in understanding this client; that no inner barriers keep him from sensing what it feels like to be the client at each moment of the relationship; and that he can convey something of his empathic understanding to the client. It means that the therapist has been comfortable in entering this relationship fully, without knowing cognitively where it will lead, satisfied with providing a climate which will permit the client the utmost freedom to become himself.

For the client, this optimal therapy would mean an exploration of increasingly strange and unknown and dangerous feelings in himself, the exploration proving possible only because he is gradually realizing that he is accepted unconditionally. Thus he becomes acquainted with elements of his experience which have in the past been denied to awareness as too threatening, too damaging to the structure of the self. He finds himself experiencing these feelings fully, completely, in the relationship, so that for the moment he *is* his fear, or his anger, or his tenderness, or his strength. And as he lives these widely varied feelings, in all their degrees of intensity, he discovers that he has experienced *himself*, that he *is* all these feelings. He finds his behavior changing in constructive fashion in accordance with his newly experienced self. He approaches the realization that he no longer needs to fear what experience may hold, but can welcome it freely as a part of his changing and developing self.

This is a thumbnail sketch of what client-centered therapy comes close to, when it is at its optimum. I give it here simply as a brief picture of the context in which I have formed my views of the good life.

A Negative Observation

As I have tried to live understandingly in the experiences of my clients, I have gradually come to one negative conclusion about the good life. It seems to me that the good life is not any fixed state. It is not, in my estimation, a state of virtue, or contentment, or nirvana, or happiness. It is not a condition in which the individual is adjusted, or fulfilled, or actualized. To use psychological terms, it is not a state of drive-reduction, or tension-reduction, or homeostasis.

I believe that all of these terms have been used in ways which imply that if one or several of these states is achieved, then the goal of life has been achieved. Certainly, for many people happiness, or adjustment, are seen as states of being which are synonymous with the good life. And social scientists have frequently spoken of the reduction of tension, or the achievement of homeostasis or equilibrium as if these states constituted the goal of the process of living.

So it is with a certain amount of surprise and concern that I realize that my experience supports none of these definitions. If I focus on the experience of those individuals who seem to have evidenced the greatest degree of movement during the therapeutic relationship, and who, in the years following this relationship, appear to have made and to be making real progress toward the good life, then it seems to me that they are not adequately described at all by any of these terms which refer to fixed states of being. I believe they would consider themselves insulted if they were described as "adjusted," and they would regard it as false if they were described as "happy" or "contented," or even "actualized." As I have known them I would regard it as most inaccurate to say that all their drive tensions have been reduced, or that they are in a state of homeostasis. So I am forced to ask myself whether there is any way in which I can generalize about their situation, any definition which I can give of the good life which would seem to fit the facts as I have observed them. I find this not at all easy, and what follows is stated very tentatively.

A Positive Observation

If I attempt to capture in a few words what seems to me to be true of these people, I believe it will come out something like this:

The good life is a *process,* not a state of being.

It is a direction, not a destination.

The direction which constitutes the good life is that which is selected by the total organism, when there is psychological freedom to move in *any* direction.

This organismically selected direction seems to have certain discernible general qualities which appear to be the same in a wide variety of unique individuals.

So I can integrate these statements into a definition which can at least serve as a basis for consideration and discussion. The good life, from the point of view of my experience, is the process of movement in a direction which the human organism selects when it is inwardly free to move in any direction, and the general qualities of this selected direction appear to have a certain universality.

THE CHARACTERISTICS OF THE PROCESS

Let me now try to specify what appear to be the characteristic qualities of this process of movement, as they crop up in person after person in therapy.

An Increasing Openness to Experience

In the first place, the process seems to involve an increasing openness to experience. This phrase has come to have more and more meaning for me. It is the polar opposite of defensiveness. Defensiveness I have described in the past as being the organism's response to experiences which are perceived or anticipated as threatening, as incongruent with the individual's existing picture of himself, or of himself in relationship to the world. These threatening experiences are temporarily rendered harmless by being distorted in awareness, or being denied to awareness. I quite literally cannot see, with accuracy, those experiences, feelings, reactions in myself which are significantly at variance with the picture of myself which I already possess. A large part of the process of therapy is the continuing discovery by the client that he is experiencing feelings and attitudes which heretofore he has not been able to be aware of, which he has not been able to "own" as being a part of himself.

If a person could be fully open to his experience, however, every stimulus—whether originating within the organism or in the environment—would be freely relayed through the nervous system without being distorted by any defensive mechanism. There would be no need of the mechanism of "subception" whereby the organism is forewarned of any experience threatening to the self. On the contrary, whether the stimulus was the impact of a configuration of form, color, or sound in the environment on the sensory nerves, or a memory trace from the past, or a visceral sensation of fear or pleasure or disgust, the person would be "living" it, would have it completely available to awareness.

Thus, one aspect of this process which I am naming "the good life" appears to be a movement away from the pole of defensiveness toward the pole of openness to experience. The individual is becoming more able to listen to himself, to experience what is going on within himself. He is more open to his feelings of fear and discouragement and pain. He is also more open to his feelings of courage, and tenderness, and awe. He is free to live his feelings subjectively, as they exist in him, and also free to be aware of these feelings. He is more able fully to live the experiences of his organism rather than shutting them out of awareness.

Increasingly Existential Living

A second characteristic of the process which for me is the good life is that it involves an increasing tendency to live fully in each moment. This is a thought which can easily be misunderstood, and which is perhaps somewhat vague in my own thinking. Let me try to explain what I mean.

I believe it would be evident that for the person who was fully open to his new experience, completely without defensiveness, each moment would be new. The complex configuration of inner and outer stimuli which exists in this moment has never existed before in just this fashion. Consequently such a person would realize that "What I will be in the next moment, and what I will do, grows out of that moment, and cannot be predicted in advance either by me or by others." Not infrequently we find clients expressing exactly this sort of feeling.

One way of expressing the fluidity which is present in such existential living is to say that the self and personality emerge *from* experience, rather than experience being translated or twisted to fit preconceived self-structure. It means that one becomes a participant in and an observer of the ongoing process of organismic experience, rather than being in control of it.

Such living in the moment means an absence of rigidity, of tight organization, of the imposition of structure on experience. It means instead a maximum of adaptability, a discovery of structure *in* experience, a flowing, changing organization of self and personality.

It is this tendency toward existential living which appears to me very evident in people who are involved in the process of the good life. One might almost say that it is the most essential quality of it. It involves discovering the structure of experience in the process of living the experience. Most of us, on the other hand, bring a preformed structure and evaluation to our experience and never relinquish it, but cram and twist the experience to fit our preconceptions, annoyed at the fluid qualities which make it so unruly in fitting our carefully constructed pigeonholes. To open one's spirit to what is going on *now,* and to discover in that present process whatever structure it appears to have—this to me is one of the qualities of the good life, the mature life, as I see clients approach it.

An Increasing Trust in His Organism

Still another characteristic of the person who is living the process of the good life appears to be an increasing trust in his organism as a means of arriving at the most satisfying behavior in each existential situation. Again let me try to explain what I mean.

In choosing what course of action to take in any situation, many people rely upon guiding principles, upon a code of action laid down by some group or institution, upon the judgment of others (from wife and friends to Emily Post), or upon the way they have behaved in some similar past situation. Yet as I observe the clients whose experiences in living have taught me so much, I find that increasingly such individuals are able to trust their total organismic reaction to a new situation because they discover to an ever-increasing degree that if they are open to their experience, doing what "feels right" proves to be a competent and trustworthy guide to behavior which is truly satisfying.

As I try to understand the reason for this, I find myself following this line of thought. The person who is fully open to his experience would have access to all of the available data in the situation, on which to base his behavior; the social demands, his own complex and possibly conflicting needs, his memories of similar situations, his perception of the uniqueness of this situation, etc., etc. The data would be very complex indeed. But he could permit his total organism, his consciousness participating, to consider each stimulus, need, and demand, its relative intensity and importance, and out of this complex weighing and balancing, discover that course of action which would come closest to satisfying all his needs in the situation. An analogy which might come close to a description would be to compare this person to a giant electronic computing machine. Since he is open to his experience, all of the data from his sense impressions, from his memory, from previous learning, from his visceral and internal states, is fed into the machine. The machine takes all of these multitudinous pulls and forces which are fed in as data, and quickly computes the course of action which would be the most economical vector of need satisfaction in this existential situation. This is the behavior of our hypothetical person.

The defects which in most of us make this process untrustworthy are the inclusion of information which does *not* belong to this present situation, or the exclusion of information which *does.* It is when memories and previous learnings are fed into the computations as if they were *this* reality, and not memories and learnings, that erroneous behavioral answers arise. Or when certain threatening experiences are inhibited from awareness, and hence are withheld from the computation or fed into it in distorted form, this too produces error. But our hypothetical person would find his organism thoroughly trustworthy, because all of the available data would be used, and it would be present in accurate rather than distorted form. Hence his behavior would come as close as possible to satisfying all his needs—for enhancement, for affiliation with others, and the like.

In this weighing, balancing, and computation, his organism would not by any means be infallible. It would always give the best possible answer for the available data, but sometimes data would be missing. Because of the element of openness to experience, however, any errors, any following of behavior which was not satisfying, would be quickly corrected. The computations, as it were, would always be in process of being corrected, because they would be continually checked in behavior.

Perhaps you will not like my analogy of an electronic computing machine. Let me return to the clients I know. As they become more open to all of their experiences, they find it increasingly possible to trust their reactions. If they "feel like" expressing anger they do so and find that this comes out satisfactorily, because they are equally alive to all of their other desires for affection, affiliation, and relationship. They are surprised at their own intuitive skill in finding behavioral solutions to complex and troubling human relationships. It is only afterward that they realize how surprisingly trustworthy their inner reactions have been in bringing about satisfactory behavior.

The Process of Functioning More Fully

I should like to draw together these three threads describing the process of the good life into a more coherent picture. It appears that the person who is psychologically free moves in the direction of becoming a more fully functioning person. He is more able to live fully in and with each and all of his feelings and reactions. He makes increasing use of all his organic equipment to sense, as accurately as possible, the existential situation within and without. He makes use of all of the information his nervous system can thus supply, using it in awareness, but recognizing that his total organism may be, and often is, wiser than his awareness. He is more able to permit his total organism to function freely in all its complexity in selecting, from the multitude of possibilities, that behavior which in this moment of time will be most generally and genuinely satisfying. He is able to put more trust in his organism in this functioning not because it is infallible, but because he can be fully open to the consequences of each of his actions and correct them if they prove to be less than satisfying.

He is more able to experience all of his feelings, and is less afraid of any of his feelings; he is his own sifter of evidence, and is more open to evidence from all sources; he is completely engaged in the process of being and becoming himself, and thus discovers that he is soundly and realistically social; he lives more completely in this moment, but learns that this is the soundest living for all time. He is becoming a more fully functioning organism, and because of the awareness of himself which flows freely in and through his experience, he is becoming a more fully functioning person.

SOME IMPLICATIONS

Any view of what constitutes the good life carries with it many implications, and the view I have presented is no exception. I hope that these implications may be food for thought. There are two or three of these about which I would like to comment.

A New Perspective on Freedom vs. Determinism

The first of these implications may not immediately be evident. It has to do with the age-old issue of "free will." Let me endeavor to spell out the way in which this issue now appears to me in a new light.

For some time I have been perplexed over the living paradox which exists in psychotherapy between freedom and determinism. In the therapeutic relationship some of the most compelling subjective experiences are those in which the client feels within himself the power of naked choice. He is *free*—to become himself or to hide behind a façade; to move forward or to retrogress; to behave in ways which are destructive of self and others, or in ways which are enhancing; quite literally free to live or die, in both the physiological and psychological meaning of those terms. Yet as we enter this field of psychotherapy with objective research methods, we are, like any other scientist, committed to a complete determinism. From this point of view every thought, feeling, and action of the client is determined by what preceded it. There can be no such thing as freedom. The dilemma I am trying to describe is no different than that found in other fields—it is simply brought to sharper focus, and appears more insoluble.

This dilemma can be seen in a fresh perspective, however, when we consider it in terms of the definition I have given of the fully functioning person. We could say that in the optimum of therapy the person rightfully experiences the most complete and absolute freedom. He wills or chooses to follow the course of action which is the most economical vector in relationship to all the internal and external stimuli, because it is that behavior which will be most deeply satisfying. But this is the same course of action which from another vantage point may be said to be determined by all the factors in the existential situation. Let us contrast this with the picture of the person who is defensively organized. He wills or chooses to follow a given course of action, but finds that he *cannot* behave in the fashion that he chooses. He is determined by the factors in the existential situation, but these factors include his defensiveness, his denial or distortion of some of the relevant data. Hence it is certain that his behavior will be less than fully satisfying. His behavior is determined, but he is not free to make an effective choice. The fully functioning person, on the other hand, not only experiences, but utilizes, the most absolute freedom when he spontaneously, freely, and voluntarily chooses and wills that which is also absolutely determined.

I am not so naive as to suppose that this fully resolves the issue between subjective and objective, between freedom and necessity. Nevertheless it has meaning for me that the more the person is living the good life, the more he will experience a freedom of choice, and the more his choices will be effectively implemented in his behavior.

Creativity as an Element of the Good Life

I believe it will be clear that a person who is involved in the directional process which I have termed "the good life" is a creative person. With his sensitive openness to his world, his trust of his own ability to form new relationships with his environment, he would be the type of person from whom creative products and creative living emerge. He would not necessarily be "adjusted" to his culture, and he would almost certainly not be a conformist. But at any time and in any culture he would live constructively, in as much harmony with his culture as a balanced satisfaction of needs demanded. In some cultural situations he might in some ways be very unhappy, but he would continue to move toward becoming himself, and to behave in such a way as to provide the maximum satisfaction of his deepest needs.

Such a person would, I believe, be recognized by the student of evolution as the type most likely to adapt and survive under changing environmental conditions. He would be able creatively to make sound adjustments to new as well as old conditions. He would be a fit vanguard of human evolution.

Basic Trustworthiness of Human Nature

It will be evident that another implication of the view I have been presenting is that the basic nature of the human being, when functioning freely, is constructive and trustworthy. For me this is an inescapable conclusion from a quarter-century of experience in psychotherapy. When we are able to free the individual from defensiveness, so that he is open to the wide range of his own needs, as well as the wide range of environmental and social demands, his reactions may be trusted to be positive, forward-moving, constructive. We do not need to ask who will socialize him, for one of his own deepest needs is for affiliation and communication with others. As he becomes more fully himself, he will become more realistically socialized. We do not need to ask who will control his aggressive impulses; for as he becomes more open to all of his impulses, his need to be liked by others and his tendency to give affection will be as strong as his impulses to strike out or to seize for himself. He will be aggressive in situations in which aggression is realistically appropriate, but there will be no runaway need for aggression. His total behavior, in these and other areas, as he moves toward being open to all his experience, will be more balanced and realistic, behavior which is appropriate to the survival and enhancement of a highly social animal.

I have little sympathy with the rather prevalent concept that man is basically irrational, and that his impulses, if not controlled, will lead to destruction of others and self. Man's behavior is exquisitely rational, moving with subtle and ordered complexity toward the goals his organism is endeavoring to achieve. The tragedy for most of us is that our defenses keep us from being aware of this rationality, so that consciously we are moving in one direction, while organismically we are moving in another. But in our person who is living the process of the good life, there would be a decreasing number of such barriers, and he would be increasingly a participant in the rationality of his organism. The only control of impulses which would exist, or which would prove necessary, is the natural and internal balancing of one need against another, and the discovery of behaviors which follow the vector most closely approximating the satisfaction of all needs. The experience of extreme satisfaction of one need (for aggression, or sex, etc.) in such a way as to do violence to the satisfaction of other needs (for companionship, tender relationship, etc.)—an experience very common in the defensively organized person—would be greatly decreased. He would participate in the vastly complex self-regulatory activities of his organism—the psychological as well as physiological thermostatic controls—in such a fashion as to live in increasing harmony with himself and with others.

The Greater Richness of Life

One last implication I should like to mention is that this process of living in the good life involves a wider range, a greater richness, than the constricted living in which most of us find ourselves. To be a part of this process means that one is involved in the frequently frightening and frequently satisfying experience of a more sensitive living, with greater range, greater variety, greater richness. It seems to me that clients who have moved significantly in therapy live more intimately with their feelings of pain, but also more vividly with their feelings of ecstasy; that anger is more clearly felt, but so also is love; that fear is an experience they know more deeply, but so is courage. And the reason they can thus live fully in a wider range is that they have this underlying confidence in themselves as trustworthy instruments for encountering life.

I believe it will have become evident why, for me, adjectives such as happy, contented, blissful, enjoyable, do not seem quite appropriate to any general description of this process I have called the good life, even though the person in this process would experience each one of these feelings at appropriate times. But the adjectives which seem more generally fitting are adjectives such as enriching, exciting, rewarding, challenging, meaningful. This process of the good life is not, I am convinced, a life for the faint-hearted. It involves the stretching and growing of becoming more and more of one's potentialities. It involves the courage to be. It means launching oneself fully into the stream of life. Yet the deeply exciting thing about human beings is that when the individual is inwardly free, he chooses as the good life this process of becoming.

Interpersonal Skills and Helping Relationships

Eileen Morley

WHY INTERPERSONAL SKILLS?

Human beings are gregarious creatures. It would be impossible for most of us to exist very long in this society without participating in a host of relationships of varying degrees of intimacy. Though the nature and intensity of these relationships vary from person to person, and from situation to situation, they are almost as much a part of our lives as the air we breathe and the clothes we wear. Furthermore we are living at a time when awareness of the importance of effective relationships and the desire for skill in cultivating them are both on the increase.

Why interpersonal skills? Because we experience interpersonal satisfaction only if we are reasonably effective in relating to other people. When the relationship is also centered on a task, whether this be raising a child, collaborating on a technical report, or winning a football game, there is a second important reason for our concern—so that the task may be completed effectively.

This is a rather pragmatic and abstract answer. At another level, interpersonal skills are important because they enable us to experience the intense joy that comes from a sense of harmony and intimacy with another person, and the pleasure and satisfaction that comes from a collaborative job well done. They also enable us to reduce the pain and conflict which we feel when important relationships go badly wrong. When we can understand something of the cause of our pain and difficulty, and of the way we may have helped create them, we can attempt to reduce them by learning to behave differently, and avoid repeating our mistakes in other situations.

The human relationships in which we are involved consist of innumerable interactions, sometimes substantial and obvious, more often minor and subtle. These interactions are fashioned out of each person's perceptions of and responses to another person's behavior.

Interpersonal effectiveness consists of engaging in this process in ways which give each relationship the best chance of continuing in a form which satisfies both the people involved. Where incompatibility exists, interpersonal effectiveness enables us to resolve, reduce, or tolerate it, so that the relationship can survive.

THE COMPLEXITY OF HUMAN INTERACTION

This effort would be relatively simple if data about people were as accessible and stable as data about technical processes. In that case we could design and lay out the interface between one person and another as we lay out the interfaces of different segments of a major engineering project. Where human behavior is concerned, however, the problem is considerably more complicated. For one thing, there is never a single "objective" view of any interpersonal situation in the way that a single view of a technical problem exists in the mind of the particular engineer who is responsible for solving it. Instead there are as many views as there are participants, each person with his own selective set of perceptions of what is going on. And in each person these perceptions are linked to a pre-existing framework of assumptions which enables the individual to create his or her own interpretative "meaning" of a given situation. As a result, relevant data is what each of us thinks is relevant. But what *we* think of as relevant may not be at all what the other person perceives as important—or even as happening! Conversely, things which look trivial to us may have immense meaning to others; may in fact touch another in a most personal and profound way.

In addition to this problem of multiple viewpoints, interpersonal behavior is complicated by the fact that individuals experience the world at varying levels of awareness. None of us is aware of all we do or feel or think. Limits to our consciousness are necessary. This is partly because we all need to protect ourselves against pain and anxiety at certain times. And it is partly because awareness of our total past experience would be an enormous neurological and psychological overload. No one could tolerate being aware of all of his or her experiencing over a lifetime. However, in a particular interpersonal situation and at a particular moment, we may need to strive for as much awareness as we are capable of in order to experience fully, and in order to give ourselves and others the best possible chance of having the relationship succeed.

Although limits to our awareness exist, they are not inflexible. We can become more conscious of a certain amount of the experiencing that usually goes on out of awareness, by actively attending to it, or by "allowing" awareness to "happen" to us. This can occur when we think deliberately about some experience in a reflective way. For instance:

> "Something went wrong in that meeting. Let me recall what happened and see if I can pin it down. Now I think about it I realize I was really upset by the way they ignored my proposal. . . ."

or

> "How did I feel when they turned down my invitation? Well, now I think about it, I was really angry!"

Awareness can also increase as the result of our "allowing" it to speak to us—for instance, in the first few moments after we wake up, or as we go about some routine task such as shaving or driving. We can cultivate awareness more actively in at least two obvious ways: by writing out our experience of something troublesome; or by talking with another sympathetic person. Expanding our awareness in one or other of these ways often produces new insights which enable us to reorganize our understanding of what we have experienced; if need be, we can then go on to use that understanding to deal with the difficulty.

In addition to that part of awareness which is available to us "for the asking," so to speak, we all have a store of unconscious memories and experiences. On the whole these are not available except under special circumstances, such as an unusual event which suddenly releases an unconscious memory or association into our conscious awareness, giving us more insight. The same thing also happens in therapy.

The reverse process is also true—ideas may move into awareness as we attend to them, and later sink back out of sight. This is normal. What is necessary in important interpersonal relationships is that we develop the skill to become more aware of problems *as* they occur, and find time to attend to aspects of them which may not be immediately obvious.

Human experience has two further complicating aspects: thought and feeling (the "cognitive" and "affective," if you wish). Because our society on the whole values the experience and expression of thought more than feelings, our training tends to emphasize the intellectual aspect of our experiencing heavily—some would say disproportionately. As a result, the feelings that were part of a particular experience tend to get separated from our thinking about it, and suppressed. To some extent this can be useful, since it is obviously necessary at times—particularly in a work setting—to talk about ideas or experiences without being flooded with associated feelings. But to some extent it is also dysfunctional, because in interpersonal relationships those feelings are very much a part of what goes on between people. They need to be expressed and understood in some appropriate way if relationships are to be rich and effective.

Just as our awareness of a particular experience increases and diminishes, so does our awareness of the feelings which were part of it. In this respect human experience is a continually flowing yet shifting process; like a river in which some channels deepen and others silt up, as the current and volume of the water change from day to day and season to season.

At the risk of seeming to oversimplify human experience into a two-dimensional diagram, let us consider these concepts visually.

In life these boundaries are never as

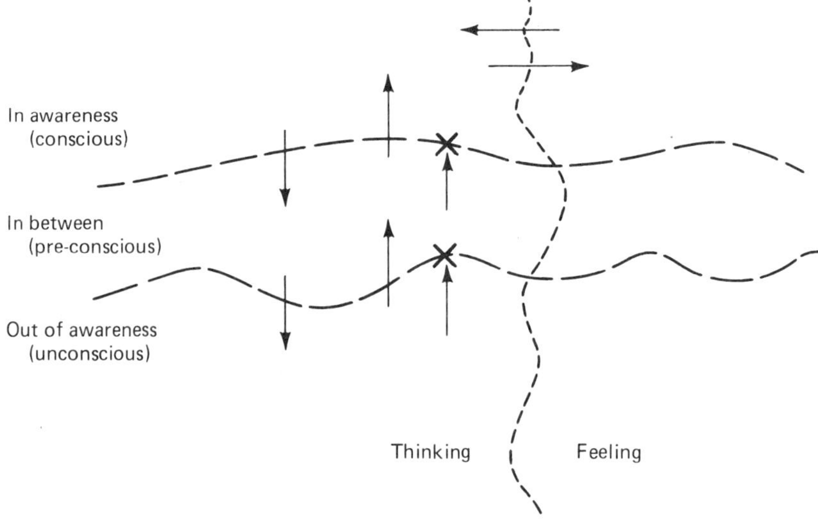

clear-cut as the diagram suggests. Boundaries shift from time to time, as certain things rise into awareness and then are forgotten again. An example of this is the heightened awareness of nonverbal communication that occurs when people first learn about body language, or of imagery and color when they first buy a camera. The awareness fades when they move to other things, though for a long time it tends to be more accessible than it was before.

People vary tremendously in the extent to which they are aware of the full flow of their present experience; the extent to which they can recall it later; and the extent to which it stimulates associated ideas and feelings. People also vary tremendously in the extent to which they can put their awareness into words. Some are so fluent that others can hardly believe that they have not "prepared" what they are saying. Others are almost totally unable to articulate their experience, even though they are fluent about other more intellectual issues. In this respect too, our abilities are influenced by the culture of the community in which we grew up or of the organization in which we work. If expression of awareness is encouraged—in our family or in some task-related way, such as theater or movie-making—then with time it becomes much easier for us to do this.

Similarly, the boundary between thought and feeling is deliberately drawn to suggest interaction between the two. For thoughts give rise to feelings, while feelings arouse images which lead to ideas. Allowing a rich interplay between the two is a powerful way of increasing our awareness of a particular experience, but again, it takes practice to enable this to happen.

If you look again at the previous diagram you will probably agree that most of us experience ourselves as "living" in the upper left quadrant much of the time. If one thinks of that quadrant as having several different aspects:

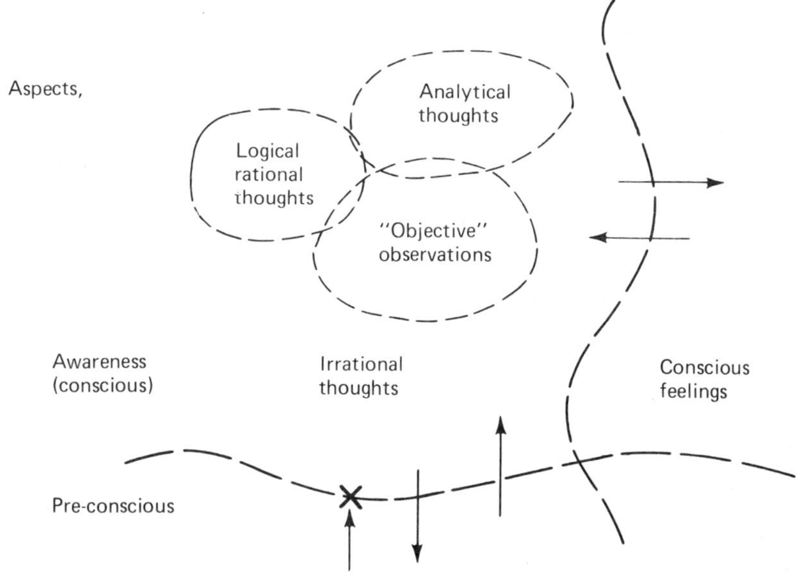

it becomes apparent that much graduate business training consists of efforts to cultivate the rational and analytical aspects of cognition which are so crucial to management. The rational-analytical process is the best means we have yet found of dealing with technical issues and problems. (Some people would say that because it is so effective, we have constructed a whole technological culture around this style of handling our environment.) In developing this ability, therefore, the student learns a highly specialized, valuable and comparatively rare skill.

If human behavior were wholly capable of intellectual analysis in the mode we described here as consciously "rational" and "logical," there would be no need for further concern with interpersonal skills. However, the experiencing of the people with whom we are in relation covers each full spectrum from thought to feeling and from awareness to non-awareness. So does our own! And it is in terms of this complexity that we need to examine the nature of interpersonal skills.

INTERPERSONAL EFFECTIVENESS

How are we to go about the process of cultivating interpersonal skills—the process of improving difficult relationships and making good ones better still? Or, when difficult relationships seem either irremediable or not worth the effort, how can we find ways to get out of them, and exchange them for something with more promise of satisfaction?

Interpersonal effectiveness involves:

- cultivating our awareness of our own experiencing;
- cultivating our understanding of the experiencing of others with whom we are in relation;
- learning to communicate with and respond to others in ways which will increase their understanding of themselves and our understanding of them, as well as their understanding of us;
- learning to behave in ways which will increase compatibility and satisfaction.

In this note we are concerned with the first three. If we can find ways to develop these capacities we can make better choices about where we want to be in relationship and how we want to behave. And in relationships where we have less immediate choice, such as those with parents and other kin, or to a reduced extent with work colleagues or neighbors, we can attempt to behave in ways which will increase harmony, effectiveness and satisfaction.

In order to improve our skills, therefore, we have to find a style which can take account of feelings as well as thought, and of different levels of awareness. For those who have worked hard to develop their rational-analytical abilities, this sometimes seems uncomfortable; a diffusion of a hard-wrought focus. It is important, however, to bear in mind that interpersonal effectiveness does not require you to give up one style for the other. That would be highly undesirable, because analytical ability is crucially important in our world. What is required is that you *add* to your repertoire a different and less directive way of relating to others.

LEARNING INTERPERSONAL SKILLS

One major element in interpersonal effectiveness is the willingness and ability to notice how relationships are working out.

If something goes wrong in a manufacturing process, something that we have no way of observing or measuring, and something which it doesn't occur to us to look for, chances are pretty slim that we will be able to locate the problem and put it right. So we develop all kinds of complex ways to monitor technical processes. As a result, when we notice something *beginning* to go wrong, we are able to correct it. Similarly with human relationships. We have to develop ways of noticing; of becoming aware of what is going on. Fortunately people have one tremendous advantage over machines. We can ask them to tell us how things are with them. "All" it takes to do this is the initiative to ask the question and the time and concern to listen to the answer. "All" is written in quotation marks because in fact this is something which many of us don't often think of doing, or if we think of, find it extraordinarily hard.

In listening to another person's answer to our question, it is necessary for us to shift out of the analytical way of thinking into a different mode of response. For we ask the question "How are you?" in order to help us understand their point of view. Instead of looking for data that *we* think are relevant to their situation, we want to know of *their* thinking and feeling. In fact, our awareness of their feeling is likely to increase our understanding of them more than our awareness of their thoughts.

If the other person is to be open with us, they need to experience us as accepting and concerned, rather than challenging, analytical or threatening. Otherwise they will quite naturally stop talking to us. They also need us to deal gently with aspects of their experience which may be highly visible to us but of which they are not fully aware. To confront or challenge them with something they are not yet ready to look at may cause them to withdraw or become defensive and so damage the relationship. Similarly they need us to refrain from judging them, and from expressing approval or disapproval, since this may not coincide with their feelings about themselves. As we listen we need to communicate our acceptance so that they will feel safe and comfortable with us, free from the anxiety that we may disagree or disapprove of what they are telling us, and the fear that we will criticize or reject them for it. This does not mean that we may never disagree or disapprove of someone else; simply that it is necessary for us to hold those opinions in abeyance and adopt an attitude of acceptance while we are listening to another person share the experience with us.

THE PROCESS OF ASSOCIATIVE THINKING AND FEELING

In addition to establishing a relationship of trust with them, there is another aspect of our interaction which is crucially important to handle well if we are to understand another person's experience adequately. When we engage in a rational analytical mode of thought, *we* decide on the definition of the problem area, and on the kind of data we need to understand it. We do this so as to introduce order, direction, and purposefulness into our thinking. However, this very purposefulness and logic excludes conscious feelings, and discourages unconscious feelings from surfacing into awareness. In attempting to understand another person's experience we need to refrain from trying to introduce our sense of order into the conversation and leave plenty of room for *their* meanings to develop.

The process in which we encourage them to engage when we do withhold our definitions and judgments (and one which we can use ourselves when we want more insight) is that of thinking by association. Associative thinking is a process of meaning-making in which one thing leads to another—not just any "other" but to the association which is the most important or powerful in a particular person's experience. Associations may run from one idea to another; from one feeling to another; or between thoughts and feelings. But all are very *personal* meanings.

For example, I recently visited a colleague's home for the first time. Sitting at the dinner table I found myself feeling much more emotionally at home than is customary for me on a first visit. Although ours was basically a professional relationship, I also found myself talking at some length about my childhood in England. Later on I noticed that the dining chairs were identical with ones which both my parents and my uncle have. Clearly their meaning for me was a feeling of "home" which had stimulated both my recollections and feeling of comfort and I mentioned this to my host.

Most of us have great difficulty in shifting to a listening mode, even for a little while. We are used to talking, not listening; to telling rather than hearing; to evaluating rather than accepting. Most difficult to acquire is the ability to allow the other person to "go where they will"—to allow one association to lead to another in a way which is meaningful, not in terms of our logic or of our perceptions of their situation, but in terms of their own inner meanings which we may not fully understand as they share them with us.

When we listen to someone talk in this way we tend to become uncomfortable because they are not "keeping to the subject" or "following a logical line of thought" in the way we have been trained to value. However, there are times when this can be extremely valuable. Some time ago I worked with a small company which I visited at irregular intervals. On these visits I would find myself responding to the president in two very different styles. When we were trying to get to the bottom of a particular problem, I would disregard his long associative trains of thought and focus on the problem under discussion. But at the beginning of each visit I would encourage him to talk associatively, so as to get a sense of what he had experienced and what he had been concerned about since I was last there. In this way I could form a picture of what was important from *his* point of view; what his current mood, frame of mind and feelings were. I also got some idea of what he did *not* want to deal with just then. All of this was valuable in setting the scene for the next step in the work.

When we respond to another person in this way, not only do we have a better chance of understanding what their current experience is like, but sometimes we enable the other person to become aware of ideas and feelings which were formerly unconscious. Most of the time our busy lives prevent this occurring. A colleague who had recently spent time away from home on a business trip, which involved living for some weeks in another country alone, commented when he returned that he had increased his awareness of himself in this period. "You forget," he said, "how living with others stops your associations from developing." For a while he had had the time and privacy to allow his to emerge. Fortunately the proximity of someone else is not always a hindrance. It is possible to interact with other people in ways which stimulate rather than discourage the emergence of associations and insights.

Patience is important because insights of this kind cannot be forced. They have to be cultivated. We can never "make" them happen. Even a well-intentioned prod on our part can be damaging if it is too aggressive or judgmental, like the way a friend described the way he had "helped" a butterfly emerge from its chrysalis. Only after he had freed it did he realize that it had begun to stiffen and then wilt as the air suddenly dried its wings before it was ready.

The ability to listen to someone else in this acceptant understanding way is a two-stage process. We need to understand how it differs from our more customary ways of interacting. And we need to develop the sensitivity and practice to engage in it successfully. In this section of the course we shall be exploring the concepts which underlie this skill and the techniques which need to be learned if we are to use it effectively.

LISTENING AS A "HELPING" INTERACTION

Listening to another person in an understanding way can have two purposes. One is to increase *our* understanding of them as we listen to them share thoughts and feelings, and as we perceive elements in their experience of which they may not be conscious. The other is to enable *them* to better understand themselves. Each is equally valid. Usually we hope that both will occur.

When the latter purpose is dominant it is often in the context of a "helping" relationship. By this we usually mean a situation where one person explicitly asks another for help with a problem in living. Sometimes the person whose help is sought is a professional who will be paid for offering it—for instance, a psychiatrist, counselor or social worker. Sometimes the help is professional but unpaid—for instance, pastoral counseling or the kind of helpful listening which we nostalgically think of the traditional family doctor as having provided in the past. Sometimes it is nonprofessional in the sense that the person who listens has no professional training but is sensitive and concerned—a close friend, neighbor, an older brother or sister, a compassionate boss. A helping relationship of this kind can also occur without a formal request. When we become aware that another person is troubled or worried and would probably benefit from a chance to talk over his concerns, we can either ask if they would like to talk about it or we can simply behave in a way which will tacitly encourage them to do so.

Clearly we all have needs at some time or other in our lives to talk over a problem or concern with someone whose sensitive responses will help us gain more insight into our own confusion, our mixed feelings or pain. In former days the presence of the extended family was an important interpersonal resource. So was a community in which one had many friends and neighbors of long standing. There was usually someone available with whom one could talk over concerns or problems, and to whom one could appropriately look for personal support and help. Today's society is lonelier, in the absolute sense that we move in and out of relationships more frequently; and in the sense that though most people have husbands or wives, children or friends, many of us find it difficult to talk openly to another about our feelings, whether of joy, perplexity, or pain.

The absence of such talk is crippling, for we best respond to problems, dilemmas and joys when we are most aware of our own experiencing. Awareness endows us with the ability to choose to be and behave as we are, or to choose to change ourselves and our behavior in whatever way we find desirable. In this sense awareness offers us the opportunity to be more fully human. Some of us are skillful in increasing our awareness through introspection, but for most people, awareness grows and insights occur more readily when we have the chance to talk over a problem with a sympathetic friend.

Today our need for supportive relationships is just as great as ever, but the resources of the family and community on which past generations counted are no longer resources for us. In a society where even the most profound relationships such as marriage and close friendship are relatively transient, there is need for us to find new ways of supplying this interpersonal support.

Why Might One Person Want to "Listen" to Another?

It may be that someone you truly care deeply about is in difficulty, and you want to help them for altruistic reasons. It may be that someone with whom you are in relationship is experiencing stress which causes their behavior to change in ways that deprive you of the fulfillment you formerly found in the relationship and perhaps even hurts you; so that you want to help them understand their difficulties for your sake as well as theirs. It may be that you need to make some decision which involves another person, and only by better understanding their experience will you be able to carry out your responsibility well. It may be that they work for you and that their difficulties are getting in the way of your task accomplishments. Whatever the dynamics, most of us sooner or later find ourselves in relation with someone else in difficulties to whom we would like to be helpful.

When we find ourselves in this situation there are several ways we can respond. Sometimes we want to solve the other person's problem for them: to "make it go away," as we soothe away the anxiety of a frightened child. We take whatever action we can think of to "fix" the problem—like putting a Band-Aid on a child's cut knee or giving another dollar to the boy who lost his pocket money. With adults this may take the form of trying to find them another job, intervening in a dispute, lending them money or trying to talk a husband or wife into returning. A second kind of reaction is to try to reassure the other person. "It's not so bad," we say. But far from helping them confront their problem, all this does is deny the reality of their feelings that it is indeed very bad. And in fact their feelings may be a truer measure of their reality than our response. Still another way is to try to legislate their bad feelings out of existence. "You shouldn't feel so bad," we say as if our giving an instruction could change their world. What we really mean is "Don't feel so bad because it makes me feel bad and I don't like that." Sometimes we retreat into intellectual analysis, as though to "analyze" the problem will solve it for them. Sometimes, in a different kind of effort to reassure them, we produce evidence that we have experienced similar problems and feelings and have survived—which simply serves to move the focus of sympathetic attention away from them and onto us.

None of these are much use. For none of them acknowledge the presence and strength of the other person's concerns and feelings, or the fact that it is the other person who "owns" the problem, and who sooner or later will have to come to grips with it. Many of the above responses would, in fact, prevent them from confronting it directly.

To be helpful in an appropriate adult way is to acknowledge the uniqueness and validity of the other person's experiencing for them. It is to help them look at and take responsibility for their problem; for their reaction to it; and for finding a solution. It is to help them grow, through the experience of confronting difficulties and coping with stress and pain.

The desire and ability to help another

person expand their understanding is obviously appropriate in all the central relationships in our lives—with husband or wife, lover, parents, children, colleagues, good friends and others who are important to us.

THE MANAGERIAL CONTEXT

The question as to how much we wish to exercise this ability in business relationships is somewhat more difficult for each of us to answer. One problem lies in the fact that a manager's role is structured around his or her ability to be directive, to give instructions, evaluate, make judgments and tell other people what to do. Many managers experience conflict about the degree of intimacy they can comfortably afford with other people whom they may later have to evaluate, perhaps adversely. Many managers have a sense that a close personal relationship will introduce a set of mutual personal obligations and commitments which sooner or later will turn out to be in conflict with those of the formal role. And most managers are concerned about the amount of time they will be distracted from their technical responsibilities.

One way of sorting out this conflict is to ask, "Who owns the problem?" Is another person involved in a difficulty which it is part of *your* job to sort out? And is their experience a part of that problem? If so, the manager needs to regard their experience as one aspect of the problem he must solve. Most employees in such situations will find it appropriate—even desirable—for a boss to ask how they feel and where they stand. In fact they are probably more likely to be resentful if he does not. Since people do not always know how they feel, or may be aware but unable to articulate feelings without help, the adoption of a listening style by the boss may be just what is needed. A listening role is equally appropriate when a manager needs to monitor people's sense of the way things are going, their morale, their satisfaction.

The conflict is greatest when a subordinate is caught in difficulties which are not directly relevant to the work at hand—a divorce, the illness of a husband or wife, anxiety over a child's defiant behavior, and so on. Here one faces the difficulty that by offering a helpful ear, a manager may be moving into a relationship of more intimacy than he is usually comfortable with—albeit temporarily. In civilian organizations where superiors are not expected to take responsibility for the personal problems of the people who work for them, each manager usually has to decide for himself where he stands on this issue, taking into account the extent to which he is willing to relax a general rule in relation to the needs of a particular person, the acuteness of a particular problem, or the personality of the individual concerned.

When we consider the nature of the relationships in which managers are typically engaged, it is also useful to make a distinction between increasing *our* understanding of others, and helping others increase *their* understanding of themselves. Though not everyone will agree that the manager's role necessarily includes the latter kind of "helping relationship," few will disagree that it is exceedingly important for a manager to know where his people are "at," either in terms of a particular issue, or in general. It is crucial for a manager to monitor the work-related experiences, opinions and feelings of those who report to him or her, so that he can understand not what he assumes them to be, but how they are actually experienced by others. And the only way to do this is first to ask, and then to listen to what is said in a way which stays with that other person's point of view and encourages them to share their experience as fully as they are able or feel to be appropriate.

Obviously such interactions take time. Every manager is continuously faced with an ongoing choice between focusing on the technical and on the human aspects of the task he has to administer. It is not often possible to attend to both at once, so that each manager has to work out her or his own answer to the question, "How much?" Obviously the answer will vary according to the interpersonal inclinations and skills of the individual; to the accessibility of the people who work for him; to the nature of the work situation and whether or not there is a private and quiet place in which to talk without interruption from colleagues, secretaries, and telephones. (Many important conversations between managers and their subordinates take place after the end of the official workday, in the privacy which occurs when most other people have gone home.)

In addition to learning how things are at a particular moment, the manager who makes the effort to explore the human side of his enterprise is making an important investment. For in attempting to understand his superiors, colleagues, and subordinates, he is signaling to them that he perceives their point of view to be genuinely relevant to his own job. Since most of us like to be personally valued rather than neglected or ignored, such interest is likely to increase the regard which others have for him. Moreover, once he has demonstrated that he perceives that an understanding of other people's points of view is a legitimate part of his role, it is likely that people will take more initiative in coming to him with problems, rather than waiting to talk about them either until he asks, or until their troubles affect both their own work and that of others, turning a personal problem into an organizational one. In this respect, a manager's ability to listen and understand other people's points of view is a necessary and useful check on the state of effective working relationships.

The purpose of this note has been to explore the ways in which feelings and thoughts contribute to personal meanings; and to consider the necessity of suspending our rational analytical style of interacting, if we want to help others increase their awareness by exploring feelings and thoughts which are on the brink of consciousness. The note has emphasized the fact that a responsive non-evaluative listening style of interaction is not a substitute for the rational analytical mode, but is supplementary—some would say complementary—to it.

In thinking about your likely future role and about the extent to which you are likely to make use of each style, you have an opportunity to give deliberate attention to something which will, for the most part, occur out of awareness. For there is usually not enough time in daily life to consider deliberately which mode we want to adopt in every single interaction with another person. Sometimes the choice does occur in awareness as a kind of snap judgment. Often it is something we usually deal with out of awareness, doing what "comes naturally." This note, this section of the course, and the course as a whole are intended to give you an opportunity to think deliberately about the kind of interpersonal styles which you would like to have come naturally to you, and the uses you will put them to; and to learn a new skill which will give you more versatility in your personal interactions with others.

Cases

Ashok Rajguru

In October 1962, Donald French, a graduate student in clinical psychology at the University of Chicago, interviewed his friend, Ashok Rajguru, a doctoral candidate in theoretical physics at Northwestern University.

Ashok Rajguru had lived in Calcutta, India, until 1960, when he had received a fellowship to continue his studies in physics at Northwestern. By the fall of 1962, Ashok had completed all the requirements for the Ph.D., except for a thesis in which he hoped to make an original contribution to quantum electrodynamics. He had not been home since first coming to this country.

Donald and Ashok had first met in June 1962 as the only summer employees at an electronics company in California. They had decided to room together and, during the summer, developed an affable relationship without ever becoming close friends. They had frequently talked about such topics as politics, literature, and economics, but had found that their social and recreational interests were quite different.

The interview was arranged by telephone one day in advance. Donald told Ashok that he wanted to practice understanding another person's point of view. Donald explained that this was part of a course at the University of Chicago, and that he would be graded on his ability to understand how someone else felt about things. Ashok readily agreed to help, without any apparent concern over whether his identity or the interview would be kept confidential.

On the day of the interview, Donald drove out to Evanston, had lunch with Ashok, and brought him back to Chicago. After a one-hour tour of the campus and some conversation about life at Chicago, Donald invited Ashok over to his room for the interview. No one else was present. Donald set up a borrowed tape recorder in the middle of the room, explaining that he wanted to listen to the discussion again so as to improve his understanding and technique. The recorder did not appear to bother Ashok, and Donald felt that the general atmosphere was one of relaxation and mutual confidence.

Donald 1: Well, as I explained before, the object is not to talk about something that interests me, but rather to talk about something that is on your mind currently.

Ashok 1: I guess I have to start somewhere!

D2: Well, what have you been thinking about lately? Is there anything particularly bothering you? [Long pause.] It doesn't have to be anything very profound. Just the kinds of things you have been thinking about; how the world is impressing you.

A2: Well, the trouble is that everything I think about nowadays is connected either with physics or politics. [Pause.] But I don't really want to talk about that.

D3: You feel you don't want to talk about physics or politics.

A3: Well, there's really no reason I shouldn't want to talk about physics, but I don't know whether that would be something of interest to you. I don't mean something technical in physics, I mean things like what you can or cannot do in physics, how far you can go, whether it is really worthwhile to be interested in this one thing to the extent that you have to forget everything else, and whether it is really worth it.

D4: Are you having some doubts about your real future in physics?

A4: Yeh! I really don't know if it is worth doing—it's quite clear that if you want to do something really worthwhile and creative, not merely in physics but in any field, then you have to think only of the field to the exclusion of everything else. And this somehow seems to me to be too great a price to pay.

D5: You feel like it would be too confining!

A5: Yes. There are just too many things in this world which one should bother about, which are interesting, to which one should pay some attention, that it isn't worthwhile to exclude everything for just one thing. I have very serious doubts as to whether it is worth it. And yet, these doubts are compounded with other doubts; such thoughts probably arise because I have done nothing significantly creative, and such doubts would probably no longer be there if I were to prove myself capable in any significant way.

D6: Uh-huh.

A6: So it's probably more basically a question of my capabilities in the field.

D7: You are wondering about your ability to do something significant?

A7: Yes, significant!

D8: And you feel like you want to do something significant.

A8: Yes. And yet it seems that, given the capabilities that I seem to have, and to do anything significant, I would have to put in much too much effort—to the exclusion of everything else.

D9: You don't feel it's possible to make contributions in physics without dedicating most of your time to it.

A9: Yes, I think it's pretty impossible. You cannot do anything significant with a peripheral attachment. I think I'm pretty much convinced of it. And I . . . [Pause.]

D10: Somehow you are hanging back.

A10: That's right. And it's very serious, because I'm at a stage where hanging back can be absolutely fatal, and I have more or less . . . one decides on a career long before one goes into a Ph.D. program—that is, when one decides to go into graduate school—and at this late stage of graduate school, to have such doubts when I should be putting in all the effort that I can, this can be pretty fatal. So it's very disturbing. I don't work as much as I should. When I do work, I have my mind half on other things. Not necessarily personal things, but things that it seems very important and relevant that I should know, things like economics and politics and modern novels. [Pause.]

D11: These things seem to be diverting your attention away from physics.

A11: Right!

D12: And you feel sort of guilty about that?

A12: I feel very guilty about that—I mean, I go into the library and read all sorts of other things, and I feel very guilty about it afterwards. And this is creating a hell of a problem for me. I just don't know what I'm going to do about it. And it's all the more painful because, after all, I've come here from another country with a specific purpose. I gave up a set of privileges which were open to me at home, I borrowed money, I came over, and made a very definite commitment.

D13: Ah yes, I see.

A13: A very definite commitment. If I were at home at this stage, I would be much freer to choose what I wanted to do. I could conceivably give this up and go into something else, but now I've more or less burned my boats—I mean, my bridges—and it's very disturbing.

D14: So the thing has some family implications as well as professional?

A14: Yes, that has some significance. I mean, part of the force which compels me to keep doing what I am is the notion that if I should at any time make a very drastic change in my career—at this stage—I would be disappointing a lot of people in the family. Not because they are very bent on seeing me as a physicist, but because they won't be very happy about the waste of time.

D15: You feel like they contributed something to your being able to come here, and that you would sort of be letting them down to cast it aside.

A15: Ah, yes, but in a somewhat different sense. That is to say, they have contributed to my coming here only to the extent that they were willing to make certain emotional sacrifices. For instance, it is very conventional in an Indian family that if the father should die, the mother should stay with one of the sons. It is just taken for granted, there is no question about it. And when I came away here, it was pretty clear that I was shirking that part of my responsibility. Clearly, my mother couldn't stay with me if such circumstances should arise. And my being willing to take this advantage and my mother being willing to let me off—she couldn't actually hold me in any sense, I mean, I was grown up—but her willingness to let me come reflected on her part a willingness to let me do whatever I should want to do. And if, having taken this opportunity to do what I want to do, I then at a late stage decide, no, it's all a waste of time and I really didn't want to do this, or I'm changing my mind, it's being capricious in a fashion which is asking too much of the other people who have made sacrifices in allowing me to do what I should want to do.

D16: So in a way, as I see it, you feel you are sort of temporarily shirking some of your responsibilities; and that this will be all right if you are able to do something successful with the time you have taken.

A16: Right! And it would not be so good if I should have nothing to show for all this time. And I really have nothing to show, but that's probably not too relevant because at this stage probably not too many people do. But quite apart from that, in going to courses and learning what I have to learn, I have by no means devoted as much attention and got as much out of being here as I could have if I were very sincere and serious. And this seems to be such a vast waste of my capabilities, of my time, of the fellowship I'm drawing on—it's a waste of everything. [Pause.] And I feel very guilty about defrauding others who are making sacrifices. Someone is giving me a fellowship so that I don't have to teach, and I should, therefore, study all the time.

D17: You feel that maybe someone else should have been given this opportunity who would hurl himself into it?

A17: Yes, someone who would get much more out of it. [Pause.] It's very bad. [Pause.] It gives you very serious feelings of guilt. It's not that I haven't worked at all. That's not it. But if I look back at the kind of work I used to do at home—by the kind of work, I mean the amount of time I would have put into serious work—it's clear that in my two years here, I could have done much, much more. That is beyond question.

D18: I see. So you really feel like there are a lot of capabilities there that you are not measuring up to?

A18: Yes. A lot of—ah—not merely capabilities, but a lot of just sheer hard work. I mean, you can't do any creative work without a lot of hard work. I'm just sort of learning this and that in a peripheral way. [Pause.] This is a very big question. I feel that I've come over here at this very important period in my life, and it's just being wasted. This is extremely undesirable. Now that I am here, I don't know what I can do about it, apart of course from telling myself that I have to work hard—and this and that. But you can tell yourself, and yet, if certain things don't work out, what can you do? Something has to be done about it.

D19: So you are fairly certain at this point that you are going to see this thing through?

A19: Yes, if for nothing else but the fact that I am sort of trapped physically. And being trapped physically, I have to make the best of it. I mean, I'm certainly not at that stage of despair where people sort of throw everything to the winds. Neither am I at that state of despair nor can I give myself up to such a state. That would be accepting defeat, and I'm not willing to. But what makes me sad is that I'm making the best of a bad bargain, whereas this could have been such a good bargain. [Pause.] I think back as to what my picture of myself here was when I was at home—you know, you project yourself forward and you think about what you'll be doing when you get there—and . . . [Pause.]

D20: It hasn't measured up to your expectations.

A20: No, it hasn't measured up at all. I compare my projections with the realities of the past two years, and there is so much lacking—much too much lacking.

D21: I gather from what you were saying before that you might leave if you were not constrained by all sorts of forces like being here, your scholarship, etc.

A21: Yeh! I think if I were in a similar situation at home, I very possibly would leave the university for a number of years. Having a master's, I could just go and teach for a while, forgetting about a Ph.D. I very possibly would have done that. And then at the end of two or three years, I possibly would have realized that my interest in the subject wasn't totally dead—rather, that it was a combination of circumstances which had covered it up somehow. [Pause.] And another thing which keeps bothering me is the lack of motivation. You know—when you are at school, people by and large have a desire to excel. They are in a group and they naturally want to stand out in the class, and this function with me is just as normal as anything else. I used to pay a lot of attention to it but . . . [Pause.]

D22: You used to be motivated, but you are not now.

A22: Now when I go to a class and have to take an exam, it just does not bother me if I am fourth in a class of seven. Whereas previously, I remember—of course, there were different circumstances—that if the difference between me and the second boy in the class was even close, it would keep me awake at night. And now this just doesn't bother me at all. Of course, at this stage it is silly to even think in those terms. But even so, that's an important element in motivation. People around you are working or getting ahead, and learning a lot, and you want to know as much as they do. If possible, you want to know a little more. Basically, very simply, that's just ego. But nowadays, that just doesn't work. I've given that up totally. Here is someone working very hard, I just say he is working hard but I'm not. So what? [Laughs.]

D23: You don't feel any competitive motivation.

A23: Right! That has vanished absolutely. It was there very strongly till the last days when I took my master's exam. [In India] it meant so much to me that I could come first in my master's exam. It was one of the strongest boosts I've ever had in my life. I worked like mad for six months. I was sick, very seriously, but that didn't matter.

D24: And you were successful.

A24: Oh, yes! All through my school and college career, there has only been one exam in which another boy beat me. This was always one of the strongest elements in my motivation. I couldn't possibly sit in a class in which other people were doing better than I, any better at all. This idea was very repugnant to me. And yet I come here and give that up totally! And yet it's quite clear to me that with a moderate amount of hard work, I can definitely be as good as the students I'm with now, if not a little better. It's not that there is a huge gap between them and me, I don't feel that at all.

D25: So by asserting yourself in the past, you could excel; and you still could, but for some reason, you just aren't doing it.

A25: Right. There was one course in which I did somehow assert myself. It became important for me to do well and I did. There were 13 or 14 people in the class, and I got either the highest or second highest mark. I don't know for what reason I did this; I think it was perhaps that I valued that one professor very much.

D26: So you still can excel if it matters.

A26: Right; if it matters. And somehow it has ceased to matter.

D27: Somehow, beating the other guys doesn't matter any more.

A27: It doesn't matter. And having lost this motivation, I seem to have lost all motivation.

D28: I see.

A28: Previously, it was not only that I should have to beat the other guys; in the process, it was also very important that I should know just for the sake of knowing. One of the strongest elements in motivation was that I should excel, but apart from that, there were other relatively minor ones—that I should know, since there were so many things to be known; I couldn't be ignorant. But now, having lost the motivation to excel, I seem to have lost the other ones too. It no longer is very important to me that I don't know all the details of quantum electrodynamics.

D29: Knowing for the sake of knowing has gone too.

A29: It has gone too. And this, more than the motivation to excel, is what bothers me. This is much more important, and this is what bothers me. I open a book in physics and read five pages and find it tough going, so I just leave it.

D30: You feel that loss of the desire to know for the sake of knowing is a more serious loss.

A30: Oh, I think so. I have no illusions as to the extent of my capabilities in physics. I realized long ago that I'm not going to be one of the very top. But to be even a moderately competent physicist, you have to know. If you are very good, then you make very good use of what you know, but even if you are going to be a moderately competent physicist, you have got to know. You have to have the desire to know. And if you don't have that, then you might as well go and be a clerk. I mean, some place where you just do routine work; where there is no question of knowing, no question of finding out, no inquiry, no interest in what you are working at.

D31: There is a kind of feeling of despair at not being readily able to be the best physicist in the country.

A31: Yeh! It is very difficult to know which came first: the realization that I was not going to be a Heisenberg or the realization that I just wasn't as interested in these things as I used to be. I think the other one came first; that is, I realized earlier what my limitations as a physicist were. That is, I realized what was the highest class to which I could aspire. And since then it has been . . . it's very difficult to say what the reasons could be.

D32: You sort of gave your all in competing with the others and went as far as you could go; as far as you felt your capabilities could carry you.

A32: Well, yes and no. [Reluctantly.] I took my capabilities as far as they could go in exams and competing with the others, but I realize that I could take them much further in terms of being a physicist rather than in terms of excelling in exams. And it is this part which I'm not fulfilling. I have fulfilled my part in terms of taking exams and that kind of thing. I'm not fulfilling what I realize are my capabilities in being a physicist; that is, in doing some good original work.

D33: I see. You feel like you did your part as a student, but now you are sort of falling down in applying it to the profession.

A33: Right. I did my part very well as a student, but I'm doing practically nothing to make myself into a competent physicist, beyond what is required of me as a student.

D34: So you are finding the conversion from student to physicist a painful and difficult one.

A34: Yes, and yet these things merge so much into one another that I don't know whether I would put it in those terms. Because you continue being a student pretty late, even after your doctorate. When you are a young postdoctoral fellow, you are still really a student. Young postdoctorals even have their offices with the graduate students. [Laughs.] So this business of growing from a student to a physicist is a slow and gradual process. It isn't as though there was an abrupt jump that I'm having trouble adjusting to. It's a very slow and gradual process, in which a person normally should have no difficulty because he really doesn't realize himself when he has ceased to be a student and when he has become a physicist.

D35: Uh-huh.

A35: And I'm still conscious of the fact that I am a student. That is, I'm still in the process where I have more learning and less original work to do, at least for a limited period, rather than less learning and more sheer work to do. I've a lot of learning yet to do. [Pause.]

D36: So you are not sure that it is the conversion from student to physicist which is bothering you.

A36: No, I think that it is something even more fundamental. It has to do with things like this. You have only one life to live. What is important and relevant in that life?

D37: It's more a hesitancy to commit yourself entirely to physics.

A37: Right. [Pause.] It probably isn't that important that I should do something creative in physics. Somehow that shouldn't be and isn't an essential ingredient in my making myself happy. It is much more important that I should be happy in quite a variety of other things. Physics just isn't as important as it used to be.

D38: So you feel like there is a wider spectrum of interests that is becoming important to you.

A38: Yes. There was a time, for example, when I used to think that it didn't matter at all if in the process of coming over here—in the process of pursuing physics—the family should be hurt. There was a time when I used to think that it was perfectly all right if I went ahead; those drags from the family should not be a factor at all. But I have ceased to think in those terms! I have come to the state where I think that human relations are much more important than I used to think even two years ago.

D39: Uh-huh.

A39: And I think basically that it is this lack of fulfillment in human relations that is at the root of all this hesitancy. If I could find satisfaction in human relations, which are more important to me than they were two years ago, then that might revive my interest in things.

D40: I see.

A40: I mean that this is my estimate of what the situation is. I have no real idea as to whether this is correct. And that is why I have the feeling that if I were at home, just because I'm so close to the family and all that, I wouldn't have felt this lack in human relations which I do feel.

D41: I see.

A41: And that is what at home partly contributed to my serious interest in the subject. I didn't realize at that stage how much these things [human relationships] meant to me. I took them for granted because they were there and, therefore, I could be totally immersed in physics. Now I feel their lack. I realize how important they were to me, and since I can't now find fulfillment, I lack interest in other things too.

D42: I see. You feel that at home, you had satisfying family and friend relationships, and that this whetted your appetite for life, for physics, for everything.

A42: Right. Right. Exactly. It was important to me that I should learn not merely because I had to learn, but because I could talk about it to my friends, because they would be interested in what I was learning, and it would raise me in their esteem. This is all a feedback process, and the feedback circuit is now absent. [Laughs.] Essentially, I have to work now in a personal vacuum, and with the absence of the feedback, it seems impossible to work up the interest that I need to. I realize more and more how important that [supportive feedback and satisfying human relationships] was, and that is why basically I have this feeling of despair, because I don't see how I can radically alter the situation, given the circumstances that I have here. I have to make the best of what I have here. But it seems to me that the best I can make of the circumstances here may not turn out to be good enough. And that is where my basic hesitancy and fear arises.

D43: So flinging yourself into physics would not permit you to satisfy this need for rich human relationships.

A43: Rather, put it the other way around. The absence of rich human relationships makes it impossible for me to fling myself!

D44: Ah! Now I understand.

A44: And I don't see how I can correct the situation with regard to human relationships so radically here.

D45: Particularly here as opposed to home.

A45: Yes. And this inability to correct human relationships won't permit me to devote the amount of attention to physics that I would want to.

D46: Because here there are some barriers to satisfying human relationships.

A46: Yes. The strongest of the barriers is the absence of family ties. I mean, ordinarily you anchor yourself to your home and then move out. And now I don't have the anchor, so I don't move out, and it all ends in a vacuum—I live by myself, etc. Of course, I have casual friends, fellows in the department, but they are not of sufficient depth to assure me of happy human relationships.

D47: So the lack of the strong, secure family ties in this country, here and now, is hurting your application to your work.

A47: Yes, that is what I think. Of course, I could be very wrong. But that is what my analysis of the situation is. And if it is correct, then it seems to me to be pretty hopeless. That is why I have been thinking of a course of action which seems to me to be the best I could do. That is, there is one language exam I have to take, and there is one advanced exam one has to take while working on the thesis in the specific field in which you are working; so I've been thinking of finishing the advanced exam, finishing the language exam I have to take, and then getting permission from here to go back home. I wouldn't have the direct contact with the professors here, but I have enough confidence in myself that given some application, the aid of the professors at home, and some correspondence with the professors here, I could turn out a thesis that they would accept here. So I've sort of been toying with that idea for a while. I would finish the requirements here and then go home. I would be left with an unfinished oral exam at the end of the thesis, but that could be worked out somehow. I don't feel like submitting myself to this void long enough so that whatever lingering interests I have in the subject would die down. It might die down to the extent that you just can't rekindle it. I don't want that to happen, and I have to do something before that.

D48: You are afraid that you might destroy your interest in physics permanently.

A48: Yes, permanently, because of this peculiar set of circumstances.

D49: And you think that would be a bad thing to have happen.

A49: Yes, that would be very bad, because so much of my respect for myself is related to my capabilities in physics. If I should just throw in the sponge, that would very seriously hurt my esteem of myself. I couldn't do it! Well, probably if I were forced I would do it, but I wouldn't want to do it. It would be too much of a personal psychological disaster. I wouldn't want to do that at all. Of course, I've been toying with that idea. [Pause.] Hopefully, if I could somehow get going—but I don't see how I could do it—then I wouldn't have to take recourse to such a drastic step. But if I were forced to, then I certainly would. Because I would be much more willing to take the step than to allow my interest in physics to die down totally.

D50: Uh-huh. Then you don't want to let your interest in physics wane because this would damage your self-respect, and that would have a detrimental effect on your whole life.

A50: Yes, a very detrimental effect. There was a stage when I used to think that creativity was the only thing a man could live for. I have given up such a drastic view of things. I used to think that nothing else mattered. I have given up such a drastic view, but I still do place a pretty large premium on creativity. If my life were to be lived without any element of creativity, I don't think that I could make it a worthwhile life. I wouldn't have enough respect for that kind of life.

D51: So your feeling about yourself is that it is still very important to you to create.

A51: Very important.

D52: And yet there are other things which are important too—in particular, worthwhile human relationships.

A52: Right. And I'm realizing how much the presence or absence of these relationships interacts with creativity.

D53: You can't separate them.

A53: You can't separate one from the other. This is something which I never realized before coming to this country, just because my need for human relationships was satisfied. And I'm beginning to see how closely they are interrelated. You can't have one without the other. You could probably have satisfying human relationships without creativity, but not the other way around, at least not for me. I've known physicists who don't care if their wives divorce them, and it happens once in a while, but I don't think that I could be that way.

D54: So you feel a need for a kind of total existence.

A54: Right!

D55: One that is rewarding on all fronts, and you can't sacrifice one for excellence in the other.

A55: And the worst part of the present situation is that the absence of one leads to the absence of the other, so that I'm in a state of total absence. [Laughs.] And yet I feel trapped. The way of doing away with this situation seems as though it should be so simple. One should have satisfying relationships, this should allow one to work, and it all should be so simple. And yet I'm in physical circumstances such that I can't put this to the test; I can't make it work.

D56: Uh-huh. So you feel that even though you have some insight into the problem, the circumstances won't let you do anything about it.

A56: That is right. [Pause.] So the problem has now resolved itself to the point that, given the fact that the circumstances won't allow me to get the best solution, I'm wondering what is the next best thing that I can do. I should be man enough to acknowledge the fact that I have to put up with something which is not the ideal solution and make the best of it. But that takes quite a while. It is a very difficult thing to do.

D57: It isn't a fully satisfying way out.

A57: No. And this period in one's life

could be so productive, it could be so satisfying. Here I am on the verge of doing creative work, at the end of the learning process, maturing from a student and adolescent into a man, and this could be such a satisfying and full period in one's life, and yet I'm living in a total vacuum. This is very unsatisfying.

D58: You sort of compare the reality with the potential and see a lot lacking.

A58: Right. You compare what it could have been and what it is and there is too much lacking. Far too much!

D59: I can certainly understand that.

A59: But I have to make a go of it. [Pause.] I have to work enough to get a decent thesis out, to learn enough to write a good thesis, and to do it fast enough so that my work will be one step ahead of the decay process. [Laughs.]

D60: Your self-respect demands that you find some way out.

A60: Right. And my self-respect also demands that I find some way out myself. I should not have to go and seek help from other people. You know, when I talk to one or two other boys about this, they say, "Your problem is psychological and you should go and see the psychological counselor." It could be psychological, but an element of my self-respect is that I should solve my problems myself. And it seems to me that I see with a fair degree of clarity just what my problems are. Half the solution to any problem lies in seeing what it is.

D61: So it's not really a question of whether he could help you or not, it's more a question of . . . you feel like you should be able to solve your problems yourself.

A61: Right. And there never has been a situation in the past in which I couldn't solve my own problems, no matter what they were. So I'm not willing to accept defeat on that count.

D62: So you don't really feel like you are beaten yet.

A62: No, certainly not! I feel that I'm down but I feel that I'll be up. [Laughs.] No, I certainly don't feel beaten at all. But I do realize that doing nothing about it for a sufficiently long time could take me to a state where I was effectively beaten, because I couldn't drag myself up. But I haven't reached that state. [Pause.] I feel reasonably confident that I can drag myself up, I don't know how, but . . . [Pause.]

D63: So you feel that at this stage of the problem, something constructive can be done, but that maybe, if you let it go on and on, it would get out of hand.

A63: Right! Right! And I even feel that at this stage, something constructive could be done by myself alone. But I'll be damned if I know what it is. [Laughs.] There is just that vague feeling of confidence in yourself, which sometimes turns out to be wrong. You know, you always tell yourself, "Heck, I've pulled myself out of ruts before and I'll do it again." But every once in a while, it doesn't happen that way, people don't pull themselves out. I only hope that I can do it but [Pause] I'll be damned if I know what I can do.

D64: So behind the problem, you still feel adequate to deal with it, but just what the solution is, you don't know yet.

A64: Basically, yes. And I don't know just what the basis of this confidence is. If someone were to ask me, "Why do you feel confident?" I wouldn't be able to give an answer. I have been told by people who have known me that, from the outside, I do look self-contained, a more or less confident individual. But, of course, inside one is never the way he seems to another person. Knowing yourself from the inside, you are never as sure of yourself as an outsider can be. In spite of that, I feel sure of myself to a certain extent. So there is no reason that I can offer for this confidence, having known myself from the inside with all the uncertainties that I have. An outsider who has known me for a while would say, "Well, of course you'll pull through, you're a more or less balanced individual, of course you'll pull yourself through." But from the inside, of course, I'm not a balanced individual. No one is if one goes deep enough. So I've no reasons to offer as to why I should feel confident except for the fact that life has gone on in such a way that nothing catastrophic has happened so far. Things seem to have worked out just right. Otherwise, I can see no reason why I should feel as confident as I do.

D65: So you sort of feel that you are not as adequate to solve this thing as other people think you are, and yet you still feel that you are adequate.

A65: Yes. I mean that other people are not willing to recognize that I do have a problem. People in the department at Northwestern, who know me fairly well, are unwilling to admit that I could have a problem—that I could be struggling this way with myself. They feel that I haven't worked hard enough in the past six months, but that this kind of thing often happens and that I'm really all right.

D66: It's sort of puzzling to you that they can't even see the war going on inside of you when it is so important.

A66: Right. Well, I can see why that should be so. I try very strongly not to reveal too much of my interior to other people, to sort of preserve an exterior, a very conscious sort of hypocrisy. It is hypocrisy, but it is conscious and I would acknowledge that, so it ceases to be a crime. So I can understand why people wouldn't see the thing either as existing or as being important.

D67: So maybe your self-respect sort of demands that you not show too much of what is going on inside.

A67: Right. I think that is a very important element in my behavior. If I have problems, I feel that I should keep them to myself. I shouldn't have to go around to people and tell them that these are my problems and ask them what to do about them. And people shouldn't come to me and say, "Jesus, man, you look like a cat with a lot of problems." [Laughs.] That is something which I certainly can't stand.

D68: You wouldn't want that to happen.

A68: I certainly wouldn't want that to happen.

D69: So you don't let them see.

A69: Yeh! And apparently I do that well enough so that they just can't see that or believe it. They don't believe that it exists. I myself have to do something about it. And I recognize what the problems are and have to do something about them.

D70: So you feel that, at least in your own mind, you have made some progress in defining the problem.

A70: Right. I think that the end of last term, I was at the stage where I didn't even know what was wrong. I was off the mark to the extent that I thought that getting away from Northwestern would be very important. You know, getting a job out someplace else. Well it was important in a very minor sense. A change of surroundings always helps. But I was foolish to think that could be important enough by itself. Toward the end of the summer and the beginning of this term, it became clear that this wasn't as important as I had thought it was. So I have overcome the total ignorance of thinking that getting away from Northwestern was the solution.

D71: You tried one solution and you realize now that that wasn't the way.

A71: Yes. That had pretty much no relevance at all. [Long pause.]

D72: So now the question in your mind is, what next?

A72: Yeh! [Pause.] Here, I just don't know. [Long pause.]

D73: And yet underneath it all, you feel like somehow or other you are going to work this thing out.

A73: Right. There is a vague notion that somehow I'm going to work it out. But it is the vaguest of notions. Somehow, I can't picture myself going to the dogs. I'll do something. [Laughs.] I just can't be stupid enough to allow that to happen.

D74: So in a way, this self-respect, which contributes to the problem by kind of locking up your feelings inside, is also the same force which is going to work things out.

A74: Yes, hopefully. Right. Probably a person without this feeling would have been tempted to give up at an earlier stage. A person without this feeling of confidence in himself would have been tempted to say, I'm not capable of solving this, or, I must go to a third person, or, I'm going to do something very drastic about it, or—I don't know. In general he might decide that he himself could not solve it. But you are right, the very element of keeping up appearances which contributes to the problem by locking things in myself is the same element which contributes to my self-confidence. Of course, it is silly to think that self-confidence alone could pull me through, because there are clear circumstances which are creating the problem. And something will have to be done about the circumstances.

D75: Uh-huh. There are external forces acting on you that are contributing to this thing also.

A75: Right. And I have to do something about them. So the problem is really deciding what I want to do about them. Then I must force myself to go through with it.

D76: So you are beginning to feel that the problem is one of adapting yourself to these external forces.

A76: Right. Right. I must tell myself, "Look, the circumstances are such that, beyond minor alterations here and there, you can't basically alter the circumstances in which you find yourself. Therefore, rather than try to adapt the circumstances to you, now try to adapt yourself to the circumstances." This is what I have not done in these two years. I have continued to be the same individual I was when I came here. The difference in the circumstances, coupled with the continuity of my "being," has caused all these difficulties. Now I realize that I can't change the circumstances—I have to do something about changing myself. At least, my reaction to the circumstances. I have come to the definite realization that "you've tried for two years, and beyond such and such, you cannot alter the circumstances." I cannot hope for, ask for, or expect very deep human attachments here. This is a fact I have to accept. This is a fact I did not accept in these two years. And you know, because I didn't have these attachments, I have been unhappy and this and that. But now I tell myself, "You've tried for two years, you haven't found it, you aren't going to find it. And you must somehow adapt yourself to work in these circumstances in which there will be a lack of human attachment. And you have to live with the circumstances and alter yourself, rather than alter the circumstances." But this is a pretty difficult thing to do. I'm 23—I was 21 when I came here—and I'm pretty grown up by this time, so it's difficult to change.

D77: You feel that you have reached an age and level of maturity at which it is difficult to make an alteration.

A77: Right. I have a more or less full-grown set of values. I don't feel that I have to alter those values basically, but I have to adjust them to new circumstances, and it is quite difficult. Very difficult, but I have to do it, and I feel vaguely confident. Of course, part of this is coupled with the fact that I like the kind of attachments I have tried to form and failed to form. I place a great premium on such attachments.

D78: That is still a basic need.

A78: Still a basic need. And therefore, to tell yourself that you have to do without them, however temporarily, is still a very difficult thing to acknowledge and work on. But it has to be done, it has to be done. People in all sorts of circumstances do it, and I will have to do it too. I feel it will take a long while but . . .

D79: So you kind of see the problem now as one of having come into a new environment with a personality structure which was well suited to the old environment, and now here you are transplanted to a new place with new forces working on you, and it is sort of necessary to adapt, but also very difficult because the old values are deeply important.

A79: Yes, deeply important. They are deeply ingrained, but more important than that, they seem to me to be the right values. If I could somehow reason myself into their inadequacy, then I would be more ready to shed them.

D80: So it is a little puzzling as to why they are not here in this new environment.

A80: Yeh! And I somehow have to adjust. [Long pause.] The difficulty has been that all these two years, I haven't made any effort to change myself—none whatsoever—and that effort has to be made.

D81: If you don't make the effort, the adjustment won't happen?

A81: No, I'm certain that it won't happen. Just by looking at the past two years. Adjustments of the type I have to make don't happen by themselves; no, you have to make a conscious effort to do it. And I just haven't made the effort at all, because I thought that the kind of personality I had was the kind of personality I would continue to like having. It fitted in pretty well with the circumstances I lived in. It seemed to me to be a personality no part of which I would like to shed. And yet here I am, and some parts of my personality just aren't relevant and have to be shed. So it's a pretty difficult process.

D82: So life was very satisfying and you were an adequate personality at home.

A82: Right. And I've ceased to be an adequate personality.

D83: Without changing at all.

A83: Without changing at all. And in the back of my mind there is this thing which keeps telling me, "Oh, no! You are an adequate personality. The circumstances are wrong." And yet, at some stage I have to realize that I cannot alter the circumstances. Therefore, the definition of the word *adequate* has to change. An adequate personality is one which copes with circumstances. And what was adequate there just isn't adequate here. There is no point in hanging onto things which were suited to a different environment and aren't suited here. Take some simple things, for example. In the type of family in which I was brought up, it was quite a virtue to be nonaggressive. By nonaggressive I don't mean anything physical. But in everyday life, just to be sort of mildly self-effacing is considered to be quite a virtue.

D84: This is the way people should behave.

A84: This is the way my father behaved. Therefore, this is the way I learned to behave. This is the way my mother has always told me is a nice way to behave. And it has always been very adequate. That is to say, I have missed nothing because of that. I have been allowed to be happy with that kind of a personality; but that doesn't work here. And yet in the back of my mind, I keep telling myself, "There was nothing wrong with that, it was quite all right, you were a decent person then, why do you have to change?" And yet circumstances are different, so I have to change. That just isn't adequate enough.

D85: So you feel that one of the ways in which you have to change is to be a little more aggressive, the way people are here.

A85: Yes. Specifically in connection with getting to know people. At home, even by being sort of mild and self-effacing, social factors worked in such a way that you still could know a lot of people. But here, unless circumstances throw you together in a special way, you do have to go out to meet people. You have to make the effort.

D86: You have to assert yourself.

A86: You have to assert yourself! If you are in a group of people, you have to make your presence felt. Otherwise, people just won't take note of you. People will take note of the person who is making the largest effort to make his presence felt. And yet I tell myself that it is crude and vulgar to make an effort to make your presence felt.

D87: Because that is the way it was at home.

A87: Yes. At home it was considered crude and vulgar if you tried to put yourself forward. And that isn't adequate here. The result is that I know very few people, apart from those I know by force of circumstances. I don't make the effort to know more people. I have been here for two years, I eat in those dining halls, I've been eating there every day for two years now, and yet, with one or two exceptions, I have never made an effort by sitting at a table where I didn't already know most of the people there. Not merely girls, but even boys. There are people whom I would like to know, who seem from a distance to be very nice people, but I just won't make the effort to go and sit down with them. They would be perfectly happy to have me there, I am certain, because . . . I have some confidence that I am not an obnoxious personality.

D88: And these people seem receptive from a distance.

A88: Yes. And yet I won't go out and make the effort.

D89: You feel that this is one of the ways in which some kind of adaptation is needed.

A89: Right. It is very necessary. There again, with regard to girls, at home it somehow happens that you don't have to go out to meet girls, you just come to know them. Your sister knows someone, or maybe there are two or three girls who live in the neighborhood and you get to know them, or your mother knows someone. You just happen to know a set of girls who are nice and whom you can go around with and talk with, without having to make the formal effort of going out and knowing girls. And you can be a very mild and nonaggressive person and yet know a lot of girls. Here, it is just the other way around. If you don't make the effort, you are out. You are just out!

D90: Getting to know girls is one of the areas in which you have to be especially aggressive.

A90: Right. There again, you tell yourself, "God, that's crude, you can't do that. [Laughs.] I mean, that's vulgar. How can you do it?" And yet it has to be done. It isn't crude and vulgar; it may have been crude and vulgar under a different set of circumstances, but here it is just the right thing. There are no absolute norms of crudity and vulgarity. It is just a question of what the norms of that particular social set are. By the norms of my social set at home, it might have been crude and vulgar, but it isn't here. I have to tell myself that since it isn't here, I have to act differently. [Long pause.] So it's a pretty difficult course of adaptation, which should have started long ago but was deferred by the illusion that circumstances could be made to change—which is pretty absurd. It's obvious that an individual can't change circumstances. That's totally beyond his control. He can only change his reaction to them. That is, he can adapt himself. That is the only thing he can do. [Pause.] I guess the realization is coming rather late, after two years.

D91: So, in a way, you are understanding what needs to be done, and yet it is a very painful thing to do.

A91: Yes, very painful. [Long pause.]

D92: And the thing has become necessary because now it is affecting your work.

A92: Right. It is necessary because now it is affecting the whole fabric of my future. That is totally dependent on my doing these things. [Pause.]

D93: So it seems like the alternatives are: Adapt in this environment and succeed, or return home and carry on with the physics where it is not necessary to adapt; and the latter is a very distasteful thing to do.

A93: Right. [Pause.] Because that would cause disappointments in people in the family and disappointments in myself. And in general, for any individual, acceptance of failure is not a very happy thing.

D94: So any particular path which you choose out of this dilemma involves some kind of pain.

A94: Right. And it seems to me that the least painful way would be that one which involved my adapting myself. For the simple reason that, once I make the initial stages of adaptation, I can get a lot of pleasure from the altered circumstances which I am missing now. I have this vague feeling and . . .

D95: So you think that the avenue of adapting would be the more rewarding one in the long run.

A95: Right. More rewarding and less painful. Quite frankly, not only will I be giving pleasure to myself, it's very possible that other people could find pleasure from my company.

D96: Uh-huh. It's probably a reciprocal thing.

A96: It is certainly true that I come from different circumstances, so there might be a variety of things others would be interested in, which they could find in me and not in other people around here.

D97: So you have some evidence that when you do begin to communicate with people, that there are certain things that they respond to.

A97: Exactly. Even in this country, whenever I have formed any acquaintances beyond the casual, it has never happened that I have not been rewarded. The first boy I got to know well enough here, this Irish boy who is no longer at Northwestern but used to be, I got to know him very well—I got to know his family, I got to know his girlfriend's family very well—and they all have reciprocated in a much fuller fashion than I expected when the friendship started out. So from the scattered instances I have gathered here, there is no reason I should fear not being rewarded—on the average—as I would like to be. There is no reason why it shouldn't work out that way.

D98: So you feel that breaking down the initial barrier is the main problem.

A98: Yes. Because where circumstances have somehow broken the barrier down, rather than myself having broken the barriers down, I have always been rewarded.

D99: Then there seem to be strong forces that make it go.

A99: Right. So if I could break the barriers down in other cases myself, where circumstances just don't happen to work the right way, or don't happen to do all the work for me—I'm sort of waiting for circumstances to do all my work for me [Laughs]; that can't always happen . . .

D100: And to do it some other way is to be "aggressive."

A100: Right. In all the cases where I have known someone relatively well, it has happened because we were thrown together. This Irish boy, I got to know him quite well because we met on registration day and then later found out that we were supposed to be in the same office with no third person. We shared the same office for a full year. So we were thrown together, and it worked out very fine.

D101: Here was just a random person, circumstances broke down the barrier, and a rewarding relationship ensued.

A101: And he is the kind of person who selects his friends very carefully. And he is also the type of person whom other people don't take to very easily. He is a cranky sort of person, very individualistic, so he formed pretty much no other attachments, with one or two possible exceptions. Later, other people shared the office, and new relationships didn't work out too well for either of us. So if he is selective and yet we could develop a fruitful relationship, then I have no reason to worry too much.

D102: You feel that if it can be done under the worst circumstances, it should be possible more often.

A102: [Long pause.] And yet it requires a change in my personality which I find very difficult. [Long pause.]

D103: Well, are you in the mood for a game of Ping-Pong?

A103: Sure, I used to be pretty good.

Chuck Lorring's Interview with Larry Baker

The following is a report which Chuck Lorring prepared on his interview with Larry Baker [See the Larry Baker (A) case in Part Two of the book]. The report was part of an assignment for a course he was taking in Interpersonal Behavior. One of Chuck's purposes in conducting the interview was to attempt to use the reflective technique in understanding Larry while helping Larry clarify whatever problems he was experiencing. We recommend that you review the Larry Baker (A) case before reading this report.

INTRODUCTION

From this mass of comments and feelings I will first concentrate on the flow of expressed feelings throughout the interview. Then I will try to organize these feelings into a logical scheme and relate them to events in his life that formed these opinions. The end result of this analysis will be a description of the interviewee as he views himself and his situation. Of course, I have my own personal opinions that I will try to substantiate, and I will try to demonstrate certain inconsistencies in his reasoning. Then the emphasis will turn to the mechanics of the interview and an evaluation of my comments. Last, I will attempt to generalize this particular case to my role as a businessman and propose some benefits possible from the experience.

FLOW OF FEELINGS

As one can see from Exhibit IV-3, the flow of expressed feelings by the interviewee was rather erratic and disorganized. After starting with an abstract issue raised by one of the cases here at school, he immediately progressed to his own feelings about that issue and what problems it posed for him. Once started on himself and his system of values, he proceeds to discuss at great length just about every facet of his business goals

Exhibit IV-3 LARRY BAKER (B)

Flow of Interviewee's Feelings throughout the Interview

Flow of Interviewee's Feelings Throughout the Interview

I am concerned over PBE.

↓

How do I draw the line between bribes and favors?

↓

I see two ways to succeed -- logic or bribes.

↓

I want a group feeling in my job.

↓

I want to be successful on the basis of my work.

↓

I want my own system.

↓

I think the underhanded people are the successful ones.

↓

I don't want to lose my values.

↓

I don't like manipulating people.

↓

I don't want to be successful at someone else's expense.

↓

I have two selfs -- my logical and my emotional.

↓

I can't resolve these two selfs and still be successful.

↓

I have faith in people and have often been disillusioned by them.

↓

I want to be at ease but I have my doubts if I can do this in business.

↓

I may have to create my own system.

↓

I haven't much time to find the right system.

↓

I just can't adapt.

↓

I like to know where I stand.

↓

I realize a need for subjective evaluation but would rather keep my personal values out.

↓

If it's impossible to find the system I'll escape but I'll always keep looking.

↓

I do realize my values will change over time but only in degree.

↓

I really do think I can find my system.

↓

I realize I have a definite need for people.

↓

I hate to have things forced on me.

↓

Leave me alone and I'll work things out.

↓

I'll just have to find my system.

and ethics. Although he spends a great deal of time discussing himself, it always seems to be at a rather objective and abstract level. Also at times, part of his seemingly disorganized manner of developing his reasoning is probably due to my directing him into certain areas. Therefore, I believe that an analysis of these feelings alone would not create the true picture of how he views himself. Hence, I have chosen to disregard the particular order in which these feelings are presented and to analyze the whole interview by a perhaps more meaningful approach. This flow chart, however, can be referred to as a helpful checkpoint in following the ensuing analysis.

SCHEMATIC ANALYSIS OF HIS POINT OF VIEW

As shown in Exhibit IV-4, I have categorized the interview comments into the events of his life, their meaning to him, and the demands of his work goals and his nonwork goals. The whole analysis follows the basic logic that, given a person's life, there are an infinite number of events that influence and shape that person's ultimate behavior. There are also certain demands that act upon the individual to further modify and determine his perception of himself.

Thus, I listed all the events of his life that he discussed. I then drew from his comments what significance each particular event had for him. The only criticism of this approach is that, although the interviewee may view these events in precisely this manner, it is rather evident from the flow chart of feelings that his perception of all of them is not nearly so clearly organized.

I then drew from additional comments two sets of demands either that he felt he was subjected to or that he voluntarily subjected himself to. The former group I called work demands and the latter I called nonwork demands. These two lists could have been expanded to include ordinary demands made of everyone in our given society, but for purposes of simplicity and validity, I confined myself to only his comments.

From all these forces that are shown acting upon the individual, I then searched the interview for evidence of conclusions on his part. Part of these data came from the summaries that I made of my comments. In several instances when I tried to express my interpretation of him from his point of view, he agreed with me very strongly. In some instances, his indication of agreement was almost unbelievable. In these cases, I felt I was justified in using my comments as material for the column, "Resulting Balance." Several comments used, however, are still only as he himself expressed them. The resulting balance then became the net result of all these forces that were shown acting upon him.

Although the same result would undoubtedly have been obtained by just discussing the interview, this method appears superior in presenting a clearer causal-relationship diagram of not only *how* the person perceives himself but some possible reasons of *why*. Again, the oversimplification of this scheme should be tempered by realizing that very likely the person's total perception of himself is not nearly so clear-cut. The important matter is that, told to reduce his perception of himself with regard to this particular situation to such an organized diagram, the interviewee could and would produce the same result.

MY OWN PERCEPTION OF HIM

Returning to my own point of view, I see the interviewee slightly different

Exhibit IV-4 LARRY BAKER (B)

Schematic Analysis of How Person Views Himself and His Situation

Schematic Analysis of How Person Views Himself and His Situation

Events of his life	Meaning of these events to him
Work experience:	
IBM →	I may have to integrate into a system to get ahead.
Ford →	If I can find a system like this I'll be able to keep my values.
job that he failed →	I want to know where I stand all the time.
business venture of his own →	I may want to create my own system.
work in factory →	I would never be happy with anything small or unchanging; I want more than that.
Military experience:	
instructor situation →	I might not be able to use logic in business like I did here.
uniform →	I don't like to have things forced on me.
Education:	
school →	I will get the tools I need to get ahead; it will open doors to new systems for me.
college in general →	This is the kind of clean competition I want in business--where I succeed on the basis of my work.
incident of final exam →	Sometimes acting according to my values hurts me; I must compete with people who don't feel as I do.
Social experience:	
changing gangs →	I have always managed to find a group with my system rather than modify my values.
California incident →	I have a definite need for association with people.
girls in class →	My logical self often conflicts with my emotional self.

→ INDIVIDUAL →

Demands of work

I will have to do good work.
I will also have to have other factors.
I may have to adapt to a system a little.
I will have to like my job.
I may have to do favors for people.
I will have to have a firm, logical approach.
I see where nice guys get squashed.

Demands of nonwork

I want to be successful and have things for my family
I want to be independent.
I want to be a self-made man.
I want to keep my value system.
I must protect myself against people who will chip away at my foundation.
I want to be at ease with both my selfs.
I don't have much time to look for my system.

Resulting balance

I will not allow myself to fall into a hole and destroy my values, but I do recognize that the degree of my values will change as I gain experience.
I recognize that there will always be a conflict between my two selfs, but I will try to keep my personal feelings out unless it is to modify my logical self so as to not hurt people.
I would prefer to be judged on my work, but I realize that there is a need for subjective evaluation and that these factors will also be important.
Although there will always be a question of whether I can find the right system, I'll always be looking for it or trying to create it.
Just as I have always managed to find the right group in the past, I think things will work out.

from the way he sees himself. Unfortunately, my association with him has been neither long enough nor deep enough to either repudiate or substantiate my views.

The basic difference centers about his rigorous devotion to his system of values. He claims to be deeply affected by these values and completely unwilling to change them in any great degree. Somehow I fail to see this result when he is faced with a permanent business situation in later years.

Perhaps I am saying that "the map is not the territory." On the one hand, he insists upon keeping his rather pure system, and yet he frankly admits his susceptibility to want of success and material possessions. He believes he can resolve this by being very mobile and relying on faith that his system does exist somewhere. I agree that he may ultimately find peace in a given system, but I do not believe that system will be as "pure" as the one he presently thinks he holds. As he himself points out, if a person wants something, he should sit down and plan how to get it. By his deciding to further his education and come to business school, I believe that he will, just as he predicts, change the degree of his values. In other words, as he pursues his education to higher limits, he also intensifies the very goal on which that education is based—to be a successful businessman. Consequently, after two years here, I believe he will leave with such high aspirations that the minor fact that he may have to do someone a favor or integrate into the system will no longer bother him as much. I do believe that he will always be somewhat of an individualist but that he will tend to "want to conform" to more trivial matters than he now lets himself admit. Add to this the pressures of time and status, and I believe his future self will be a bit tempered.

ANALYSIS OF INTERVIEW STRUCTURE

Using a scheme suggested by experts in the field, I categorized all my comments to his remarks in the manner shown in Exhibit IV-5. I must admit that the task was very difficult and was done from my point of view. Therefore, some decisions might be questioned by another person's different interpretation. However, by accepting at least the general trends, one can see that, basically, the interviewee talked about himself, and the interviewer clarified or accepted his expressed feelings. The two most common errors I fell into were interpreting what he said from my point of view and clarifying his unexpressed feelings. Of these two, the latter was more common and, in my opinion, produced the greater risk of damaging the interview results. Fortunately, most of these instances were accepted by him, and he made no effort to defend himself or inhibit his flow of feelings. A very good example is C18, where I interrupted him to say, "But you don't like to do that." I was taking the risk that this was how he felt when I really should have waited to let him express it. Fortunately, he accepted it quite well.

Another criticism, not brought out by this exhibit, was my preoccupation with trying to make him have a problem. I suppose this was due to the context in which I had studied the whole interview approach—all the reading material used examples of people confronted with problems. A good example of this tendency to concentrate on or develop a problem is C27, where I steered him back to the logical versus emotional conflict.

On the whole, for my first experience with such a technique, I thought that the results were very good. There were many

Exhibit IV-5 LARRY BAKER (B)

A Classification of an Interviewer's Responses

Among other subjects, the interviewee may talk about:	Among other possibilities, an interviewer may: A. Give the interviewer's opinions, experiences, advice, etc.	B. Interpret what the interviewee says from the interviewer's point of view.	Clarify or accept: C. The (intellectual) content of what the interviewee says.	D. The interviewee's expressed feelings.	E. The interviewee's unexpressed feelings.	
1. Objects, concepts, events, etc.	49, 52 (2)	8, 14 (2)		20, 32, 34, 36 (4)		8
2. Other people.				1, 9, 12 (3)		3
3. Himself.	27, 35 (2)	11, 21, 22, 26, 31, 40 (6)	39 (1)	2-6, 15-17, 23-24, 29-30, 33, 37-38, 41-44, 46-47 (21)	7, 10, 13, 18, 19, 25, 28, 45, 48 (9)	39
	4	8	1	28	9	

Note: 50 and 51 were direct questions.

instances in which I could have easily taken issue with him because of my own feelings, but I successfully avoided doing so. I also believe that more depth could have been achieved if I had had a closer relationship with the interviewee.

WHAT I LEARNED

As I objectively look back over the whole process of interviewing and analyzing, I try to pick out what generalities it all has to offer that I might possibly use as a future business executive. I suppose I am most aware of the value such a process would mean to me if either this person or someone precisely like him were one of my subordinates. In other words, what has this process taught me about this person that would enable me to better guide, supervise, and motivate him?

Basically, I would have the benefit of these main points:

1. I would never try to force anything on him.

2. I would give him as much free rein as possible in accomplishing his work.

3. I would appeal to him on a very logical basis, since this part of him takes the fore.

4. I would make it a point to provide him with as challenging and varied assignments as possible.

5. I would assure him that he would be evaluated primarily on the basis of his work.

In general, I found the whole experience a very interesting and enlightening one.

PART FIVE

CHOICES IN INTERPERSONAL RELATIONSHIPS

Introduction

A book like this can come to an end in a number of ways. Some would prefer an intellectual synthesis of the concepts used, others an emotional appeal on behalf of the use of these concepts. We can certainly understand the attraction of either. But our purpose here is to open up rather than provide closure.

Our experience is that the important learnings a reader takes away from a book like this are those that are personal, unique, and often private. These learnings come together in different ways for different people and they have unresolved different issues. They are not the kind of learnings that can be summed up in the last section of a book.

Our purpose in what remains of this book is to explore some choices and questions most of us face in living and working with others. The final chapter does offer a summary of sorts but not of what is important to remember from prior chapters. Rather, it presents what we see as the important limitations of what this book has had to offer. It also reports some of our own experience in trying to use the ideas of this book and what direction our own learning is taking beyond these learnings. Our intention in doing this is to point to further possibilities and choices. It is also to remind the reader, as well as ourselves, that the primary characteristic of the kind of learnings we have attempted to foster is their ongoingness.

We have also selected a number of readings we think are provocative and useful in exploring choices in interpersonal relationship. These readings are about ambivalence, responsibility, values, and success. The intention is partly to resolve some uneasy questions we suspect the book has raised. But it is mainly to encourage the asking of new ones. We suggest you read what follows not to find closure, but rather to move beyond what you already have learned.

Chapter Twelve

Beyond These Learnings

It may well have occurred to you that we have presented for the most part quite simple ways of thinking about very complex phenomena. Certainly, there are available theories of individual personality, as well as models of interpersonal relationships, that are much more complex than ones we have used. In one sense, our preference for simple "maps" and respect for the complexity of the "territory" tells something about us. In another, it tells even more about our experience over the years with varied learners other than ourselves. And we think it tells something too about the state of the art at this relatively early stage in the development of psychological ideas.

In any event, even the relatively simple ways of thinking presented here may have seemed difficult to use well. Had our primary goal been to increase your knowledge *about* ways of thinking *about* relationships, this book would have been very different. But our central goal was to some extent to increase your conscious and intuitive *skill*—that is, the *use* of knowledge. That is a very different and often much more difficult thing, and we are glad you got this far.

Whether one uses simple or complex "maps," relationships are not, in fact, the models we use to conceptualize them. They are to us what water is to fish. We live in them. They are a large part of what it means to be human, to be alive, to be becoming. They are still more often a mystery to us than they are understood. Sometimes we are stunned at their influence upon us, sometimes we despair of ever "making them work," sometimes we are gratefully awed at their potential for love. This is, of course, especially true when it is *our* relationships we consider. Other people's have a way of seeming much more clear to us than our own. And yet, so close to our trees that we can't see our forest, we need whatever help we can use in better living in our own relationships. To whatever extent previous material may have made a small contribution to you, we are pleased.

Yet, as we end, we want to add a caveat and a suggestion. What we have been trying to do for you may have been a useful, even necessary step on your personal and professional journey, but our experience is that it is probably insufficient, for some very good reasons.

First, *the limits of theory, or ways of thinking.* At this stage, only adherents with misplaced religious fervor *believe* in psychological thinking. They are ideas to be used, tested, refined, and over time replaced by even more useful ideas. In short, it is unwise to believe in a theory any more than one believes in a shovel. Both are to be used, have limitations, and will yet be improved. The test is what works best for you, given your purpose.

Second, *the demands of role.* Most of us will not be professionally focused upon individual development. Indeed, as managers, the demands of task, the needs of groups of people, and the realities of economics will press justifiably for our attention. Relationships will be very important, but not always the most important variable.

Third, *the limits of awareness.* It is clear that much that we and others experience and do is related to what is not conscious for us or them. Our behavior often results from forces not in our awareness. Attention to the behavior, and the discovery of patterns in it, may help us infer what is hidden from us. But it would be naive to assume that even a full-time commitment to knowing about ourselves or others would result in our really being in complete charge of ourselves or our relationships. Much about us remains a mystery to us. Remember that good therapists also go to therapists when they need them.

Fourth, *the limits of the psychological metaphor.* As we have worked over the years with psychological ideas, it has come to us that, collectively, they are a metaphor for man. And as Gregory Bateson told us, "Truths lurk in metaphors." But one metaphor is not likely to shelter all the truths we need or seek.

Given some of the limits of the psychological metaphor, we have found it necessary to ask, "Well, if I can understand only in part what is going on inside me, and between me and others, and inside others, how do I go about making judgments about how to behave?"

Over the years it has become more clear to us that when an impasse is reached in our own lives, when the use of psychological ideas seems to have led us into a blind alley, the way out of the fix is to switch from the "psychological" metaphor to what, for lack of a less loaded word, we call the "spiritual" metaphor. By "spiritual," we do not refer to the institutional expressions of such insights, although many people find their formal religious experience most meaningful. We refer instead to those ideas, those teachings, that nearly all formal religions in Western culture share, and that many Eastern religions teach too. And again, we like to keep it simple.

For example, over thousands of years, people have found that there are certain "character flaws," sometimes called "sins," that are worth avoiding because they diminish the quality of living. The "seven deadly sins" of pride, greed, lust, anger, gluttony, envy, and sloth are for us very helpful ideas. A short case may help explain what we mean.

A man we know had for years devoted a good deal of his considerable energy to sexual conquest. He had assumed that more sex is better than less, and regarded any day without one or two new partners a failure. As he gave himself over to the endless pursuit of sex, he found himself less and less satisfied in every way. Finally, he slid into a serious depression and sought professional help. Several years of individual and group therapy banished the depression, brought to awareness the pain of the many rejections he had to endure to find new partners who were willing, and slowly surfaced the interpretation that the problem was his closeness to his mother and inability to "leave" her. It was thought that whenever he became fond of a particular woman, having sex with her became impossible, because he associated her with his mother and thus experienced unconsciously the taboo of incest. A modern Don Juan problem. He decided to seek out a relationship with one woman, to face his unconscious fears with her, and to become capable of enjoying a close relationship. He moved away from New York City, found a woman, and lived with her.

It didn't work. It appeared the problem was not to be solved within the metaphor that diagnosed it. The way out for him was to seek the experience of love, not the management of lust. And to seek love, it was useful to switch metaphors. He joined a very active community center and got much involved in activities to benefit the very young and the elderly. In those "caring relationships" he seemed to discover loving feelings inside himself that were not erotic. Slowly, those feelings began to exist for women who were possible sexual partners, and after a number of affairs, he became more comfortable sexually in a loving relationship. But he still has to pay attention to lust as a kind of addiction and avoid acting on it, and he still has to encourage his loving feelings through active community work.

The point is that the psychological diagnosis was insufficient. It offered insight but not an effective action plan.

We could easily illustrate the other six "deadly sins," but perhaps considering the most troublesome one will be sufficient. Pride is generally listed first because it is so often the most damaging.

In our society, the first half of life seems dedicated to the strengthening of the ego into a competent, confident manager of ourselves. All too easily, that can slip over into arrogance and overweaning pride—especially in a secular society, which suggests that each person should become his or her own "god." When we experience no power larger than ourselves except the impersonal impact of random events, which is frequently the experience of agnostics and atheists, we necessarily assume that *we* are the only force we can trust to take care of ourselves. That turns us into little "gods" who fail ourselves all too often. And these failures really hurt. We not only fail to overpower our problem directly (the man described above), but we confront our relative powerlessness as a local "god." A double loss.

Even if we "succeed," the price paid by those who believe it is all their doing (plus maybe a little luck) is one of a relatively high state of anxiety. They know extreme highs and lows but experience little peace, ease, comfort, and serenity between the relatively infrequent intensity of wins and losses. They seem more likely to suffer the stress-related diseases discussed in one of the readings in this section. And the impact on their relationships can be as troublesome as on themselves.

If you were to pick only two or three cases in this text and ask yourself the role pride played in the difficulties described (in "Knowlton" or "Neely," for example), you might see the extent to which egos functioning as local "gods"—that is, pride—contributed to the problems.

To consider oneself one person among other persons, doing the best one knows how within human limits, aspiring to spiritual as well as other goals, seems to provide a view of self, others, and the world that enhances the probabilities of a satisfying, productive, and growth-filled life.

When we think we understand a problem we have in relationships, and it still sits there and stares at us, we have found it useful (note that our test is pragmatic—what *works*) to switch to a spiritual metaphor.

We discovered this reluctantly. We were not religious "believers." But our "belief" in rationality was such that it was increasingly difficult to ignore the data. Those people who also use the spiritual metaphors seem to live better than those who do not. It then came clear that those "nonbelievers" who use spiritual metaphors *as if* they were real, in order to test the outcomes pragmatically, came to feel a lot more comfortable with themselves. Some came to believe in traditional forms. Others came to believe only in the utility of the ideas. Both experienced improvement in their lives.

The truths in the psychological metaphor are ones we value. All we wish to add here is that our own journey has led us to the place where we find the truths in the spiritual metaphor powerful too. The use of *both* has begun to transform our relationships with others. We wanted to share that in brief, even if it runs the risk of sounding discontinuous with what has gone before, or appears irritatingly "religious" or idealistic to some. Our experiencing of it has been far more an outcome of pragmatism than dogmatism and has led so far to a belief in the utility of the spiritual metaphor. We suggest you test it, in your way, for yourself and see what you find.

In any event, we hope you end this book with an open mind, using the ideas in it as a walking stick to explore your relationships across the years to come. We wish you well as one of the pilgrims on the journey.

Readings

Intentionality and Ambivalence

James F.T. Bugental

Dr. May has given us a brilliant and evocative development of William James's fertile sowing. It is dismaying that two generations have intervened between these two creative approaches to such a fundamental issue in human experience. Will and intention, key processes by which we men guide our lives, would seem of such self-evident centrality of concern that it is almost incredible that a science supposedly dedicated to human behavior and experience could have ignored them while concerning itself with how pigeons peck or rats turn corners! Perhaps it is a part of our culture-wide psychosis which also finds expression in concern about the lengths of young men's hair while being unconcerned about training 30,000 of these young men each month to kill their fellows. May I say before leaving this aside that I mean my reference to a culture-wide psychosis quite literally?

This paper was presented as a part of an American Psychological Association program on "The Unfinished Business of William James," as a comment on an address by Rollo May, Washington, D.C., September 2, 1967.

Reprinted by permission of the author.

Now I would like to summarize briefly one portion of Dr. May's wide-ranging contributions. Then I will, with his permission, develop at some length an aspect which especially seems promising to me. Hopefully I will be able to show some further implications which I think are generally consonant with both James's and Dr. May's views and which seem to me exceedingly important to our understanding of this matter of intentionality.

The aspect on which I want to center my attention is the conception of *intentionality* which Dr. May has advanced. You will recall that he has told us that intentionality is "man's capacity to have intentions. Intentionality is the structure which gives meaning to experience." Now this conception seems to me eminently valuable—although, to be sure, I would prefer to call intentionality a "process" rather than a "structure", however, that issue is not pivotal at this point.

I believe that Dr. May's conceptualization of intentionality has an important further significance—a significance which makes it central to our whole understanding of the human experiences of wanting, ambivalence, and choice.

TWO FORMS OF AMBIVALENCE

To try to make this more tangible, let us look at Mable, who is caught in a hell of ambivalence, which is to say of contradictory intentions. Her situation, in grossly oversimplified fashion, is this:

> At 42, Mable had been married for 17 years to a man whom she loved deeply and with whom she had much that was meaningful and satisfying. Then, through a series of circumstances not important here, she found herself also very much in love with another man, a widower, and he returned her feeling. She had not lost her love for her husband, Greg, nor did she want only a simple "fling" with the other man, Hal.
>
> Now, let me assure you that, as her therapist, I am convinced that her feelings for both Greg and Hal were genuine expressions of Mable's nature and not to be dismissed by calling them either "infatuation" or "middle-aged restlessness." With each of these men, Mable recognized she could actualize a different aspect of her potentialities as a human being. Yet, being a part of our culture, she knew she could not realize both. Greg meant a deepening and broadening of a long and meaningful relationship and of an aspect of herself that was rich in personal significance and in emotional promise. Hal, on the other hand, extended the possibility of developing heretofore latent potentialities within herself, potentialities which she now realized she deeply wanted to explore. Her choice, she came to realize in our work together, was as much between contrasting ways of having her own life as between Greg and Hal.

Let me make explicit now some of the implicit points in Mable's situation which require our attention: First, the therapeutic process brought her to recognize that her conflict was at root a choice within herself, a choice of what she would *intend* to actualize in her own life. Second, as I have just indicated by my language, she was faced with two incompatible intentions. Both were conscious, and both were expressions of Mable's intentionality—that is, of her capacity to have intentions. Finally, it will be useful to have a word to designate Mable's situation; that word is, of course, "ambivalence." It is with the experience of ambivalence and its relation to intentionality that I wish to deal now.

I believe it was Raimy who first clarified and empirically demonstrated that there are two forms of ambivalence. One form is sequential ambivalence; the other is simultaneous ambivalence. In sequential ambivalence, we experience first one and then the other of two conflicting intentions, but we do not feelingfully know both at the same time. While one is dominant in awareness, the other is perceived only abstractly or detachedly. Thus, Mable, for a time, when she was at home with Greg would be very aware of how rich her life was with him and would wonder that she could be tempted to overturn it with all the pain, guilt, and disruption of her own and his futures that would be involved. Then when she was with Hal, or perhaps just away from Greg, she would be swept by anguish as she knew how vital was her feeling for Hal and her yearning for the different life she would have were she to go to him.

In simultaneous ambivalence, however, one confronts the conflict of intentions directly, and both are experienced feelingfully. This Mable could not at first tolerate. It is an extremely excruciating experience. Indeed, in fear, exasperation, and great pain, Mable would rail at me when I kept interpreting her attempts to suppress one or the other of her intentions and to try, by what Dr. May called the exercise of "Victorian will power," to end the ambivalence and force a decision. Thus, at one time she resolved to give up her marriage and venture into the fresh areas of her own potential that Hal symbolized. At another point, she firmly insisted that the only possible course was to dismiss Hal from her thoughts and feelings and make her marriage richer and more meaningful. On both of these occasions and their several repetitions, I pointed out and she reluctantly recognized the suppression and denial in which she was engaging.

When Mable was seeking to avoid pain through handling her ambivalence sequentially, she seemed to be demonstrating Dr. May's point that a person "cannot permit himself to see the trauma until he is ready to take a stand toward it." She was refusing to see the imminent trauma of choosing Hal while she was with Greg because she was unable to take a stand toward that trauma and to decide for a life with one or the other. And of course, the same refusal to see the looming trauma was present when she was thinking of being with Hal.

Now these thoughts bring me to another point of great importance in Dr. May's paper, and a point that I want to develop somewhat further than did he. He says, "The world can literally be too overwhelming if we are not able to take a stand toward a traumatic happening but also are unable to escape seeing it." He goes on to warn against the therapist forcing an obvious truth on the unready patient.

When, as in Mable's plight, sequential ambivalence is resulting in blocking out some of one's reality, the therapeutic need is not—as May warns—that of forcing that reality directly on the patient, but it is the therapist's task to expose the patient's resistance to facing the whole of his situation. While this may seem a quibble to those not familiar with the therapeutic situation, it is, I can assure you, a tremendously different experience for the patient when his therapist presses an unwelcome insight, as compared with the therapist simply confronting the patient with the ways he is blocking himself from confronting that which is already within him, so to speak. Thus, when Mable was intently arguing that she had outgrown her husband and owed it to him and herself to break up a stultifying relation, I did not tell her she was not letting herself know how much she really loved Greg, but I did repeatedly point out how her manner was rigid and forced, how she seemed to need to be defiant, and how she was weeping as though grief-filled, though her words were about objective recognition of facts and optimistic plans for life with Hal.

Now, obviously my intent is to help Mable change her sequential ambivalence to simultaneous ambivalence. This is in keeping with my belief that sequential ambivalence is neurotic and simultaneous ambivalence may be existential. Sequential ambivalence, it seems to me, expresses a resistance to open or authentic being, a resistance arising from dread of the existential anxiety of choice. It is no light matter, this anxiety of choice. Such words as "excruciating," "anguish," and "dread" hardly do justice to the torment someone in Mable's position experiences. Thoughts of suicide or psychosis or of abandoning the entire seemingly intolerable situation are inevitably part of it, for one realizes that one's whole life is indeed hanging in the balance. This is existential crisis in its truest form.

RESOLUTION OF THE AMBIVALENCE

I believe, however, that when the person in the crisis is able to "stay with it" as wholly and with as little distortion or suppression as possible, then the stage is set for a truly creative resolution of the dilemma. (As an aside, let me note how very essential it is for the therapist—if there is one involved—to avoid diluting either the pain or the autonomy of his patient in this crisis.)

In saying that the stage is set for a truly creative solution, I am saying three things: First, this direct confrontation of the ambivalence with its inherent pain and anxiety is a way of "taking a stand" in the terms Dr. May introduced. Second, I think the thoughts of suicide, psychosis, or disappearance are expressions of a striving for radical reorganization of the self-and-world outlook. They are not apt to be acted on, in my experience, so long as the confrontation is as authentic and as nearly total as possible.

Third, I believe that the person who is fully mobilized in such a crisis will find eventually some resolution which is uniquely his own and which preserves his values and even enhances his life as compared to its pre-crisis fullness or meaningfulness. What I am trying to convey was beautifully caught in an aphorism of George Kelly's, whose untimely death this spring has saddened many of us seeking to develop a truly humanistic psychology. Kelly remarked that "the key to man's destiny is his ability to reconstrue that which he cannot deny."

This is an observation of such significance for the human condition that it can well serve as a cornerstone for a whole edifice of psychology—as Kelly himself began building. What was lacking in his structure, to my mind, is supplied by Dr. May's conception of intentionality as we are here developing it. For the capacity to have intentions provides the dynamic, the force, to bring about the reconstruing which turns the key of man's destiny.

I want to restate this point because it is central to my whole thesis here, and yet it is a point that is difficult to convey in its full significance. The point is this: When a person faces a seemingly impossible conflict in his life and when he brings to that confrontation all of his feelingful awareness, then he will create some solution which is an innovation, a new possibility which, for him at least, did not exist before. Let me illustrate this by returning to Mable's struggle.

> After a seemingly endless time of misery of a depth which she felt almost unendurable, Mable began talking differently of her dilemma. No longer was it cast solely in terms of the choice between Greg and Hal. Now she spoke more often of her own needs and fears, her own potentialities, her own opportunities to choose her life.

This change in her outlook seems to have been possible because Mable had genuinely, without suppression or repression, confronted her contradictory intentions. What this means, so far as I can render it explicit, is that she had done three things emotionally:

First, Mable had come to realize her own identity as someone separate from either Greg or Hal. That is, she saw how all along subtly she had used her husband to define her own being and how she had come near to doing the same with Hal. Now she discovered that her sense of selfhood could be freed of either of these men. This did not mean she would cease to love or need her husband, with whom she chose to remain, but it did mean that she was not faced with devastation when she thought of life without him.

Second, Mable experienced fully her massive feelings of guilt toward her husband, toward Hal, and then toward herself. She recognized how she had brought hurt to each and how she had failed to realize her own potential with both men and in her own life. This recognition brought great waves of pain. After a time, however, she began to be able to see past the pain and to find the intention to live her life in such a way that she did not continue to add to the guilt and pain. She moved, in short, from preoccupation with the guilty past and an impossible future (for which she wanted both men) to facing the living present.

So, third, she was able to make the Jamesian fiat, "Be it so!" She was able, in Dr. May's words, "to throw [her] weight on" the possibility of life with Greg rather than with Hal and say, "Let this be the reality for me!" As Dr. May notes, this is commitment. I will add that this is the betting of one's life which is the basis for taking charge of one's life. It is diametrically opposite to the sort of blind, desperate plunging toward a false decision which Mable attempted when she was caught in sequential ambivalence. In the resolution which emerges from confronting simultaneous ambivalence, there is a genuine relinquishment as well as a positive choice.

> It is important to grasp the full significance of this change. It was pervasive of all levels of Mable's being from broad life decisions of place to live, manner of investing her talents, and ways of relating to her husband to differences in her ways of talking with her children, of using a free afternoon, or of choice of friends. Moreover, her manner when talking with me and with the therapy group of which she as a member was so much more open, quietly assured, and oriented in terms of values which she clearly felt deeply.
>
> I do not mean to convey a "happy-ever-after" picture. Mable, even some time later, would feel a sudden surge of pain and loss when unexpectedly the thought of Hal would come to mind. Moreover, she knew gradually diminishing times of misgivings about her decision, as well as incidents of fear, anger, and even despair when she realized how irrevocably left behind was the life she had so nearly had with Hal. Nevertheless her whole being was evolving in a direction of her intention, and she was becoming a much more whole person in charge of her own life.

Now the important point to recognize in Mable's resolution of her dilemma—and one on which Dr. May insisted, you will recall, when he distinguished intentionality from simple voluntarism and again as he said, "Will consists of listening rather than manipulation"—is that no wise counselor could have provided her with the course she eventually worked out, nor could Mable herself have objectively planned it before going through the full confrontation of her ambivalence. As Dr. May described, conception requires a readiness to take a stand, and only the confrontation could prepare the way for her new stance. To be sure, such a wise counselor or even Mable could have specified all the objective aspects of the resolution, but it would have been quite futile because it would not have involved Mable's intentionality.

You will have noted, perhaps, that I have several times spoken of Mable's *resolution* of her ambivalence. "Resolution" is a term that I prefer in some ways to "will." It seems to me to have less of the flavor of Victorian will power, and it has two affirmative meanings that commend it. "Resolution" signifies a releasing of the conflict of ambivalence, and "resolution" denotes the taking a stand of which Dr. May speaks and which is the focusing of intentionality essential to the creative outcome of the crisis.

CONCLUSION

So now we come to take one more look at this intentionality which is so crucial an element in determining our human experience. It is, as we've noted repeatedly, the capacity to have intentions, but it is more than that. Intentionality is the process through which we bring to focus our being. Through our intentionality we may direct the diffuse array of our wants and needs, our information and interests, our talents and strengths, our hopes and fears—in short, our whole being. Much of the time our intentionality is spread through a variety of specific intentions, some consonant, some diverse or even contradictory. It is only at times of life crisis—often, as in Mable's experience, occasioned by the incompatibility of major life intentions—that we bring ourselves to something approaching a full mobilization of our intentionality. Such occasions are nearly always instances of tremendous emotional stress, which is in itself a part of the mobilization of intentionality. They are, however, also the occasions on which one may truly claim and remake his life.

REFERENCES

BUGENTAL, J.F.T., *The Search for Authenticity.* New York: Holt, Rinehart & Winston, 1965.

KELLY, G.A., "Personal Construct Theory and Psychotherapy." Lectures for the Second Los Angeles Society of Clinical Psychologists Post-Doctoral Institute, 1959.

———*The Psychology of Personal Constructs.* New York: Norton, 1955.

RAIMY, V.C., "The Self-Concept as a Factor in Counseling and Personality Organization." Unpubl. Doct. dissert., Ohio State University, 1943.

Someone Needs to Worry: The Existential Anxiety of Responsibility and Decision

James F.T. Bugental

The older woman smiled understandingly but with a trace of sadness at the girl as she said, "I certainly understand now why you did as you did, but you see I really have no choice in the matter. If I made an exception for you now, then I'd have to make an exception for everyone else who had good reasons for breaking the rules. Pretty soon the rules would be meaningless, wouldn't they? So, although I really am sorry about it, the situation is clear, and it calls for you to be restricted to campus for the next month."

The student looked appreciatively at the dean through her tears. "It helps to know that you understand, but somehow it just doesn't seem fair under the circumstances. This will mean I'll lose my job, and I don't know whether Dad will be able to keep me in school or not."

The dean was sympathetic but made it evident that she had no choice. She did promise to try to help the student find another job. The student left with confused feelings of gratitude and resentment. She was guilty for the resentment and told herself that she was unfair and probably selfish to feel it since the dean had been so understanding.

When the student was gone, Dean Stoddart sat back in her chair for a minute, herself swept by contradictory feelings. On the one hand, she felt a certain satisfaction that she had finally trained her feelings and her judgment to the point at which she could stand firm when the regulations required it. For so many years she had found herself carried away by her sympathies so that she almost never was able to combine understanding with consistent application of the rules. She was always getting into hot water in those days, forever accused of being inconsistent or even of being undemocratic in having as many ways of administering the rules as there were people who came into her office.

Ruefully, Margaret Stoddart reflected

Reproduced by permission of the author. From the *Journal of Contemporary Psychotherapy*, Vol. 2, No. 1 (Summer 1969), 41-53.

that it had been a real struggle to be able to handle a situation as she had just handled this one. Yet, and here the irony came in, somehow she wasn't content. Somehow, she felt vaguely uneasy even as she reassured herself that she had done the job well. Later in the day, on the couch in my office, she found herself ruminating: "I don't know what it is that keeps bothering me about that interview. The student has probably forgotten it by now, but I feel restless whenever I think about it. And I keep thinking about it. It's like there's something I've overlooked, but I can't think what it might be . . ."

And of course, Margaret is right. She *has* overlooked something. She has overlooked something just as our whole culture tends to overlook that something more and more. She has overlooked the student's and her own *humanity*. She has made herself and the student objects controlled by the rules. She didn't administer the rules. The rules administered her!

Now that may seem a pretty drastic thing to say. Certainly, one might argue that Margaret was just doing her job and doing it with kindness but with responsibility too. How can I say that she is the object of the rules rather than their subject, that she was not truly a person in that interview? And I *do* say those things. I say further that she was non-being, pragmatically dead, in that conversation with the student and that this deadness is what makes her have the headaches and the sleeplessness that bring her every Tuesday, Thursday, and Friday afternoon to lie on the couch in my office and talk about her life.

This is a sweeping statement, and so now I want to support it. It will help to clarify what I mean if we take apart what she said to the student. First we heard,

> I certainly understand now why you did as you did, but you see I really have no choice in the matter.

Margaret is here expressing thoughts which are repugnant to her when she comes to make them explicit in my office, and yet they are ideas that she recognizes as part of her unverbalized thinking. They may be phrased this way: "Human understanding is not truly significant; if it were, my understanding would be some help to you now. Human empathy is ultimately impotent; the impersonal structure of which we are both parts is stronger. I am not choosing; if I or my feelings counted, the outcome would be different."

Clearly what is involved here is Margaret's—and our culture's—confused and contradictory values about what is important in making decisions.

She next told the student:

> If I made an exception for you now, then I'd have to make an exception for everyone else who had good reasons for breaking the rules.

Gradually Margaret recognizes that in saying this she is expressing her feelings that "Consistency is more important than is human understanding or human need. If I exercise choice now and set aside the rules, I will lose the power of choice in the future. Precedent will take control. Reasons—even good reasons—are less influential than rules and precedent. Rules and precedents transcend human considerations."

Finally Margaret said,

> Pretty soon the rules would be meaningless, wouldn't they? So, although I am really sorry about it, the situation is clear, and it calls for you to be restricted to campus for the next month.

Now the underlying message is, "Rules have meanings in themselves. We must respect those meanings no matter how we feel. You can see I'm sorry, but my being sorry doesn't have any weight against the meanings in the rules. Also, the situation has an implicit meaning apart from us who are concerned with it or my feelings and your reasons. The situation and the rules together dictate your punishment. It's nothing personal."

How very unfair my analysis is, one may well think. Certainly, I recognize that it is kind of relentless, and I realize I am practicing the same kind of impersonal application of the rules (this time the rules of logic) that I am pointing out Margaret engaged in. But that does not negate the implications we have traced. It does make it clear that I cannot content myself alone with what I am doing in applying that logic. But more of this later.

The matter that I want to discuss in this paper is the issue that Margaret confronts in her life and which our whole society, knowingly or not, is confronting in its life. There is no single name for it which will adequately identify it for all readers. Some of the names I can use may help to point the general direction, however. Thus, I can speak of the problem of existential choice, of the subject-object dichotomy, of the conflict between behavioristic and humanistic psychologies, of the threat to individual dignity which is potential in the population explosion, or of the dilemma of those in authority over others in balancing respect for law and order against appreciation of the individual's needs and problems, and of their roles as administrators in contrast to their roles as counselors. All of these matters are aspects of the same nuclear issue or question: What is the nature of man, and how can many men live together in fulfillment of their individual beings? Our culture, our whole world as we know it, is one answer—in many ways one of the most successful answers of which we have knowledge—yet, manifestly it is an incomplete answer, and it may well prove to be tragically inadequate.

The issue which I am characterizing by these diverse labels is by no means an academic one or one only of concern to philosophers or existential psychotherapists. Around the ebb and flow of the conflicts involved in this issue hang all that we hold dear and quite possibly, our lives themselves. Our form of government, our stance in international affairs, our relations with those we love, and our feelings are intimately bound up in these matters. They are not abstract problems. They are very concrete and literally vital.

I want to enlarge on how I see these issues, recognizing that I will only be able to deal with some aspects of what is a much more complex and embracing perspective on our human experience.

Man, we may recognize, may be viewed from either of two major perspectives: the inner, subjective, experience-centered or the outer, objective, behavior-centered. Let me be clear right here: We need both perspectives. Yet what we see, how we interpret man's nature, what we think is good for man, varies with which perspective we adopt at any given moment.

OBJECTIVE VIEW OF MAN

The objective view of man sees him as an object, as the name implies. "Object" here is used as it is in grammar, to refer to the thing done to, the recipient of the action. The objective view therefore looks for stimuli impinging on the organism, takes note of behaviors emitted from the organism, discounts or denies anything purported to be occurring inside the organism, and seeks causes residing outside the organism. The objective view is useful in thinking about matters such as rapid transit, employment trends, public health, and megakill.

On the other hand, the subjective view of man sees him as the subject of his own life. And "subject" here means, as in grammar, the doer, the one taking action, the one acting upon objects. The subjective view tries to understand how things look to the person, what it is the person wants to experience, how the person can change the environment to fit his wants; and thus this perspective speaks of reasons, not of causes. The subjective view is essential to understanding particular persons in the midst of their own lives and to helping those persons to make their lives more fulfilling.

With these contrasting conceptions in mind, it will be evident, I think, why the population increase puts continually greater pressure on all of us to think in terms of the objective perspective. It is a shorter step from a census of 3,000,000,000 to the concept of an "acceptable casualty rate of 15,000,000" than from a campus of 300 to a concept of individualized application of campus regulations.

A key idea differentiating the two perspectives is that of *interchangeability*. The objective view sees men as interchangeable; individuality is not recognized as such. The subjective view insists on the uniqueness of each person.

Having described these two perspectives which affect how we see and deal with our lives, let me be quite explicit: I am not arguing that one or the other is the right one and that the other should be discarded. It is essential, at least at this stage of our evolution, that we have both available. What I am concerned about (and anxious to bring others to be concerned about with me) is the tendency for one, the objective, to be advanced as *the correct* and the *only* correct perspective.

To my way of thinking, the situation is clearly one for which we may borrow a concept from the physicists, the concept of *complementarity*. This was developed to account for the fact that two apparently mutually exclusive but noncompeting theories were necessary to make sense of the known phenomena of light: the volley theory and the wave theory. Neither is sufficient in itself; each serves usefully to describe some of the important phenomena of light but is inadequate for other phenomena. So with the subjective and the objective perspectives of man: Each is important and helps us to understand more about ourselves and others than would either by itself.

Now, just to set matters straight, let me make explicit that I am strongly identified with the humanistic approach in psychology and thus with the subjective perspective on man. This does not refute what I said earlier, that we do, indeed, need both perspectives. My contention is simply that in psychology, as in the broader culture, there is a disproportionate emphasis on the objective frame-of-reference and a dangerous under-recognition of the subjective aspect of man's living.

Only ultra-zealous behaviorists and others of extreme positions would really disagree with my general thesis that we need both the subjective and the objective perspectives. It is when we come to particular issues, to the point of making concrete choices, that the conflict becomes so pointed and painful. This is what Margaret Stoddart experiences with increasing awareness. This is what I want to examine further here. But first I want to give the matter more focus by considering instances in which the subjective perspective is clearly appropriate but often lost, i.e., within the individual's own life. Having some understanding about this, we will be better able to examine the issue in larger perspective, for we will understand a powerful, and often unconscious, influence affecting how we deal with ourselves and others.

In my book called *The Search for Authenticity*[1] I have described the observations which lead me to believe that most

[1]New York: Holt, Rinehart & Winston, 1965.

of us are seldom fully alive in all the potential vitality we possess. I find it hard to convey how much deeper and richer that potential seems to me to be than we customarily realize. Perhaps I can indicate something of how it appears to me if I say that I think that the loss of our human resources is much greater than all other waste of natural resources combined. Every man or woman with whom I've worked intensively has more than once disclosed further reaches of latent possibility containing much of richness, meaningfulness, and beauty. Nor can such evidence be dismissed because it comes from "neurotics," for many of the people I am talking about are functioning personally, socially, and professionally well above the average of the general population.

Now, why should this be? It is my belief that we have drawn back from forthright confrontation of certain conditions of our being and that this withdrawal has meant a loss of access to our own fullness. Let me try to illustrate:

> Jennifer is an honor graduate student in one of the humanities. She is now working on her doctoral dissertation. In doing this, she has gone through a very painful emotional crisis. She wanted very much to undertake an offbeat problem which she had found exciting in her studies. However, no adequate methods for investigating such a topic exist. She was dubious about winning faculty support for the necessarily exploratory and inconclusive study which would be all she could hope to accomplish at this point. Discreet inquiries of her chairman and others confirmed her misgivings. She is reluctantly discarding her interest and choosing a "safe" topic for which well-established procedures exist.
>
> Newton is now thirty-seven. He has not married. He did not complete college. He has never worked in one position more than 15 months. Newton repeatedly thinks of leaving therapy, although we both know he has barely begun on the task. But Newton doesn't want to "get hooked" on therapy—or anything else. He makes quite a point of how he has kept from being tied down to anything so that now he is "free." He came to therapy only to help him "get set" so that when he was ready, he could really choose wisely. If I ask him what he is free to do, Newton becomes uneasy and tries to change the subject. He well knows what he is free *from* but not at all what he is free *for*.

Jennifer and Newton are people in flight from their lives. I have described them in ways which make very evident how it is that they flee, but we all do this sort of evading in some degree. We pull back from the fact that we are constantly changing and try to achieve and maintain constancy as though we were solid things rather than the flowing processes which constitute our truer nature. We shrink from the omnipresent intrusions of chance into our plans and our hopes and our fears. We dread being blamed, so that we deny our responsibilities, not realizing that thereby we often close off our opportunities as well. Because no one value rules all hearts, we feel frightened by the complexities of choice and look for rules and guides outside of ourselves. We hesitate to give ourselves fully in relation with others and are forever haunted by the specter of loneliness.

Yet when we can meet these same conditions of being—change, contingency, responsibility, autonomy, and apartness—with directness, we find they lead to the experiences of wholeness, faith, identity, creativity, and love.

I want to expand on these views and show how this matter of whether one is subject or object in his own life comes to be so very significant. In my work with people in intensive therapy, it has proven useful to my thinking to recognize five attributes of our lives which seem fundamental to all else. These five are that:

1. We are embodied physically.
2. We are finite, limited in all major di-

mensions (e.g., in how long we will live, in how much we can know, in how much we can do).

3. We are capable of acting; we are not merely passive observers.

4. We have choice as to the actions we will take; we are not governed solely by tropisms or instincts.

5. We are each a part of all other people and yet always apart from them at the same time.

These I have found to be useful descriptions of our being. When we live in accord with them, we live authentically and we are truly alive. When, as is always the case in some measure, we try to evade these conditions of our being, we are in that degree non-being.

TO LIVE AUTHENTICALLY

What does it mean to live authentically in accord with the conditions of our being? I think it means to meet each of those conditions with all its implications without distortion. It means to confront and incorporate the anxiety of being (i.e., the existential anxiety) which each of these conditions arouses. This process of confrontation and incorporation is the affirmation or expression of our subjecthood.

Let me try to make all this a bit more evident by using the following somewhat over-simplified pattern. Each of the conditions of being, I believe, contains a certain amount of threat or what is called existential anxiety. When we, consciously or not, encounter that anxiety, we are at a fork in the road. To the extent that we come to it directly and make it a part of our being alive, of our whole way of being in the world, we move toward greater authenticity. To the degree that we shrink from that confrontation, we become less vital in our lives. Now let us see how this works out for each of the five conditions of being that I listed earlier.

To be embodied physically means many things, but it is the experience of continual and inevitable *change* in one's self which is of particular significance. Often we try to deny that inexorable changingness and then we experience illness, either physical or psychological or both. When we can accept into our very being the fact of our continual change, then we come to experience wholeness.

Our being finite confronts us with the degree to which *contingency*—the unexpected and the uncontrolled—can enter into our lives. We realize we can never be sure of the future. This confrontation is one from which we may pull back, with the result we may experience the terror of feelings of powerlessness. (Sometimes this is masked by its inverse form, the implicit or explicit claim to omnipotence.) When we can accept our finitude, we come to a new sense of faith. This is not necessarily faith in something or somebody; it is rather a condition of inner living characterized by a feeling of integrity within one's own life.

The third of our basic conditions of being is our ability to take actions. This confronts us with *responsibility.* Too many of us equate responsibility with blame and thus pull back from it. This is the neurotic response. When we are able to meet that fact of responsibility, we can emerge with a feeling of commitment in our living which is the very stuff of our identities.

The recognition that I have some autonomy among the actions I will and will not take brings me to deal with a *choice.* This may seem a glad opportunity or a fearsome burden. Often I seek some external agency to relieve me of the load. Then I come to dread absurdity. On the other hand, when I can accept that choicefulness, I discover my potential for creativity.

Finally, the paradoxical condition of man in relation to his fellows is that he is at once separate from them but yet linked to them. This confrontation I have called *"a-partness,"* implying a pun which carries the double meaning of being "apart-from" and yet "a-part-of" others. Flight from such a-partness ends in estrangement; acceptance leads to the experience of love.

It is this aspect of our being that is peculiarly important when we look to the issue of subjectivity and objectivity in relation to others. When we emphasize the "a-part-of" aspect of our being, we tend to adopt the subjective frame of reference. We find in fiction, biography, conversation, companionship, and similar experiences confirmation of ourselves in the presence of others who share our experiences. When, on the other hand, we emphasize the "apart-from" aspect, we move into the objective frame of reference, and we talk in institutional terms about numbers and groups of people.

Now the key significance I want to emphasize in these instances is that the existential confrontation is at that point at which one decides to what extent to be a subject and to what extent an object in his own life. Avoiding the confrontations leads to illness, powerlessness, blame, absurdity, and estrangement. These are the characteristics of the human object. Acceptance of the confrontations and their incorporation leads to wholeness, faith, identity, creativity, and love. These are the attributes of true subjecthood.

Having this view of the intrapersonal dynamics of the subject-object problem, we need to turn once again to a broader perspective. Let me point out that in doing so, we are practicing the very philosophy we preach. The look at intrapersonal dynamics was certainly within the subjective perspective. Now we need to make use of the objective perspective as well.

By this time, some are certainly asking, "What's the answer? What should Margaret Stoddart have done? What should I do?" And here's the rub. Here's the part a good number of us are likely to fail to hear, or, hearing, fail to remember: *There is no answer.* When we seek for an answer in that fashion, we engage in the very same displacement of subjecthood that Margaret did in the application of the rules in the interview in which we first met her. If there were an answer, then there would be no need of the person. A person is an answer*er*, but if he only answers in terms of the rules, then there is no need of the person: Pragmatically he does not exist. Existentially he is nonbeing!

"What does he want, chaos, anarchy?" some will ask now, with a bit of annoyance. One may well say to himself, "You can't run a school of 200, 2,000, or 20,000 as though it were a family of five."

As to what I want, I'd answer, "I want to cling to my being subject of my own life. I want to call on others to recognize how they may be being displaced in the centers of their own lives and how they may be, unwittingly, aiding the displacement of still others from their personhood." I don't have a prescription. I think the problem is extremely difficult, challenging, and immensely exciting when we are really alive to it.

But, having said that, I must offer my agreement: Indeed, you can't—so far as I know—run a school of 200, 2,000, or 20,000 purely subjectively. I think we have practically no technology or methodology for dealing with large numbers of *subjects.* We only know how to deal with large numbers of objects. Many times it's the only way to proceed—with the present stage of our development being what it is. I might well do just as Margaret did were I in her place. I hope I might also be anxious to find some way to put back into life a little of the vitality I had perforce killed in it. This is existential guilt and restitution.

It's a lot like the way I eat steaks with gusto, but sometimes feel concern that it is after all a kind of cannibalism. It's like my willingness to go on each day with my own life when I am a part of a state that still uses capital punishment, a nation that has armies and atom bombs. I hope I never get adjusted to these facts, even though I can't change them.

One thing I do about my own guilt is to make restitution. I do that here by writing in this way, trying to enliven others. "Trying to spread his guilt around," I imagine some will say. And that would be almost right. I'm not spreading my guilt. I can't, and I hope I wouldn't. It's too vital a part of me. But I am trying to awaken others to their own guilt and thus to their own vitalness, their own being alive.

I'm one of that odd breed of psychotherapists who often seem to try to make their patients anxious and guilty rather than to help them rid themselves of those feelings, as all therapists once were supposed to do. I do try to help my patients hurt better, weep better, cuss better, love and hate more fully, live and die more vitally. I hope my patients will leave me less well "adjusted" than they might have been before or than many other people are. This is what I mean when I call myself an existential psychotherapist.

As Erich Fromm[2] has so well demonstrated, man has but recently evolved to a concept and partial experience in which the individuality of each person is recognized in some measure and is beginning to be valued. Saying it differently, for most of man's history, he regarded himself primarily as a part of a larger whole. That larger whole might be the company of the faithful, the serfs of a particular baron, the legions of Caesar, the citizens of Paris, the field hands of Colonel Prentiss, the members of the Nazi party; in short, the objects of some subject. There were, of course, the individuals favored by birth, talents, wealth, or position who became separate persons in their own and others' eyes, but they were the exceptions. The human experience was implicitly that of being an interchangeable part of some larger whole.

I believe that the concept of individuality is an evolutionary mutation. It is incompletely realized today, to be sure. We are in a time of trying whether it is viable. It certainly is not a dominant trend yet in our species. There are many forces which seek to eliminate it.

Let us examine just two of the forces strongly opposed to individuality and subjectivity: First are the intrapsychic threats we have already described, which must be borne by the individual person and which urge him to displace onto other agencies (as did the Germans in supporting Hitler). The second force is the weight of man's history as embodied in all institutions. Social institutions by their very nature are objective in large part. And I do mean all: education, religion, entertainment, government, and so on. Each, insofar as we have conceived them, treats persons objectively—indeed, we value that in many of our institutions. We enshrine justice as blindfolded. Yet that means persons are seen as interchangeable, and individuality is deemed inappropriate as a consideration.

But in referring to formal institutions, I have by no means exhausted the matter. Let us look at language, one of the most basic of our institutions, our means for communicating with others and even for thinking subjectively within ourselves. By and large, our language is objective. The only distinctions recognized, for the most part, are those of gender, number,

[2] *Escape from Freedom* (New York: Holt, Rinehart & Winston, 1941).

and in some languages, familiarity between the speaker and the one to whom he speaks. Now, that is not completely so, of course, and we do develop more subjective languages in many situations. Lovers have their own special words and meanings. Any group that works together gets its private "in" jokes and signals. Still, language that is "proper" and is taught in the schools is objective language, and we are given little help and often some discouragement from developing subjective language.

If we broaden our perspective once more to life in general, then we must recognize that none of us has any real idea what a truly subjectively oriented world would be like. It certainly would be radically different than anything we now know. Efficiency would probably not be a very high value; consistency, a by-product at best. Uniformity would be a vice, or at least a serious fault. Objectivity and impersonality about human experience clearly would be perversions and quite probably would be felt to be obscene.

To talk of a truly subjectively oriented world is really to engage in fancies, however. What we are concerned with in our own very real world is the relative balance between regard for the objective and attention to the subjective. We have pointed out how the balance seems to be on the objective side. Yet there is another side to the story, as I suggested above. We are in the midst of increasing turmoil which has many roots and many meanings but which may usefully be viewed from the perspective of the conflict between subjectivity and objectivity, between the values inherent in the emergence of individuality and the values inherent in the social good.

What view do you take of the following pictures from recent and current history? Governor Wallace stands in a schoolhouse doorway defying federal law. In many cities and on many college campuses, there are student and black riots. The anti-draft demonstrators burn their draft cards. The New York transit workers defy a court injunction by their strike. A single judge berates the transit workers and the transit authority for disregarding the law in settling that strike.

The list could be endlessly lengthened. It could be extended to other realms also: What is happening to our sexual mores? A large percentage of college graduates and even those with advanced degrees make many errors in writing and speaking English. How often does a husband open the car door for his wife? Some parents seem delighted that their daughters are chosen to pose naked in a national circulation magazine. Uniform retirement rules brush aside the elderly into elaborate playpens called retirement communities. The major sources of entertainment, radio, television, and the movies, are consistently berated by critics for producing more mediocre and inferior fare.

All of this may be the ferment of change, of evolution, or even of revolution. Or these may be the death throes of a dying culture. Who can say for sure which? Or are those really the same thing?

THE ULTIMATE GOOD

Some are going to read me as subscribing to lawlessness. I am not. But neither am I saying that obedience to the law is the ultimate good. I don't know what the ultimate good is. But man does have a choice, whether he recognizes it or not. And if he is to be truly alive, man must choose knowingly. For man chooses, whether he knows it or not. Choice is not a good; it is simply a fact of life. It is a fact of life more basic than any we can link to birds and bees, and one about which we get less training than the child of the most inhibited home gets about sex.

Still, the hope of subjecthood is deep within us. At Nuremberg we enunciated that hope, in the doctrine that men had a higher responsibility than obedience to the state. They had, we and our allies maintained, a loyalty to life, to man himself. On this basis we tried, condemned, and executed men who had been faithfully obeying the laws of their country. Yet, in negation of this very same principle, today we try, condemn, and imprison men who state their allegiance to that same higher responsibility and refuse obedience to the laws of our own country.

Repeatedly I find myself seeking an answer to this dilemma of the human condition: our treasured subjecthood and the sheer weight of the necessity to accept objectness for ourselves and others. I know I won't find *the answer.* Indeed, the very idea of an ultimate answer is a contradiction in itself. I know further that the matter is not one in which either subjectivity or objectivity can, must, or should ultimately triumph. The paradox must be embraced, not resolved away.

But I am convinced also that we are far too over-balanced on the side of the objective, that there is too much trend toward going even further in that direction and too little counterforce to preserve our subjectivity. I believe the whole technology of our lives is too much in the domain of the objective. We are at such an early stage of developing ways of recognizing, furthering, and celebrating our subjecthood.

I want to join my voice to those of others who insist that we need not yield up our humanity, our subjective sovereignty, to the destroyer that is blind, unrestrained objectivity. Moreover, I want to urge others, especially those in the crucially important positions at the crossroads of human lives, to work to preserve these values for themselves and for those whom they touch.

It is time to return to Margaret Stoddart and to the difficult job she has at the frontier between the subjective and the objective.

Margaret Stoddart has completed her therapy with me, but her problem is still with her. Therapy did not solve it. It is the problem of being human. What therapy did do was very important, though. It helped Margaret confront her problem more directly. It did this in several ways. One of the very important ways was to help her recognize that it was appropriate for her to be troubled when she found herself in conflict between the rules on the one hand and an individual on the other.

The point of this is that Margaret had felt that it was an evidence that something was wrong with her for her to feel this conflict. She had had the image that if only she were as she should be, she wouldn't feel distress when she insisted that the rules must apply to an offending student, or she wouldn't feel misgivings when she decided to set the rules aside in another instance. She really believed that there was a right way to handle every case and that, if she were only the person she should be, she would know that right way. What therapy helped Margaret to recognize was that she would never get to such a point; indeed, that she should be suspicious if she ever found she was not concerned about her decisions. One of the most important things Margaret brought to her work was the very fact of her concern, her human feelings.

With the misgivings about those feelings reduced, Margaret could do a better job of being concerned about the issue which was valid: How much could she respect the individual while yet protecting the group? In this she asserted her own subjecthood while yet fostering others in doing likewise.

We have to have rules and laws. Traffic signals make freedom possible by limiting it. But the dean of women who is only the enforcer of rules is the creature of those rules even as she tries to make others creatures of them also.

Too often the dean's job is seen as that of transforming the deviant subject into the compliant object, as that of helping to make the machine run without the hitches of individual differences.

Some deans cling to a different interpretation: They see their jobs as that of bringing the impersonal machine to recognize that individuality is still a cherished value. Such deans are probably in the minority, and they are in real jeopardy. Indeed, their days are numbered if the object-proponents have their way.

Earlier I conducted a rather ruthless analysis of what the underlying meanings were in Margaret's interview with the student. Now it is time for me to accept the responsibility of trying to phrase what might be a more authentic subjective monologue:

> I can make or not make exceptions. I am the subject, not the object of the rules.
>
> Whether I make an exception for you will grow out of our meeting, whether I feel it is more authentic to do so or not to do so. Whether or not I make an exception for you is not going to become my master. The next person in a similar situation to yours (there are no identities here) will have to present his need, and I will have to meet him as best I can.
>
> I will make mistakes. I will even be unfair, unknowingly, at times. I have prejudices and blind spots that you will be hurt by but that I will try to overcome or at least to reduce in time.

In very brief, this is the message I want to present: Two significant perspectives on any human situation are the subjective and the objective. They may or may not agree in the implications they suggest. No rule is adequate to decide between them. Only a living person ought to do that. The person who must make such decisions will be troubled, and ought to be troubled. That is why he is there. A rule and a machine applying it would not be troubled. It is important to the preservation of important human values that someone be troubled this way. I hope to reduce a secondary distress by the reassurance that such a person need not be troubled about being troubled. The uniquely human function is to be *concerned.* That concern is one of the most important human contributions.

So it comes down to this: What I do is to urge awareness of the matter. One may find this an uneasy awareness. I usually do. But I still encourage the acceptance of that uneasiness, that quest. It's the price of one's own dignity, one's own humanity, one's own subjecthood.

The Aircraft Brake Scandal: A Cautionary Tale in Which The Moral Is Unpleasant

Kermit Vandivier

The B.F. Goodrich Company is what business magazines like to refer to as "a major American corporation." It has operations in a dozen states and as many foreign countries; and of these far-flung facilities, the Goodrich plant at Troy, Ohio, is not the most imposing. It is a small, one-story building, once used to manufacture airplanes. Set in the grassy flatlands of west-central Ohio, it employs only about six hundred people. Nevertheless, it is one of the three largest manufacturers of aircraft wheels and brakes, a leader in a most profitable industry. Goodrich wheels and brakes support such well-known planes as the F111, the C5A, the Boeing 727, the XB70, and many others.

Contracts for aircraft wheels and brakes often run into millions of dollars, and ordinarily a contract with a total value of less than $70,000, though welcome, would not create any special stir of joy in the hearts of Goodrich sales personnel. But purchase order P-237138—issued on June 18, 1967, by the LTV Aerospace Corporation, ordering 202 brake assemblies for a new air force plane at a total of $69,417—was received by Goodrich with considerable glee. And there was good reason. Some ten years previously, Goodrich had built a brake for LTV that was, to say the least, considerably less than a rousing success. The brake had not lived up to Goodrich's promises, and after experiencing considerable difficulty, LTV had written off Goodrich as a source of brakes. Since that time, Goodrich salesmen had been unable to sell so much as a shot of brake fluid to LTV. So in 1967, when LTV requested bids on wheels and brakes for the new A7D light attack aircraft it proposed to build for the air force, Goodrich submitted a bid that was absurdly low, so low that LTV could not, in all prudence, turn it down.

Goodrich had, in industry parlance, "bought into the business." The company did not expect to make a profit on the initial deal; it was prepared, if necessary, to lose money. But aircraft brakes are not something that can be ordered off the shelf. They are designed for a particular aircraft, and once an aircraft manufacturer buys a brake, he is forced to purchase all replacement parts from the brake manufacturer. The $70,000 that Goodrich would get for making the brake would be a drop in the bucket when compared with the cost of the linings and other parts the air force would have to buy from Goodrich during the lifetime of the aircraft.

There was another factor, besides the low bid, that had undoubtedly influenced LTV. All aircraft brakes made today are of the disk type, and the bid submitted by Goodrich called for a relatively small brake, one containing four disks and weighing only 106 pounds. The weight of any aircraft part is extremely important: The lighter a part is, the heavier the plane's payload can be.

The brake was designed by one of Goodrich's most capable engineers, John Warren. A tall, lanky, blond graduate of Purdue, Warren had come from the Chrysler Corporation seven years before and had become adept at aircraft brake design. The happy-go-lucky manner he usually maintained belied a temper that exploded whenever anyone ventured to offer criticism of his work, no matter how small. On these occasions, Warren would turn red in the face, often throwing or slamming something and then stalking from the scene. As his co-workers learned the consequences of criticizing him, they did so less and less readily, and when he submitted his preliminary design for the A7D brake, it was accepted without question.

Warren was named project engineer for the A7D, and he, in turn, assigned the task of producing the final production design to a newcomer to the Goodrich engineering stable, Searle Lawson. Just turned twenty-six, Lawson had been out of the Northrop Institute of Technology only one year when he came to Goodrich in January 1967. He had been assigned to various "paper projects" to break him in, and after several months spent reviewing statistics and old brake designs, he was beginning to fret at the lack of challenge. When told he was being assigned to his first "real" project, he was elated and immediately plunged into his work.

The major portion of the design had already been completed by Warren, and major subassemblies for the brake had already been ordered from Goodrich suppliers. Naturally, however, before Goodrich could start making the brakes on a production basis, much testing would have to be done. Lawson would have to determine the best materials to use for the linings and discover what minor adjustments in the design would have to be made.

Then, after the preliminary testing and after the brake was judged ready for production, one whole brake assembly would undergo a series of grueling, simulated braking stops and other severe trials called qualification tests. These tests are required by the military, which gives very detailed specifications on how they are to be conducted, the criteria for failure, and so on. They are performed in the Goodrich plant's test laboratory, where huge machines called dynamometers can simulate the weight and speed of almost any aircraft.

A DISMAL BEGINNING

Searle Lawson was well aware that much work had to be done before the

A7D brake could go into production, and he knew that LTV had set the last two weeks in June 1968 as the starting dates for flight tests. So he decided to begin testing immediately. Goodrich's suppliers had not yet delivered the brake housing and other parts, but the brake disks had arrived, and using the housing from a brake similar in size and weight to the A7D brake, Lawson built a prototype. The prototype was installed in a test wheel and placed on one of the big dynamometers in the plant's test laboratory. Lawson began a series of tests, "landing" the wheel and brake at the A7D's landing speed and braking it to a stop. The main purpose of these preliminary tests was to learn what temperatures would develop within the brake during the simulated stops and to evaluate lining materials tentatively selected for use.

During a normal aircraft landing, the temperatures inside the brake may reach 1,000 degrees, and occasionally a bit higher. During Lawson's first simulated landings, the temperature of his prototype brake reached 1,500 degrees. The brake glowed a bright cherry-red and threw off incandescent particles of metal and lining material as the temperature reached its peak. After a few such stops, the brake was dismantled and the linings were found to be almost completely disintegrated. Lawson chalked this first failure up to chance and, ordering new lining materials, tried again.

The second attempt was a repeat of the first. The brake became extremely hot, causing the lining materials to crumble into dust.

After the third such failure, Lawson, inexperienced though he was, knew that the fault lay not in defective parts or unsuitable lining material but in the basic design of the brake itself. Ignoring Warren's original computations, Lawson made his own, and it didn't take him long to discover where the trouble lay—the brake was too small. There simply was not enough surface area on the disks to stop the aircraft without generating the excessive heat that caused the linings to fail.

The answer to the problem was obvious, but far from simple—the four-disk brake would have to be scrapped, and a new design using five disks, would have to be developed. The implications were not lost on Lawson. Such a step would require junking the four-disk brake subassemblies, many of which had now begun to arrive from the various suppliers. It would also mean several weeks of preliminary design and testing and many more weeks of waiting while the suppliers made and delivered the new subassemblies.

Yet, several weeks had already gone by since LTV's order had arrived, and the date for delivery of the first production brakes for flight testing was only a few months away.

Although John Warren had more or less turned the A7D over to Lawson, he knew of the difficulties Lawson had been experiencing. He had assured the young engineer that the problem revolved around getting the right kind of lining material. Once that was found, he said, the difficulties would end.

Despite the evidence of the abortive tests and Lawson's careful computations, Warren rejected the suggestion that the four-disk brake was too light for the job. He knew that his superior had already told LTV, in rather glowing terms, that the preliminary tests on the A7D brake were very successful. Indeed, Warren's superiors weren't aware at this time of the trouble on the brake. It would have been difficult for Warren to admit not only that he had made a serious error in his calculations and original design but that his mistakes had been caught by a green kid, barely out of college.

Warren's reaction to a five-disk brake

was not unexpected by Lawson, and, seeing that the four-disk brake was not to be abandoned so easily, he took his calculations and dismal test results one step up the corporate ladder.

At Goodrich, the man who supervises the engineers working on projects slated for production is called, predictably, the projects manager. The job was held by a short, chubby, bald man named Robert Sink. Some fifteen years before, Sink had begun working at Goodrich as a lowly draftsman. Slowly, he worked his way up. Despite his geniality, Sink was neither respected nor liked by the majority of the engineers, and his appointment as their supervisor did not improve their feelings toward him. He possessed only a high-school diploma, and it quite naturally rankled those who had gone through years of college to be commanded by a man whom they considered their intellectual inferior. But, though Sink had no college training, he had something even more useful: a fine working knowledge of company politics.

Puffing on a meerschaum pipe, Sink listened gravely as young Lawson confided his fears about the four-disk brake. Then he examined Lawson's calculations and the results of the abortive tests. Despite the fact that he was not a qualified engineer in the strictest sense of the word, it must certainly have been obvious to Sink that Lawson's calculations were correct and that a four-disk brake would never work on the A7D.

But other things of equal importance were also obvious. First, to concede that Lawson's calculations were correct would also mean conceding that Warren's calculations were incorrect. As projects manager, not only was he responsible for Warren's activities, but, in admitting that Warren had erred, he would have to admit that he had erred in trusting Warren's judgment. It also meant that, as projects manager, it would be he who would have to explain the whole messy situation to the Goodrich hierarchy, not only at Troy but possibly on the corporate level at Goodrich's Akron offices. And having taken Warren's judgment of the four-disk brake at face value, he had assured LTV, not once but several times, that about all there was left to do on the brake was pack it in a crate and ship it out the door.

There's really no problem at all, he told Lawson. After all, Warren was an experienced engineer, and if he said the brake would work, it would work. Just keep on testing and probably maybe even on the very next try, it'll work out just fine.

Lawson was far from convinced, but without the support of his superiors there was little he could do except keep on testing. By now, housings for the four-disk brake had begun to arrive at the plant, and Lawson was able to build a production model of the brake and begin the formal qualification test demanded by the military.

The first qualification attempts went exactly as the tests on the prototype had. Terrific heat developed within the brakes, and after a few short simulated stops, the linings crumbled. A new type of lining material was ordered and once again an attempt to qualify the brake was made. Again, failure.

Experts were called in from lining manufacturers, and new lining "mixes" were tried, always with the same result. Failure.

It was now the last week in March 1968, and flight tests were scheduled to begin in seventy days. Twelve separate attempts had been made to qualify the brake, and all had failed. It was no longer possible for anyone to ignore the glaring truth that the brake was a dismal failure and that nothing short of a major design change could ever make it work.

On April 4, the thirteenth attempt at qualification was begun. This time no attempt was made to conduct the tests by the methods and techniques spelled out in the military specifications. Regardless of how it had to be done, the brake was to be "nursed" through the required fifty simulated stops.

Fans were set up to provide special cooling. Instead of maintaining pressure on the brake until the test wheel had come to a complete stop, the pressure was reduced when the wheel had decelerated to around 15 mph, allowing it to "coast" to a stop. After each stop, the brake was disassembled and carefully cleaned, and after some of the stops, internal brake parts were machined in order to remove warp and other disfigurations caused by the high heat.

By these and other methods, all clearly contrary to the techniques established by the military specifications, the brake was coaxed through the fifty stops. But even using these methods, the brake could not meet all the requirements. On one stop the wheel rolled for a distance of 16,000 feet, or over three miles, before the brake could bring it to a stop. The normal distance for such a stop was around 3,500 feet.

NURSING IT THROUGH

On April 11, the day the thirteenth test was completed, I became personally involved in the A7D situation.

I had worked in the Goodrich test laboratory for five years, starting first as an instrumentation engineer, then later becoming a data analyst and technical writer. As part of my duties, I analyzed the reams and reams of instrumentation data that came from the many testing machines in the lab, then transcribed all of it to a more usable form for the engineering department. When a new-type brake had successfully completed the required qualification tests, I would issue a formal qualification report.

Qualification reports are an accumulation of all the data and test logs compiled during the qualification tests and are documentary proof that a brake has met all the requirements established by the military specifications and is therefore presumed safe for flight testing. Before actual flight tests are conducted on a brake, qualification reports have to be delivered to the customer and to various government officials.

On April 11, I was looking over the data from the latest A7D test, and I noticed that many irregularities in testing methods had been noted on the test logs.

Technically, of course, there was nothing wrong with conducting tests in any manner desired, so long as the test was for research purposes only. But qualification test methods are clearly delineated by the military, and I knew that this test had been a formal qualification attempt. One particular notation on the test logs caught my eye. For some of the stops, the instrument that recorded the brake pressure had been deliberately miscalibrated so that, while the brake pressure used during the stops was recorded as 1,000 psi (pounds per square inch)—the maximum pressure that would be available on the A7D aircraft—the pressure had actually been 1,100 psi.

I showed the test logs to the test lab supervisor, Ralph Gretzinger, who said he had learned from the technician who had miscalibrated the instrument that he had been asked to do so by Lawson. Lawson, said Gretzinger, readily admitted asking for the miscalibration, saying he had been told to do so by Sink.

I asked Gretzinger why anyone would want to miscalibrate the data-recording instruments.

"Why? I'll tell you why," he snorted. "That brake is a failure. It's way too small for the job, and they're not ever going to get it to work. They're getting desperate, and instead of scrapping the damned thing and starting over, they figure they can horse around down here in the lab and qualify it that way."

An expert engineer, Gretzinger had been responsible for several innovations in brake design. It was he who had invented the unique brake system used on the famous XB70. "If you want to find out what's going on," said Gretzinger, "ask Lawson; he'll tell you."

Curious, I did ask Lawson the next time he came into the lab. He seemed eager to discuss the A7D and gave me the history of his months of frustrating efforts to get Warren and Sink to change the brake design. "I just can't believe this is really happening," said Lawson, shaking his head slowly. "This isn't engineering, at least not what I thought it would be. Back in school, I thought that when you were an engineer, you tried to do your best, no matter what it cost. But this is something else."

He sat across the desk from me, his chin propped in his hand. "Just wait," he warned. "You'll get a chance to see what I'm talking about. You're going to get in the act too, because I've already had the word that we're going to make one more attempt to qualify the brake, and that's it. Win or lose, we're going to issue a qualification report!"

I reminded him that a qualification report could be issued only after a brake had successfully met all military requirements, and therefore, unless the next qualification attempt was a success, no report would be issued.

"You'll find out," retorted Lawson. "I was already told that regardless of what the brake does on test, it's going to be qualified." He said he had been told in those exact words at a conference with Sink and Russell Van Horn.

This was the first indication that Sink had brought his boss, Van Horn, into the mess. Although Van Horn, as manager of the design engineering section, was responsible for the entire department, he was not necessarily familiar with all phases of every project, and it was not uncommon for those under him to exercise the what-he-doesn't-know-won't-hurt-him philosophy. If he was aware of the full extent of the A7D situation, it meant that Sink had decided not only to call for help but to look toward that moment when blame must be borne and, if possible, shared.

Also, if Van Horn had said, "Regardless of what the brake does on test, it's going to be qualified," then it could only mean that, if necessary, a false qualification report would be issued. I discussed this possibility with Gretzinger, and he assured me that under no circumstances would such a report ever be issued.

"If they want a qualification report, we'll write them one, but we'll tell it just like it is." he declared emphatically. "No false data or false reports are going to come out of this lab."

On May 2, 1968, the fourteenth and final attempt to qualify the brake was begun. Although the same improper methods used to nurse the brake through the previous tests were employed, it soon became obvious that this too would end in failure.

When the tests were about half completed, Lawson asked if I would start preparing the various engineering curves and graphic displays that were normally incorporated in a qualification report. I flatly refused to have anything to do with the matter and immediately told Gretzinger what I had been asked to do. He was furious and repeated his previous declaration that under no circumstances would any false data or other matter be issued from the lab.

"I'm going to get this settled right now, once and for all," he declared. "I'm going to see Line [Russell Line, manager of the Goodrich Technical Services Section, of which the test lab was a part] and find out just how far this thing is going to go!" He stormed out of the room.

In about an hour, he returned and called me to his desk. He sat silently for a few moments, then muttered half to himself, "I wonder what the hell they'd do if I just quit?" I didn't answer and I didn't ask what he meant. I knew. He had been beaten down. He had reached the point when the decision had to be made. Defy them now while there was still time—or knuckle under, sell out.

"You know," he went on uncertainly, looking down at his desk, "I've been an engineer for a long time, and I've always believed that ethics and integrity were every bit as important as theorems and formulas, and never once has anything happened to change my beliefs. Now this. . . . Hell, I've got two sons I've got to put through school and I just . . . " His voice trailed off.

He sat for a few more minutes, then, looking over the top of his glasses, said hoarsely, "Well, it looks like we're licked. The way it stands now, we're to go ahead and prepare the data and other things for the graphic presentation in the report, and when we're finished, someone upstairs will actually write the report.

"After all," he continued, "we're just drawing some curves, and what happens to them after they leave here—well, we're not responsible for that."

I wasn't at all satisfied with the situation and decided that I too would discuss the matter with Russell Line, the senior executive in our section.

Tall, powerfully built, his teeth flashing white, his face tanned to a coffee-brown by a daily stint with a sunlamp, Line looked and acted every inch the executive. He had been transferred from the Akron offices some two years previously, and he commanded great respect and had come to be well liked by those of us who worked under him.

He listened sympathetically while I explained how I felt about the A7D situation, and when I had finished, he asked me what I wanted him to do about it. I said that as employees of the Goodrich Company we had a responsibility to protect the company and its reputation if at all possible. I said I was certain that officers on the corporate level would never knowingly allow such tactics as had been employed on the A7D.

"I agree with you," he remarked, "but I still want to know what you want me to do about it."

I suggested that in all probability the chief engineer at the Troy plant, H.C. "Bud" Sunderman, was unaware of the A7D problem and that he, Line, could tell him what was going on.

Line laughed, good-humoredly, "Sure, I could, but I'm not going to. Bud probably already knows about this thing anyway and if he doesn't, I'm sure not going to be the one to tell him."

"But why?"

"Because it's none of my business, and it's none of yours. I learned a long time ago not to worry about things over which I had no control. I have no control over this."

I wasn't satisfied with this answer, and I asked him if his conscience wouldn't bother him if, say, during flight tests on the brake, something should happen resulting in death or injury to the test pilot.

"Look," he said, becoming somewhat exasperated, "I just told you I have no control over this. Why should my conscience bother me?"

His voice took on a quiet, soothing tone as he continued. "You're just getting all upset over this thing for nothing. I just do as I'm told, and I'd advise you to do the same."

I made no attempt to rationalize what I had been asked to do. It made no difference who would falsify which part of the report or whether the actual falsification would be by misleading numbers or misleading words. Whether by acts of commission or omission, all of us who contributed to the fraud would be guilty. The only question left for me to decide was whether or not I would become a party to the fraud.

Before coming to Goodrich in 1963, I had held a variety of jobs, each a little more pleasant, a little more rewarding than the last. At forty-two, with seven children, I had decided that the Goodrich Company would probably by my "home" for the rest of my working life. The job paid well, it was pleasant and challenging, and the future looked reasonably bright. My wife and I had bought a home and we were ready to settle down into a comfortable, middle-aged, middle-class rut. If I refused to take part in the A7D fraud, I would have either to resign or be fired. The report would be written by someome anyway, but I would have the satisfaction of knowing I had had no part in the matter. But bills aren't paid with personal satisfaction, nor house payments with ethical principles. I made my decision. The next morning, I telephoned Lawson and told him I was ready to begin on the qualification report.

I had written dozens of qualification reports, and I knew what a "good" one looked like. Resorting to the actual test data only on occasion, Lawson and I proceeded to prepare page after page of elaborate, detailed engineering curves, charts, and test logs, which purported to show what had happened during the formal qualification tests. Where temperatures were too high, we deliberately chopped them down a few hundred degrees, and where they were too low, we raised them to a value that would appear reasonable to the LTV and military engineers. Brake pressure, torque values, distances, times—everything of consequence was tailored to fit.

Occasionally, we would find that some test either hadn't been performed at all or had been conducted improperly. On those occasions, we "conducted" the test—successfully, of course—on paper.

For nearly a month we worked on the graphic presentation that would be a part of the report. Meanwhile, the final qualification attempt had been completed, and the brake, not unexpectedly, had failed again.

We finished our work on the graphic portion of the report around the first of June. Altogether, we had prepared nearly two hundred pages of data, containing dozens of deliberate falsifications and misrepresentations. I delivered the data to Gretzinger, who said he had been instructed to deliver it personally to the chief engineer, Bud Sunderman, who in turn would assign someone in the engineering department to complete the written portion of the report. He gathered the bundle of data and left the office. Within minutes, he was back with the data, his face white with anger.

"That damned Sink's beat me to it," he said furiously. "He's already talked to Bud about this, and now Sunderman says no one in the engineering department has time to write the report. He wants us to do it, and I told him we couldn't."

The words had barely left his mouth when Russell Line burst in the door. "What the hell's all the fuss about this damned report?" he demanded.

Patiently, Gretzinger explained. "There's no fuss, Sunderman just told me that we'd have to write the report down here, and I said we couldn't. Russ," he went on, "I've told you before that we weren't going to write the report. I made my position clear on that a long time ago."

Line shut him up with a wave of his hand and, turning to me, bellowed, "I'm getting sick and tired of hearing about this damned report. Now, write the goddamn thing and shut up about it!" He slammed out of the office.

Gretzinger and I just sat for a few seconds looking at each other. Then he spoke.

"Well, I guess he's made it pretty clear, hasn't he? We can either write the thing or quit. You know, what we should have done was quit a long time ago. Now, it's too late."

Somehow, I wasn't at all surprised at this turn of events, and it didn't really make that much difference. As far as I was concerned, we were all up to our necks in the thing anyway, and writing the narrative portion of the report couldn't make me more guilty than I already felt myself to be.

Within two days, I had completed the narrative, or written portion, of the report. As a final sop to my own self-respect, in the conclusion of the report I wrote, "The B.F. Goodrich P/N 2-1162-3 brake assembly does not meet the intent or the requirements of the applicable specification documents and therefore is not qualified."

This was a meaningless gesture, since I knew that this would certainly be changed when the report went through the final typing process. Sure enough, when the report was published, the negative conclusion had been made positive.

One final and significant incident occurred just before publication.

Qualification reports always bear the signature of the person who has prepared them. I refused to sign the report, as did Lawson. Warren was later asked to sign the report. He replied that he would "when I receive a signed statement from Bob Sink ordering me to sign it."

The engineering secretary who was delegated the responsibility of "dogging" the report through publication told me later that after I, Lawson, and Warren had all refused to sign the report, she had asked Sink if he would sign. He replied, "On something of this nature, I don't think a signature is really needed."

NEAR CRASHES

On June 5, 1968, the report was officially published and copies were delivered by hand to the air force and LTV. Within a week, flight tests were begun at Edwards Air Force Base in California. Searle Lawson was sent to California as Goodrich's representative. Within approximately two weeks, he returned because some rather unusual incidents during the tests had caused them to be canceled.

His face was grim as he related stories of several near crashes during landings—caused by brake troubles. He told me about one incident in which, upon landing, one brake was literally welded together by the intense heat developed during the test stop. The wheel locked, and the plane skidded for nearly 1,500 feet before coming to a halt. The plane was jacked up and the wheel removed. The fused parts within the brake had to be pried apart.

That evening I left work early and went to see my attorney. After I told him the story, he advised that, while I was probably not actually guilty of fraud, I was certainly part of a conspiracy to defraud. He advised me to go to the Federal Bureau of Investigation and offered to arrange an appointment. The following week he took me to the Dayton office of the FBI, and after I had been warned that I would not be immune from prosecution, I disclosed the A7D matter to one of the agents. The agent told me to say nothing about the episode to anyone and to report any further incidents to him. He said he would forward the story to his superiors in Washington.

A few days later, Lawson returned from a conference with LTV in Dallas and said that the air force, which had previously approved the qualification report, had suddenly rescinded that approval and was demanding to see some of the raw test data. I gathered that the FBI had passed the word.

Omitting any reference to the FBI, I told Lawson I had been to an attorney and that we were probably guilty of conspiracy.

"Can you get me an appointment with your attorney?" he asked. Within a week, he had been to the FBI and told them of his part in the mess. He too was advised to say nothing but to keep on the job, reporting any new development.

Naturally, with the rescinding of air

force approval and the demand to see raw test data, Goodrich officials were in a panic. A conference was called for July 27, a Saturday morning affair at which Lawson, Sink, Warren, and I were present. We met in a tiny conference room in the deserted engineering department. Lawson and I, by now openly hostile to Warren and Sink, ranged ourselves on one side of the conference table while Warren sat on the other side. Sink, chairing the meeting, paced slowly in front of a blackboard, puffing furiously on a pipe.

The meeting was called, Sink began, "to see where we stand on the A7D." What we were going to do, he said, was to "level" with LTV and tell them the "whole truth" about the A7D. "After all," he said, "they're in this thing with us, and they have the right to know how matters stand."

"In other words," I asked, "we're going to tell them the truth?"

"That's right," he replied. "We're going to level with them and let them handle the ball from there."

"There's one thing I don't quite understand, " I interjected. "Isn't it going to be pretty hard for us to admit to them that we've lied?"

"Now, wait a minute," he said angrily. "Let's don't go off half-cocked on this thing. It's not a matter of lying. We've just interpreted the information the way we felt it should be."

"I don't know what you call it," I replied, "but to me it's lying, and it's going to be damned hard to confess to them that we've been lying all along."

He became very agitated at this and repeated, "We're not lying," adding, "I don't like this sort of talk."

I dropped the matter at this point, and he began discussing the various discrepancies in the report.

We broke for lunch, and afterward, I came back to the plant to find Sink sitting alone at his desk, waiting to resume the meeting. He called me over and said he wanted to apologize for his outburst that morning. "This thing has kind of gotten me down," he confessed, "and I think you've got the wrong picture. I don't think you really understand everything about this."

Perhaps so, I conceded, but it seemed to me that if we had already told LTV one thing and then had to tell them another, changing our story completely, we would have to admit we were lying.

"No," he explained patiently, "we're not really lying. All we were doing was interpreting the figures the way we knew they should be. We were just exercising engineering license."

During the afternoon session, we marked some forty-three discrepant points in the report; forty-three points that LTV would surely spot as occasions where we had exercised "engineering license."

After Sink listed those points on the blackboard, we discussed each one individually. As each point came up, Sink would explain that it was probably "too minor to bother about," or that perhaps it "wouldn't be wise to open that can of worms," or that maybe this was a point that "LTV just wouldn't understand." When the meeting was over, it had been decided that only three points were "worth mentioning."

Similar conferences were held during August and September, and the summer was punctuated with frequent treks between Dallas and Troy and demands by the air force to see the raw test data. Tempers were short, and matters seemed to grow worse.

Finally, early in October 1968, Lawson submitted his resignation, to take effect on October 25. On October 18, I submitted my own resignation, to take effect on November 1. In my resignation, addressed to Russell Line, I cited the A7D report and stated, "As you are aware, this report contained numerous deliberate and willful misrepresentations which, according to legal counsel, constitute fraud and expose both myself and others to criminal charges of conspiracy to defraud .... The events of the past seven months have created an atmosphere of deceit and distrust in which it is impossible to work .... "

On October 25, I received a sharp summons to the office of Bud Sunderman. Tall and graying, impeccably dressed at all times, he was capable of producing a dazzling smile or a hearty chuckle or immobilizing his face into marble hardness, as the occasion required.

I faced the marble hardness when I reached his office. He motioned me to a chair. "I have your resignation here," he snapped, "and I must say you have made some rather shocking, I might even say irresponsible, charges. This is very serious."

Before I could reply, he was demanding an explanation. "I want to know exactly what the fraud is in connection with the A7D and how you can dare accuse this company of such a thing!"

I started to tell some of the things that had happened during the testing, but he shut me off saying, "There's nothing wrong with anything we've done here. You aren't aware of all the things that have been going on behind the scenes. If you had known the true situation, you would never have made these charges." He said that in view of my apparent "disloyalty" he had decided to accept my resignation "right now," and said it would be better for all concerned if I left the plant immediately. As I got up to leave he asked me if I intended to "carry this thing further."

I answered simply, "Yes," to which he replied, "Suit yourself." Within twenty minutes, I had cleaned out my desk and left. Forty-eight hours later, the B.F. Goodrich Company recalled the qualification report and the four-disk brake, announcing that it would replace the brake with a new improved, five-disk brake at no cost to LTV.

Ten months later, on August 13, 1969, I was the chief government witness at a hearing conducted before Senator William Proxmire's Economy in Government Subcommittee. I related the A7D story to the committee, and my testimony was supported by Searle Lawson, who followed me to the witness stand. Air force officers also testified, as well as a four-man team from the General Accounting Office, which had conducted an investigation of the A7D brake at the request of Senator Proxmire. Both air force and GAO investigators declared that the brake was dangerous and had not been tested properly.

Testifying for Goodrich was R.G. Jeter, vice-president and general counsel of the company, from the Akron headquarters. Representing the Troy plant was Robert Sink. These two denied any wrongdoing on the part of the Goodrich Company, despite expert testimony to the contrary by air force and GAO officials. Sink was quick to deny any connection with the writing of the report or directing of any falsifications, claiming to have been on the West Coast at the time. John Warren was the man who had supervised its writing, said Sink.

As for me, I was dismissed as a high-school graduate with no technical training, while Sink testified that Lawson was a young, inexperienced engineer. "We tried to give him guidance," Sink testified, "but he preferred to have his own convictions."

About changing the data and figures in the report, Sink said, "When you take data from several different sources, you have to rationalize among those data what is the true story. This is part of your engineering know-how." He admitted that changes had been made in the data, "but only to make them more consistent with the overall picture of the data that is available."

Jeter pooh-poohed the suggestion that anything improper occurred, saying, "We have thirty-odd engineers at this plant . . . and I say to you that it is incredible that these men would stand idly by and see reports changed or falsified . . . . I mean you just do not have to do that working for anybody . . . . Just nobody does that."

The four-hour hearing adjourned with no real conclusion reached by the subcommittee. But the following day, the Department of Defense made sweeping changes in its inspection, testing, and reporting procedures. A spokesman said the changes were a result of the Goodrich episode.

The A7D is now in service, sporting a Goodrich-made five-disk brake, a brake that works very well, I'm told. Business at the Goodrich plant is good. Lawson is now an engineer for LTV and has been assigned to the A7D project, possibly explaining why the A7D's new brakes work so well. And I am now a newspaper reporter.

At this writing, those remaining at Goodrich—including Warren—are still secure in the same positions, all except Russell Line and Robert Sink. Line has been rewarded with a promotion to production superintendent, a large step upward on the corporate ladder. As for Sink, he moved up into Line's old job.

Modern Stress: Stratagems for Self-Awareness

Luise Cahill Dittrich

AMERICA THE DANGEROUS

We Americans as a culture reinforce certain stable values—achievement, stamina, competitiveness. Yet these same values, which have made our nation productive and powerful, exact their price from us. For we often strive too mightily. We plan obsessively for tomorrow, and so find it difficult to enjoy today or remember yesterday. And in all our contending, reaching, and planning, we subject ourselves to strains on body and mind so intense that one-third of our yearly deaths are from heart attack, and countless of us suffer stress-related afflictions, from ulcers and colitis to alcoholism and depression. Within reasonable limits, the values that make ours a great nation can help make us a healthy, fulfilled people. But allowed to run away with us, these same values can make us discontented, and even dangerously ill.

Many Americans function in a milieu of anxiety. Internal pressures plague us—"perform, measure up, succeed." In addition, the external pressures of modern life multiply daily, with accelerating change, megalopolitan crisis and eco-disturbance. In such an anxiety-charged environment, the daily stuff of living—marriage and childrearing, earning a living, human interaction—becomes subject to, and often the cause of, very real stress-induced dangers. The victims of such undue stress are numerous and recognizable. The executive suicide. The alcoholic. The man in the golf cart, trying to take it easy after his first heart attack. The chronic depressive who slow-motions his way through viscous days.

But what is stress? Is it always harmful? Can we learn to cope better with the inevitable stress in modern life?

HOW MUCH IS TOO MUCH?

According to Hans Selye, M.D. [15],[1] stress is the "sum of all nonspecific

[1]Numbers refer to bibliographical sources; see final page of this article.

changes caused by function or damage," or simply, "the rate of wear and tear in the body." Stress is a state of bodily alertness to any kind of exposure—exposure to nervous tension, for instance, or to temperature extremes, or to physical injury. A stress reaction can be a general body response. When threatened with aggression, the body gears itself up for "fight or flight"; adrenalines pour into the circulatory system, heartbeat and breathing quicken, blood pressure increases. Later, when the threat disappears, so does the stress reaction, and the body slows to normal. Or a stress reaction can be localized in various parts of the body. Antibodies fighting off viral invasion; a shiver to prevent loss of body heat; one's hand darting back from a hot stove; muscle fatigue from carrying a heavy suitcase—all these are examples of the many local stress reactions by which the body protects itself.

Stress reactions, then, are natural, inevitable and invaluable to us as biological organisms. However, too great a stress reaction, or too many stress-inducing situations, are harmful. As we have said, the total-body "fight or flight" reaction is a biological device to help combat danger. Yet unlike our early ancestors, few of us are routinely endangered by wild animals or the elements. Our "dangers" more likely are emotional, or abstract: an intimidating superior, a marital quarrel, a flat tire when one is already late. And so the "fight or flight" reaction with its biological extremes is often an *over*-reaction to its stimulus, and becomes to some extent inappropriate. Nevertheless, it can still be seen in the reaction of an employee to a fierce memo from an intimidating boss, or in the reaction of a student to continued badgering from a teacher.

In situations of prolonged stress overload, we place severe strain upon our body sub-systems. Soldiers in combat, for instance, operating at peak levels of stress for extended periods of time, can begin to suffer "long-range strain," a behavior breakdown that Alvin Toffler [17] describes:

> Mental deterioration often began with fatigue ... followed by confusion and nervous irritability. The man became hypersensitive to the slightest stimuli .... He showed signs of bewilderment .... He became tense, anxious, and heatedly irascible. His comrades never knew when he would flail out in anger, even violence ... [in] the final stage of emotional exhaustion ... the soldier ... gave up the struggle to save himself, to guide himself rationally through the battle.

Despite man's remarkable adaptive abilities, he is still a finite biosystem, and cannot charge this system beyond its limits. And just as stress overload can wear down a combat soldier, so can it wear down a harried professional who crowds life with obligations, deadlines and tensions. "Long-range strain," after all, is actually another version of the civilian experience often called "nervous breakdown."

Besides being the result of prolonged stress situations, stress overload can occur suddenly. Overwhelming sudden grief or loss can precipitate what has been called "giving-up syndrome," in which the loss creates such profound feelings of helplessness or hopelessness that the individual collapses in illness or death. "He died of a broken heart" is perhaps a proverbial way of explaining the buckling—or giving-up—of the individual under the catastrophic loss of a loved one, or of some cherished aspect of his life. Douglas Colligan [2] writes:

> Grief [has been found] to be one of the most common reasons for the "giving-up complex," and in his catalog of sudden deaths Dr. [George] Engel found that a huge portion of them happened to grief-stricken individuals. [In] a famous study ... entitled "Broken Heart," ... British re-

searchers studied the mortality rate of 4,500 widowers within six months of their wives' deaths. Compared with other men the same age, the widowers studied had a mortality rate that was 40 per cent higher.

Toffler [17] feels that our mass culture itself is another major source of stress overload. He defines "future shock" as

> . . . the distress, both physical and psychological, that arises from an overload of the human organism's physical adaptive systems and its decision-making processes . . . future shock is the human response to over-stimulation.

The stress overload in our culture, "future shock," appears everywhere: it appears in the many and frequent "massive life changes" thrust upon us by our transience and rapid pace; it appears in our "serial career" patterns;[2] it appears in the bombardment of our senses by media and other incessant sources of stimulation; it appears in the "decisional overstimulation" that results from redoubling amounts of new information.

Reactions to "future shock" vary with individuals, and with the intensity of their stress overload, Toffler says. Symptoms range from "anxiety, hostility to helpful authority, and seemingly senseless violence, to physical illness, depression and apathy." Sometimes, to avoid the countless decisions our culture insists upon, "future shock" victims withdraw—intellectually, socially and emotionally. Withdrawal, like "giving-up syndrome" and "long-range strain," are adaptive responses to intolerably high degrees of anxiety or tension.

Toffler suggests that the key to combating "future shock" is "not to suppress change, but to manage it." Change, most likely, is here to stay. But how do we "manage" it? First, says Toffler, we can insure our own "personal stability zones" by

> . . . consciously maintaining longer-term relationships with the various elements of our physical environment. Thus, we can refuse to purchase throw-away products. We can hang onto the old jacket for another season . . . we can resist when the salesman tells us it's time to trade in our automobile . . . .
>
> We can use the same tactic with respect to people and the other dimensions of experience . . . . We can consciously disconnect . . . .

Such maneuvers as these are not the same as withdrawal. Instead, they are deliberate attempts to determine in part one's own rate of change, one's own pace of life. Whereas withdrawal is a refusal to confront reality, maintaining "personal stability" is seen as an attempt to manage part of that reality.

Toffler also suggests periodic self-evaluation to search out signs of how well or how poorly we are reacting to our own environment:

> Heart palpitations, tremors, insomnia or unexplained fatigue may well signal overstimulation, just as confusion, unusual irritability, profound lassitude and a panicky sense that things are slipping out of control are psychological indications. By observing ourselves, looking back over the changes in our recent past, we can determine whether we are operating comfortably within our adaptive range or pressing its outer limits . . . .
>
> Having done this, we can also begin consciously to influence it—speeding it up or slowing it down—first with respect to small things, the micro-environment, and then in

[2]Toffler writes, "When *Fortune* magazine in the mid-1960's surveyed 1,003 young executives employed by major American corporations, it found that fully one out of three held a job that simply had not existed until he stepped into it. Another large group held positions that had been filled by only one incumbent before them. Even when the name of the occupation stays the same, the content of the work is frequently transformed, and the people filling the jobs change."

terms of the larger, structural patterns of experience.

If unavoidable tensions exist in American society (and in industrialized society as a whole), why don't we *all* fall victim to "future shock"? Why don't even more of us withdraw, or give up? The neurosurgeon and race-car driver can thrive on their high-stress occupations; the same degree of stress in the lives of other persons might undo them utterly. Some of us find a roller-coaster ride thrilling, while others find it terrifying. Obviously, there is an enormous range of stress tolerance in human beings. Each of us fits—somewhere—into that range. And each of us *needs* a certain amount of stress in his life. Too little stress is just as harmful as too much, as Nancy Gross [6] explains:

> . . . stress is a prime requisite of health . . . the human body seems to find it almost impossible to tolerate too little stress for any appreciable period . . . .
>
> To dedicate your life to the avoidance of stress is both pointless and dangerous. For the body, in its instinctive wisdom, seeks constantly to maintain its proper stress level . . . .

The result of too little stress in one's life is atrophy: mental dullness, physical disabilities, evaporation of spirit. Avoidance of these pitfalls is as crucial to individual fulfillment as avoidance of overstimulation and excessive change.

TYPES OF STRESS: HELPFUL VS. HARMFUL

One of our basic needs as human beings is the need to work. Psychologist Harry Levinson [11] asserts that work provides us, not only with money, but with other gratifications: psychological balance, social ties with others, clarification of identity, and feelings of mastery over self and environment. Selye [15] identifies two additional human needs: "the thirst for approval" and the need for completion. He writes:

> The great practical lesson is to realize the deep-rooted biologic necessity for completion, the fulfillment of all our smallest needs and greatest aspirations, in harmony with our hereditary make-up.

These various human needs all find expression in another need—the need for achievement. This need to achieve is closely related to our creative impulse, the impulse to *become* rather than just *be*, to actualize our aspirations. The achievement need is, of course, monumentally strong in some, while others are content to carve a small (but nevertheless recognizable) niche in society.

In his research on achievement motivation, David C. McClelland [14] has cited the Protestant work ethic as a nurturer of achievement aims. In countries that espouse the Protestant ethic, achievement needs ("n Achievement") are strongly reinforced, both in the family unit and in the larger society. It is no surprise, then, that we Americans are highly motivated to achieve.

Yet such a need arouses stress in the human body. Is it harmful? Lee Smith [16] differentiates between "satisfying" and "unsatisfying" stress. The stress imposed by achieving goals, by creating, by working, is the deeply "satisfying" stress upon which men and women thrive. (Kenneth Lamott [10] concurs, adding that "people who enjoy their work tend to stave off disease much longer than those who don't.") On the other hand, "unsatisfying" stress is the stress of frustration and failure. The person who is laid off his job; the person who cannot attain a long-sought goal; the person who cannot live up to her own expectations; the unchallenged person whose work is rote; these are people who encounter harmful stress in their lives.

Thus, another type of stress overload is too much of the *wrong kind* of stress. An adulthood spent in a harmfully stressful way—i.e., full of frustration and unsuccessful struggle—is not only unhappy; it is also physically dangerous. We have seen how stress overload can lead to various behavior breakdowns. Stress overload can also lead to physical breakdowns, with symptoms ranging from warts to ulcers, dermatitis to hypertension, bleeding gums to heart attacks. Clearly the stress-related illness of greatest concern to Americans—because it strikes us so virulently—is heart attack. To be sure, coronary heart disease has many physical causes (e.g., hypertension, diabetes, hypothyroidism), as well as a host of strongly suspected causes (e.g., high-cholesterol diet, cigarette smoking, lack of exercise, obesity). But cardiologists Meyer Friedman and Ray H. Rosenman [4] offer compelling evidence that "emotional stress" (our "harmful" stress) is "a relevant component of coronary heart disease." Convinced of the connection between emotional stress and such heart-disease-related problems as increased serum cholesterol level, hypertension and heart attack itself, Friedman and Rosenman describe a premature heart attack behavior "type"—"Type A."[3]

Type A is a highly stressful behavior pattern that is, in fact, an exaggeration of the very desirable need for achievement. Type A behavior has certain characteristics: an *excessive* competitiveness; aggressiveness so strong it borders on hostility; an exaggerated sense of time urgency; and considerable impatience. The Type A personality experiences most life events in terms of chronic struggle—with time, with others—and so invites the inevitable frustration inherent in harmful stress. Constant struggle takes its toll in chemical strain on the body, as Friedman and Rosenman explain:

> When a man [or woman] . . . is engaged in any sort of struggle, the emotional repercussions of this struggle induce [a] series of signals . . . [a] complex of nervous and endocrine gland hormones are secreted . . . large amounts of various pituitary and adrenal hormones, testosterone [or estrogen], thyroxine, and insulin . . . the Type A . . . is engaged in a chronic, more or less continuous . . . struggle . . . . Type A subjects too often are exposing their arteries to "high voltage" chemicals even during the "low voltage" periods of their daily living.

While competitiveness is a natural enough component of the desire to achieve, the Type A person competes even in situations where competition is unneccessary or even inappropriate. A friendly card game, for instance, might become as much of a competitive proving ground as a board meeting. Often this drive to compete springs from the Type A person's strong need to prove to *himself* that he is valuable, capable and worthy; the Type A often strives—throughout his lifetime, perhaps—to prove his self-worth. Thus an element of insecurity fuels his excessive aggressiveness. Additionally, Type A aggressiveness usually has a significant component of free-floating hostility; anger can be easily aroused by a myriad of situations, from a serious conflict with a peer to the minor inefficiency of a supermarket checkout clerk.

Another major element of Type A behavior is an obsessive "hurry sickness." Now, everyone is sometimes frustrated by the limitations of time in our country, especially since Americans place a high premium on both speedy efficiency and perfectionistic thoroughness, often two intrinsically contradictory demands. But the Type A's frustration is chronic, and his tendency is to do constant battle with deadlines. If a Type A businesswoman

[3]All discussion of Type A behavior in this note is derived from Meyer Friedman and Ray H. Rosenman, *Type A Behavior and Your Heart.*

wrote her annual report in four weeks last year, she might try to write it in three weeks this year. If a Type A motorist drives to work in 17 minutes today, he'll try for 15 minutes tomorrow (and woe to any slowpoke who gets in his way; Type A's are easily frustrated behind the wheel). A second manifestation of "hurry sickness" is polyphasic behavior (i.e., undertaking multiple tasks simultaneously). The businessman who shaves, dictates letters or drinks coffee while driving to work is engaging in polyphasic activity. Here again, the person tries to overcome those physical limitations imposed by the archvillain, time. A corollary obsession to "hurry sickness" is number accumulation. The Type A person is fascinated by the acquisition of *numbers* of things: the investor, by numbers of dollars; the scientist, by numbers of discoveries; the writer, by numbers of publications. And on it goes.

Yet the Type A's chronic struggle with time, with peers, and with his own limitations is not restricted, or even peculiar, to any profession or sex. Male or female taxi drivers or lawyers, dry cleaners or stockbrokers might tend equally to exhibit Type A characteristics. (Friedman and Rosenman do assert that a housewife is less likely to be Type A than a woman doctor, since those competitive and deadline-racing tendencies are less often reinforced in the home than outside it.)

However, participation or even success in the marketplace is not a sure sign of Type A behavior. As Friedman and Rosenman point out, the same taxi drivers and stockbrokers can just as likely be "Type B":

> The ... Type B Behavior Pattern is the exact opposite of ... Type A. [The Type B subject] is rarely harried by desires to obtain a wildly increasing number of things or participate in an endlessly growing series of events in an ever decreasing amount of time. His ambition may be as great [as] or even greater than that of his Type A counterpart ... but [his drive] is such that it seems to steady him, give confidence and security to him, rather that to goad, irritate, and infuriate, as with the Type A .... The Type B person is far more aware of his capabilities than concerned about what peers and superiors may think of his actions.

Theoretically, while the Type A person hurries obsessively, the Type B person hurries when it is appropriate to hurry; and while the Type A is driven to compete irrationally, the Type B draws upon his competitive drive when it is useful. And just because a person is Type B, he needn't be thought of as indifferent to success and achievement. In fact, plenty of executives and other persons motivated towards achievement are closer to Type B than to Type A. (In reality, of course, few persons are either pure Type A or pure Type B; but many of us are "closer" to one type than to the other.)

In American society, the chief component of Type A behavior, "competitive overdrive," is a "socially acceptable—indeed, often praised—form of conflict." Type A behavior runs so deeply in our value system that it is usually considered normal and desirable. American economic opportunity insists upon the need for competition. Then, too, the American emphasis on speed and acquisition also supports Type A behavior. In fact, one might almost say that American society, as a whole, exhibits Type A characteristics.

But despite its almost universal reinforcement in American society, severe Type A behavior can be debilitating, even devastating, to the body. Friedman and Rosenman's clinical evidence strongly links stress-filled Type A behavior to high blood cholesterol, hypertension and activities (or situations) that are hazardous to the heart:

> Type A subjects show a higher serum cholesterol, a higher serum fat, more diabetic-

like traits or precursors, smoke more cigarettes, exercise less (because they can't find time to do so), are "over-driving" certain of their endocrine glands in a manner that can be expected to damage their coronary arteries, eat meals rich in cholesterol and animal fat, and also suffer more from high blood pressure that Type B subjects.

How can a severely Type A person alter his behavior, and thereby reduce his risk of premature heart disease? First, like all of us, he can heed the customary caveats: Reduce cholesterol intake, maintain reasonable weight level, exercise moderately and refrain from smoking. Next, he can undertake a plan of behavior modification to defuse the "overcharged" aspects of his personality. Such a plan, say Friedman and Rosenman, should begin with an honest and thorough self-evaluation (advice not unlike Toffler's), in which the Type A person considers such matters as his intelligence, perceptiveness, creativity, sense of humor, attitude towards change, aesthetic involvement, level of hostility, courage, ethics and life priorities. A total self-appraisal of this kind gives one a greater independence from the opinions of others, and lessens the compulsion to acquire as a measure of self-worth. Further behavior modification strategies to release one's personality from the grip of Type A behavior include:

Concentrating on Enjoying Events and Experiences as They Take Place. In the hustle and hassle of his life, the Type A seldom pauses to observe the various ongoing enjoyments of life—from the company right now of a loved one to the rising of the sun, both of which can be spiritually enriching. In Thornton Wilder's *Our Town*, Emily recounts some small but miraculous pleasures of life:

> ... clocks ticking ... and ... sunflowers. And food and coffee. And new-ironed dresses and hot baths ... and sleeping and waking up.

Establishing Reasonable Life Goals, Both Professional and Private. Attempting to cram too much activity into too little time, the Type A typically makes life unreasonable for himself. His professional goals are unattainable, while his personal goals are vague. The Type A should establish what is and is not worth his striving; he should allow himself to relax. According to Gross [6]:

> ... You owe yourself the indulgence of a sense of humor through which you can cut ... annoyances down to size. You owe yourself the indulgence of the patience that permits you to ignore pressures and delays .... You owe yourself the indulgence of vacations, of aspirin when you are coming down with a cold, of hours of peaceful privacy, of relaxation, of occasional bursts of the extravagance ... that give[s] color to life. You owe yourself the responsibility of using your body and your mind in the interests of the constructive realities and aspirations that mean the most to you. You owe yourself a pace ... which meets your temperamental needs, which neither hurries you nor holds you back.

Accepting the Incompleteness of Life. No Type A ever accomplishes all that he sets out to accomplish. No Type A is ever fully satisfied with what he does accomplish. Part of his "hurry sickness" is a race to get more things done than he can, in fact, do. On this point, Friedman and Rosenman address the Type A person directly:

> ... part of ... liberating yourself from ... Type A behavior is to recognize and to accept the fact that your life must be ... maintained by incompleted processes, tasks, and events. You must ... accept your life as a melange of activities in which only some of the many processes manage to get finished ... this unfinishedness ... is your reassurance that you are living.

Re-engineering "Hurry Sickness." The Type A person should find time for the avocational interests that can make him a fuller human being. He should revise his daily schedule in order to discard extra activities and find time for rest. Above all, he should find in his daily life a time and place for aloneness. Fromm [5] writes:

> The most important step in learning concentration is to learn to be alone with oneself without reading, listening to the radio, smoking or drinking . . . Paradoxically, the ability to be alone is the condition for the ability to love. Anyone who tries to be alone with himself will discover how difficult it is. . . .

Re-engineering Hostility. If a Type A is hostile towards others, he should first identify that the emotion does exist in him. Then he is in a position to alter this essentially antagonistic stance. When hostility surfaces, he should try to reason himself out of it. Particularly helpful in dissipating anger is a sense of humor, which sees the absurdity in many supposedly "serious" situations. And while the Type A person is learning to check his volatility, he should, if possible, avoid persons and situations that arouse his hostility.

Establishing New Habits to Replace Unacceptable Ones. A Type A person *can* learn to engage in monophasic behavior to check his desire to compete, to listen more patiently. He needs to identify the habits that cause his life to be unnecessarily stressful, and then practice the new patterns until they become habitual. (Exhibit V-1 is a self-test for Type A behavior pattern.)

Awareness of one's emotions and bodily limitations, plus a systematic attempt to alter Type A behavior (as in the guidelines above), can yield a less stressful style of life, as well as reduced risk of coronary heart disease and stress-related illness. To Americans, plagued as we are with heart attack, hypertension and the other afflictions linked with stress, the promise of a longer life, more satisfying all the way through, is encouraging indeed.

STRESSFUL ROLES

Harmful stress, then, can originate from within the human body, from certain styles and paces of life, from within the human personality. Such stress can also originate from the multitude of pressures applied to us as social creatures. In order to function, society must restrict individual behavior, must steer that behavior into socially meaningful roles. Sidney M. Jourard [9] points out that

> . . . no social system can use all of every man's self and yet keep the social system functioning well. This is what roles are for—sex roles as well as as occupational, age, and familial roles.

The traditional "male" and "female" roles of American society have imposed certain emotional stresses upon individuals. For example, the American male role has asked that a man be aggressive, undemonstrative, and unassailable. In reality, of course, men also are passive, expressive and vulnerable. Yet a man who is aware of such experiencing or expression has usually been constrained by his role to hide such alleged "weakness" from others and ultimately, perhaps, from himself. As a result, men have typically encountered difficulties, Jourard feels, in certain personal and interpersonal processes: self-disclosure (lack of "openness"), insight (lack of "self-knowledge"), empathy (inability to identify with others), and even the capacity to love and be loved:

> . . . men, in spite of good intentions to promote the happiness and growth of others by loving actions, will often "miss the target." . . . The obverse of this situation is likewise true. If a man is reluctant to make

Exhibit V-1

TEST FOR TYPE A BEHAVIOR PATTERN

YOU POSSESS TYPE A BEHAVIOR PATTERN:

1. If you have (a) a habit of explosively accentuating various key words in your ordinary speech even when there is no real need for such accentuation, and (b) a tendency to utter the last few words of your sentences far more rapidly than the opening words. The vocal explosiveness betrays the excess aggression or hostility you may be harboring. The hurrying of the ends of sentences mirrors your underlying impatience with spending even the time required for your own speech.

2. If you always move, walk, and eat rapidly.

3. If you feel (particularly if you openly exhibit to others) an impatience with the rate at which most events take place. You are suffering from this sort of impatience if you find it difficult to restrain yourself from hurrying the speech of others and resort to the device of saying very quickly, over and over again, "Uh huh, uh huh," or, "Yes yes, yes yes," to someone who is talking, unconsciously urging him to "get on with" or hasten his rate of speaking. You are also suffering from impatience if you attempt to finish the sentences of persons speaking to you before they can.

   Other signs of this sort of impatience: If you become unduly irritated or even enraged when a car ahead of you in your lane runs at a pace you consider too slow; if you find it anguishing to wait in a line or to wait your turn to be seated at a restaurant; if you find it intolerable to watch others perform tasks you know you can do faster; if you become impatient with yourself as you are obliged to perform repetitious duties (making out bank deposit slips, writing checks, washing and cleaning dishes, and so on), which are necessary but take you away from doing things you really have an interest in doing; if you find yourself hurrying your own reading or always attempting to obtain condensations or summaries of truly interesting and worthwhile literature.

4. If you indulge in polyphasic thought or performance, frequently striving to think of or do two or more things simultaneously. For example, if while trying to listen to another person's speech you persist in continuing to think about an irrelevant subject, you are indulging in polyphasic thought. Similarly, if while golfing or fishing you continue to ponder your business or professional problems, or if while using an electric razor you attempt also to eat your breakfast or drive your car, or if while driving your car you attempt to dictate letters for your secretary, you are indulging in polyphasic performance. This is one of the commonest traits in the Type A man. Nor is he always satisfied with doing just two things at one time. We have known subjects who not only shaved and ate simultaneously, but also managed to read a business or professional journal at the same time.

5. If you find it always difficult to refrain from talking about or bringing up the theme of any conversation around to those subjects which especially

Exhibit V-1

TEST FOR TYPE A BEHAVIOR PATTERN (continued)

interest and intrigue you, and when unable to accomplish this maneuver, you pretend to listen but really remain preoccupied with your own thoughts.

6. If you almost always feel vaguely guilty when you relax and do absolutely nothing for several hours to several days.

7. If you no longer observe the more important or interesting or lovely objects that you encounter in your milieu. For example, if you enter a strange office, store, or home, and after leaving any of these places you cannot recall what was in them, you no longer are observing well - or for that matter enjoying life very much.

8. If you do not have any time to spare to become the things worth being because you are so preoccupied with getting the things worth having.

9. If you attempt to schedule more and more in less and less time, and in doing so make fewer and fewer allowances for unforeseen contingencies. A concomitant of this is a chronic sense of time urgency, one of the core components of Type A Behavior Pattern.

10. If, on meeting another severely afflicted Type A person, instead of feeling compassion for his affliction you find yourself compelled to "challenge" him. This is a telltale trait because no one arouses the aggressive and/or hostile feelings of one Type A subject more quickly than another Type A subject.

11. If you resort to certain characteristic gestures or nervous tics: For example, if in conversation you frequently clench your fist, or bang your hand upon a table or pound one fist into the palm of your other hand in order to emphasize a conversational point, you are exhibiting Type A gestures. Similarly, if the corners of your mouth spasmodically, in tic-like fashion, jerk backward slightly exposing your teeth, or if you habitually clench your jaw, or even grind your teeth, you are subject to muscular phenomena suggesting the presence of a continuous struggle, which is, of course, the kernel of the Type A Behavior Pattern.

12. If you believe that whatever success you have enjoyed has been due in good part to your ability to get things done faster than your fellow men and if you are afraid to stop doing everything faster and faster.

13. If you find yourself increasingly and ineluctably committed to translating and evaluating not only your own but also the activities of others in terms of "numbers."

himself known to another person, even to his spouse—because it is not manly to be psychologically naked—then it follows that *men will be difficult to love.*

Jourard saw the traditional male role, with its insistence on hiding so much of the self, as a serious handicap to living authentically or congruently. This restriction of a man's natural self and emotions imposes some degree of stress upon the individual. And while men have not traditionally been able to define themselves in terms of their emotions (as women in large part have), they have often defined themselves in terms of their work. For gainful employment was, and still is, a major part of male identity. Colligan [2] quotes psychologist Martin Seligman as saying:

> Deprive a man of work and you may remove his most meaningful source of instrumental control. In our society your work is your identification. Take that away from most people and you remove the most important thing in their lives.

Since so much of his self-esteem and self-identification come from his work, for a man to lose his job is a major blow. Dorothea and Benjamin Braginsky [1] report the statements of a laid-off technical-engineering writer:

> You have no friends when you're unemployed. They think it's a disease that is contagious. . . . I've found open resentments, like, "I'm glad it happened to you and not me, brother." Without my [personal] writing I would be out . . . with the rest of the boys in a tavern drinking and drowning my troubles. If a man is gainfully employed, and then you take away his employment, he's just like . . . an idle tool. It's like being in a prison. If a man is going to contribute to society, he has to be gainfully employed.

The stress of being unemployed is keenly felt by many men. And for the aging man in retirement, this kind of stress can be insidious. Jourard states:

> . . . men in our society, following retirement, will frequently disintegrate and die not long after they assume their new life of leisure . . . men can see themselves as manly, and life worthwhile . . . so long as they are engaged in gainful employ, or are sexually potent, or have enviable social status. . . . Thus if man's sense of masculine identify, as presently culturally defined, is a condition for continued existence, and if this is easily undermined by the vicissitudes of aging or . . . of a changing social system, then . . . the male role has an added lethal component.

Most of us know of a newly-retired man who visibly withers while trying to adjust to his "reduced" status, or of the recent widower who cannot seem to rally after his wife's death. By contrast, Jourard has observed that newly-widowed women (culturally permitted to experience a greater degree of authenticity throughout their emotional lives), "though affected by the husbands' . . . death[s], managed to find new grounds and meaning for continued existence, and got on with living."

Clearly, the traditional male role, while helping to perpetuate American achievement, has done so at expense to the authentic being of the individual male, forcing him to base his identity too much outside of himself.

Women, for their part, seem to have been dealt a tricky hand by their role in American society. The traditional "female" role (which, like the traditional male role, in some subcultures has already altered considerably) of docile competence, supportiveness and unassertiveness was cloaked in paradox, which Matina Horner [7] describes:

> We have an educational system that ostensibly encourages and prepares men and women identically for careers that social

and . . . internal psychological pressures really limit to men.

There has been a contradiction, then, between women's training (which funneled them towards achievement aims) and the female role (which discouraged that very desire for achievement). Like men, women internalize early the American values that promote achievement, self-reliance and development of personal resources (values that have led some social scientists to characterize American culture as "masculine"); yet in a confusing about-face, women have learned via their female role that achievement need in *them* is overly aggressive, "unfeminine." So women also internalized the need to repress assertive tendencies. (Freud perhaps overstated this as, "The whole essence of femininity lies in repressing aggressiveness.")

Until very recently, society seemed to consider femininity and personal achievement as "two desirable but mutually exclusive ends." It is small wonder that women who *do* pursue career and other achievement goals so often experience anxiety and guilt. The traditional restrictions of the female role still produce stress for the woman who transcends those restrictions. Often, as if to compensate for their "unfeminine" desire to achieve, Horner observes, career women go to great lengths to display their femininity.

Horner also makes the point that a psychological barrier (the "motive to avoid success") persists despite women's now legal right to participate fully in American society. Women's "fear of success" remains because they expect "that success in achievement situations will be followed by . . . social rejection and the sense of losing one's femininity." Whereas a man's achievement goals have always reinforced his sense of "manliness," the same achievement goals in a woman might have evidenced her "lack of femininity." Thus, almost until the present, in a ploy that was largely self-protective, the high school coed hid her brainpower from her boyfriend; and later, the adult woman declined to compete in "man's world." Displaying her true potential was dangerous for the female; she risked losing the approval of her boyfriend or her spouse, or even other women. "Women," wrote David Riesman in 1964, "as with many minority groups, bitterly resent and envy those among them who break out of confinement." More than a decade after Riesman's words, women's risks are diminishing, but have by no means disappeared.

As evidence that more contemporary women seek to redefine the female role, Marsha Dubrow [3] describes women's "assertiveness training" groups that now exist in many American cities. Such training involves behavior modification techniques to replace passivity and self-denigration (traits inherent in the traditional female role) with self-assertion and belief in one's abilities. Assertiveness training is a step towards discarding the stressful guilt and apprehensiveness that the culturally defined female role fostered.

Thus, the traditional roles of both sexes imposed, and to some extent still impose, stress upon American men and women. "Unsatisfying stress" has attended both the male's invulnerable, unemotional façade, and the female's passive unassertiveness; the male role has not met men's need for authenticity, and the female role has not met women's need for achievement. As we know, of course, the traditional "male" and "female" roles are currently in transition, a rapid and profound transition that parallels that of American culture itself. (Even the descriptions quoted in this section are already obsolete in certain sub-cultures. But change in a country so large and diverse as ours is uneven. Sex roles among urban graduate students might barely resemble those among farm families, for example.) This transition in our role definitions currently imposes another type of "unsatisfying stress," which many have encountered: the stress of uncertainty and lack of precedent. For, defining sex roles means breaking new cultural ground, exploring new ways of relating to ourselves, each other, and our environment. Yet as varied, altered roles become more established and familiar, it is hoped by those encouraging change that a greater amount of "satisfying stress"—the stress of achieving goals, of meeting challenges, while living authentically—will be more present in the lives of both men and women.

EMOTIONAL IMPACT OF STRESS

Many emotional symptoms can be linked with harmful stress. Earlier we touched upon the "nervous breakdown"[4] as one result of stress overload. Breakdown is one of the major maladaptive reactions to stress. Another of these maladaptions is addiction—a troubling word that actually means any obsessive dependence (although its medical application is to specific physiologic dependence). In a stress-filled environment, addiction is a method of displacement or withdrawal. The nicotine addict, for instance, displaces his daily anxieties in the act of smoking and in its attendant "rituals"; the very familiarity of the various actions, from lighting the cigarette to flicking the ashes, is powerfully comforting. Technically a stimulant, the cigarette nevertheless becomes a pacifier in times of stress. In addition, the body's dependence on nicotine is also powerful; thus the addiction involves the interplay of emotional and physiologic needs.

Human beings, in our infinite variety, can be "addicted" to almost anything: narcotics, caffeine, tranquilizers, gambling, television, eating. In American life, one of the most noxious physiologic addictions—since it is so widely tolerated and so difficult to define—is alcoholism. To the alcoholic, alcohol is medicine. It is his method of curing pain, of withdrawing from the intolerable nature of some dimension of his life. The cause of the pain might be marital unhappiness, a high-stress occupation, self-disappointment and anger, and, of course, the physical compulsion for alcohol itself. (There is some, but not conclusive, evidence that alcoholics often tend to be persons for whom self-assertion is particularly difficult.) Whatever the cause, alcohol brings the desired result: a flight from pain, from confronting "intolerable" realities. Use of alcohol brings the alcoholic relief from stress, at least temporarily. Yet the price the alcoholic pays—in medical and human terms—for his temporary oblivion is immense. Medically, the body develops the same physiologic dependence on alcohol that the smoker develops for nicotine. Alcohol destroys body cells, poisons the bloodstream, weakens resistance to disease. But besides being physically damaging, alcohol wreaks emotional havoc. Two items from an Alcoholics Anonymous pamphlet [8] hint at the destructiveness of alcoholism:

> Has Your Drinking Problem Become Progressively More Serious During the Past Year?
>
> All the available medical evidence indicates that alcoholism is a *progressive* illness. Once a person's drinking gets out of control, the problem gets worse, never fades away. An alcoholic has only these final alternatives: 1) to drink himself to death or

[4]The term "nervous breakdown" is actually a catch-all label for a variety of breakdown reactions. Any emotional response that precludes the normal functioning of an individual (e.g., depression, mental paralysis, obsessive fear, psychotic episode) can be called a "nervous breakdown."

be committed to an institution, or 2) to stay away from alcohol in any form.

Has Your Drinking Created Problems at Home?

> Many of us [i.e., members of A.A.] used to assert that we drank *because* of unpleasant or annoying home situations. It rarely occurred to us that problems of this type are aggravated, rather than solved, by our uncontrolled drinking.

These questions point to the tremendous damage alcoholism causes, to the health and well-being of the alcoholic himself, and to the whole fabric of his family life. The types of questions Alcoholics Anonymous asks can help an individual to test himself or herself for problem drinking, perhaps for alcoholism. (See Exhibit V-2 for more questions relating to problem drinking. They are included here because there is evidence of an increase in the incidence of youthful alcoholism.) But even so, the defini-

Exhibit V-2

TEN QUESTIONS FROM ALCOHOLICS ANONYMOUS

TEN QUESTIONS FROM ALCOHOLICS ANONYMOUS

1. Have You Ever Tried to Stop Drinking for a Week (or Longer) Only to Fall Short of Your Goal?

2. Do You Resent the Advice of Others Who Try to Get You to Stop Drinking?

3. Have You Ever Tried to Control Your Drinking by Switching from One Alcoholic Beverage to Another?

4. Have You Taken a Morning Drink During the Past Year?

5. Do You Envy People Who Can Drink Without Getting Into Trouble?

6. At Social Affairs Where Drinking Is Limited, Do You Try to Obtain "Extra" Drinks?

7. Despite Evidence to the Contrary, Have You Continued to Assert that You Can Stop Drinking "on Your Own" Whenever You Wish?

8. During the Past Year, Have You Missed Time from Work as a Result of Drinking?

9. Have You Ever Functioned Somehow (Yet Had No Memory Afterwards) During Your Drinking?

10. Have You Ever Felt You Could Do More With Your Life if You Did Not Drink?

tion of "alcoholic" is elusive and subjective, and alcoholism continues to ravage large numbers of Americans who find the stress imposed by their problems and fears initially eased, but eventually much worsened, by drinking.

Alcoholism is sometimes a sign of self-directed anger. Depression—another emotional problem related to stress overload—is always in part a sign of anger, usually with oneself. According to Levinson [13] one major cause of depression is the self-anger that results from failure. Levinson suggests that "the person who blames himself repeatedly for defects and losses in his life may eventually plunge into . . . severe depression . . . and become suicidal."

Levinson [12] says that the man or woman with depressive tendencies typically possesses high aspirations ("ego ideals") but a low self-image (feels inadequate to reach ego ideals). Many external pressures can increase already high ego ideals—parental, teacher, or supervisor expectations, for instance, or competition for desirable positions in school or job. Such pressure can lead to a person's creating impossible goals for himself. And with impossible goals, failure is, by definition, inevitable. For this type of person, failure is a constant threat, and when it occurs, the person succumbs to feelings of inadequacy, self-criticism, guilt and depression. Failure (real or imagined) can lower his self-image even further, and can kindle self-directed rage (or perhaps *re*-kindle; often self-anger is a holdover from infant rage that the child guiltily perceived as his own fault, the result of his own inadequacy).

For a person with intolerably high aspirations, the alternatives to failure—and to the continual stress his aspirations induce—might seem very limited. To admit to problems and depression is "weak"; to sensibly seek psychiatric help is not only "weak," it is also "crazy." Often, therefore, the depressive develops psychosomatic symptoms. Or else he unconsciously attacks himself by having "accidents" (the car; the lawnmower; the boat); and by making "mistakes" (on the job; in the marriage; with the kids). In severe cases, the depressive might even commit suicide, thinking that death is his only escape from failure.

In order to "cope with threats to the self-image that may precipitate depression and, eventually, self-destructive behavior," Levinson recommends that (1) one should cultivate a range of interests, rather than overidentify with one field ("The more the person has . . . organized his life around one activity, the more vulnerable he is"); (2) one should seek from a peer or superior "accurate, honest, and frequent performance appraisal . . . to maintain a perspective on himself"; (3) one should learn to break a problem down into its components, so that it does not seem insurmountable.

And in order to become aware of self-anger in *others*, Levinson suggests that one become sensitive to unusual behavior changes:

> Be alert to signs of depression . . . loss of appetite and substantial weight loss, sleeplessness or excess fatigue, heavy drinking, excessive use of tranquilizers or energizers, inability to complete work because of mental paralysis or reverie, increasing irritability, slowness and dull quality in speech, physical symptoms that have no physical basis, repeated deep sighing, and talk of suicide.

Along with family members and colleagues, managers are often in the position to notice such telltale changes in the behavior of their subordinates:

> Senior executives should try to relieve irrational pressures of guilt or responsibility that people express—but not by dismissing

> [them] with . . . "Don't let it bother you" or "Forget it." One constructive way to avoid a buildup of pressures is through clarification of . . . the subordinate's responsibility . . . It may be helpful if the superior recounted his own past problems . . . to help his subordinate accept the human quality of imperfection in himself and others.

Levinson urges managers not to send their troubled subordinates off on vacations or "rests," since this kind of respite only gives the person greater latitude in which to extend his depression and guilt. The depressive should, instead, be supported by his work atmosphere and the involvement of his colleagues and superiors. "Above all, a seriously depressed person must be treated professionally."

The depressive, like the alcoholic and the chain smoker, is a victim of the emotional havoc of stress. When unchecked, these emotional problems result in the sufferer's inability to function, and possibly in his death. The alcoholic, the heavy smoker, can die from their addictions. And the depressive can be desperate enough to take his own life. So the dangers of stress overload in our lives are real enough, and should not be ignored. But neither should they be feared as unmanageable and overpowering. For we can learn to cope with too much, or the wrong kind of, stress.

SELF-AWARENESS IS SELF-DEFENSE

In our attempts to reduce harmful and excessive stress, lack of self-awareness is our biggest (and most needless) impediment. The Type A person who won't admit he is driving himself too hard, the alcoholic who insists he is a social drinker, the depressive who doesn't see his insomnia and irritability as symptoms of trouble—all of these persons, who are already encountering stress-related difficulties, run added risks from their lack of self-contact. Yet anyone can learn to become more self-aware, through closer contact with one's feelings and perceptions, and through closer contact with one's own body.

Total body awareness usually varies with age. The teenager is intensely—often painfully—aware of his changing body, and waits for his twenties in order to feel "grown up." The person in his twenties largely loses this high degree of awareness; his body is mostly mature, after all, and he tends to assume that his physical construct is more or less permanent *as it is*. But by the time a person reaches his thirties, he starts to notice subtle visual changes in his body; a change of texture in skin, perhaps, or a new tendency to thicken around the middle. This perception of change becomes more metaphysical in the late thirties and early forties, as a person realizes his own finiteness; death, he begins to see, *is* an inevitability, not merely an abstraction that happens to other people. As a result of this realization, the forties can become a decade of caution. The smoker of twenty years will try to stop. Or the overweight person will try to reduce. The hard-driving person will try to slow down (especially if he sees one of his hard-driving friends succumb to early heart disease; the perception of death as real begins to be actualized by one's forties, and the lesson indeed comes home).

People generally do not deliberately cultivate this kind of overall body awareness; it exists instead as part of one's metaphysical self-consciousness. It is not an "ability." But the specific awareness of body signals, especially *body distress signals*, is an ability to be developed. A body distress signal is a message from the body that says "something is wrong." The man who drives to work each morning with a knot in his stomach, and yet insists that he is enjoying life, is ignoring a blatant distress signal. These signals are multitudinous—headaches, muscular tenseness, depression, loss of libido, insomnia, irritability, menstrual irregularity, heart palpitations, lassitude; in fact, any significant departure from one's normal healthy state. (Selye [15] asserts, in fact, that stress is a component in every illness, and a major component in a mild illness. Even a head cold, then, might be a body distress signal, pointing to stress.)

The chief method for coping with the stress that almost invariably causes these symtoms is the ability to "read" them as distress signals, to recognize in them cues to feeling states. Erich Fromm [5] discusses the ability to interpret physical (and emotional) signals:

> One [should be] aware . . . of a sense of tiredness or depression, and instead of giving in to it and supporting it by depressive thoughts . . . one asks oneself "what happened?" Why am I depressed? The same is done by noticing when one is irritated or angry, or tending to daydreaming, or other escape activities. In each of these instances the important thing is to be aware of them and not to rationalize them in the thousand . . . ways in which this can be done; furthermore to be open to our own inner voice, which will tell us—often rather immediately—why we are anxious, depressed, irritated.

The process Fromm describes—that of sifting through one's consciousness to find the cause of stress-related symptoms—is the first step in reducing harmful stress in daily life. For in psychoanalytic theory, knowledge is indeed power, the power to dispel an unwanted behavior or experiencing by first identifying its root causes.

Boredom is a major symptom of too little stress. Boredom dulls the body, mind and spirit. It leads to chronic fatigue, inactivity, apathy—all of which, of course, lead to more boredom.

Another dimension of body awareness is the most basic, and perhaps, the most important: care and feeding. What-you-do-with-your-body and what-goes-into-your body are interrelated. One's sensitivity to his bodily needs, limitations and responses begins here, in attention to such fundamental matters as nutrition, sleep, exercise and the thousand small details of one's physical well-being. Consider, for example, Selye's advice [15] with respect to activity and sleep.

> Try not to overwork any part of your body or mind disproportionately by repeating the same actions to exhaustion. Be especially careful to avoid the senseless repetition of the same task when you are already exhausted. A moment of objective self-analysis will . . . convince you that the same work could be done much more easily after a night's sleep . . . if you get . . . in a rut you may not be able to stop, and mentally you will keep on repeating your routine throughout the night . . . never allow . . . yourself to be under the kind of stress during the day that may automatically go on through the night. This self-perpetuating kind of stress may be the result of a heavy meal, whiskey, emotional upsets. . . .

Caring for one's body also includes seeking help appropriately. The most obvious preventive measure for body care is the medical checkup. While not totally effective in averting illness, a physical examination is nevertheless the best way of remaining ahead of serious medical problems. Similarly, one should seek psychological help in times of emotional distress—when awareness of one's body signals is simply insufficient to the task of working through the emotional problem.

Self-awareness, then, is a sensitivity to the urgings of both body and mind: It is the ability to be symptom-aware; it is proper attention to caring for oneself. Self-awareness is actually our first line of defense against the numerous dangers of a changing, unpredictable world, and, of course, against our self-induced dysfunctional stresses. Through self-awareness we can reduce unnecessary stress in our daily lives, and cope more effectively with the desirable stress that remains in well-balanced, healthful living.

SUMMARY

The key points in this note gather around the issue of stress in contemporary American life:

- the traditional values, the strong achievement needs internalized by many of us, and the high degree of change in American society all impose considerable anxiety and stress;
- some stress is a natural, desirable, necessary component of our lives;
- too much stress, however, is harmful: stress overload symptoms include "long-range strain," "giving-up syndrome," "future shock";
- too little stress is also harmful: lack of stress dulls the mind, spirit and body;
- individual stress tolerance varies widely: what is exhilarating to one person is intolerable to another;
- "satisfying stress" (achieving goals, meeting challenges) is the type of stress upon which people thrive;
- "unsatisfying stress" (the stress of frustration and failure) is physically and emotionally debilitating;
- "unsatisfying," frustration-stress is inherent in the struggle-oriented pattern called "Type A";
- both "male" and "female" roles have traditionally imposed "unsatisfying stress" upon Americans;
- as sex roles alter, the stress of change is currently greater; in the future this stress might become more satisfying;
- there are major maladaptive reactions to harmful stress: "nervous breakdown," alcoholism, depression, hypertension, heart attack.
- self-awareness comprises body awareness, emotional awareness, physical self-care, recognition of when help is needed, action to get that help;
- self-awareness is self-defensive in reducing harmful stress.

Some of the above points, especially those relating to physical care and body awareness, might seem tiresome to strong, alert young adults. Why, one might ask, are we being told all this? Do we really need to know these things? Quite probably, everyone needs to know this type of information *eventually*, some persons sooner than others. The idea behind this chapter is that one should "store" the learning until it is needed—if a life change causes disorientation; if one becomes depressed; if a physical stress-symptom rears its insistent head. We are all creatures of our needs, which change as our lives change. And as stress becomes felt in our lives, one of our strong needs is (or will be) the ability to manage it, to channel it productively with minimal wear and tear on our total selves, in order to live well all life long.

BIBLIOGRAPHY

BRAGINSKY, D. D., and B. M. BRAGINSKY, "Surplus People: Their Lost Faith in Self and System," *Psychology Today*, August 1975.

COLLIGAN, DOUGLAS, "That Helpless Feeling: The Dangers of Stress," *New York Magazine*, July 14, 1975.

DUBROW, MARSHA, "Female Assertiveness: How a Pussycat Can Learn to be a Panther," *New York Magazine*, July 28, 1975.

FRIEDMAN, MEYER, and RAY H. ROSENMAN, *Type A Behavior and Your Heart.* Greenwich, Connecticut, 1974.

FROMM, ERICH, *The Art of Loving.* New York, 1956.

GROSS, NANCY E., *Living with Stress.* New York, 1958.

HORNER, MATINA S., "Femininity and Successful Achievement: A Basic Inconsistency," Chapter 3 of *Feminine Personality and Conflict*, by JUDITH M. BARDWICK, ELIZABETH DOUVAN, MATINA S. HORNER, and DAVID GUTMANN. Belmont, California, 1970.

Is A.A. For You? pamphlet of Alcoholics Anonymous World Services, Inc., New York, 1954.

JOURARD, SIDNEY M., "Some Lethal Aspects of the Male Role," in *The Transparent Self.* Princeton, New Jersey, 1964.

LAMOTT, KENNETH, "What to Do When Stress Signs Say You're Killing Yourself," *Today's Health*, January 1975.

LEVINSON, HARRY, *Executive Stress.* New York, 1964.

———, "On Executive Suicide," *Harvard Business Review*, July/August 1975.

———, "What Killed Bob Lyons?" *Harvard Business Review*, January/February 1963.

MCCLELLAND, DAVID C., *The Achieving Society.* Princeton, New Jersey, 1961.

SELYE, HANS, *The Stress of Life.* New York, 1956.

SMITH, LEE, "What Kills Executives?" *Dun's Review*, March 1975.

TOFFLER, ALVIN, *Future Shock.* New York, 1970.

The Secret of Success

Fritz J. Roethlisberger

I have chosen to talk to you tonight on the question, "What is the secret of success?" From my point of view this question is silly, meaningless, and unanswerable, and frankly I have no intention of answering it. However, as some people have a tendency to ask themselves silly, meaningless, and unanswerable questions—for which I don't hold myself responsible in the slightest— it seems to me that it is not the answers, but the tendency to ask such questions, that needs attention.

Most of us in academic circles would profit from a consideration of this problem, because after all we spend a good bit of our time in an environment where questions are being asked that are never quite satisfactorily answered. Instructors ask you questions which you don't answer, at least to the instructor's satisfaction. You ask questions of instructors who in turn do not give answers that satisfy you. This, as you know, can be a most frustrating experience.

Now, this frustrating experience can be easily remedied, theoretically at least. Everyone is so concerned with the answers to questions that no one bothers to look carefully at the questions they are asking. Everyone seems to assume that there must be an answer to any question which any damn fool can ask. Our whole educational process is committed to trying to give answers to silly questions. Very few students are taught to scrutinize with as much care the questions they ask or are asked as the answers they give or that are given to them. As a result they become steadily more and more disillusioned with themselves and their instructors.

Let me therefore start by examining carefully the question, "What is the secret

This paper is a partially edited version of a talk given by Professor Roethlisberger to students at Harvard Business School in 1948. Reprinted by permission of the publishers from *Man-in-Organization: Essays of F.J. Roethlisberger* (Cambridge, Mass.: The Belknap Press of Harvard University Press, 1968).

of success?" I suppose most of you feel you know what success means. "*Success is success. Period.*" But just stop and reflect a moment.

* * *

"Success," like many words, has many meanings, not just one meaning. It is absurd to think that because there is one word, there is one thing to which it refers. There are probably as many meanings as there are people who use the word and situations to which the word is referred. Probably ninety out of a hundred times when the word is used it has little or no meaning, apart from the personal situation and feelings of the person who used it. In the experience I described above I gave an extreme example of a situation where failure and success are so inextricably intertwined that some people have difficulty in knowing that when they have failed, they have succeeded. I can also think of situations where the more successful you are in one respect, the more you have failed in another respect.

PREOCCUPATION AND ADAPTATION

There is one aspect of this problem in which I have been interested for some time and that is the preoccupation about success with which so many students are concerned. For many years I have been interested in this preoccupation with the future which prevented so many able young people from relating themselves effectively to the present. About fifteen years ago it was part of my job to interview a good many students—very good and able students—in the University. In my many discussions with them and especially at the business school, the topic of "success" was frequently brought up. Everything including "going to bed early at night," "taking regular exercise," "not drinking coffee or smoking cigarettes," "getting good grades," and "sticking to one thing" was proposed as having a good deal to do with, or constituting the essence of, success. One student I remember kept a collection of maxims about success. Perhaps you would like to hear some of these maxims. Let me read from his notebook.

1. The expert should be on tap, not on top.

2. Qualities necessary to success: ambition with a will to work.

3. Requisites of success: strong arm, clean mind, brave heart.

4. The essence of success: health, ability, and character.

5. The secret of success [now we have it] is for a person to be ready for opportunity when it comes.

6. The best substitute for brains is silence.

7. The person who wakes up and finds fame hasn't been asleep.

8. If you are a self-starter, the boss won't have to be a crank.

As you can imagine, this student had a difficult time in living up to all these rules. This rat race for success left him in a perpetual state of agitation and with little opportunity to attend to his immediate surroundings. It has always interested me to observe that the more preoccupied people are with this "success," the more unsuccessful they are likely to be in relating themselves to people here and now. This was particularly true of the student I just mentioned. He had few friends. All his life he felt he had lacked personal and intimate relationships with his peers. This was particularly true in his relations to women. This inability to relate himself to women was well reflected in his notebook, which also contained maxims on the topic of "women." When I read you some of these maxims I think that most of you, without being psychiatrists, will be able to see that he was better acquainted with the *word* "woman" than with the many particular and different creatures to whom this word refers. Here are some.

> 1. There are two places where to be a coward is the worst of all things: one is in war, the other in love.
>
> 2. Let your words be as clean as those from the lips of a good woman and as few as those from an Indian.
>
> 3. You gaze at a star for two motives, because it is luminous, because it is impenetrable. You have by your side a sweeter radiance, a greater mystery, woman.
>
> 4. The hardest thing for a man to forgive in a woman is that of falling in love with him when he doesn't want her to and the hardest thing for a woman to forgive in a man is not falling in love with her when she wants him to.
>
> 5. Sexual intercourse is something "no gentleman would propose nor no gentleman would refuse."

It is needless to go on with this list of maxims. They well illustrate two uniformities in experience I have frequently observed: (1) excessive preoccupations about success prevent rather than facilitate the process of giving and sustaining one's attention to the present, and (2) people with such preoccupations do not seem to have the capacity for easy, intimate, and friendly association with other people. Like the student I mentioned above, they become enamored about words rather than the things to which words refer. As a result they have a greater facility in relating themselves to words and abstractions than to concrete events, things, and people.

There is a third uniformity which is also worthy of comment. An excessive preoccupation about success always seems to be accompanied by an equally excessive preoccupation about failure. I have frequently encountered these alternating preoccupations of success and failure by means of which some people tend to isolate themselves from their social surroundings. For some people there is nothing which lies between success and failure. They interpret their own activities as well as the activities of others in terms of these irreducible categories. Anything which is not completely successful is failure. One man I knew, for example, used to spend considerable time in picturing himself as one who had achieved high eminence and authority in his chosen field of endeavor and imagining how his associates and the people back home would then regard him. Maybe he could be president of the United States? Then wouldn't he make things hum! On the other hand, when he was depressed and probably more fatigued, he would be convinced that he would never amount to much. His life had been one failure after another. Then he would picture himself as a butler in a very wealthy family where he could have close contact with luxury and conveniences. Or maybe he could get arrested and sent to jail where the state would take care of him. Between viewing life from the White House or "behind bars" there was no middle point of vantage. In the thinking of such people, the notion of adventure is lacking. There is little or no place for exploration and experiment. They work so hard in preventing themselves from making mistakes that they never learn anything at all.

WHAT PREVENTS GROWTH AND ADJUSTMENT

Instead of asking the question, "What is the secret of success?" it might be more sensible to ask, "What prevents me from adjusting to and and growing in my situation here and now?" or, "What prevents me from learning here and now?" To these questions, experience can give a partial answer.

It should be obvious that growth, adjustment, and learning take place in the present. One cannot adjust easily to the past or future. The past is gone and the future is uncertain. If a person therefore is excessively preoccupied with the past or future, he or she ceases to pay attention to the present where growth, learning, and adjustment are most likely to take place. To be overly preoccupied with the mistakes, failures, and sins of the past or to be overly preoccupied with vague, absolutistic, and unrealistic goals is the best way I know of preventing growth, learning, and adjustment here and now. This statement is an induction from experience which can be checked in your own experience as well as in the experience of others. It points to the two chief sources of interference with the adequacy of relationship to your present situation.

(1) One source of interference comes from the past. We may bring to our present situation erroneous meanings derived from past experiences. We may have understood and misinterpreted our past experience. This is something which the advocates of "learning from experience" often ignore. It is just as likely that we learn the wrong as the right lessons from experience. The experience of most of us is limited and insufficient. Moreover, experience doesn't speak or reveal its significance or meaning in the raw, so to speak. It has to be constantly and continuously cross-examined if misunderstanding and misinterpretation are not to result. One never learns from experience by asking silly and unanswerable questions of it. What I am trying to say has been well expressed in a truism with which most of you are familiar. "It's not what people don't know that causes trouble; it's what they do know that ain't so that prevents learning and growth." Too many of us know too many things that ain't so. It is this factor as much as any that makes the teaching of administrative practices difficult. It takes many years for most of us to see the significance of our experience and to draw from it correctly the lessons it teaches. Elton Mayo, with whom I was associated for many years, used to put this idea tersely by saying, "People are not born sane or insane. Sanity, particularly in our modern complex world, is a difficult achievement."

(2) The second source of interference to adequacy of relationship to one's present situation comes, peculiarly enough, from the future. It comes from the vague, unrealistic, and absolutistic goals we set for ourselves, in terms of which we constantly frustrate our daily sense of accomplishment. "Success," as envisaged by some, is one of such goals. It is a word with such a vague, unrealistic, and absolutist referent that it prevents growth and adjustment here and now. I know of no word which has gotten more people into more trouble. To go around asking of life, "Am I a success or a failure?" is one of those silly questions which people ask which has no answer. It's like asking, "Am I a man or a mouse?"—another one of those questions which make many students miserable. The closest we can come to an answer is one which is unsatisfactory for most people. Everyone is both a success and a failure. Everyone is both a man and a mouse. This is the lesson which experience, when sufficiently cross-examined, teaches—for many of us, the hard way. This applies to you as well as your professors. I hope I'm not disillusioning some of you too quickly. Curiously enough, however, these statements, once they have been emotionally accepted, release you from a silly and fret-

ful worry. You can go to bed at night and chuckle instead of stewing about the "riddle of the universe."

PRESENT AND FUTURE

This brings me to the last point I want to make. It will be the most difficult one for most of you to accept. It makes more sense at the age of forty than at the age of twenty. But then you know when life begins, particularly for Harvard professors, who take a longer time than most people to grow up. In spite of their erudition from books, they too have to learn some things the hard way.

Some of you, I fear, tend to think of the present as a means and the future as an end. Many of you treat the business school, for example, as a means, to some glorious end—"success." You go through the dreary round of case discussion merely as a routine preparation for that great day when you will be finally in touch with that brute and stubborn reality called "business" where you will find "success." As a result, some of you don't learn very much while you are here. I suspect that for some of you, this state of affairs may continue. Each job you have will be viewed merely as a stepping stone to the next higher job in the ladder to "success."

What if I suggested to you that the future is the means, and the present is the end? Would that sound too silly? Before throwing it out as absurd, however, let's consider it for a moment. You can't live in the past or in the future, can you? And when the future comes, it is a "present," isn't it? When a businessman retires at the age of sixty-five he doesn't have the same organism he had when he was twenty. Isn't it likely—or am I just daydreaming?—that he won't be able to enjoy at the age of sixty-five some of the things he thought he would enjoy at the age of twenty? Why is it then that so many of us feel that we can't settle down and enjoy the present until we have achieved success? Why do we constantly take all meaning and significance out of the present and put it in the future? Isn't it because we treat the present as a means and the future as an end? Aren't we assuming that when we arrive at this point, everything will be "hunky-dory"? But isn't it likely that if this is our basic attitude, we will continue to act in our old way? When the future comes, it will be a present, and as we have taught ourselves to treat the present as insignificant, won't we have to posit more and new goals, bigger and better goals to strive for—ad infinitum?

The question I am raising is this: Are there not two different kinds of goals?—(1) one kind of goal which takes all significance and meaning out of the present, and (2) another kind of goal which makes the present more meaningful and significant.

(1) A good example of the first kind of goal is the excessive preoccupation about success of which I have been speaking. By means of it we make ourselves miserable in the present. We prevent ourselves from learning and growing here and now. In this frame of reference we create a target just in order to shoot at it and we make ourselves miserable every time we fail to hit the bull's-eye.

(2) In the case of the second kind of goal, we create a target in order to perfect our shooting here and now. This kind of goal works for us. It makes meaningful and significant the present. It facilitates growth, learning, the sense of adventure and exploration. In this frame of reference, hitting the bull's-eye isn't an end in itself. The bull's-eye merely becomes a means for correcting the source of error here and now. Are not such goals treating the future as a means and the present as an end? If so, what are these goals which allow us to retain our

zest for growth and learning and adaptation until the day we die? This question, I suggest, rather than the goal of "success" might be an appropriate subject for your mature reflection.

CONCLUSION

Curiously enough, in the process of debunking the word "success" I have made certain statements about how to deal successfully with the present. These statements can be summarized as follows:

(1) Stop right here and now asking yourself unanswerable questions. Avoid this practice as you would the plague. Give up the notion that every question has an answer. Trying to answer unanswerable questions has more serious consequences than many so-called "vices." People who indulge in this pastime fill our mental hospitals and educational institutions. Some of them may even become "successes" and get to be political and business leaders. But so what?

(2) Stop right here and now trying to answer the silly and unanswerable questions that are asked of you. Do this to the point of rudeness if you have to, but in most cases all you will need to do is to listen politely. You will find, as you get more experience in this technique, that the last thing a person wants is your answer to his silly question anyway.

(3) Only ask questions to which experience can give you an answer here and now—not a final answer but a tentative answer which will facilitate new and better discriminations here and now. Keep cross-examining experience with better questions. As you put less effort into answering unanswerable questions, begin to put more effort into finding one good question worth asking of experience here and now. There are not too many lying about; so don't rush. Take it easy.

(4) Stop reflecting morbidly about the mistakes of the past and the goals of the future. As Professor Meriam has told you, the business school provides a wonderful opportunity, if you will avail yourself of it, for making mistakes and learning. If I understand him correctly, what he is saying to you is: Don't let your eagerness for future high passes and distinctions prevent you from learning here and now. Don't make of "grades" a goal which deprives the work you do here and now of being interesting, stimulating, and fun. If you have to hitch your wagon to a star, don't choose a star for its inscrutability, impenetrability, and sweet mystery—like the grades you get, for example. That, as you well know, is the road to despair. Choose a star—preferably a few—that will partially illuminate and reinforce the significance of your present experience. Excessive preoccupation about grades and "success" won't do this for you.

(5) What will? Most fortunately for me, my time is running short, so that I won't have the time to answer this question I am probably raising in your minds. How can we choose goals which will allow us to retain a zest for living in the present until the day we die? Is this an unanswerable question? In part I think it is. The question contains quite a few vague words. In it the word "choose" is crucial. Most of us don't choose our goals. We live with goals that have been borrowed or handed down to us by our parents and society. Nevertheless I think this is a better question than the one with which we started, "What is the secret of success?" It is less absolutistic. It at least implies that the satisfactions we get from the present are relative to the expectations we have and the demands we make of the present situation. It also implies that goals are not static things—like most other matters, they are subject to change. It suggests that occasionally they need renovation and that they can be reno-

vated in the direction of making the present more significant if we so choose. Unfortunately, many people do not choose to tinker with their goals in this way. They use their borrowed goals to make themselves miserable. Lastly, I think that this is a better question in that it is one to which at least each person can obtain a partial answer for him- or herself in his or her own experience.

I hope I have amply demonstrated to you the difficulty of asking a sensible question.

Index